2

POLITICS ⒤ STATES ⓐ COMMUNITIES

THIRTEENTH EDITION

Thomas R. Dye
Florida State University, Emeritus

Susan A. MacManus
University of South Florida

With the assistance of
Kristine Zooberg
Andrew F. Quecan
Ralph Reid
Research Associates

PEARSON
Prentice
Hall

Upper Saddle River, New Jersey 07458

Library of Congress Cataloging-in-Publication Data

Dye, Thomas R.
  Politics in states and communities / Thomas R. Dye, Susan
A. MacManus with the assistance of Kristine Zooberg.—13th ed.
    p. cm.
  Includes bibliographical references and index.
  ISBN-13: 978-0-13-602535-1
  ISBN-10: 0-13-602535-8
  1. State governments—United States. 2. Local government—
United States. I. MacManus, Susan A. II. Zooberg, Kristine. III. Title.
  JK2408.D82 2009
  320.80973—dc22   2008001078

Executive Editor: Dickson Musslewhite
Associate Editor: Rob DeGeorge
Editorial Assistant: Synamin Ballatt
Marketing Manager: Ann Stypuloski
Marketing Assistant: Liz Hoens
Production Liaison: Lynn Savino Wendel
Supplements Editor: Virginia Livsey
Permissions Coordinator: Lisa M. Black
Senior Operations Specialist: Mary Ann Gloriande
Art Director/Cover and Interior Design: Ilze Lemesis
Senior Art Director: Maria Lange
Cover Illustration/Photo: Lars Howlett/Contributor/Aurora/Getty Images, Inc.
Director, Image Resource Center: Melinda Reo
Manager, Rights and Permissions: Zina Arabia
Manager, Visual Research: Beth Brenzel
Manager, Cover Visual Research & Permissions: Karen Sanatar
Image Permission Coordinator: Debbie Hewitson
Photo Researcher: David Tietz
Composition/Full-Service Project Management: Bruce Hobart/Pine Tree Composition, Inc.
Printer/Binder: Quad/Graphics-Taunton
Cover Printer: Coral Graphics

Credits and acknowledgments borrowed from other sources and reproduced, with permission, in this textbook appear on page 627.

Pearson Education LTD., London
Pearson Education Singapore, Pte. Ltd
Pearson Education, Canada, Ltd
Pearson Education—Japan
Pearson Education Australia PTY, Limited

Pearson Education North Asia Ltd
Pearson Educación de Mexico, S.A. de C.V.
Pearson Education Malaysia, Pte. Ltd
Pearson Education, Upper Saddle River, New Jersey

To Joann
and
to Cameron,
Allison,
Susan,
and Genelle

10 9 8 7 6 5
ISBN-10: 0-13-602535-8
ISBN-13: 978-0-13-602535-1

CONTENTS

4. PARTICIPATION IN STATE POLITICS 104

5. PARTIES AND CAMPAIGNS IN THE STATES 144

6. LEGISLATORS IN STATE POLITICS 182

7. GOVERNORS IN STATE POLITICS 226

PREFACE

Politics in States and Communities is distinguished by:

Its focus on politics.

Its comparative approach.

Its concern with explanation.

Its interest in policy.

Its focus is on conflicts in states and communities and the structures and processes designed to manage conflict.

This "conflict management" theme emphasizes the sources and nature of conflict in society, how conflict is carried on, how key decision makers in states and communities act in conflict situations, and how "politicos" emerge and determine "who gets what." The political conflict management theme guides the discussion of formal governmental structures: federalism, state constitutions, parties and primaries, apportionment, legislative organizations, gubernatorial powers, court procedures, nonpartisanship, mayor and manager government, metropolitan government, community power, school boards and superintendents, tax systems, budget making, and so on.

An equally important theme is that states and communities in America play an important role in the political life of the nation. State and local governments do more than merely provide certain services such as education, road building, or fire protection. They also perform a vital political function by helping to resolve conflicts of interest in American society.

NEW TO THE THIRTEENTH EDITION

The thirteenth edition presents more in-depth and up-to-date coverage of the following:

- Campaigns and elections—federal oversight, the touch screen and paper ballot controversy, the Netroots and You Tube revolutions, the growing muscle of state parties (e.g., front loading of presidential primary elections); the rise of "convenience voting"; uncontrollable spending on ads by 527s (advocacy groups); the "Oprah" approach—using talk shows to reach casual voters.

- The segmentation of the media—voters and candidates choosing media in line with their own ideology.

- Money in politics—the rising costs of campaigns at all levels; self-financed candidates; new court rulings; use of the Internet and growth in the small donor ranks (the "democratization" of fund-raising).

- Immigration—the pros and cons, the economic and political impact on states, and conflicts over immigration reform.

- Pocketbook issues—the growing gap between the rich and the poor; the affordable housing and health insurance crises, and the increase in tax protests.

- Federal mandates and preemptions—an increase in the nationalization of public policies; the controversial Real ID Act.

- Minority politics—the extension of the federal Voting Rights Act; co-ethnic voting (the tendency of ethnics to vote for someone from their racial/ethnic group) and the conditions under which it occurs; the rise of minority media and its impact on minority voting; minority politicians on the national stage.

- Term limits—a close look at their intended and unintended consequences both on governing and representation.
- The growth of the lobbying industry and special interest politics; attempts (and failures) to regulate.
- Running for office—difficulties; motivations; younger face of candidates; strategic decision-making on when to run and who governors are picking as running mates.
- The changing world of state and local employees—the impact of citizen negativism and budget cutbacks, performance measurement and management fads, morale boosters.
- Changes in the judicial system—court shopping, growing interest in rehabilitation; slippage in support for death penalty, increase in legal challenges to execution methods; reconsideration of mandatory sentencing laws due to prison overcrowding.
- The changing face, shape, and politics of metropolitan America—shrinking middle-class neighborhoods in older areas; the decline of "first suburbs"; the rise of edge cities; the emergence of newly-urbanized micropolitan statistical areas.
- A more in-depth look at the role of the media—in exposing corruption; interactions with legislators, lobbyists, staffers, and bureaucrats.
- Land use fights at the local level—growth versus no growth; economic development versus the environment; the growing clout of professional planners; the decline of affordable housing and its consequences; citizen protests against government use of eminent domain.
- Transportation policy—roads, mass transit, subsidies, public safety issues including cell phone usage.
- Environmental policy—the greening of the states; air, water, and land pollution.
- Education policy—racial balancing; the controversy over testing and the federal No Child Left Behind Act; the changing world of higher education politics; the interface between religion and schools.
- Civil rights policy—the expansion of civil rights battlefields beyond just race to gender, disability, and sexual preference issues; the increased political clout of minorities; new court rulings on race and gay rights.
- Health care policy—the growing ranks of the uninsured; the impact of the rising costs of Medicare and Medicaid on other government programs; tough decisions about managed care.
- Welfare policy—reassessment of welfare reforms; identification of flaws in the incentive system.
- Managing during periods of economic decline—tapping new revenue sources, cutback management techniques; ways of avoiding financial disaster.

We begin each chapter with real-life situations designed to make the materials that follow more relevant. Individuals featured in our "People in Politics" come from a wider variety of backgrounds, states, and positions than those in previous editions. We feature state legislative leaders, new governors, outstanding state employee winners, an African American female supreme court justice, local officials, and elected officials seeking national office. We have more "What Do You Think?" features, including the following: "Identity Crisis: Federalism and the Real ID Act"; "Homeowners Associations: 'Buddies' or 'Bullies'?"; "Should Cash Strapped-States Lease Toll Roads to Private Investors?"; "Is Welfare Reform a Success?" Some new "Did You Know?" features inform students about new trends: "Bureaucrats Challenged to "Write It Simple!"; "Same-Sex Marriage in the States"; 'Three Sure Roads to Financial Disaster."

Among the popular features that have been revised and retained: "What Are the Most Livable States?"; "Getting into Politics"; "Religion and Politics: The Culture Wars

Intensify"; "Are Term Limits a Good Idea?"; "Federalism and the Drinking Age: Why 21 and Not 18?"; "Today's High Tech Campaigns Have a Vocabulary All Their Own"; "Informal Rules of the [Legislative] Game"; "How to Win at the Budget Game"; "America's Most Crime-Ridden Big Cities"; "Can Punishment Deter Crime?"; "Exposing Political Corruption"; "Sexual Harassment"; "Battles over Abortion"; "The Debate over School Vouchers"; and "'Diversity' in Universities."

As in previous editions, special attention has been given to racial and ethnic conflict, including new material on Hispanic, Asian, and Native American population growth and political power. The racial/ethnic-related subjects covered in each chapter are as follows: Chapter 1: "Race and Ethnicity," and "The Politics of Immigration"; Chapter 2: "The Politics of State Initiatives" (including affirmative action and racial preferences); Chapter 3: "Federalism's Faults" (Hurricane Katrina); Chapter 4: "Race, Ethnicity, and Political Participation," "Securing the Right to Vote" (ending discriminatory voting practices), and "Minorities in State Politics" (affirmative racial gerrymandering; racial polarization; Hispanic power); Chapter 5: racial/ethnic makeup of political party supporters; Chapter 6: "Minorities and Women in State Legislatures"; Chapter 7: "The Making of a Governor—Race and Ethnicity," "Minority and Women Governors"; Chapter 8: "Bureaucracy, Democracy, Representativeness, and Responsiveness" (minority employee presence); Chapter 9: "The Politics of Death Sentences," hate crimes, and racial issues in jury selection; race and the death penalty. Chapter 10: "Minorities and Women in Community Politics," minority representation and local election systems, "Growing Diversity in Metropolitan Areas"; Chapter 11: minority mayors and councilors, multiracial voting coalitions, and multilingual communicators in city hall; Chapter 12: "Ethnic and Racial Diversity in Metropolitan Areas," the racial composition of cities and suburbs, the concentration of social problems in the inner city (racial tensions and rioting), racial politics in consolidation efforts; Chapter 13: the relocation of poor minorities, the racial composition of neighborhoods; Chapter 14: The Impact of Budget Cuts on Minorities; Chapter 15: "Politics and Civil Rights," a variety of topics, including racial balance in schools, affirmative action battles, Hispanic politics, Native Americans and tribal government, Americans with disabilities, gender equality, sexual harassment, and abortion; Chapter 16: "Education," racially biased educational testing, racial differences in dropout rates, and black representation on school boards.; Chapter 17: the disproportionate number of minorities who are poor, on welfare, and without adequate health care.

Finally, the thirteenth edition continues the popular feature *"Rankings of the States"* on topics such as population growth, income and education, Hispanic and African American populations, reliance on federal aid, voter turnout, women and minorities in state legislatures, governors' institutional and personal powers, government spending and employment, special district governments, crime and law enforcement, road mileage and gasoline taxes, tax burdens, state spending and borrowing, educational performance (SATs, high school and college graduates), poverty, heath insurance coverage, and financing public schools.

INSTRUCTIONAL FEATURES

This book includes multiple instructional features designed to provide timeliness and relevance, to capture students' attention and interest, to involve students interactively with political questions, and to aid in the study of state and local politics. While the instructional features should aid in teaching state and local politics, the text material is not "dumbed down." It still includes the most important research by scholars in the field.

"Questions to Consider" Each chapter opens with a set of questions for students to think about as they read through the material. These questions include factual queries as well as opinion surveys, which are deliberately designed to inspire debate. For example, students are asked to consider whether states should deny welfare benefits to illegal aliens or whether they generally favor affirmative action. Many of these interactive questions are also found on our Web site (*www.prenhall.com/dye*). After students answer the questions online, they can immediately see how their peers around the country answered the same questions.

"People in Politics" These features are designed to personalize politics for students, to illustrate to them that the participants in the struggle for power are real people. They discuss where prominent people in politics went to school, how they got started in politics, how their careers developed, and how much power they came to possess. Examples include California Governor Arnold Schwarzenegger; Los Angeles Mayor Antonio Villaraigosa; Rudolph Giuliani; Massachusetts Governor Deval Patrick; Florida Supreme Court Justice Peggy Quince; New York City Mayor Michael Bloomberg; Florida's state party chairwomen Karen Thurman (D); Texas state party chairwoman Tina Benkiser (R); and the late Dr. Martin Luther King, Jr.

"Up Close" These features illustrate the struggle over who gets what. They range over a wide variety of current political conflicts, such as federalism and the drinking age, state constitutions and the right to bear arms, the firing of state employees, political corruption, and the rise and fall of TennCare.

"Rankings of the States" Comparative analysis is used throughout the text both to describe and to explain differences among states and communities in governmental structure, political processes, and public policy. Through the *Rankings of the States* boxes, students can observe their own state in relation to all other states.

"Did You Know?" These features, designed to be both instructive and entertaining, inform students about various aspects of American states and communities—everything from state birds, songs, flowers, and nicknames to ratings for the "most livable" and best-educated states.

Chapter Pedagogy Each chapter contains a running glossary in the margin and Web information designed to help students better master the information as they read and review the chapters.

SUPPLEMENTARY PACKAGE

Instructor's Resource Manual with Test Item File

For each chapter in the book, the *Instructor's Resource Manual* contains a chapter outline, lecture suggestions, and a list of suggested classroom activities and discussion topics. The thoroughly revised *Test Item File* includes questions in multiple choice, true/false, and essay format.

Prentice Hall Test Generator

A computerized version of the test item file, this program allows full editing of the questions and the addition of instructor-generated test items. Other special features include random generation, scrambling question order, and test preview before printing. Available in Windows and Macintosh formats.

MyPoliSciKit

mypoliscikit www.mypoliscikit.com

MyPoliSciKit provides study modules to help students review their understanding of content through multiple choice, true-false, fill-in-the-blank, and essay questions for each chapter.

OneSearch: Evaluating Online Sources with *Research Navigator*™

This brief guide focuses on developing the critical thinking skills necessary to evaluate and effectively use online sources. It also provides an access code and instruction on using *Research Navigator*™, a powerful research tool that provides access to exclusive databases of reliable source material.

Research Navigator™

This exciting new Internet resource helps students make the most of their research time. From finding the right articles and journals to citing sources, drafting and writing effective papers, and completing research assignments, *Research Navigator*™ simplifies and streamlines the entire process. Contact your local Prentice Hall sales representative for more details or take a tour on the Web at *http://www.researchnavigator.com*.

ACKNOWLEDGMENTS

We are deeply indebted to the research scholars whose labors produced the insight and understanding that we try to convey to our readers. This text contains more than 500 research citations relevant to state and local politics in America. Hundreds of scholars have contributed to this impressive body of literature. We have tried our best to accurately describe and interpret their work; we apologize for any errors in our descriptions or interpretations.

The following reviewers provided helpful suggestions for this edition: Rebecca Tatman Klase, Greensboro College; and Ronald Pettus, St. Charles Community College.

Thomas R. Dye

Susan A. MacManus

POLITICS IN STATES AND COMMUNITIES

CHAPTER ONE

POLITICS IN STATES AND COMMUNITIES

QUESTIONS TO CONSIDER

What is the most important responsibility of state and local government in the United States?
- ■ Providing public services
- ■ Managing social conflicts
- ■ Both equally important

Do you think states should encourage citizens to voluntarily patrol borders to control illegal immigration?
- ■ Yes   ■ No

How would you describe your state politically?
- ■ Conservative
- ■ Liberal
- ■ Moderate

What is the most costly state and local government function?
- ■ Education
- ■ Welfare
- ■ Highways

3

A POLITICAL APPROACH TO STATES AND COMMUNITIES

Politics is the management of conflict. Disagreements are often fierce at the state and local levels over everything from the death penalty, stem cell research, and student testing, to which neighborhood will get a new park, what taxes to impose, and how to deal with race and religious controversies. An understanding of "politics" in American states and communities requires an understanding of the major conflicts confronting society and an understanding of political processes and governmental organizations designed to manage conflict. State and local governments do more than provide public services such as education, highways, police and fire protection, sewage disposal, and garbage collection. These are important functions of government to be sure; but it is even more important that government deal with racial tensions, school disputes, growth problems, economic stagnation, minority concerns, poverty, drugs, crime, and violence. These problems are primarily *political* in nature; that is, people have different ideas about *what* should be done, or *whether* government should do anything at all.

Moreover, many of the service functions of government also engender political conflict. Even if "there is only one way to pave a street," political questions remain. Whose street will get paved? Who will get the paving contract? Who will pay for it? Shouldn't we build a new school instead of paving the street?

THE COMPARATIVE STUDY OF STATES AND COMMUNITIES

The task of political science is not only to *describe* politics and public policy in American states and communities, but also to *explain* differences encountered from state to state and community to community through comparative analysis. We want to know *what* is happening in American politics, and we want to know *why*. Which states allow their citizens to vote directly on controversial issues and which states don't? Which states place limits on abortion? Which states tax their citizens heavily and which states have no income tax? What are the most influential lobbying groups in the states? Which states generally vote Democratic and which states can usually be counted on by Republicans? In which states are women most successful in winning office? Which states spend the most for schools? Which states have the death penalty and actually use it? Which cities are leading the "wi-fi" revolution and creating wireless communities? Why do some states *lead* while others *lag* in tackling tough issues? What we really want to understand is the "whos, whats, whens, wheres, hows, and whys" of state and local politics. Most of us will move to vastly different locations several times in our lifetime and will likely encounter situations that upset us to the point where we want to get involved and hold *somebody* accountable. It is hard to fix blame if you do not have a clue about how politics works in different states and communities.

In the past, the phrase *comparative government* applied to the study of foreign governments, but American states and communities provide an excellent opportunity for genuine **comparative study**, which is comparing political institutions and behaviors from state to state and community to community in order to identify and explain similarities or differences.

We want to know what is happening in American politics, and we want to know why.

COMPARATIVE POLITICAL STUDY

Comparing political institutions and behaviors from state to state and community to community in order to identify and explain similarities or differences.

Comparison is a vital part of explanation. Only by comparing politics and public policy in different states and communities with different socioeconomic and political environments can we arrive at any comprehensive explanations of political life. Comparative analysis helps us answer the question *why*.

American states and communities provide excellent "laboratories" for applying comparative analysis. States and communities are not alike in social and economic conditions, in politics and government, or in their public policies. These differences are important assets in comparative study because they enable us to search for relationships between different socioeconomic conditions, political system characteristics, and policy outcomes. For example, if differences among states and communities in educational policies are closely associated with differences in economic resources or in party politics, then we may assume that economic resources or party politics help "explain" educational policies.

State politics are often affected by unique historical circumstances. (See Figure 1–1 and Table 1–1.) Louisiana is distinctive because of its French–Spanish colonial background, and the continuing influence of this background on its politics today. For nine years Texas was an independent republic (1836–1845) before it was annexed as a state by Congress. Eleven southern states were involved in a bloody war against the federal government from 1861 to 1865. Hawaii has a unique history and culture, combining the influence of Polynesian, Chinese, Japanese, and haole civilizations. Alaska's rugged climate and geography and physical isolation set it apart. Wisconsin and Minnesota reflect the Scandinavian influences of their early settlers. Four states—Pennsylvania, Massachusetts, Kentucky, and Virginia—call themselves **"commonwealths,"** but this title has no legal meaning. Life in Florida is more tourist oriented than anywhere else. Michigan is the home of the automobile industry. West Virginia is noted for its mountains and its coal mines. Utah was initially settled by members of the Church of Jesus Christ of Latter-Day Saints, popularly known as the Mormons, and it retains much of its distinctly Mormon culture today.

These unique historical and cultural settings help to shape state political systems and public policies. However, the mere identification of unique traits or histories does not really "explain" why politics or public policy differs from state to state. Ad hoc explanations do not help very much in developing general theories of politics. For example, only Texas has the Alamo and only New York has the Statue of Liberty, but these characteristics do not explain why New York has a state income tax and Texas does not. Students of state politics must search for social and economic conditions that appear most influential in shaping state politics over time in all the states. Despite the uniqueness of history and culture in many of our states, we must *search for explanations* of why state governments do what they do.

Since it is impossible to consider all the conditions that might influence state politics, we must focus our attention on a limited

Each state's politics reflects its own unique history and culture. Hawaii's elected officials wear with pride clothing and flowered leis that have come to symbolize the state, just as many Texas officials love to don cowboy hats.

FIGURE 1–1 **State Histories**

By the Treaty of Paris, 1783, England gave up claim to the thirteen original Colonies, and to all land within an area extending along the present Canadian border to the Lake of the Woods, down the Mississippi River to the thirty-first parallel, east to the Chattahoochie, down that river to the mouth of the Flint, east to the source of the St. Mary's, down that river to the ocean. Territory west of the Alleghenies was claimed by various states but was eventually all ceded to the nation.

In 1803 President Thomas Jefferson engineered the Louisiana Purchase from France; it was the largest acquisition of territory in U.S. history, more than doubling the size of the nation.

American invasions of Canada were failures in both the Revolutionary War and the War of 1812. In the Rush–Bagot Treaty of 1817, the border between the United States and Canada was demilitarized and fixed at the forty-ninth parallel. Later, in 1846, the British relinquished their claims to the Oregon territory south of the forty-ninth parallel.

In 1819 Spain ceded Florida to the United States in the Adams–Onis Treaty, after General Andrew Jackson and his Tennessee volunteers invaded the territory in a war with the Seminole Indians.

Following battles at the Alamo in San Antonio and at the San Jacinto River, Texas declared its independence from Mexico in 1836, but the Mexican government refused to recognize the new Republic. In 1845 Congress annexed Texas at the Republic's request, ending nine years of independence. In 1846 Congress declared war on Mexico and, following the American army's capture of Veracruz and Mexico City, forced that nation to cede the territories that became California, Nevada, Utah, Arizona, and New Mexico. Later, in 1853, the Gadsden Purchase from Mexico extended the U.S. border further south.

Beginning with South Carolina on December 20, 1860, eleven southern states seceded from the United States of America, forming their own Confederate States of America. They were readmitted to the Union following their defeat in the Civil War, after they agreed to ratify the Thirteenth Amendment, abolishing slavery (1865), and later the Fourteenth Amendment, guaranteeing equal protection of the laws (1868), and the Fifteenth Amendment, preventing denial or abridgment of the right to vote on account of "race, color, or previous condition of servitude."

Twice the size of Texas, Alaska was purchased from Russia for $7.2 million in 1867. (At the time Secretary of State William Henry Seward was criticized for his extravagance, and Alaska was dubbed "Seward's folly" and "Seward's icebox.") Hawaii was annexed to the United States by congressional resolution in 1898 without consulting its residents.

Following victories in the Spanish American War in 1898, Spain ceded Puerto Rico, Samoa and Guam, and the Philippines, which remained a U.S. territory until granted independence in 1946. The Virgin Islands were purchased from Denmark in 1917.

TABLE 1–1   The States of the Union

State	Capital	Date Admitted to Union	Chronological Order of Admission to Union
Alabama	Montgomery	Dec. 14, 1819	22
Alaska	Juneau	Jan. 3, 1959	49
Arizona	Phoenix	Feb. 14, 1912	48
Arkansas	Little Rock	June 15, 1836	25
California	Sacramento	Sept. 9, 1850	31
Colorado	Denver	Aug. 1, 1876	38
Connecticut	Hartford	Jan. 9, 1788[a]	5
Delaware	Dover	Dec. 7, 1787[a]	1
Florida	Tallahassee	March 3, 1845	27
Georgia	Atlanta	Jan. 2, 1788[a]	4
Hawaii	Honolulu	Aug. 21, 1959	50
Idaho	Boise	July 3, 1890	43
Illinois	Springfield	Dec. 3, 1818	21
Indiana	Indianapolis	Dec. 11, 1816	19
Iowa	Des Moines	Dec. 28, 1846	29
Kansas	Topeka	Jan. 29, 1861	34
Kentucky	Frankfort	June 1, 1792	15
Louisiana	Baton Rouge	April 30, 1812	18
Maine	Augusta	March 15, 1820	23
Maryland	Annapolis	April 28, 1788[a]	7
Massachusetts	Boston	Feb. 6, 1788[a]	6
Michigan	Lansing	Jan. 26, 1837	26
Minnesota	St. Paul	May 11, 1858	32
Mississippi	Jackson	Dec. 10, 1817	20
Missouri	Jefferson City	Aug. 10, 1821	24
Montana	Helena	Nov. 8, 1889	41
Nebraska	Lincoln	March 1, 1867	37
Nevada	Carson City	Oct. 31, 1864	36
New Hampshire	Concord	June 21, 1788[a]	9
New Jersey	Trenton	Dec. 18, 1787[a]	3
New Mexico	Santa Fe	Jan. 6, 1912	47
New York	Albany	July 26, 1788[a]	11
North Carolina	Raleigh	Nov. 21, 1789[a]	12
North Dakota	Bismarck	Nov. 2, 1889	39
Ohio	Columbus	March 1, 1803	17
Oklahoma	Oklahoma City	Nov. 16, 1907	46
Oregon	Salem	Feb. 14, 1859	33
Pennsylvania	Harrisburg	Dec. 12, 1787[a]	2
Rhode Island	Providence	May 29, 1790[a]	13
South Carolina	Columbia	May 23, 1788[a]	8
South Dakota	Pierre	Nov. 2, 1889	40
Tennessee	Nashville	June 1, 1796	16
Texas	Austin	Dec. 29, 1845	28 *(continued)*

	TABLE I–I	(Continued)		
State	**Capital**	**Date Admitted to Union**	**Chronological Order of Admission to Union**
Utah	Salt Lake City	Jan. 4, 1896	45
Vermont	Montpelier	March 4, 1791	14
Virginia	Richmond	June 25, 1788[a]	10
Washington	Olympia	Nov. 11, 1889	42
West Virginia	Charleston	June 20, 1863	35
Wisconsin	Madison	May 29, 1848	30
Wyoming	Cheyenne	July 10, 1890	44

[a] Date of ratification of U.S. Constitution.
Source: Derived from *Book of the States*, 2007, pp. 556–557.

STATE ECONOMIC DEVELOPMENT

Broadly defined as population growth and the income and educational levels of a state's population.

number of variables. We can begin with economic development—one of the most influential variables affecting state politics and public policy. **Economic development** is defined broadly to include three closely related components: population growth, income, and education.

Population Growth

America has always been a rapidly changing society. As its people change—in numbers, race, ethnicity, income, education, culture—new conflicts arise, some old conflicts burn out, and other conflicts reignite.

The total population of the United States grew by 13.3 percent between 1990 and 2000. But states grew unevenly. California, already the nation's largest state, gained the most numbers of new residents—4.1 million; Texas gained almost as many—3.9 million, followed by Florida—3.0 million. Texas leapt ahead of New York in state rankings by total population.

Population growth *rates*—the percent population increase over the decade—may be better indicators of the changing requirements of state governments to provide public services, as well as the changing politics in the states. The fastest growing states between 1990 and 2000 were the "Sunbelt" states of the West and South. Twelve states, led by Nevada and Arizona, grew by more than 20 percent. In contrast, population growth was sluggish in the "Rustbelt" states of the East and Midwest. Ten of these states grew by less than 6 percent, less than half of the national growth rate. (Louisiana was the only southern state in the slow growth category.) The Census Bureau predicts that by 2011, Florida will edge past New York into third place in total population. The top five fastest-growing states between 2000 and 2030 are projected to be Nevada (114 percent), Arizona (109 percent), Florida (79 percent), Texas (60 percent), and Utah (56 percent). (See "*Rankings of the States:* Population Size and Projected Growth Rate, 2010–2030.")

INCOME

Money that is received as a result of the normal business activities of an individual or a business (e.g., wages).

Income

Rising personal **income** is a key component of economic development. It indicates increased worker productivity and the creation of wealth. Per capita personal income in the United States grew from about $4,000 in 1970 to about $28,500 in 2000. Income is not evenly distributed throughout the states (see "*Rankings of the States:* Income and Education"). Per capita personal income in Connecticut is more than $47,000, but it is less than $25,000 in Louisiana.

Population Size and Projected Growth Rate, 2010–2030

of the STATES

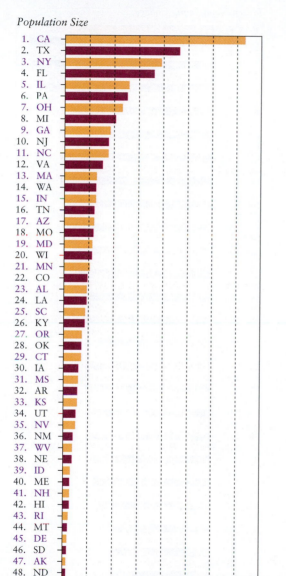

Population Size

1. CA
2. TX
3. NY
4. FL
5. IL
6. PA
7. OH
8. MI
9. GA
10. NJ
11. NC
12. VA
13. MA
14. WA
15. IN
16. TN
17. AZ
18. MO
19. MD
20. WI
21. MN
22. CO
23. AL
24. LA
25. SC
26. KY
27. OR
28. OK
29. CT
30. IA
31. MS
32. AR
33. KS
34. UT
35. NV
36. NM
37. WV
38. NE
39. ID
40. ME
41. NH
42. HI
43. RI
44. MT
45. DE
46. SD
47. AK
48. ND
49. VT
50. WY

0   10,000   20,000   30,000   40,000

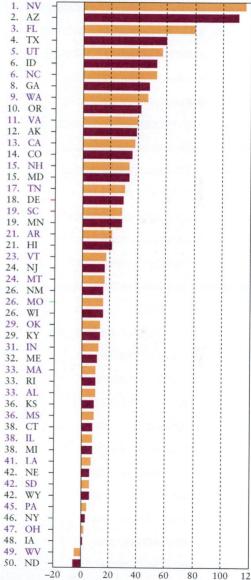

Growth Rate
Percentage Change, 2010–2030

1. NV
2. AZ
3. FL
4. TX
5. UT
6. ID
6. NC
8. GA
9. WA
10. OR
11. VA
12. AK
13. CA
14. CO
15. NH
15. MD
17. TN
18. DE
19. SC
19. MN
21. AR
21. HI
23. VT
24. NJ
24. MT
26. NM
26. MO
26. WI
29. OK
29. KY
31. IN
32. ME
33. MA
33. RI
33. AL
36. KS
36. MS
38. CT
38. IL
38. MI
41. I.A
42. NE
42. SD
42. WY
45. PA
46. NY
47. OH
48. IA
49. WV
50. ND

-20   0   20   40   60   80   100   12

Note: Data are for 2005, in thousands.
Source: U.S. Census Bureau, *Statistical Abstract of the United States 2007.* Available at http://www.census.gov/prod/2006pubs/07statab/pop.pdf, Table 17

Source: U.S. Census Bureau, *Statistical Abstract of the United States 2007.* Available at http://www.census.gov/prod/2006pubs/07statab/pop.pdf, Table 19

RANKINGS
of the STATES

Income and Education

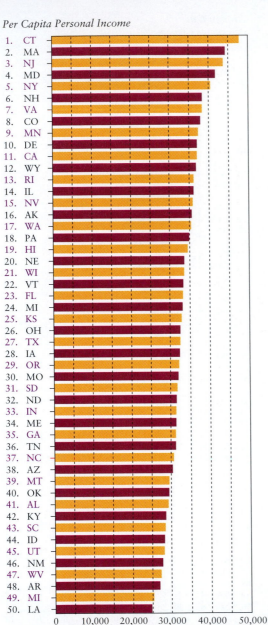

Per Capita Personal Income

1. CT
2. MA
3. NJ
4. MD
5. NY
6. NH
7. VA
8. CO
9. MN
10. DE
11. CA
12. WY
13. RI
14. IL
15. NV
16. AK
17. WA
18. PA
19. HI
20. NE
21. WI
22. VT
23. FL
24. MI
25. KS
26. OH
27. TX
28. IA
29. OR
30. MO
31. SD
32. ND
33. IN
34. ME
35. GA
36. TN
37. NC
38. AZ
39. MT
40. OK
41. AL
42. KY
43. SC
44. ID
45. UT
46. NM
47. WV
48. AR
49. MI
50. LA

0   10,000   20,000   30,000   40,000   50,000

Note: Data are for 2005, in current dollars.
Source: U.S. Census Bureau, *Statistical Abstract of the United States 2007.* Available at http://www.census.gov/prod/2006pubs/07statab/income.pdf, No. 660

Percent Completing College

1. CT
2. MA
3. MD
3. NJ
5. CO
6. VT
7. MN
8. NH
9. WA
10. VA
11. HI
12. CA
12. KS
14. NY
15. UT
16. IL
17. RI
18. OR
19. AK
20. AZ
21. ND
21. NM
23. GA
24. ID
25. PA
26. DE
27. FL
28. MT
28. NC
28. TX
31. NE
31. WI
31. SD
34. MO
35. MI
36. IA
37. ME
37. SC
39. OK
40. NE
41. OH
42. IN
43. WY
44. MS
45. TN
46. AL
47. LA
48. KY
49. AR
50. WV

0   5   10   15   20   25   30   35   4

Note: Data are for 2005.
Source: U.S. Census Bureau, *Statistical Abstract of the United States 2007.* Available at http://www.census.gov/prod/2006pubs/07statab/educ.pdf, No. 218.

Education

An economically developed society requires educated workers. Many economists have asserted that economic growth involves an upgrading in the workforce, the development of professional managerial skills, and an increase in the volume of research. These developments obviously involve a general increase in the *educational levels* of the adult population. In 1970 about 11 percent of the adult population of the United States had completed four years or more of college; by 2000 that figure had risen to over 25 percent. But high levels of educational attainment do not prevail uniformly throughout the states (see "*Rankings of the States:* Income and Education").

The extent to which economic development—population growth, income, and education—affects the politics of the states is an important question, which we will return to again in the chapters that follow.

RACE AND ETHNICITY

States differ in the racial and ethnic composition of their populations. These differences account for much of the variation in the politics of states and cities throughout the nation. Later we will be examining racial and ethnic cleavages in voting behavior and political participation (Chapter 4), state legislative politics (Chapter 6), community politics (Chapter 11), and civil rights policy (Chapter 15).

African Americans

Today the nation's 37 million blacks comprise 13 percent of the total population of the United States. (The distribution of blacks among the fifty states in 2000 is shown in "*Rankings of the States:* Hispanic and African American Populations.") In 1900, most African Americans (89.7 percent) were concentrated in the South. But World Wars I and II provided job opportunities in large cities of the Northeast and Midwest. Blacks could not cast ballots in most southern counties, but they could "vote with their feet." The migration of blacks from the rural South to the urban North was one of the largest internal migrations in our history. But blacks have steadily been moving back to the South. Today, 55 percent of the nation's black population lives in the South.

African American candidates have been increasingly successful in winning city and county offices and state legislative seats in the southern states and in big cities throughout the nation. (See Chapter 4 for a discussion of voting rights laws and their impact on the election of minorities.) The largest numbers of black elected officials are found in the southern states. In 1989 the nation's first elected black governor, Douglas Wilder, moved into Virginia's statehouse, once the office of Jefferson Davis, president of the Confederacy. Black candidates have also been increasingly successful in winning elections in large cities throughout the nation. Later in this book we will describe black representation in city councils (see Chapter 11) and in state legislatures (see Chapter 6), as well as civil rights policy (see Chapter 15).

Hispanics

Perhaps the most significant change in the nation's ethnic composition over the last decade is the growth in the numbers and percentage of Hispanic Americans. In 2000, Hispanics became the nation's largest minority. More than one in eight people in the United States are of Hispanic origin. (The term *Hispanic* refers to persons of Spanish-speaking ancestry and culture, regardless of race, and includes Mexican Americans, Cuban Americans,

RANKINGS
of the STATES

Hispanic and African American Populations

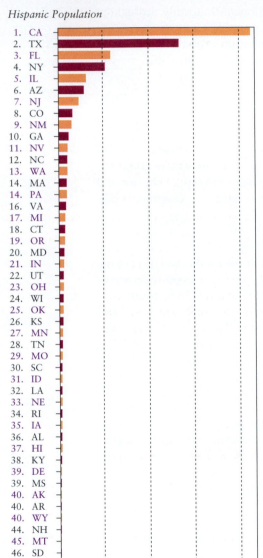

Hispanic Population

1.	CA	
2.	TX	
3.	FL	
4.	NY	
5.	IL	
6.	AZ	
7.	NJ	
8.	CO	
9.	NM	
10.	GA	
11.	NV	
12.	NC	
13.	WA	
14.	MA	
14.	PA	
16.	VA	
17.	MI	
18.	CT	
19.	OR	
20.	MD	
21.	IN	
22.	UT	
23.	OH	
24.	WI	
25.	OK	
26.	KS	
27.	MN	
28.	TN	
29.	MO	
30.	SC	
31.	ID	
32.	LA	
33.	NE	
34.	RI	
35.	IA	
36.	AL	
37.	HI	
38.	KY	
39.	DE	
39.	MS	
40.	AK	
40.	AR	
40.	WY	
44.	NH	
45.	MT	
46.	SD	
47.	WV	
48.	ME	
49.	ND	
50.	VT	

0   3,000   6,000   9,000   12,000

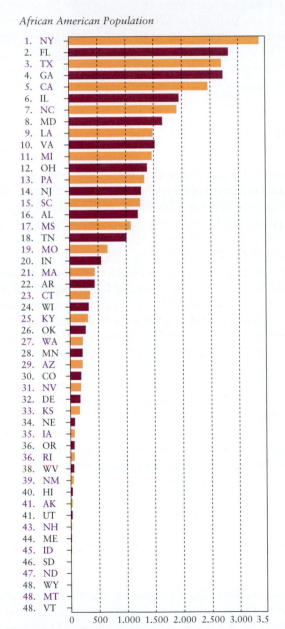

African American Population

1.	NY	
2.	FL	
3.	TX	
4.	GA	
5.	CA	
6.	IL	
7.	NC	
8.	MD	
9.	LA	
10.	VA	
11.	MI	
12.	OH	
13.	PA	
14.	NJ	
15.	SC	
16.	AL	
17.	MS	
18.	TN	
19.	MO	
20.	IN	
21.	MA	
22.	AR	
23.	CT	
24.	WI	
25.	KY	
26.	OK	
27.	WA	
28.	MN	
29.	AZ	
30.	CO	
31.	NV	
32.	DE	
33.	KS	
34.	NE	
35.	IA	
36.	OR	
36.	RI	
38.	WV	
39.	NM	
40.	HI	
41.	AK	
41.	UT	
43.	NH	
44.	ME	
45.	ID	
46.	SD	
47.	ND	
48.	WY	
48.	MT	
48.	VT	

0   500 1,000 1,500 2,000 2,500 3,000 3.5

Note: Data are for 2005, in thousands.
Source: U.S. Census Bureau, *Statistical Abstract of the United States 2007.* Available at http://www.census.gov/prod/2006pubs/07statab/pop.pdf, No. 23

Central and South Americans, and Puerto Ricans.) Today Hispanics slightly outnumber African Americans in the U.S. population (see "*Rankings of the States:* Hispanic and African American Populations"). The largest subgroup are Mexican Americans, some of whom are descendants of citizens living in Mexican territory that was annexed to the United States in 1848 (see Figure 1–1), but most of them have come to the United States in accelerating numbers in recent years. The largest Mexican American populations are found in New Mexico, California, Texas, and Arizona. The second largest subgroup are Hispanics from Central and South America, who are concentrated in the Northeast, South, and West. The third largest

Ethnic-based holidays are often adopted by the community-at-large. In Texas, Cinco de Mayo (5th of May) celebrations, commemorating the victory of the Mexicans over the French at the Battle of Puebla in 1862, are quite popular. Cinco de Mayo festivities feature music, dance, food, and beverages unique to Mexico and reflect the influence that Mexican American immigrants have had on the culture and politics of the state.

subgroup are the Puerto Ricans, many of whom retain ties to the Commonwealth and move back and forth from the island to the mainland, especially to New York City and now central Florida. The fourth largest subgroup are Cubans, most of whom have fled from Castro's Cuba. They live mainly in the Miami metropolitan area. While these groups share a common language and faith (Catholic), they often differ in their political leanings and participation rates due to varied cultural backgrounds and length of residency in the United States[1] (see Chapter 15).

Asians and Pacific Islanders

The Asian population of the nation, nearly 14 million (5 percent of the nation's total), is actually growing more rapidly than any other minority. One-half of Asians and Pacific Islanders live in the West. California has the largest Asian population (4.6 million) but Asians are a majority (58 percent) of the population of Hawaii, the only state with a "majority minority" population. Asians, like Hispanics, are not a monolithic group either ethnically or politically.[2] There are significant language and cultural differences among Chinese, Japanese, Koreans, Cambodians, Malaysians, Pakistanis, Filipinos, Thais, Hmong, Laotians, and Vietnamese Americans. Pacific Islanders, those with origins in Hawaii, Guam, Samoa, or other Pacific Islands, also have unique heritages.

Asians, like Hispanics, are not a monolithic group either ethnically or politically.

Native Americans

It is estimated that 10 million Native Americans (American Indians and Alaska Natives) once inhabited the North American continent. By 1900 the Native American population had been reduced to barely a half million by wars, diseases, and forced privations inflicted upon them. Today Native Americans number over 2.5 million, or 1 percent of the U.S. population. There are more than 562 Indian tribes and Alaska Native groups that speak more than 250 languages. Each tribe has its own culture, history, and identity.[3] The ten largest American Indian tribal groups are the Cherokee, Navajo, Latin American Indian, Choctaw, Sioux, Chippewa, Apache, Blackfeet, Iroquois, and Pueblo. The four largest Alaska native tribal groups are Eskimo, Tlingit-Haida, Alaska Athabascan, and Aleut. The eleven states with the largest Native American populations are, in descending order, California, Oklahoma, Arizona, Texas, New Mexico, New York, Washington, North Carolina, Michigan, Alaska, and Florida (see Chapter 15). Approximately half of all Native Americans live on semiautonomous reservations in various states.

THE POLITICS OF IMMIGRATION

America is a nation of immigrants, from the first "boat people," the Pilgrims, to the latest Haitian and Cuban refugees. Americans are proud of their immigrant heritage and the freedom and opportunity the nation has extended to generations of "huddled masses yearning to breathe free"—words emblazoned upon the Statue of Liberty in New York's harbor. Continuing immigration, together with differences in birth and death rates, is expected to change the ethnic composition of the nation considerably over the next half-century (see Figure 1–2).

Most immigrants come to the United States for economic opportunity. Others come to escape oppression and discrimination. Most personify the traits we typically think of as American—opportunism, ambition, perseverance, initiative, and a willingness to work hard. As immigrants have always done, they frequently take dirty, low-paying, thankless jobs that other Americans shun. When they open their own businesses, they often do so in blighted, crime-ridden neighborhoods long since abandoned by other entrepreneurs.

FIGURE 1–2 Current and Projected Racial and Ethnic Characteristics of U.S. Population

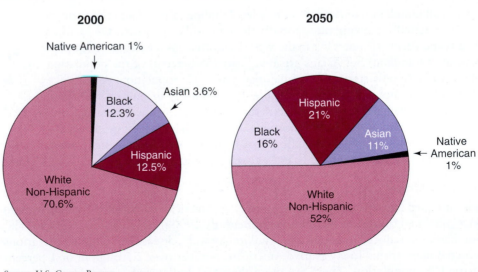

2000

Native American 1%
Black 12.3%
Asian 3.6%
Hispanic 12.5%
White Non-Hispanic 70.6%

2050

Hispanic 21%
Black 16%
Asian 11%
Native American 1%
White Non-Hispanic 52%

Source: U.S. Census Bureau

National Immigration Policy

Immigration policy is a responsibility of the national government. Today, roughly a million people per year are admitted *legally* to the United States as "lawful permanent residents" (persons who have needed job skills or who have relatives who are U.S. citizens) or as **"political refugees"** (persons with "a well-founded fear of persecution" in their country of origin). In addition, each year more than 25 million people are awarded temporary visas to enter the United States for study, business, or pleasure. Finally, it is estimated that 2 to 3 million *illegal* immigrants come to America each year.

Immigration "reform" was the announced goal of Congress in the Immigration Reform and Control Act of 1986, also known as the Simpson–Mazzoli Act. It sought to control immigration by placing principal responsibility on employers; it set fines for knowingly hiring **illegal aliens**. However, it allowed employers to accept many different forms of easily forged documentation and at the same time subjected them to penalties for discrimination against legal foreign-born residents. To win political support, the act granted **amnesty** to illegal aliens who had lived in the United States since 1982. But the act failed to reduce the flow of either legal or illegal immigrants.

Illegal Immigration

In theory, a sovereign nation should be able to maintain secure borders, but in practice the United States has been unwilling and unable to do so. Estimates of **illegal immigration** vary wildly, from the official **U.S. Immigration and Customs Enforcement** (ICE) estimate of 400,000 per year (about 45 percent of the legal immigration), to unofficial estimates ranging up to 3 million per year. ICE estimates that about 4 million illegal immigrants currently reside in the United States; unofficial estimates range from 12 to 15 million or more. Many illegal immigrants slip across U.S. borders or enter ports with false documentation, while many more overstay tourist or student visas.

AMERICA'S MIXED MESSAGE...

POLITICAL REFUGEE

Those residing in the U.S. because they have "a well-founded fear of persecution" in their country of origin.

ILLEGAL ALIENS

Persons residing illegally in a nation, sometimes referred to as undocumented residents.

ALIENS

Persons residing in a nation who are not citizens.

AMNESTY

Government forgiveness of a crime, usually granted to a group of people.

ILLEGAL IMMIGRATION

The unlawful entry of people from other nations into the United States.

IMMIGRATION AND CUSTOMS ENFORCEMENT (ICE) AGENCY

Federal agency responsible for the enforcement of immigration and customs laws.

Border control is an expensive and difficult, but not impossible, task. Localized experiments in border enforcement have indicated that illegal immigration can be reduced by half or more with significant increases in ICE personnel and technology. However, political opposition to increased border enforcement and reduced immigration comes from a variety of sources. Large numbers of Americans identify with the aspirations of people striving to come to America, whether legally or illegally. Many Americans still have relatives living abroad who may wish to immigrate. Hispanic groups have been especially concerned about immigration enforcement efforts that may lead to discrimination against all Hispanic Americans. Powerful groups benefit from the availability of illegal immigrants, such as the agriculture, restaurant, clothing, and hospital industries; they regularly lobby in Washington to weaken enforcement efforts. Some employers prefer hiring illegal immigrants (*los indocumentados*) because they are willing to work at hard jobs for low pay and few if any benefits. Even "high-tech" firms have found it profitable to bring in English-speaking immigrants as computer programmers.

Immigration and Federalism

Although the federal government has exclusive power over immigration policy, its decisions have very significant effects on states and communities.

Although the federal government has exclusive power over immigration policy, its decisions have very significant effects on states and communities—on their governmental budgets, on the use of their public services, and even on their social character. Immigration is by no means uniform across the states. On the contrary, legal and illegal immigration are concentrated in relatively few states. California, Hawaii, New York, Florida, and Texas have the highest proportions of legal immigrants among their populations. And these states, together with Arizona, New Mexico, Colorado, Illinois, and New Jersey, probably have the highest numbers of illegal immigrants as well. (See Figure 1–3.) Moreover, the populations of particular cities—such as Los Angeles, Miami, El Paso, and San Antonio—may be one-third to one-half foreign born.

Occasionally states and cities have attempted to enact their own versions of immigration reform. In 1994 California voters approved a referendum, Proposition 187, which would have barred welfare and other benefits to persons living in the state illegally. A federal court later declared major portions of Proposition 187 unconstitutional. And the U.S. Supreme Court has held that a state may not bar the children of illegal immigrants from attending public schools. Some cities with politically liberal electorates (for example, San Francisco) have declared themselves to be **"sanctuary" cities**, ordering their police officers not to enforce federal immigration laws or even to ask suspects about their immigration status. Some cities with more conservative voters have adopted ordinances making it illegal for landlords to rent to illegal immigrants or employers to hire them. Federal courts have invalidated most of these laws as an unconstitutional interference in the exercise of federal power.[4]

Federal immigration policies impose expensive unfunded mandates on the states. (For a general discussion of unfunded mandates, see Chapter 3.) Although family "sponsors" may have pledged support of immigrants, and immigrants who become a "public charge" may be deported legally, these provisions of the law are almost never enforced. States and cities are obliged to provide educational, health, and social services to immigrants, both legal and illegal. Thus, federal immigration policy heavily impacts state and local budgets, especially in California, Florida, Texas, and other states with disproportionate numbers of immigrants.

FIGURE 1–3 Estimates of Undocumented Migrant Population by State

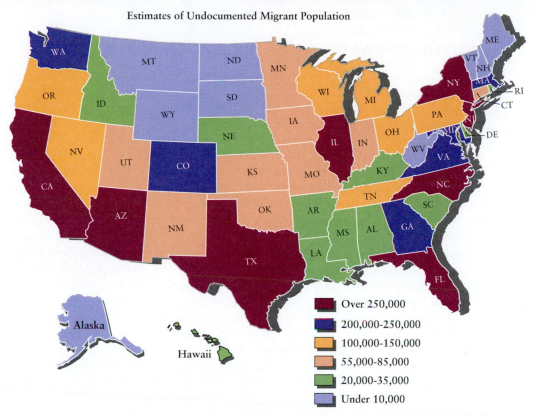

Estimates of Undocumented Migrant Population

■ (Over 250,000)	Over 250,000
■ (200,000-250,000)	200,000-250,000
■ (100,000-150,000)	100,000-150,000
■ (55,000-85,000)	55,000-85,000
■ (20,000-35,000)	20,000-35,000
■ (Under 10,000)	Under 10,000

Source: Pew Hispanic Center estimates based on March 2002, 2003, and 2004 Current Population Surveys.

Conflict over Immigration Reform

Conflict in Washington over immigration policy is intense. To date, this conflict has prevented any effective action to halt illegal immigration or to determine the status of millions of illegal immigrants or to decide how many aliens should be admitted each year and what the criteria for their admission should be. Congress and President George W. Bush wrestled with these questions in a comprehensive 789-page bill in 2007. The bill tried to compromise diverse interests—employers seeking to keep immigration as open as possible, millions of illegal immigrants seeking a legal path to citizenship, citizens seeking border security and opposed to any form of amnesty for illegal aliens. The bill's major provisions included: strengthening border enforcement, including funding of 700 miles of fencing along the 2000-mile Mexican border; granting legal status to millions of undocumented immigrants currently living in the country; providing a path to citizenship that included criminal background checks, paying fines and fees, and acquiring English proficiency; establishing a temporary (two-year) guest worker program; and shifting the criteria for legal immigration from

Citizens opposed to giving amnesty to illegal immigrants currently in the U.S. complain that "illegals" receive services like health care for free while they do not.

It does appear that some states have developed historical traditions of Democratic and Republican party affiliation, as well as cultural patterns of liberal and conservative politics, that are indepen-dent of any demo-graphic features of their populations.

family-based preferences to a greater emphasis on skills and education. Opponents of one or another of these various provisions, both Democrats and Republicans, united to defeat the bill in the U.S. Senate.

LIBERALISM AND CONSERVATISM IN THE STATES

State politics differ in their prevailing ideological predispositions—that is, whether they are predominantly "liberal" or "conservative." There are various ways of defining and measuring ideological predispositions.[5] Liberal and conservative states might be identified in terms of their policy enactments. For example, "policy liberalism" might be defined as the adoption of relaxed eligibility standards for receipts of welfare and medical benefits, decriminalization of marijuana possession and an absence of the death penalty, extensive regulation of business, state ratification of the Equal Rights Amendment, and the adop-tion of progressive state income taxes; "policy conservatism" would be defined as the opposite of these enactments. Scholars frequently construct new policy liberalism rank-ings for states based on key ideological issues of the day. One such index includes state positions on five issues: gun control, abortion laws, welfare eligibility and work require-ments, tax progressivity, and unionization.[6] (See "*Rankings of the States:* State Policy Liberalism.") The most liberal states are California, New York, Vermont, Massachusetts, Connecticut, Minnesota, and Oregon. Mississippi, Arkansas, Louisiana, Georgia, Tennessee, Florida, Wyoming, and the Dakotas are among the most conservative.

The ideological profiles of the fifty states can also be constructed using voters' self-identification.[7] A common question in opinion polls is, "How would you describe your views on most political matters? Generally do you think of yourself as liberal, moder-ate, or conservative?" Nationally, among voters, 21 percent describe their ideological disposition as liberal, 45 percent as moderate, and 34 percent as conservative.[8] Historically, researchers have found that the ideological identification of the voters in the states correlates closely with measures of policy liberalism and conservatism.[9]

Ethnic Influences

Patterns of immigration in the states have left their mark. It should come as no surprise that Canada is the leading country of origin for the states on our north-ern border, and Mexico is the leading country of origin for the states on our southern border. The Spanish heritage in Texas, New Mexico, Arizona, and southern California is important politically as well as culturally. Likewise, the Cuban heritage in southern Florida creates the cultural background for politics in that state. Ethnicity-based political cultures throughout the nation show dis-tinctive patterns based on the prevalence of "Nordic" (e.g., Wisconsin, Min-nesota, North Dakota), "Hispanic" (e.g., Texas, New Mexico, Arizona), "Mormon" (e.g., Utah), and other cultural influences.[10]

State Political Cultures

Do the states exhibit separate and identifiable political cultures? That is, are there political differences among the states that cannot be accounted for by demographic characteristics, for example, race, ethnicity, income, or education? It does appear that some states have developed historical traditions of Demo-cratic and Republican party affiliation, as well as cultural patterns of liberal and

State Policy Liberalism

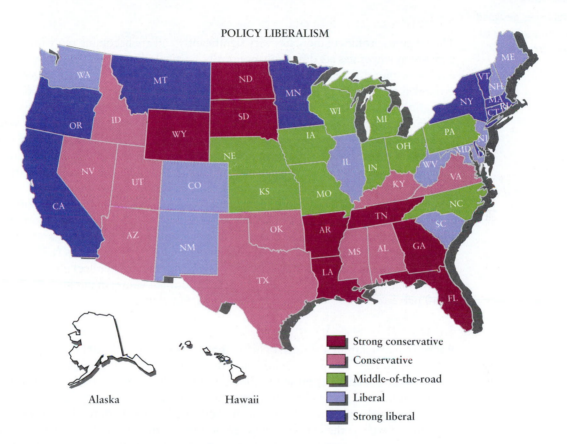

POLICY LIBERALISM

Alaska   Hawaii

Legend:
- Strong conservative
- Conservative
- Middle-of-the-road
- Liberal
- Strong liberal

Note: Data are for 2002. Ranked 1 = most liberal, 48 = most conservative.
Source: Data from "Public Opinion, Public Policy and Organized Interests in the American States" by Virginia Gray, David Lowery, Matthew Fellowes, and Andrea McAtee, *Political Research Quarterly*, Volume 57, No. 3 (2004), pp. 411–420. Copyright © 2004. Reprinted by permission of Sage Publications, Inc.

POLITICAL CULTURE

Historical styles and traditions in states' politics that cannot be directly attributed to demographic factors.

WEDGES

Moral issues designed to cause someone to cross party lines.

conservative politics, that are independent of any demographic features of their populations. For example, Minnesota has developed a liberal and Democratic tradition, Indiana a conservative and Republican tradition, and neither can be fully explained by the socioeconomic composition of their populations. The liberal politics of Massachusetts, Rhode Island, and Oregon, as well as the conservative politics of Tennessee, North Dakota, and Utah, are not fully explained by characteristics of these states' populations or by specific historical events. So we attribute to **"political culture"** the unexplained variation in partisan affiliations and ideological predispositions that we cannot explain by social or economic factors.

Religion in the States

The religious profiles of the states vary significantly and are becoming more important in explaining why states act differently politically, particularly on highly divisive, politically explosive moral issues.[11] A voter's position on these media-grabbing issues may be grounded in religious beliefs and may be a stronger voting cue than one's political party affiliation, although the two are often related.[12] Consequently, moral issues (like same-sex marriage) are increasingly being used by political parties and candidates as **wedges**, designed to cause someone to cross party lines on those hot-button issues alone. Putting such issues on the ballot in the form of an amendment is seen as a way to boost turnout among religious conservatives, regardless of whether they are Republicans or Democrats. Liberals, in turn, use such amendments as tools to turn out their own voters, many of whom are more concerned about the blurring of church and state than the issue itself.

Actually, it is the frequency of a person's religious service attendance more than an individual's specific faith that is often the best determinant of his or her stance on moral issues. (See "*Up Close:* Religion and Politics: The Culture Wars Intensify.") According to a Gallup poll, 71 percent of Americans who attend religious services on a weekly basis believe that the government should promote traditional values in our society compared to 40 percent of those who seldom or never attend church.[13]

Leadership

Political leadership in a state also helps shape its politics and public policy. While we can systematically examine the influence of population size and growth, income, education, race, and ethnicity on state politics, we must also remind ourselves that from time to time individual leaders have brought about political change in their states—change that might not have occurred without their efforts. Electoral politics in states and communities as well as the nation encourage political entrepreneurship—that is, electoral politics provide incentives for candidates to propose policy innovations in order to publicize themselves and win votes.

POLICY RESPONSIBILITIES OF STATES AND COMMUNITIES

Despite the glamour of national politics, states and communities carry on the greatest volume of public business, settle the largest number of political conflicts, make the majority of policy decisions, and direct the bulk of public programs. They have the major responsibility for maintaining domestic law and order, for educating the children, for moving Americans from place to place, and for caring for the poor and the ill.

up CLOSE

Religion and Politics:
The Culture Wars Intensify

"There are two things we don't talk about outside the home—religion and politics." This parental advice, common in days past, is rarely heeded by either parents or their offspring in today's tumultuous times. Increasingly, religion and politics are closely linked in the rough-and-tumble world of politics as moral issues become more prevalent. The "culture wars" or values battles get massive media attention. Citizens' views on issues like stem cell research, medicinal marijuana, same-sex marriage, abortion, euthanasia, gambling, public posting of the Ten Commandments, and the word *God* in the pledge of allegiance often stem from deeply held religious convictions or fervent beliefs about the separation of church and state.

Roughly six in ten Americans see religion as "very important" in their lives. Overall, 57 percent of Americans describe themselves as Protestant (Baptist, Lutheran, Methodist, Presbyterian, Episcopalian, Pentecostal, Jehovah's Witness, Church of Christ), 23 percent as Roman Catholic, 2 percent as Jewish, 2 percent Mormon, 1 percent Orthodox Church (Greek or Russian), 2 percent Other, and 11 percent as no religion. But there is widespread variation in religious preferences across the states. The most religious states are those "in the traditional Bible Belt—from Texas stretching eastward to the Carolinas and northward to Kentucky and West Virginia. . . . The least religious states consist of the 'Left Coast'—California, Oregon, and Washington—almost all of the New England States, and Minnesota."[1]

Gallup polls show that Rhode Island is the most Catholic of any state, Utah the most Mormon, New York the most heavily Jewish, Alabama the most heavily Protestant, and Oregon the most heavily secular (nonreligious). Regionally, the highest proportion of Protestants lives in the southern states, Catholics in the northeast; Jews in the northeast; Mormons in Utah; and atheists and agnostics (secularists) in the West, especially in Oregon, Idaho, and Washington.

Actually, the fervor with which one embraces religion (frequency of attendance at religious services; importance of religion in one's life) is often a better predictor of issue preferences than one's actual religious preference. Public opinion surveys reveal that more religiously engaged persons see moral issues, like same-sex marriage, stem cell research, abortion, public display of the Ten Commandments, and euthanasia, differently than less religiously active persons. This is precisely why political analysts and campaign consultants take a careful state-by-state look at a population's religiosity in crafting campaign strategies and in trying to understand policy differences.

Religious Commitment Affects Views on Moral Issues

Moral Issue	Religious Commitment*		
	Low (%)	Moderate (%)	High (%)
More important not to destroy embryos than to conduct stem cell research	20	30	53
Believe it is proper to display the Ten Commandments in government buildings	56	78	84
Oppose allowing homosexuals to marry legally	43	57	79

*Note: Commitment is an index combining respondents' attendance of religious services and importance of religion in their lives.

Stem-cell researcher.

[1]Analysis based on a study by The Pew Research Center For The People & The Press ("The 2004 Political Landscape") and reported by Jody Brown, "Poll Reveals Religious Beliefs Critical Factor in Political Preferences," accessed at www.catholicexchange.com/vm/PFarticle.asp?vm_id=31&art_id=21891&sec_id=41759, May 10, 2005.
Sources: Jeffery M. Jones, "Tracking Religious Affiliation, State by State," The Gallup Organization, June 22, 2004; The Pew Research Center For The People & The Press, "GOP The Religion-Friendly Party," August 24, 2004.

They regulate the provision of water, gas, electric, and other public utilities; share in the regulation of insurance and banking enterprises, regulate the use of land; and supervise the sale of ownership of property. Their courts settle by far the greatest number of civil and criminal cases. In short, states and communities are by no means unimportant political systems. Each state determines for itself via the state constitution or state laws whether a function will primarily be funded and performed by the state government or by various local governments—cities, counties, school districts, or other local entities. In many instances, both state and local government dollars help support a specific service.

Education

Education is the most costly function of state and local governments (combined). (See Figure 1–4.) Local governments spend a larger portion of their budget on education than state governments, but each helps fund this critical activity. States and communities are responsible for decisions about what should be taught in the public schools, how much should be spent on the education of each child, how many children should be in each classroom, how often they shall be tested, how much teachers should be paid, how responsibilities in education should be divided between state and local governments, what qualifications teachers must have, what types of rates and taxes shall be levied for education, and many other decisions that affect the life of every child in America. Support for higher education, including funds for state and community colleges and universities, is now a major expenditure of state governments.

Education is the most costly function of state and local governments (combined).

Education is one of the most costly functions performed by state and local governments. Some of the most intense fights in state legislatures are over how much money to spend on K–12 education versus higher education (community colleges and universities).

FIGURE 1–4 **How State and Local Governments Spend Their Money**

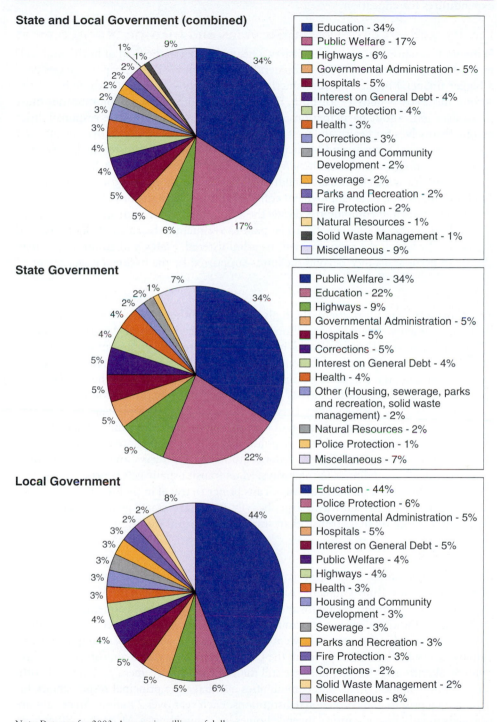

State and Local Government (combined)

- Education - 34%
- Public Welfare - 17%
- Highways - 6%
- Governmental Administration - 5%
- Hospitals - 5%
- Interest on General Debt - 4%
- Police Protection - 4%
- Health - 3%
- Corrections - 3%
- Housing and Community Development - 2%
- Sewerage - 2%
- Parks and Recreation - 2%
- Fire Protection - 2%
- Natural Resources - 1%
- Solid Waste Management - 1%
- Miscellaneous - 9%

State Government

- Public Welfare - 34%
- Education - 22%
- Highways - 9%
- Governmental Administration - 5%
- Hospitals - 5%
- Corrections - 5%
- Interest on General Debt - 4%
- Health - 4%
- Other (Housing, sewerage, parks and recreation, solid waste management) - 2%
- Natural Resources - 2%
- Police Protection - 1%
- Miscellaneous - 7%

Local Government

- Education - 44%
- Police Protection - 6%
- Governmental Administration - 5%
- Hospitals - 5%
- Interest on General Debt - 5%
- Public Welfare - 4%
- Highways - 4%
- Health - 3%
- Housing and Community Development - 3%
- Sewerage - 3%
- Parks and Recreation - 3%
- Fire Protection - 3%
- Corrections - 2%
- Solid Waste Management - 2%
- Miscellaneous - 8%

Note: Data are for 2003. Amount in millions of dollars.
Source: U.S. Census Bureau, *Statistical Abstract of the United States 2007*; Accessed at http://www.census.gov/compendia/statab/2007edition.html, No. 425.

The federal government has never contributed more than 10 percent of the nation's total expenditures for education.

Health and Welfare (Social Services and Income Maintenance)

States and communities continue to carry a heavy burden in the field of health and welfare—despite an extensive system of federal grants-in-aid for this purpose. States bear a bigger financial burden for this function than local governments, although it is the second most costly activity for both. (See Figure 1–4.) States and communities must make decisions about participation in federal programs and allocate responsibilities among themselves for health and welfare programs. While the federal government itself administers Social Security and Medicare, state governments administer the largest public assistance programs—Temporary Assistance for Needy Families (cash aid, formerly Aid to Families with Dependent Children), Medicaid (health care for the poor), and food stamps, as well as unemployment compensation. Within the broad outlines of federal policy, states and communities decide the amount of money appropriated for health and welfare purposes, the benefits to be paid to recipients, the rules of eligibility, and the means by which the programs will be administered. States and communities may choose to grant assistance beyond the limits supported by the national government.

Transportation

Transportation—more particularly, highways—is another key function of state and local governments. There are 4 million miles of surfaced roads in America, and over 230 million registered motor vehicles in the nation. States and communities must make decisions about the allocation of money for streets and highways, sources of funds for highway revenue, the extent of gasoline and motor vehicle taxation, the regulation of traffic on the highways, the location of highways, the determination of construction policies, the division of responsibility between state and local governments for highway financing administration, the division of highway funds between rural and urban areas, and other important issues in highway politics. While the federal government is deeply involved in highway construction, federal grants for highways amount to less than 30 percent of all expenditures for highways. Mass transit usually gets short-changed next to highways because a majority of Americans prefer to travel in their own car over riding buses or taking the subway. Large, heavily urbanized states generally spend proportionately more on mass transit than smaller, more rural states.

Public Safety

States and communities have the principal responsibility for public safety in America (see "*People in Politics:* Rudy Giuliani: From New York City Mayor to the White House?"). State police have important highway safety responsibilities and cooperate with local authorities in the apprehension of criminals. However, community police forces continue to be the principal instrument of law enforcement and public safety. Local governments employ nearly half a million police in the United States today, and almost as many firefighters. Sheriffs and their deputies are still the principal enforcement and arresting officers in rural counties. States and communities also have the principal responsibility for maintaining prisons and correctional institutions. Each year over 2 million Americans are prisoners in jails, police stations, juvenile homes, or penitentiaries. More than 90 percent of these prisoners are in state and local rather than federal institutions.

Rudy Giuliani: From the Mayor's Mansion to the White House?

In recent years, the most successful path to the White House has been through the governor's office. Rarely has a big city mayor even attempted to make a run for president. So it was quite newsworthy when former New York City Mayor Rudy Giuliani made it official in 2007 that he was running for president. At the same time, it was not surprising that he would make a run, in light of his high name recognition and his experience in crisis management.

In the aftermath of September 11, 2001, New York City Mayor Rudy Giuliani led his city—and the nation—through a horrendous period of turmoil. His efforts inspired *Time* magazine to name him Person of the Year. When major crises, from natural disasters to terrorist attacks, strike at America, it is *state and local government officials* who bear the major responsibility for ensuring the public's safety.

As the grandson of Italian immigrants, Giuliani rose from Catholic high school in Brooklyn, through Manhattan College in the Bronx, to New York University Law School, graduating magna cum laude in 1968. He served in various federal prosecutor positions prior to being appointed U.S. Attorney for the Southern District of New York in 1983. He became a national figure during his successful prosecution of the bosses of New York's notorious Mafia "Five Families" in 1986. Later he successfully prosecuted Wall Street white-collar criminals. He lost a race for mayor of New York City in 1989 but came back to win that post in 1993.

As New York's Mayor, Giuliani quickly established himself as a leader who would govern the city previously declared "ungovernable" by scholars and commentators. He introduced the "broken windows" crime-fighting strategy to the city then ranked among the most crime-ridden in the nation. He insisted on arrests for petty offenses (e.g., subway turnstile jumping, graffiti, vandalism and aggressive panhandling) in order not only to improve the quality of life in the city but also to lead to the capture of suspects wanted for more serious crimes. The strategy was coupled with the use of the latest computer mapping technology to track crime statistics and pinpoint unusual activity in specific neighborhoods.

The introduction of these hard-line tactics created more than a little controversy among civil libertarians and many minority group leaders. But over a five-year period, the city's overall crime rate fell by an unprecedented 57% and murders fell by 65 percent. New York City became the safest big city in the country. Although a Republican in an overwhelming Democratic city, Giuliani was re-elected in 1997 by a wide margin.

On September 11, 2001, Giuliani raced to the World Trade Center Towers even before the second plane hit. He was nearly trapped inside a makeshift command center when the towers imploded. He then led a platoon of city officials through ash and smoke to set up a new command center. He took to the airwaves to calm and reassure New Yorkers and made hundreds of rapid-fire decisions about security and rescue operations. His charismatic presence, compassionate words, and reassuring messages won him the acclamation "Mayor of the World."[a]

Following his two terms as New York City's mayor, Giuliani founded a security consulting business, Giuliani Partners. Later he would join a law firm, Bracewell and Giuliani. He campaigned across the country for Republican candidates, including President George W. Bush (the former governor of Texas) in his 2004 re-election race. He declined an offer by Bush to become Secretary of Homeland Security and turned down an opportunity to challenge Democrat Hillary Clinton for her U.S. Senate seat in 2006. But his personal life could best be described as unstable. He has been married three times. He suffered tabloid coverage of his messy divorces from his first two wives.

Giuliani announced his intention to run for president in November 2006, two full years before the 2008 presidential election. In early 2007, he confirmed his candidacy on *Larry King Live*. Early polls showed him with the highest name recognition and most support as the front runner in the race for the Republican nomination. Yet his position on several hot button social issues remained a problem for him among some conservative Republication voters. Giuliani is on record as a pro-choice supporter of abortion rights, a supporter of gun control,

(continued)

and friendly toward gay rights. In early debates among Republican presidential candidates, he appeared uneasy in defending his positions on moral issues but confident in articulating his stances on homeland security, emergency management, and national defense.

[a]Eric Pooley, "Mayor of the World," *Time* Person of the Year, from the December 31–January 7, 2002 issue, www.time.com/time/poy2001/winner3.html, © 2002, Time Inc. Reprinted by permission.

Civil Rights

The national government has defined a national system of civil rights, but these rights cannot become realities without the support of state and local authorities. States and communities must deal directly with racial problems, such as racial isolation in the public schools, job discrimination, and the existence of segregated housing patterns in the cities. They must also deal directly with the consequences of racial tension, including violence. But in the twenty-first century, civil rights battles are not just racial in nature. Claims of discrimination are on the upswing from older workers, gays and lesbians, women, disabled persons, and immigrants.

Physical Environment

Local governments have the principal responsibility for our physical environment. They must plan streets, parks, and commerical, residential, and industrial areas and provide essential public utilities for the community. The waste materials of human beings—rubbish, garbage, and sewage—exceed one ton every day per person. The task of disposal is an immense one; the problem is not only collecting it, but finding ways to dispose of it. If it is incinerated, it contributes to air pollution; and if it is carried off into streams, rivers, or lakes, it contributes to water pollution. A community's water supply may also be contaminated if pollutants and toxins are buried. Thus, communities are largely responsible for two of the nation's most pressing problems: air and water pollution.

Taxation

To pay for these programs, states and communities must make important decisions about taxation: They must decide about levels of taxation and what tax burdens their citizens can carry. They must determine how much to rely upon income, sales, or property taxation. States and communities must raise nearly $2 trillion per year and at the same time compete with one another to attract industry and commerce. If taxes are too high, businesses and residents alike may leave along with jobs. But if taxes are too low, the quality of life may deteriorate with the same result: loss of jobs and residents. Finding the right level of taxation is one of the toughest jobs facing state and local officials . . . and one of the most perilous politically.

How did the states become states? The original thirteen states did so by ratifying the U.S. Constitution.

"STATES," "DISTRICTS," AND "TERRITORIES"

How did the states become states? The original thirteen states did so by ratifying the U.S. Constitution. The first new states to be admitted were Vermont in 1791 and Kentucky in 1792. States that sought admission began by petitioning Congress to allow them to elect delegates and draw up a state constitution.

Congress granted this permission in a series of enabling acts. Later, when the territorial voters approved the new constitution, the territory formally applied for admission and presented its constitution to Congress for approval. Congress accepted the application by a joint resolution of both houses, and a new star was added to the flag. The last admissions were Alaska and Hawaii in 1959.

Of course, from a political perspective, admission was not always an easy process. Long before the Civil War (or "The War Between the States," as it is still called in parts of the Old South), states were admitted roughly in pairs of free and slave states, so as not to upset the delicate balance in the U.S. Senate. Iowa and Wisconsin were admitted as free states in 1846 and 1848, while Florida and Texas were admitted in 1845 as slave states. When California was admitted as a free state in the famous Compromise of 1850, the balance was tilted toward the free states. The balance was further tipped when Minnesota was admitted in 1858 and Oregon in 1859. The Civil War followed in 1861.

Eleven states seceded from the Union that year—Alabama, Arkansas, Florida, Georgia, Louisiana, Mississippi, North Carolina, South Carolina (December 1860), Tennessee, Texas, and Virginia. Although the Supreme Court later voided the acts of secession as unconstitutional, Congress required all of these states to reapply for admission to the Union. These states were under military occupation by United States troops. The military governments drew up new state constitutions, registered black voters, and sent black representatives to Congress. Congress required these governments to ratify the Thirteenth, Fourteenth, and Fifteenth Amendments in order to be readmitted to the Union. The "reconstructed" southern state governments did so, and all were readmitted by 1870.

When Texas was admitted in 1845, Congress granted it a special privilege: The state might, if it wished, divide itself into four states. This provision recognized that Texas was a separate nation when it chose to become a state. A conservative Congress initially rejected Arizona's constitution because it included the progressive notion of popular recall of judges; the state obligingly changed its constitution, was admitted in 1912, and then promptly amended the constitution to put recall back in. Once admitted, there was nothing the Congress could do about Arizona's recalcitrance.

Hawaii and Alaska were the last states admitted to the Union (1959). Hawaii is the only state with an Asian majority population (64 percent). For many years following its annexation to the United States in 1898, Hawaii's economy depended primarily on sugar and pineapple exports. But today its economy depends heavily on tourism, not only from "the mainland" but also from Japan. Living costs in both Hawaii and Alaska are very high; these states frequently appear at or near the top of state rankings based on dollar amounts.

The District of Columbia

The U.S. Constitution, Article I, Section 8, specified in 1787 that "the seat of the government of the United States" shall be in a "district not exceeding ten square miles" ceded to the federal government by the states (Maryland and Virginia). The District of Columbia (DC) was to be governed by the Congress. In defense of a separate district, Alexander Hamilton wrote

> [Congressional control] of the seat of government . . . is an indispensable necessity. Without it not only the public authority may be insulted and its proceedings interrupted with impunity, but a dependence of the members of the general government of the state comprehending the seat of government . . . might bring the national councils an imputation of awe or influence . . . dishonorable to the government.[14]

Hamilton's language is stiff and formal, but his meaning is clear: Making Washington, DC a state would generate undue local pressure on Congress.

Politically, Washington, DC is heavily Democratic, liberal, and black. Its 607,000 residents are likely to support larger social welfare programs, an expanded bureaucracy, and increased federal spending. Opponents of these policies are not likely to be enthusiastic about DC representation in Congress.

The Twenty-Third Amendment, ratified in 1961, gives Washington, DC full participation in presidential elections. Congress has also granted by law full home rule to the city so it has its own elected mayor and city council. In 1978, Congress passed another constitutional amendment that would grant the District full congressional representation and the right to vote on ratification of future constitutional amendments. However, the necessary three-quarters of the states failed to ratify this amendment. So while DC residents can vote in presidential elections, they are not represented

District of Columbia residents frequently take to the streets to call attention to the fact that they are taxed but have no elected representatives in the U.S. Congress. They want Congress to admit the District to the Union as a state. In the past, a proposed constitutional amendment to give DC full congressional representation failed because the required three-fourths of the states did not ratify it. Some of the reluctance came from states fearing some of the federal funds they then received would go to DC residents. Other states hesitated, citing "not ready for prime time" reasons, namely the inept governance of the District of Columbia by local elected officials.

by voting members in the U.S. Senate or House of Representatives.

Having failed to gain congressional representation by constitutional amendment, District residents and their supporters in Congress turned to a new strategy—calling on Congress to admit the District to the Union as a state. (While the Constitution specifies that Congress shall govern over "such District not exceeding ten miles square . . . as the seat of the government," presumably Congress could satisfy this constitutional mandate by reducing "the seat of the government" to a few blocks surrounding the capitol, while admitting the bulk of the District as a state.) This strategy not only reduces the barrier in Congress from a two-thirds vote to a simple majority vote of both houses, but, more importantly, eliminates the need to secure ratification by three-quarters of the states. Nonetheless, so far Congress has refused to vote for District statehood (presumably the state would be named "Columbia"). Troubles with District self-government have convinced many Congress members that Washington is not ready for statehood. But the District's residents and its shadow (nonvoting) representative in Congress never quit trying.

The Commonwealth of Puerto Rico

Nearly 4 million people live on the Caribbean island of Puerto Rico. They are American citizens, and the government of Puerto Rico resembles a state government, with a constitution and an elected governor and legislature. However, Puerto Rico has no voting members of the Congress and no electoral votes in presidential elections.

The population of Puerto Rico is greater than that of twenty-three states. Over 1 million Puerto Ricans have migrated over the years to the U.S. mainland, particularly to New York City. Median family income in Puerto Rico is the highest in the Caribbean, but it is only half that of the poorest state in the United States. The population is largely Spanish speaking; as citizens they can move anywhere in the United States; and they have been subject to the draft in wartime. The United States seized Puerto Rico in 1898 in the Spanish–American War. In 1950, its voters chose to become a "commonwealth," and self-governing commonwealth status was officially recognized in 1952. In a 1967 plebiscite, 60 percent of Puerto Ricans voted to remain a commonwealth, 39 percent voted for statehood, and less than 1 percent voted for independence. In nonbinding referenda in 1993 and 1998, Puerto Ricans continued to support commonwealth status, but opinion today appears to be almost equally divided between statehood and commonwealth status, with independence as a distant third option.

Puerto Rico is a territory of the U.S. Puerto Ricans who permanently move to the U.S. are entitled to register to vote immediately because all territorial residents are full U.S. citizens. Consequently, candidates running in states with sizable Hispanic populations are more likely to target newly arrived Puerto Ricans than Hispanics from Colombia, Venezuela, Mexico, or other Latin American countries who must first become naturalized citizens before they are eligible to register to vote.

Under "commonwealth" status Puerto Ricans pay no U.S. income tax, although local taxes are substantial. Yet they receive all of the benefits that U.S. citizens are entitled to—Social Security, public assistance, food stamps, Medicaid, Medicare, and so forth. If Puerto Rico was to become a state, its voters could participate in presidential and congressional elections; but its taxpayers would not enjoy the same favorable cost–benefit ratio they enjoy under commonwealth status. Some Puerto Ricans fear that statehood would dilute the island's cultural identity and perhaps force English upon them as the national language. Puerto Rico has its own Olympic team and competes in the Miss Universe pageant as an independent nation.

U.S. Territories

In addition to the Commonwealth of Puerto Rico, the United States has twelve "territories," also known as possessions. The major territories are the U.S. Virgin Islands, American Samoa, Guam, and the Northern Mariana Islands. The residents of all U.S. territories are full U.S. citizens (with the exception of those on American Samoa, who are U.S. nationals but not citizens). These residents possess all the rights and obligations of United States citizens, including Social Security payments and benefits and service in the armed forces, *except for* the right to vote in presidential elections or to vote for representatives in the U.S. Congress. (However, both the Democratic and Republican parties seat voting delegations from the territories at their presidential nominating conventions.)[15]

How the American States Got Their Names

Alabama—Indian for tribal town, later a tribe (Alabamas or Alibamons) of the Creek confederacy.

Alaska—Russian version of Aleutian (Eskimo) word, *alakshak,* for "peninsula," "great lands," or "land that is not an island."

Arizona—Spanish version of Pimo Indian word for "little spring place," or Aztec *arizuma,* meaning "silver-bearing."

Arkansas—French variant of Kansas, a Sioux Indian name for "south wind people."

California—bestowed by the Spanish conquistadors (possibly by Cortez). It was the name of an imaginary island, and earthly paradise, in "Las Serges de Esplandian," a Spanish romance written by Montalvo in 1510. Baja California (Lower California, in Mexico) was first visited by the Spanish in 1533. The present U.S. state was called Alta (Upper) California.

Colorado—Spanish, red, first applied to Colorado River.

Connecticut—From Mohican and other Algonquin words meaning "long river place."

Delaware—Named for Lord De La Warr, early governor of Virginia; first applied to river, then to Indian tribe (Lenni-Lenape), and the state.

District of Columbia—For Columbus, 1791.

Florida—Named by Ponce de Leon on Pascua Florida, "Flowery Easter," on Easter Sunday, 1513.

Georgia—For King George II of England by James Oglethorpe, colonial administrator, 1732.

Hawaii—Possibly derived from native word for homeland, Hawaiki or Owhyhee.

Idaho—A coined name from an **invented** Indian word meaning "gem of the mountains," originally suggested for the Pike's Peak mining territory (Colorado), then applied to the new mining territory of the Pacific Northwest. Another theory suggests Idaho may be a Kiowa Apache term for the Comanche.

Illinois—French for *Illini* or land of *Illini,* Algonquin word meaning "men" or "warriors."

Indiana—Means "land of the Indians."

Iowa—Indian word variously translated as "one who puts to sleep" or "beautiful land."

Kansas—Sioux word for "south wind people."

Kentucky—Indian word variously translated as "dark and bloody ground," "meadow land," and "land of tomorrow."

Louisiana—Part of territory called Louisiana by Sieur de La Salle for French King Louis XIV.

Maine—From Maine, ancient French province. Also: descriptive, referring to the mainland in distinction to the many coastal islands.

Maryland—For Queen Henrietta Maria, wife of Charles I of England.

Massachusetts—From Indian tribe named after "large hill place" identified by Capt. John Smith as near Milton, MA.

Michigan—From Chippewa words *mici gama,* meaning "great water," after the lake of the same name.

Minnesota—From Dakota Sioux word meaning "cloudy water" or "sky-tinted water" of the Minnesota River.

Mississippi—Probably Chippewa; *mici zibi,* "great river" or "gathering-in of all the waters." Also: Algonquin word, *messipi.*

Missouri—Algonquin Indian tribe named after Missouri River, meaning "muddy water."

Montana—Latin or Spanish for "mountainous."

Nebraska—from Omaha or Otos Indian word meaning "broad water" or "flat river," describing the Platte River.

Nevada—Spanish, meaning "snow-clad."

New Hampshire—Named in 1629 by Capt. John Mason of Plymouth Council for his home county in England.

New Jersey—The Duke of York, 1664, gave a patent to John Berkeley and Sir George Carteret to be called Nova Caesaria, or New Jersey, after England's Isle of Jersey.

New Mexico—Spaniards in Mexico applied term to land north and west of Rio Grande in the sixteenth century.

New York—For Duke of York and Albany who received patent to New Netherland from his brother Charles II and sent an expedition to capture it in 1664.

North Carolina—In 1619 Charles I gave a large patent to Sir Robert Heath to be called Province of Carolana, from *Carolus,* Latin name for Charles. A new patent was granted by Charles II to Earl of Clarendon and others. Divided into North and South Carolina, 1710.

North Dakota—Dakota is Sioux for "friend" or "ally."

Ohio—Iroquois word for "fine or good river."

Oklahoma—Choctaw coined word meaning "red man," proposed by Rev. Allen Wright, Choctaw-speaking Indian.

Oregon—Origin unknown. One theory holds that the name may have been derived from that part of the Wisconsin River shown on a 1715 French map as "Ouaricon-sint."

Pennsylvania—William Penn, the Quaker, who was made full proprietor by King Charles II in 1681, suggested Sylvania, or woodland, for his tract. The king's government owed Penn's father, Admiral William Penn, £16,000, and the land was granted in part settlement, the king added the Penn to Sylvania, against the desires of the modest proprietor, in honor of the admiral.

Puerto Rico—Spanish for Rich Port.

Rhode Island—Exact origin is unknown. One theory notes that Giovanni de Verazano recorded an island about the size of Rhodes in the Mediterranean in 1524, but others believe the state was named Roode Eylandt by Adriaen Block, Dutch explorer, because of its red clay.

South Carolina—See *North Carolina*.

South Dakota—See *North Dakota*.

Tennessee—Tanasi was the name of Cherokee villages on the Little Tennessee River. From 1784 to 1788 this was the State of Franklin, or Frankland.

Texas—Variant of word used by Caddo and other Indians meaning "friends" or "allies," and applied to them by the Spanish in eastern Texas. Also written *texias, tejas, teysas*.

Utah—From a Navajo word meaning "upper," or "higher up," as applied to a Shoshone tribe called Ute. Spanish form is Yutta, English Uta, or Utah. Proposed name

Deseret, "land of honeybees," from the Book of Mormon, was rejected by Congress.

Vermont—From French words *vert*/green, and *mont*/mountain. The Green Mountains were said to have been named by Samuel de Champlain. The Green Mountain Boys were Gen. Stark's men in the Revolution. When the state was formed in 1777, Dr. Thomas Young suggested combining *vert* and *mont* into Vermont.

Virginia—Named by Sir Walter Raleigh, who fitted out the expedition of 1584, in honor of Queen Elizabeth, the Virgin Queen of England.

Washington—Named after George Washington. When the bill creating the Territory of Columbia was introduced in the 32nd Congress, the name was changed to Washington because of the existence of the District of Columbia.

West Virginia—So named when western counties of Virginia refused to secede from the United States, 1863.

Wisconsin—An Indian name, spelled Quisconsin and Mesconsing by early chroniclers. Believed to mean "grassy place" in Chippewa. Congress made it Wisconsin.

Wyoming—The word was taken from Wyoming Valley, PA, which was the site of an Indian massacre and became widely known by Campbell's poem "Gertrude of Wyoming." In Algonquin, "large prairie place."

Source: By permission of The Smithsonian Institution Press, Smithsonian Institution, Washington, DC.

A major source of information on state and local government in the United States is the annual publication of the Bureau of the Census, *Statistical Abstract of the United States*, the latest edition of which can be found in the reference section of most libraries. The Census Bureau also maintains one of the most interesting Web sites on the Internet at **www.census.gov.** This home page of the Census Bureau directs visitors to a wide variety of information on "People," "Business," and "Geography" (including maps). The Census Bureau updates the estimated population of the United States on this page every five minutes!

Many of the *"Rankings of the States"* figures in this book are taken from Census Bureau data. For example, if you wish to observe the latest estimates of median family income for each state, click *people*, then *income*, then *median family income by state*. (The states are listed alphabetically with their median family income; you will have to rank them yourself.) From the Census Bureau home page, you can also "select a state" and "get a state profile." Try it for your home state.

www.governing.com

The official Web site of *Governing* magazine—dedicated to the coverage of states and localities (today's news, legislatures, politics, government information technology).

www.firstgov.com

The one-stop shopping site; it is the official gateway, or link, to millions of Web pages from federal, state, local, and tribal governments. It also has a Spanish-language Web portal.

www.newsdirectory.com

This site lets you read virtually every daily newspaper in the United States online, no subscription required.

www.stateline.org

A favorite of professional journalists, state officials, students, and ordinary citizens; covers a wide range of issues—crime, economy, education, energy, environment, health care, homeland security, politics, social policy, taxes and budget, technology, and transportation.

www.ice.gov

Official site of the federal Immigration and Customs Enforcement (ICE) Agency.

CHAPTER TWO

DEMOCRACY AND CONSTITUTIONALISM IN THE STATES

2

QUESTIONS TO CONSIDER

Should same-sex marriages be prohibited by state constitutions?
■ Yes   ■ No

Should voters decide key policy questions themselves in referenda elections, or should voters allow their elected representatives to make these decisions and then reward or punish these representatives in the next election?
■ Voters should decide policy.
■ Elected representatives should decide policy.

Should state constitutions limit the types and amounts of taxes that a state can levy on its citizens?
■ Yes   ■ No

Should state constitutions limit how many terms state legislators can serve?
■ Yes   ■ No

CONSTITUTIONAL GOVERNMENT IN THE STATES

Think state constitutions are dull, unimportant, antiquated documents that are only read by law school students, judges, and an occasional politician? Think that what is in state constitutions cannot easily be changed and is pretty much "set in cement"? Think state constitutions are more interesting to historians than campaign consultants and candidates? Think again! State constitutions are frequently the center of intense, hard-fought, multimillion-dollar political battles over everything from school vouchers, medical malpractice, and gambling to cigarette taxes and sexual assault. Constitutions contain principles worth fighting for—or against. And they are much easier to amend than the U.S. Constitution. Constitutions govern governments. They set forth the structure and organization of government; they distribute powers among branches of government; they prescribe the rules by which decisions will be made. Most important, constitutions limit the powers of government and protect the rights of citizens. All fifty states have written constitutions.

Limited Government

The true meaning of constitutionalism is limited government.

The true meaning of **constitutionalism** is limited government. Today most of the world's governments, including even the most authoritarian regimes, have written constitutions that describe the formal structure of government. But the constitutions of authoritarian regimes rarely place any restrictions on the powers of government. In the English and American political heritage, constitutionalism means that the power of government over the individual is clearly limited, that there are some aspects of life that even majorities cannot regulate, and that government itself is restrained by a higher law. Constitutional government places individual liberty beyond the reach of governments, even democratic governments. Thus, if a majority of voters wanted to prohibit communists, or atheists, or racists, from writing or speaking or organizing themselves, they could not do so under a constitutional government that protects free speech and press and assembly.

All fifty state constitutions limit the powers of state government and protect individual liberty. While we have come to rely principally on the U.S. Constitution for the protection of individual liberty, every state constitution also contains a bill of rights that protects individuals in each state from deprivations of personal liberty by their state government. Most of these state constitutional guarantees merely reiterate rights guaranteed to all Americans in the U.S. Constitution, but some state documents extend rights *beyond* the federal guarantees.

Legal Status

State constitutions are the supreme law of the state. They take precedence over any state *law* in conflict with them. Since constitutions govern the activities of governments themselves, they are considered more fundamental than the ordinary laws passed by governments.

The U.S. Constitution is the *supreme law* of the nation. State constitutions take precedence over state law, but they are subordinate to the U.S. Constitution and the laws of the United States. The U.S. Constitution mentions state constitutions only once, and it does so to assert the supremacy of the U.S. Constitution and the laws and treaties of the United States. Article VI states:

> This constitution, and the laws of the United States which shall be made in pursuance thereof; and all treaties made, or which shall be made, under the authority of the

United States, shall be the supreme law of the land; and the judges in every state shall be bound thereby, *anything in the constitution or laws of any state to the contrary notwithstanding.* (italics added)

Origins of Written Constitutions

Probably no other people in the world are more devoted to the idea of written constitutions than are Americans. This devotion has deep roots in national traditions. In 1215 a group of English lords forced King John to sign a document, later known as the Magna Carta, which guaranteed them certain feudal rights and set a precedent for constitutional government. Although the British political tradition eventually rejected formal written constitutions, the idea of a written constitution was strongly reinforced by the experience in the American colonies. The colonies were legally established by charters given to companies establishing settlements in America. These charters became more elaborate as the colonial ventures succeeded, and dependence on a written code for the regulation of government organization and operation became strongly entrenched in the American colonies.

Probably no other people in the world are more devoted to the idea of written constitutions than are Americans.

Colonial History

The charters, or **"constitutions,"** were granted by royal action, either by recognizing proprietary rights, as in Maryland, Delaware, and Pennsylvania, or by granting royal commissions to companies to establish governments, as in Virginia, Massachusetts, New Hampshire, New York, New Jersey, Georgia, and North and South Carolina. Only in Connecticut and Rhode Island was there much popular participation in early constitution making. In these two colonies, royal **charters** were granted directly to the colonists themselves, who participated in drawing up the charter for submission to the Crown. The important point is that these charters, whatever their origin, were present in all the colonies, and many political traditions and expectations grew up around them.

All the colonies were subject to royal control. Yet colonists looked to their charters for protection against British interference in colonial affairs. This was particularly true in Connecticut and Rhode Island, which had elected governors and legislatures whose acts were not subjected to a royal governor's veto, nor sent to England for approval. The political importance of these early charters is illustrated by the conflict over the Fundamental Orders of Connecticut. In 1685 King James issued an order for the repeal of Connecticut's charter. In 1687 Sir Edmund Androse went to Hartford and in the name of the Crown declared the government dissolved. The charter was not surrendered, however, but hidden by Captain John Wadsworth in an oak tree, which is now displayed for sightseers. Immediately after the English revolution of 1688, the document was taken out of the "Charter Oak" and used again as the fundamental law of the colony. Succeeding British monarchs silently permitted this colonial defiance. After the Declaration of Independence, new constitutions were written in eleven states; Connecticut retained its charter as the fundamental law until 1818, and Rhode Island kept its charter until 1842. The colonial experience, together with the earlier English heritage, firmly implanted the tradition of written consitutions.

State Constitutional Politics

Theoretically, constitutional decision making is deciding *how to decide.* It is deciding on the rules for policymaking; it is not policymaking itself. Policies are to be decided later, according to the rules set forth in a constitution.

CONSTITUTION

The legal structure establishing governmental bodies, granting their powers, determining how their members are selected, and prescribing the rules by which they make their decisions. Considered basic or fundamental, a constitution cannot be changed by ordinary acts of governmental bodies.

COLONIAL CHARTERS

Documents granted to American colonies by English kings establishing governments; fostered the American tradition of written constitutions.

But realistically, all state constitutions not only specify organizations and processes of decision making, they also undertake to determine many substantive policy questions. Unlike the U.S. Constitution, state constitutions contain many policy mandates on topics as diverse as tax rates, utility regulation, labor–management relations, insurance regulation, debt limits, educational funding, gambling, and a host of other policy matters. In nearly every election, voters are asked to decide on proposed amendments to their state constitutions. Most of these amendments deal with policy questions about which the voters have little knowledge or information. The result, of course, is that most state constitutions have become ponderous tomes that look more like law books than constitutions. While the U.S. Constitution contains only about 8,700 words, the average state constitution contains 26,000, and some run to over 100,000 (see Table 2–1). Length itself is not the problem, but, rather, that these constitutions are laden with detailed policy decisions.

Interest Group Influence

Why have so many policy mandates crept into state constitutions? Inasmuch as constitutions govern the actions of governors, legislators, executive agencies, and courts, many special interest groups as well as citizen movements have sought to place their own policy preferences in constitutions. This places these preferences beyond the immediate reach of government officials, who are bound by constitutional mandates. If a policy preference is enacted into state law, it can be changed by ordinary actions of the legislature and governor. But if a policy preference is written into the state constitution, it can be changed only by extraordinary procedures—for most states a two-thirds vote in both houses of the legislature and majority approval of the voters in a statewide referendum. So interest groups frequently strive to "constitutionalize" their policy preferences.

Interest groups frequently strive to "constitutionalize" their policy preferences.

Citizens' Movements

Moreover, grassroots citizen movements in the United States have frequently displayed a distrust of elected officials. Citizens have frequently sought to bind officials by constitutional mandates. Indeed, referenda on proposed state constitutional amendments confront voters in many states in almost every election. Over the years, specific constitutional amendments seeking to tell legislatures and governors what they can and cannot do have been accumulated in lengthy documents. The more detailed and specific a state's constitution, the more likely it is to require more amendments to meet changing circumstances over time, thus leading to an even longer document.

Reformers' Influence

Constitutional reformers and "good government" groups have sought for many years to take policy matters out of the state constitution. They argue that governors and legislators should not be bound by constitutional details, that they need flexibility in confronting new challenges, and that state government should be strengthened, not weakened, in the modern era. These reform efforts have met with some success; newer state constitutions tend to be shorter than older ones. But it has become more difficult for reformers to convince politicians or the public that a state's constitution needs a complete overhaul.

			Number of Amendments			
State	**Number of Constitutions***	**Dates of Adoption**	**Effective Date of Present Constitution**	**Estimated Length**	**Submitted to Voters**	**Adopted**	**Passage Rate (%)**
Alabama	6	1819, 1861, 1865, 1868, 1875, 1901	1901	340,136	1088 [a]	794	73
Alaska	1	1956	1959	15,988	41	29	71
Arizona	1	1911	1912	28,876	254	141	56
Arkansas	5	1836, 1861, 1864, 1868, 1874	1874	59,500	190	92	48
California	2	1849, 1879	1879	54,645	870	514	59
Colorado	1	1876	1876	74,522	315	150	48
Connecticut[b]	4	1818, 1965	1965	17,256	30	29	97
Delaware	4	1776, 1792, 1831, 1897	1897	19,000	N/A[c]	138	N/A
Florida	6	1839, 1861, 1865, 1868, 1886, 1968	1969	51,456	141	110	78
Georgia	10	1777, 1789, 1798, 1861, 1865, 1868, 1877, 1945, 1976, 1982	1983	39,526	86	66	77
Hawaii	1	1950	1959	20,774	128	108	84
Idaho	1	1889	1890	24,232	206	119	58
Illinois	4	1818, 1848, 1870, 1970	1971	16,510	17	11	65
Indiana	2	1816, 1851	1851	10,379	78	46	59
Iowa	2	1846, 1857	1857	12,616	57	52	91
Kansas	1	1859	1861	12,296	123	93	76
Kentucky	4	1792, 1799, 1850, 1891	1891	23,911	75	41	55
Louisiana	11	1812, 1845, 1852, 1861, 1864, 1868, 1879, 1898, 1913, 1921, 1974	1975	54,112	210	150	71
Maine	1	1819	1820	16,276	203	171	84
Maryland	4	1776, 1851, 1864, 1867	1867	46,600	257	221	86
Massachusetts	1	1780	1780	36,700	148	120	81
Michigan	4	1835, 1850, 1908, 1963	1964	34,659	66	28	42
Minnesota	1	1857	1858	11,547	214	119	56

TABLE 2–1   General Information on State Constitutions

(*continued*)

TABLE 2-1 (Continued)

State	Number of Constitutions*	Dates of Adoption	Effective Date of Present Constitution	Estimated Length	Number of Amendments		
					Submitted to Voters	Adopted	Passage Rate (%)
Mississippi	4	1817, 1832, 1869, 1890	1890	24,323	158	123	78
Missouri	4	1820, 1865, 1875, 1945	1945	42,600	170	109	64
Montana	2	1889, 1972	1973	13,145	54	30	56
Nebraska	2	1866, 1875	1875	20,048	344	224	65
Nevada	1	1864	1864	31,377	226	134	59
New Hampshire	2	1776, 1784	1784	9,200	287	145	51
New Jersey	3	1776, 1844, 1947	1948	22,956	74	41	55
New Mexico	1	1911	1912	27,200	284	155	55
New York	4	1777, 1822, 1846, 1894	1895	51,700	291	216	74
North Carolina	3	1776, 1868, 1970	1971	16,532	42	34	81
North Dakota	1	1889	1889	19,130	262	149	57
Ohio	2	1802, 1851	1851	48,521	275	163	59
Oklahoma	1	1907	1907	74,075	340	175	51
Oregon	1	1857	1859	54,083	477	238	50
Pennsylvania	5	1776, 1790, 1838, 1873, 1968	1968	27,711	36	30	83
Rhode Island[b]	3	1842, 1986	1843	10,908	11	10	91
South Carolina	7	1776, 1778, 1790, 1861, 1865, 1868, 1895	1896	22,300	679	492	72
South Dakota	1	1889	1889	27,675	223	213	96
Tennessee	3	1796, 1835, 1870	1870	13,300	61	38	62
Texas	5	1845, 1861, 1866, 1869, 1876	1876	90,000	614	439	71
Utah	1	1895	1896	11,000	158	107	68
Vermont	3	1777, 1786, 1793	1793	10,286	211	53	25
Virginia	6	1776, 1830, 1851, 1869, 1902, 1970	1971	21,319	51	43	84

(continued)

TABLE 2-1 (Continued)

State	Number of Constitutions*	Dates of Adoption	Effective Date of Present Constitution	Number of Amendments			Passage Rate (%)
				Estimated Length	Submitted to Voters	Adopted	
Washington	1	1889	1889	33,564	170	97	57
West Virginia	2	1863, 1872	1872	26,000	121	71	59
Wisconsin	1	1848	1848	14,392	193	144	75
Wyoming	1	1889	1890	31,800	123	97	79

*The constitutions referred to in this table include those Civil War documents customarily listed by the individual states.

[a]The Alabama constitution includes numerous local amendments that apply to only one county.

An estimated 70 percent of all amendments are local.

A 1982 amendment provides that after proposal by the legislature to which special procedures apply, only a local vote (with exceptions) is necessary to add them the the constitution.

[b]Colonial charters with some alterations served as the first constitutions in Connecticut (1638, 1662) and in Rhode Island (1663).

[c]Proposed amendments are not submitted to the voters in Delaware.

Source: For more detailed information, see Book of the States, 2007 (Lexington, KY: Council on State Governments, 2007). Data as of January 1, 2007.

BILL OF RIGHTS

In state constitutions, written protections for basic freedoms; most resemble the Bill of Rights in the U.S. Constitution but some extend these rights.

Growth of State Constitutional Law

Along with interest groups and citizens' movements, lawyers and judges have also contributed to the growth of state constitutional law. In a significant number of cases, state court judges have interpreted their own constitutions independently of the U.S. Constitution regarding civil rights and other controversies (see "The New Judicial Federalism" in Chapter 9). An emerging body of state constitutional law is a reminder of the legal importance of state constitutions.

STATE CONSTITUTIONS: AN OVERVIEW

Bill of Rights

All state constitutions have a bill of rights, which asserts the basic freedoms of speech, press, religion, and assembly. (See "*Up Close:* State Constitutions and the Right to Bear Arms.") There are frequent references to basic procedural rights, such as the writ of habeas corpus, trial by jury, protection against double jeopardy and self-incrimination, as well as prohibitions against ex post facto laws, imprisonment for debt, unreasonable searches and seizures, and excessive bail. Most of these protections merely duplicate the guarantees of the U.S. Constitution. However, frequently one finds in the state constitutions interesting "rights," which are not found in the national Constitution. For example, the Florida Constitution guarantees "every natural person the right to be let alone and free from government intrusion into his private life"; Mississippi guarantees the right of victims of crime to speak in court and receive restitution; Indiana prohibits "unnecessary rigor" in punishment for crime. Some state constitutions have "little ERAs"— equal rights amendments—guaranteeing sexual equality under law. Moreover, a *state* supreme court may place a different interpretation on a state constitutional right than the *federal* courts place on the same guarantee in the U.S. Constitution. (See "Judicial Federalism" in Chapter 9.)

SEPARATION OF POWERS

The constitutional allocation of powers among the three branches of the state government: legislative, executive, and judicial.

Separation of Powers

All state constitutions reflect the American political tradition of separation of powers, with separate legislative, executive, and judicial articles establishing these separate branches of government and ensuring a system of **checks and balances.** Generally, however, state constitutions emphasize legislative power over executive power. The historical explanation for this is that governors were appointed by the king in most colonies and the early constitutions reflected the colonists' distaste for executive authority. Yet the fact that constitutions are usually written by legislatures, legislative commissions, or constitutional conventions that resemble legislatures may also explain why legislative power is emphasized. Finally, the curtailment of executive power may reflect the desires of important interest groups in the states, who would prefer to deal with independent boards and commissions in the executive branch rather than with a strong governor. (See Chapter 7 for further discussion.)

CHECKS AND BALANCES

Constitutional provisions giving each branch of state government certain checks over of other branches.

Weak Governors

Whether the reasons are historical or political, the executive branches of most state governments are weakened and divided by state constitutions. Executive powers are divided among the governor and many separately elected executive officers—attorney general, secretary of state, treasurer, auditor, lieutenant governor, state school superintendent, and others. State constitutions also curtail executive authority by establishing a multitude of boards or commissions to head executive departments. Membership on these boards and commissions is generally for long overlapping terms, which are not identical to the term of the governor.

Legislative Powers

Only the Nebraska Constitution provides for a unicameral legislature. All other state legislatures are **bicameral**—divided into an upper and a lower chamber—making a total of ninety-nine state legislative bodies. In many states the basis for apportioning these bodies is set forth in the state constitution. However, since the guarantee of the U.S. Constitution that no state shall deny to any person the "equal protection of the laws" takes precedence over state constitutions, federal courts require state legislative apportionment in both houses to meet the constitutional standard of one person, one vote. (See Chapter 6.)

Local Governments

All state constitutions have provisions regarding the organization and powers of local government. Local governments are really subdivisions of state governments; they are not independent governmental bodies. State constitutions generally describe the organization of counties, cities, towns, townships, boroughs, school districts, and special districts. They may delegate responsibilities to them for public safety, police, fire, sanitation, sewage and refuse disposal, hospitals, streets, and public health. State constitutions may establish tax and debt limits for local governments, describe the kinds of taxes they may levy, and prescribe the way in which their funds may be spent. In the absence of constitutional provisions governing local governments, these subordinate units must rely upon state legislatures for their organization and powers. In recent years there has been a movement toward greater home rule for communities. More than half the states have provided for some semblance of home rule, which removes some of the internal affairs of communities from the intervention of state legislatures. Of course, when a "home rule" charter is granted to a community by an act of the legislature, it can be readily withdrawn or revised by the legislature. Constitutional home rule is a more secure grant of power to communities than legislative home rule. (See Chapter 10 for further discussion.)

Local governments are really subdivisions of state governments; they are not independent governmental bodies.

Interest Group Regulation

Since state constitutions take precedence over state laws and are more difficult to amend, interest groups prefer to see special protections written into the state's fundamental document. This prevents legislatures from meddling in important business affairs each legislative session. Even reformers sometimes support the inclusion of regulatory language in the state's constitution, out of fear that later lobbying efforts by business could easily change state laws. So most state constitutions include long sections on regulation of insurance, utilities, corporations, alcoholic beverages, railroads, mining, medicine, real estate, the state bar association, and so forth.

Interest groups prefer to see special protections written into the state's fundamental document.

up CLOSE

State Constitutions and the Right to Bear Arms

The Second Amendment to the U.S. Constitution states: "A well-regulated Militia, being necessary to the security of a free State, the right of the people to keep and bear Arms, shall not be infringed." What is meant by the right of the people "to keep and bear arms"?

The Right of States to Maintain Militias

Many constitutional scholars argue that the Second Amendment protects only the *collective* right of the states to form militias—that is, their right to maintain National Guard units. They focus on the qualifying phrase "a well-regulated Militia, being necessary to the security of a free State." The Second Amendment merely prevents Congress from denying the states the right to organize their own military units. If the Founders had wished to create an individual right to bear arms, they would not have inserted the phrase about a "well-regulated militia." (Opponents of this view argue that the original definition of a militia included all free males over age eighteen.) Interpreted in this fashion, the Second Amendment does *not* protect private groups who form themselves into militias, nor does it guarantee citizens the right to own guns.

The Right of Individuals to Bear Arms in Self-Defense

However, another view is that the Second Amendment confers on Americans an *individual* constitutional right, like the First Amendment freedom of speech or press; that is, the right to own and bear arms. The history surrounding the adoption of the Second Amendment reveals the concern of colonists with attempts by despotic governments to confiscate the arms of citizens and render them helpless to resist tyranny. James Madison wrote in the *Federalist Papers* No. 46 that "the advantage of being armed which the Americans possess over the people of almost every other nation, forms a barrier against the enterprise of [tyrannical] ambition."

Thomas Jefferson wrote, "No free man shall ever be debarred the use of arms" in the Virginia Constitution; and he later argued that "Laws that forbid the carrying of arms . . . make things worse for the assaulted and better for the assailants . . . for an unarmed man may be attacked with greater confidence than an armed man."[a]

Gun Control

Federal gun control legislation frequently follows murders or assassination attempts on prominent figures. The Federal Gun Control Act of 1968 was a response to the assassinations of Senator Robert F. Kennedy and Martin Luther King, Jr., in that year. It banned mail-order sales of handguns and required that manufacturers place serial numbers on all firearms, that dealers record all sales, and that dealers be licensed by the Bureau of Alcohol, Tobacco and Firearms. In 1993, Congress passed the Brady Act, requiring a seven-day waiting period for the purchase of a handgun. The act is named for James S. Brady, former press secretary to President Ronald Reagan, who was severely wounded in the 1981 attempted assassination of the president. The Crime Control Act of 1994 banned the manufacture or sale of "assault weapons," generally defined to

include both automatic and semiautomatic rifles and machine pistols.

Proponents of gun control cite the U.S. Supreme Court decision in *United States* v. *Miller* (1939). In this case, the Court considered the constitutionality of the federal National Firearms Act of 1934, which, among other things, prohibited the transportation of sawed-off shotguns in interstate commerce. The defendant claimed that Congress could not infringe upon his right to keep and bear arms. But the Court responded that a sawed-off shotgun had no "relationship to the preservation or efficiency of a well-regulated militia."[b] The clear implication of this decision is that the right to bear arms refers only to a state's right to maintain a militia. But even if an individual has a constitutional right to own a gun,

the Supreme Court is likely to approve of reasonable restrictions on that right, including waiting periods for purchases, reporting, and registration. No constitutional right is viewed as absolute.

State Gun Laws

Many state constitutions include a provision guaranteeing the right to bear arms. Most of these state guarantees do not refer to a militia, but rather to the specific right of people to bear arms in self-defense. For example, Florida's constitution says: "The right of the people to keep and bear arms in defense of themselves and of the lawful authority of the state shall not be infringed." Voters in state referenda have consistently approved of the individual's right to bear arms.

[a]See Stephen P. Halbrook, *That Every Man Be Armed: The Evolution of a Constitutional Right* (Albuquerque: University of New Mexico Press, 1984).
[b]*United States* v. *Miller*, 307 U.S. 174 (1939).

Taxation and Finance

All state constitutions have articles on taxation and finance. Frequently these place severe restrictions on the taxing power of state and local governments. Taxpayer groups distrust state legislatures and wherever possible seek to restrict taxing powers by constitutional mandate. Many referenda votes are designed to amend the state's constitution to limit tax burdens. (See Chapter 14.) Local governments may also be limited in state constitutions to specific tax sources and upper limits or "caps" on local taxation. Certain classes of property may be protected, such as that devoted to religious, educational, or charitable uses; government property; some agricultural or forestry land; and even "**homesteads,**" that is, owner-occupied homes. Some constitutions may grant tax exemptions to new industries in order to attract industrial development. Constitutions may "earmark" certain tax revenues for specific purposes; for example, gasoline taxes may be earmarked for highway use only.

HOMESTEAD
An owner-occupied home; many states grant tax breaks to this type of property.

Debt Limitation

Most state constitutions limit debt that can be incurred by the state only or by local governments. Many states *must* have a balanced operating budget. (Although such a constitutional command does not always succeed, on the whole, state governments are less burdened by debt than is the federal government.) Local governments are frequently limited to a debt that cannot exceed a fixed percentage of the value of property in the community. Moreover, state constitutions generally require a local referendum to approve any increase in local debt. Occasionally, however, state and local governments devise ways to get around constitutional debt limits; for example, they may pledge the revenues of a new project ("revenue bonds") to pay off the debt, rather than taxes ("full faith and credit bonds"). (See Chapter 14.)

CONSTITUTIONAL CHANGE IN THE STATES

The U.S. Constitution has been amended only twenty-seven times in 200 years (and the first ten amendments, the Bill of Rights, were really part of the process of ratifying the original document). But state constitutions are so detailed and restrictive that they must be amended frequently. Nearly every year state voters must consider constitutional amendments on the ballot.

Throughout the fifty states, there are now four methods of constitutional change:

- *Legislative proposal:* Amendments are passed by the state legislature and then submitted to the voters for approval in a referendum. This method is available in all states. (However, in Delaware, amendments passed by the legislature need not be submitted to the voters.)
- *Popular initiative:* A specific number of voters petition to get a constitutional amendment on the ballot for approval by the voters in a referendum. This method is available in seventeen states.
- *Constitutional revision convention:* Legislatures submit to the voters a proposal for calling a constitutional convention, and if voters approve, a convention convenes, draws up constitutional revisions, and submits them again for approval by the voters in a referendum. This method is available in at least forty-one states.
- *Constitutional commission:* Constitutional commissions may be created by legislatures to study the constitution and recommend changes to the state legislature, or in the case of Florida (only), to submit its recommendations directly to the voters in a referendum.

Over the years, the record of voters' response to state constitutional amendments (Table 2–2) shows that voters are more accepting of individual amendments submitted to them by *state legislatures* than any other method of constitutional change. In contrast, most citizen initiatives are defeated at the polls, as are most amendments proposed by constitutional conventions. These figures affirm the key role that state legislatures play in constitutional change. While it is true that many legislative proposals are merely "editorial," voters seem to prefer limited, step-by-step, constitutional change, rather than sweeping reform initiated by citizens.

Legislative Proposal

LEGISLATIVE PROPOSAL

The state legislature places a constitutional amendment on the ballot for voter approval.

The most common method of amending state constitutions is by **legislative proposal**. Many states require that a constitutional amendment receive a two-thirds vote in both chambers of the legislature before submission to the voters; a few states require a three-fifths majority in both houses, while others require only simple legislative majorities. Some states require that a constitutional amendment be passed by two successive legislative sessions before being submitted to the voters. Every state except Delaware requires constitutional amendments proposed by the legislature to be submitted to the voters for approval in a referendum. (See Table 2–3.)

Popular Initiative

POPULAR INITIATIVE

Registered voters sign a petition to place a constitutional amendment on the ballot for voter approval.

Popular initiative for constitutional revision was introduced during the Progressive Era at the beginning of the twentieth century. These states usually require that an initiative

TABLE 2–2   The Success of State Constitutional Amendments by Method of Initiation

Method of Initiation	Total Proposals						Percent Adopted					
	1996–1997	1998–1999	2000–2001	2002–2003	2004–2005	2006	1996–1997	1998–1999	2000–2001	2002–2003	2004–2005	2006
All Methods	233	296	212	232	166	166	76	77	72	71	68	75
Legislative Proposal	193	266	180	208	127	133	82	79	91	75	75	86
Popular (Citizen) Initiative	40	21	32	24	39	33	48	52	41	36	44	33
Constitutional Convention												
Constitutional Revision Commission		9						89				

Source: The Book of the States 2007, volume 39, page 3.

petition be signed by 5, 10, or 15 percent of the number who voted in the last governor's election. The petition method allows citizens to get an amendment on the ballot *without the approval of the state legislature*. It is not surprising that measures designed to reduce the powers of legislators—for example, *tax limitation* measures and *term limits* for legislators—have come about as a result of citizen initiatives.

Constitutional Convention

While there has been only one national Constitutional Convention (in 1787), there have been over 230 state constitutional conventions. State constitutional conventions are generally proposed by state legislatures, and the question of whether or not to have a convention is generally submitted to the state's voters. (Some state constitutions require periodic submission to the voters of the question of calling a constitutional convention.) The legislature usually decides how convention delegates are to be elected and the convention organized. More important, the legislature usually decides whether the convention's work is to be *limited* to specific proposals or topics, or *unlimited* and free to write an entire new constitution.

In recent years, however, neither legislators nor voters have shown much enthusiasm for state constitutional conventions. No state conventions were held in the 1990s. (The Louisiana legislature convened itself as the "Louisiana Convention of 1992," but the meeting was really only a special session of the legislature; moreover, its proposed constitutional revision failed by a wide margin at the polls.) Hawaii voters came close to calling a convention in 1996; they cast more "Yes" than "No" votes but not the necessary majority of *all* votes after blank votes were counted. Indeed, voters have regularly *rejected* convention calls in the states that require periodic votes on whether or not to hold a convention.

TABLE 2–3   State Constitutional Amendment by Legislatures

	Legislative Vote Required for Proposal	Consideration by Two Sessions Required	Referendum Vote Required for Ratification
Alabama	3/5	No	Majority vote on amendment
Alaska	2/3	No	Majority vote on amendment
Arizona	Majority	No	Majority vote on amendment
Arkansas	Majority	No	Majority vote on amendment
California	2/3	No	Majority vote on amendment
Colorado	2/3	No	Majority vote on amendment
Connecticut	(a)	(a)	Majority vote on amendment
Delaware	2/3	Yes	Not required
Florida	3/5	No	Majority vote on amendment
Georgia	2/3	No	Majority vote on amendment
Hawaii	(b)	(b)	Majority vote on amendment
Idaho	2/3	No	Majority vote on amendment
Illinois	3/5	No	(c)
Indiana	Majority	Yes	Majority vote on amendment
Iowa	Majority	Yes	Majority vote on amendment
Kansas	2/3	No	Majority vote on amendment
Kentucky	3/5	No	Majority vote on amendment
Louisiana	2/3	No	Majority vote on amendment
Maine	2/3	No	Majority vote on amendment
Maryland	3/5	No	Majority vote on amendment
Massachusetts	Majority	Yes	Majority vote on amendment
Michigan	2/3	No	Majority vote on amendment
Minnesota	Majority	No	Majority vote on amendment
Mississippi	2/3	No	Majority vote on amendment
Missouri	Majority	No	Majority vote on amendment
Montana	2/3	No	Majority vote on amendment
Nebraska	3/5	No	Majority vote on amendment
Nevada	Majority	Yes	Majority vote on amendment
New Hampshire	3/5	No	2/3 vote on amendment
New Jersey	(d)	(d)	Majority vote on amendment
New Mexico	Majority	No	Majority vote on amendment
New York	Majority	Yes	Majority vote on amendment
North Carolina	3/5	No	Majority vote on amendment
North Dakota	Majority	No	Majority vote on amendment
Ohio	3/5	No	Majority vote on amendment
Oklahoma	Majority	No	Majority vote on amendment
Oregon	Majority	No	Majority vote on amendment
Pennsylvania	Majority	Yes	Majority vote on amendment
Rhode Island	Majority	No	Majority vote on amendment
South Carolina	2/3	Yes	Majority vote on amendment
South Dakota	Majority	No	Majority vote on amendment
Tennessee	2/3	Yes	Majority vote in election
Texas	2/3	No	Majority vote on amendment

TABLE 2–3 (Continued)

	Legislative Vote Required for Proposal	Consideration by Two Sessions Required	Referendum Vote Required for Ratification
Utah	2/3	No	Majority vote on amendment
Vermont	Majority	Yes	Majority vote on amendment
Virginia	Majority	Yes	Majority vote on amendment
Washington	2/3	No	Majority vote on amendment
West Virginia	2/3	No	Majority vote on amendment
Wisconsin	Majority	Yes	Majority vote on amendment
Wyoming	2/3	No	Majority vote in election

[a] 3/4 vote at one session, or majority vote in two sessions between which an election has intervened.

[b] 2/3 vote at one session or majority vote in two sessions.

[c] Majority voting in election or 3/5 voting on amendment.

[d] 3/5 vote at one session or majority vote in two sessions.

Source: Derived from *The Book of the States*, 2007 edition.

Political leaders and citizens alike appear wary of calling a constitutional convention. They are suspicious of "reform" and fearful about "runaway" conventions making unwanted changes in the political system. This is true of voters despite the fact that they always have the opportunity of later voting on the constitutional changes proposed by a convention. The current fear of conventions may also be a product of low levels of trust and confidence in government, as well as a lack of political consensus on many "hot-button" issues such as abortion, affirmative action, gambling, gun control, tax limitations, and so forth. Advocates on both sides of these kinds of issues may be unsure of the outcome of a convention and therefore unite to oppose calling for one. Rhode Islanders reflected these concerns when they defeated such a call by a 52%–48% margin in 2004. Comments by one citizen blogger (Web logger) analyzed the dilemma well: "I guess it's a matter of cynicism. If you think an honest group of engaged citizens can get together and debate good reforms for our government, vote yes. If you're worried that a slate of unaccountable insiders will stack the delegate deck or simple majorities will want to roll back things like gay rights or reproductive rights, vote no."[1]

Constitutional Revision Commissions

Constitutional revision commissions are supposed to "study and recommend" constitutional changes. These commissions are established by the legislature and report their recommendations back to the legislature. (Only in Florida do the recommendations of the Constitutional Revision Commission go directly to the voters for ratification.) Legislatures generally prefer constitutional revision commissions to a constitutional convention, because a commission can only study and report to the legislature. A commission can relieve the state legislature of a great deal of work. The typical commission is appointed by an act of the legislature, and its membership usually includes legislators, executive officials, and prominent citizens. Its recommendations are usually handled in the legislature like regular constitutional amendments, although they may be more sweeping than ordinary amendments.

Constitutional revision commissions have also been declining in number in recent years. (However, three of the nation's largest states—California, New York, and Florida—together with Arkansas and Utah created constitutional revision commissions in the 1990s.) The value of these commissions is in their supposed ability to review fundamental governmental processes, to inspire citizen participation in this review, and perhaps to provide an opportunity for legislatures to shift some especially controversial issues away from themselves and onto the shoulders of independent bodies.[2] And, of course, legislatures still retain control of the revision process, since commissions must usually make their recommendations to their legislatures, which then decide whether to place them on the ballot for voter approval. More often than not, legislators have ignored commission recommendations or watered them down before submitting them to the voters.

DEMOCRACY IN THE STATES

DEMOCRACY

Popular participation in government. (The Greek root of the word means "rule by the many.")

REPRESENTATIONAL DEMOCRACY

Popular participation in government through the selection of public officials by vote of the people in periodic, competitive elections in which candidates and voters can freely express themselves.

DIRECT DEMOCRACY

Popular participation in government through direct voter initiation of policy (usually by petition) and voter approval or rejection of policy decisions by popular vote.

Democracy means popular participation in government. (The Greek root of the word means "rule by the many.") But popular participation can have different meanings. To our nation's Founders, who were quite ambivalent about the wisdom of democracy, it meant that the voice of the people would be *represented* in government. **Representational democracy** means the selection of government officials by vote of the people in periodic elections open to competition in which candidates and voters can freely express themselves. (Note that "elections" in which only one party is permitted to run candidates, or where candidates are not free to express their views, do not qualify as democratic.) The Founders believed that government rests ultimately on the consent of the governed. But their notion of "republicanism" envisioned decision making by representatives of the people, rather than direct decision making by the people themselves. The U.S. Constitution has no provision for direct voting by the people on national policy questions.

"Direct democracy" means that the people themselves can initiate and decide policy questions by popular vote. The Founders were profoundly skeptical of this form of democracy. They had read about direct democracy in the ancient Greek city-state of Athens, and they believed that "the follies" of direct democracy far outweighed any virtues it might possess. It was not until over one hundred years after the U.S. Constitution was written that widespread support developed in the American states for direct voter participation in policymaking. Direct democracy developed in states and communities, and it is to be found today *only* in state and local government.

History of Direct Democracy in the States

At the beginning of the twentieth century, a strong populist movement in the midwestern and western states attacked railroads, banks, corporations, and the political institutions that were said to be in their hands.[3] The populists were later joined by progressive reformers who attacked "bosses," "machines," and parties as corrupt. The populists believed that their elected representatives were ignoring the needs of farmers, debtors, and laborers. They wished to bypass governors and legislatures and directly enact popular laws for railroad rate regulation, relief of farm debt, and monetary expansion. They believed that both the Democratic and Republican parties of their era were controlled by the trusts and monopolies. The progressives and reformers viewed politics as distasteful. They did not believe that government should be involved in resolving conflicts among competing interests or striving for compromises in public policy. Instead, government should serve "the public interest"; it should seek out the "right" answer to public questions; it should replace politicians with managers and administrators. The progressive reform movement was supported by many upper-middle-class, white, Anglo-Saxon, Protestant groups, who felt that political "machines" were catering to the votes of recent immigrants such as the Irish, Italians, eastern and southern Europeans, working-class people, Catholics, and Jews.[4] The progressive reform movement brought about many changes in the structure of municipal government. (See "Reformers and Do-Gooders" in Chapter 11.) The movement also brought about some interesting innovations in state government.

In order to reduce the influence of "politics," "parties," and "politicians," the populists and progressives advocated a wide range of devices designed to bypass political institutions and encourage direct participation by voters in public affairs. They were largely responsible for replacing party conventions with the primary elections we use today. They were also successful in bringing about the Seventeenth Amendment to the U.S. Constitution, which requires that U.S. senators be directly elected by the voters rather than chosen by state legislatures. They supported woman's suffrage, civil service, and restrictive immigration laws.

The populists and progressives were also responsible for the widespread adoption of three forms of direct democracy: the initiative, referendum, and recall. These reforms began in the farm states of the Midwest and the mining states of the West. The populists provided much of the early support for these devices, and the progressives and reformers carried them to fruition. President Woodrow Wilson endorsed the initiative, referendum, and recall, and most adoptions occurred prior to World War I.

Initiative

The initiative is a device whereby a specific number or percent of voters, through the use of a petition, may have a proposed state constitutional amendment or a state law placed on the ballot for adoption or rejection by the electorate of a state. This process bypasses the legislature and allows citizens to both propose and adopt laws and constitutional amendments. Table 2–4 lists the states that allow popular initiatives for constitutional amendments and those that allow popular initiatives for state law. Note that Alaska, Idaho, Maine, Utah, Washington, and Wyoming permit citizen initiatives for state *laws*, but not for constitutional *amendments*.

Referendum

The referendum is a device by which the electorate must approve decisions of the legislature before these become law or become part of the state constitution. As we noted earlier, most states require a favorable referendum vote for a state constitutional amendment. Referenda on state laws may be submitted by the legislature (when legislators want to shift decision-making responsibility to the people), or referenda may be demanded by popular petition (when the people wish to change laws passed by the legislature).

Recall

Recall elections allow voters to remove an elected official before his or her term expires. Usually a recall election is initiated by a petition. The number of signatures required is usually expressed as a percentage of votes cast in the last election for the official being recalled (frequently 25 percent). Currently eighteen states provide for recall election for some or all of their elected officials (see Table 2–4). Although officials are often

INITIATIVE

A device by which a specific number or percentage of the voters may petition to have a constitutional amendment or law placed on the ballot for adoption or rejection by the electorate; found in some state constitutions but not in the U.S. Constitution.

REFERENDA

Proposed laws or constitutional amendments submitted to the voters for their direct approval or rejection; found in some state constitutions but not in the U.S. Constitution.

RECALL

An election to allow voters to decide whether or not to remove an elected official before his or her term expires.

TABLE 2–4 Initiative and Recall in the States

Initiative for Constitutional Amendments (Signatures Required to Get on Ballot)[a] (*n* = 18)	Statutory Initiative (for State Laws) (*n* = 21)	Recall (Signatures Required to Force a Recall Election)[b] (*n* = 18)
Arizona (15%)	Alaska	Alaska (25%)
Arkansas (10%)	Arizona	Arizona (25%)
California (8%)	Arkansas	California (12%)
Colorado (5%)	California	Colorado (25%)
Florida (8%)	Colorado	Georgia (15%)
Illinois (8%)	Idaho	Idaho (20%)
Massachusetts (3%)	Maine	Kansas (40%)
Michigan (10%)	Massachusetts	Louisiana (33%)
Mississippi (12%)	Michigan	Michigan (25%)
Missouri (8%)	Missouri	Minnesota (25%)
Montana (10%)	Montana	Montana (10%)
Nebraska (10%)	Nebraska	Nevada (25%)
Nevada (10%)	Nevada	New Jersey (25%)
North Dakota (4% of state population)	North Dakota	North Dakota (25%)
Ohio (10%)	Ohio	Oregon (15%)
Oklahoma (15%)	Oklahoma	Rhode Island (15%)
Oregon (8%)	Oregon	Washington (25%)
South Dakota (10%)	South Dakota	Wisconsin (25%)
	Utah	
	Washington	
	Wyoming	

[a]Figures expressed as percentage of vote in last governor's election unless otherwise specified; some states also require distribution of votes across counties and districts.

[b]Figures are percentages of voters in last general elections of the official sought to be recalled.

Source: Statutory and Constitutional Initiative Powers from National Conference of State Legislatures, http://www.ncsl.org/programs/legismgt/elect/irstates. February 27, 2007; recall powers from National Conference of State Legislatures, http://www.ncsl.org/programs/legismgt/elect/recallprovision.htm, March 21, 2006.

publicly threatened with recall, rarely is anyone ever removed from office through this device. A recall of a state elected official requires an expensive petition drive as well as a campaign against the incumbent. The "granddaddy of all recalls" removed California Governor Gray Davis from office in 2003. *The Terminator*, movie star Arnold Schwarzenegger, was voted in as his replacement. (See "*People in Politics:* Arnold! From Maverick to Moderate.")

DIRECT VERSUS REPRESENTATIVE DEMOCRACY

The U.S. Constitution has no provision for national referenda. Americans as a nation cannot vote on federal laws or amendments to the national constitution. But voters in the *states* can express their frustrations directly in popular initiatives and referenda voting.

Arguments for Direct Democracy

Proponents of direct democracy make several strong arguments on behalf of the initiative and referendum devices.[5]

- Direct democracy enhances government responsiveness and accountability. The threat of a successful initiative and referendum drive—indeed sometimes the mere circulation of a petition—encourages officials to take popular actions.
- Direct democracy allows citizen groups to bring their concerns directly to the public. Taxpayer groups, for example, who are not especially well represented in state capitols, have been able through initiative and referendum devices to place their concerns on the public agenda.
- Direct democracy stimulates debate about policy issues. In elections with important referendum issues on the ballot, campaigns tend to be more issue oriented. Candidates, newspapers, interest groups, and television news are all forced to directly confront policy issues.
- Direct democracy stimulates voter interest and improves election-day turnout. Controversial issues on the ballot—the death penalty, abortion, gun control, taxes, gay rights, English only, and so on—bring out additional voters. There is some limited evidence that elections with initiatives on the ballot increase voter turnout by three to five percentage points over elections with no initiatives on the ballot.[6]
- Direct democracy increases trust in government and diminishes alienation. While it is difficult to substantiate such a claim, the opportunity to directly affect issues should give voters an increased sense of power.

Arguments for Representative Democracy

Opponents of direct democracy, from our nation's Founders to the present, argue that representative democracy offers far better protection for individual liberty and the rights of minorities than direct democracy. The Founders constructed a system of checks and balances not so much to protect against the oppression of a ruler, but to protect against the tyranny of the majority. Opponents of direct democracy echo many of the Founders' arguments:

- Direct democracy encourages majorities to sacrifice the rights of individuals and minorities. This argument supposes that voters are generally less tolerant than elected officials, and there is some evidence to support this supposition. However, there is little evidence that public policy in states with the initiative and referendum is any more oppressive than public policy in states without these devices. Nonetheless, the potential of majoritarian sacrifice of the liberty of unpopular people is always a concern.
- Direct democracy facilitates the adoption of unwise and unsound policies. Although voters have rejected many bad ideas, frequently initiatives are less well drafted than legislation.
- Voters are not sufficiently informed to cast intelligent ballots on many issues. Many voters cast their vote in a referendum without ever having considered the issue before going into the polling booth.
- A referendum does not allow consideration of alternative policies or modifications or amendments to the proposition set forth on the ballot. In contrast, legislators devote a great deal of attention to writing, rewriting, and amending bills, and seeking out compromises among interests.
- Direct democracy enables special interests to mount expensive initiative and referendum campaigns. Although proponents of direct democracy argue that these devices allow citizens to bypass special-interest-group-dominated legislatures, in fact only a fairly well-financed group can mount a statewide campaign on behalf of a referendum issue. And the outcomes of the vote may be heavily influenced by paid television advertising. So money is important in both "representational" and "direct" democracy.

Arnold! From Maverick to Moderate

The State of California is the second largest government in the U.S.—second only to the federal government in revenues, spending, and employment. California's population and economy are larger than those of most nations in the world. When Californians voted to recall (oust) Democratic Governor Gray Davis, Republican political novice Arnold Schwarzenegger beat out more than 135 candidates who had filed to become Davis's replacement. It was the nation's most widely publicized recall election; it was big news nationally and internationally. But by the time Arnold sought re-election in 2006 and won quite handily, he had become an experienced, moderate politico rather than a maverick conservative.

Arnold Schwarzenegger had never held political office before his election to the governorship of California in 2003. "Ahnold" (a play on his Austrian accent) came to office in a rare recall election of his predecessor, Gray Davis. (Eighteen states include recall provisions in their constitutions—petitions signed by a specific number of voters that force incumbent officials to face an election that risks their being ousted before the end of their term.)

Arnold's father had been a local police chief in Austria and a Nazi Party member before World War II. Arnold donated hundreds of thousands of dollars to the Simon Wiesenthal Center, a Jewish human rights organization that investigated his father's activities and found no evidence that he had committed any war crimes. Arnold spent his teenage years developing his body in the hope of one day becoming Mr. Universe. At age 20 he fulfilled his dream, becoming the youngest-ever Mr. Universe; he would go on to win that title four more times.

Schwarzenegger moved to the United States in 1968, speaking little English. He continued to win bodybuilding titles, later admitting to the use of performance-enhancing anabolic steroids. Arnold had long planned to move from bodybuilding into movie stardom. He appeared in a few early forgotten films in the 1970s and finally made his breakthrough movie *Conan the Barbarian* in 1982. He followed this success with another box office hit, *The Terminator*, in 1984. In subsequent films, Schwarzenegger tried comedy, but he returned to action hero in *Total Recall* in 1990, a widely praised science-fiction motion picture.

Arnold married Maria Shriver in 1986. She is the niece of President John F. Kennedy and a successful television newscaster and commentator. They have four children.

Arnold, a registered Republican, revealed an interest in politics by becoming involved with the Special Olympics and serving on President George H. W. Bush's Council on Physical Fitness. As a candidate in the 2003 recall election, Schwarzenegger enjoyed the most name recognition in the crowded field of candidates. He offered few specifics in his campaign for governor: "I am a man of the people." He won 48.6 percent of the vote; under the California Constitution, no runoff was required.

Arnold was initially successful in repealing an unpopular vehicle registration fee but later began to feel a backlash when powerful state unions opposed his various initiatives. He came up against political reality in a special referendum in 2005 in which four ballot measures he sponsored were defeated. His approval ratings sank to dangerous lows. He referred to his Democratic opponents in the legislature as "girlie men." But his political fortunes rose again as he campaigned for re-election in 2006. Despite a poor year nationally for Republicans, Schwarzenegger won re-election with 56 percent of the vote. His victory enhanced his political influence nationwide. He abandoned partisan attacks on the Democratic legislature and transformed himself into a consensus builder. He negotiated agreements on increasing the minimum wage, increasing school spending, cutting air pollution, and saving energy. (He customized his 800-horsepower Hummer into an environmentally clean vehicle.) He restructured his image as an independent-minded governor. "I'm for the people," he said, inferring he was putting party aside. Some described Schwarzenegger as having gone from a maverick to a moderate in his politics. One thing is for sure: Initially he made nearly everyone aware of how the recall process worked.

The Decline of Representative Government

Direct, popular participation in government in the American states has been growing in strength at the expense of representative democracy. State legislatures, and indeed state governments generally, are perceived by the American public as largely unresponsive, frequently unethical, and dominated by special interests. Whether or not this popular image is accurate, it drives the political movement toward increasing numbers of popular initiatives and referenda votes. National surveys report overwhelming support for "laws which allow citizens to place initiatives directly on the ballot by collecting petition signatures."[7] In American state and local government, "Participatory democracy is here to stay; there is no turning back."[8] Citizens have, in effect, become "Election Day lawmakers."[9]

THE POLITICS OF STATE INITIATIVES

In theory the initiative device is ideologically neutral; both liberal and conservative groups can use this device to bypass state legislatures. During the progressive era at the beginning of the twentieth century, many *liberal* reforms were advanced by popular initiative. In recent years, as the general public has moved in a *conservative* direction, many citizen initiative efforts have reflected conservative themes. It is true, however, that the ideological makeup of a state affects the type of initiatives that end up on the ballot. This explains why citizens in the more liberal states, like Oregon, Colorado, and California, sign petitions to put medicinal marijuana issues on the ballot while those in the more conservative Deep South states put amendments defining marriage as solely between a man and a woman up for approval (see Table 2–5).

Tax Limitation Initiatives

The nation's "tax revolt" got its start with citizen initiatives in the states, beginning with California's **Proposition 13** in 1978, a constitutional amendment initiative to reduce property taxes. "Prop 13" was funded by real estate developers, business, and agricultural interests. Opposition was led by public officials who believed the amendment would cripple public services. The political establishment was joined by public employee unions, teachers, and environmental groups in making dire predictions about the impact of the amendment. But California voters went to the polls in record numbers to give approval to Proposition 13 by better than a two-to-one margin. By 1980 Democrats and Republicans across the nation were campaigning as "tax cutters." Later President Ronald Reagan would interpret it as part of a general mandate for lower taxes and less government, and as a forerunner to his own federal income tax cuts. But not all states joined in the "tax revolt."

Steep property tax increases, often due to higher land valuations, frequently generate citizen protests and often result in tax limitation ballot initiatives. Tax revolts have long characterized politics in America, beginning with the Boston Tea Party.

TABLE 2–5   State Votes on Selected Propositions in the 2000s

Taxes		Outcome
Colorado (2004)	Raise cigarette tax from 20 to 84 cents a pack.	Pass
Maine (2004)	Limit property taxes to 1% of assessed value of property.	Fail
Oklahoma (2004)	Create property tax exemption for disabled veterans and surviving spouses.	Pass
Oregon (2004)	Treat mobile homes as homes and not as vehicles for tax purposes.	Pass
Alaska (2006)	Tax commercial passenger ships visiting the state.	Pass
Colorado (2006)	Prohibit tax deduction of wages paid to illegal aliens.	Pass
Civil Rights		
Arizona (2004)	Require proof of citizenship to register to vote; require state agencies to check the immigration status of program beneficiaries.	Pass
Arkansas (2004)	Define marriage as solely the union between one man and one woman.	Pass
Nevada (2000)	Prohibit same-sex marriages.	Pass
Michigan (2006)	Prohibit racial preferences/affirmative action.	Pass
Rhode Island (2006)	Give voting rights to felons.	Pass
Drugs		
Alaska (2004)	Legalize persons age 21 or older to grow, sell, use, or give away marijuana.	Fail
Colorado (2000)	Allow marijuana for medicinal purposes.	Pass
Montana (2004)	Allow marijuana for medicinal purposes.	Pass
Nevada (2006)	Legalize possession of one ounce of marijuana.	Fail
Arizona (2006)	Limit probation for methamphetamine convicts.	Pass
Education		
California (2000)	Establish school voucher system.	Fail
Michigan (2000)	Establish school voucher system.	Fail
South Dakota (2004)	Allow state to provide food and transportation funding for children who attend religious schools.	Fail
Ohio (2006)	Allow slot machines; dedicate revenue for college scholarships.	Pass
Abortion		
Colorado (2000)	Require waiting period for abortions.	Fail
Florida (2004)	Authorize legislature to pass a law requiring parental notification when teens seek an abortion.	Pass
Oregon (2006)	Require a waiting period and parental notification for abortion by minor.	Fail
Other		
Alaska (2004)	Prevent intentional baiting and feeding of bears.	Fail
Georgia (2006)	State must preserve the "tradition of fishing and hunting."	Pass
Louisiana (2006)	Restrict use of eminent domain for private projects.	Pass
Oklahoma (2006)	Prohibit paying legislators in jail.	Pass
Missouri (2006)	Allow stem cell research.	Pass
Oklahoma (2006)	Allow sale of alcohol on election day by package stores.	Pass
Ohio (2006)	Ban smoking in many public places except bars.	Fail

Source: *The Book of the States*, annual publication.

In the years since Proposition 13, however, almost as many states have *defeated* tax limitation referenda as passed them. And California voters surprised antitax forces in 1998 by approving a citizen initiative to raise cigarette taxes by 50 cents a pack. (In Chapter 14 we will devote more discussion to the politics of taxation.) Scholars have tried to distinguish between states in which tax revolts are successful and those where they are not. It turns out that the states with constitutional provisions for citizen initiatives are more likely to join the "tax revolt"—that is, to pass tax limitation constitutional amendments—than states without provisions for citizen initiatives.[10] Cigarette tax increases are the exception—they seem to pass nearly everywhere, especially if the tax is earmarked for health programs for the poor.

The states with constitutional provisions for citizen initiatives are more likely to join the "tax revolt"—that is, to pass tax limitation constitutional amendments—than states without provisions for citizen initiatives.

Crime and Drugs

"Getting tough on crime" has generally been popular with referendum voters. The death penalty has been approved everywhere it has appeared on the ballot, including Massachusetts, although New Jersey's *legislature* banned it in 2007.

Yet recent referendum votes suggest that citizens are far less enthusiastic about the "War on Drugs" than most politicians proclaim to be. Governors and legislators apparently feel uncomfortable taking the lead in reducing penalties for drug possession or allowing marijuana use for medicinal purposes.

But voters in California approved an initiative statute, placed on the ballot by citizen petition, that substitutes treatment for prison for drug possession and use. This initiative requires judges to impose probation and drug treatment, not incarceration, for possession, use, or transportation of controlled substances. Only the manufacture and sale of drugs remains a prison offense. Moreover, the initiative authorizes the dismissal of charges after completion of drug treatment.

And voters in Arizona, California, Alaska, Colorado, Nevada, Oregon, Montana, and Washington have approved referenda allowing the medical use of marijuana. Hawaii and Maine also allow marijuana for medical use. (However, the federal government has not changed *its* laws prohibiting the use of marijuana for medical purposes, and the U.S. Supreme Court has held that federal law prevails over state law in drug regulation.)

Constitutional amendments allowing medical use of marijuana have been approved by voters in several states. However, federal law prohibits it and the U.S. Supreme Court has held that federal law prevails over state law in drug regulation.

Abortion and Physician-Assisted Suicide

Both abortion and physician-assisted suicide remain controversial issues among both citizens and legislators. In some states, referendum votes have prohibited the use of state funds for abortion, while in other states such a prohibition has failed. (The U.S. Congress, in its controversial "Hyde Amendment," prohibits the use of federal funds for abortions, except to protect the life of a woman or in cases of rape or incest. See "Battles over Abortion" in Chapter 15.) Limits on abortion have been hotly contested in various state referendum votes; abortion opponents have lost more of these referendum votes than they have won. And no consensus appears to have developed in the states regarding physician-assisted suicide. Voters in Michigan defeated an initiative allowing it in 1998, but voters in Maine approved it in 2000.

Prohibiting Same-Sex Marriages

Following a decision by the Supreme Court of Vermont that recognized the validity of same-sex marriages in that state, several states moved quickly to amend their constitutions to prohibit such marriages and to deny recognition to them. When a Massachusetts Supreme Judicial Court ruled in February 2004 that the state's prohibition against gay marriage violated the state constitution, a number of other states rushed to put amendments outlawing same-sex marriages on their ballots. Referendum voters have approved such prohibitions almost everywhere they have appeared on the ballot.

School Vouchers

Proposals to grant school vouchers to parents to spend at any school they choose, including private schools, have met with voter disapproval in several key referendum votes including California (in 1993 and again in 2000) and Michigan. These losses have set back the advocates of "school choice." (See "Reinventing Education" in Chapter 16.)

Affirmative Action and Racial Preferences

Michigan voters approved an amendment prohibiting public institutions like the University of Michigan from giving preferential treatment on the basis of race. Many college students protested against the proposed amendment.

No referendum issue has generated more controversy than the California Civil Rights Initiative, approved by the voters in that state in 1996. Proposition 209 bans "granting preferential treatment to any individual or group" on the basis of "race, sex, color, ethnicity or national origin" in state employment, education, or contracting. Arizona's Proposition 200 amendment, passed in 2004 (56 percent Yes vote), was nearly as explosive. It requires people registering to vote to prove their citizenship and those voting in person on Election Day to show identification. It also requires proof of citizenship or of legal residency when applying for nonfederally funded public assistance and establishes fines for state and local government employees who fail to check. Proponents (Protect Arizona Now) saw it as a way to discourage illegal immigrants from influencing Arizona elections. Opponents (Hispanic groups like the League of United Latin American Citizens [LULAC], the Mexican American League Defense and Educational Fund [MALDEF], and the National Council of La Raza) viewed the Proposition as harassment against immigrants—both legal and illegal. Even the Mexican government weighed in against it, predicting it "will lead to discrimination based on racial profiling while limiting access to basic health and educational services."[11] The anti-racial-preference issue extended to Michigan when in 2006 voters there also approved such an amendment. Proposal 2 prohibits public institutions like the University of Michigan from giving preferential treatment on the basis of race.

Immigration

The rising costs of illegal immigrants have put more fiscal pressure on state and local governments than on the federal government since states and localities deliver most of the services. Arizona voters approved denying bail to illegal immigrants charged with committing a serious felony and prohibited them from collecting punitive damages from civil suits. Colorado's voters ratified an amendment directing the state attorney general to sue the federal government to get it to enforce existing federal immigration laws.

Eminent Domain

Local governments have the power to "take" private property to use for public purposes (e.g., roads, schools), although the property owner must be paid for the land taken by the government. But when the U.S. Supreme Court ruled that private property could be condemned via **eminent domain** proceedings and used for economic development purposes (which might mean taking private property for private sector gain if a developer were involved), citizens in many states were outraged. In 2006 alone, a number of constitutional amendments restricting such practices were approved by the voters.

Initiative Campaigns

Over time, initiative campaigns have become more sophisticated and costly. Supporters of an initiative must first of all circulate their petitions, often using paid as well as volunteer workers to obtain the necessary signatures.[12] Television, radio, and newspaper advertising usually accompanies the drive for signatures. Once on the ballot, an initiative campaign can become very expensive, with television "infomercials," celebrity endorsements, and get-out-the-vote work on election day. There are political consulting firms that specialize in developing campaign strategies for the passage or defeat of ballot initiatives rather than candidates.

EMINENT DOMAIN

Government's condemnation (taking) of private property for public use; landowner must be compensated.

There are political consulting firms that specialize in developing campaign strategies for the passage or defeat of ballot initiatives rather than candidates.

A U.S. Supreme Court ruling (*Kelo v. City of New London*, 2005) that local governments could use their eminent domain powers to condemn private property, then, in turn, allow the property to be used for *private gain* under the guise of "economic development" has prompted many state legislatures to place anti-taking amendments on the ballot. Property rights groups keep a close eye on these proposals; most have passed easily.

Some initiative campaigns are sponsored by "special interests"—specific businesses or industries; labor unions, including government employees; religious organizations; environmental groups; and public interest groups.[13] The gambling industry, for example, often backs "citizens' initiatives" to legalize gambling. Many of the designated sponsoring groups for petitions—for example, "Citizens for Tax Justice" (tax limits) and "Eight is Enough" (term limits)—are organized and funded by established lobbying groups that have failed to accomplish their goals through the legislative process.

Opposition campaigns to initiatives may also be well funded by organized interests. Lobbying groups that are well entrenched in state capitals—public employee unions, teachers' unions, and utility, insurance, and liquor industries (see Chapter 6)—are usually leery of citizens' initiatives. Political officeholders are also generally skeptical of citizen initiatives, even though they may occasionally endorse particularly popular ones. After all, the initiative process is designed to *bypass* the state capital and its power holders. A proposal in New Jersey in 1992 to adopt the initiative process was successfully defeated by a strong coalition of well-established interest groups that mounted "an unprecedented joint lobbying effort."[14] Occasionally opposition groups have resorted to the "counterinitiative"—deliberately adding an initiative to the ballot that is designed to undermine support for a popular citizen initiative. There is a tendency for voters to vote against initiatives when the issues are complex and confusing. Occasionally state supreme courts have denied an initiative a place on the ballot, not only for procedural reasons, but also because in the court's opinion it violated the U.S. Constitution.

Initiatives Impact a Candidate's Campaign

Candidates for office are certainly attentive to issues that will be listed on the same ballot as they are for two reasons. First, they will undoubtedly have to take a public stand on them. One well-known political consultant warns that "Political candidates fool themselves into thinking campaigns are about the candidates and not the issues."[15] A candidate's stance on a high-profile ballot issue is often an important determinant of whether that candidate will get a voter's support.[16] Second, ballot initiatives can "skew voter turnout and create competition for money, interests, and votes."[17] Turnout in nonpresidential election years is higher, particularly among regular *party-line* voters, when there is a high-profile citizen initiative on the ballot.[18]

The Threat of Initiatives

Legislatures may be goaded at times into enacting legislation by the threat of a popular initiative. Recognizing that a popular initiative may gain a position on the ballot and win voter approval, legislatures may prefer to preempt an initiative movement by writing their own version of the policy. Indeed there is some evidence that legislature in initiative states are more sensitive to majority preferences among voters than legislatures in states without the initiative device.[19]

Reform Proposals

Reformers have argued that initiative voting is becoming too common, that multiple initiatives on the ballot overload and confuse voters, that initiatives are often poorly drafted, and that voters are often poorly informed about the real purposes and intent of an initiative. They often urge that neutral voter guides be printed by the state, summarizing arguments for and against initiative questions; that the names and affiliations of major contributors to initiative campaigns be published; and that courts scrutinize titles on initiatives to ensure that they accurately reflect their purposes and intent.

Americans overwhelmingly support the initiative process. Indeed, 64 percent of Americans say that it is a good idea to let citizens place issues directly on the ballot by collecting petition signatures:

> Q. Many states have laws which allow citizens to place initiatives directly on the ballot by collecting petition signatures. If the initiative is approved by voters on Election Day, it becomes law. Is this a good idea?[20]

Yes	64%
No	17%
Not sure	19%

Yet only eighteen states currently have a statewide constitutional initiative process (see Table 2–4). Despite the popularity of the initiative and referendum process, legislators in a majority of states are unlikely to grant initiative rights to their citizens in the near future.

Citizens' Initiatives and Term Limits

Citizen initiatives to limit the terms of public officials—Congress members, state legislators, and other state and local officials—have enjoyed great success whenever they have appeared on the ballot. The U.S. Supreme Court has held that a state *cannot* impose term limits on *members of Congress*. However, states, and citizens in states with the popular initiative and referenda, can limit the terms of their own *state legislators*. And indeed, term limits have usually won by landslide margins whenever they have appeared on referenda ballots (see Table 2–6).

Opponents of term limits, including state legislators themselves, have pursued the two-pronged strategy against the measure: First try to persuade the voters to reject it, and if that fails try to persuade a court to declare it unconstitutional. Supporters of term limits clearly have public opinion on their side. (See "*What Do You Think? Are Term Limits a Good Idea?*") And voters are not at all supportive of legislators' efforts to relax term limits once they have been voted in. In 2004, citizens of Arkansas and Montana overwhelmingly rejected proposals to allow legislators to serve longer before being "term-limited" out of office.

Constitutional arguments against term limits have led to prolonged litigation in the courts. Opponents argued that term limits placed an unconstitutional barrier on the right to be a candidate for public office, and that they violated the right of voters to cast their ballots for candidates of their choice. These arguments were rejected first by the California Supreme Court, and later by the U.S. Court of Appeals (together with

TERM LIMITS

Constitutional limits on the number of terms or the number of years that a public official can serve in the same office.

Groups in favor of term limits want "citizen legislators" rather than career politicians. They feel that long-time officeholders care more about how issues play out in the media or in polls than how they affect the daily lives of their constituents back home. Those who oppose term limits cite the right of every voter to elect his or her candidate of choice, regardless of how long that person may have served in elective office.

TABLE 2–6   Term-Limited State Legislators

State	Year Enacted	House			Senate			Percent Voted Yes
		Limit	Year of Impact		Limit	Year of Impact		
Maine	1993	8	1996		8	1996		67.6
California	1990	6	1996		8	1998		52.2
Colorado	1990	8	1998		8	1998		71
Arkansas	1992	6	1998		8	2000		59.9
Michigan	1992	6	1998		8	2002		58.8
Florida	1992	8	2000		8	2000		76.8
Ohio	1992	8	2000		8	2000		68.4
South Dakota	1992	8	2000		8	2000		63.5
Montana	1992	8	2000		8	2000		67
Arizona	1992	8	2000		8	2000		74.2
Missouri	1992	8	2002		8	2002		75
Oklahoma	1990	12	2004		12	2004		67.3
Nebraska	2000	n/a	n/a		8	2006		56
Louisiana	1995	12	2007		12	2007		76
Nevada	1996	12	2010		12	2010		70.4

Source: National Conference on State Legislatures, 2007. Available at http://www.ncsl.org/programs/legismgt/about/states.htm.

the argument that voters did not understand what they were voting for on term limits referenda).[21] The U.S. Supreme Court has declined to hear appeals of cases upholding the constitutionality of term limits.[22]

U.S. Supreme Court Rejection of Congressional Term Limits by States

When the voters of Arkansas adopted a state constitutional amendment in 1992 setting term limits for their U.S. senators and representatives, the U.S. Supreme Court ruled in 1995 that this action violated the U.S. Constitution by setting forth qualifications for Congress members beyond those found in Article I. Only three qualifications are specified in the U.S. Constitution: age, citizenship, and residence. (The Arkansas term limit amendment actually set qualifications for eligibility for name placement on the ballot; Arkansas argued that this was a permissible exercise of power to regulate "times, places and manner of holding elections" granted to the states in Article I. But the Court dismissed this argument as an "indirect attempt to accomplish what the Constitution prohibits.") The Court held that a state cannot limit the terms of members of Congress:

> Allowing individual states to adopt their own qualifications for Congressional service would be inconsistent with the framers' vision of a uniform national legislature representing the people of the United States. If the qualifications set forth in the text of the Constitution are to be changed, that text must be amended.[23]

Justice John Paul Stevens, writing for the majority in the controversial 5–4 decision, set forth two key arguments in opposition to state-imposed congressional term limits: first, that the power to do so is *not* among the powers reserved to the states by the

Are Term Limits a Good Idea?

Distrust of politicians and declining confidence in the ability of government to confront national problems fueled grassroots movements in many states to limit the terms of public officials—both Congress members and state legislators. However, the enthusiasm of the general public for term limits was seldom matched by legislators—either in Washington or in state capitals—who were reluctant to limit their own legislative careers. Hence, citizens in states with the popular initiative and referenda turned to these instruments of direct democracy.

Arguments for Term Limits

Proponents of term limits argue that "citizen-legislators" have largely been replaced by career "professional politicians." People who have held legislative office for many years become isolated from the lives and concerns of average citizens. Career politicians respond to the media, to polls, to interest groups, but they have no direct feeling for how their constituents live. Term limits, proponents argue, would force politicians to return home and live under the laws that they make.

Proponents also argue that term limits would increase competition in the electoral system. By creating "open seat" races on a regular basis, more people would be encouraged to seek public office. Incumbents do not win so often because they are the most qualified people in their districts, but rather because of the many electoral advantages granted by incumbency itself—name recognition, campaign contributions from special interests, pork barrel projects and casework, office staff, and so on (see "The Great Incumbency Machine" in Chapter 6). These incumbent advantages discourage good people from challenging officeholders.

Arguments against Term Limits

Opponents of term limits argue that they infringe on the voters' freedom of choice. If voters are upset with the performance of their state legislators, they can always "throw the rascals out." If they want to limit a legislator's term, they can do so simply by not reelecting him or her. But if voters wish to keep popular, able, experienced, and hard-working legislators in office, they should be permitted to do so. Experience is a valuable asset in state capitals; voters may legitimately desire to be represented by senior legislators with knowledge and experience in public affairs.

Opponents also argue that inexperienced legislators would be forced to rely more on the policy information supplied to them by bureaucrats, lobbyists, and staff people. Term limits, they argue, would weaken the legislature, leaving it less capable of checking the power of the special interests. But proponents counter this argument by observing that the closest relationships in state capitals develop between lobbyists and senior legislators who have interacted professionally and socially over the years, and that most powerful lobbying groups strongly oppose term limits.

Tenth Amendment, and second, that the Founders intended age, citizenship, and residency to be the *only* qualifications for members of Congress.

Term Limits Kick In

Term limits are beginning to take their toll on state legislatures across the country. In 2000 significant numbers of state legislators were "termed-limited" out of office. The result in a number of states (Arizona, California, Florida, Maine, Michigan, Missouri, Ohio, Oregon, and South Dakota) was an increase in the number of "freshman" legislators.

State legislators themselves are strongly opposed to term limits. The National Conference of State Legislatures reports that 83 percent of state legislators polled oppose term limits. Even many of those who originally favored limits now say they were mistaken: "Originally, I believed that fresh blood would be good; however, experience, understanding of the process and historical knowledge are lost. The same debates occur year after year."[24] Another complaint is that eight-year terms encourage early and continuing political jousting for leadership positions (e.g., Speaker of the House, presiding officer of the Senate, key committee chairs). A majority of legislators say that term limits have added to the influence of legislative staff and lobbyists. However, interestingly, both staffers and lobbyists themselves oppose term limits; staffers fear losing their jobs when new legislators bring in their own new staffers, and lobbyists must work to establish new relationships with new legislators rather than rely on old acquaintances in the legislature. Some legislatures report taking proactive steps to mitigate the inexperience of new legislators by initiating presession training in the legislative process. Legislators also feel term limits strengthen the governor's power at their expense.

did YOU know?

Nicknames of the States

One of the less important, yet sometimes very heated, issues that confront state legislatures is the selection of official nicknames for their state as well as official birds, flowers, trees, songs, and the like. If you think you know about the American states (or if you pass your driving time reading license plates), try to match the state with its official nickname without looking at the answers.

Easy Ones	Answers	Hard Ones	Answers
Heart of Dixie	Alabama	Land of Opportunity	Arkansas
Grand Canyon State	Arizona	Constitution State, Nutmeg State	Connecticut
Golden State	California	First State, Diamond State	Delaware
Centennial State	Colorado	Gem State	Idaho
Peach State, Empire State of the South	Georgia	Prairie State	Illinois
		Sunflower State	Kansas
Sunshine State	Florida	Pelican State	Louisiana
Aloha State	Hawaii	Pine Tree State	Maine
Hawkeye State	Iowa	Old Line State, Free State	Maryland
Hoosier State	Indiana	North Star State, Gopher State	Minnesota
Bluegrass State	Kentucky	Magnolia State	Mississippi
Bay State, Old Colony	Massachusetts	Treasurer State	Montana
Great Lake State, Wolverine State	Michigan	Silver State	Nevada
Show Me State	Missouri	Granite State	New Hampshire
Cornhusker State	Nebraska	Garden State	New Jersey
Empire State	New York	Land of Enchantment	New Mexico
Tar Heel State	North Carolina	Sioux State, Flickertale State	North Dakota
Buckeye State	Ohio	Keystone State	Pennsylvania
Sooner State	Oklahoma	Palmetto State	South Carolina
Beaver State	Oregon	Coyote State	South Dakota
Little Rhody	Rhode Island	Beehive State	Utah
Volunteer State	Tennessee	Green Mountain State	Vermont
Lone Star State	Texas	Evergreen State	Washington
Old Dominion	Virginia	Equality State	Wyoming
Mountain State	West Virginia	The Last Frontier	Alaska
Badger State	Wisconsin		

www.camlaw.rutgers.edu/statecon

The site for the Center for State Constitutional Studies at Rutgers, the State University of New Jersey at Camden has an excellent collection of papers and publications on state constitutions.

http://www.stateconstitutions.umd.edu/index.aspx

Home for the NBER/Maryland State Constitutions Project. Searchable and indexed text for many state constitutions from 1776 to the present as well as quantitative databases on the characteristics of state constitutions.

Several national organizations are promoting initiatives and referenda votes in multiple states.

www.termlimits.org

The Web site for U.S. term limits; provides arguments and information designed to promote term limits for all public officials.

www.acri.org

The American Civil Rights Institute, a group that promotes state constitutional initiatives designed to end racial preferences in affirmative action programs.

www.iandrinstitute.org

An outstanding Web site sponsored by the Initiative & Referendum Institute at the University of Southern California; quick facts, up-to-date state-by-state information on the initiative process; access to publications on initiative and referendum issues around the world.

http://ncsl.org/programs/legman/about/amend_US_Const.htm

A detailed, step-by-step description of the process to amend the U.S. Constitution.

STATES, COMMUNITIES, AND AMERICAN FEDERALISM

3

QUESTIONS TO CONSIDER

Would the nation be better off with a single national government passing uniform laws and providing uniform services throughout the country rather than fifty state governments with different laws and programs?
■ Yes   ■ No

Should the definition of marriage be the same in all states?
■ Yes   ■ No

Which level of government does the best job of dealing with the problems it faces?
■ Federal
■ State
■ Local

Should violence against women be a *federal* crime?
■ Yes   ■ No

WHAT IS FEDERALISM?

Federalism requires that the powers of the national and subnational governments be guaranteed by a constitution that cannot be changed without the consent of both national and subnational populations.

Virtually all nations of the world have some units of local government—states, republics, provinces, regions, cities, counties, or villages. Decentralization of the administrative burdens of government is required almost everywhere. But not all nations have federal systems of government.

Federalism is a system of government in which power is divided between national and subnational governments with both exercising separate and autonomous authority, both electing their own officials, and both taxing their own citizens for the provision of public services. Moreover, federalism requires that the powers of the national and subnational governments be guaranteed by a constitution that cannot be changed without the consent of both national and subnational populations.[1]

The United States, Canada, Australia, India, the Federal Republic of Germany, and Switzerland are generally regarded as federal systems. But Great Britain, France, Italy, and Sweden are not. While these nations have local governments, they are dependent on the national government for their powers. They are considered **unitary systems** rather than federal systems, because their local governments can be altered or even abolished by the national governments acting alone. In contrast, a system is said to be a **confederation** if the power of the national government is dependent upon local units of government. While these terms—unitary and confederation—can be defined theoretically, in the real world of politics it is not so easy to distinguish between governments that are truly federal and those that are not. Indeed, as we shall see in this chapter, it is not clear whether the U.S. government today retains its federal character.

What is clear is that this rather unique arrangement often creates interesting politics between the two levels of government. Some draw parallels between national–state government relationships and family interactions. Sometimes the two levels get along famously (a "love-in"), most notably when Washington sends millions to state capitols to fund everything from highways to health care to disaster relief. Other times, they are at one another's throats (a "family feud"), like when the U.S. Department of Defense proposes to close more military bases in one state than another. Or when the national government orders states to revamp their driver's licenses or purchase new voting machines but doesn't give them sufficient funds to do so. When certain types of issues arise, the two would rather go their separate ways ("live and let live"). Individual states may like to set their own policies on taxing out-of-state Internet sales or defining "marriage," "life," and "privacy rights" without being overruled by Congress or the federal courts who might see these issues as more national in scope. As with families, interactions among the various levels of government are constantly changing as the players change. And the most intense conflicts, by far, are over money, power, and control.

WHY FEDERALISM?

Why have state and local governments anyway? Why not have a centralized political system with a single government accountable to national majorities in national elections—a government capable of implementing uniform policies throughout the country?

FEDERALISM

A constitutional arrangement whereby power is divided between national and subnational governments, each of which enforces its own laws directly on its citizens and neither of which can alter the arrangement without the consent of the other.

UNITARY SYSTEM

Constitutional arrangement whereby authority rests with the national government; subnational governments have only those powers given to them by the national government.

"Auxiliary Precautions" against Tyranny

The nation's Founders understood that "republican principles," while they should be nurtured and cherished, would not be sufficient in themselves to protect individual liberty. Periodic elections, party competition, voter enfranchisement, and political equality may function to make governing elites more responsive to popular concerns. According to the Founders, "A dependence on the people is, no doubt, the primary control of government, but experience has taught mankind the necessity of auxiliary precautions." (James Madison, *The Federalist No. 51*).

Among the most important "auxiliary precautions" devised by the Founders to control government are federalism—dividing powers between the national and state governments—and **separation of powers**—the dispersal of power among the separate executive, legislative, and judicial branches of government.

> In the compound republic of America, the power surrendered by the people is first divided between two distinct governments, and then the portion allotted to each subdivided among distinct and separate departments. Hence a double security arises to the rights of the people. The different governments will control each other, at the same time that each will be controlled by itself.[2]

Dispersing Power

Decentralization distributes power more widely among different sets of leaders. Multiple leadership groups are generally believed to be more democratic than a single set of all-powerful leaders. Moreover, state and local governments provide a political base of offices for the opposition party when it has lost national elections. In this way state and local governments contribute to party competition in America by helping to tide over the losing party after electoral defeat so that it may remain strong enough to challenge incumbents at the next election. And finally, of course, state and local governments provide a channel of recruitment for national political leaders. National leaders can be drawn from a pool of leaders experienced in state and local politics.

Increasing Participation

Decentralization allows more people to participate in the political system. There are more than 87,000 governments in America—states, counties, townships, municipalities, towns, special districts, and school districts. Nearly a million people hold some kind of public office. Most are elected at the state and local levels. (Only 542 are federal officials—one President, one Vice President, 100 U.S. Senators [two from each state], 435 U.S. Representatives, four Delegates to the House of Representatives from U.S. territories and the District of Columbia, and one Resident Commissioner from the Commonwealth of Puerto Rico.) State and local governments are widely regarded as being "closer to the people." Thus, by providing more opportunities for direct citizen involvement in government, state and local governments contribute to the popular sense of political effectiveness.

Improving Efficiency

Decentralization makes government more manageable and efficient, especially in a very diverse nation where a "one size fits all" approach to delivering services does not always work very well. Imagine the bureaucracy, red tape, and confusion if every government activity in every local community in the nation—police, schools, roads, firefighting,

CONFEDERATION
Constitutional arrangement whereby the national government is created by and relies on subnational governments for its authority.

SEPARATION OF POWERS
The dispersal of power among the separate executive, legislative, and judicial branches of government.

garbage collection, sewage disposal, and so forth—were controlled by a centralized administration in Washington. If local governments did not exist, they would have to be invented. Government becomes arbitrary when a bureaucracy far from the scene directs a local administrator to proceed with the impossible—local conditions notwithstanding. Decentralization softens the rigidity of law.

Ensuring Policy Responsiveness

Decentralized government encourages policy responsiveness. Multiple competing governments are more sensitive to citizen views than monopoly government. The existence of multiple governments offering different packages of benefits and costs allows a better match between citizen preferences and public policy. People and businesses can "vote with their feet" by relocating to those states and communities that most closely conform to their own policy preferences. Americans are very mobile. In a given year, some 14 percent of Americans move. Of those, 59 percent move within the same county, 19 percent to a different county within the same state, 19 percent to a different state, and 3 percent from abroad. Business and industry are also increasingly mobile. Mobility not only facilitates a better match between citizen preferences and public policy, it also encourages competition between states and communities to offer improved services at lower costs.

Encouraging Policy Innovation

Federalism encourages policy experimentation and innovation. Federalism may be perceived today as a "conservative" idea, but it was once viewed as the instrument of "progressivism." A strong argument can be made that the groundwork for Franklin Delano Roosevelt's (FDR's) New Deal in the 1930s was built in state policy experimentation during the Progressive Era earlier in the century. Federal programs as diverse as the income tax, unemployment compensation, countercyclical public works, Social Security, wage and hour legislation, bank deposit insurance, and food stamps all had antecedents at the state level. Indeed, the compelling phrase "laboratories of democracy" is generally attributed to the great progressive jurist, Supreme Court Justice Louis D. Brandeis, who used it in defense of state experimentation with new solutions to social and economic problems.[3] Competition among governments provides additional incentives for inventiveness and innovation in public policy.[4]

Managing Conflict

Political decentralization frequently reduces the severity of conflict in a society. Decentralization is a classic method by which different peoples can be brought together in a nation without engendering irresolvable conflict. Conflicts between geographically defined groups in America are resolved by allowing each to pursue its own policies within the separate states and communities; this avoids battling over a single national policy to be applied uniformly throughout the land.

FEDERALISM'S FAULTS

Federalism is not without its faults. It may create confusion as to what level of government is responsible for action. (See "*Up Close:* Hurricane Katrina: Federalism Fails.") Federalism can also obstruct action on national issues. Although decentralization may reduce conflict at the national level, it may do so at the price of "sweeping under the rug" some serious, national injustices.

Hurricane Katrina: Federalism Fails

When the disastrous Hurricane Katrina, a category 4 storm with its 145-mile-per-hour winds and 20-foot storm surge, caused levees to break and the city of New Orleans to be flooded, government officials at all levels blamed each other for the chaos that emerged. The flaws of federalism were laid bare for all to see as television cameras vividly portrayed the human miseries and sufferings of those who could not—or did not—evacuate the city:

> As the city became paralyzed by water and by lawlessness, so did the response by government. The fractured division of responsibility—Governor Blanco controlled state agencies and the National Guard, Mayor Nagin directed city workers, and Mr. Brown, the head of FEMA, served as the point man for the federal government—meant that no one person was in charge.[a]

"Accusations shot back and forth from New Orleans to Baton Rouge to Washington, and blame settled on all."[b] The public criticized officials at every level for failing to provide for the public safety and general welfare of desperate and needy Americans in a time of crisis.[c] In the eyes of the public, politicians and government bureaucrats seemed to stand idly by, waiting for others to take action, and then quickly pointed fingers when they did not. Government officials themselves were hesitant to take charge, fearing they would be perceived as "stepping on the jurisdictional toes" of others: The Blame Game.

The Mayor of New Orleans, C. Ray Nagin, attacked FEMA (Federal Emergency Management Agency) officials, Pentagon officials, and President Bush for failing to grasp the urgency and magnitude of needed people, supplies, and equipment. He criticized the president and Congress for failing to appropriate enough federal funds

to fix the levee system and for failing to address poverty and racial inequities over the years. He even criticized Louisiana Governor Kathleen Blanco, a fellow Democrat, for inaction.

Louisiana Governor Blanco blasted FEMA, the President, and other national officials for their sluggish responsiveness to her requests for federal help, particularly military personnel to help save lives and restore order. "We need your help. We need everything you've got," she pleaded.[d] She was critical of the New Orleans mayor for not issuing more timely evacuation orders, saying it was his responsibility, not hers.

The head of FEMA, Michael Brown, also criticized the Mayor for failing to issue voluntary, then mandatory, evacuation orders in a timely fashion. (The Mayor declared a mandatory evacuation only 24 hours before the hurricane hit in spite of forecasts by the National Hurricane Center "that Katrina was a monster that would trigger a huge storm surge, likely swamp New Orleans' levees and cause catastrophic flooding."[e]) The FEMA chief also blamed the disorganization and disarray on years of corruption in local government hiring, firing, and contracting. (Brown ultimately resigned from FEMA after having been removed from his Katrina oversight role by his boss, the director of the Department of Homeland Security. Brown came to symbolize the inefficiency and ineptness of the FEMA response.)

Federal officials pointed fingers at state and local officials who they perceived were lax in utilizing the powers they had under the U.S. Constitution and federal statutes. They were quick to point out that "in the U.S. federal system, state and local governments are the first line of defense, simply because the first responders—police, fire[fighters], emergency medical services—report to mayors and governors,"[f] not to FEMA or the President of the United States. They criticized Mayor Nagin for failing to implement his city's own emergency management plan. Images of some 2,000 submerged school buses that could have been used to evacuate poor, elderly, and disabled residents who had no means of transportation, lent legitimacy to this criticism.

Following the exposure of federalism-related flaws in our system of governance, discussions began on Capitol Hill about who should be given the clear "lead responsibility" to take charge in such situations in the future—the same debate the Founders had when writing the U.S. Constitution.

Some homeland security specialists testified that "a bigger and faster federalized effort, particularly in

(continued)

large-scale disasters" is needed. They proposed that the lead role be played by the U.S. Department of Defense. Randall Larsen, a retired Air Force colonel and homeland security specialist argued that "there are certain circumstances where the state and locals are so decimated that the feds have to take over for a time" because "only the armed forces can carry a complete new infrastructure—food, water, power, shelter, security, and communications—into an area where every essential has been swept away."[g]

A number of state and local officials strongly disagreed, vehemently arguing that they know their communities better, are in command of National Guard units, and are not limited by Posse Comitatus.[h] Former Virginia Governor James Gilmore, founder of the National Council on Readiness and Preparedness cautioned against a military takeover because "practically speaking, they're not going to get there for 72 hours" and because "the same mobile city of supplies that makes the military so useful in disasters is also so big that it takes time to deploy."[i]

And so one of the nation's oldest debates—federal versus states' rights (centralization v. decentralization) continues.

[a]Eric Lipton, Christopher Drew, Scott Shane and David Rohde, "Breakdowns Marked Path From Hurricane to Anarchy," *The New York Times*, September 11, 2005; accessed at www.nytimes.com/2005/09/11/national/nationalspecial/11response.html?pagewanted=print, September 11, 2005.
[b]Sydney J. Freedberg, Jr., "Learning From Mistakes: Federal Leadership and Local Initiative Are Both Essential," *National Journal*, September 9, 2005; accessed at http//nationaljournal.com/scripts/printpage.cgi?members/news/2005/09/0909nj1.htm, September 9, 2005.
[c]In a poll by the Associated Press/Ipsos Public Affairs, 54 percent gave low marks to the president, nearly 75 percent to state officials, 67 percent to local officials, and 63 percent to the federal government in general. Gwen Glazer and Erin Madigan, "The Katrina Effect: Public Has Little Confidence in Bush, Government's Disaster Response Capabilities," *NationalJournal.com*, September 12, 2005; accessed at http://nationaljournal.com/scripts/printpagecgi?members/pollstrack, September 12, 2005.
[d]Susan B. Glasser and Michael Grunwald, "The Steady Buildup to a City's Chaos," *The Washington Post*, September 11, 2005, p. 101.
[e]"Catastrophic Failure," *Florida Today*, September 11, 2005; accessed at www.floridatoday.com/apps/pbcs.dll/article?AID+/20050911/OPINION/509110311/1004, September 11, 2005.
[f]George Melloan, "What Are the Lessons of Katrina?" *The Wall Street Journal Online*, September 13, 2005; accessed at http://online.wsj/article_print/0,,SB112657951035438991,00.html, September 13, 2005.
[g]Sydney J. Freedberg, Jr., "Learning From Mistakes: Federal Leadership and Local Initiative Are Both Essential," *National Journal*, September 9, 2005; accessed at http//nationaljournal.com/scripts/printpage.cgi?members/news/2005/09/0909nj1.htm, September 9, 2005.
[h]The Posse Comitatus Act, circa 1878, "bars the Army from conducting police activities on U.S. soil without a waiver." Bradley Graham, "Storm Renews Debate Over Federal Role in Disaster," *The Washington Post*, September 9, 2005; accessed at http://info.mgnetwork.com/printthispage.cgi?url=http%3A//tampatrib.com/News/MGBORWVXDD . . . , September 9, 2005.
[i]Sydney J. Freedberg, Jr., "Learning From Mistakes: Federal Leadership and Local Initiative Are Both Essential," *National Journal*, September 9, 2005; accessed at http//nationaljournal.com/scripts/printpage.cgi?members/news/2005/09/0909nj1.htm, September 9, 2005.

Protecting Slavery and Segregation

Federalism in America remains tainted by its historical association with slavery, segregation, and discrimination. An early doctrine of "nullification" was set forth by Thomas Jefferson in the Virginia and Kentucky Resolution of 1798, asserting states' right to nullify unconstitutional laws of Congress. Although the original use of this doctrine was to counter congressional attacks on a free press in the Alien and Sedition Acts, the doctrine was later revived to defend slavery. John C. Calhoun of South Carolina argued forcefully in the years before the Civil War that slavery was an issue for states to decide and that under the Constitution of 1787, Congress had no power to interfere with slavery in the southern states or in the new western territories.

In the years immediately following the Civil War the issues of slavery, racial inequality, and black voting rights were nationalized. The Thirteenth, Fourteenth, and Fifteenth Amendments to the Constitution were enforced with federal troops in the southern states during Reconstruction. But following the Compromise of 1876 federal troops were withdrawn from the southern states and legal and social segregation of blacks became a "way of life" in the region. Segregation was *denationalized;* this reduced national conflict over race, but the price was paid by black Americans. Not until the 1950s and 1960s were questions of segregation and equality again made into national issues. The civil rights movement asserted the supremacy of national law, especially the U.S. Supreme Court's decision in *Brown* v. *Board of Education Topeka, Kansas,* 1954, that segregation violated the Fourteenth Amendment's guarantee of equal protection of the law, and later the national Civil Rights Act of 1964. Segregationists asserted the states' rights argument so often in defense of racial discrimination that it became a code word for racism.

Indeed, only now that *national* constitutional and legal guarantees of equal protection of the law are in place is it possible to reassess the true values of federalism. Having established that federalism will not be allowed to justify racial inequality, we are now free to explore the values of decentralized government.

Obstructing National Policies

Federalism allows state and local officials to obstruct action on national problems. It allows local leaders and citizens to frustrate national policy, to sacrifice the national interest to local interests. Decentralized government provides an opportunity for local citizen activist "NIMBYs" (not in my back yard) to obstruct airports, highways, waste disposal plants, public housing, and many other projects in the national interest.

Racing to the Bottom?

Yet another concern is that competition among the states, a major feature of federalism, may lead to a "race to the bottom" among the states with regard to welfare assistance and other programs for the poor. States may be encouraged to continuously reduce benefit levels in order to avoid becoming "welfare magnets," that is, to avoid the migration of the poor to states with more generous welfare programs. But despite many scholarly studies, there is little direct evidence of poor families moving to states for higher benefit levels, or other states lowering benefits to avoid the migration of poor people.[5]

Allowing Inequalities

Finally, under federalism the benefits and costs of government are spread unevenly across the nation. For example, some states spend over twice as much on the education of each child in the public schools as other states (see Chapter 16). Welfare benefits in some states are over twice as high as in other states (see Chapter 17). Taxes in some states are over twice as high per capita as in other states (see Chapter 14).

THE STRUCTURE OF AMERICAN FEDERALISM

In deciding in 1869 that a state had no constitutional right to secede from the union, Chief Justice Salmon P. Chase described the legal character of American federalism:

> The preservation of the states and the maintenance of their governments, are as much within the design and care of the constitution as the preservation of the union and the maintenance of the national government. The constitution, in all of its provisions, looks to an indestructible union, composed of indestructible states.[6]

DELEGATED, OR ENUMERATED, POWERS

Powers specifically mentioned in the Constitution as belonging to the national government.

NECESSARY AND PROPER CLAUSE

Clause in Article I, Section 8, of the U.S. Constitution granting Congress the power to enact all laws that are "necessary and proper" for carrying out those responsibilities specifically delegated to it. Also referred to as the Implied Powers Clause.

IMPLIED POWERS

Powers not mentioned specifically in the Constitution as belonging to Congress but inferred as necessary and proper for carrying out the enumerated powers.

NATIONAL SUPREMACY CLAUSE

Clause in Article VI of the U.S. Constitution declaring the constitution and laws of the national government "the supreme law of the land" superior to the constitutions and laws of the states.

What is meant by "an indestructible union, composed of indestructible states"? American federalism is an indissoluble partnership between the states and the national government. The Constitution of the United States allocated power between two separate authorities, the nation and the states, each of which was to be independent of the other. Both the nation and the states were allowed to enforce their laws directly on individuals through their own officials and courts. The Constitution itself was the only legal source of authority for the division of powers between the states and the nation. The American federal system was designed as a strong national government, coupled with a strong state government, in which authority and power are shared, constitutionally and practically.

The framework of American federalism is determined by (1) the powers delegated by the Constitution of the national government, and the declared supremacy of that government; (2) the constitutional guarantees reserved for the states; (3) the powers denied by the Constitution to both the national government and the states; (4) the constitutional provisions giving the states a role in the composition of the national government; and (5) the subsequent constitutional and historical development of federalism.

Delegated Powers and National Supremacy

Article I, Section 8, of the U.S. Constitution lists eighteen grants of power to Congress. These "delegated" or "enumerated" powers include authority over matters of war and foreign affairs, the power to declare war, raise armies, equip navies, and establish rules for the military. Another series of delegated powers is related to control of the economy, including the power to coin money, to control its value, and to regulate foreign and interstate commerce. The national government has been given independent powers of taxation "to pay the debts and provide for the common defense and general welfare of the United States." It has the power to establish its own court system, to decide cases arising under the Constitution and the laws and treaties of the United States and cases involving certain kinds of parties. The national government was given the authority to grant copyright patents, establish post offices, enact bankruptcy laws, punish counterfeiting, punish crimes committed on the high seas, and govern the District of Columbia. (See Table 3–1.) Finally, after seventeen grants of express power came the power "to make all laws which shall be necessary and proper for carrying into execution the foregoing powers, and all other powers vested by this constitution in the government of the United States or in any department or officer thereof." This is generally referred to as the **Necessary and Proper Clause** or the **Implied Powers Clause**.

These delegated powers, when coupled with the National Supremacy Clause of Article VI, ensured a powerful national government. The National Supremacy Clause was quite specific regarding the relationship between the national government and the states. In questions involving conflict between the state laws and the Constitution, laws, or treaties of the United States,

> This constitution, and the laws of the United States which shall be made in pursuance thereof; and all treaties made or which shall be made under the authority of the United States shall be the supreme law of the land; and the judges in every state shall be bound thereby, anything in the constitution or laws of any state to the contrary notwithstanding.

Reserved Powers

Despite these broad grants of power to the national government, the states retained a great deal of authority over the lives of their citizens. The Tenth Amendment reaffirmed

TABLE 3–1 Original Constitutional Distribution of Powers

Under the Constitution of 1787, certain powers were delegated to the national government, other powers were shared by the national and state governments, and still other powers were reserved for state governments alone. Similarly, certain powers were denied by the Constitution to the national government, other powers were denied to both the national and state governments, and still other powers were denied only to state governments. Later amendments especially protected individual liberties. Article and section numbers of the U.S. Constitution are shown in parentheses.

Powers Granted by the Constitution

National Government Delegated Powers

Military Affairs and Defense

- Provide for the common defense (I-8)
- Declare war (I-8)
- Raise and support armies (I-8)
- Provide and maintain a navy (I-8)
- Define and punish piracies (I-8)
- Define and punish offenses against the law of nations (I-8)
- Provide for calling forth the militia to execute laws, suppress insurrections, and repel invasions (I-8)
- Provide for organizing, arming, and disciplining militia (I-8)
- Declare the punishment of treason (III-3)

Economic Affairs

- Regulate commerce with foreign nations, among the several states, and with Indian tribes (I-8)
- Establish uniform laws on bankruptcy (I-8)
- Coin money and regulate its value (I-8)
- Fix standards of weights and measures (I-8)
- Provide for patents and copyrights (I-8)
- Establish post offices and post roads (I-8)

Governmental Organization

- Constitute tribunals inferior to the Supreme Court (I-8, III-1)
- Exercise exclusive legislative power over the seat of government and over certain military installations (I-8)
- Admit new states (IV-3)
- Dispose of and regulate territory or property of the United States (IV-3)

"Implied" Powers

- Make necessary and proper laws for carrying expressed powers into execution (I-8)

National and State Governments Concurrent Powers

- Levy taxes (I-8)
- Borrow money (I-8)
- Contract and pay debts (I-8)
- Charter banks and corporations (I-8)
- Make and enforce laws (I-8)
- Establish courts (I-8)
- Provide for the general welfare (I-8)

State Government Reserved to the States

- Regulate intrastate commerce
- Conduct elections
- Provide for public health, safety, and morals
- Establish local government
- Maintain militia (National Guard)
- Ratify amendments to the federal Constitution (V)
- Determine voter qualifications (I-2)

"Reserved" Powers

- Powers not delegated to national government nor denied to the States by the Constitution (X)

(continued)

TABLE 3–1 (Continued)

Powers Denied by the Constitution

National Government

- Give preference to ports of any state (I-9)
- Impose tax or duty on articles exported from any state (I-9)
- Directly tax except by apportionment among states on population basis (I-9), now superseded as to income tax (Amendment XVI)
- Draw money from Treasury except by appropriation (I-9)

National and State Governments

- Grant titles of nobility (I-9)
- Limit suspension of habeas corpus (I-9)
- Issue bills of attainder (I-10)
- Make ex post facto laws (I-10)
- Establish a religion or prohibit free exercise of religion (Amendment I)
- Abridge freedom of speech, press, assembly, or rights of petition (Amendment I)
- Deny right to bear arms protected (Amendment II)
- Restrict quartering of soldiers in private homes (Amendment III)

- Conduct unreasonable searches or seizures (Amendment IV)
- Deny guarantees of fair trials (Amendment V, Amendment VI, and Amendment VII)
- Impose excessive bail or unusual punishments (Amendment VII)
- Take life, liberty, or property without due process (Amendment V)
- Permit slavery (Amendment XIII)
- Deny life, liberty, or property without due process of law (Amendment XIV)
- Deny voting because of race, color, previous servitude (Amendment XV), or sex (Amendment XIX), or age if 18 or over (Amendment XXVI)
- Deny voting because of non-payment of any tax

State Governments

Economic Affairs

- Use legal tender other than gold or silver coins (I-10)
- Issue separate state coinage (I-10)
- Impair the obligation of contracts (I-10)
- Emit bills of credit (I-10)

- Levy import or export duties, except reasonable inspection fees, without consent of Congress (I-10)
- Abridge privileges and immunities of national citizenship (Amendment XIV)
- Make any law that violates federal law (VI)
- Pay for rebellion against United States or for emancipated slaves (Amendment XIV)

Foreign Affairs

- Enter into treaties, alliances, or confederations (I-10)
- Make compact with a foreign state, except by congressional consent (I-10)

Military Affairs

- Issue letters of marque and reprisal (I-10)
- Maintain standing military forces in peace without congressional consent (I-10)
- Engage in war, without congressional consent, except in imminent danger or when invaded (I-10)

RESERVED POWERS

Powers not granted to the national government or specifically denied to the states in the Constitution that are recognized by the Tenth Amendment as belonging to the state governments. This guarantee, known as the Reserved Powers Clause, embodies the principle of American federalism.

the idea that the national government had only certain delegated powers and that all powers not delegated to it were retained by the states:

> The powers not delegated to the United States by the constitution, nor prohibited by it to the states, are reserved to the states respectively, or to the people.

The states retained control over the ownership and use of property; the regulation of offenses against persons and property (see "*Up Close:* Federalizing Crime"); the regulation of marriage and divorce; the control of business, labor, farming, trades, and professions; the provision of education, welfare, health, hospitals, and other social welfare activities; and provision of highways, roads, canals, and other public works. The states retained full authority over the organization and control of local government units. Finally, the states, like the federal government, possessed the power to tax and spend for the general welfare.

Powers Denied to the Nation and States

The Constitution denies some powers to both national and state governments; these denials generally safeguard individual rights. Both nation and states are forbidden to pass

up CLOSE   Federalizing Crime

Political office holders in Washington are continually pressured to make a "federal crime" out of virtually every offense in society. Neither Democrats nor Republicans, liberals nor conservatives, are willing to risk their political futures by telling their constituents that crime fighting is a state and local responsibility. So Washington lawmakers continue to add common offenses to the ever lengthening list of federal crimes.

Traditionally, federal crimes were limited to a relatively narrow range of offenses, including counterfeiting and currency violations; tax evasion, including alcohol, tobacco, and firearm taxes; fraud and embezzlement; robbery of federally insured banks; murder or assault of a federal official; and violations of customs and immigration laws. While some federal criminal laws overlapped state laws, most criminal activity—murder, rape, robbery, assault, burglary, theft, auto theft, gambling, sex offenses, and so on—fell under state jurisdiction. Indeed, the *police power* was believed to be one of the "reserved" powers states referred to in the Tenth Amendment.

But over time Congress has made more and more offenses *federal* crimes. Today federal crimes range from drive-by shootings to obstructing sidewalks in front of abortion clinics. Any violent offense motivated by racial, religious, or ethnic animosity is a "hate crime" subject to federal investigation and prosecution. **"Racketeering"** and **"conspiracy"** (organizing and communicating with others about the intent to commit a crime) is a federal crime. The

greatest impact of federal involvement in law enforcement is found in drug-related crime. Drug offenders may be tried in either federal or state courts or both. Federal drug laws, including those prohibiting possession, carry heavier penalties than those of most states.

The effect of federalizing crime is to subject citizens to the possibility of being tried twice for the same crime—in federal court and in state court for an offense that violates both federal and state criminal codes. The U.S. Supreme Court has held that such multiple prosecution does *not* violate the Double Jeopardy Clause of the Fifth Amendment, "nor shall any person be subject for the same offense to be twice put in jeopardy of life or limb."[a] In the well-publicized Rodney King case, a California state jury acquitted police officers of beating King, but a federal court jury later convicted them of violating King's civil rights.

Only recently has the U.S. Supreme Court recognized that federalizing crime may impinge upon the reserved powers of states. In 1994 Congress passed a popular Violence Against Women Act that allowed victims of "gender-motivated violence," including rape, to sue their attackers for monetary damages in federal court. Congress defended its constitutional authority to involve itself in crimes against women by citing the Commerce Clause, arguing that crimes against women interfered with interstate commerce, the power over which is given to the national government in Article I of the Constitution. But in 2000 the Supreme Court said, "If accepted, this reasoning would allow Congress to regulate any crime whose nationwide, aggregate impact has substantial effects on employment, production, transit, or consumption. Moreover, such reasoning will not limit Congress to regulating violence, but may be applied equally as well to family law and other areas of state regulation since the aggregate effect of marriage, divorce, and childbearing on the national economy is undoubtedly significant. The Constitution requires a distinction between what is truly national and what is truly local, and there's no better example of the police power, which the Founders undeniably left reposed in the states and denied the central government, than the suppression of violent crime in vindication of its victims."[b] In Justice Scalia's opinion, allowing Congress to claim that violence against women interfered with interstate commerce would open the door to federalizing all crime: "would allow general federal criminal laws, because all crime affects interstate commerce."

RACKETEERING AND CONSPIRACY

Organizing and communicating with others about the intent to commit a crime.

---

[a] *Health* v. *Alabama* 474 U.S. 82 (1985).
[b] *U.S.* v. *Morrison*, May 15, 2000.

ex post facto laws or bills of attainder. The first eight of the ten amendments to the Constitution, known as "the Bill of Rights," originally applied to the *federal* government, but the Fourteenth Amendment, passed by Congress in 1866, provided that the *states* must also adhere to fundamental guarantees of individual liberty. "No state shall make or enforce any law which shall abridge the privileges or immunities of the citizens of the United States; nor shall any state deprive any person of life, liberty or property without due process of law; nor deny to any person within its jurisdiction equal protection of the laws."

Some powers were denied only to the states, generally as a safeguard to national unity, including the powers to coin money, enter into treaties with foreign powers, interfere with the obligations of contracts, levy duties on imports or exports without congressional consent, maintain military forces in peacetime, engage in war, or enter into compacts with foreign nations or other states.

The National Government's Obligations to the States

The Constitution imposes several obligations on the national government in its relations with the states. First of all, the states are guaranteed *territorial integrity:* No new state can be created by Congress out of the territory of an existing state without its consent. (Nonetheless, Congress admitted West Virginia to the Union in 1863 when the western counties of Virginia separated from that state during the Civil War. Later a "reconstructed" Virginia legislature gave its approval.) The national government must also guarantee to every state *"a republican form of government."* A republican government is a government by democratically elected representatives. Presumably this clause in the Constitution means that the national government will ensure that no authoritarian or dictatorial regime will be permitted to rule in any state. Apparently this clause does *not* prohibit popular initiatives, referenda, town meetings, or other forms of direct democracy. The Supreme Court has never given any specific meaning to this guarantee. Each state is also guaranteed *equal representation in the U.S. Senate.* Indeed, the Constitution, Article V, prohibits any amendments that would deprive the states of equal representation in the Senate. Finally, the national government is required to *protect each state against foreign invasion and domestic violence.* The protection against foreign invasion is unequivocal, but the clause dealing with domestic violence includes the phrase "upon application of the legislature or the Executive (when the legislature cannot be convened)." Governors have called upon the national government to intervene in riots to maintain public order. But the national government has also intervened *without* "application" by state officials in cases where federal laws are being violated. Perhaps the most important direct intervention was President Dwight Eisenhower's decision to send federal troops to Little Rock High School in Arkansas in 1956 to enforce the Supreme Court's desegregation decision in *Brown* v. *Board of Education of Topeka, Kansas* (see Chapter 15).

State Role in National Government

The states also play an important role in the composition of the national government. U.S. representatives must be apportioned among the states according to their population every ten years. Governors have the authority to fill vacancies in Congress, and every state must have at least one representative regardless of population. The Senate of the United States is composed of two senators from each state regardless of the state's population. The times, places, and manner of holding elections for Congress are determined by the states. The president is chosen by electors, allotted to each state on the basis of the number of its senators and representatives. (See Figure 3–1.)

Finally, amendments to the U.S. Constitution must be ratified by three-fourths of the states. (See Figure 3–2.)

FIGURE 3–1 States Drawn in Proportion to Electoral Votes

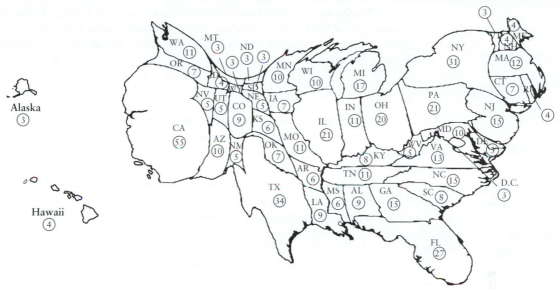

Source: Michael Gastner, Cosma Shalizi, and Mark Newman. Maps and Cartograms of the 2004 U.S. Presidential Election Results. University of Michigan. Accessed at www.personal.umich.edu/~mejn/election, November 13, 2005. The number of electoral college votes by state is available at http://www.archives.gov/federal-register/electoral-college/2004/allocation.html

FIGURE 3–2 The States' Role in Constitutional Amendment

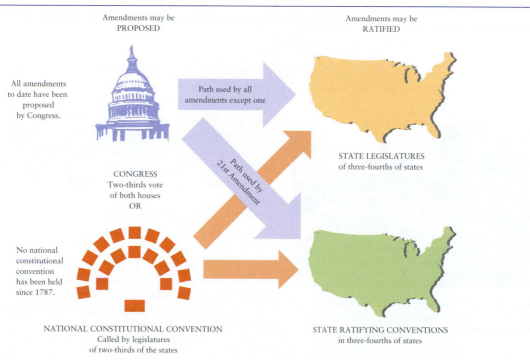

Amendments may be PROPOSED

All amendments to date have been proposed by Congress.

CONGRESS
Two-thirds vote of both houses
OR

No national constitutional convention has been held since 1787.

NATIONAL CONSTITUTIONAL CONVENTION
Called by legislatures of two-thirds of the states

Path used by all amendments except one

Path used by 21st Amendment

Amendments may be RATIFIED

STATE LEGISLATURES
of three-fourths of states

STATE RATIFYING CONVENTIONS
in three-fourths of states

The Constitution cannot be amended without the approval of three-fourths of the states.

BATTLES IN THE STATES OVER CONSTITUTIONAL AMENDMENTS

The power of the states in the American federal system has been demonstrated in several battles over constitutional amendments passed by Congress. According to Article V of the U.S. Constitution, the Constitution cannot be amended without the approval of three-fourths of the states, either by their state legislatures or by state constitutional ratifying conventions.

The Defeat of ERA

ERA (EQUAL RIGHTS AMENDMENT)

A constitutional amendment proposed by Congress but never ratified by the necessary three-fourths of the states. It would have guaranteed "equality of rights under law" for women and men.

In 1972 when Congress sent the **Equal Rights Amendment** (**ERA**) to the states for ratification, it did so with overwhelming support of both Democrats and Republicans in the House and the Senate. National opinion polls and most national leaders, including Presidents Nixon, Ford, and Carter, strongly endorsed the simple language of the proposed amendment: "Equality of rights under law shall not be denied or abridged by the United States or by any State on account of sex."

The ERA won quick ratification in about half of the states. By 1978, thirty-five state legislatures had ratified the ERA. (See Figure 3–3.) (However, five states voted to rescind their earlier ratification. While there is some disagreement about the validity of these "rescissions," most constitutional scholars do not believe a state can rescind its earlier ratification of a constitutional amendment; there is no language in the Constitution referring to rescissions of constitutional amendments.) Leaders of the ERA movement called upon Congress to grant an unprecedented extension of time beyond the traditional seven years to continue the battle for ratification. (The Constitution, Article V, does not specify how long states can consider a constitutional amendment.) In 1978, Congress (by simple majority vote) granted the ERA an unprecedented additional three years for state ratification; the new limit was 1982, a full ten years after Congress proposed the original ERA.

The "Stop ERA" movement gained strength in the states over time. Under the leadership of conservative spokeswoman Phyllis Schlafly, an active group of women successfully lobbied *against* the ERA in state legislatures. In spite of overwhelming support for the ERA from Democratic and Republican presidents and Congresses, leading celebrities from television and films, and even a majority of Americans surveyed by national polling organizations, these "ladies in pink" were influential in the defeat of the ERA. (The phrase "ladies in pink" refers to a common practice of anti-ERA women lobbyists wearing pink, dressing well, baking apple pies for legislators, and otherwise adopting the traditional symbols of femininity.) Most of the lobbying against the ERA in state legislatures was done by women's groups. While not as well organized as the leading feminist groups (National Organization of Women [NOW], the League of Women Voters, the Women's Political Caucus, and so on), the "ladies in pink" were very much in evidence when state legislatures considered ratification of the ERA.[7]

Louisiana ERA supporters march through New Orleans's historic French Quarter to publicize their ERA ratification campaign.

80 CHAPTER 3

FIGURE 3–3 **ERA in the States**

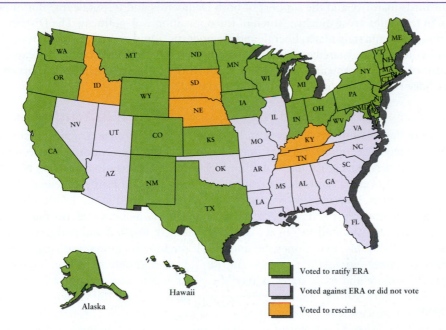

Voted to ratify ERA

Voted against ERA or did not vote

Voted to rescind

Three-quarters of the states *must* concur in a constitutional amendment. This is a powerful tool of the states in our federal system. The wording of the Constitution cannot be altered without the approval of the states, regardless of how much support such a change in wording may have in Washington. Despite national support for the ERA, the amendment fell *three states short* of ratification by the necessary thirty-eight states. Last-ditch attempts to pass the ERA in states where the battle was close (Florida, Illinois, and North Carolina) failed in 1982. But there is a renewed effort in a number of states to ratify the amendment. "All we need is three," is the rallying cry of current-day supporters of the ERA. The biggest problem they face is the belief by many citizens that there already *is* an equal rights amendment in the U.S. Constitution. It is less likely that state legislators will put a high priority on its passage without pressure from the grassroots.

The Defeat of the District of Columbia Amendment

The Constitution grants Congress the power to govern the District of Columbia, but over time Congress has delegated considerable home rule to the District. Washington elects its own mayor and council, levies city taxes, and provides municipal services to its residents. The Twenty-Third Amendment, ratified by the states in 1961, gives Washingtonians three *presidential* electors, but residents of the city have never had voting members of Congress. (The District's only congressional representation is its *nonvoting* delegates to the House and Senate, who may serve on committees and participate in debates on the floor.) In 1978 Congress passed and sent to the states a constitutional amendment to grant the District of Columbia two U.S. senators and as many representatives as their population would warrant if it were a state (currently one). Congress placed a seven-year time limit on ratification by the states in the amendment itself, thus preventing a time extension by simple majority vote of the House and Senate.

The DC amendment passed both houses of Congress with well over the necessary two-thirds majority and the support of both Democrats and Republicans. But opposition in the states arose quickly. Much of the opposition was political: The District was seen as predominately black, liberal, and Democratic. Only about 8 percent of the District's voters are registered as Republicans. The District itself has a less-than-reassuring record of self-government. By the 1985 deadline only sixteen states, well short of the necessary thirty-eight, had ratified the amendment.

The Surprise Passage of the Twenty-Seventh Amendment

As part of the Bill of Rights, Congress in 1789 sent to the states an amendment that would prohibit a pay raise for members of Congress until after the intervention of an election for House members. The amendment had no time limit for ratification attached to it. But only six of the original thirteen states ratified Madison's pay raise amendment, and it was largely forgotten. However, as congressional scandals mounted in the 1980s and public confidence in Congress plummeted, the old amendment was rediscovered. (By one account, a University of Texas student ran across the amendment in 1982 and realized it had no time limit. Using his own money, he undertook a national campaign that resulted in twenty-six states ratifying the amendment. But he received only a "C" on his research paper.)[8] As more and more states ratified the two-hundred-year-old amendment, Congress should have realized that their behavior was under scrutiny. But Congress proceeded in 1989 to vote itself a 50 percent pay raise, touching off a storm of protest. (Nationwide polls indicated that 82 percent of Americans opposed the pay increase.) Angry voters looked for ways to rein in an arrogant Congress. Fifteen additional states rushed to ratify Madison's amendment.

Some scholars, as well as leaders in Congress, argued that ratification of the amendment after 203 years did not meet "the standard of timeliness." They argued that even though the Constitution itself placed no time limits on ratification, Article V "implied" that ratification should occur within a "reasonable" time. But when the archivist of the United States, Don Wilson, officially certified the adoption of the Twenty-Seventh Amendment in 1992 as he was authorized to do by law, congressional leaders were stymied. Although they were irate over the archivist's action, they were unable to reverse it. Individual members of Congress raced to join in the popular sentiment, fearing that any effort to undo the amendment would be dealt with severely by the voters in the next election. Both houses voted nearly unanimously to endorse the amendment. The states had succeeded in administering an unexpected reprimand to Congress.

HOW MONEY SHIFTED POWER TO WASHINGTON

Today there are really no segments of public activity fully "reserved" to the states or the people.

Over the years the national government has acquired much greater power in the federal system than the Founders originally envisioned. (See "*Up Close:* Historic Landmarks in the Development of American Federalism.") The "delegated" powers of the national government are now so broadly defined—particularly the power to tax and spend for the general welfare—that the government in Washington is involved in every aspect of American life. (The argument that constitutionally Congress can tax and spend only in support of its *enumerated* powers was rejected by the Supreme Court.)[9] Today there are really no segments of public activity fully "reserved" to the states or the people.

up CLOSE

Historic Landmarks in the Development of American Federalism

The American federal system is a product of more than its formal constitutional provisions. It has also been shaped by interpretations by the courts of constitutional principles as well as the history of disputes that have occurred over state and national authority.

Marbury v. *Madison* (1803): Expanding Federal Court Authority

Chief Justice John Marshall, who presided over the Supreme Court from 1801 to 1835, became a major architect of American federalism. Under John Marshall, *the Supreme Court assumed the role of arbiter in disputes between state and national authority*. It was under John Marshall that the Supreme Court in *Marbury* v. *Madison* assumed the power to interpret the U.S. Constitution authoritatively. The fact that the referee of disputes between state and national authority has been the *national* Supreme Court has had a profound influence on the development of American federalism. Since the Supreme Court is a *national* institution, one might say that in disputes between nation and states, one of the members of the two contending teams is also serving as umpire. Constitutionally speaking, then, there is really *no* limitation on national as against state authority *if* all three branches of the national government—the Congress, the president, and the Court—act together to override state authority.

McCulloch v. *Maryland* (1819): Expanding Implied Powers of the National Government

In the case of *McCulloch* v. *Maryland*, Chief Justice John Marshall provided a broad interpretation of the Necessary and Proper Clause:

> Let the end be legitimate, let it be within the scope of the Constitution, and all means which are appropriate, which are plainly adopted to the end, which are not prohibited but consistent with the letter and the spirit of the Constitution, are constitutional.[a]

The *McCulloch* case firmly established the principle that the Necessary and Proper Clause gives Congress the right to choose its means for carrying out the enumerated powers of the national government. Today, Congress can devise programs, create agencies, and establish national laws on the basis of long chains of reasoning from the most meager phrases of the constitutional text because of the broad interpretation of the Necessary and Proper Clause.

Secession and the Civil War (1861–1865): Maintaining the "Indestructible Union"

The Civil War was, of course, the greatest crisis of the American federal system. Did a state have the right to oppose national law to the point of secession? In the years preceding the Civil War, John C. Calhoun argued that the Constitution was a compact made by the *states* in a sovereign capacity rather than by the *people* in their national capacity. Calhoun contended that the federal government was an agent of the states, that the states retained their sovereignty in this compact, and that the federal government must not violate the compact, under the penalty of state nullification or even secession from the Union.

The issue was decided in the nation's bloodiest war. What was decided on the battlefield between 1861 and 1865 was confirmed by the Supreme Court in 1869: "Ours is an indestructible union, composed of indestructible states."[b] Yet the states' rights doctrines, and political disputes over the character of American federalism, did not disappear with Lee's surrender at Appomattox. The Thirteenth, Fourteenth, and Fifteenth Amendments, passed by the Reconstruction Congress, were clearly aimed at limiting state power in the interests of individual freedom. The Thirteenth Amendment eliminated slavery in the states; the Fifteenth Amendment prevented states from discriminating against blacks in the right to vote; and the Fourteenth Amendment declared that "no State shall make or enforce any law which shall abridge the privileges or immunities of citizens of the United States; nor shall any state deprive any person of life, liberty, or property without due process of law; nor deny to any person within its jurisdiction the equal protection of the laws." These amendments delegated to Congress the power to secure their enforcement. Yet for several generations these amendments were narrowly construed and added little, if anything, to national power.

National Labor Relations Board v. *Jones and Laughlin Steel Corp.* (1937): Expanding Interstate Commerce

The Industrial Revolution in America created a *national* economy with a nationwide network of transportation and communication and the potential for national economic depressions. Yet for a time, the Supreme Court placed obstacles in the way of national authority over the

(continued)

economy, and by so doing the Court created a "crisis" in American federalism. For many years, the Court narrowly construed interstate commerce to mean only the movement of goods and services across state lines, insisting that agriculture, mining, manufacturing, and labor relations were outside the reach of the delegated powers of the national government. However, when confronted with the Great Depression of the 1930s and President Franklin D. Roosevelt's threat to "pack" the Court with additional members to secure approval of his New Deal measures, the Court yielded. In *National Labor Relations Board* v. *Jones and Laughlin Steel Corporation* in 1937, the Court recognized the principle that production and distribution of goods and services for a national market could be regulated by Congress under the Interstate Commerce Clause. The effect was to give the national government effective control over the national economy.

Brown v. Board of Education of Topeka, Kansas (1954): Guaranteeing Civil Rights

After World War I, the Supreme Court began to build a national system of civil rights that was based on the Fourteenth Amendment. In early cases, the Court held that the Fourteenth Amendment prevented states from interfering with free speech, free press, or religious practices. Not until 1954, in the Supreme Court's landmark desegregation decision in *Brown* v. *Board of Education of Topeka, Kansas*, did the Court begin to call for the full assertion of national authority on behalf of civil rights.[c] The Supreme Court's use of the Fourteenth Amendment to ensure a national system of civil rights supported by the power of the federal government was an important step in the evolution of the American federal system.

Voting Rights Act (1965) and Bush v. Gore (2000): Federal Oversight of Elections

The Voting Rights Act of 1965 plunged the federal government into direct oversight of state and local as well as federal elections in an effort to end discriminatory practices. The Act and subsequent amendments to it require the Justice Department to approve any election law changes in states and communities covered by the Act. It provides that intent to discriminate need not be proven if the results demonstrate a discriminatory impact on minorities.

In the contested presidential election of 2000, the U.S. Supreme Court confirmed national oversight of Electoral College voting and vote counting in *Bush* v. *Gore*. In this landmark case the Court reversed a Florida Supreme Court interpretation of that state's election laws and ruled that voting and vote counting are entitled to Equal Protection and Due Process under the Fourteenth Amendment.

The U.S. Supreme Court's controversial decision in *Bush* v. *Gore*, issued in December 2000, effectively determined the outcome of the 2000 presidential election. It also affirmed that voting and vote counting processes in states must adhere to equal protection and due process under the Fourteenth Amendment to the U.S. Constitution.

[a]*McCulloch* v. *Maryland*, 4 Wheaton 316.
[b]*Texas* v. *White*, 7 Wallace 700 (1869).
[c]*Brown* v. *Board of Education of Topeka, Kansas*, 347 U.S. 483 (1954).

The Earliest Federal Aid

It is possible to argue that even in the earliest days of the Republic, the national government was involved in public activities that were not specifically delegated to it in the Constitution.[10] The first Congress of the United States in the famous Northwest Ordinance, providing for the government of the territories to the west of the Appalachian Mountains, authorized grants of federal land for the establishment of public schools, and by so doing, showed a concern for education, an area "reserved" to the states by the Constitution. Again in 1863, in the Morrill Land Grant Act, Congress provided grants of land to the states to promote higher education.

Money, Power, and the Income Tax

The year 1913, when the Sixteenth Amendment gave the federal government the power to tax income directly, marked the beginning of a new era in American federalism. Congress had been given the power to tax and spend for the general welfare in Article I of the Constitution. However, the Sixteenth Amendment helped to shift the balance of financial power from the states to Washington, when it gave Congress the power to tax the incomes of corporations and individuals on a progressive basis. The income tax gave the federal government the power to raise large sums of money, which it proceeded to spend for the general welfare as well as for defense. It is no coincidence that the first major grant-in-aid programs (agricultural extension in 1914, highways in 1916, vocational education in 1917, and public health in 1918) all came shortly after the inauguration of the federal income tax.

Federal Grants-in-Aid

The federal "grant-in-aid" has been the principal instrument in the expansion of national power. More than one-third of all state and local government expenditures are currently from monies derived from federal grants. This money is paid out through a staggering number and variety of programs. (See Table 3–2.) Federal grants may be obtained to assist in everything from the preservation of historic buildings, the development of

TABLE 3–2 Selected State/Local Government Programs Receiving Federal Grants
Child nutrition
Food stamp administration
Special supplemental food program (WIC, or Women, Infants, and Children)
Collaborative Forest Restoration
Water to At-Risk Natural Desert Terminal Lakes
Adult education for the disadvantaged
Economic development administration
Public Television Station Digital Transition
National Guard centers—construction
Healthy Communities
Community Action for a Renewed Environment
Community-Based Abstinence Education
Food Safety and Security Monitoring
Wastewater treatment facilities
FEMA disaster relief
Welfare cash payments (Temporary Assistance to Needy Families)
Children and family services (Head Start)
Foster care and adoption assistance
Low-income home energy assistance
Medicaid
Centers for Disease Control
Substance abuse and mental health
(continued)

TABLE 3–2 (Continued)
Section 8 housing assistance
Job Training Partnership Act
Unemployment insurance and services
Justice Institute grants
Highway trust fund
Airport trust fund
Federal transit administration
Emergency shelters
Veterans' state nursing home care
Community-based child abuse prevention
Voting access for individuals with disabilities
Incarcerated youth offenders
Law Enforcement Terrorism Prevention Program

Source: Catalog of Federal Domestic Assistance, 2007 (www.cfda.gov).

minority-owned businesses, the education of the disabled, the construction of airports, to the funding of disaster relief and tree preservation.

The largest portion of federal grant-in-aid money (46 percent) is devoted to health, especially Medicaid's health care for the poor, and welfare, especially Temporary Assistance to Needy Families. Only about 11 percent is used for highways and transit, and only about 13 percent for education, training, employment, and social services. (See Figure 3–4.)

FIGURE 3–4 Federal Grants-in-Aid by Major Function

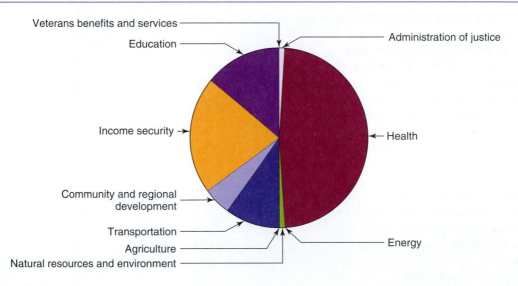

Note: Data are for 2006.
Source: Calculated from U.S. Census Bureau, *Statistical Abstract 2007*, No. 422. Available at http://www.census.gov/prod/2006pubs/07statab/stlocgov.pdf

Money with Strings Attached

Today, grant-in-aid programs are the single most important source of federal influence over state and local activity. A **grant-in-aid** is defined as payment of funds by one level of government (national or state) to be expended by another level (state or local) for a specified purpose, usually on a matching-funds basis (the federal government puts up only as much as the state or locality) and "in accordance with prescribed standards or requirements." No state or local government is *required* to accept grants-in-aid. Participation in grant-in-aid programs is voluntary. So in theory, if conditions attached to the grant money are too oppressive, state and local governments can simply decline to participate and pass up these funds. Yet it is often asserted that states are "bribed" by the temptation of much-needed federal money and "blackmailed" by the thought that other states will get the money, which was raised in part by federal taxes on the state's own citizens. (See "*Up Close:* Federalism and the Drinking Age.")

Currently, federal grants-in-aid can be described as either **"categorical grants"** or **"block grants,"** depending on the extent of federal oversight of how the money is spent.

Categorical grants: Grants for specific, narrow projects. Each project must be approved by a federal administrative agency. Most federal aid money is distributed in the form of categorical grants. Categorical grants can be distributed on a project basis or a formula basis. Grants made on a project basis are distributed by federal administrative agencies to state or local governments that compete for project funds in their applications. Federal agencies have a great deal of discretion in selecting specific projects for support, and they can exercise direct control over the projects. However, some categorical grants are distributed to state or local governments according to a fixed formula set by Congress. Federal administrative agencies may require reports and adherence to rules and guidelines, but they do not choose which specific projects to fund.

Block grants: Grants for a general governmental function, such as health, social services, law enforcement, education, or community development. State and local governments have fairly wide discretion in deciding how to spend federal block grant money within a functional area. For example, cities receiving "community development" block grants can decide for themselves about specific neighborhood development projects, housing projects, community facilities, etc. All block grants are distributed on a formula basis set by Congress.

Grantsmanship

Federal money flows unevenly among the states (see "*Rankings of the States:* Reliance on Federal Aid"). The federal grant system is not neutral in its impact on the states, nor is it intended to be. Many grant programs are based on formulas that incorporate various indications of need and financial ability. Federal aid is supposed to be "targeted" on national problems.[11] The effect of differential grant allocations among the states, combined with differences among state populations in federal tax collections, is to *redistribute* federal money throughout the nation. The big winners in the federal grant game are generally rural states; the losers are the urban states. But not always—a prime exception being funding for homeland security. Funding battles are always a principal source of conflict between governments—"the time-honored bone of intergovernmental contention."[12]

The rush to Washington to ensure that states and cities receive their "fair share" of federal grant money, together with concerns over federal interference in the conduct

GRANTS-IN-AID

Payments of funds from the national government to state or local governments or from a state government to local governments for specific purposes, usually on a matching basis.

CATEGORICAL GRANTS

Federal grants-in-aid to state or local governments for specific purposes or projects.

BLOCK GRANTS

Federal grants-in-aid for general governmental functions, allowing state and local governments to exercise some flexibility in use with a function.

Federalism and the Drinking Age: Why 21 and Not 18?

Nowhere among Congress's enumerated powers in the U.S. Constitution do we find the power to regulate the consumption of alcoholic beverages. Traditionally, the "reserved" powers of the states included the protection of the health, safety, and well-being of their own citizens. And every state set minimum drinking age laws of its own.

In the early 1970s most states lowered their drinking age to eighteen, influenced perhaps by the Twenty-Sixth Amendment giving eighteen-year-olds the right to vote. But in the early 1980s, the states individually began to raise the drinking age, as part of a national movement against drunk driving. By 1984 about half of the states had changed the legal drinking age to twenty-one (such as California); other states chose nineteen (including New York, Florida, and Texas) or twenty (such as Massachusetts and Connecticut); and still other states (such as Colorado and Kansas) allowed eighteen-year-olds to buy beer and wine but required a person to be twenty-one in order to buy "distilled spirits." Only a few states (Vermont, Rhode Island, Louisiana, and Hawaii) retained a general eighteen-year-old drinking age.

The minimum drinking age became a national issue largely as a result of emotional appeals by groups such as Mothers Against Drunk Driving (MADD). Politically these appeals were more effective than any scientific studies of alcohol-related deaths. Nonetheless, statistical evidence presented to Congress by the National Transportation Safety Board showed that teenagers were more likely to be involved in alcohol-related traffic deaths than non-teenagers. Indeed, drunk driving was (and remains) the leading cause of death among teenagers.[a] The National Student Association, restaurant owners, and the liquor industry countered that teenagers were no worse offenders than those in the twenty-one to twenty-five age group and that the selection of all teenagers for special restrictions was age discrimination. But the tragic stories told at televised committee hearings by grieving mothers of dead teenagers swept away the opposition.

Federalism arguments were also swept away. Several senators argued that a national drinking age infringed on the powers of the states in a matter traditionally under state control. However, the new law did not directly mandate a national drinking age. Instead, it ordered the withholding of 10 percent of all federal highway funds from any state that failed to raise its minimum drinking age to twenty-one. States retained the right to ignore the national drinking age and give up a significant portion of their highway funds. Opponents of this device labeled it "federal blackmail" and a federal intrusion into state responsibilities. For some state officials the issue was not teen drinking but rather the preemption of state authority.

Constitutionally, Congress was exercising its powers to spend money for the general welfare. Congress was not directly legislating in an area "reserved" to the states—protection of health, safety, and well-being. Instead, Congress was threatening to withhold some federal highway grant monies from states that did not meet a federal requirement.[b] Technically states remain free to set their own minimum drinking age. Despite heated arguments in many state legislatures, all adopted the twenty-one-year-old national drinking age by 1990. Money is power; this axiom holds true in the American federal system as in politics generally.

[a]*Congressional Quarterly Weekly Report* (June 30, 1984): 1557. National Highway Transportation Safety Administration, Federal Accident Report, July 1996. See also www.madd.org on the Internet.
[b]*South Dakota* v. *Dole* 438 U.S. 203 (1987).

of state and local government, has produced a great deal of intergovernmental lobbying at the nation's capital. Most individual states now maintain offices in Washington with staff committed to looking after their interests. Cities have also hired Washington-based lobbyists to look after their interests in the federal grants game, particularly since during the Bush administration, more federal aid was directed at local governments than in the past.[13]

Reliance on Federal Aid

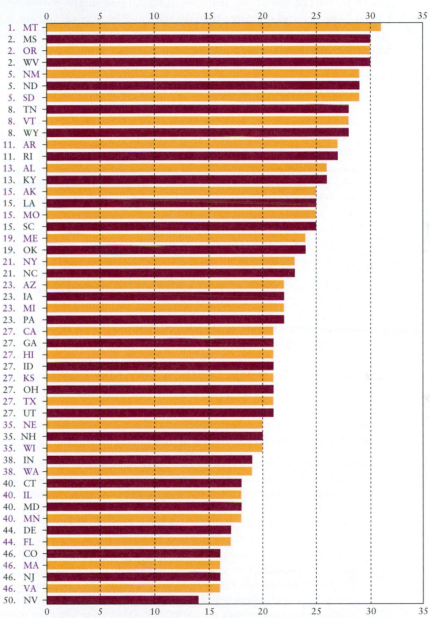

Rank	State	
1.	MT	
2.	MS	
2.	OR	
2.	WV	
5.	NM	
5.	ND	
5.	SD	
8.	TN	
8.	VT	
8.	WY	
11.	AR	
11.	RI	
13.	AL	
13.	KY	
15.	AK	
15.	LA	
15.	MO	
15.	SC	
19.	ME	
19.	OK	
21.	NY	
21.	NC	
23.	AZ	
23.	IA	
23.	MI	
23.	PA	
27.	CA	
27.	GA	
27.	HI	
27.	ID	
27.	KS	
27.	OH	
27.	TX	
27.	UT	
35.	NE	
35.	NH	
35.	WI	
38.	IN	
38.	WA	
40.	CT	
40.	IL	
40.	MD	
40.	MN	
44.	DE	
44.	FL	
46.	CO	
46.	MA	
46.	NJ	
46.	VA	
50.	NV	

Percent of State and Local Government Revenue from Federal Government

Note: Data are for 2002.
Source: U.S. Census Bureau, *Statistical Abstract 2007*, No. 431. Available at http://www.census.gov/prod/2006pubs/07statab/stlocgov.pdf

THE POLITICS OF GRANTS-IN-AID

From the earliest days of the Republic, Americans have argued over federalism. In recent years, political conflict over federalism—over the decision between national versus state and local responsibilities and finances—has tended to follow traditional "liberal" and "conservative" political cleavages. Generally, liberals seek to enhance the power of the *national* government because they believe that people's lives can be changed—and bettered—by the exercise of national governmental power. The government in Washington has more power and resources than do state and local governments, which many liberals regard as too slow, cumbersome, weak, and unresponsive. Thus liberalism and centralization are closely related in American politics.

The liberal argument for national authority can be summarized as follows:

- There is insufficient awareness of social problems by state and local governments. The federal government must take the lead in civil rights, equal employment opportunities, care for the poor and aged, the provision of adequate medical care for all Americans, and the elimination of urban poverty and blight. Grants-in-aid permit the government to set national goals and priorities in all levels of government.

- Grants-in-aid provide the necessary impetus for social change. It is difficult to achieve change when reform-minded citizens must deal with fifty state governments and over 80,000 local governments. Change is more likely to be accomplished by a strong central government.

- Finally, grants-in-aid provide an opportunity for the national government to ensure a uniform level of public service throughout the nation—for example, federal grants-in-aid help ensure a minimum level of existence for the poverty-stricken regardless of where they live. This aspect of federal policy assumes that in some parts of the nation, state and local governments are unable, or perhaps unwilling, to devote their resources to raising public service levels to minimum national standards. (See Figure 3–4.)

Conservatives, in contrast, are skeptical about the "good" that government can do and believe that adding to the power of the national government is not an effective way of resolving society's problems. On the contrary, they often argue that "government is the problem, not the solution." Excessive federal government regulation, burdensome taxation, and big spending combine to restrict individual freedom, penalize work and savings, and destroy incentives for economic growth. Government should be kept small, controllable, and close to the people.

Conservative objections to federal grant-in-aid programs can be summarized as follows:

- Grassroots government promotes a sense of self-responsibility and self-reliance. State and local governments can better adapt public programs to local needs and conditions. Federal grants-in-aid are invariably accompanied by federal standards or "guidelines," which must be adhered to if states and communities are to receive their federal money. While no state is required to accept a federal grant and its restrictions, it is very difficult for states and communities to resist the pressure to accept federal money.

- Federal grants cause state and local officials to overspend what looks to them like "free" money. Overspending on programs or services that local residents would not be willing to pay for out of their *own* tax revenues creates waste and inefficiency and contributes to the overall growth of government. Federal money is not "free": It comes from the *nation's* taxpayers. Local governments are sometimes pressured to apply for funds for projects they do not really need, simply because federal funds are available.

- Finally, the grant-in-aid system assumes that federal officials are better judges of goals and priorities at all levels of government than are state or local officials. In many grant programs federal officials must approve each funded project—a housing project in Des Moines, a sewage disposal system in Baton Rouge, an urban renewal project in Alabama. Block grants, which allocate federal funds on a formula basis to states and communities for general purposes like "community development" or "mental health," provide more flexibility than project grants. But Congress cannot resist attaching strings and guidelines for the use of these grants.

Americans are divided over the merits of these arguments. (See "*Up Close:* Which Government Does the Best Job?") Most national opinion surveys reveal greater trust and confidence in state and local governments than in the federal government. But many Americans believe that the federal government can do a better job handling specific issues such as protecting civil rights. There is no way to settle these arguments about federalism; they have been heard for over 200 years in American politics.

FEDERALISM: VARIATIONS ON THE THEME

The relative strength of the national government versus state and local governments has constantly changed over the course of American history.

Dual Federalism (1787–1913)

For the nation's first hundred years, the pattern of federal–state relations has been described as dual federalism. Under this pattern, the states and the nation divided most governmental functions. The national government concentrated its attention on the "delegated" powers—national defense, foreign affairs, tariffs, commerce crossing state lines, coining money, establishing standard weights and measures, maintaining a post office and building post roads, and admitting new states. State governments decided the important domestic policy issues—slavery (until the Civil War), education, welfare, health, and criminal justice. This separation of policy responsibilities was once compared to a "layer cake,"[14] with local governments at the base, state governments in the middle, and the national government at the top.

Cooperative Federalism (1913–1964)

The Industrial Revolution and the development of a national economy, the income tax, which shifted financial resources to the national government, and the challenges of two world wars and the Great Depression, all combined to end the distinction between national and state concerns. The new pattern of federal–state relations was labeled cooperative federalism. Both the nation and the states exercised responsibilities for welfare, health, highways, education, and criminal justice. This merging of policy responsibilities was compared to a "marble cake." "As the colors are mixed in a marble cake, so functions are mixed in the American federal system."[15]

The Great Depression of the 1930s forced states to ask for federal financial assistance in dealing with poverty, unemployment, and old age. Governors welcomed massive federal public works projects. In addition, the federal government intervened directly in economic affairs, labor relations, business practices and agriculture. Through the grant-in-aid device, the national government cooperated with the states in public assistance, employment services, child welfare, public housing, urban renewal, highway building, and vocational education.

DUAL FEDERALISM

Early concept of federalism in which national and state powers were clearly distinguished and functionally separate.

COOPERATIVE FEDERALISM

Model of federalism in which national, state, and local governments work together exercising common policy responsibilities.

up CLOSE   Which Government Does the Best Job?

Americans appear to be ambivalent about federalism. On the one hand, most surveys show that Americans have greater confidence in their state and local governments than in the federal government. In general, they would prefer that power be concentrated at the state rather than the federal level. They believe that state and local officials get more done than the federal government.

Yet at the same time most Americans want the federal government, rather than state or local governments, to run programs in many specific policy areas, like health care and the environment.

Trust and Confidence

Generally speaking, which of the following cares more about the important problems that affect you personally?

The governor, my state legislature	52
The President and Congress	36
Neither	10
Don't know/refused	2

And which level of government gets more done?

Local	37
State	31
Federal	27
Don't know/refused	5

For each issue, tell me whether the state government or the federal government should take the lead.

Issue	Federal	State	DK/Ref. (Don't Know/Refuse to Answer)
Education	24	75	
Highways and roads	27	73	
Health care	72	27	1
Crime	27	72	1
Environment	72	28	1
Jobs and the economy	56	43	1

Source: "Immigration, Federalism," Andres McKenna Research. January 15–25, 2004. N = 800 registered voters.

CENTRALIZED FEDERALISM

Model of federalism in which the national government assumes primary responsibility for determining national goals in all major policy areas and directs state and local government activity through conditions attached to money grants.

Yet even in this period of shared national–state responsibility, the national government emphasized cooperation in achieving common national and state goals. Congress generally acknowledged that it had no direct constitutional authority to regulate public health, safety, or welfare.

Centralized Federalism (1964–1980)

Over the years it became increasingly difficult to maintain the fiction that the national government was merely assisting the states in performing their domestic responsibility. By the time President Lyndon B. Johnson launched the "Great Society" in 1964, the federal government clearly set forth its own "national" goals. Virtually all problems confronting American society—from solid-waste disposal and water and air pollution to consumer safety, home insulation, noise abatement, and even metric conversion—were declared to be national problems. Congress legislated directly on any matter it chose, without regard to its "enumerated powers" and without pretense to financial assistance. The Supreme Court no longer concerned itself with the "reserved" powers of the states; the Tenth Amendment lost most of its meaning. The pattern of national–state relations became centralized. As for the cake analogies, one commentator observed, "The frosting had moved up to the top, something like a pineapple upside-down cake."[16]

New Federalism (1980–1985)

From time to time efforts have been made to reverse the flow of power to Washington and return responsibilities to state and local government. The phrase "New Federalism" originated in the administration of President Richard M. Nixon, who used it to describe **general revenue sharing**—federal sharing of tax revenues with state and local governments with few strings attached. Later, "New Federalism" was used by President Ronald Reagan to describe a series of proposals designed to reduce federal involvement in domestic programs and encourage states and cities to undertake greater policy responsibilities themselves.

General Revenue Sharing (GRS) was begun in 1972 as a conservative alternative to categorical grants by federal agencies for specific projects. It was argued that unrestricted federal money grants to state and local government was preferable to centralized bureaucratic decision making in Washington. GRS promised to reverse the flow of power to federal bureaucrats, end excessive red tape, and revitalize state and local governments. GRS was strongly supported by state and local government officials, who were happy to have the federal government collect tax money and then turn it over to them to spend. But the Reagan administration, confronting high federal deficits and wanting to reduce Washington's role in domestic policy, undertook a long and eventually successful effort in 1986 to end General Revenue Sharing.

Another Reagan approach to cutting federal strings in grant-in-aid programs was greater reliance on the block grant. Congress endorsed many block grants in the early 1980s, but the struggle between categorical grant interests (liberals and Democrats) and the consolidationists (Reagan and the Republicans) was really a draw. Many categorical grant programs were merged (notably in health services; alcohol, drug abuse, and mental health; social services; maternal and child health; community services; community development; and education), but many others remained independent.

Another accomplishment of the Reagan administration's New Federalism was a temporary reversal of the historical trend of the greater dependence of state and local governments on federal money. In the years prior to 1980, state and local governments had become increasingly dependent on federal grants as sources of revenue. Federal grants rose to over one-quarter of all state–local expenditures in 1980 (see Table 3–3). Total federal aid dollars continued to rise during the Reagan years, but not at the same

TABLE 3–3	Trends in Federal Grants-in-Aid		
		Federal Grants as a Percent of	
	Total Federal Grants (Billion Dollars)	Total Federal Spending	State and Local Expenditures
1980	91	15.5	39.9
1985	106	11.2	29.6
1990	135	10.8	25.2
1995	225	14.8	31.5
2000	285	15.9	27.2
2003	387	17.9	31.0
2006, est.	449	16.6	(NA)

Source: U.S. Census Bureau, *Statistical Abstract of the United States 2007*, No. 421.

Available at http://www.census.gov/prod/2006pubs/07statab/stlocgov.pdf

rate as in previous years. The result was a decline in state/local dependence on federal money to less than 20 percent.

However, it is not likely that presidents or Congress members or candidates for these national offices will ever be moved to restrain national power. People expect federal officials to "do something" about virtually every problem that confronts individuals, families, communities, or the nation. Politicians gain very little by telling their constituents that a particular problem is not a federal problem. Indeed, by the 1990s under Republican President George H. W. Bush as well as Democratic President Bill Clinton, the flow of federal aid dollars to the states accelerated. Reversing the trend of the 1980s, state and local government dependence on federal revenue rose somewhat.

Representational Federalism (1985–1996)

Despite centralizing tendencies, it was still widely assumed prior to 1985 that the Congress could not directly legislate how state and local governments should go about performing their *traditional* functions. However, in its 1985 *Garcia* decision,[17] the U.S. Supreme Court appeared to remove all barriers to direct congressional legislation in matters traditionally reserved to the states. The case arose after Congress directly ordered state and local governments to pay minimum wages to their employees. The Court dismissed arguments that the nature of American federalism and the Reserved Powers Clause of the Tenth Amendment prevented Congress from directly legislating in state affairs. The Court declared that there were *no* "a priori definitions of state sovereignty," *no* "discrete limitations on the objects of federal authority." and *no* protection of state powers in the U.S. Constitution. According to the Court: "State sovereign interests . . . are more properly protected by procedural safeguards inherent in the structure of the federal system than by judicially created limitations on federal power." It said that the only protection for state powers was to be found in the states' role in electing U.S. senators, members of the U.S. House of Representatives, and the president.

The Supreme Court's *Garcia* case ruling became known as "representational federalism"—a denial that there is any constitutional division of powers between states and nation and an assertion that federalism is defined by the role of the states in electing members of Congress and the president. The United States is said to retain a federal system because national officials are selected from subunits of government— the president through the allocation of Electoral College votes to the states, and the Congress through the allocation of two Senate seats per state and the apportionment of representatives to states based on population. Whatever protection exists for state power and independence must be found in the national political process—in the influence of state and district voters on their senators and Congress members. Representational federalism does not recognize any constitutionally protected powers of the states.

However, the Supreme Court may be unwilling to jettison altogether the notion of federalism as the division of power between nation and states. Justice Sandra Day O'Connor, a former Arizona legislator and appellate court judge, was a staunch defender of federalism on the U.S. Supreme Court. Quoting from the *Federalist* and citing the Tenth Amendment, Justice O'Connor wrote the majority opinion in a case considering whether Congress's Age Discrimination Employment Act invalidated a provision of the Missouri Constitution requiring judges to retire at age seventy.[18] She cited the "constitutional balance of federal and state powers" as a reason for upholding the Missouri Constitution. Only a "clear statement" by Congress of its intent to override a traditional state power would justify doing so. This "clear statement" rule presumably governs federal laws that may be in conflict with state laws or constitutions. The rule does not prevent Congress from directly regulating state government activity, but it requires Congress to say unambiguously that this is its intent.

Coercive Federalism: Preemptions and Mandates (1997–present)

Can Congress *directly* regulate the traditional functions of state and local governments? We know that Congress can influence the actions of state and local governments by offering them grants of money and then threatening to withdraw them if they do not meet federal rules, regulations, or "guidelines." But can Congress, in the exercise of its broad constitutional powers, legislate directly about traditional functions of state and local governments—schools, streets, police and fire protection, water and sewers, refuse disposal? Can the national government by law treat the states as administrative units required to carry out the mandates of Congress?

Certainly the historical answer to this question was "No." A typical nineteenth-century description of federalism by the U.S. Supreme Court asserted that the federal government could not intrude or interfere with the independent powers of state governments and vice versa:

> There are within the territorial limits of each state two governments [state and national], restricted in their spheres of action, but independent of each other, and supreme within their respective spheres. Each has its separate departments, each has its distinct laws, and each has its own tribunes for their enforcement. Neither government can intrude within the jurisdiction of the other or authorize any interference therein by its judicial officers with the action of the other.[19]

Perhaps this separation and independence never really characterized relations between the national government and the state governments. But at least state governments were viewed as independent authorities that could not be directly coerced by the national government in their traditional functions. Today, many state officials believe their independence is slowly being whittled away by actions of Congress and the federal courts. Federalism scholars agree with this assessment. The federal government has continued centralizing and nationalizing policy in major areas formerly controlled by states and localities (education testing, sales tax collection, emergency management, infrastructure, and election administration) through use of mandates and preemptions. Some have labeled this "opportunistic federalism" on the part of the federal government.[20]

■ *Congressional regulation of state taxes.* More than a century ago, the U.S. Supreme Court held that Congress could not levy taxes on the states or on their bonds or notes.[21] Inter-governmental tax immunity was believed to be an integral part of the Tenth Amendment's guarantee of the reserved powers of the states. The states could not tax federal bonds and the nation could not tax state bonds. But in 1987 the U.S. Supreme Court shocked state and local officials and the municipal bond market by holding that Congress could if it wished levy taxes on the interest received from state and local bonds. In a dissent, Justice Sandra Day O'Connor observed that "the Court has failed to enforce the constitutional safeguards of state autonomy and self-sufficiency that may be found in the Tenth Amendment and the Guarantee Clause, as well as in the principles of federalism implicit in the Constitution."[22]

PREEMPTIONS

In federal–state relations, the federal government's assumption of regulatory powers in a particular field to the partial or full exclusion of state powers.

MANDATES

In federal–state relations, the federal government's orders to state (and local) governments to provide particular services or perform specific services.

■ *Federal preemptions.* The supremacy of federal laws over those of the states, spelled out in the Supremacy Clause of the Constitution, permits Congress to decide whether or not state laws in a particular field are preempted by federal law. To date, Congress has passed over 500 preemption statutes and the number is on the rise.[23] **Total preemption** refers to the federal government's assumption of all regulatory powers in a particular field—for example, copyrights, bankruptcy, railroads, and airlines. No state regulations in a totally preempted field are permitted. **Partial preemption** stipulates that a state law on the same subject is valid as long as it does not conflict with the federal law in the same area. For example, the Occupational Safety and Health Act of 1970 specifically permits state regulation of any occupational safety or health issue on which the federal Occupational Safety and Health Administration (OSHA) has *not* developed a standard; but once OSHA enacts a standard, all state standards are nullified.

■ *Federal mandates.* Federal **mandates** are orders to state and local governments to comply with federal laws. Federal mandates occur in a wide variety of areas—from civil rights and voter rights laws to conditions of jails and juvenile detention centers, minimum wage and worker safety regulations, air and water pollution controls, and requirements for access for disabled people. (See Table 3–4.) State and local governments frequently complain that compliance with federal "unfunded mandates" imposes costs on them that are seldom reimbursed.

TABLE 3–4   Selected Federal Mandates

Examples of Federal Mandates to State and Local Governments

- *Age Discrimination Act 1986* Outlaws mandatory retirement ages for public as well as private employees, including police, firefighters, and state college and university faculty.
- *Asbestos Hazard Emergency Act 1986* Orders school districts to inspect for asbestos hazards and remove asbestos from school buildings when necessary.
- *Safe Drinking Water Act 1986* Establishes national requirements for municipal water supplies; regulates municipal waste treatment plants.
- *Clean Air Act 1990* Bans municipal incinerators and requires auto emission inspections in certain urban areas.
- *Americans with Disabilities Act 1990* Requires all state and local government buildings to provide access for individuals with physical disabilities.
- *National Voter Registration Act 1993* Requires states to register voters at driver's licensing, welfare, and unemployment offices.
- *No Child Left Behind Act 2001* Requires states and their school districts to test public school pupils and provide vouchers to pupils from consistently below average scoring schools.
- *Help America Vote Act 2002* Requires states to modernize registration and voting procedures and voting technology.
- *Homeland Security Act 2002* Requires states and communities as "first responders" to train, equip, and prepare for terrorist attacks.
- *REAL ID Act 2005* Designed to prevent terrorism, reduce fraud, and improve the reliability and accuracy of identification documents that state governments issue. The REAL ID Act requires that a REAL ID driver's license be used for "official purposes," as defined by the Department of Homeland Security.

Note: Some of these mandates are partially funded by the federal government but state and local officials still see them as "unfunded" because they are not totally funded.

- *"Unfunded" mandates.* Federal mandates often impose heavy costs on states and communities. When no federal monies are provided to cover these costs, the mandates are said to be unfunded mandates. Governors, mayors, and other state and local officials (including Bill Clinton, when he served as governor of Arkansas) have often urged Congress to stop imposing unfunded mandates on states and communities. Private industries have long voiced the same complaint. Regulations and mandates allow Congress to address problems while pushing the costs of doing so onto others. In 1995 Congress finally responded to these complaints by requiring that any bill imposing unfunded costs of $58 million on state and local governments (as determined by the Congressional Budget Office) would be subject to an additional procedural vote; a majority must vote to waive a prohibition against unfunded mandates before such a bill can come to the House or Senate floor.

Many state and local officials see the federal Homeland Security Act as an example of an "underfunded" mandate. Fights over the formula for distributing federal Homeland Security funds to states and localities are ongoing in Congress.

Federal officials often define "unfunded mandates" differently than state officials. A Congressional Budget Office report in the early 2000s concluded that only two unfunded mandates exceeding the Unfunded Mandates Reform Act of 1995 have been passed by Congress (an increase in the federal wage in 1996, a reduction in federal reimbursement of state Food Stamp administrative costs in 1998). But the National Governors Association disagrees. It regards as "unfunded" any *under*funded grants-in-aid that state and local governments cannot realistically reject or opt out of once they are passed by Congress.[24] The Homeland Security, No Child Left Behind, the Help America Vote, and Real ID Acts are seen by many state officials as examples of underfunded, de facto mandates. (See *What Do You Think? Identity Crisis? Federalism and the Real ID Act.*)

UNFUNDED MANDATES

Mandates that impose costs on state and local governments (and private industry) without reimbursement from the federal government.

CONGRESS AND DEVOLUTION

Controversy over federalism—what level of government should do what and who should pay for it—is as old as the nation itself. Beginning in 1995, debates over federalism were renewed. The new term was devolution—the passing down of responsibilities from the national government to the states.[25]

DEVOLUTION

Passing down of responsibilities from the national government to the states.

Devolution and Welfare Reform

Welfare reform turned out to be the key to devolution. Bill Clinton once promised "to end welfare as we know it," but it was a Republican Congress in 1996 that did so. After President Clinton had twice vetoed welfare reform bills, he and Congress finally agreed to merge welfare reform with devolution by

- Ending a sixty-year-old federal entitlement program for cash welfare aid (Aid to Families with Dependent Children), and substituting block grants with lump-sum allocations to the states for welfare payments (now known as Temporary Assistance to Needy Families)

Identity Crisis?
Federalism and the Real ID Act

Should the federal government require the states to provide uniform and secure driver's licenses in order to protect national security? If so, should the federal government pay the costs?

Congress passed the Real ID Act of 2005 as part of a wider effort at protecting homeland security. The Act requires the states to provide uniform, tamper-proof driver's licenses and ID cards by 2010. (The deadline for compliance was initially set for May 11, 2008 but was later extended by the Department of Homeland Security.) It sets standards for the documentation required to obtain a driver's license (birth certificates, immigration status, address, Social Security number, etc.). Each state must maintain a licensing database and share it with the federal government and all other states. The Act threatens to halt persons without a real ID from flying on commercial aircraft or entering federal buildings or nuclear power plants, and it promises to cut off federal transportation funds to noncomplying states.

The Real ID Act is an unfunded mandate. Insufficient federal funds have been allocated to the states to pay the estimated $11 billion dollars required to implement the Act. Licenses that meet the Act's security requirements may cost $100 each or more. The National Governors Association (NGA) recommended extending the deadline for implementation and called for the provision of federal funds necessary for state compliance. The NGA argued that issuing new complying licenses to every driver in the nation will create a bureaucratic nightmare. The cost must be either aided by increasing license fees or allocating tax funds to the states.

Opponents of the Real ID Act argue that it creates a national ID card that Americans have never before been required to carry. And they argue that driver's licensing has always been a state responsibility, and that federalism protects against congressional mandates in fields reserved to the states. Supporters of the Real ID Act argue that the federal government is responsible for national security and that current threats to security require national standards for identification. What do you think?

REAL ID ACT OF 2005

Requires states to provide uniform, tamper-proof driver's licenses and ID cards and maintain a licensing database to be shared with the federal government and other states.

ID verification will cost state and local governments lots of money. Proponents say it is worth it to prevent fraud.

- Granting the states broad flexibility in determining eligibility and benefit levels for persons receiving such aid
- Allowing states to increase welfare spending if they choose to do so but penalizing states that reduce their spending for cash aid below 75 percent of their 1996 levels
- Allowing states to deny additional cash payments for children born to women already receiving welfare assistance and allowing states to deny cash payments to parents under age eighteen who do not live with an adult and attend school

Devolution resulted in a dramatic reduction of welfare caseloads—an average of more than 50 percent throughout the states, although part of this reduction may be due to the healthy national economy. (For more information on welfare policy, see Chapter 17.)

Political Obstacles to Federalism

It is not likely that presidents or members of Congress will ever be motivated to restrain their own power. Even when they recognize that they may be overstepping the enumerated powers of the national government, political pressures on them to "DO SOMETHING!" about virtually every problem that confronts individuals, families, or communities inspire them to propose federal interventions. Politicians gain very little by telling their constituents that a particular problem—violence in the schools, domestic abuse, physician-assisted suicide, and so forth—is not a federal responsibility and should be dealt with at the state or local level of government.

THE SUPREME COURT AND THE REVIVAL OF FEDERALISM

The U.S. Supreme Court reconsidered the nature of American federalism in several recent cases. For the first time in many years, the Court declared laws of Congress unconstitutional because they exceeded the enumerated powers of Congress in Article I and tread upon the powers reserved to the states in the Tenth Amendment to the Constitution.

Federalism Revived

When a student, Alfonso Lopez, was apprehended at his high school carrying a .38-caliber handgun, federal agents charged him with violating the federal Gun-Free School Zones Act of 1990. He was convicted and sentenced to six months in prison. His attorney appealed on the ground that it was beyond the constitutionally delegated powers of Congress to police local school zones. In *U.S. v. Lopez* (1995) the U.S. Supreme Court issued its first opinion in more than sixty years that recognized a limit to Congress's power over interstate commerce and reaffirmed the Founders' notion that the federal government has only the powers enumerated in the U.S. Constitution. Attorneys for the federal government argued that the Gun-Free School Zones Act was a constitutional exercise of its interstate commerce power because "possession of a firearm in a school zone may result in violent crime and that violent crime can be expected to affect the functioning of the national economy." But the Court rejected this argument, holding that such reasoning would remove virtually all limits to federal power. "To uphold the Government's contentions here, we would have to pile inference upon inference in a manner that would bid fair to convert congressional activity under the Commerce Clause to a general police power of the sort retained by the states."[26]

The U.S. Supreme Court again invalidated a provision of a law of Congress—the Brady Handgun Violence Prevention Act—by deciding that its command to local law enforcement officers to conduct background checks on gun purchasers violated "the very principle of separate state sovereignty." The Court affirmed that the "federal government may neither issue directives requiring the states to address particular problems, nor command the state's officers, or those of their political subdivisions, to administer or enforce a federal regulatory program."[27]

HORIZONTAL FEDERALISM

Relationships between the states.

FULL FAITH AND CREDIT

The clause in the U.S. Constitution requiring states to legally recognize the official acts of other states.

States Shielded from Lawsuits

The Supreme Court ruled in 1996 in *Seminole Tribe* v. *Florida* that the Eleventh Amendment shields states from lawsuits by private parties that seek to force states to comply with federal laws enacted under the commerce power.[28] And by the same division of votes (Majority: Rehnquist, O'Connor, Scalia, Kennedy, Thomas; Minority: Stevens, Souter, Ginsburg, Breyer), the Court held in 1999 in *Aldin* v. *Maine* that states were also shielded in their own courts from lawsuits in which private parties seek to enforce federal mandates. In an opinion that surveyed over 200 years of American federalism, Justice Kennedy wrote, "Congress has vast power but not all power. . . . When Congress legislates in matters affecting the states, it may not treat these soverign entities as mere prefectures or corporations."[29] But in 2003, the court took a slightly different direction. In a 6–3 ruling, it held that state employees could sue their state in federal court to enforce rights granted by the federal Family and Medical Leave Act of 1993 (*Nevada Department of Human Resources* v. *Hibbs*).[30]

Limits on the Commerce Power

In 2000, to the surprise of many observers, the Supreme Court held that Congress's Violence Against Women Act was an unconstitutional extension of federal power into the reserved police powers of states. Citing its earlier *Lopez* decision, the Court held that noneconomic crimes are beyond the power of the national government under the Interstate Commerce Clause. "Gender-motivated crimes of violence are not, in any sense, economic activity." The Court rejected Congress's argument that the aggregate impact of crime nationwide has a substantial effect on interstate commerce. "The Constitution requires a distinction between what is truly national and what is truly local, and there is no better example of the police power, which the Founders undeniably left reposed in the States and denied the central government, than the suppression of violent crime and vindication of its victims."[31]

Federalism's Future

It may be too early to judge the impact of these decisions on federalism—whether they represent the return to the traditional notions of enumerated powers of Congress and reserved powers of the states. These decisions invalidated very popular laws of Congress—laws with broad political support across the country. And these decisions were made by a 5–4 vote of the justices, suggesting that the replacement of a single justice might reverse this current trend toward federalism by the Supreme Court.

INTERSTATE RELATIONS, HORIZONTAL FEDERALISM

Full Faith and Credit

The U.S. Constitution provides that "full faith and credit shall be given in each state to the public acts, records, and judicial proceedings of every other state." As more Americans move from state to state, it becomes increasingly important that the states recognize each other's legal instruments. This constitutional clause is intended to protect the rights of individuals who move from one state to another, and it is also intended to prevent individuals from evading their legal responsibilities by crossing state lines. Courts in Illinois must recognize decisions made by courts in Michigan. Contracts entered into in New York may be enforced in Florida. Corporations chartered in Delaware should be permitted to do business in North Dakota. One of the more serious problems in interstate relations today is the failure of the states to meet their obligations under the Full Faith and Credit Clause in the area of domestic relations, including divorce, alimony, child support, and custody of children. The result is now a complex and confused situation in domestic relations law. Full faith and credit-based battles in courtrooms across the United States are destined to intensify, as states pass sharply different laws defining marriage, life, privacy, and guardianship rights. Legal scholars are already arguing about whether same-sex marriages in some states will be recognized in other states where marriage is defined as solely between a man and a woman.

When the State of Massachusetts approved gay marriages, a number of other states amended their constitutions to define marriage as between a man and a woman. The issue is likely headed to the U.S. Supreme Court since the U.S. Constitution requires that "full faith and credit shall be given in each state to the public acts, records, and judicial proceedings of every other state."

Privileges and Immunities

The Constitution also states: "The citizens of each state shall be entitled to all privileges and immunities of citizens in the several states." Apparently the Founders thought that no state should discriminate against citizens from another state in favor of its own citizens. To do so would seriously jeopardize national unity. This clause also implies that citizens of any state may move freely about the country and settle where they like, with the assurance that as newcomers they will not be subjected to unreasonable discrimination. The newcomer should not be subject to discriminatory taxation; nor barred from lawful occupations under the same conditions as other citizens of the state; nor prevented from acquiring and using property; nor denied equal protection of the laws; nor refused access to the courts. However, states have managed to compromise this constitutional guarantee in several important ways. States establish residence requirements for voting and holding office, which prevent newcomers from exercising the same rights as older residents. States often require periods of residence as a prerequisite for holding a state job or for admission into professional practice such as law or medicine. States discriminate against out-of-state students in the tuition charged in public schools and colleges. Finally, some states are now seeking ways to keep "outsiders" from moving in and presumably altering the "natural" environment.

PRIVILEGES AND IMMUNITIES
The clause in the U.S. Constitution preventing states from discriminating against citizens of other states.

EXTRADITION
The surrender by one state of a person accused or convicted of a crime in another state.

Extradition

The Constitution also provides that "a person in any state with treason, felony, or other crime who shall flee from justice and be found in another state, shall on the demand of the executive authority from the state from which he fled, be delivered up, to be removed to the state having jurisdiction of the crime." In other words, the Constitution requires governors to extradite fugitives from another state's justice.

Governors have not always honored requests for extradition, but since no state wants to harbor criminals of another state, extradition is seldom refused. Among reasons advanced for the occasional refusals are (1) the individual has become a law-abiding citizen in his

What Are the "Most Livable" States?

Spirited debates are often engendered by rankings of states (or cities) by "livability." Each year the Morgan Quitno Press attracts both publicity and controversy with its livability ratings (shown below for the states). These ratings are calculated from each state's ranking on forty-three separate factors ranging from crime rates, infant mortality rates, deaths by suicide, and poverty rates (negative factors) to growth in personal income, home ownership rates, job growth, percent of population graduated from college, and percent of days that are sunny.

Rank	State	Livability Rating	Rank	State	Livability Rating
1	New Hampshire	34.66	26	Illinois	25.36
2	Minnesota	33.32	27	Florida	25.27
3	Wyoming	32.86	28	Rhode Island	25.05
4	Utah	32.05	29	New York	25.02
5	New Jersey	31.16	30	California	24.61
6	Iowa	30.84	31	Washington	24.34
7	Vermont	30.41	32	Arizona	24.16
8	Massachusetts	30.30	33	Pennsylvania	23.70
9	South Dakota	29.95	34	Missouri	23.18
10	Connecticut	29.86	35	Indiana	22.91
11	Nebraska	29.84	36	Ohio	22.30
12	Virginia	29.68	37	New Mexico	22.02
13	North Dakota	29.32	38	Michigan	22.00
14	Idaho	28.89	39	Texas	21.55
15	Maryland	28.82	40	Oklahoma	21.30
16	Maine	28.27	41	Georgia	21.09
17	Kansas	28.00	42	Alabama	20.86
18	Colorado	27.36	43	North Carolina	20.86
19	Hawaii	26.73	44	Tennessee	20.11
20	Wisconsin	26.09	45	West Virginia	18.93
21	Delaware	25.98	46	South Carolina	18.84
22	Montana	25.82	47	Kentucky	18.66
23	Oregon	25.77	48	Arkansas	18.59
24	Alaska	25.75	49	Louisiana	18.39
25	Nevada	25.70	50	Mississippi	15.86

Note: Data are from 2007.

Source: "Most Livable States Award," from http:www.cqpress.com/product/City-Crime-Rankings-14th Edition.html, Morgan Quitno Press, now CQ Press. Copyright © 2007 by CQ Press, a division of Congressional Quarterly, Inc. Reprinted by permission of CQ Press.

or hir new state; (2) a northern governor did not approve of the conditions in Georgia chain gangs; (3) a black returned to a southern state would not receive a fair trial; and (4) the governor did not believe that there was sufficient evidence against the fugitive to warrant his or her conviction in the first place.

Interstate Compacts

The Constitution provides that "no state shall without the consent of Congress . . . enter into any agreement or compact with another state." Over 150 interstate compacts now serve a wide variety of interests, such as interstate water resources; conservation of natural resources, including oil, wildlife, and fisheries; the control of floods; the development of interstate toll highways; the coordination of civil defense measures; the reciprocal supervision of parolees; the coordination of welfare and institutional care programs; the administration of interstate metropolitan areas; and the resolution of interstate tax conflicts. The average number of compacts a state is involved in is twenty-five.[32] Two compacts involve all fifty states: the Interstate Compact on the Placement of Children and the Uniform Interstate Compact on Juveniles. In practice, Congress has little to do with these compacts; the Supreme Court has held that congressional consent is required only if the compact encroaches upon some federal power. Otherwise, the negotiation and ratification of interstate compacts lies with the legislatures of the states involved.

Conflicts between States

States are not supposed to make war on each other, although they did so from 1861 to 1865. They are supposed to take their conflicts to the Supreme Court. The Constitution gives the U.S. Supreme Court the power to settle all cases involving two or more states. In recent years the Supreme Court has heard disputes between states over boundaries, the diversion of water, fishing rights, and the disposal of sewage and garbage.

ON THE WEB

Most states can also be accessed directly by inserting the state's postal abbreviation in the following address: **www.state.us** for example,

www.state.ca.us for California

www.state.va.us for Virginia

The exception is South Carolina (**myscgov.com**).

Perhaps the most important single source of comparative information on the states is provided by the Council of State Governments in its annual publication *The Book of the States*. This publication is not online, but it can be found in most university library reference sections. The Council of State Governments Web site is found at **www.csg.org**

The site provides a daily review of state government news to all viewers and access to state data archives for paid members as well as authorized state officials.

The official Web site of The DC Voting Rights Movement is **www.dcvote.org**

CHAPTER FOUR

PARTICIPATION IN STATE POLITICS

4

QUESTIONS TO CONSIDER

Are you registered to vote in your state?
- ☐ Yes   ☐ No

What political activities have you undertaken in your state's most recent election?
- ☐ Worked in party or campaign
- ☐ Wore button or applied a bumper sticker to your car
- ☐ Visited a candidate's Web site
- ☐ Voted
- ☐ Did not participate

Do you believe an interest group should be allowed to make campaign contributions to candidates who may later vote on bills affecting the group's interests?
- ☐ Yes   ☐ No

Is it ever right to deliberately violate a law that you believe is unjust?
- ☐ Yes   ☐ No

Do you ever expect to run for public office?
- ☐ Yes   ☐ No

THE NATURE OF POLITICAL PARTICIPATION

Recent elections have seen a modest upswing in voter participation in most states. More Americans than ever register and vote, log on to political Web sites, attend politically oriented events (concerts, movies, rallies, meet-ups, protests), wear their political preferences (shirts, hats, buttons, wristbands, flip-flops), and give money to candidates and politically oriented advocacy groups. Civic engagement is seen by many as on the upswing—at least in presidential election years. But political participation rates lag in nonpresidential election years, when many states and localities elect their officials.

Historically, campaigns have turned to the young for energy and innovation. It is certainly the case in the twenty-first century as young voters are being heavily targeted by both Democratic and Republican candidates. Because college students are more likely to get engaged in political discussions and activities than their non-college-attending friends,[1] candidates at all levels (federal, state, local) are visiting college campuses more than at any time since the 1960s. The candidates are not always just combing for votes. They seek young volunteers to help them design their Web sites; survey potential voters going door-to-door, recording their responses using "high-tech" hand-held PDAs; work phone banks; stuff envelopes; organize campus forums; make signs; pass out leaflets; chalk sidewalks; drive candidates to/from airports; staff large political rallies; and do anything else that comes to mind.

Popular participation in politics is the very definition of democracy. Individuals can participate in politics in many ways. They may run for, and win, public office; participate in marches, demonstrations, and sit-ins; make financial contributions to political candidates or causes; attend political meetings, speeches, and rallies; write letters or send e-mail to public officials or to newspapers; wear a political button or place a bumper sticker on a car; belong to organizations that support or oppose particular candidates or take stands on public issues; attempt to influence friends while discussing candidates or issues; vote in elections; or merely follow an issue or a campaign in the media.

This listing probably constitutes a ranking of the forms of political participation in order of frequency. (See Figure 4–1.) Less than one percent of the population *ever* runs for public office (see "*Up Close:* Getting into Politics"). Typically, only around half of the voting age population votes in presidential elections. Far fewer vote in state and local elections. Over one-third of the population is politically apathetic: They do not vote at

FIGURE 4–1 Political Participation

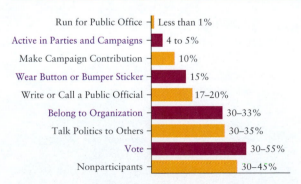

Source: National Election Studies Cumulative File.

all, and they are largely unaware of the political life of the nation. Ironically, many who do not consider themselves "political" participate in the life of their community as volunteers for various groups and organizations. They are unaware that volunteering at a local soup kitchen or tutoring disadvantaged elementary school kids are both examples of civic participation that make one's community a better place in which to live.

Sustained political participation—voting consistently in election after election for state and local offices as well as Congress and the president—is very rare. One study of voter participation over ten elections (including presidential, congressional, gubernatorial, and state and local legislative elections) showed that only 4 percent of the voting age population voted in nine or all ten of the elections; only 26 percent voted in half of the ten elections; and 38 percent did not vote in any election.[2] Age is the best predictor of sustained political activity; older citizens are more likely than young people to be regular voters. Knowing this, candidates often target their campaigns to older voters, which, in turn, further alienates younger voters,[3] especially in state and local elections when younger voter turnout is considerably lower than that of persons age fifty and older. On the other hand, younger citizens are more likely than many older voters to participate in community volunteer efforts.[4]

Older citizens are more likely than young people to be regular voters.

EXPLAINING VOTER TURNOUT

A sign of the times: A bumper sticker reads, "DON'T VOTE. IT JUST ENCOURAGES THEM." Around half of America's eligible voters stay away from the polls, even in a presidential election. Voter turnout is even lower in congressional elections, where turnout falls to about 35 percent of the voting age population in the off years (when presidential candidates are not on the ballot). Turnout rates in gubernatorial elections are roughly similar to turnout rates for congressional races, rising and falling depending on whether the election is held simultaneously with a presidential election (see Figure 4–2). City and county elections, when they are held separately from national elections, usually produce turnouts of 25 to 35 percent. However, turnout can shoot up sharply if a local contest features interesting and unique candidates or centers on highly contentious moral or pocketbook issues. Such situations tend to spark more media coverage and prompt more "get out the vote" efforts by candidates and advocacy groups.

Is Voting Rational?

Why is voter turnout so low? Actually, we could reverse the question and ask why people vote at all. A "rational" voter (one who seeks to maximize personal benefits and minimize costs) should vote only if the costs of voting (the time and energy spent first in registering, then in informing oneself about the candidates, and finally going to the polls on Election Day) are exceeded by the expected value of having the preferred candidate win (the personal benefits to be received from the winner) multiplied by the probability that one's own vote will be the deciding vote.[5] But under this "rational" notion, not many people would vote: Few Americans receive direct personal and tangible benefits from the election of one candidate versus another. And most Americans know that the likelihood of one vote determining the outcome of the election is very remote. Yet millions of Americans vote anyway.

FIGURE 4–2 The Trend in Voter Turnout

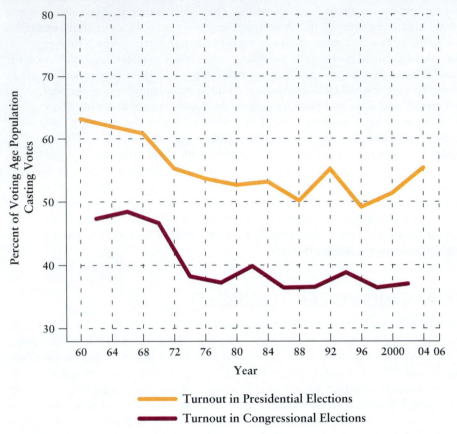

Turnout in Presidential Elections

Turnout in Congressional Elections

Source: Federal Election Commission. Data drawn from Congressional Record Service reports, Election Data Services Inc., and State Election Offices.

In order to rescue the "rational" model, political theorists have added "the intrinsic rewards of voting" to the equation.[6] These rewards include the ethic of voting, patriotism, a sense of duty, and allegiance to democracy. In other words, people get psychic rewards from voting itself rather than tangible benefits, and these psychic rewards do not depend on who wins or whether a single vote determines the outcome. So more people vote out of a sense of civic duty and commitment to democracy than on a purely rational basis.

Why People Stay at Home: Top Twelve Reasons

Millions of Americans stay at home on Election Day. Why? There are many answers to this question, but among the twelve most common (not necessarily in order of importance) are the following:

- *Burdensome and confusing registration requirements.* Registration procedures vary from state to state. While it is getting easier to register (some states now allow online registration), the timetables for registration differ. If voters are unaware of these differences, they may end up missing the cutoff date for a specific election. This often happens to people

up CLOSE   Getting into Politics

Politics attracts both "amateurs" and "professionals." Amateurs may be defined as people who continue in a full-time job or occupation while engaging in politics part time, mainly for friendship and association or out of a sense of civic duty. Professionals are people who devote all their time and energy to politics, running for and occupying public office themselves, or working for candidates with the expectation of appointment to office upon the victory of their chosen candidate.

Get Involved

The most common way to get into politics is to get involved in the community. Look into various organizations in your community, including

- Neighborhood associations
- Chambers of commerce, business associations
- Churches and synagogues (become an usher, if possible, for visibility)
- Political groups (Democratic or Republican clubs, League of Women Voters, and so on)
- Parent Teacher Associations (PTAs)
- Service clubs (Rotary, Kiwanis, Civitan, Toastmasters)
- Recreation organizations (Little League, flag football, soccer leagues, running and walking clubs, for example, as participant, coach, or umpire)

You can find out when and where such groups meet by looking in the neighborhood section of your local newspaper, watching the community calendar on TV, or listening to it on the radio. Become an active member and gain some visibility in your community.

Learn about Public Affairs

It is essential that you learn about the public issues confronting your community and state as well as the duties and responsibilities of various government offices. You should

- Attend meetings of your council or commission or attend state legislative sessions and committee hearings.
- Become familiar with current issues and officeholders, and obtain a copy of and read the budget.
- Learn the demographics of your district (racial, ethnic, and age composition; occupational mix; average incomes; neighborhood differences, and so on).

Run for Public Office

Many rewards come with elected office—the opportunity to help shape public policy; public attention and name recognition; and many business, professional, and social contacts. But there are many drawbacks as well—the absence of privacy; a microscopic review of one's past; constant calls, meetings, interviews, and handshaking; and perhaps most onerous of all, the continual need to solicit campaign funds. Before deciding to run, potential candidates should seriously consider the tremendous amount of work required. If you decide to run, begin by contacting your county elections department and try to obtain the following:

- Qualifying forms and information
- Campaign financing forms and regulations
- District and street maps for your district
- Recent election results in your district
- Election-law book or pamphlet
- Voter registration lists (usually sold as lists, labels, or tapes)

Also contact your party's county chairperson and ask for advice and assistance. Convince the party's leaders that you can win. Ask for a copy of their list of regular campaign contributors.

Raise Money

Perhaps the most difficult task in politics is that of raising campaign funds. The easiest way to finance a campaign is to be rich enough to provide your own funds. Failing that, you must

- Establish a campaign fund, according to the laws of your state.
- Find a treasurer/campaign-finance chairperson who knows large numbers of wealthy, politically involved people.
- Identify, call, and meet personally with potential contributors and solicit pledges, or better yet, checks.
- Invite wealthy, politically involved people to small coffees, cocktail parties, dinners; give a brief campaign speech and then have your finance chairperson solicit contributions.
- Be outgoing in confronting potential contributors; use the direct approach (e.g., "I know you want to help, Jim. How much can I put you down for?").
- Follow up fundraising events and meetings with personal phone calls.
- Be prepared to continue fundraising activities throughout your campaign; file accurate financial disclosure statements as required by law in your state.

(continued)

Organize Your Campaign

Professional campaign managers and management firms almost always outperform volunteers. (Many firms advertise in the monthly magazine *Campaigns and Elections*, which can be accessed online at www.campaignline.com.) If you cannot afford professional management, you must rely on yourself or trusted friends to perform the following:

- Prepare and memorize a brief (preferably less than seven seconds) answer to the question, "Why are you running?"
- Ask trusted friends from various clubs, activities, neighborhoods, churches, and so on, to meet and serve as a campaign committee. If your district is racially or ethnically diverse, make sure all groups are represented on your committee.
- Decide on a campaign theme; research issues important to your community; develop brief, well-articulated positions on these issues.
- Open a campaign headquarters with desks and telephones. Buy a cell phone; use call forwarding; stay in contact. Use your garage if you can't afford an office.
- Arrange to meet with newspaper editors, editorial boards, TV station executives, and political reporters. Be prepared for tough questions.
- Hire a media consultant or advertising agency, or appoint a volunteer media director who knows television, radio, and newspaper advertising.
- Arrange a press conference to announce your candidacy. Notify all media well in advance. Arrange for an overflow crowd of supporters to cheer and applaud.
- Produce eye-catching, inspirational fifteen- or thirty-second television and radio ads that present a favorable image of you and stress your campaign theme.
- Prepare and print attractive campaign brochures, signs, and bumper stickers.
- Prepare a schedule of community events, meetings, and other public happenings, and plan to make an appearance.
- If funds permit, hire a local survey-research firm or pollster to conduct continuous telephone surveys of voters in your district, asking what they think are the most important issues, how they stand on them, whether they recognize your name and your theme, and how they plan to vote. Be prepared to change your theme and your position on issues if survey results show strong opposition to your views.

Campaign Hard

Fundraising, organizing, developing issues, writing speeches, and polling continue up to Election Day. Campaigns themselves may be primarily *media centered* or primarily *door-to-door* ("retail") or some combination of both.

- Attend every community gathering possible, just to be seen, even if you do not give a speech. Keep all speeches *short*. Focus on one or two issues that your polls show are important to voters.
- Recruit paid or unpaid volunteers to canvass neighborhoods door-to-door to hand out literature and whenever possible to engage potential voters in friendly, favorable conversations about you. Record names and addresses of voters who say they support you.
- Do door-to-door canvassing yourself with a brief (seven-second) self-introduction and statement of the reason you are running. Canvassing may also include offices, factories, coffee shops, shopping malls—anywhere you find a crowd—as well as neighborhoods. Use registration lists to identify members of your own party, and try to address them by name.
- Organize a phone bank, either professional or volunteer. Prepare *brief* introduction and phone statements. Your phone bank should become increasingly active as the election nears. Call only persons on election lists registered in your party. Record names of people who say they support you.
- Know your opponent: Research his or her past affiliations, indiscretions, if any, previous voting record, and public positions on issues.
- Be prepared to "define" your opponent in negative terms. Negative advertising works. But be fair: Base your comments about your opponent on supportable facts.

On Election Day

Turning out *your* voters is the key to success. Election Day is the busiest day of the campaign for you and especially your staff. But don't forget to encourage your supporters to vote absentee or early if they cannot make it to the polls on Election Day.

- Use your phone bank to place as many calls as possible to your party members in your district (especially those who have indicated in previous calls and visits that they support you). Remind them to vote; make sure your phone workers can tell each voter where to go to cast their vote. Ask if they need a ride to the polls.
- Prepare volunteer drivers to take anyone to the polls that needs a ride. Send cars to condominiums, nursing homes, neighborhoods, and so on, clearly marked with your name but willing to assist anyone.
- Assign workers to as many polling places as possible. Most state laws require that they stay a specified distance from the voting booths. But they should be in evidence with your signs and literature to buttonhole voters before they go into the booth.
- Show up at city or county election offices on election night with a prepared victory statement thanking supporters and voters and pledging your service to the district, city, county, or state. (Also prepare a courteous concession statement pledging your support to the winner, in case you lose.)
- Attend the victory party with your supporters; meet many "new" friends.

Voter Turnout Rate

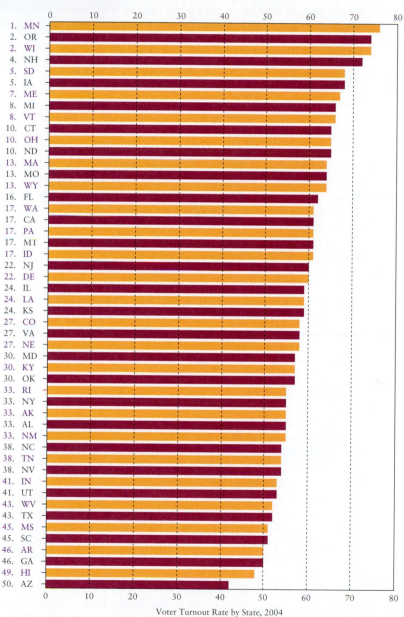

Rank	State
1.	MN
2.	OR
2.	WI
4.	NH
5.	SD
5.	IA
7.	ME
8.	MI
8.	VT
10.	CT
10.	OH
10.	ND
13.	MA
13.	MO
13.	WY
16.	FL
17.	WA
17.	CA
17.	PA
17.	MT
17.	ID
22.	NJ
22.	DE
24.	IL
24.	LA
24.	KS
27.	CO
27.	VA
27.	NE
30.	MD
30.	KY
30.	OK
33.	RI
33.	NY
33.	AK
33.	AL
33.	NM
38.	NC
38.	TN
38.	NV
41.	IN
41.	UT
43.	WV
43.	TX
45.	MS
45.	SC
46.	AR
46.	GA
49.	HI
50.	AZ

Voter Turnout Rate by State, 2004

Note: Data are for 2004. Turnout is the percent of registered voters who voted.
Source: Committee for the Study of the American Electorate 2004 Election Report. Available at http://www.fairvote.org/reports/CSAE2004electionreport.pdf

who have moved since the last election—which lots of Americans do every year. (The Census Bureau estimates that over 40 million move annually.) Several states have Election Day registration or no registration. Predictably, turnout is higher in these states. (See *"Rankings of the States:* Voter Turnout Rate.")

■ *Voter unawareness of the availability of alternatives to voting in person: absentee voting, early voting (in some states).* Some states are better than others at making it easy to vote absentee and at publicizing such information. Younger voters away at college, voters with sight or mobility limitations, often senior citizens, and people whose jobs take them on the road a lot or who work shifts often don't vote because they are unaware of how to vote before Election Day.

■ *Lack of competition ("no suspense").* Competition increases turnout. If it is a "no brainer" as to who is going to win, and if a voter does not believe his or her vote may make a difference, it is easy to decide not to vote, especially if one's schedule is quite hectic on Election Day.

■ *No high-profile races featuring interesting candidates or "hot" issues.* Turnout typically goes up when media coverage escalates. The media, especially television, is more likely to cover fascinating candidates (e.g., the first woman or minority candidate for mayor, a professional wrestler running for governor) and controversial issues (e.g., gay rights, stem cell research, casino gambling, gun control, abortion).

■ *No personal contact by a candidate or political party.* The failure of candidates or political parties to personally encourage voters to go to the polls—either by phone or in person via candidate appearances—reduces the likelihood that a person will vote. But this is often difficult to do in large states and metropolitan areas, which is why candidates often turn to bulk mail and television to encourage people to vote instead of the old-fashioned door-to-door and "meet-and-greet" methods. (Half of all Americans said no one contacted them to register or vote in the 2004 election cycle.)

■ *Purely personal reasons.* Individuals have their own reasons for not voting, such as feeling that one doesn't know enough about the candidates or the issues on the ballot; unexpected Election Day occurrences—illness, accident, travel, work schedule; language barriers; fear of not knowing *where* to vote, especially if you have moved; first-time voters getting cold feet at the last minute, fearing embarrassment if they had to admit to a poll worker that they do not know *how* to actually cast a ballot (e.g., new voting technologies replacing punch-card ballots).

■ *Social and cultural attributes and experiences.* Voting studies have found that a person's income, education, age, gender, race or ethnicity, health status, attachment to a community, marital status, length of time in the United States (if a naturalized citizen), and religion and frequency of religious service attendance, as well as a person's participation in community and political organizations and their civic attachments, can affect their likelihood of voting—or not voting.

■ *Psychological "disconnects" with the political system.* Some voters are angry at all politicians, regardless of what party label they are running under or what office they are seeking. Others are highly cynical of the whole process and don't believe that their vote will make any difference or that those elected will pay any attention to their concerns. And some immigrants have come to America from cultures where politics was reserved for society's elites.

■ *The way the media covers elections.* Citizens often complain that the media focuses more on the "horse race" (who's winning) than on the issues. Other complaints are that the "down ballot" (low-profile) races get far too little coverage, especially by television, so voters do not have enough information on them. Voters also routinely complain about the bias of political reporters and their "gotcha" style of journalism, along with the large number of debates, and the tendency of reporters to give more time in their stories to political pundits than to the candidates themselves. Another common complaint is that voters are so barraged with campaign ads that by Election Day, they have had it!

- *A decline in the quality and quantity of high school civics and government classes.* Not everyone goes to college. For many, high school is the end of the road for their civics instruction. Surveys of young adults tell us that many of these courses last only one semester, focus almost exclusively on the national government, or spend too much time discussing tedious processes such as how a bill becomes a law. Rarely do they learn about the mechanics of voting (registering, changing one's place of registration, voting absentee) or how to get involved in state and local politics. This helps explain why voter turnout rates in state and local elections are often far lower than in presidential elections. Many civic education–oriented groups across the United States are actively trying to change this picture.

- *The weather.* Rain and snow keeps well-intentioned voters at home—Democrats more than Republicans.[7]

- *The location of the polling place.* Changes in the location of a voter's polling place (precinct) may cause a voter to say "forget it" if he or she shows up at the wrong precinct on Election Day and is instructed to go to a new location. If the polling place is located a considerable distance from the voter's residence, that, too, may dampen voting if the citizen waited until Election Day to cast a ballot instead of voting early or via absentee ballot.[8]

Who Fails to Vote

The profile of nonvoters has remained fairly stable when it comes to education, income, and age. For years, studies have found that the young, the poor, the unemployed, and the least educated are the least likely to vote and the most likely to feel alienated or turned off by politics.[9] (See Table 4–1.)

Nonvoters are also more prevalent among

- First-generation immigrants, especially non–English speaking[10]
- Those who seldom participate in organized religious activities
- Newcomers to a community[11]
- People with little or no interest in politics, little trust in government, no belief that voting is a civic duty, and no belief they can make a difference by voting
- Persons with physical disabilities[12]
- Blue-collar and service-sector workers
- Asians and Latinos
- Single parents living in poor neighborhoods
- Independents
- Persons who have not been contacted by a candidate or party
- Renters (versus homeowners)

Socioeconomic Explanations

Much of the variation in voter turnout among the states can be explained by socioeconomic characteristics of their residents—their overall educational level, income, racial and ethnic mix, and age profile. For example, income and educational levels are higher, and the white population is larger, in Minnesota and Wisconsin. Turnout is much higher in these states than in many Deep South states, whose populations are poorer, less educated, younger, and more racially diverse. (Rising turnout rates among these southern states has been attributed somewhat to socioeconomic shifts—more newcomers from the North—and to federal civil rights laws and black voter mobilization efforts.)

TABLE 4–1   Characteristics of Voters: 2000 versus 2004

Characteristics	2000 Percent Reporting They Voted	2004 Percent Reporting They Voted
Sex		
Male	53.1	56.3
Female	56.2	60.1
Race		
White	56.4	60.3
Black	53.5	56.3
Hispanic	27.5	28.0
Asian	N/A	29.8
Age		
18–20	28.4	41.0
21–24	24.2	42.5
25–34	43.7	46.9
35–44	55.0	56.9
45–64	64.1	66.6
65 & Over	67.6	68.9
Employment		
Employed	55.5	60.0
Unemployed	35.1	46.4
Education		
8 Years	26.8	23.6
High School Graduate	49.4	52.4
College Graduate	72.0	74.2

Sources: Statistical Abstract of the United States 2001, p. 251. 2004 data were calculated from U.S. Census "Voting and Registration in the Election of November 2004," Tables 1, 4a, 4b, 6, and 7.

Differences in Party Strength

States vary in the proportion of their voters who either register as independents or describe themselves as weak party identifiers. One presidential election study concluded that "turnout has declined most in states which once had strong traditional party organizations."[13] The question is "Why?" There are several answers. First, independents are less likely to vote than staunch partisans. Second, party organizations play a key role in "get out the vote" efforts. Party volunteers make phone calls, send out voting reminders, and take people to the polls.

Differences in Registration Procedures

Voter registration procedures differ significantly across the fifty states. Several states allow Election Day registration (Maine, Minnesota, Wisconsin, Wyoming, New Hampshire, and Idaho). One state has no registration requirement at all (North Dakota). A sizable number of states require a person to register fifteen to thirty days in advance of the election in order to give election officials time to prepare voter lists for each voting precinct's poll workers. Such requirements are designed to reduce voter fraud and maintain the integrity of the voting process. Today, it is far easier to register than in days past.

The question is, "How helpful are these variations in registration procedures in explaining state turnout variations?" Many advocacy groups are convinced they make a lot of difference, especially in fast-growing states. New residents may incorrectly assume that registration procedures in their new home state are the same as in the one they left, but they may not be. The truth is that "the overall evidence does not support the argument that Election Day registration is the answer to America's turnout problems."[14]

Federally Mandated "Motor Voter" Law

Although Congress had previously passed voting rights laws designed to protect minorities, it had never directly intervened in the general process of state election administration prior to 1993. But with strong Democratic support, Congress passed the National Voter Registration Act of 1993, popularly known as the "motor voter" act. It mandates that the states offer people the opportunity to register when they apply for a driver's license or apply for welfare services. States must also offer registration by mail, and they must accept a simplified registration form prepared by the Federal Election Commission. Finally, the Act bars states from removing the names of people from registration lists for failure to vote.

What is the impact of the motor voter law on voter turnout in the states? Early studies showed that states that had enacted their own motor voter registration laws before the federal mandate appear to have increased their turnout rates by doing so.[15] However, although the law has increased voter *registration*, the evidence is mixed as to whether it adds significantly to *turnout* on Election Day.[16] Why? "Making registration easier does not provide citizens with a reason to vote."[17] What seems to be more effective are **post-registration laws**, which require each voter to be mailed a sample ballot and information about polling place location, providing a longer voting day, and requiring firms to give their employees time off to vote. One study has found that most of these increase young voter turnout.[18]

Party Competition

Voter participation rates can also be affected by the degree of interparty competition in a state. The more fierce the competition between the parties, the greater the interest of citizens in elections, and the larger the voter turnout. When parties and candidates compete fiercely, they make news and are given a large play via the mass media. Thus, a setting of competitive politics tends to have a greater amount of political stimuli available in the environment than does a setting with weak competition. More money is spent in campaigning. People are also more likely to perceive that their votes count in a close, competitive contest, and thus they are more likely to cast them.[19]

Voting Time, Place, Equipment, Ballots, Poll Workers

There is tremendous variation across the states in how easy each makes it for a voter to cast a ballot. Many believe that turnout can be increased by

- Making it easier to vote absentee (no excuse required) or to vote *before* Election Day (early voting, voting by mail)
- Making it easier to vote *on* Election Day: provisional ballots for those who believe they are registered and have erroneously been kept off of the precinct list of registered voters; voting by Internet
- Making polling places more accessible to persons with physical disabilities (curbside voting, selection of more accessible polling places and voting booths)

PARTY COMPETITION
The competitiveness of the two major parties, usually measured by the closeness of the vote for various offices.

POST-REGISTRATION LAWS
Methods to enhance voter turnout after a person registers. Most effective with young voters.

- Selecting better voting equipment (touch-screen or optical scan voting machines, not punch-card machines)
- Designing better ballot layouts (no more "butterfly ballots"; Braille ballots and large print for visually impaired voters)
- Better training of America's 1.4 million poll workers in how to assist voters, especially first-time voters
- Implementing easier procedures for restoring the voting rights of felons
- Implementing better voter education programs targeted at all age groups, but especially among younger citizens (e.g., Kids Vote, State Mock Elections)

Many of these suggestions emerged in the aftermath of the presidential election in 2000, the closest race in modern American history, when the need to revamp many state election codes became obvious. Several state associations, along with a number of prominent commissions, such as the National Commission on Federal Election Reform co-chaired by former presidents Jimmy Carter and Gerald Ford, and the U.S. Congress all conducted analyses that came to the same conclusion—America's state election systems needed to be overhauled. In response, Congress ended up passing the Help America Vote Act in 2002, which mandated states to reform their election systems.[20] The nation's aging electorate—and the growing number of voters with sight, hearing, and/or mobility limitations—has also prompted states to reexamine the location of their polling places, along with the accessibility of their voting booths, ballot design, and voting technology, and to place more emphasis on training poll workers. So, too, has the federal Voting Accessibility for the Elderly and Handicapped Act (VAEHA), enacted in 1984. Under the Act, states are responsible for ensuring that polling places for federal elections are accessible to elderly voters and voters with disabilities.

Media Predicting Winners

Election 2000 also reopened some other debates about the impact of media coverage on voter turnout in different time zones.[21] The network practice of using exit polls to "call" elections before the polls have closed everywhere has long been under attack, especially by political parties and candidates on the West Coast. The National Commission on Federal Election Reform recommended this practice be stopped, at least in the forty-eight contiguous states. Although the national television networks were more cautious in 2004 and did not call a state until all its polls were closed (important in states with multiple time zones), they still refused to wait until all polls in every state were closed to report projections. Will it ever happen? Doubtful. The news media is a highly competitive business and, let's be honest, voters want to know the results as soon as possible.

Counting Ballots

The failure of many states to have uniform procedures in place with regard to counting the votes was another flaw that surfaced in the post-election court battles surrounding Election 2000. What is a legally cast ballot? When, who, and how are recounts conducted? What procedures are in place to guarantee that the absentee ballots cast by military personnel and citizens living overseas are counted in a timely fashion? Answers to these questions often were not clear due to "fuzzy" election laws. Ballot spoilage rates varied from state-to-state, and from county-to-county, even within the same state. The Help America Vote Act has pushed states to enact legislation addressing these problems. Some states, like Florida, Georgia, and Maryland, have done so much more quickly than others, which have lagged behind.[22]

The major criticisms of touch-screen voting machines (left) are fears of tampering (fraud) and the lack of a paper trail to use if a recount is needed. Both concerns have led some states and localities to abandon touch screens in favor of optical scan voting machines (right). Regardless of the type of voting equipment used, voters can still make mistakes, mostly by ignoring instructions.

Voting Equipment Controversies

Americans cast their ballots on a wide variety of voting equipment. A survey by Election Data Services reported the breakdown of voting equipment in use at the nation's 181,209 voting precincts in 2006 was optical scan (41 percent), Direct Recording Electronic (DRE) touch-screen machines (39 percent), punchcards (3 percent), mechanical lever machines (10 percent), paper ballots (less than 1 percent), and a combination (7 percent).[23] This breakdown is constantly changing as states comply with the Help America Vote Act's push to eliminate punch-card ballots and lever voting machines (voters pull a lever next to their ballot choice). But that will not end controversies over voting equipment. The reliability of computerized voting machines is under attack. Critics of touch-screen voting equipment are demanding a paper trail to allow a citizen to confirm that a vote was recorded correctly and, if necessary, to verify results in case a recount is needed. But there has been little agreement on how best to do it,[24] other than by buying lots of new printers or abandoning touch-screen machines altogether, both of which are expensive. (Florida chose to abandon its touch screens in favor of optical scan equipment in time for the 2008 presidential election.) Disabled voters, a group with growing political clout, are monitoring paper trail proposals very carefully to make sure their rights to a secret ballot are not jeopardized. The Director of the Disability Vote Project of the American Association of People with Disabilities has testified that electronic touch-screen machines are the only "certified, tested, and proven equipment" that provide full access to disabled voters.[25] Concerns about fraud in the election system are also escalating.

Internet Voting: Promoting Democracy or Permitting Fraud?

As the number of Americans online continues to increase, the question arises as to whether voting online will promote democracy or permit fraud. Some analysts believe it will substantially increase voter turnout because of its convenience. They argue it will give voters more time to think about how to vote on complex ballot initiatives and confusing bond referenda. Others are more skeptical about voting online. They worry about how to verify a voter's eligibility and identification and how to prevent hackers from "stealing" an election. Another concern is the "digital divide" that exists between rich and poor in America and between men and women.[26]

RACE, ETHNICITY, AND POLITICAL PARTICIPATION

Racial and ethnic minorities are growing in numbers and percentages of the U.S. population (see "Race and Ethnicity" in Chapter 1) and in political power.

African Americans

For years, black voter turnout rates lagged behind white turnout, primarily due to discrimination. (More will be said about this later in the chapter.) But this gap has closed in recent years. Now, black voter turnout often exceeds white turnout, especially in areas where blacks make up a sizable portion of the voting age population, when a minority is a candidate in a high-profile election or the first minority to run for the office, and in places where black churches are very proactive in voter mobilization and education.[27]

Hispanics

Voter participation rates among Hispanics still trail black and white turnout. However, when controls are made for education, income, age, and mobility, this turnout gap almost disappears.[28] Nonetheless, Hispanic voter participation is still relatively weak. In the 2004 presidential election, despite constituting over 11 percent of the voting age population, Hispanics cast only 8 percent of the total vote. In contrast, African Americans, who comprise 12 percent of the voting age population, cast 11 percent of the total vote. Hispanics, like blacks, are more likely to vote for Latinos—a practice known as "co-ethnic voting."[29]

Various explanations have been advanced for the lower voter participation of Hispanics. For starters, language can be a rather steep hurdle to jump, especially for newly arrived immigrants. The good news is that the emergence of Spanish-speaking television, radio, and newspapers is helping candidates reach out to this population more easily than in the past.[30] So, too, is the availability of ballots in Spanish. Hispanic voter turnout is also affected by one's country of origin. There is less interest among immigrants from certain Latin and South American countries where politics is largely reserved for elites and for men (patriarchal societies). It is no surprise that naturalized Hispanic citizens, with the exception of Cuban Americans, still vote at lower rates than their American-born peers. But this is changing rapidly as the Hispanic population continues to explode in the United States.[31]

As Hispanics emerge as the nation's largest minority, both Democratic and Republican parties vie for their votes. It is especially important for the Republicans to win over a substantial

Hispanics, the nation's fastest growing ethnic group, are becoming more active politically. Democrats and Republicans alike have stepped up their voter education and get-out-the-vote programs targeted at this large bloc of potential supporters.

TABLE 4–2	Minority Voting in the 2000 and 2004 Presidential Elections		
2000	**White**	**African American**	**Latino**
Share of Total 2000 Vote	80%	10%	7%
Republican Bush	54	8	35
Democrat Gore	42	90	62
Independent Nader	3	2	3
2004	**White**	**African American**	**Latino**
Share of Total 2004 Vote	77	11	8
Republican Bush	58	11	44
Democrat Kerry	41	88	53
Independent Nader	0	0	2

Source: Voter News Service exit poll, November 2000; National Election Poll (or NEP) Exit Poll, conducted by Edison/ Mitofsky, November 2004 (available at http://www.cnn.com/ELECTION/2004/pages/results/states/US/P/00/epolls.0.html).

portion of Hispanic voters, inasmuch as African American voters are solidly Democratic. In the 2004 presidential election, 88 percent of the African American vote was cast for Democratic candidate John Kerry. (See Table 4–2.) The Latino vote in 2004 split 53 percent for Democrat Kerry to 44 percent for Republican George W. Bush (a gain of 9 percent over 2000). The Republican Bush brothers (President George W. Bush and his brother, Florida Governor Jeb Bush) made special efforts to recruit Hispanic voters to their party. Both speak Spanish (Jeb better than George W.). Both brothers attempted to deal with Hispanic concerns as governors of their states, Texas and Florida, and both succeeded in winning over substantial portions of the Hispanic voters in those states. By the 2008 Election, Democrats had geared up to recapture some of the Hispanic vote.

As Hispanics emerge as the nation's largest minority, both Democratic and Republican parties vie for their votes.

Asians

Asian and Pacific Islanders make up a relatively small portion of the U.S. population (3.6 percent and 0.1 percent, respectively). Asian participation rates lag behind white, black, and Hispanic rates.[32] Some attribute high levels of nonvoting to more pervasive language and cultural barriers faced by Asians. Others point to the higher-than-average tendency of newly registered Asians to register as independents, rather than Democrats or Republicans.[33] (As noted previously, partisans are higher turnout voters than independents.)

SECURING THE RIGHT TO VOTE

The only mention of voting requirements in the Constitution of the United States as it was originally adopted is in Article I: "The electors in each state shall have the qualifications requisite for electors for the most numerous branch of the state legislature." Of course, "electors" (voters) for the most numerous branch of the state legislature are determined by *state* laws and constitutions. The effect of this constitutional provision was to leave to the states the power to determine who is eligible to vote in both state and federal elections. Over the years, however, a combination of constitutional amendments, congressional actions, and Supreme Court decisions has largely removed control over voting from the states and made it a responsibility of the national government.

Elimination of Property Qualifications

Early in American history, voting was limited to males over twenty-one years of age, who resided in the voting district for a certain period and owned a considerable amount of land or received a large income from other investments. So great was the fear that the "common man" would use his vote to attack the rights of property owners that only 120,000 people out of 2 million were permitted to vote in the 1780s. Men of property felt that only other men of property had sufficient "stake in society" to exercise their vote in a "responsible" fashion. Gradually, however, Jeffersonian and Jacksonian principles of democracy, including confidence in the reason and integrity of the common man, spread rapidly in the new Republic. Most property qualifications were eliminated by the states themselves in the early nineteenth century.

Fifteenth Amendment

The first constitutional limitation on state powers over voting came with the ratification of the Fifteenth Amendment: "The right of the citizens of the United States to vote shall not be denied or abridged by the United States or any state on account of race, color, or previous condition of servitude." The object of this amendment, passed by the Reconstruction Congress and adopted in 1870, was to extend the vote to former black slaves and prohibit voter discrimination on the basis of race. The Fifteenth Amendment also gives Congress the power to enforce black voting rights "by appropriate legislation." Thus, the states retained their right to determine voter qualifications *as long as they do not practice racial discrimination*, and Congress was given the power to pass legislation ensuring black voting rights.

Nineteenth Amendment

Following the Civil War many of the women who had been active abolitionists, seeking to end slavery, turned their attention to the condition of women in America. They had learned to organize, conduct petition campaigns, and parade and demonstrate, as abolitionists, and later they sought to improve the legal and political rights of women. In 1869 the Wyoming territory adopted woman's suffrage; later several other western states followed suit. But it was not until the Nineteenth Amendment to the U.S. Constitution in 1920 that women's voting rights were constitutionally guaranteed.

The "White Primary"

For almost 100 years after the adoption of the Fifteenth Amendment, white politicians in the southern states were able to defeat its purposes. Social and economic pressures and threats of violence were used to intimidate many thousands of would-be voters. There were also many "legal" methods of disenfranchisement.

For many years the most effective means of banning black voting was a technique known as the "**white primary**." So strong was the Democratic party throughout the South that the Democratic nomination for public office was tantamount to election. This meant that *primary* elections to choose the Democratic nominee were the only elections in which real choices were made. If blacks were prevented from voting in Democratic primaries, they could be effectively disenfranchised. Thus southern state legislatures resorted to the simple device of declaring the Democratic party in southern states a private club and ruling that only white people could participate in its elections, that is, in *primary* elections. Blacks would be free to vote in "official," general elections, but all whites tacitly agreed to support the Democratic, or "white man's," party, in general elections, regardless of their differences in the primary. Not until 1944, in *Smith* v. *Allright*, did the Supreme Court declare this practice unconstitutional.[34]

Discrimination

Black voting in the South increased substantially after World War II. (From an estimated 5 percent of voting age blacks registered in southern states in the 1940s, black registration rose to an estimated 20 percent in 1952, 25 percent in 1956, 28 percent in 1960, and 39 percent in 1964.) But as late as 1965 black voter turnout rate was little more than half of the white rate. In hundreds of rural counties throughout the South, blacks were prevented from registering and voting. Despite the Fifteenth Amendment, many local registrars in the South succeeded in barring black registration by means of an endless variety of obstacles, delays, and frustrations. Application forms for registration were lengthy and complicated; even a minor error would lead to rejection, such as underlining rather than circling in the "Mr.–Mrs.–Miss" set of choices as instructed. Literacy tests were the most common form of disenfranchisement. Many a black college graduate failed to interpret "properly" the complex legal documents that were part of the test. White applicants for voter registration were seldom asked to go through these lengthy procedures.

Civil Rights Act of 1964

The Civil Rights Act of 1964 made it unlawful for registrars to apply unequal standards in registration procedures or to reject applications because of immaterial errors. It required that literacy tests be in writing and made a sixth-grade education a presumption of literacy.

Twenty-Fourth Amendment

The Twenty-Fourth Amendment to the Constitution was ratified in 1964, making poll taxes unconstitutional as a requirement for voting in national elections. In 1965 the Supreme Court declared poll taxes unconstitutional in state and local elections as well.[35]

Voting Rights Act of 1965

In Selma, Alabama, in early 1965, civil rights organizations effectively demonstrated that local registrars were still keeping large numbers of blacks off the voting rolls. Registrars closed their offices for all but a few hours every month, placed limits on the number of applications processed, went out to lunch when black applicants appeared, delayed months before processing applications from blacks, and discovered a variety of other methods to keep blacks disenfranchised. In response to the Selma march, Congress enacted a strong Voting Rights Act (VRA) in 1965. The U.S. attorney general, upon evidence of voter discrimination, was empowered to replace local registrars with federal registrars, abolish literacy tests, and register voters under simplified federal procedures.[36] However, it turned out that federal registrars were sent to only a small number of southern counties. Many southern counties that had previously discriminated in voter registration hurried to sign up black voters just to avoid the imposition of federal registrars. The Voting Rights Act of 1965 has been extended and amended several times: 1970, 1975, 1982, and 2006.

(The "Fannie Lou Hamer, Rosa Parks, and Coretta Scott King Voting Rights Act Reauthorization and Amendments Act of 2006" extends the VRA for 25 more years, until 2031.) Hispanics and other language minorities were added to the Act's coverage in the 1975 revisions. The impact of the Act has been to largely eliminate discrimination in registration and voting. It has also increased the opportunity of black and Latino voters to elect representatives of their choice by providing a vehicle for challenging discriminatory election methods that may dilute minority voting strength. The Act has been called "the single most effective piece of civil rights legislation ever passed by Congress."[37]

Eighteen-Year-Old Voting

Before 1970 only three of the fifty states permitted residents eighteen to twenty-one years of age to vote—Georgia, Kentucky, and Alaska. All other states, in the exercise of their constitutional responsibility to determine the qualifications of "electors," had set the voting age at twenty-one. The movement for eighteen-year-old voting received its original impetus in Georgia in 1944 under the leadership of Governor Ellis Arnall, who argued successfully that eighteen-year-olds were then being called upon to fight and die for their country in World War II and, therefore, deserved to have a voice in the conduct of government. However, this argument failed to convince adult voters in other states; qualifications for military service were not regarded as the same as qualifications for rational decision making in elections. In state after state, voters rejected state constitutional amendments designed to extend the vote to eighteen-year-olds.

Congress intervened on behalf of eighteen-year-old voting with the passage of the Twenty-Sixth Amendment to the Constitution in 1971.[38] The states quickly ratified this amendment, during a period of national turbulence over the Vietnam War. Many supporters of the amendment believed that protests on the campuses and streets could be reduced if youthful protesters were given the vote. Moreover, Democrats

Congress passed and President Bush signed into law the Fannie Lou Hamer, Rosa Parks, and Coretta Scott King Voting Rights Act Reauthorization and Amendments Act of 2006, extending the federal Voting Rights Act until 2031. Each of the women played a vital role in the battle for civil rights for African Americans.

believed that their party would gain from the youth vote, and liberal candidates believed that idealistic young voters would spark their campaigns.

It turned out, however, that young people cast their votes for parties and candidates in the same proportions as older voters. The image of the idealistic, activist student is not an accurate image of the young voter in America. Less than one-third of people age eighteen to twenty-four are in college. More than half of this age group are working and either living with their parents or are married and living in their own households. College students achieve greater visibility in the news media at election time than young working people because they turn out to vote at higher rates.

The federal Voting Rights Act protects the voting rights of language minorities. Election officials are responsible for translating ballot language to reflect their area's population composition.

MINORITIES IN STATE POLITICS

Racial and ethnic conflict remains a central factor in the politics of nearly every state. In recent years, conflict over voting and representation has centered on the effects of various institutional arrangements on minority influence in government.

Diluting Minority Votes

Congress strengthened the Voting Rights Act in 1982 by outlawing any electoral arrangements that had the *effect* of weakening minority voting power. This "effects" test replaced the earlier "intent" test, which required black plaintiffs to prove that a particular arrangement was adopted with the specific intent of reducing black voting power.[39] (An "intent" test invalidates laws or practices only if they are designed to discriminate; an "effects" test invalidates laws or practices that adversely affect racial minorities regardless of the original intent.) For example, at-large elections or multimember districts for city councils, county commissions, or state legislative seats may have the effect of weakening minority voting power if a white majority in such districts consistently prevents blacks or Hispanics from winning office. Congress stopped short of directly outlawing such districts but established a "totality of circumstances" test to be used to determine if such districts had a discriminatory effect. The "circumstances" to be considered by the courts include whether or not there has been a history of racial polarization in voting and whether minority candidates have ever won election to office in the district.[40]

Affirmative Racial Gerrymandering

The U.S. Supreme Court requires states and cities to provide minorities with a "realistic opportunity to elect officials of their choice." In the key case of *Thornburg* v. *Gingles*,[41] the Court interpreted the Voting Rights Act Amendments of 1982 to require state legislatures to draw election district boundary lines in a way that guarantees that minorities can elect minority representatives to governing bodies. The burden of proof was shifted

AFFIRMATIVE RACIAL GERRYMANDERING

Drawing election district boundaries to provide maximum opportunities for the election of minorities.

GERRYMANDERING

Drawing election district boundaries to give an advantage to a party, candidate, or racial or ethnic group.

MAJORITY-MINORITY DISTRICTS

Districts in which minority racial or ethnic group members constitute a majority of voters.

from minorities to show that district lines diluted their voting strength to state lawmakers to show that they have done everything possible to maximize minority representation. The effect of the Court's decision was to inspire affirmative racial gerrymandering—the creation of predominately black and minority districts wherever possible.

Racial **gerrymandering** dominated the redistricting process in all of the large states following the 1990 census. In many states Republican legislators allied themselves with black and Hispanic groups in efforts to create minority districts; Republicans understood that "packing" minority (usually Democratic) voters into selected districts would reduce Democratic votes in many other districts.[42] The U.S. Justice Department also pressed state legislatures to maximize the number of **"majority-minority" congressional and state legislative districts**. With the assistance of sophisticated computer models, state legislatures and federal courts drew many odd-shaped minority congressional and state legislative districts.

Continuing Constitutional Doubts

Yet the U.S. Supreme Court has expressed constitutional doubts about bizarre-shaped districts based solely on racial composition. In a controversial 5–4 decision, Justice Sandra Day O'Connor wrote, "Race gerrymandering, even for remedial purposes, may balkanize us into competing racial factions. . . . A reapportionment plan that includes in one district individuals who have little in common with one another but the color of their skin bears an uncomfortable resemblance to political apartheid."[43] (See Figure 4–3.) Later the Court held that the use of race as the "predominant factor" in dividing district lines is unconstitutional: "When the state assigns voters on the basis of race, it engages in the offensive and demeaning assumption that voters of a particular race, because of their race, think alike, share the same political interests and will prefer the same candidates at the

FIGURE 4–3 **Affirmative Racial Gerrymandering**

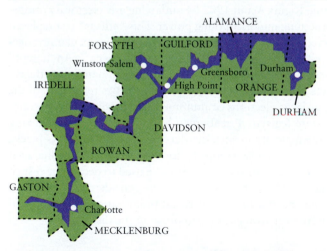

Note: North Carolina's Twelfth Congressional District was drawn up to be a "majority-minority" district by combining African-American communities over a wide region of the state. The U.S. Supreme Court in *Shaw v. Reno* (1993) ordered a court review of this district to determine whether it incorporated any common interest other than race. The North Carolina legislature redrew the district in 1997, lowering its black population percentage from 57 to 46, yet keeping its lengthy connection of black voters from Charlotte to Greensboro.

polls."[44] But the Court stopped short of saying that all race-conscious districting is unconstitutional. Several states redrew the boundaries of majority-minority districts trying to conform to the Court's opinions. Incumbent African-American Congress members managed to hold on to their seats in these states. But the constitutional status of affirmative racial gerrymandering remains unclear.

Increased Black Representation

Black representation in state and local government, as well as in the U.S. Congress, rose dramatically in the 1990s. New minority districts in many states boosted black representation in state legislatures. Today roughly 7 percent of all 7,382 state legislators in the nation are African Americans. There are almost 1,000 black elected officials at the county level, over 4,000 at the municipal level, and nearly 20,000 black school board members across the U.S. We will return to the question of minority representation in state legislatures in Chapter 6 and on city councils in Chapter 11.

Racial Polarization

Increases in the number of African-American officeholders in state and local government are primarily the result of the creation of more black majority districts in cities and states. Few blacks win office in majority white city council, county commission, school board, or state legislative districts, although the number is increasing over time. In legislative districts where the black population is 65 percent or more, black candidates win 98 percent of the legislative seats. Majority white districts elect black candidates to about 2 percent of their legislative seats. While a few notable black political leaders have won electoral support across racial lines, racial polarization in voting remains a fact of life in many communities, but not all.[45]

Hispanic Power

The progress of Hispanics in state and local politics in recent years is reflected in the election of several governors and increasing numbers of state legislators, city and county commission members, and school board members. However, Hispanic political influence in the states is still very limited. Latinos make up 3 percent of all state legislators. Latinos have been more successful at capturing school board seats—over 1,600 and municipal offices—over 1,000. More than 400 have also been elected to county posts. Hispanic voter turnout is much lower than that for other ethnic groups in America. Many Hispanics are resident aliens and therefore not eligible to vote. Language barriers may also present an obstacle to full participation. Finally, Hispanic voters divide their political loyalties. Cuban Americans tend to vote Republican. They are economically very successful; they are concentrated in the Miami area, and they are a major force in city and state politics in Florida. The largest Hispanic group, Mexican Americans, tends to vote Democratic; their power is concentrated in California, Texas, Arizona, and New Mexico.[46]

WOMEN IN STATE POLITICS

Traditionally women did not participate in politics as much as men. Women were less likely than men to contribute money, lobby elected officials, and run for or win public office.

Why was this so? Several explanations have been offered: (1) Women were socialized into more "passive" roles from childhood; (2) women with children and family responsibilities could not fully participate in politics; and (3) women did not have educations, occupations, and incomes equivalent to those of men. Perhaps all of these factors were at work in reducing female political participation, but today they are less important than they once were.

Women in State Offices

Women have made impressive political gains in state politics in recent years. Almost one-fourth of the nation's 7,382 state legislators are women. Women hold 21 percent of the 1,971 state senate seats and 24 percent of the 5,411 state house or assembly seats. Twenty-nine women have served as governors of 22 states.[47] Seventy-six of the 315 statewide executive offices across the country (almost 25 percent) are held by women. (In the 110th Congress—2007–2009—seventy women are serving in the House and sixteen in the Senate.) (See Table 4–3.) While these figures are modest indeed, they represent significant advances over the recent past. In 1969 only 4 percent of the nation's state legislators were women.

Until the election of Ella Grasso (D.–Connecticut) and Dixy Lee Ray (D.–Washington) in the late 1970s, no woman had won election to that office on her own; earlier women governors had succeeded their husbands to that office. Women are making even more rapid gains in city and county offices. The total number of women officeholders in local government has more than tripled over the last decade. Of the 249 mayors of U.S. cities with populations over 100,000, 12 percent are women; of the 1,150 mayors of cities with populations over 30,000, 16 percent are females.[48] This influx of women at the grassroots level over the last decade is now contributing to the success of women in running for and winning higher state and national offices.

Election Challenges Confronting Women

Women continue to confront special challenges when running for office.[49] In some places, political party leaders still tend to assist male more than female candidates.[50] In general, female candidates enjoy a slight advantage over male candidates in public perceptions of honesty, sincerity, and caring. However, women candidates are often perceived as "not tough enough" to deal with hard issues like drugs and crime. When women candidates seek to prove that they are "tough," they risk being branded with adjectives like "strident" or "abrasive."

TABLE 4–3 Women in National and State Elective Offices (Percent of Total)

Level of Office	1985	1987	1989	1991	1993	1995	1997	1999	2001	2003	2005	2007
U.S. Congress	5	5	5	6	10	10	11	12	14	14	15	16
Statewide Elective	14	14	14	18	22	26	26	28	28	26	25	24
State Legislatures	15	16	17	18	21	21	22	22	22	22	23	24

Source: Women in Elective Office 2007; Center for Women and Politics; Rutgers University, the State University of New Jersey, 2007. Available at http://www.rci.rutgers.edu/~cawp/Facts/Officeholders/elective.pdf

The Political Gender Gap

The **gender gap** in politics refers to differences between women and men in political views, party affiliation, and voting choices. This gap has narrowed slightly in recent years, with women currently more likely to identify with the Democratic party and men as Republicans. Indeed, at the presidential level, national polls indicate that the majority of men voted for Republicans George H. W. Bush in 1992, Bob Dole in 1996, and George W. Bush in 2000 and 2004, and that a majority of women favored Bill Clinton in 1992 and 1996, Al Gore in 2000, and John Kerry in 2004. This gender gap extends into state politics as well, with women frequently giving Democratic gubernatorial candidates five to ten more percentage points than men, although the gap does vary across states.

Women and Policymaking

Do greater numbers of women in state and local elected offices make any significant difference in public policy? Political scientists have attempted to learn whether or not increases in female elected officials actually bring about any significant policy changes. The evidence on this question is mixed. Male legislators support feminist positions on ERA, abortion, employment, education, and health just as often as female legislators. However, there is some evidence that women legislators give higher *priority* to these issues. Women are more likely than men to have as their "top legislative priority" bills focusing on women's and children's issues. However, state legislatures with larger percentages of women do *not* pass feminist legislation any more often than state legislatures with fewer women legislators.[51] (Women's priority issues are discussed in Chapter 15.)

There may also be gender-based attitudinal differences that affect a wide range of policy issues. For example, women state legislators may be more likely to view social problems such as crime in a larger societal context, leading them to focus on preventive and interventionist policies. Male legislators may view crime as an individual act that can be curtailed by certain swift and severe punishment. Over time as women increase their numbers in state legislatures and city councils, we might expect subtle changes in both the style and substance of policymaking.[52]

YOUNG AND OLD IN STATE POLITICS

Generational conflict is intensifying in the nation and the states. The **generation gap** in politics—differences between young and old in political views and policy preferences—may not yet be as great as differences among races and ethnic groups or among educational and income classes, but serious studies of generational politics conclude that "age will take on an equal or greater weight [in politics] in the not too distant future.[53]

Senior Power

Senior citizens are the most politically powerful age group in the population. They constitute 28 percent of the voting-age population, but because of their high voter turnout rates, they constitute more than one-third of the voters on Election Day. Persons over age sixty-five average a 69 percent turnout rate in presidential elections and a 61 percent rate in congressional elections. In contrast, the turnout rate for those who are age eighteen to twenty-four is 42 percent in presidential elections and 19 percent in congressional elections. In short, the voting power of senior citizens is twice that of young people. No elected official can afford to offend the seniors, although the senior vote is less monolithic than it used to be.[54]

Generational Policy Agendas

There is actually a great deal of misunderstanding about the priorities of the different generations and a lot of mislabeling, such as "greedy geezers," "selfish GenXers," or "Me-Millennials." (GenXers were born 1965–1981; Me-Millenials were born 1982–2000.) In reality, on state and local issues, the young and the old often agree on what are the big problems. Where they differ is on which problem should be tackled first. Surveys have shown that the priorities of different age cohorts often vary:

On economics:

- Young: economy and jobs
- Old: taxes and government spending

On noneconomic domestic issues:

- Young: education, environment, crime, moral issues
- Old: health, social services, crime, moral issues

These same surveys have shown that the generations also differ on the causes and cures of problems:

- Young: identify economic causes; favor solutions with a preventive emphasis
- Old: Point to lapses in individual responsibility as major cause; favor reactive approaches

Exit survey data from the fifty states collected in 2004 support these generalizations. Younger and older voters were generally concerned about the same issues. (For example, 22 percent of the 18- to 29-year-olds identified "moral values" as the single most important issue for them, exactly the same rate as in the electorate overall.) But their views on what to do about a specific moral value issue—gay marriage—were very different: 41 percent of voters age 18–29 supported same-sex marriage compared to just 16 percent of those age 60 and older. Young voters were more concerned about education and less concerned about terrorism than older voters. And more younger than older voters had experienced a job loss.[55]

INTEREST GROUPS IN STATE POLITICS

Both interest groups and political parties organize individuals to make claims upon government, but these two forms of political organizations differ in several respects. An interest group seeks to influence specific policies of government—not to achieve control over government as a whole. A political party concentrates on winning public office in elections and is somewhat less concerned with policy questions. An interest group does not ordinarily run candidates for public office under its own banner, although it may give influential support to party candidates. Finally, the basic function of a political party in a two-party system is to organize a *majority* of persons for the purpose of governing. In contrast, an interest group gives political expression to the interests of *minority* groups.

Interest groups arise when individuals with a common interest decide that by banding together and by consolidating their strength they can exercise more influence over public policy than they could as individuals acting alone. The impulse toward organization and collective action is particularly strong in a society of great size and complexity. Over time, individual action in politics gives way to collective action by giant organizations of businesspeople, professionals, and union members, as well as racial, religious, and ideological groups.

INTEREST GROUPS

People who come together to exercise influence over government policy.

Lobbyists, the people who represent the thousands of groups and individuals hoping to get their priorities adopted into law, are often regarded negatively by Americans. The public's general impression is that lobbyists buy votes on issues from elected officials through wining and dining. This is a very narrow view of lobbying. In today's world of highly complex and technical issues, lobbyists often play a critical role in providing elected officials with information that they could not possibly gather on their own. The important thing to remember is that on virtually every issue, legislators are getting lobbied by groups representing both sides of the issue. (For every lobbyist favoring "x," there is another opposed to it.)

Organized Interests

Groups may be highly organized into formal organizations with offices and professional staffs within the capitals of every state: The U.S. Chamber of Commerce, the National Association of Manufacturers, the AFL-CIO, and the National Education

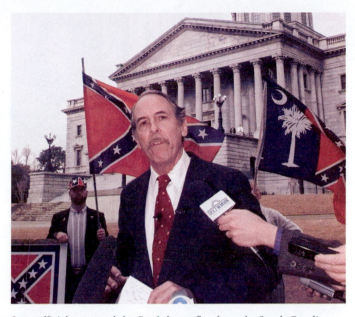

State officials removed the Confederate flag from the South Carolina Capitol Dome following massive pressure from the National Association for the Advancement of Colored People (NAACP). The group had called for a tourism boycott of the state. Tourism is a vital sector of South Carolina's economy.

Association are examples of highly organized interest groups that operate in every state. Other groups have little formal organization and appear at state capitals only when an issue arises of particular concern to them, for example, when motorcyclists assemble to protest mandatory helmets or when commercial fishermen come to complain about banning of nets.

Interest groups may be organized around *occupational or economic interests* (e.g., the Association of Real Estate Boards, the Association of Broadcasters, the Bankers Association, the Automobile Dealers Association, the Cattleman's Association, the Home Builders Association, the Insurance Council, the Association of Trial Lawyers), or on *racial or religious* bases (e.g., the National Association for the Advancement of Colored People, the Christian Coalition, the National Council of Churches, the Anti-Defamation League of B'nai B'rith), or around *shared experiences* (e.g., the American Legion, the Veterans of Foreign Wars, the League of Women Voters, the Automobile Association of America), or around *ideological positions* (e.g., Americans for Democratic Action, Common Cause, Americans for Constitutional Action). *Labor unions*, especially those representing employees of governments and school districts (e.g., the National Education Association; the American Federation of Teachers; and the American Federation of State, County, and Municipal Employees), as well as industrial unions and the state AFL-CIO federation, are well organized and well represented in virtually all state capitals.[56] *Government officials* and governments themselves organize and help exert pressure on higher levels of government (e.g., the National Governors' Conference, the Council of State Governments, the National League of Cities, U.S. Conference of Mayors, the National Association of Chiefs of Police, and the National Association of Counties). Even the *recipients of government services* have organized themselves (e.g., the American Association of Retired Persons [AARP]).

LOBBYISTS
Individuals, groups, or organizations that actively seek to influence government policy.

LOBBYING
Communications directed at government decision makers with the purpose of influencing policy.

Global warming—not a real problem. (Photo by Ken Adachi, educate-yourself.org)

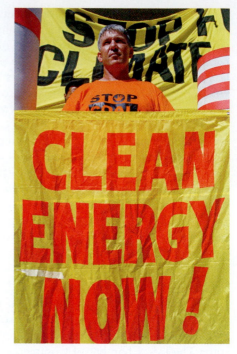

Global warming—a real problem.

Overall, economic interests are more frequently encountered in state politics than noneconomic interests. But certainly the proliferation of active noneconomic groups in America, from the environmentalists' Sierra Club to the senior citizens' AARP and the liberal-oriented Common Cause, testifies to the importance of organization in all phases of political life. Particularly active at the state level are the businesses subject to extensive regulation by state governments. Banks, truckers, doctors and lawyers, insurance companies, the gaming industry, utilities, hospitals, and liquor interests are consistently found to be among the most highly organized groups in state capitals. Chapters of the National Education Association are also highly active in state capitals, presenting the demands of educational administrators and teachers. And local governments and local government officials are well organized to present their demands at state capitals.

A national survey of interest group activity in all fifty state capitals identified groups that were rated very "effective" in the states (see Table 4–4).

> *Particularly active at the state level are the businesses subject to extensive regulation by state governments.*

Professional Lobbyists

Often groups and corporations choose to be "represented" in state capitals by professional lobbyists. Many successful professional lobbyists are former legislators (see Chapter 6), or former executive officials, or former top gubernatorial or legislative aides, who have turned their state government experience into a career. They "know their way around" the capital. They offer their services—access to legislative and executive officials, knowledge of the lawmaking process, ability to present information and testimony to key policymakers at the right time, political skills and knowledge, personal friendships, and "connections"—to their clients at rates that usually depend on their reputation for influence. Occasionally their compensation

TABLE 4–4 Heavy Hitters: The Twenty-Five Most Influential Interests in the States

Rank	Interest	Number of States in Which Interest Seen as Very Effective
1	General business (state chamber of commerce, etc.)	40
2	School teachers' organizations (National Education Association [NEA] and American Federation of Teachers [AFT])	37
3	Utility companies and associations (electric, gas, water, telephone/telecommunications)	24
4	Insurance; general and medical (companies and associations)	21
5	Hospital/nursing home associations	21
6	Lawyers (predominately trial lawyers, state bar associations)	22
7	Manufacturers (companies and associations)	18
8	General local government organizations (municipal leagues, county organizations, elected officials)	18
9	Physicians/state medical associations	17
10	General farm organizations (state farm bureaus, etc.)	16
11	Bankers' associations	15
12	Traditional labor associations (predominately AFL-CIO)	13
13	Universities and colleges (institutions and employees)	13
14	State and local government employees	11
15	Contractors/builders/developers	13
16	Realtors' associations	13
17	K–12 education interests (other than teachers)	9
18	Individual labor unions (Teamsters, United Auto Workers [UAW], etc.)	8
19	Truckers and private transport interests (excluding railroads)	9
20	Sportsmen/hunting and fishing (includes anti-gun-control groups)	9
21	Gaming interests (racetracks/casinos/lotteries)	9
22	Environmentalists	6
23	Agricultural commodity organizations (stockgrowers, grain growers, etc.)	7
24	Retailers (companies and trade associations)	8
25	Individual banks and financial institutions	6

Source: P. 122, "Interest Groups in the Fifty States" by Clive S. Thomas and Ronald J. Hrebenar in *Politics in the American States: A Comparative Analysis*, 8th ed. edited by Virginia Gray and Russell H. Hanson. Copyright © 2004 by CQ Press, a division of Congressional Quarterly, Inc Reprinted by permission of CQ Press.

is tied to their success in getting a bill passed; a six-figure fee may rest on the outcome of a single vote. Some professional lobbyists are attached to law firms or public relations firms and occasionally do other work; others are full-time lobbyists with multiple clients.

Most professional lobbyists publicly attribute their success to hard work, persistence, information, and ability to get along with others: "Being prepared, personal credibility"; "Legislators know I'm going to present the facts whether they're favorable to my client or not"; "I'm a forceful advocate—determined"; "Doing my homework on the issues"; "Knowledge of the issues I'm dealing with and knowledge of the system"; "I try to understand the political pressures on elected officials." Yet in more candid moments professional lobbyists will acknowledge that their success is largely attributable to personal friendships, political experience, and financial contributions: "Close friends I made in the legislature while I served as Speaker of the House"; "I raise a lot of money for people"; "My client has the largest political action committee in the state."[57]

Lobby Registration

It is very difficult to get a comprehensive picture of interest group activity in state capitals. Many organizations, businesses, legal firms, and individuals engage in interest group activity of one kind or another, and it is difficult to keep track of their varied activities. Most states require the registration of "lobbyists" and the submission of reports about their membership and finances. These laws do not restrain lobbying (that would probably violate the First Amendment freedom to "petition" the government for "redress of grievances"). Rather, they are meant to spotlight the activities of lobbyists. However, many hundreds of lobbyists never register under the pretext that they are not *really lobbyists*, but, instead, businesses, public relations firms, lawyers, researchers, or educational people. Usually, only the larger, formal, organized interest groups and professional lobbyists are *officially* registered as lobbyists in their states. Some states are more rigorously monitoring the registration and reporting of lobbyists. But often it is the news media that is the most intense "lobbyist watchdog." On the other hand, statehouse reporters are the first to admit they rank lobbyists as great sources of information about what is going on in the legislature.[58]

FUNCTIONS AND TACTICS OF INTEREST GROUPS

Interest group techniques are as varied as the imaginations of their leaders. Groups are attempting to advance their interests when a liquor firm sends a case of bourbon to a state legislator; when the League of Women Voters distributes biographies of political candidates; when an insurance company argues before a state insurance commission that rates must be increased; when the National Education Association provides state legislators with information comparing teachers' salaries in the fifty states; when railroads ask state highway departments to place weight limitations on trucks; or when the American Civil Liberties Union supplies lawyers for civil rights demonstrators.

Typical Tactics

Typical lists of lobbying activities as supplied by lobbyists themselves usually begin with testifying at legislative committee hearings, contacting legislators directly, and helping to draft legislation. These lists usually go on to include getting constituents to contact legislators, inspiring letter-writing and e-mail campaigns, and entering coalitions with other groups to lobby about particular pieces of legislation. Somewhat fewer lobbyists admit to making monetary contributions to legislators and performing personal and political favors for them, but we know from campaign contribution records and anecdotal evidence that these practices are very common. Some lobbying organizations focus more on filing lawsuits or otherwise engaging in court litigation; indeed, some larger organizations have semiautonomous "legal defense" branches to carry on such activity. Relatively few interest groups resort to protests and demonstrations. None admit to direct bribery, but, as we shall see, reports of direct payments to legislators or their campaign funds in exchange for votes are not uncommon.

Bill Monitoring

More time is spent by lobbyists on monitoring the content and progress of bills affecting their clients and members than on any other activity. Just "keeping tabs" on what is going on each day in government is a time-consuming task. Lobbyists must be aware of any provisions of any bills affecting their clients, even provisions that are buried in a bill that does not mention them in its title or summary. Typically lobbyists may identify 100 or more bills that might affect their clients or members each legislative session, although they are likely to closely monitor the progress of only twenty or thirty bills that have a chance of becoming enacted.[59] (Less than 25 percent of bills introduced in a legislature are ever enacted in any form into law; see Chapter 6.) Lobbyists must be watchful: Nothing is more embarrassing to a lobbyist than to find that the legislature has passed a bill adversely affecting their client's interests without their ever knowing about it.

Lobbying

Lobbying is defined as any communication, by someone acting on behalf of a group, directed at a government decision maker with the hope of influencing that person. Direct persuasion is usually more than just a matter of argument or emotional appeal to the lawmaker. Often it involves the communication of useful technical and political information. Many public officials are required to vote on, or decide about, hundreds of questions each year. It is impossible for them to be fully informed about the wide variety of bills and issues they face. Consequently, many decision makers depend on skilled lobbyists to provide technical information about matters requiring action, and to inform them of the policy preferences of important segments of the population. (See "Lobbying in State Legislatures" in Chapter 6.)

The behavior of lobbyists depends on the interests they represent and the characteristics of the state political system in which they function. Some interests hire full-time lobbyists; others rely on attorneys or firms who lobby on behalf of more than one group. Still other interests rely on volunteers. Some maintain active contact with legislators or make campaign contributions. Some formulate a legislative agenda each session and trace the progress of bills in which they are interested. Indeed, one study of lobbying on behalf of the aging in four separate states revealed much variation in lobbying activity even on the same issues.[60]

"Schmoozing"

"Schmoozing" usually refers to informal contacts between lobbyists and legislators—at local bars, restaurants, country clubs, testimonial dinners, and occasionally during vacation travel. Typically lobbyists pick up the bill for these activities. This is not an illegal

"SCHMOOZING"
Informal contacts between lobbyists and legislators.

BRIBERY

Offering anything of value to government officials with the purpose of influencing them in the performance of their duties.

GRASSROOTS LOBBYING

Influencing legislators by contacting their constituents and asking them to contact their legislators.

practice, although many states now require officially registered lobbyists to list such expenditures. Gifts are occasionally given by lobbyists to legislators, but states usually require legislators to report gifts over specified dollar values.

Bribery and Corruption

Lobbying in state capitals may be somewhat cruder—if not more corrupt—than lobbying in Washington. In interviewing lobbyists and legislators in Washington, Lester Milbrath found that they considered state lobbying much more corrupt than national lobbying. " 'Lobbying is very different before state legislators; it is much more individualistic. Maybe this is the reason they have more bribery in state legislatures than in Congress.' 'In the state legislatures, lobbying is definitely on a lower plane. The lobbyists are loose and hand out money and favors quite freely.' 'Lobbying at the state level is cruder, more basic, and more obvious.' "[61] Needless to say, it is difficult to document such statements. However, it seems reasonable to believe that state legislators might be more subject to the appeals of organized interest groups than members of Congress.

State legislators, unlike most members of Congress, are only part-time lawmakers. They must manage their own business, professional, and investment interests in addition to their legislative duties. They may have personal business or professional or real estate or legal ties with the same interests that are seeking to influence their legislative behavior. Such "conflicts of interest"—legislators voting in committee or on the floor on issues in which they have a personal financial interest—are not uncommon. Indeed, some interests occasionally seek to establish business or professional ties with legislators just to win their support.

Bribery is the offering of anything of value to government officials to influence them in the performance of their duties. Vote buying is illegal, but not unheard of in state capitals. Instead of bribery, organized interests may contribute to a legislator's campaign chest without mentioning any specific quid pro quo.

Grassroots Lobbying, Media Campaigns, and Public Relations

Most people think of interest group tactics as direct attempts to influence decision makers, but many groups spend more of their time, energy, and resources in general public relations activities than anything else. The purpose of a continuing public relations campaign is to create an environment favorable to the interest group and its program. It is hoped that a reservoir of public goodwill can be established, which can be relied on later when a critical issue arises.

Lobbyists know that legislators pay attention to their constituents. Grassroots lobbying involves interest group efforts to get constituents to call or write their legislator on behalf of the group's position on pending legislation. Grassroots campaigns are now highly professional. They "rely totally on mass marketing, high technology, and public relations ploys reminiscent of political campaigns."[62] Form letters supplied to constituents by interest groups to sign and send to their legislator may not be very effective. But direct calls and personal letters, faxes, and e-mails, especially from constituents who have previously contributed to a legislator's campaign, are seldom ignored.

Media campaigns are very effective, but also very expensive. These involve paid advertisements on radio or television designed to influence public opinion on pending legislation. Heavy media campaigns are more likely to be undertaken by lobbyists in Washington, DC, than in state capitals. Only about 20 to 30 percent of lobbyists in the states report having directly advertised in the media.[63]

Political Action Committees (PAC) Money in the States

Political campaigns are very expensive, and it is always difficult for a candidate to find enough money to finance a campaign. This is true for officeholders seeking reelection as well as new contenders. It is perfectly legal for an interest group to make a contribution to a candidate's campaign fund. Ordinarily, a respectable lobbyist would not be so crude as to exact any specific pledges from a candidate in exchange for a campaign contribution. He or she simply makes a contribution and lets the candidate figure out what to do when in office to ensure further contributions to the candidate's next campaign. (For further discussion, see "Money in State Politics" in Chapter 5.) There is, however, some evidence that contributions do influence a legislator's vote *if* the "vote means the difference between a contributing group's success or defeat on a bill."[64] The organizational strength of a group can also affect public policy. One study of the impact of labor unions on state public policy found that the greater the organizational strength of labor, the more states spend on welfare and education.[65]

Interest groups, operating through political action committees, or PACs, are becoming a major source of campaign funding for state office. As campaign costs increase, reliance on PAC money increases. In large urban states such as California and New York, where campaigns for state legislature may cost $100,000 or more, PAC contributions are the largest source of campaign funding.

PACs are politically sophisticated contributors. They do not like to back losers. Since incumbent members of state legislatures running for reelection seldom lose (see "The Great Incumbency Machine" in Chapter 6), PAC contributions are heavily weighted in favor of incumbents over challengers and candidates from the political party that controls each house of the legislature.

In states where there are campaign contribution limits, interest groups find other ways to support their preferred candidate. They may spend money on an advocacy ad, give an endorsement, or contribute to the state political party of which the candidate is a member.[66]

COMPARING INTEREST GROUP POWER IN THE STATES

How do interest group systems in the states differ? Why do some states have strong, influential interest groups shaping public policy, while in other states the influence of interest groups is moderated by group competition, party rivalry, and electoral politics?

We might define overall interest group influence in a state as "the extent to which interest groups as a whole influence public policy when compared to other components of the political system, such as political parties, the legislature, the governor, etc."[67] Using this definition researchers have attempted to categorize the states as having a "dominant," "complementary," or "subordinate" interest group system, in terms of its policy impact relative to the parties and the branches of government (see Figure 4–4).

Over time interest group influence appears to be increasing in all of the states. A major factor in this strengthening of interest groups is their increasing role in campaign finance. The more money coming from interest groups to political candidates, the greater is the influence of the interest group system.

Yet interest group influence in some states is greater than in other states, and our task is to search for explanations. One thing to remember is that some types of interest groups are powerful in one state, but not another. In such instances, these powerhouses often

---

PACs

Political action committees; organizations formed to raise and distribute campaign funds to candidates for public office.

INTEREST GROUP INFLUENCE

The extent to which interest groups as a whole influence public policy as compared with other components of the political system.

FIGURE 4–4 Overall Impact of Interest Groups

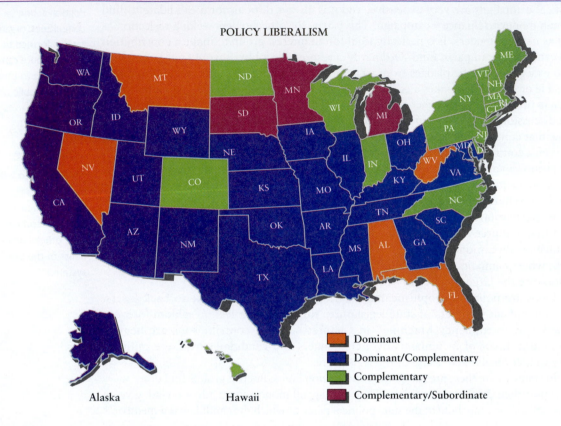

POLICY LIBERALISM

Dominant
Dominant/Complementary
Complementary
Complementary/Subordinate

Alaska   Hawaii

Note:
Dominant: Interest groups as a whole are the overwhelming and consistent influence on policy making.
Complimentary:
Interest groups tend to work in conjunction with or are constrained by other aspects of the political system (such as the party system, a strong executive branch, group competition, political culture, or a combination of these).
Subordinate:
Interest group system is consistently subordinated to other aspects of the policy making process.
Dominant/Complementary:
Interest group system in place in a state combines elements of both or alternates between the two situations, or is in the process of moving from one to the other.
Complementary/Subordinate:
Interest group system in place in a state combines elements of both or alternates between the two situations, or is in the process of moving from one to the other.
Source: Clive S. Thomas and Ronald J. Hrebenar, "Interest Groups in the Fifty States," in Virginia Gray and Russell L. Hanson, *Politics in the American States: A Comparative Analysis*, 8th ed. (Washington, DC: CQ Press, 2004), 122.

reflect key components of a state's economy (e.g., automobile lobbying groups in Michigan, tobacco interest groups in North Carolina, mining industry groups in Montana and West Virginia).

The Economic Diversity Explanation

Wealthy urban industrial states (Connecticut, Massachusetts, Michigan, New Jersey, New York, Rhode Island) have weaker interest group systems because of the diversity and complexity of their economies. No single industry can dominate political life.

Instead, multiple competing interest groups tend to balance each other, and this cancels the influence of interest groups generally. In contrast, in rural states with less economic diversity, a few dominant industries (oil and gas in Louisiana, coal in West Virginia) appear to have more influence. The reputation for influence for particular industries in these states causes them to be viewed as strong pressure group states.

The Party Explanation

According to political scientist Sarah McCally Morehouse, "Where parties are strong, pressure groups are weak or moderate; where parties are weak, pressure groups are strong enough to dominate the policy-making process."[68] Where competitive political parties are strong—where the parties actively recruit candidates, provide campaign support, and hold their members accountable after the election—interest groups are less powerful. Policymakers in these states look to the party for policy guidance rather than to interest groups. Interest group influence is channeled through the parties; the parties are coalitions of interest groups; no single interest group can dominate or circumvent the party. Strong party states (Connecticut, New York, Minnesota, North Dakota, Rhode Island, Wisconsin, Massachusetts, Colorado) have weak interest group systems. Weak party states (primarily the one-party southern states) have strong interest group systems. Party competition is discussed earlier in this chapter.

Strong governors and strong legislative leadership, exercising their influence as party leaders, can provide a check on the lobbying efforts of interest groups. When the special interests lose, it is usually on issues on which the governor and the party leadership have taken a clear stand[69] or when the governor is of one party and the legislature is controlled by the other (divided control) and the governor vetoes a piece of legislation.

The Professionalism Explanation

State legislatures are becoming more professional over time. In Chapter 6 we define a professional legislature as a well-paid, full-time, well-staffed body, as opposed to an amateur legislature, which meets only a few weeks each year, pays its members very little, and has few research or information services available to it. Professional legislatures have less turnover in members and more experience in lawmaking. Clearly, these characteristics of legislatures affect the power of interest groups. Interest groups are more influential when legislatures are *less* professional. When members are less experienced, paid less, and have little time or resources to research issues themselves, they must depend more on interest groups, and interest groups gain influence. Interest groups also frequently have more clout in states with legislative term limits, which have the effect of creating less-experienced lawmakers who turn more to interest groups to help them draft bills and raise campaign funds.[70]

The Governmental Fragmentation Explanation

It is also likely that states with weak governors, multiple independently elected state officials, and numerous independent boards and commissions have strong interest group systems. In states with fragmented executive power (Florida, South Carolina), interest groups have additional points of access and control, and executive officials do not have counterbalancing power. Strong governors (as in New York, Massachusetts, New Jersey, Connecticut, Delaware, and Minnesota) are better able to confront the influence of interest groups when they choose to do so. (We will discuss governors' powers in Chapter 7.)

PROFESSIONALISM

In legislatures, the extent to which members have the services of full-time, well-paid staff, as well as their access to research and sources of information.

PROTEST

In politics, public activities designed to call attention to issues and influence decision makers.

NETROOTS REVOLUTION

Grassroots-level protests use the Internet; can involve a large number of like-minded citizens.

ELECTRONIC ACTIVISM

Organizing citizens via the Internet.

Fortunately, we do not have to choose one explanation to the exclusion of others. Economic diversity, party strength, professionalism, and governmental fragmentation all contribute to the explanation of interest group strength in the states.

PROTEST AS POLITICAL PARTICIPATION

Organized protests—marches, demonstrations, disruptions, civil disobedience—are important forms of political activity. Protest marches and demonstrations are now nearly as frequent at state capitols and city halls as in Washington. It is a lot easier to travel to the state capitol than all the way to DC. Even more common are protests via the Web—the **"netroots" revolution**.

It is important to distinguish between *protest, civil disobedience*, and *violence*, even though all may be forms of political activity. Most *protests* do *not* involve unlawful conduct and are protected by the constitutional guarantee of the First Amendment to "peaceably assemble and petition for redress of grievances." A march on city hall or the state capitol, followed by a mass assembly of people with speakers, sign-waving, songs, and perhaps the formal presentation of grievances to whichever brave official agrees to meet with the protesters, is well within the constitutional guarantees of Americans.

Protest

Protest refers to direct, collective activity by persons who wish to obtain concessions from established power holders. Often the protest is a means of acquiring bargaining power by those who would otherwise be powerless. The protest may challenge established groups by threatening their reputations (in cases in which they might be harmed by unfavorable publicity), their economic position (in cases in which noise and disruption upset their daily activity), or their sense of security (when the threat exists that the protest may turn unruly or violent). The strategy of protest may appeal especially to powerless minorities who have little else to bargain with except the promise to stop protesting.

Protests may also aim at motivating uncommitted "third parties" to enter the political arena on behalf of the protesters. The object of the protest is to call attention to the existence of some issue and urge others to apply pressure on public officials. Of course, this strategy requires the support and assistance of the news media. If protests are ignored by television and newspapers, they can hardly be expected to activate support. However, the news media seldom ignore protests with audience interest; protest leaders and journalists share an interest in dramatizing "news" for the public.

Protests do not necessarily have to take place "in the streets." The Internet has made it possible for interest groups to protest electronically via highly organized e-mail campaigns to public officials. Some have labeled this new form of protest as **"electronic activism."** "You can hear the netroots screaming," wrote one columnist for the *New York Times* who was describing an Internet poll being taken by a protest group.[71]

ONLINE ACTIVISM: LET YOUR VOICE BE HEARD

It's easy to join Planned Parenthood's online Action Network: just click here. Our online activist alert system keeps you up-to-date on all the latest news pertaining to reproductive justice and it also allows you to speak out with the simple click of a button.

Many interest groups now organize lobbying and protest activities via the Internet. This online activism is often referred to as "electronic activism."

Civil Disobedience

Civil disobedience is a form of protest that involves breaking "unjust" laws. Civil disobedience is not new: It has played an important role in American history, from the Boston Tea Party to the abolitionists who illegally hid runaway slaves, to the suffragettes who demonstrated for women's voting rights, to the labor organizers who picketed to form the nation's major industrial unions, to the civil rights workers of the early 1960s who deliberately violated segregation laws. The purpose of civil disobedience is to call attention, or to "bear witness," to the existence of injustice. In the words of Martin Luther King, Jr., civil disobedience "seeks to dramatize the issue so that it can no longer be ignored."[72] There should be no violence in true civil disobedience, and only "unjust" laws are broken. Moreover, the law is broken "openly, lovingly" with a willingness to accept the penalty. Punishment is actively sought rather than avoided, since punishment will help to emphasize the injustice of the law. The object is to stir the conscience of an apathetic majority and win support for measures that will eliminate injustices. By willingly accepting punishment for the violation of an unjust law, people who practice civil disobedience demonstrate their sincerity. They hope to shame public officials and make them ask themselves how far they are willing to go to protect the status quo.

Civil disobedience acts, which often result in arrest, are designed to call attention to the existence of injustice. People for the Ethical Treatment of Animals (PETA) has used this tactic quite frequently in its effort to stop local stores from selling furs.

As in all protest activity, the participation of the news media, particularly television, is essential to the success of civil disobedience. The dramatization of injustice makes news; the public's sympathy is won when injustices are spotlighted; and the willingness of demonstrators to accept punishment is visible evidence of their sincerity. Cruelty or violence directed *against* the demonstrators by police or others plays into the hands of the protesters by further emphasizing injustices.[73]

Violence

Violence can also be a form of political participation. To be sure, it is criminal, and it is generally irrational and self-defeating. However, political assassination; bombing and terrorism; and rioting, burning, and looting have occurred with uncomfortable frequency in American politics. Violence is a tool used by groups on both the left and the right ends of the political spectrum. For example, violent protests at the 1999 World Trade Organization meeting in Seattle mostly came from the left whereas violence against abortion clinics in the 1990s came from the right. The plane crashes into the Twin Towers of the World Trade Center in New York and the Pentagon on September 11, 2001 were an even more recent reminder that violence is often the primary way extremist groups call attention to their political agendas.

It is important to distinguish violence from protest and civil disobedience. Peaceful protest is constitutionally guaranteed. Most protests are free of violence. Occasionally there is an implicit *threat* of violence in a protest—a threat that can be manipulated by protesters to help gain their ends. However, most protests harness frustrations and hostilities and direct them into constitutionally acceptable activities. Civil disobedience should also be distinguished from violence. The civil disobedient breaks only "unjust" laws, openly and without violence, and willingly

CIVIL DISOBEDIENCE
A form of protest that involves peaceful nonviolent breaking of laws considered to be unjust.

It is important to distinguish violence from protest and civil disobedience.

Violence (e.g., bombing, assassination, terrorism, sabotage, rioting, burning, looting) is a form of political participation, but one that is a criminal act. State and local law enforcement agencies must be prepared for such incidents, with well-trained officers and proper equipment, such as this bomb disposal robot used by the Massachusetts State Police. State and local governments may use their federal Homeland Security grant monies to purchase such equipment.

accepts punishment without attempting escape. Rioting, burning, and looting—as well as bombing and assassination—are clearly distinguishable from peaceful protest and even civil disobedience.

News Media

The real key to success in protest activity is found in the support or opposition of the news media to protest group demands. Virtually all of the studies of protest activity have asserted that it is the response of "third parties," primarily the news media, and not the immediate response of public officials, that is essential to success.[74] This is a plausible finding, because, after all, if protesters could persuade public officials directly, there would be no need to protest. Indeed, one might even distinguish between "interest groups," which have a high degree of continuous interaction with public officials, and "protest groups," which do not regularly interact with public officials and must engage in protest to be heard. Furthermore, to be heard, reports of their protests must be carried in newspapers and on television, which increasingly are reporting protests taking place in the **blogosphere**.

The Effectiveness of Protests

Several conditions must be present if protest is to be effective.[75] First, there must be a clear goal or objective of the protest. Protesters must aim at specific concessions or legislation they desire; generally, complex problems or complaints that cannot readily be solved by specific governmental action are not good targets for protest activity. Second, the protest must be directed at some public officials who are capable of granting the desired goal. It is difficult to secure concessions if no one is in a position to grant them. Third, the protest leaders must not only organize their masses for protest activity, but they must also simultaneously bargain with public officials for the desired concessions. This implies a division of labor between "organizers" and "negotiators."

Official Responses to Protests

Finally, we might note in this discussion the strategies available to public officials who are faced with protest activity. They may greet the protesters with smiles and reassurances that they agree with their objectives. They may dispense *symbolic* satisfaction without actually granting any tangible payoffs. Once the "crisis" is abated, the bargaining leverage of the protest leaders diminishes considerably. Public officials may dispense *token* satisfactions by responding, with much publicity, to one or more specific cases of injustice, while doing little of a broad-based nature to alleviate conditions. Or public officials may *appear to be constrained* in their ability to grant protest goals by claiming that they lack the financial resources or legal authority to do anything—the "I-would-help-you-if-I-could-but-I-can't" pose. Another tactic is to *postpone action* by calling for further study while offering assurances of sympathy and interest. Finally, public officials may try to *discredit* protesters by stating or implying that they are violence-prone or unrepresentative of the real aspirations of the people they seek to lead. This tactic is especially effective if the protest involves violence or disruption or if protest leaders have "leftist" or criminal backgrounds.

State and Local Governments Bear Costs of Protests

Protests—peaceful and violent—occur in a particular state and locality. The targeted audience of the protesters may extend beyond where the protest is taking place (to national or international television audiences). But it is the responsibility of the state or local government serving the area where the protest is occurring to protect the public and to respond when tragedies strike. Sometimes these situations can break the budget. Early estimates of the costs of the attacks on the World Trade Center in New York were in the billions. And even though Congress approved a substantial amount of federal fiscal assistance, the costs to both the State of New York and the City of New York created tremendous fiscal pressures on their budgets. In other words, state and local governments—and their tax payers—bear the major costs of protests.

ON THE WEB

The Internet offers yet another form of political participation. Virtually all serious candidates for national and statewide office—president, Congress, governor, and so on—open Web sites early in their campaigns. Typically campaign Web sites offer flattering profiles of the candidates together with their public records and policy statements (and, of course, addresses to send campaign contributions).

www.politicaljunkie.com

A good starting point for seeking out political information relevant to your state (or to particular issues or interest groups or election results). This is a comprehensive Web site with direct links to political news sources, columnists, candidates, parties, interest groups, lobbyists, PACs, think tanks, and much more (including political humor). It offers state-by-state links under "How to Register by State" and "Key Dates for Each State."

www.politico.com

A Web-based "newspaper" featuring political news and blogs written by a wide variety of reporters and columnists.

www.lwv.org

The League of Women Voters' official Web site.

www.vote-smart.org

Project Vote Smart Web site; offers the opportunity to track the public records of candidates and elected officials, including the president, members of Congress, governors, and state legislators. If you do not know who represents you in Congress or your state legislature, you can simply enter your ZIP code where indicated and Project Vote Smart will provide that information.

Most major interest groups maintain national Web sites that include addresses and often direct links to state affiliates. And for most major interest groups, joining up is just a click away. See, for example,

American Association of Retired Persons (AARP) at **www.aarp.org**

Common Cause at **www.commoncause.org**

Christian Coalition at **www.cc.org**

www.fairvote.org

The official Web site of Fair Vote, an organization that promotes voter turnout, fair representation, and election reforms such as instant runoff voting, proportional voting, direct election of the president, and automatic voter registration.

www.electionline.org

Produced by the Election Reform Information Project, the Web site is described as "the nation's only nonpartisan, nonadvocacy Web site providing up-to-the-minute news and analysis on election reform." An easily accessible Interactive Map allows one to access detailed information on a specific state, county, or township.

www.eac.gov

The official Web site of the United States Election Assistance Commission, an independent bipartisan commission created by the Help America Vote Act of 2002 (HAVA).

CHAPTER FIVE

© Daryl Cagle

PARTIES AND CAMPAIGNS IN THE STATES

5

QUESTIONS TO CONSIDER

Do you believe that the Democratic and Republican parties in your state offer clear policy alternatives to the voters?

■ Yes   ■ No

In politics, with which of the following do you generally identify yourself?

■ Democrat
■ Republican
■ Independent

Should candidates be limited in the amount of money they can spend on their campaigns?

■ Yes   ■ No

From where do you get most of your news about politics and campaigns?

■ Newspaper
■ Television
■ Internet
■ Late-night entertainment/comedy shows

AMERICAN POLITICAL PARTIES: IN DISARRAY OR EXPERIENCING A REBIRTH?

For every news story that proclaims political parties to be dying—irrelevant and out of touch with most voters—there is another that points to the heightened role that state and local political party organizations play in registering voters and in GOTV—getting-out-the-vote—operations. News operations (and political scientists, too) routinely "color" states and counties red (Republican) or blue (Democrat) to visually describe which party has the most registrants or to report which party's candidate won the most votes in an election contest.

Throughout the often-heated campaign season, pollsters repeatedly take snapshots of potential voters "sliced and diced" by age, race/ethnicity, gender, education, income, religious affiliation, and ideology. Their main purpose is to see who is identifying themselves with the two major parties (Democrat, Republican), with minor parties (such as Libertarian, Green, Reform), or as independents (no party affiliation) and how they plan to vote on Election Day (strictly along party lines, for the other party's candidates, or by splitting their vote between the parties).

After a major election, *academics and scholars* at various think tanks analyze the links between voter attributes, party identification, and voting patterns. Their primary goal is to determine if there have been any seismic shifts in the composition of political parties in the nation at large and in specific states and localities. New typologies (categories) of the electorate generally emerge as the quality and quantity of data improves, along with the software used to probe the data. Such was the case after the 2004 presidential election when the Pew Research Center, with much fanfare, unveiled its widely cited three group-nine category typology. (See Table 5–1.) Voters are sorted into homogeneous groups based on their values, political beliefs, and party affiliation.[1]

Post-election analyses by *party activists and professional campaign consultants* tend to focus more on trying to understand why one party's candidates won and another's lost. Here the bulk of the attention is on analyzing and comparing the effectiveness of state and local party organizations. How well did each do in recruiting volunteers, energizing the electorate (registering voters, promoting absentee balloting, getting people to the polls), identifying solid core supporters and the undecideds, organizing local political forums and rallies, and raising money?

Political parties are still central features on the American political landscape, although more Americans, particularly younger voters, are describing themselves as "independents." In some families, party loyalties are a way of life, passed on like religion. In others, there is little discussion about politics at home, which leaves the establishment of party loyalty, if any, more in the hands of schools, social networks, or the mass media.

Staunch supporters of political parties today often cite scholars who have concluded that were it not for parties, there would be no democracy: "Political parties created modern democracy and modern democracy is unthinkable save in terms of parties."[2] While many agree with this broad assessment, there is less consensus about whether today's political parties have successfully played all the roles that early party supporters proclaimed that they could. There is an ongoing debate between the "purists" and the "realists" about the degree to which political parties do all that was initially expected of them or whether it really matters.[3] Others debate whether the American system of government is more party centered or more candidate centered. Do voters pay

TABLE 5–1   Partisanship and the New Political Typology

	Party Identification[a]			Independents Who "Lean" Included[b]	
	Rep. (%)	Dem. (%)	Ind. (%)	Rep./lean R. (%)	Dem./lean D. (%)
Total	31	34	35	45	46
Republican Groups					
Enterprisers: staunch conservatives	81	1	18	98	1
Social conservatives: religious, critical of business	82	0	18	97	1
Pro-gov't conservatives: struggling social conservatives	58	2	40	86	3
Middle Groups					
Upbeats: positive outlook and moderate	39	5	56	73	14
Disaffected: working class and discouraged	30	2	68	60	10
Bystanders: democracy's dropouts	22	22	56	39	38
Democratic Groups					
Conservative Democrats: secular and antiwar	0	89	11	0	98
Disadvantaged Democrats: social welfare loyalists	0	84	16	0	99
Liberals: latter-day New Dealers	1	59	40	2	92

[a]Independents include respondents who say they have no preference.

[b]Respondents who do not initially choose a party identification are asked "as of today do you lean more to the Republican Party or more to the Democratic Party?" These columns include these leaners with those who choose a party initially.

Source: Pew Center for The People and The Press, *The 2005 Political Typology*, p. 8. Available at http://people-press.org/reports/display .php3?PageID=943. Copyright © 2005. Reprinted by permission of the publisher.

more attention to the party affiliation of a candidate or to the candidate's personal attributes—age, looks, gender, race, campaign style, political ads, debate skills, and so forth?

The Responsible Party Model

Initially, political parties were viewed as the principal instrument of majority control of public policy. "Responsible parties," as perceived by the "purists," are supposed to (1) develop and clarify alternative policy positions for the voters; (2) educate the people about the issues and simplify choices for them; (3) recruit candidates for public office who agree with the parties' policy positions; (4) organize and direct their candidates' campaigns to win office; (5) hold their elected officials responsible for enacting the parties' policy positions after they are elected; and (6) organize legislatures to ensure party control of policymaking. In carrying out these functions, responsible parties are supposed to modify the demands of special interests, build a consensus that could win

RESPONSIBLE PARTY MODEL

A party system in which each party offers clear policy alternatives and holds their elected officials responsible for enacting these policies in office.

majority support, and provide simple and identifiable, yet meaningful, choices for the voters on Election Day. In this way, disciplined, issue-oriented, competitive parties are seen as the principal means by which the people would direct public policy and hold elected officials accountable.

Problems with the Model

Over the years, the "realists" have outlined many shortcomings of the "responsible party" model. Among the most commonly cited are the following:

- *The parties do not offer the voters clear policy alternatives.* Instead, each tries to capture the broad center of most policy dimensions, where it believes most Americans can be found. There is no incentive for parties to stand on the far right or far left when most Americans are found in the center. So the parties echo each other, and critics refer to them as Tweedledee and Tweedledum.
- *Voter decisions are not motivated primarily by policy considerations.* Most voters cast their votes on the basis of candidate "image," the "goodness" or "badness" of the times, and traditional voting habits. This means there is little incentive for either parties or candidates to concentrate on issues. Party platforms are seldom read by anyone. Modern campaign techniques focus on the image of the candidate—compassion, warmth, good humor, experience, physical appearance, ease in front of a camera, and so forth—rather than positions on the issues.
- *American political parties have no way to bind their elected officials to party positions or even their campaign pledges.* Parties cannot really discipline members of Congress or state legislatures for voting against the party position. Party cohesion, where it exists, is more a product of likemindedness among Democratic or Republican legislators than it is of party control.

The Rise of Candidate-Centered Elections

In addition to these underlying problems, over time candidate-centered politics has been on the upswing due to the following:

- *The rise of primary elections.* Party organizations cannot control who the party's nominee shall be. Nominations are won in primary elections. The progressive reformers who introduced primary elections at the beginning of the twentieth century wanted to undercut the power of party machines in determining who runs for office, and the reformers succeeded in doing so. Nominees now establish personal organizations in primary elections and campaign for popular votes; they do not have to negotiate with party leaders, especially if they are self-financed candidates. Of course, the party organization may endorse a candidate in a primary election, but this is no guarantee of success with the party's voters.
- *The decline of* **party identification**. Democratic and Republican party loyalties have been declining over the years. Most people remain registered as Democrats or Republicans in order to vote in party primary elections, but increasing numbers of people identify themselves as "independent" and cast their vote in general elections without reference to party. **Split-ticket voting** (where a single voter casts his or her vote for a Democrat in one race and a Republican in another) has also increased.
- *More focus on the candidate, less on his or her party affiliation.* Primary elections, the decline in party identification, and the importance of direct media communication with the voters have all combined to create a **candidate-centered style of political campaigning**. Candidates raise their own campaign funds, create their own personal organizations, and hire professional consultants to produce their own ads (many no longer even include their party affilation in the advertising[4] or, if they do, the party label is minimized so as not to call attention to it).

PARTY IDENTIFICATION

Self-described identification with a political party, usually in response to the question, "Generally speaking, how would you identify yourself: as a Republican, Democrat, independent, or something else?"

SPLIT-TICKET VOTING

A citizen votes for a Democrat in one race and a Republican in another in the same election.

CANDIDATE-CENTERED POLITICS

Individual candidates rather than parties raise funds, create personal organizations, and rely on professional consultants to direct their campaigns.

- *The influence of the mass media, particularly television.* Candidates can come directly into the voter's living room via television (broadcast, cable) and into a citizen's computer, personal digital assistant (PDA), or cell phone via the Internet (Web sites, e-mail). Campaigning electronically (via the airwaves and phones lines) has become more essential, particularly in large, fast-growing states where it is more difficult to reach a large proportion of the voters by going door-to-door (**shoe leather campaigning**).

- *The decline of patronage.* Civil service reforms, at the national, state, and even city levels, have reduced the tangible rewards of electoral victory. Party "**professionals**"—who work in political campaigns to secure jobs and favors for themselves and their friends—are now being replaced by political "**amateurs**"—who work in political campaigns for the emotional satisfaction of supporting a "cause." Amateurs work intensely during campaigns, but professionals once worked year-round, off-years and election years, building party support with small personal favors for the voters. These party "regulars" are disappearing.

- *The rise of single-issue interest groups, PACs, and "527s."* Parties have always coexisted with broad-based interest groups, many of whom contribute money to both Democratic and Republican candidates in order to ensure access regardless of who wins. But many of the more militant single-issue groups require a "litmus test" of individual candidates on single issues— abortion, gun control, and so forth. Their support and money hinge on the candidate's position on a single issue. Most PAC (political action committee) money goes directly to candidates, although some does go to state party organizations. The newest type of group, a "527" (named after the portion of the IRS tax code that covers it), can spend unlimited amounts of money on campaign ads or activities but is expressly prohibited from coordinating its efforts with either a party or a candidate. (Examples of 527s are MoveOn.org, Swift Boat Veterans for Truth.)

A growing number of Americans do not identify with either the Republican or Democratic Party. Consequently, in many states, there has been a surge in the number of voters who either register as independents or with third parties (Libertarian, Reform, Green, Socialist, and others).

Parties are Survivors

Despite the debate over whether we *should* have a pure responsible party system, the bottom line is that we do not have one for all the reasons laid out above. Nonetheless, American political parties "have demonstrated amazing adaptability and durability."[5] The political reality is that both the major parties (Democratic and Republican) and various minor or third parties continue to perform important political functions:

- *Parties organize elections and narrow the choices of political office seekers confronting the voters.* In most state elections, the field of candidates in the November general election is narrowed to the Democratic and Republican party nominees. Very few independents are ever elected to high political office in the states. Only four governors in recent decades— Angus King and James Longley of Maine, Walter Hickel of Alaska, and Lowell Weicker of Connecticut—have been elected as independents. Jesse Ventura, the Reform party candidate, won election as governor of Minnesota over his Democratic and Republican opponents. There are fewer than a dozen independent state legislators in the nation. Nebraska has the nation's only nonpartisan state legislature. Party nominees—for governor, attorney general, and other statewide executive offices, as well as state legislative seats—are selected in party primary elections in most states.

"SHOE LEATHER CAMPAIGNING"
Door-to-door campaigning by candidates or party workers.

PARTY PROFESSIONALS
Those who participate in campaigns and party politics year-round, often to get jobs for themselves or their friends and to strengthen their party.

POLITICAL AMATEURS
Part-timers who participate in campaigns and party politics primarily during elections usually to support a specific candidate or cause.

DEALIGNMENT

A decline in party
loyalty among voters
and a rise in indepen-
dent and split ticket
voting.

CORE VOTERS

Those who always
vote the party line.

- *Parties continue to play an important role in voter choice.* It is true that political parties have lost much of their attractiveness to voters—a development described as **dealignment**. That is, fewer people identify themselves as "strong" Democrats or as "strong" Republicans; more people call themselves "Independents," and more people split their votes between candidates of different parties, although this is less the case in highly competitive, evenly divided states. Party labels remain an important influence on voter choice. People who identify themselves as Democrats tend to vote for Democratic candidates, just as people who identify themselves as Republicans vote for Republican candidates. Nationwide the Democratic and Republican parties have inspired popular images of themselves (see Table 5–2). Both parties maintain fairly stable coalitions of supporters—called **core voters**. These national images and coalitions extend into the politics of most, but certainly not all, states. Party identifiers in some states are more conservative or more liberal than their counterparts in others.

- *Party organizations and activists in the states play an important role in guiding their party and in shaping its image with the voters.* Party activists are the people who serve on city, county, or state party committees, or who serve on the staffs of these committees. They regularly work in campaigns and serve on their state's delegation to the national party conventions. Democratic and Republican state party organizations are found in every state. (Each national party's Web site typically has links to the individual state party organizations and the state party Web site to local party organizations.) In some states these organizations are more powerful than in other states, but in all fifty states, party organizations are becoming increasingly efficient and more professional in their operations.

- *Finally, the Democratic and Republican parties perform the central task of organizing state legislatures.* Only Nebraska has an official nonpartisan legislature. But in every other state, legislative leadership—for example, the house speaker and senate president—as well as committee chairs, are selected on a party basis. The majority party regularly votes for its own candidates for these posts. (See Chapter 6.)

TABLE 5–2 Democratic and Republican Party Supporters Nationwide

	Supporters[a]	
	Republican (%)	Democratic (%)
All Voters	30	33
Gender		
Male	31	29
Female	28	37
Race/Ethnicity		
White	34	29
Black	6	63
Hispanic	20	40
Ideology		
Conservative	51	22
Moderate	22	36
Liberal	8	51
Age Group		
18–29	25	29
30–49	31	32
50–64	29	35
65+	32	40

TABLE 5-2 (Continued)

	Supporters[a]	
	Republican (%)	Democratic (%)
Education		
Less than high school	21	40
High school graduate	28	33
Some college	32	31
College graduate and above	33	32
Income		
Under $20,000	19	42
$20,000–$30,000	24	37
$30,000–$50,000	30	34
$50,000–$75,000	36	29
$75,000 and above	38	29

Note: [a]Row percentages do not add to 100% because independents are excluded from the table.
Source: Pew Research Center for The People and The Press, *Trends 2005*, p. 9. Copyright © 2005. Reprinted by permission of the publisher.

PARTIES AND PRIMARIES

Party primary elections nominate most candidates for public office in America. For the nation's first century, candidates were nominated by party conventions, not primary elections, and as a result party organizations were far more influential than they are today. Primary elections were a key reform in the progressive movement of the early twentieth century. Primaries "democratized" the nomination process and reduced the power of party bosses.

Filing

Primary elections are governed by state law; anyone can *file* a petition with a minimum number of voter signatures, pay a small fee, and have his or her name placed on the primary ballot of either party for practically any public office. A candidate does *not* have to have experience in the party, or even the support of party officials, in order to file for elective office.

Endorsements

Primaries, then, reduce the influence of party organizations in the political process. It is possible, of course, for party organizations at the city, county, or state levels to *endorse*, officially or unofficially, candidates in primary elections. The importance of endorsements varies with the strength and unity of party organizations. Where party organizations are strong at the city or county level, the word can be passed down to precinct committee members to turn out the party's faithful for the endorsed candidate. Party endorsement in a statewide race appears to have less value.

Closed and Open Primaries

Primary elections in most states are **closed**—that is, only voters who have *previously* registered as members of a party may vote in that party's primary. (See Table 5–3.) Only registered Democrats vote in the Democratic primary, and only registered Republicans vote in the Republican primary. **Semiclosed** primaries allow voters to change party

PRIMARY ELECTION

An election held to decide a political party's nominee for public office.

CLOSED PRIMARIES

Primary elections in which voters must declare (or have previously declared) their party affiliation and can cast a ballot only in their own party's primary election.

SEMICLOSED PRIMARIES

Primary elections in which voters must declare (or have previously declared) their party affiliation and can cast a ballot only in their own party's primary election; voters can change party registration on primary election day.

TABLE 5–3 Primary Elections in the States

Types of Primaries (First Primary)

Closed: Proper Party Registration Required	Semiclosed: Voters May Register or Change Party on Election Day	Semiopen: Voters Request Party Ballot	Open: Voter Decides in Which Primary to Vote in Voting Booth	Nonpartisan	Runoff (Second Primary)[j]
Connecticut[a]	Alaska[d]	Alabama[h]	Hawaii	Louisiana	Alabama
Delaware	Arizona[c]	Arkansas[h]	Idaho		Arkansas
Florida	California[d]	Georgia[h]	Michigan		Georgia
Kentucky[a]	Colorado[e]	Illinois[h]	Minnesota		Louisiana
Maine	Iowa[e]	Indiana[h]	Missouri		Mississippi
Nebraska	Kansas[c]	Mississippi[h]	Montana		North Carolina
Nevada	Maryland[d]	Ohio[h]	North Dakota		Oklahoma
New Jersey	Massachusetts	South Carolina[h]	Vermont		South Carolina
New Mexico	New Hampshire[c]	Tennessee[i]	Wisconsin		Texas
New York	North Carolina	Texas			
Oklahoma	Oregon[d]	Virginia[h]			
Pennsylvania	Rhode Island[c]				
South Dakota	Utah[f]				
Wyoming[b]	West Virginia[g]				

[a]At present, unaffiliated voters may not participate, but parties can adopt rules to permit participation by unaffiliated voters by party rule.
[b]Same-day registration permits any voter to declare or change party affiliation at the polls and reverse the change after voting.
[c]Independent voters may choose either party ballot, which registers them with the party.
[d]Unaffiliated voters may vote in primaries, if permitted by party rule.
[e]Voters may declare party affiliation at the polls, which enrolls them with a party.
[f]No public record kept of independent voters' choice of party primary.
[g]Independents may vote in Republican primary only.
[h]Voter's choice of party is recorded and parties have access to the lists.
[i]No public record kept of voter choice of party primary.
[j]Held if no candidate receives or gets a majority of the votes in the first primary.
Source: Virginia Gray and Russell Hanson, "Parties and Elections," in *Politics in the American States: A Comparative Analysis*, 8th ed. (Washington, DC: CQ Press, 2004), 83. Reprinted by permission of Federal Election Committee.

OPEN PRIMARIES

Primary elections in which a voter may cast a ballot in either party's primary election.

BLANKET PRIMARY

Voters can vote for one party's candidate for one office and for another party's candidate for another office; now illegal.

registration on Election Day. Primaries in other states are **open**—voters can choose when they enter the polling place which party primary they wish to vote in. In Louisiana, all candidates run in the same primary election (often referred to as a *nonpartisan* statewide primary election). If a candidate gets over 50 percent of the vote, he or she wins the office; otherwise, the top two vote-getters run again in the general election. At one time, Alaska, California, and Washington had **blanket** primaries in which voters could vote in *both* party primaries simultaneously—voting for one party's candidate for one office, and for another party's candidate for another office. But the U.S. Supreme Court ruled blanket primaries unconstitutional in 2000,[6] which thrilled leaders in both parties who did not like them because they allowed "outsiders" to influence the nomination of their party's candidate.

Party leaders generally prefer the closed primary because they fear crossovers and raiding. **Crossovers** are voters who choose to vote in the primary of the party that they usually do not support in the general election. **Raiding** is an organized attempt to cross over and vote in order to defeat an attractive candidate running for the opposition party's nomination. However, there is no evidence that large numbers of voters connive in such a fashion.

Runoff Primaries

In most states, the **plurality** winner of the party's primary election—the candidate receiving the most votes, whether a majority or not—becomes the party's nominee. But in some states, a candidate must win a **majority** of votes in a primary election to become the party's nominee. If no candidate succeeds in winning a majority in the first primary, a **runoff primary** is held between the top two vote-getters in the first primary.

Runoff primaries are linked to the traditional one-party politics of the southern states. Runoff primaries prevent a candidate with a minority of party voters from capturing the nomination in a race with three or more contenders. Presumably the runoff primary encourages candidates to seek majority support and prevents extremist candidates from winning nominations. No one can win a nomination by relying on splits among multiple opponents.

First primary front-runners have a better-than-even chance of winning the runoff. Overall, front-runners win about two-thirds of runoff primaries for state legislative seats, although they win only slightly more than half of the runoffs for governor and U.S. senator.[7]

Runoff primaries have been attacked as racially discriminatory. In districts where there is a large but less than majority black population and a history of racial block voting, black candidates who win a plurality of votes in the first primary may be defeated in the runoff if white voters unite behind the white runner-up. (It is possible, of course, for the reverse to occur in a majority black district.) One study of local runoff primaries in Georgia found that black plurality winners in the first primary were somewhat less likely to win a runoff against a white runner-up (50 percent black runoff victories) than white plurality winners against a black runner-up (84 percent white runoff victories).[8] However, more extensive and recent studies have concluded that runoff elections do not have the racially discriminatory impact that they were once perceived to have.[9] Race aside, because turnout in runoff primaries is often quite low while the costs remain high, some states, like Florida, have eliminated them.

Conventions

State conventions continue in a handful of states. In New York and Connecticut, statewide **party conventions** nominate candidates; however, candidates can "challenge" the convention nominee to a primary election if the challenger receives a specified share of the convention vote (25 percent in New York, 20 percent in Connecticut).

Statewide party organizations seldom have much influence over primary outcomes. State party chairs and state party committee members generally don't like to publicly "take sides," often seeing it as equivalent to having to pick which of your offspring you love the most. Plus by avoiding endorsements during the primary stage of an election, it makes it easier to mount a united front behind the party's nominee in the general election.

CROSSOVER VOTING

Voters affiliated with one party casting votes in the other party's primary election.

"RAIDING"

An organized attempt to cross over and vote in another party's primary in order to defeat an attractive candidate.

PLURALITY WINNER

The candidate receiving the most votes, whether a majority or not.

MAJORITY WINNER

The candidate receiving fifty percent plus one of the vote.

RUNOFF PRIMARY

An additional (second) primary held between the top two vote-getters in a primary.

PARTY CONVENTION

Delegates chosen by party members choose the party's nominee, write the party's platform, and rally party support.

Presidential Primaries and Caucuses

Every four years, state parties play a major role in nominating the party's candidate for president. In most states, each party holds a **presidential primary election**, usually, but not always, on the same day. But in some states, like Iowa, parties may use caucuses to select the presidential candidate they would like to see officially nominated at the national party convention. A **party caucus** is a meeting of voters at some officially designated location for the purpose of choosing who they prefer as their party's standard bearer in the race for president. Beginning with the 2008 presidential election cycle, a number of states began moving up the date of their primaries (front-loading)—even defying national party calendar rules—to have more influence over the selection of the nominee.

Presidential primary elections play an integral part in the nomination process which helps explain why so many states want to be "first." In 2008, South Carolina was one of the earliest states to hold a primary so naturally, the leading Democratic candidates were there early . . . and often.

STATE PARTY ORGANIZATIONS AND ACTIVISTS

State party organizations are "highly variable, elusive to find, difficult to define, and frustrating to study."[10] Indeed, both Democratic and Republican party organizations at the state and local levels are ill-defined, fluid, and very often "unoccupied," particularly right after an election. It is more difficult to get people to engage in party activities between elections than in the heat of a "campaign season." Then it is fairly easy to fill party posts, especially in a highly competitive, two-party state.

Nonetheless, a small core of Democratic and Republican party activists willing to be involved year-round can be found in every state. They occupy positions on city, county, and state Democratic and Republican committees, and in the county and state conventions of their party. They represent their party on the national party committees and in the national party presidential nominating conventions. At the lowest level, they continue to keep in contact with neighbors, urging residents to register and vote, handing out party literature, inviting newcomers to get involved, and perhaps even trying to do small favors for their loyal voters.

Activists as Ideologues

Whereas parties may be pushed toward the ideological center in order to win elections, the activists in the parties tend to be strong ideologues—people who take consistently "liberal" or "conservative" positions on the issues. Republican party activists in most states are more conservative than Democratic party activists. Indeed, Republican party activists tend to be more conservative than the general public, and Democratic party activists tend to be more liberal than the general public. This is true even though activists in both parties will tend to be more conservative in a conservative state and more liberal in a liberal state.[11]

In the southern and border states, as the Republican party has grown in strength, Democratic and Republican party activists have clearly separated themselves along ideological lines. Today there are fewer conservatives among Democratic party activists in the South than in previous eras. As conservatives drift toward the Republican party, the liberal strength within the Democratic party increases. Blacks have assumed increasingly active and influential roles in southern Democratic party organizations, while fundamentalist white Protestants have become an increasingly active force in Republican circles.[12] The result is greater ideological cleavage between the parties.

Activists as Potential Candidates

Party activists—people who serve on party posts as committee members or chairpersons at the city, county, or state level, or as delegates to party conventions—constitute a recruitment pool for candidates for public office. Often these people initially volunteered for party work with the expectation of eventually running for public office. Their party activity provides technical knowledge as well as personal contacts that become useful in their own future campaign. Party workers generally have voter registration lists available to them as well as information regarding ballot access, filing dates, campaign expenditure reporting, and other useful information. And, of course, party workers come into personal contact with key campaign contributors.

State Party Organizations

American political parties are decentralized in their organization. Power flows from the bottom up, not the top down. (See Figure 5–1 and "*Up Close*: Texas Party Organizations.") It is not really surprising in the American system of federalism—when only the president and vice president have *national* constituencies, and senators, representatives, governors, state legislators, and county and city officials all have *state and local* constituencies—that the American parties are decentralized.

At the national level, the Democratic and Republican parties consist of a national committee; a House and Senate party conference; and various national clubs, such as Young Democrats and Young Republicans. There are also *fifty state parties*, which are composed of state committees and county and city organizations. This structure is tied together very loosely. State committees are generally involved in important statewide elections—governors, U.S. senators, and representatives in the smaller states. City and county committees are generally responsible for county and municipal offices, state legislative seats, and congressional seats in the larger states. The Democratic and Republican National Committees exist primarily for the purpose of holding national conventions every four years to select the party's presidential candidate. Since each level of party organization has "its own fish to fry," each operates quite independently of the other levels.

State Laws Govern Parties

Party affairs are governed largely by the laws of the states. Each state sets forth the conditions that an organization must meet to qualify as a political party and to get its

PARTY CAUCUS
A meeting of voters at some officially designated location for the purpose of nominating party candidates.

PARTY ACTIVISTS
People who serve in city, county, or state party organizations, or who regularly work in campaigns.

STATE COMMITTEES
Governing bodies of state party organizations.

COUNTY COMMITTEES
Governing bodies of county party organizations.

FIGURE 5–1 Political Parties Are Built from the Bottom Up

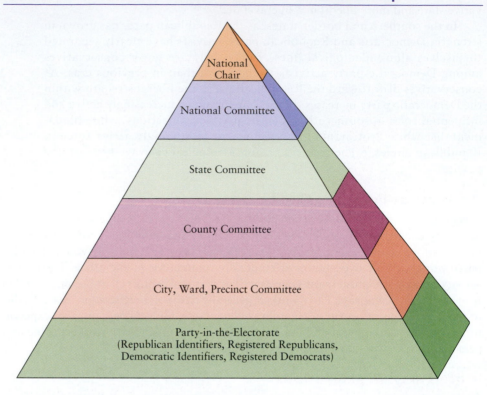

National Chair

National Committee

State Committee

County Committee

City, Ward, Precinct Committee

Party-in-the-Electorate
(Republican Identifiers, Registered Republicans,
Democratic Identifiers, Registered Democrats)

Each state sets forth the conditions that an organization must meet to qualify as a political party and to get its candidates' names printed on the official election ballots.

candidates' names printed on the official election ballots. Each state sets the qualifications for membership in a party and the right to vote in the party's primary election. State laws determine the number, method of selection, and duties of various party officials, committees, and conventions. The states, rather than the parties themselves, decide how the parties shall nominate candidates for public office. Most states require that party nominations be made by direct primaries, but several states still nominate by party caucuses or conventions. Most states also attempt to regulate party finances, although with little success.

State Committees

State party organizations officially consist of a "state committee," a "state chairman," or "chairwoman," and perhaps a state executive director and an office staff working at the state capitol. Democratic and Republican state committees vary from state to state in composition, organization, and function. Membership on the state committee may range from about a dozen up to several hundred. The members may be chosen through party primaries or by state party conventions. Generally, representation on state committees is allocated to counties, but occasionally other units of government are recognized in state party organization. A state party chairman or chairwoman generally serves at the head of the state committee; these people are generally selected by the state committee, but their selection is often dictated by the party's candidate for governor.

up CLOSE — Texts Party Organizations

The Democratic and Republican party organizations in Texas are not unlike those of many states. Texas law provides for open primaries; voters can decide to cast their ballots in either the Democratic or Republican party primary without prior registration as party members. There are 254 counties in Texas and more than 8,700 local voting precincts. Many party committee posts are vacant or occupied by people who do little or nothing for their party. But some party activists devote a great deal of time and energy to their jobs. Some county committees meet only irregularly and have a difficult time getting a quorum of members to attend. Other counties (mostly in the state's larger cities) have active committees, office headquarters, and professional staff. The Democratic and Republican state committees have sixty-four members; these members are selected by party conventions held in each state senate district. The state Democratic and Republican party chairs and vice-chairs are selected at state party conventions held every two years. These conventions also adopt state party platforms, but party candidates are chosen by voters in primary elections.

Source: Thomas R. Dye, L. Tucker Gibson, Jr., and Clay Robinson, *Politics in America*, Texas Edition, 7th ed. (Upper Saddle River, NJ: Prentice Hall, 2007).

In recent years state party organizations have strengthened themselves, despite the rise of candidate-centered politics. They have become "service agencies"[13] providing an array of technical services to their candidate—modern telephone polling facilities, Web site designs, lists of potential contributors, direct mail and telemarketing systems, links to media outlets throughout the state (with reporters' names and phone numbers listed), access to campaign and media consultants, Spanish-language training, advice on election law complaince and campaign finance reporting, research (including **"oppo research"** on the weaknesses of opponents), and even seminars on campaign techniques. Virtually all state parties now have permanent headquarters in the state capital. Most state parties today have full-time professional staff in addition to part-time help and volunteers. They are geared up to hold press conferences and issue press releases on a moment's notice, often in response to some activity or pronouncement by the opposition party.

Yet state party organizations are only a part of the broader network that includes candidate organizations, interest groups regularly aligned with the party (unions and teacher organizations are especially important to Democrats), professional political campaign consultants, and professional fundraisers.

It is difficult to assess whether or to what extent the strength of state party organizations contributes to electoral success in a state. So many other factors affect electoral success that it is difficult to estimate the *independent* effect, if any, of party organizational strength. But it is widely believed among party activists that sophisticated organizations improve prospects of victory for the party's candidates.

OPPO RESEARCH

Searching for information about the weaknesses of an opponent, often via newspapers, public records, and the Internet.

State Party Chairpersons

State party chairpersons are by no means political hacks. Most state chairpersons have been successful business people, lawyers, or public officials who may even serve their posts without salaries to satisfy their interest in politics and public affairs. Republican chairpersons are more likely to have held important positions in business and management, while Democratic chairpersons are more likely to be lawyers who have held political office previously. Some come up through the ranks of local party organizations and have never held elective office; others started in elective politics. While in that position, they routinely interact with local party leaders who then become their supporters when they seek the state party chair position. (See "*People in Politics:* Two Powerful Women, Two Different Paths to Becoming State Party Chair.")

State party chairpersons can play different roles from state to state. Some see themselves as mere "political agents" of their governor; others are independently powerful. In general, chairpersons of the party out of power have more independence and power than those of the party in power. The latter are overshadowed by their governor. Party chairpersons do not hold on to their jobs very long—the average is less than three years.[14]

County Committees

Party organizations at the county level can be found almost everywhere. The organizations include the following:

- An active chairperson and executive committee, plus a few associated activists, who in effect make most of the decisions in the name of the party, who raise funds, who occasionally seek out candidates to fill out the party's slate in the general election (or approve the candidates who select themselves), and who speak locally for the party.

- A ward and precinct organization in which only a few local committee members are active and in which there is little door-to-door canvassing or other direct voter contact.

- The active participation in organizational matters of some of the party's elected public officials, who may share effective control of the organization with the official leadership of the party organization.

- Financial contributors to the party and its candidates, together with leaders of local interest groups that generally ally themselves with the party.

Republican and Democratic county chairpersons probably constitute the most important building blocks of party organization in America. City and county party officers and committees are chosen locally and cannot be removed by any higher party authority. In short, authority is not concentrated in any single statewide organization but is divided among many city and county party organizations.

Local Party Organizations

Very few local organizations have a full-time staff, or a permanent headquarters, or even a telephone listing,[15] but they may have a Web site. (Many local parties get young party activists to design these.) Most rely on volunteers—precinct and county committee members—who seldom meet in nonelection years. Few local organizations have any budget. Most engage in election year efforts at distributing campaign literature, organizing campaign events, putting up posters and lawn signs, conducting registration drives, and even some door-to-door canvassing. The role of local party organizations is mostly supplementary to that of the candidates' own organizations.

Party volunteers operate phone banks which often survey party members about what issues they regard as the most important for candidates to address. These grassroots volunteers are also critical to Get-Out-The-Vote (GOTV) efforts—reminding voters to go to the polls or to vote absentee and even offering rides to the polls.

Two Powerful Women, Two Different Paths to Becoming State Party Chair

Becoming state party chairperson is quite an accomplishment, especially in the nation's third and fourth largest states. But with the honor comes a lot of responsibility. Texas's Tina Benkiser (R) and Florida's Karen Thurman (D) are up to the task. Each has a long history of involvement in partisan affairs, but they have taken very different paths to the top party spot. Thurman's route was via elective office while Benkiser's was up through the ranks of local and state party committees.

Thurman started her professional life as a middle school math teacher in a city of 2,000. She got involved in local politics, at the prompting of her students, in an effort to save a local beach. Her political career was textbook-like in its progression: city council member (1974–1982), mayor (1979–1981), state senator (1983–1993), then U.S. Congress member (1993–2003). Her congressional district was considered to be the most competitive in the state, yet she easily won reelection for a decade. Thurman was skilled at representing a very diverse constituency—gun owners in the rural parts of the district, liberal college professors at the University of Florida. After Thurman lost her congressional seat, she kept active in state Democratic Party politics, frequently appearing at party events. When the state party chair

decided to step down and make a run for governor in 2005, Thurman stepped up to run for the post and won easily. She acknowledged the job would be difficult. Her big challenge? To rebuild a party "that over the last decade has fallen from its once dominant, century-long place atop statewide government."[a]

Benkiser is a Houston lawyer specializing in corporate transactions, business formation, intellectual property, and sports and entertainment law. Her party activism credentials are impressive, earned through many years of volunteering "in the trenches": three terms on the State Republican Executive Committee, precinct chair, election judge, volunteer on federal, state, and local campaigns, activist in the local Republican Women's Club, and frequent delegate to the Texas Federation of Republican Women's state conventions. Benkiser become only the second woman party head in the history of the Texas GOP. Building enthusiasm for party activities is a big part of being a state party chair, but especially in Texas— a state with an "attitude." In promoting the party's straw poll for the 2008 election, she said: "We are so excited to give our grassroots leaders the opportunity to kick the tires and look under the hoods of these presidential candidates. Plus our GOP events are just fun and no one does it as big as Texas."[b]

[a]Raghuram Vadarevu, "Thurman Drawn Back to Political Limelight," *St. Petersburg Times*, May 1, 2005.
[b]*The Lantern*, Summer 2007.

However, when it comes to statewide races (gubernatorial, U.S. Senate, presidential contests), local party organizations are often seen as a vital part of state party-driven GOTV efforts. Thousands of volunteers are needed to chair precinct committees, call potential supporters urging them to vote, and wave signs and give last minute pitches for their party's candidates at every polling place.

REPUBLICAN AND DEMOCRATIC PARTY FORTUNES IN THE STATES

Throughout history, Democratic and Republican party fortunes have swung back and forth. National public opinion polls show that for many years, a greater percentage of Americans have identified themselves as Democrats than Republicans, although the gap between the parties has fluctuated, with Republicans gaining in the 1990s. (See Table 5–4.)

TABLE 5–4	Party Identification Among All Americans											
	1937 %	1960 %	1972 %	1984 %	1988 %	1994 %	1996 %	1998 %	2000 %	2002 %	2004 %	2006 %
Democrats	50	47	43	40	42	40	38	30	34	34	38	35
Independents	16	23	29	29	28	34	33	36	36	32	27	40
Republicans	34	30	28	31	30	26	29	26	30	34	35	24

Source: Gallup Polls.

However, neither major party can claim it is the majority party due to the growing number of self-identified "independents" in recent years. The result in state politics has been a rise in party competitiveness, especially in the southern states, which at one time were solidly Democratic.

Party Registration

In states that register voters by party, the Democratic party does better in registration figures than it does in opinion polls.[16] The tendency for many independents and even some Republicans to register as Democrats is more pronounced in the southern states. Voters choose to register in the traditionally dominant party for several reasons: perhaps because the dominant party's primary is more interesting insofar as the winner is more likely to go on to win office; or perhaps because people seeking political favors (like jobs, contracts, zoning decisions) wish to be identified publicly with the dominant party; or perhaps because of social pressures and a desire to be seen as a member of the dominant party, or just because they haven't gotten around to changing their party registration. Because the Democratic party was traditionally the dominant party in most states, registration figures remain skewed toward the Democrats. This makes it important to look at voting patterns in addition to party registration to get an accurate read of a state's party leanings.

Changing Party Fortunes in Gubernatorial Races

The Republican party enjoyed its greatest resurgence in nearly half a century in congressional and state politics in 1994. In that year Republicans captured control of the U.S. House of Representatives for the first time since 1954. At the state level, the GOP gained a majority of governorships for the first time in over three decades (see Figure 5–2). Following the 2004 elections, Republicans occupied governor's chairs in twenty-eight states, including four of the nation's five largest states—California, New York, Texas, and Florida. But by 2006, the pendulum had swung back to the Democrats.

Changing Party Fortunes in State Legislatures

The Democratic party long enjoyed dominance over state legislatures. In the mid-1970s, the Democratic party controlled over thirty state legislatures, while the Republican party controlled only four. But the Republican party's fortunes in state legislatures improved significantly in the 1990s (see Figure 5–3). Following the 2004 state legislature elections, Republicans controlled twenty-one legislatures, Democrats seventeen, with eleven split between the parties. But, as with governors, control shifted back to Democrats in 2006.

FIGURE 5–2 Party Control of Governorships

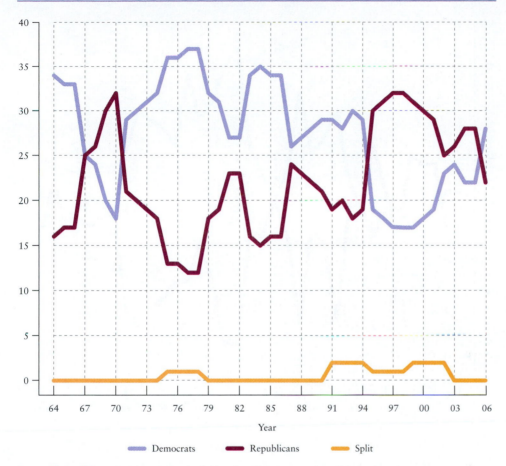

Year

— Democrats   — Republicans   — Split

Source: National Governors Association. Available at http://www.nga.org/portal/site/nga/menuitem
.216dbea7c618ef3f8a278110501010a0/?vgnextoid=21cca0ca9e3f1010V gnVCM1000001a01010aRCRD

DIVIDED PARTY GOVERNMENT IN THE STATES

Overall, the frequency of **divided party government** (where the executive branch is controlled by one party and one or both houses of the legislative branch are controlled by the other party) rose in the American states in the 1980s. Since 1984 more than half of the states have had divided government; the high was thirty-one states after both the 1988 and 1996 elections. But that trend has tapered off somewhat in recent years.

Unified Party Government

A **unified party government**—where the same party controls both houses of the legislature as well as the governorship—is often *presumed* to be better able to enact its program into law. More importantly, perhaps, voters are better able to attribute praise or blame for the direction of state government. Under a unified party government, the

DIVIDED PARTY GOVERNMENT

In state politics, where the governorship is controlled by one party and one or both houses of the legislature is controlled by the other party.

UNIFIED PARTY GOVERNMENT

In state politics, where the governorship and both houses of the state legislature are controlled by the same party.

FIGURE 5–3 Democratic and Republican Control of State Legislatures

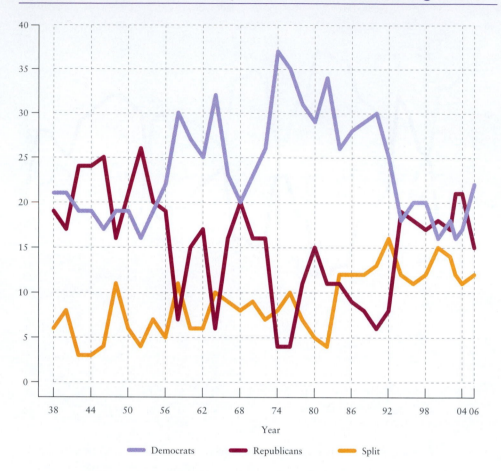

Source: National Conference of State Legislatures; 2007 Partisan Composition of State Legislatures. Available at http://www.ncsl.org/statevote/partycomptable2007.htm

dominant party cannot escape responsibility for poor performance by blaming it on the opponent party's control of one house or branch of state government.[17] When that does occur, it is usually because of *intraparty* squabbles. The greater the control one party has, the more likely it is that factions will emerge within that party's elected officials, usually along ideological or geographical lines or both.

Does Divided Government Mean "Gridlock"?

Legislative gridlock—the failure to enact significant pieces of legislation—is often attributed to divided party government. Studies of state legislatures have shown that the overall output of a legislature (the number of bills passed) is *not* affected by divided party government. However, it has been shown that divided party government makes the passage of *controversial* legislation more difficult. When a governor faces a legislature with one or more houses controlled by the opposite party, it becomes more difficult to pass legislation in areas where there are high levels of conflict, often welfare,

**LEGISLATIVE
"GRIDLOCK"**

The failure to pass controversial legislation, often due to divided control.

crime, education, moral issues, and the environment. (See "Divided Government: Governor versus the Legislature" in Chapter 7.) Legislative gridlock under divided government is worse in states with strong interest group systems. Yet in less controversial areas of legislation, such as agriculture, economic development, and transportation, divided party government does not appear to impede the passage of legislation.[18]

PARTY COMPETITION AND POLICY DIFFERENCES WITHIN THE STATES

Party competition within the fifty states is uneven and dynamic. A state's competitiveness may change as the composition of its population shifts. But just exactly how competitive are the political parties in each of the fifty states? The answer to the question differs according to how one is measuring competition. One way of measuring party competitiveness is to track how often there is a change in the party affiliation of the winning candidate (*party turnover*) for top-of-the-ticket offices—president, governor, U.S. senator, or other statewide executive officials—or how wide is the winning candidate's *margin of victory*. Another is to count how often the governor is from one political party at the same time both houses of the state legislatures are controlled by the other party (*divided control*). Comparing the *percentage of voters who register with (or identify with) each party* is also a means of determining competitiveness—the more equal the percentages, the more competitive the party system is assumed to be.

Party leaders, campaign strategists, and political analysts use each of these measures to gauge the odds they will face in any campaign. Relying on just one could be rather deceiving and short-sighted. For example, Florida is not competitive if one merely uses the divided control measure but it is very competitive if one uses margin of victory or party registration/identification parity measures. (Table 5–5 groups states by one measure of competition—the degree of divided control of the governorship and upper and lower houses of the state legislature—while Figure 5–4 groups states by citizen vote preference prior to the 2008 presidential election as measured by polls.) The perceived level of competition affects a party's ability to recruit candidates (particularly for down ballot races), raise money (both inside and outside the state), and engage volunteers.

Republican party strength is greatest in states in the South and Mountain West while Democratic party strength is strongest in states in the Northeast, Rust Belt, and Pacific Coast. However, states change as their demographic makeup shifts. For example, some states in the Mountain West have become more Democratic following an influx of Californians. Generally, however, party competition in the states is stronger today than at any time in recent history, paralleling the high incidence of people moving from one state to another.

Parties' Policy Differences

Party competition is most likely to produce policy differences if there is a bimodal distribution of voters' preferences in a state; and if the parties have strong organization and ideologically motivated activists, then the parties in that state will offer clear policy alternatives. This notion can be diagrammed as follows: where there is a **bimodal distribution of opinion** (voters divide into liberals and conservatives) and the parties take the policy positions of their different groups of constituents.

UNIMODAL DISTRIBUTION OF OPINION

This occurs when most voters prefer moderate or centrist policies, thereby causing the parties to move closer together in their policy positions.

BIMODAL DISTRIBUTION OF OPINION

This occurs when most voters are clearly divided in their policy preferences, thereby causing the parties to take divergent policy positions.

Bimodal Distribution of Opinion

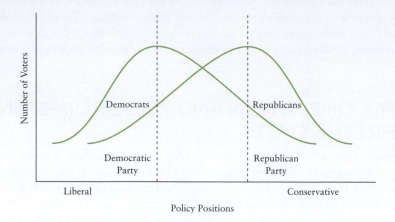

<table>
<tr><td colspan="3" style="text-align:left">

TABLE 5–5 Unified and Divided Party Government in the States

</td></tr>
</table>

Unified and Divided Party Legislative Government in the States

Republican	Democratic	Divided Party Government
Alaska	Alabama	Delaware
Arizona	Arkansas	Kentucky
Florida	California	Minnesota
Georgia	Colorado	Montana
Idaho	Connecticut	Nevada
Iowa	DC	New York
Indiana	Hawaii	Oklahoma
Kansas	Louisiana	Oregon
Michigan	Maine	Tennessee
Missouri	Maryland	
New Hampshire	Massachusetts	
North Dakota	Mississippi	
Ohio	New Jersey	
Pennsylvania	New Mexico	
South Carolina	North Carolina	
South Dakota	Rhode Island	
Texas	Vermont	
Utah	Washington	
Virginia	West Virginia	
Wisconsin		
Wyoming		

Note: Nebraska retains its nonpartisan legislature.
Source: National Conference of State Legislatures; State Vote 2006. Available at http://www.ncsl.org/statevote/statevotemaps2006.htm

FIGURE 5–4 **"Color-Coded" State Party Competitiveness in National Elections**

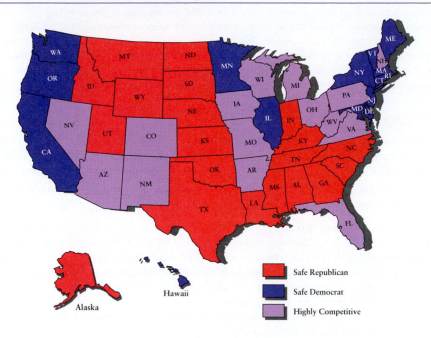

Legend:
- Safe Republican
- Safe Democrat
- Highly Competitive

Note: Color code applies to presidential elections.
Source: Louis Jacobson, Stateline.org columnist. "2008 may come down to Ohio—again." July 19, 2007. Available at http://www.stateline.org/live/printable/story?contentId=225442. Reprinted by permission of the author and publisher.

Few candidates for governor, senator, or any other statewide office rely exclusively on the party organization to handle their campaigns. Most create their own campaign organizations and then turn to the whole new "image industry" to manage their mass media campaigns, which often seem to be nonstop.

Party conflict over policy questions is most frequent in those states in which the Democratic party represents central-city, low-income, ethnic, and racial constituencies, and the Republican party represents middle-class, suburban, small-town, and rural constituencies. In these states, the Democratic and Republican parties will tend to disagree over taxation and appropriations, welfare, education, moral values, and regulation of business and labor—that is, the major social and economic controversies that divide the national parties.[19] These schisms make it easier for professional campaign consultants to target a party's key, core constituents.

PROFESSIONAL MEDIA CAMPAIGNS

Professional public relations specialists, pollsters and focus group gurus, creative webmasters, and advertising geniuses now play a bigger role in the design and management of political campaigns than they used to before the professionalization of campaigns.[20] Few candidates for governor, senator, or any other statewide office rely exclusively on the party organization to handle their campaigns. Most create their own campaign organizations and then turn to the whole new "image industry" to manage their mass media

MEDIA CAMPAIGN

Contacting potential voters and soliciting their support primarily through television, radio, newspaper and Internet advertising.

campaigns, which often seem to be nonstop. Political campaign communication experts describe the pervasiveness of campaigns in today's media-dominated world:

> Whether we like it or not . . . we can scarcely avoid taking part in the campaign process. Those who choose not to participate directly become involved at some level even if it is only to explain to friends why they are refusing to respond to a candidate's telephone survey, or why they are turning off the television to avoid political programs and advertisements. . . . Somebody is always seeking elective office. . . . The modern campaign knows no season. It seems that as one ends, another begins.[21]

"Marketing" Candidates

If marketing, advertising, and public relations firms can sell cars, pain relievers, and hair products, why not political candidates? Indeed, today marketing and media specialists have largely taken over political campaigns for most important offices. Modern professional campaign management involves techniques that strongly resemble those employed in commercial product marketing, including the following:

- Computerized mailing lists for fundraising and the preparation and mailing of slick brochures to the voters. Knowing that 75 percent of all direct mail ends up in the trash can unopened, consultants have become more adept at creating outer envelopes that entice the recipient to open them. Color and size matter most.[22] In states with Early Voting, mail pieces are often sent as early as eight weeks before Election Day. Mail sent earliest is most likely to influence active, frequent voters who make up their minds early. Late mail is targeted to late deciders and designed to remind them to vote and to give them a simple-to-grasp contrast between the candidates.[23]

- Computerized voter lists that include occupation, age, race, interests, memberships, and so on, of each voter, so that special statements by the candidate can be delivered to special groups of voters, which is microtargeting. For example, in past elections, Republican consulting firms identified as many as thirty-two categories of voters, each identifiable by income, magazine subscriptions, favorite television shows, consumer buying patterns, and hobbies. This detailed information made it easy to target each voter with a tailored message.[24]

- Public opinion polling on a regular basis throughout the campaign, which enables candidates to identify their opponents' weaknesses as well as their own and to assess the voters' moods and opinion shifts throughout the campaign. Consultants advise spending between 10 and 15 percent of a candidate's campaign budget on different types of polling: To know your opponent, you need a short *vulnerability* poll (answers the question "Should I run against this opponent?"). To know yourself, commission a larger *benchmark* poll (find out what and how strongly do they think about me, my message theme, my targeting, and my media). And to know your race when it matters most, buy at least two *tracking* polls (answer the questions "How am I doing, how is my opponent doing, and what do I need to do to win?").[25]

- The preparation of video ads, television ads, radio broadcasts, signs, bumper stickers, clothing lines, automated recorded phone calls ("robo" calls) and so on, which emphasize the candidate's "theme." (See *Did You Know?* "Today's 'High-Tech' Campaigns Have a Vocabulary All Their Own.")

- Developing "media events" that will attract the attention of television and newspapers, for example, walking across the state, working a day in the lettuce fields, and so forth. These events do not always need to be aimed at newscasts. The "Oprah" approach calls for candidates to appear on talk shows to reach those who normally don't watch much news.[26] For some, local newscasts are seen as just another player in election politics, while for others, they are the primary source of political news.[27]

Public Relations Firms

Professional public relations firms come in different sizes and shapes. Some are all-purpose organizations that plan the whole campaign; select a theme; monitor the electorate with continuous polling; produce television tapes for commercials, newspaper advertisements, and radio spots; select clothing and hairstyles for their candidates; write speeches and schedule appearances (or avoid them if the candidates cannot speak well); and even plan the victory party. Other organizations limit themselves to particular functions, such as polling or television production. Some firms specialize by party, handling only Democratic or Republican candidates; a few firms specialize by ideology, handling liberal or conservative clients. Still other firms are strictly professional, providing services to any candidate who can afford them.

Polling

Frequently, polling is at the center of strategic campaign decision making. At the beginning of the campaign, polls test the "recognition factor" of the candidate and assess what political issues are uppermost in the minds of voters. Special polling techniques can determine what a "winning candidate profile" looks like in a district. The results of these polls will be used to determine a general strategy—developing a favorable "image" for the candidate and focusing on a popular campaign "theme." Early polls can also detect weaknesses in the candidate, which can then be overcome in advertising (too rich—then show her in blue jeans reading to young children in a poor neighborhood; too intellectual—then show him in a hog-calling contest; and so on). Polls can tell whether the party is stronger than the candidate (then identify the candidate as loyal to the party) or whether the candidate is stronger than the party (then stress the candidate's independent thinking).

During the campaign the polls can chart the progress of the candidate and even assess the effectiveness of specific themes and "media events." A **"media event"** is an activity generated to attract news coverage, for example, walking the entire length of the state to show "closeness to the people," or carrying around a broom to symbolize "house cleaning," or spending occasional days doing manual work in a factory or on a farm. Finally, polls can identify the undecided vote toward the end of the campaign and help direct the time and resources of the candidate.

Name Recognition

The first objective in a professional campaign is to increase the candidate's name recognition among the voters. Years ago, name recognition could only be achieved through years of service in minor public or party offices (or owning a well-known family name). Today, expert media advisors (and lots of money) can create instant celebrity. "Exposure" is the name of the game, and exposure requires attracting the attention of the news media. (As one commentator observed, "To a politician there is no such thing as indecent exposure. Obscurity is a dirty word and almost all exposure is decidedly decent.") A millionaire land developer (former Governor and later U.S. Senator Bob Graham of Florida) attracted attention by simply working a few days as ditch-digger, busboy, bulldozer operator, and so on, to identify with the "common people" and receive a great deal of news coverage.

Campaign Themes

The emphasis of the professional public-relations campaign is on simplicity: a few themes, brief speeches, uncluttered ads, quick and catchy spot commercials. Finding the right theme or slogan is essential; this effort is not greatly different from that of launching an

POLLING
Questioning a representative sample of the population (or of likely voters) to determine public opinion about candidates and issues.

NAME RECOGNITION
The likelihood that people recognize a candidate's name when questioned in opinion polls.

MEDIA EVENT
An activity designed to attract news coverage of a candidate (free media).

Interest groups, like political parties, play an important role in grassroots campaigning. A politically active organization, like the Teamsters Union, sends an activist member to the door of a fellow member with instructions to get that person to vote on Election Day.

advertising campaign for a new detergent. A campaign theme should not be controversial. It might be as simple as "A leader you can trust"; the candidate would then be "packaged" as competent and trustworthy. Equally important is to make sure a candidate "stays on message." Why? Message discipline makes those phrases more potent and consistency increases the likelihood that voters will believe what you are saying.[28]

Personality, Not Policy

A professional media campaign generally focuses on the personal qualities of the candidate rather than his or her stand on policy issues. Professional campaigns are based on the assumption that a candidate's image is the most important factor affecting voter choice. This image is largely devoid of issues, except in very general terms; for example, "tough on crime," "stands up to the special interests," "fights for the taxpayer." And a favorite campaign tactic is to associate one's opponent with *un*popular policy positions whenever possible.

Grassroots Campaigning

Door-to-door campaigning (personal contacting) by candidates or party workers is very effective when used, but it is labor and time intensive, and limited in the proportion of voters who can be reached. This is why statewide candidates have to rely more on mass media-based campaign techniques. However, local party organizations may play the role of surrogates for the candidate, walking through neighborhoods handing out their brochures, leaving door hangers for those not home, and contacting potential supporters by

Television may consume up to three-quarters of all campaign costs.

phone or e-mail.[29] But grassroots campaigning by statewide candidates themselves is less common than "shoe leather campaigning" by candidates for the state legislature or other local offices.

Media Campaigning

Media campaigning concentrates on obtaining the maximum "free" exposure on the evening news, as well as saturating television and newspapers with paid commercial advertising. To win favorable news coverage, candidates and their managers must devise attractive media events with visuals and sound bites too good for the television news to ignore. News coverage of a candidate is more credible than paid commercials. So candidates must do or say something interesting and "newsworthy" as often as possible during the campaign.

Television "spot" advertisements incur costs in both production and broadcast time. Indeed, television may consume up to three-quarters of all campaign costs; about one-third of TV costs go for production of ads and two-thirds to buying time from television stations. The Federal Communications Commission requires broadcasters to make available broadcast time to political candidates for federal office at the same rates charged to product advertisers but this does not apply to candidates for state and local offices. Ads are big business for professional campaign consultants and for local television stations. The estimated cumulative spending on TV political ads by presidential, state, and local candidates, political parties, and independent political groups in a single election cycle is in the billions. No surprise here. The average cost

Political party mascots capture the attention of young and old alike. They also often end up in local television and newspaper stories highlighting a campaign event.

of a *single* thirty-second spot aired on prime-time network television can cost in the hundreds of thousands of dollars. (To put things in perspective, the average rate for a thirty-second spot during the Super Bowl is well over $2.5 *million*.)

Deciding where to "run" an ad is becoming more difficult as the media habits of Americans change, especially across different generations. (See Table 5–6.) No single source of news today is as dominant as network news was in the early 1990s.[30] Increasingly, candidates are turning to cable television and radio because they are cheaper and more easily targeted to specific groups of voters (they reach more segmented audiences). Web-based advertising is also on the upswing as more Americans are going on-line for campaign information.

Many Americans are choosing the news they wish to watch on the basis of the perceived ideological bent of specific broadcast and cable news outlets, their anchors, news magazine show hosts, and their reporters. The same holds true for what radio stations they select and which Internet Web sites they visit, and whose e-mail lists they would like to be on. (Review Table 5–6.)

Negative Ads

Professional media campaigns have increasingly turned to the airing of television commercials and Internet video ads depicting the opponent in negative terms. The original negative TV ad is generally identified as the 1964 "daisy-picking" commercial, aired by the Lyndon B. Johnson presidential campaign, which portrayed Republican opponent Barry Goldwater as a nuclear warmonger. Over time the techniques of negative ads have been refined; weaknesses in opponents are identified and dramatized in emotionally forceful

Hand-held cameras make it easy to grab footage of exciting campaign events which can, in turn, be used in candidate ads and posted on-line at candidate and political party Web sites.

TABLE 5–6 Regular News Sources Differ by an Individual's Age and Ideology

Program	All (%)	Age		Ideology		
		18–49 (%)	50+ (%)	Conservative (%)	Moderate (%)	Liberal (%)
Local TV news	71	69	75	73	73	70
Local daily newspaper	54	48	64	56	57	54
Network evening news	46	41	54	47	49	44
Fox News Channel	43	41	46	52	40	34
Cable News Network (CNN)	39	38	42	34	44	41
Network morning shows	34	33	36	32	38	34
National Public Radio	28	28	28	22	29	42
News from Google, Yahoo, etc.	25	31	17	22	28	33
News magazines	23	21	25	20	26	27
TV news websites	22	26	17	19	26	25
O'Reilly Factor	17	14	22	26	14	11
Daily Show, Colbert Report	16	18	14	12	16	26
NewsHour with Jim Lehrer	14	11	18	12	14	20
Major newspaper Web sites	12	13	9	8	12	20
Online news discussion blogs	11	11	11	9	13	16
Rush Limbaugh's radio show	8	6	10	13	7	3

Note: Respondents were asked, "Now I'd like to know how often you watch, listen to, or read some different news sources. Do you _____ regularly, or not?"

Source: From *What Americans Know: 1989–2007* by the Pew Research Center for The People and The Press. Copyright © 2007. Reprinted by permission of the publisher. http://people-press.org/reports/pdf/319.pdf

thirty- and twenty-second spots. There is little agreement over whether an ad is negative or unfair: What one person labels a "negative" ad, another person may say is "true" depending on their own partisan or ideological bent.

Although reformers bemoan "mudslinging," negative advertising can be very effective. Such advertising seeks to "define" an opponent in negative terms. Many voters cast their ballots *against* candidates they have come to dislike. Research into the opponent's public and personal background, often via "googling" or "yahooing," provides the data for **negative campaigning**. Previous speeches or writings can be mined for embarrassing statements, and previous voting records can be scrutinized for unpopular policy positions. Personal scandals can be exposed as evidence of "character." Victims of negative ads can be expected to counterattack with charges of "mudslinging" and "dirty" politics. If candidates fear that their personal attacks on opponents might backfire, they may "leak" negative information to reporters and hope that the media will do their dirty work for them. Analyses of the impact of negative ads show it varies by who is delivering the message, who is receiving the message, and by whether the criticism is a personal attack or an attack on a candidate's issue position. Negative ads focusing on issues have a greater impact than attacks on a candidate's personal qualities, incumbents are criticized more for running them than challengers, and negative information about a candidate from the press is more harmful to a candidate than negative television ads aimed at that candidate. They also find that political novices are more influenced by negative ads than "old hands."[31]

Although reformers bemoan "mudslinging," negative advertising can be very effective.

NEGATIVE CAMPAIGNING

Soliciting voter support by attacking one's opponent.

Free Air Time

Candidates also seek free air time on public service programs and televised debates. Underfunded candidates are more dependent upon these opportunities than their more affluent opponents. Thus, well-funded and poorly funded candidates may argue over the number and times of public debates and who is eligible to participate. (Many local television stations limit debate participation to candidates who receive a certain level of support from voters surveyed by a major polling firm.)

Campaigning on the Web

A well-designed Web site is now a must for candidates. Web masters have become critical members of campaign staffs charged with designing

New Hampshire law requires that the state's presidential primary election be the first in the nation. Republican candidates running for their party's presidential nomination in 2008 were more than happy to take part in a televised debate sponsored by one of the state's leading newspapers—the *Union Leader*.

and updating the Net-based portion of a candidate's campaign. The more interactive the site, the better. Web sites play a big part in soliciting volunteers, raising money, informing voters about upcoming campaign events, and keeping enthusiastic supporters on the bandwagon. Major news media (television, radio, newspapers) routinely promote links to candidate Web sites in their regular news coverage. A particularly clever Web site feature might well be the centerpiece of a prime-time story—free media for the candidate.

MONEY IN STATE POLITICS

Running for public office costs money. Running for statewide offices in large states may cost millions; but even running for city council and school board seats can cost thousands. Candidates who do not have enough personal wealth to finance their own campaigns must find contributors. Fundraising is one of the least pleasant aspects of politics. The mere thought of having to ask family, friends, and strangers for money keep many citizens from running for office. However, there are firms that specialize in fundraising to help with this—if a candidate can afford them—or friends who are experienced in raising money for local charities and organizations and have good "money networks" who can help. The prevailing rule of thumb is this: "Raising money is about asking. It is a numbers game. The more people you ask for money, the more money you will raise. . . . You must ask the right people the right way. That takes preparation, coordination, and organization."[32]

What Money Can Do

Can money buy elections? Not always, but money can make a significant difference in the outcome. Let us summarize what research has shown about the effects of campaign spending:

- Campaign spending is generally more important in contested primary elections than general elections. In primary elections where candidates are from the same party and the electorate is more easily influenced by the kinds of campaigning that money can buy.

- "Early money"—a sizable campaign treasury available at the beginning of the campaign—is usually more valuable than money coming in later and closer to Election Day. A candidate who can raise a lot of money early is perceived as a more credible, viable candidate than one who cannot. In the early stages of a campaign, the press routinely compares the fundraising totals of the various candidates.
- Campaign spending in primary elections is closely related to electoral outcome where the party organizations are weak; where they are strong and they endorse a primary candidate, money is less important.[33] Primary voters are more likely than general election voters to be more ardently partisan.
- Campaign spending is more important in larger jurisdictions, where face-to-face campaigning is not possible and mass media appeals are essential. Television ads cost more in big markets and so does direct mail because it must be sent to many more voters.
- After a certain level of campaign spending is reached, additional expenditures do not produce the same effect. A law of diminishing returns seems to operate to reduce the impact of very heavy campaign spending.[34]
- Incumbent officeholders have a very strong advantage over challengers in soliciting and receiving campaign contributions.[35]
- However, the advantage of incumbency itself is greater than the advantage of heavy campaign spending. While it is true that incumbents have an easier time obtaining campaign contributions than challengers, only part of the advantage of being an incumbent derives from easier access to money. Most of the incumbent's advantage is in name recognition and greater news media coverage.[36]
- Candidates who outspend their opponents win in two out of three elections. Of course, the higher-spending candidates are usually incumbents, and incumbents tend to win even when they are outspent. But in elections in which there is no incumbent seeking reelection, the candidate who spends the most money can be expected to win two of every three of these open-seat contests.[37]
- Most contributors want to be personally asked for money by the candidate. A major time commitment by the candidate is needed to raise money (some call it "dialing for dollars").

Fundraising

The need to raise millions of dollars for political campaigns, especially for costly television advertising, has stimulated the development of many new fundraising techniques. Campaign financing has moved beyond the small, face-to-face circle of contributing friends, supporters, and partisans. An important source of campaign money now is the political action committees, or PAC, which mobilizes group financial support for candidates. PACs have been organized by corporations, unions, trade and professional associations, environmental groups, and liberal and conservative ideological groups. The wealthiest PACs are based in Washington, but PAC contributions are becoming increasingly important in state gubernatorial and legislative campaigns as well.[38]

Individual contributions are now sought through a variety of solicitation techniques, including the Internet, direct mail to persons designated by computer programs to be likely contributors, direct telephone solicitation by a candidate or via a recorded message, and live appeals by workers at telephone banks. About 10 percent of the population now claims to have ever contributed to candidates running for public office. But less than one-half of one percent contribute in any particular election cycle. Contributors disproportionately represent high-income, well-educated, older political partisans, although Internet

Contributors disproportionately represent high-income, well-educated, older political partisans, although Internet appeals have prompted the younger, less well-heeled to give.

appeals have prompted the younger, less well-heeled to give. There are, indeed, networks of contributors.[39] Some candidates have been able to tap into these networks through specialized mailing lists, telephone directories, and e-mail network list serves.

These specialized techniques supplement the more traditional fundraising dinners, barbecues, fish frys, and cocktail parties. A successful fundraising dinner usually includes an appearance by a national political figure, perhaps even the president, or an appearance by a show business celebrity. Tickets are sold in blocks to PACs and to wealthy, individual contributors who will give even more to have a "photo-op" with the famous guest. Successful techniques may vary with the political culture of the state; for example, celebrity rock concerts in California versus barbecues in Texas.

Big Money in the States

Where does the big money come from? States vary somewhat in their principal sources of campaign money because they differ in their economic bases and population makeup. Table 5–7 details the pattern of contributions in four states (two large, two small) in the 2006 election cycle. In virtually every state, lawyers and lobbyists and real estate are among the top ten categories of contributors, although the rank order is different. Individual self-financed candidates and state political parties are also consistently big money sources in state elections. States differ in the degree to which other types of contributors play a major role in state elections, reflecting differences in their economies: livestock in Montana, unions in California and New York, food processing and sales in Vermont.

Campaign Spending in the States

Campaign spending in the state elections varies enormously from state to state. A gubernatorial campaign in a small state may cost only $2 to $5 million, but campaigns in California, New York, Texas, and Florida can easily top $20 million just in a party primary alone.[40] Special elections can cost even more because the candidates have to reach a lot of voters in a hurry and that spells television advertising. The 77-day California gubernatorial recall election campaign generated an astounding $82.4 million in campaign contributions.[41]

State legislative campaigns may range in cost from $5,000 to over $500,000, depending on their competitiveness and the size of the district. Political scientist Frank Sorauf reports that California leads in campaign spending, not only because of its size, but also because of its sophisticated political culture. (The 191 candidates for the California state legislature in 2000 spent an average of $275,000.) In contrast, in the 2003 election cycle, candidates for the Mississippi state senate on average spent $25,367 while those running for the state house spent $14,191 each.[42]

Critics of current campaign finance laws argue that the growing amount of money pouring into campaigns is having a corrupting influence on politics, or at the very least, adding to the public's perception of corruption and their cynicism toward politics in general.

STATE CAMPAIGN FINANCE REFORM

The cost of running for public office rises every year. (The total price of the congressional and presidential elections runs into the billions.) Public opinion surveys consistently show that the public thinks too much money is spent on political campaigns. They also

TABLE 5–7 Big Money Sources in State-Level Elections: Selected States

California

Population Size 36,039,000
Total, 2006 $808,730,651
Dem. Percent 55
Rep. percent 43

Top 10 Categories of Contributors

Candidate Self-Finance
Party Committees
Lawyers & Lobbyists
Real Estate
Public Sector Unions
General Trade Unions
Health Professionals
Insurance
Securities & Investment
Telecom Services & Equipment

New York

Population Size 19,258,000
Total, 2006 $153,080,448
Dem. Percent 70
Rep. percent 27

Top 10 Categories of Contributors

Real Estate
Party Committees
Candidate Committees
Lawyers & Lobbyists
General Trade Unions
Public Sector Unions
Securities & Investment
Candidate Self-Finance
Insurance
Health Professionals

Vermont

Population Size 631,000
Total, 2006 $1,215,387
Dem. Percent 60
Rep. percent 29

Top 10 Categories of Contributors

Party Committees
Real Estate
Leadership PACs
Telecom Services & Equipment
Lawyers & Lobbyists
Candidate Self-Finance
General Contractors
Candidate Committees
Automotive
Food Processing & Sales

Montana

Population Size 933,000
Total, 2006 $3,207,058
Dem. Percent 47
Rep. percent 53

Top 10 Categories of Contributors

Candidate Self-Finance
Lawyers & Lobbyists
Retired
Party Committees
Civil Servants/Public Officials
Health Professionals
Education
Democratic Officials, Candidates,
   & Former Members
Real Estate
Livestock

Note: Figures are for state executive, legislative, and judicial races, ballot measures, and political party committees. Data are for 2006.

Source: From *State at a Glance: State 2006,* National Institute on Money in State Politics. Http://www.followthemoney.org. Copyright © 2007. Reprinted by permission of The National Institute on Money in State Politics.

believe that lobbyists and big donors "buy" elections and that after the election, these "money bags" gain greater access to elected officials than is available to the average citizen. These attitudes have prompted many states to pass legislation addressing the money side of political campaigns.

To many voters, far too much money is spent on campaigns. They are convinced that all most candidates want when they contact a voter by mail, e-mail, phone, or in person is MONEY! But in fact, campaigns do cost a lot of money, largely because of the high costs of television advertising and direct mail.

State Campaign Finance Laws

Most states have enacted laws designed to bring greater "ethics" into political campaigning and reduce the importance of large campaign contributions. Generally these laws attempt to do one or more of the following:

- *Limit the size of campaign contributions to a specific race by certain groups* (usually corporations and unions) and individuals (excluding the candidate); thirty-seven states limit the amount of contributions to candidates by individuals, political parties, and political action committees; forty-five states regulate corporate contributions to candidates (twenty-six states set limits on the amount that can be contributed; nineteen states prohibit any corporate contribution).[43]

- *Limit the overall spending of candidates and parties;* usually applies when candidates take public funds for their campaign (e.g., Florida's spending cap for a candidate for statewide office is $20 million if the candidate decides to accept available public matching funds; Michigan's is $2 million); several have voluntary limits—such as Hawaii and Colorado; but less than half the states impose spending limits.

- *Require financial disclosure of a candidate's personal finances as well as campaign contributions and expenditures*—"Who gave it? Who got it?" All states require some disclosure from candidates, committees, and political parties, but some require more detail than others and for reports to be filed in a more timely fashion, often electronically via the Internet.

- *Establish public funding of campaign expenses.* Eleven states currently have some type of public financing programs for candidates and/or political parties. But in every case, participation in such programs is optional. Funds are generated in many different ways, depending on the state: tax check-offs, voluntary surcharges, tax credits, or direct state appropriations. Two states with well-established public financing programs are Minnesota and New Jersey. Three states, Arizona, Maine, and Vermont, have "Clean Elections" programs. This variation on public campaign financing allows gubernatorial and legislative candidates to finance their campaigns almost entirely with public funds. Once a candidate qualifies by collecting a specified number of small contributions (perhaps as low as $10 or $25), he or she agrees not to collect any more contributions from private sources, but instead to receive a grant from the state to finance his or her campaign.

- *Establish regulatory agencies, or "commissions," to oversee campaign practices.*

The fact that the specifics of federal and state laws differ considerably creates confusion and misunderstanding among citizens as well as among candidates running for offices at different levels (federal, state, local), particularly since federal campaign finance laws get markedly more publicity than state laws.

Federal Campaign Finance Laws

The initial model for the various campaign finance-related state laws was the Federal Election Campaign Act of 1974, which placed limits on the size of individual campaign contributions, required disclosure of campaign finances, provided for public funding of presidential elections through a tax check-off on federal income tax returns, and established a Federal Elections Commission to supervise presidential elections and distribute public funds to candidates.

In 2002, Congress passed the **Bipartisan Campaign Reform Act** (BCRA), also known as the McCain–Feingold bill. The specifics of this Act apply to federal elections (presidential, congressional):

- **Soft money** contributions to the *national* parties are prohibited. However, state and local parties can solicit soft money contributions of up to $10,000 for get-out-the-vote activities in federal elections. "Soft money" refers to contributions made to parties rather than directly to the campaign chests of candidates. Soft money is supposed to be spent for "party-building" activities, get-out-the-vote drives, or general party advertising (e.g., "Vote Republican" or "Vote Democratic"). But state and local parties cannot use soft money for activities directly affecting federal elections.
- Contributions from individuals to federal candidates are limited to $2,000 (raised from $1,000). Limits can be raised for candidates facing wealthy opponents who pay for their own campaigns.
- Campaign ads by corporations, unions, and interest groups, in support of federal candidates, cannot be run sixty days before a general election, thirty days before a primary election.
- Expenditures by independent groups made on the candidates' behalf must be reported to the Federal Elections Commission. Individuals, corporations, and organizations may not pay for any "**electioneering communication**," which is defined as any broadcast that refers to a candidate for federal office that is aired within thirty days of a federal primary election or sixty days of a federal general election.

The U.S. Supreme Court and Campaign Finance

The U.S. Supreme Court has recognized that limitations on campaign *contributions* help further a compelling government interest—"preventing corruption and the appearance of corruption" in election campaigns. But the Court has been reluctant to allow governments to limit campaign *expenditures*, because paying to express political views is necessary in the exercise of free speech. In an important early case, *Buckley* v. *Valeo* (1976), the Court held that limiting a candidate's campaign expenditures that are made from one's own personal funds violated the First Amendment's guarantee of free speech.[44]

Later, when called upon to consider the constitutionality of the BCRA, the Court upheld limitations on contributions directly to candidates and to national parties.[45] It also upheld limits on "soft money" contributions to state and local parties, recognizing that these provisions were designed to prevent circumventions of valid prohibitions on campaign contributions. And the Court also upheld a prohibition on spending for "electioneering communications" by individuals and interest groups that are controlled or coordinated with parties or candidates. The Court struck down an attempt by Congress to prohibit children from making campaign contributions.

But still later, the U.S. Supreme Court reconsidered the BCRA's provisions limiting individual and organization electioneering communications. The Court distinguished between "**express advocacy**" on behalf of a candidate or party and "**issue ads**" that are not the functional equivalent of express advocacy.[46] (In other words, ads that do not urge viewers or listeners to vote for or against a particular candidate or party.) "When it comes to defining what speech qualifies as the functional equivalent of express advocacy, the Court should give the benefit of the doubt to speech, not censorship." The effect of the decision is to permit political contributors to support organizations unaffiliated with a candidate or party, including nonprofit "527" organizations, that air television ads not *expressly* endorsing a candidate right up to Election Day.

These decisions not only affect federal campaign finance laws but also the laws of state and local jurisdictions. The Supreme Court has also held that a state law that places too low a limit on how much individuals can contribute to a candidate or party violates the First Amendment's guarantee of free speech. When Vermont placed a $200 limit on campaign contributions for offices in that state, the Court held that limits could not be so low as to prevent challengers from mounting effective campaigns. Vermont's limits were held to be "disproportionately severe."[47]

Do Campaign Finance Reforms Work?

It is not clear whether state campaign finance laws actually succeed in limiting overall spending in elections. Experience suggests that in reality "If you squeeze money out of one arena, it will ooze into another."[48] Reforms often squeeze money out of candidates' hands and into the hands of self-proclaimed voter education groups with narrow agendas and obscure memberships. These groups spend large amounts of money urging voters to support one candidate or another.

Note also that, under *Buckley*, any candidate can spend unlimited personal wealth on his or her own election campaign, and individuals can spend any amount to advertise their own personal views, as long as they do not spend their money through a party or campaign organization. If anything, the personal wealth of the candidate has become an even more important qualification for successful campaigning. And in states with spending limits tied to public funding of campaigns, more candidates are simply refusing public funds, which means they must raise even more money from donors.

The overall conclusion is one that affirms what many Americans have always believed: "Money always finds a way into the system. . . . Twenty years from now reformers will be screaming for something else. Stay tuned."[49]

EXPRESS ADVOCACY

An ad for a federal candidate paid for by an individual or interest group that asks a voter to support (or reject) a particular candidate or party.

ISSUE AD

Campaign ad paid for by an individual or group that does not ask voters to vote for or against a specific candidate or party.

Today's "High-Tech" Campaigns Have a Vocabulary All Their Own

Campaign "lingo" is constantly evolving to adapt to technological innovations, new demographic patterns, and changing media habits. Here are examples of new words in the vocabularies of campaign strategists and consultants that surfaced in recent election cycles:

Meet-ups	Internet-organized, volunteer-run meetings of persons with similar interests, candidate preferences; www.Meetup.com.
Observancy gap	Turnout rate and candidate preference differences between persons who regularly attend a religious service and those who seldom or never do; the more frequently one attends worship services, the more likely one is to vote Republican.
Battleground state	Competitive state; candidates highly likely to visit because the state could tip in either direction; a swing state; lots of TV ads likely to be run by presidential candidates.
Fly-over state	One-party state; candidates not likely to visit because the outcome seems pretty obvious; no presidential TV ads.
GOTV	Get-out-the-vote; used to describe a campaign's multipart strategy to mobilize voters on Election Day—or before if a state has Early Voting.
Computerized "robo" call	Automated phone call, often features the voice of a celebrity, the candidate, or a famous relative.
IVR call	Interactive voice response call; a recorded voice asks various questions to which the person receiving the "survey" responds; considered very cost-efficient by consultants.
Microtargeting	Aiming direct mail, cable TV ad buys, phone calls at narrow "slices" of the population defined by individual consumer buying patterns and television watching habits (e.g., theater-goers—Democrats; Fox News viewers—Republicans).
Web video ad	A political video sent via email by a candidate, party, or interest group; considerably cheaper than an ad run on broadcast television; if well done, generates lots of news coverage; best at reaching young, educated, professional citizens; unregulated by federal campaign finance law provisions.
LUR	Lowest unit rate; refers to cost of a television ad to a candidate for federal office; is the same rate given to a station's most favored advertisers; does *not* apply to state and local candidates.
Virtual precinct	A voter's own group of friends and family organized via the Internet to contact others on behalf of a candidate.
Viral marketing	Running an online spot ad or virtual video or creating a Web site that is so catchy and clever that an Internet user forwards it to others; also gets media attention.
Web-based petition	Circulated via the Internet; is often a tool used to raise money, recruit volunteers, and/or force a candidate to take position; also used to grab media attention.
Convergence media	Television station and newspaper owned by the same firm in the same media market; often share facilities and a Web site.
Anger points	"Hot-button" issues that make a voter mad and more likely to turn out to vote; often are identified by polls then used by consultants to develop ads.

"Googling"/"Yahooing"	A method of researching a candidate or opponent to find out the "good, bad, and ugly" information about the person that is readily available via the Web.
72-hour campaign	All the GOTV activities in the three days prior to Election Day; a term originally coined by Republicans.
PDA canvassing	Party workers and volunteers using personal data assistants to record comments, preferences of potential voters they meet while going door-to-door; data are uploaded into central file.
Podcasting	An online audio recording sent by a candidate via digital audio players.
Blogging	A Web log. Candidates regularly post short catchy, diary-like entries about the events of the day in which they participated while on the campaign trial.
"You-Tubing"	A popular Web video-sharing Web site that lets anyone, including political candidates, upload short videos for public (and private) viewing; became popularized when CNN featured You Tube videos in presidential debates.
Web2.0	A "term" used by techies to refer to an expanded role for the Web that includes more interactive uses by individuals such as participatory blogs, social networks, podcasts, Facebook, You Tube, Flickr, Wikipedia, and MySpace.
"Netroots"	Grassroots political activism organized through Internet media such as meet-ups, blogs, and social networking sites.

Information on state political parties can usually be accessed via links on national party Web sites. These party sites offer encouragement to participate in party affairs, campaigns and elections, and, of course, campaign fundraising.

www.democrats.org

Democratic National Committee (DNC)

www.rnc.org

Republican National Committee (RNC)

www.reformparty.org

Reform Party of the United States of America

www.gp.org

Green Party of the United States

www.lp.org

Libertarian Party

Want to know why the donkey and elephant are the symbols of the Democratic and Republican parties, respectively? Go to

www.c-span.org/questions/week174.htm

www.vetcentric.com/magazine/magazineArticle.cfm?ARTICLEID=1655

Popular Web sites that track money and campaign finance reform efforts include the following:

www.opensecrets.org

The official Web site for the Center for Responsible Politics; it tracks campaign contributions to candidates for *federal* offices.

http://www.tray.com

The Political Money Line, a free Internet news site dedicated to the topic of political money, is maintained by a private company. It tracks campaign contributions to *federal* candidates and has excellent data and graphics showing contributions by parties, PACs, and individuals by state.

http://followthemoney.org

This Web site of the nonpartisan Institute on Money in State Politics allows one to track contributions in all fifty states to state political party committees, state-level candidates (governor, Supreme Court), and ballot measures. For each state, it also reports the average dollars per voter contributed along with the top twenty contributors broken down by economic sector.

http://www.publicampaign.org

Public Campaign is a nonpartisan group whose goal is to dramatically reduce the role of big special interest money in American politics; initiated the Clean Money Campaign Reform movement.

LEGISLATORS IN STATE POLITICS

6

QUESTIONS TO CONSIDER

How would you rate the job your own state legislature is doing?

- ■ Excellent
- ■ Good
- ■ Average
- ■ Poor

Can you follow the path of a bill through the legislative process in your state?

- ■ Yes
- ■ No

Do full-time, well-paid professional legislatures with large staffs generally make better policies than those with part-time, lower-paid, citizen members?

- ■ Yes
- ■ No

Would you prefer legislators who act as "trustees" and use their own best judgment in voting or "delegates" who will vote the way a majority of their constituents wish?

- ■ Prefer "trustee" representation
- ■ Prefer "delegate" representation
- ■ Prefer "politico" representation (some of each, depending on issue)

Should the redrawing of state senate and house districts be done by state legislators, an independent redistricting commission, or the state Supreme Court?

- ■ By the elected state legislators
- ■ By an appointed independent redistricting commission
- ■ By the state Supreme Court

FUNCTIONS OF STATE LEGISLATURES

Most Americans generally are aware of the fact that legislators make law. The problem is that they call *all* lawmakers—in Washington, DC, and in their own state capitals—"Congressmen." Obviously, this is not correct for several reasons. First, Congress is the legislative body for the *national* government, while a state legislature (or assembly as it is called in some states) is the legislative body for the *state* government. And obviously not all legislators are men! There is yet another big difference. In some states, there are limits as to how many terms a state senator or representative may serve, but there are no term limits for members of Congress. Still, there are a lot of similarities in the "job responsibilities" of Congress members and state lawmakers.

If you were to ask state legislators themselves what the job of the legislature is, they typically say, "Our job is to pass laws," or "We have to help the people who live in the districts we represent," or "We have to make policy." All the answers are correct, but none by itself tells the whole story.

Enacting Laws

It is true that, from a *legal viewpoint*, the function of state legislatures is to "pass laws," that is, to enact statutory law. A legislature may enact more than a thousand laws in a single legislative session. The average legislator introduces ten to twelve bills each year. Many are never expected to pass. They are introduced merely as a favor to a constituent or an interest group, or to get a headline in a newspaper back home, or to create awareness of an issue.

The nation's fifty state legislatures collectively consider more than 160,000 bills each session, and they pass nearly 25,000. The range of subject matter of bills considered by a legislature is enormous. A legislature may consider authorization of $50 billion of state spending, or it may argue whether or not inscribing license plates with "The Poultry State" would cause the state to be called "chicken." Obviously, these considerations range from the trivial to the vital.

Among the recent issues confronting state legislatures: the rising costs of drugs for the poor and for seniors, identity theft, highway safety, student achievement tests, abandoned babies, the manufacture and use of methamphetamines, and the monitoring of sexual predators. Flurries of new state laws have dealt with seatbelts and children's safety seats. A number of states have approved laws allowing young mothers to leave their babies at hospitals without fear of prosecution, an effort to save abandoned babies. New laws against identity theft—when someone's credit and personal information is misused—have passed in many states, as have laws requiring that the whereabouts of sexual predators be made known to citizens. And, of course, legislatures continue to address trivial matters: Kentucky made the Appalachian dulcimer the state's official musical instrument; Arkansas made the Dutch oven the official state cooking pot; Florida finally made the orange the sunshine state's official fruit.

Considering Constitutional Amendments, Gubernatorial Appointments, and State Courts

In addition to the enactment of statutory law, legislatures share in the process of state constitutional revision (see "Constitutional Change in the States" in Chapter 2) and consider amendments to the U.S. Constitution. (See "Battles in the States over Constitutional Amendments" in Chapter 3.) Many governors' appointments to high state offices require legislative approval (see "The Governor's Managerial Powers" in Chapter 7). The legislature also makes laws authorizing and funding the establishment of new courts and more judges as needed.

Approving Budgets

Perhaps their single most important function is the passage of the appropriation and tax measures in the state budget. No state monies may be spent without a legislative appropriation, and it is difficult to think of any governmental action that does not involve some financial expenditure. Potentially, a legislature can control any activity of the state government through its power over appropriations.

Perhaps their single most important function is the passage of the appropriation and tax measures in the state budget.

Serving Constituents

Legislators spend a great deal of time answering requests from constituents—**"servicing the district."** Many letters and phone calls will come from interest groups in their districts—business, labor, agriculture, school teachers, municipal employees, and so on. These communications may deal with specific bills or with items in the state budget. Other communications may come from citizens who want specific assistance or favors—help with getting a state job, help with permits or licenses, voicing an opinion about whom the state university should hire as a new football coach, asking for state funding for a new road or museum in their community, and so forth.

CONSTITUENTS

Residents of a legislator's district; the people who are represented by a legislator.

Overseeing State Agencies

Legislative "oversight" of state agencies and programs is another important function. Legislators frequently challenge state administrators to explain why they are doing what they do. Frequently, committee hearings and budget hearings, in particular, provide opportunities for legislators to put administrators "through the wringer" about programs and expenditures. Lately child welfare agency administrators in many states have been called to explain their agency's difficulty in curbing the rising incidences of runaway children and child abuse by foster parents. Often embarrassed administrators feel harassed at these meetings, but the true purpose is to remind state administrators that elected representatives of the people are the final legal authority.

Most states now have **"sunset" laws** that call for their legislatures to reenact programs every few years or else see them go out of existence (sunset). Few programs or agencies are ever sunseted, but such laws force periodic legislative reexamination and evaluation of the performance of state bureaucracies.

SERVICING THE DISTRICT

Legislators spend a great deal of time answering requests from constituents.

LEGISLATIVE OVERSIGHT

The monitoring of the activities of state agencies by the legislature and its committees.

THE MAKING OF A STATE LEGISLATOR

State legislators are not "representative" of the population of their states in the sense of being typical cross-sections of them. On the contrary. the nation's 7,382 state legislators are generally selected from the better-educated, more prestigiously employed, middle-class segments of the population.

SUNSET LAWS

Laws that fix termination dates for programs and agencies in order to force the legislature to renew them if the legislators wish the programs to continue.

Status

Social background information on state legislators indicates that legislators tend to come from the "upwardly mobile" sectors of the population. This places many of them among the "second-rung" elites in the status system rather than the established wealthy.

Although the sons and daughters, grandsons and granddaughters of distinguished old families of great wealth frequently enter presidential and gubernatorial politics in the states, they seldom run for the state legislature. Legislators are frequently among the middle-status groups for whom politics is an avenue of upward mobility.

Occupation

Legislators must come from occupational groups with flexible work responsibility or from the ranks of retired persons. The lawyer, the farmer, or the business owner can adjust his or her work to the legislative schedule, but the office manager cannot. The overrepresented occupations are those involving extensive public contact. The lawyer, real estate agent, insurance agent, and merchant establish in their business the wide circle of friends necessary for political success. Physicians and educators interface with persons from all walks of life. In short, the legislator's occupation should provide free time, public contacts, and social respectability.

Education

State legislators are generally well educated. More than three-quarters of them are college educated, compared to only one-quarter of the general population.

Age

The average age of a state legislator is 53. Legislators have gotten slightly younger in recent years, thanks to term limits. Retirees as a proportion of state legislators are obviously higher in states with larger senior populations (see Figure 6–1, Nevada).

FIGURE 6–1 Legislators' Occupations: A Two-State Comparison

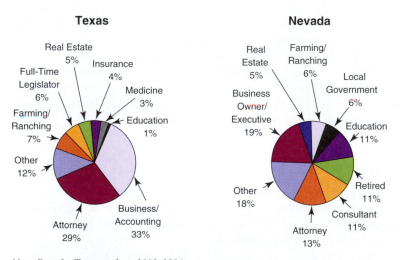

Note: Data for Texas are from 2003–2004.
Source: Texas Legislative Reference Library; Texas Senate; Texas House.
Note: Data for Nevada are from 2005.
Source: "Membership Profile of the 2005 Nevada Legislature," Nevada Legislative Counsel Bureau Research Division; January 28, 2005.

Personal Wealth

Legislators frequently claim that public service is a financial burden. While this may be true, legislators are generally recruited from among the more affluent members of society, and they become even more affluent during their tenure. Indeed, there is evidence that (1) the average **net worth** of new legislators is increasing over time, and (2) the average legislator increases his or her net worth while serving in the legislature. (Net worth is the total value of all assets—houses, autos, stocks, bonds, property, etc.—after subtracting the total value of all outstanding debts—mortgages, loans, etc.) For example, in Florida, the average legislator more than *tripled* his or her net worth in ten years of legislative service. Asked to explain these increases in personal wealth, one legislator said, "Maybe they do well because they're achievers. That's why they win when they run for office and that's why they make money."[1] But it's more likely that legislative service, and the public name recognition that comes with it, enhances one's legal practice, real estate or insurance business, as well as investment opportunities.

Lawyers

Attorneys no longer dominate most state legislatures, although most citizens still believe they do. (See Figure 6–1.) According to the National Conference of State Legislatures, only about 15 percent of legislators are attorneys, down considerably from the 1970s, when one-fourth of all legislators were lawyers.[2] However, lawyers are still overrepresented in legislative bodies at all levels of government relative to their proportional makeup in the population at large. It is sometimes argued that the lawyer brings a special kind of skill to politics. The lawyer's occupation is the representation of clients, so he or she makes no great change in occupation when going from representing clients in private practice to representing constituents in the legislature. Lawyers are trained to deal with public policy as it is reflected in the statute books, so they may be reasonably familiar with public policy before entering the legislature. Moreover, service in the legislature can help a lawyer's private practice through free public advertising and opportunities to make contacts with potential clients.

There are also important institutional advantages for lawyers to enter state politics—specifically, the availability of a large number of highly valued "lawyers-only" posts in state government, such as judge and prosecuting attorney. Lawyers are eligible for many elective and appointive public jobs from which nonlawyers are excluded. State legislative seats are viewed by lawyers as stepping-stones to these posts—appellate court judge, Supreme Court justice, attorney general, regulatory commissioner, and so on. The post-legislative careers of lawyers show that over half go on to other public offices, compared to less than one-third of the nonlawyer legislators.[3]

Do lawyers behave any differently from nonlawyers in the legislature? Lawyers do *not* vote any differently from nonlawyers on most issues; lawyers are neutral "contractors" for parties, interest groups, constituents, and others. Generally, they do not vote together as a bloc. However, lawyers do act together in legislatures to protect the legal profession. The opposition of trial lawyers to insurance reform, including "no-fault" insurance, and their opposition to "**tort reform**" (a tort is a civil wrong that results in damages) has kept both from passing in many state legislatures where reforms have been introduced. This, in turn, has prompted more doctors and small business owners to run for the state legislature.

NET WORTH
The total value of all assets after subtracting the total value of all outstanding debts.

TORT
A civil wrong that results in damages.

FULL-TIME LEGISLATORS

Those for whom service in the legislature is their primary occupation. In states with full-time legislators, legislator salaries are typically higher.

"CITIZEN LEGISLATOR"

Legislators who spend a few months in the state capitol during the regular session, then return home to their own business or profession.

Today, African Americans occupy about 7 percent of all state legislative seats in the nation, Hispanics occupy about 3 percent of these seats, and women occupy about 24 percent.

Amateurs

Most state legislatures are still part-time bodies. There are constitutional limits to the length of legislative sessions in most states; the most common limit is sixty days per year. Most state legislatures put in fewer than 100 working days a year. It is true that interim committee meetings and other legislative responsibilities may add to the duties of legislators, and over the years sessions have grown longer. But most state legislators have other occupations, and few rely on their legislative compensation alone.[4]

In recent years, however, an increasing number of state legislators are **full-time representatives**. The "**citizen legislator**" who spends two months in the state capitol and then returns home to his or her own business or profession still predominates in the states, but the proportion of full-time legislators is growing. Full-time legislators (those who have no other occupation) are more frequent in large states with better-paid legislatures, such as California, New York, and Michigan. However, the truth is that the line between full-time and part-time has been blurred. All legislators are spending more time on the job, whether their legislature is formally full-time or not.[5]

MINORITIES AND WOMEN IN STATE LEGISLATURES

Minorities and women have made impressive gains in American state legislatures in recent decades. Today, African Americans occupy about 7 percent of all state legislative seats in the nation, Hispanics occupy about 3 percent of these seats, and women occupy about 24 percent.[6] (See Rankings of the States; African Americans, Hispanics and Women in State Legislatures.)

African American Representation in State Legislatures

Black voter mobilization, stemming initially from the Voting Rights Act of 1965 and later from federal court enforcement of amendments to that act following the 1990 census (see "Minorities in State Politics" in Chapter 4), has resulted in the election of substantial numbers of African-American state legislators. Most are elected from majority black districts. Southern states, with larger black populations, have the largest percentages of African-American state legislators. Nonetheless, nationwide the percentage of African-American state legislators (7 percent) is somewhat less than the percentage of African Americans in the voting-age population (11.3 percent).

Black legislators in the states have had a significant impact on public policy, especially where they have become committee chairs.[7] Their voting on civil rights and welfare issues is clearly distinguishable in southern states.[8] White legislators, even those with substantial numbers of black constituents, are not as strong in support of these issues as black legislators. The National Black Caucus of State Legislators (NBCSL), established in 1977, has been instrumental in helping its members develop policy initiatives on a wide range of topics, from HIV/AIDS and education reform, to equity in home ownership.

Hispanic Representation in State Legislatures

Hispanic membership in state legislatures is significant in a number of states. The largest Hispanic delegations are found in those states with the largest Hispanic populations—New Mexico, Texas, Arizona, Colorado, and California. However, Hispanic representation in state legislatures remains well below what we would expect given the growing Hispanic percentage of the nation's population. Nationwide, 3 percent of all state legislators are Hispanic, but Latinos make up 10.9 percent of the voting-age population. When citizenship is considered, Hispanics or Latinos make up a smaller proportion (7.4 percent) of the citizen voting-age population. The current underrepresentation of Hispanics differs from state to state and is generally a product of the same forces that appear to reduce Hispanic political participation generally. (See "Minorities in State Politics" in Chapter 4.)

Like African-American legislators, Hispanic state legislators have their own association. The National Hispanic Caucus of State Legislators (NHCSL) was founded in 1989 to organize Latino state lawmakers and strengthen the voice of Hispanic America. Improving educational outcomes for Latino children is a top priority for the group.

Members of California's Legislative Black Caucus celebrate the group's fortieth anniversary. For the first time in 1966, California's State Legislature included five black Assembly Members and its first black Senator. In 1967, these legislators organized into the California Legislative Black Caucus, the first caucus of its kind in the nation. The Caucus produces an annual report on the State of Black California to guide their legislative objectives each year. *Source*: LearnCalifornia.Org; available at www.learncalifornia.org/doc/asp?id=2698

Women in State Legislatures

While women today occupy only about 24 percent of all state legislative seats in the nation, this is a significant increase over the scant 4 percent female state legislators in 1969, although the percentages have flattened off somewhat (see Figure 6–2). Minority women comprise over one-third of all female legislators. Black, Latino, and Asian women legislators make up a higher proportion of their racial/ethnic group's legislative representation than white or American Indian female legislators. Of all blacks serving in state legislatures across the U.S., 37 percent are females. Women legislators comprise 31 percent of Hispanic legislators, 31 percent of Asian legislators, 21.3 percent of white legislators, and 21 percent of American Indian females.[9]

Like their male counterparts, female legislators tend to come from politically active families, to have lived in their communities for a long time, to be representative of their district in race and ethnicity, and to enjoy somewhat higher social status than most of their constituents. Women are somewhat better represented in the New England and western states with less "professional" legislatures; the large urban industrial states with more "professional" legislatures have fewer female representatives.[10] Southern states also tend to have fewer female legislators.

Among the factors associated with increased representation of women are the female percentage of the labor force and the proliferation of active women's organizations in the states.[11] Certain cultural forces in the states, notably religious fundamentalism, may also be an obstacle to women gaining political office.[12] But another "obstacle" is the growing attractiveness of city and county elective offices that pay better than the state legislature, are less likely to have term limits, and allow one to stay home rather than having to split time between one's home town and the state capital.[13]

RANKINGS of the STATES

African Americans, Hispanics, and Women in State Legislatures

Rankings of the States
Women and Minority Legislators

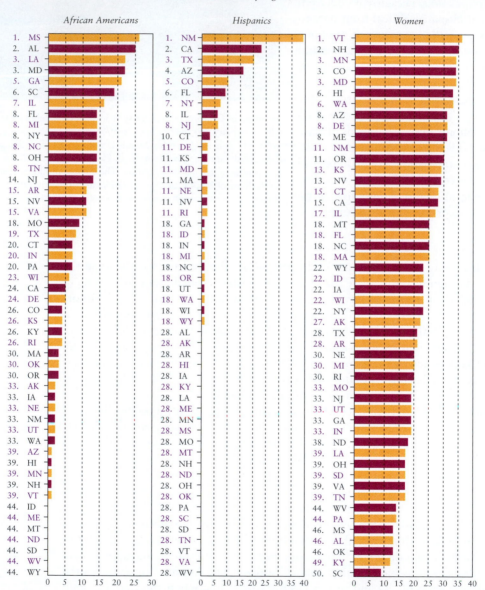

African Americans	Hispanics	Women
1. MS	1. NM	1. VT
2. AL	2. CA	2. NH
3. LA	3. TX	3. MN
3. MD	4. AZ	3. CO
5. GA	5. CO	3. MD
6. SC	6. FL	6. HI
7. IL	7. NY	6. WA
8. FL	8. IL	8. AZ
8. MI	8. NJ	8. DE
8. NY	10. CT	8. ME
8. NC	11. DE	11. NM
8. OH	11. KS	11. OR
8. TN	11. MD	13. KS
14. NJ	11. MA	13. NV
15. AR	11. NE	15. CT
15. NV	11. NV	15. CA
15. VA	11. RI	17. IL
18. MO	18. GA	18. MT
19. TX	18. ID	18. FL
20. CT	18. IN	18. NC
20. IN	18. MI	18. MA
20. PA	18. NC	22. WY
23. WI	18. OR	22. ID
24. CA	18. UT	22. IA
24. DE	18. WA	22. WI
26. CO	18. WI	22. NY
26. KS	18. WY	27. AK
26. KY	28. AL	28. TX
26. RI	28. AK	28. AR
30. MA	28. AR	30. NE
30. OK	28. HI	30. MI
30. OR	28. IA	30. RI
33. AK	28. KY	33. MO
33. IA	28. LA	33. NJ
33. NE	28. ME	33. UT
33. NM	28. MN	33. GA
33. UT	28. MS	33. IN
33. WA	28. MO	38. ND
39. AZ	28. MT	39. LA
39. HI	28. NH	39. OH
39. MN	28. ND	39. SD
39. NH	28. OH	39. VA
39. VT	28. OK	39. TN
44. ID	28. PA	44. WV
44. ME	28. SC	44. PA
44. MT	28. SD	46. MS
44. ND	28. TN	46. AL
44. SD	28. VT	46. OK
44. WV	28. VA	49. KY
44. WY	28. WV	50. SC

Note: Data for African Americans and Hispanics are for 2003; data for women are for 2007.

Source: National Conference of State Legislatures, "Numbers of African-American Legislators 2003." Available at http://ncsl.org/programs/legman/about/aframer.htm; National Conference of State Legislatures; "Latino Legislators 2003." Available at http://ncsl.org/programs/legman/about/latino.htm; Center for American Women and Politics, "Women in State Legislatures Fact Sheet 2007." Available at www.cawp.rutgers.edu/Facts/Officeholders/stleg.pdf

FIGURE 6–2 **Women in State Legislatures**

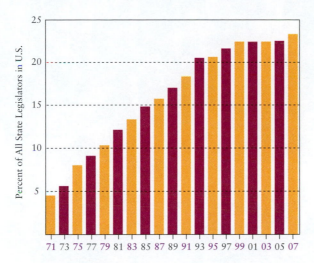

Note: Data are for 2007.
Source: Center for American Women and Politics; Women in State Legislatures Fact Sheet 2007; available at http://www.cawp.rutgers.edu/Facts/Officeholders/stleg.pdf

Women candidates are just as successful in primary and general elections as men.[14] Voters are *not* predisposed to cast ballots either for or against female candidates.[15] Incumbency gives all officeholders an electoral advantage; since more males held office in the past, women challengers have faced the obstacle of incumbency. But women and men fare equally in races for open seats and there is no evidence they drop out of races any more often than male candidates.[16] So why are women underrepresented in state legislatures?

Fewer women than men run for state legislative seats. Scholars frequently cite women's traditional family roles of wife and mother as obstacles to a political career. Female legislative candidates with young children are very rare; newly elected women legislators are four years older on the average than newly elected male legislators—a fact generally attributed to women waiting until their children are older.[17] Many women who confront conflicts between family life and political activity choose in favor of their families. One study found that more women serve in the legislatures of states whose capitals are located close to the major population centers than in the legislatures of states whose capitals are isolated and require long commutes from home.[18] Some researchers believe that gender-role attitudes about the "proper role" of women in politics vary among the states, and these attitudes independently affect the gender gap in state legislative representation.[19]

Women in Legislative Leadership Positions

Although there continue to be a lot of "firsts" in the various states—first woman speaker of the house, first woman president of the senate, first woman majority or minority leader, and so on—over time women have gained a fair share of leadership posts. Those

Women now make up almost one-fourth of all state legislators. They come from a variety of backgrounds and political persuasions. While fewer women than men run for the state legislature, women who run are just as successful as men at winning primary and general elections. Once elected, female legislators tend to emphasize consensual, cooperative, and inclusive decision making slightly more than their male counterparts.

who have done so, however, believe that they had to work harder, study the issues more closely, and overcome more stereotyping than their male counterparts in order to win respect in their chambers.[20]

Women have also won their fair share of committee chairs; that is, in most states they occupy as many or more committee chairs than the percentage of women in the legislative body would indicate.[21] Indeed, they chair a disproportionate number of education, health, and human service committees, while at the same time, they chair a fair share of the key budget and taxation committees.

Women have also ascended into major leadership posts in each chamber: presidents and president pro tems of the Senate, speakers or speaker pro tems of the House, and majority leaders, minority leaders, floor leaders, and whips in each chamber.

The Effect of Electing Women to State Legislatures

What, if any, changes have been brought about by increasing numbers of women serving in state legislatures? Most of the evidence to date indicates that women exhibit unique priorities, particularly in the area of women's issues.[22] Women legislators are more liberal in their policy attitudes and they exhibit greater commitment to the pursuit of feminist initiatives and legislation incorporating issues of concern to women, including education, health, and welfare. In law enforcement, women are more likely to favor rehabilitative approaches, while men are more likely to prefer punishment. The growing presence of women's caucuses in state legislatures accentuates gender-based voting behavior by women legislators. But women are just as likely as men to secure the passage of legislation that they introduce.[23]

There is also evidence that women go about law making somewhat differently than men. Traditionally, male legislative behavior (described as competitive, bargaining, log-rolling, and confrontational) was regarded as the norm in legislative institutions. Some research suggests that women are slowly transforming legislative processes by emphasizing consensual, cooperative, and inclusive decision making.[24] But other research has found more differences among women or among men than differences *between* the sexes. One study of legislators in Arizona and California found that female representatives do not weigh the concerns, needs, or demands of their constituents more heavily than their male counterparts, nor do women devote any less time and energy to legislative duties and the policymaking process than men. But women legislators do forge closer ties to their female constituents.[25]

GETTING TO THE STATE CAPITOL

The state legislature is a convenient starting place for a political career. About one-half of the state legislators in the nation never served in public office before their election to the legislature, and a greater percentage of new members are in the lower rather than upper chambers. The other half had only limited experience on city councils, county commissions, and school boards.

Getting into Politics

Why does a legislator decide to run for office in the first place? It is next to impossible to determine the real motivations of political office seekers—they seldom know themselves. Legislators will usually describe their motivations in highly idealistic terms: "I felt that I could do the community a service"; "I considered it a civic duty." Only seldom are reasons for candidacy expressed in personal terms: "Oh, I just think it's lots of fun." Gregariousness and the desire to socialize no doubt contribute to the reasons for some office seekers. Politics can have a special lure of its own: "It gets into your blood and you like it." For some, particular issues may mobilize a political career. For others, activity in organizations that are deeply involved in politics often leads to candidacy.

Political Experience

States with stronger parties are more likely to nominate people who have worked for the party in some previous appointed or elective office. States with weaker parties are more likely to elect "amateurs" with no previous political experience. The stronger the

> *The state legislature is a convenient starting place for a political career. About one-half of the state legislators in the nation never served in public office before their election to the legislature.*

party organization, the more likely a legislative candidate will have to serve a political apprenticeship in some local or party offices. However, as party organizations weaken, the easier it becomes for individuals with little or no prior governmental experience, and with more personal wealth, to win legislative seats.

Raising Campaign Money

The first challenge that an aspiring legislator faces is raising money to finance his or her campaign. In some states with small legislative districts, nonprofessional legislatures, and largely rural constituencies, a state legislative race may cost only $10,000 to $25,000. But large urban state legislative races may cost upward of several hundred thousand dollars, especially in quite competitive races. Senate contests cost more than house contests, and winners spend more than losers. Money allows a candidate to produce commercials, buy television and radio time, buy newspaper ads, travel around the district, and distribute bumper stickers and campaign buttons. Some state legislative candidates employ professional campaign management firms. Most state legislative campaigns are relatively amateurish, but they still cost money. When campaigns are relatively inexpensive, the candidate and his or her friends contribute most of the money. But in more expensive races, candidates may turn to PACs. Corporate, labor, environmental, and ideological PACs are becoming increasingly active in state capitals, particularly in the larger states. (See "Money in State Politics" in Chapter 5.) Perhaps as much as one-quarter to one-third of money for state legislative campaigns now comes from PAC contributions, most of which goes to incumbents. But a growing source of money is the **"527" type organization**—an independent advocacy group that can spend money for or against a candidate, with no limit, but stopping short of saying "Vote for candidate X."[26] In general, incumbents have an easier time raising money; so, too, do moderates as opposed to ideologically extreme candidates.[27]

Facing the Primaries

Candidates face two important obstacles when they decide to run for the state legislature: the primary and the general election. A seat in the legislature depends on how much competition a candidate encounters in these elections. First, let us consider **competition** in the primary elections. More than half of the nation's state legislators are *unopposed* for their party's nomination in **uncontested** primary elections. Many legislators who do face primary competition have only token opposition. Most primary competition occurs in a party's **"safe"** districts, some competition occurs in **"close"** districts, and there is a distinct shortage of candidates in districts where the party's chances are poor. In other words, primary competition is greater where the likelihood of victory in the general election is greater. Primary competition is also stiffer when there is an open seat and in states with more professional (full-time) legislatures.[28]

Some states require runoff elections when no candidate wins a majority in the first primary. (See Chapter 5.) Thus, some candidates face three elections on their way to the legislature—a first primary, a runoff primary, and the general election.

The General Election

The culmination of the recruitment process is in the general election, yet in many legislative constituencies one party is so entrenched that the voters have little real choice at the general election. In some districts, the minority party is so weak that it fails to run candidates for legislative seats. Overall about one-third of state legislative general elections are uncontested; that is, one or another of the major parties does not even field a candidate.[29]

"Competition" implies more than a name filed under the opposition party label. Generally a **competitive election** is one in which the winning candidate wins by something less than two to one. In light of this more realistic definition of competition, the absence of truly competitive politics in state legislative elections is striking. Overall, more than half of the nation's legislators are elected in *noncompetitive* general elections, where their opponents are either nonexistent or receive less than one-third of the vote. Even in competitive states, such as California, Michigan, Minnesota, New York, Pennsylvania, and Wisconsin, over half the state legislators face only token opposition in the general election.[30] Moreover, competition is *declining* over time, as more legislators are winning by lopsided margins.[31] Some blame this on the redistricting process whereby legislators draw themselves fairly "safe," noncompetitive districts. (More will be said about this later in the chapter.) But others point to the growing financial advantage incumbents have over challengers and to the fact that "Americans are increasingly living in communities and neighborhoods whose residents share their values and they are increasingly voting for candidates who reflect those values."[32]

COMPETITIVE ELECTION

An election in which the loser receives at least one-third of the votes.

INCUMBENTS

Persons currently serving in elective or appointed positions in government.

QUALITY CHALLENGERS

People who have won previous state or local elections and can raise campaign funds.

THE GREAT INCUMBENCY MACHINE

Legislators who choose to run for re-election (**incumbents**) are seldom defeated. Indeed, they are usually unopposed in the primary election, and sometimes unopposed in the general election. Potential **challengers** are discouraged by the record of success of incumbents.[33] Nearly 90 percent of incumbent state legislators who seek re-election are successful. Aspiring newcomers in politics are advised to wait for incumbents to leave office voluntarily or until an incumbent is term limited and cannot run again. Redistricting also opens up legislative seats and occasionally forces incumbents to run against each other, but in most states that only happens every ten years. Although there is some evidence that "**quality challengers**"—people who have won previous state or local elections and can raise campaign funds—have a better chance than newcomers to defeat incumbents, nonetheless, the likelihood of defeating an incumbent in either the primary or general election is very low.[34]

Nearly 90 percent of incumbent state legislators who seek re-election are successful.

Visibility

Why do incumbents win? First, they enjoy greater visibility and name recognition in their districts: "The reason I get 93 percent victories is what I do back home. I stay highly visible. No grass grows under my feet. I show I haven't forgot from whence I came."[35] Incumbents spend a major portion of their time throughout their term of office campaigning for re-election: "I have the feeling that the most effective campaigning is done when no election is near. During the interval between elections you have to establish every personal contact you can." Legislators regularly appear at civic clubs, social and charitable events, churches, and many other gatherings: "Personally, I will speak on any subject. I talk on everything whether it deals with politics or not." Indeed, many legislators spend more time campaigning for reelection than lawmaking. Few challengers can afford to spend two or four years campaigning.

Resources of Office

As legislatures become more professional over time—employing large professional staffs; providing offices, expense accounts, and travel budgets to legislators; and increasing their pay—incumbents acquire greater resources to assist them in servicing constituents. **Constituent service** or "casework" is growing in state legislatures; legislators are increasingly involved in assisting constituents in dealing with state bureaucracies, providing information, and doing small favors at the capital. Over time this form of "retail" politics gradually builds a network of grateful voters.

Legislators in professionalized legislatures are given large sums to subsidize what are really campaign activities—printing and mailing of newsletters; press rooms and video studios; travel reimbursement; and aides, assistants, staffers, and interns who spend much of their time on constituent services.

Professionalized legislatures enjoy abundant resources, sometimes referred to as the five S's: space, salary, session length, staff, and structure. There is evidence that these resources contribute to incumbent reelection.[36] It is increasingly difficult for challengers to confront incumbents with these resources, and access to the five S's encourages incumbents to remain in office.

Money

Finally, and perhaps most importantly, incumbents attract much more in the way of campaign contributions than challengers. Interest group contributions go overwhelmingly to incumbents. (See "Money in State Politics" in Chapter 5.) These groups are seeking access and influence with decision makers, so they direct their contributions to people in office. Moreover, group leaders know that incumbents are rarely defeated and they do not want to antagonize incumbents by contributing to challengers. Incumbents can build a "war chest" over time; often the size of the war chest itself is enough to discourage potential challengers from entering races against them. When incumbent state legislators decide to run for Congress (often because they have been "termed out of office"[37] or are smart enough to run only in races that they are most likely to win), they are much better at attracting money, especially early on in primary battles, than their opponents.[38]

Professionalism and Careerism

Professionalism in state legislatures encourages **careerism**. It encourages people who view politics as a career to seek and win a seat in the state legislature. Higher pay makes the job more attractive and allows legislators to devote all their time to politics and policymaking.[39] Year-round sessions discourage people who cannot take leave from their business or profession. Greater resources available to legislators allow them to perform more casework for constituents and to build a personal organization devoted to keeping themselves in office. Additional resources make life at the state capital more comfortable, especially for party leaders.[40] There is less voluntary turnover in professional legislatures, and less likelihood that an incumbent will be defeated. Political scientist Alan Rosenthal writes, "One quality that distinguishes the new breed of full-time, professional politicians from the old breed of part-time, citizen legislators is ambition. The latter were content to spend a few years in legislative office and then return to private careers. The former, by contrast, would like to spend most of their careers in government and politics. They find public office appealing and the game of politics exhilarating."[41]

LEGISLATIVE APPORTIONMENT AND DISTRICTING

Legislative apportionment refers to the allocation of seats to specific populations. When state legislative and congressional district boundary lines have to be redrawn after each census, several factors are taken into consideration: compliance with the "one-person, one-vote," adherence to federal Voting Rights Act requirements to protect minorities, and respect for a state's **traditional redistricting principles**—such as compactness, contiguity, maintaining communities of interest, and minimizing the splitting of counties, cities, and precincts. These factors have become more critical over the years, primarily through court rulings.[42]

Prior to 1962, malapportionment was common in American state legislatures. **Malapportionment** occurs when there are differing numbers of people in legislative districts that receive the same number of seats. Malapportionment creates inequality of representation: If one single-member district has twice the population of another, the value of a vote in the larger district is only half the value of a vote in the smaller district. Small minorities of the population could elect a majority of the house or senate or both in most of the states. Generally, it was the rural voters in a state who controlled a majority of legislative seats, and it was the urban voters who were discriminated against in the value of their vote. Finally, the U.S. Supreme Court intervened and the "one person, one vote" principle prevailed.

Supreme Court Intervention

After years of avoiding the issue of malapportionment, the U.S. Supreme Court acted in 1962 in the landmark case of *Baker* v. *Carr*.[43] This case involved the complaint of urban residents in Tennessee, where the largest district in the lower house was twenty-three times larger than the smallest district. The Supreme Court decided that such inequalities in state apportionment laws denied voters "equal protection of the laws" guaranteed by the Fourteenth Amendment and that the federal courts should grant relief from these inequalities. The Supreme Court did not decide on any firm mathematical standard of correct apportionment, holding only that "as nearly as practicable, one man's vote should be equal to another's."[44] The Supreme Court required that *both* houses of the state legislature be apportioned on the basis of population; the Court rejected the federal analogy of a senate based on geographic units: "Legislators represent people, not trees or acres. Legislators are elected by voters, not farms or cities or economic interests."[45] State after state was forced to reapportion its legislature under the threat of judicial intervention. In addition to requiring population equality in legislative districting, the Supreme Court also required population equality in congressional districting by state legislatures. The philosophy underlying these decisions was expressed by the Court: "The conception of political equality from the Declaration of Independence to Lincoln's Gettysburg Address, to the Fourteenth, Fifteenth, Seventeenth, and Nineteenth Amendments, can mean only one thing—one person, one vote."[46]

The Impact of Reapportionment

The reapportionment revolution of the 1960s significantly increased the representation afforded urban interests in state legislatures. Reapportionment also seemed to bring younger, better-educated, more prestigiously employed people

APPORTIONMENT
The determination of how many residents should live in a representative's district.

TRADITIONAL REDISTRICTING PRINCIPLES
Compactness; contiguity; keeping communities of interest, counties, towns, and precincts together.

MALAPPORTIONMENT
Unequal numbers of people in legislative districts creating inequality of representation.

"The conception of political equality from the Declaration of Independence to Lincoln's Gettysburg Address, to the Fourteenth, Fifteenth, Seventeenth, and Nineteenth Amendments, can mean only one thing—one person, one vote."

into state legislatures. It also brought many "new" people into legislative politics—people who had little or no previous experience in public office.

Standards of Equality among Districts

Today there is very little inequality in the number of people in legislative districts in any state, and "one person, one vote" is the prevailing form of representation. But federal courts have not always been consistent or precise in determining exactly *how equal* congressional and state legislative districts must be. In several early cases, federal courts calculated an "ideal" district by dividing the total population of the state by the number of legislative seats and then comparing all district populations to this ideal district. Variations of more than 2 percent in any district from the ideal often led to federal court invalidation of a state's redistricting plan. Later the federal courts began calculating an "overall range" by adding the deviations of the largest district and the smallest district from the ideal, disregarding the plus and minus signs. (Thus if the largest district was 2 percent larger than the ideal, and the smallest district 1 percent smaller than the ideal, the "overall range" would be 3 percent.)

With regard to *congressional* districts, the U.S. Supreme Court has required strict standards of equality. Indeed, no population inequality that "could practically be avoided" is permitted in congressional districts; a New Jersey plan with an overall range of 0.70 percent was struck down upon presentation of evidence that the legislature could have reduced the range to 0.45.[47]

However, the U.S. Supreme Court has been somewhat more lenient in considering *state legislative* districting plans. The Court has refused to set any specific mathematical standards of equality for legislative districts. Nonetheless, districting plans with an overall range of more than 10 percent "create a prima facie case of discrimination and therefore must be justified by the state."[48] Federal courts will allow some deviations from absolute equality in order to recognize political subdivision (e.g., city, county) boundaries. Some citizens do not agree with this philosophy. Several states were sued about the population deviations in their post-2000 Census plans, most notably New York and Georgia. In Georgia, the federal court overturned the state's legislative plans.[49]

Districting: Partisan and Incumbent Gerrymandering

Districting refers to the drawing of boundary lines for legislative districts. While malapportionment refers to inequality in representation, gerrymandering refers to the drawing of district lines for political advantage. The population of districts can be equal, yet the districts drawn in such a fashion as to give advantage to one party or group over another. Consider a very simple example:

For a city that is entitled to three representatives, the eastern third of the city is Republican while the western two-thirds are Democratic. If the Republicans draw the district lines, they will draw them along a north–south direction to allow them to win in one of the three districts; if Democrats draw the district lines, they will draw them along an east–west direction to allow them to win all three districts by diluting the Republican vote. (See Figure 6–3.) Often, gerrymandering is not as neat as our example; district lines may twist and turn and create grotesque geographic patterns.

Gerrymandering can be accomplished by the combined methods of splintering and packing. **Splintering** involves dividing up and diluting a strong minority to deny it the power to elect a representative. **Packing** involves the concentration of partisan voters in a single district in order to "waste" their votes in large majorities for a single

FIGURE 6–3 Two Different Draws, Two Different Partisan Outcomes

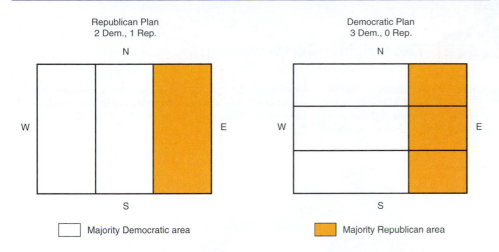

Republican Plan
2 Dem., 1 Rep.

Democratic Plan
3 Dem., 0 Rep.

☐ Majority Democratic area   ■ Majority Republican area

representative and thereby protect modest majorities in other districts (see "*Up Close: The Original Gerrymander*"). Some describe the redistricting process as "the most naked exercise of political power in the states."[50]

As long as districts are equal in population, **partisan gerrymandering** does *not* violate federal court standards for "equal protection" under the Fourteenth Amendment of the U.S. Constitution. There is no constitutional obligation to allocate seats "to the contending parties in proportion to what their anticipated statewide vote will be."[51] However, the federal courts may intervene in political gerrymandering if it "consistently degrades a voter's or a group of voters' influence on the political process as a whole." This vague standard set forth by the U.S. Supreme Court keeps the door open to judicial intervention in particularly grievous cases of political gerrymandering. But so far, the Court has continued to keep the door shut, much to the dismay of some.[52] A partisan-gerrymandering-based legal challenge to Pennsylvania's redistricting was rejected by a 5–4 decision of the U.S. Supreme Court in *Vieth* v. *Jubelirer* (2004).[53] After years of trying to establish a standard for partisan gerrymandering, the Supreme Court gave up. It firmly rejected the notion that districting had to be "fair" to the parties. " 'Fairness' is not a judicially manageable standard." The Court reaffirmed that partisan gerrymandering was a *nonjusticiable* issue—it could not be decided by courts.

Incumbent gerrymandering sometimes supplements traditional partisan gerrymandering. The object of incumbent gerrymandering is to protect the seats of incumbents. Often if party control of state government is divided, thus preventing the passage of a partisan gerrymander, legislators will agree to protect themselves. This explains why some citizens refer to some redistricting maps as nothing more than "incumbency protection" plans, particularly if the legislators themselves draw the lines.

The Seats–Votes Relationship

One way to determine whether partisan gerrymandering has short-changed a party is to compare the total statewide vote compiled by all of the party's candidates with the proportion of legislative seats it won.[54] For example, if a party's candidates won 55 percent of the total votes cast in all legislative elections but won only 45 percent of the

PARTISAN GERRYMAN-DERING

The drawing of electoral district boundary lines to grant political advantage to a particular party, therefore increasing the number of winning candidates within that party.

up CLOSE   The Original Gerrymander

The term *gerrymander* immortalizes Governor Elbridge Gerry (1744–1814) of Massachusetts, who in 1812 redistricted the state legislature to favor Democrats over Federalists. A district north of Boston was designed to concentrate and thus waste Federalist votes. The district was portrayed in a political cartoon in the *Boston Gazette* on March 26, 1812, as a "gerrymander."

seats, we might conclude that partisan gerrymandering was to blame. This comparison is not always valid, however, especially when it is understood that a party that wins a slight majority of votes would normally be expected to win a much larger proportion of seats. For example, a party that wins 52 percent of total votes cast in all legislative elections might win 65 percent of the seats; theoretically it could win 100 percent of the seats in the unlikely event that its 52 percent of the votes was spread evenly in every legislative district. The U.S. Supreme Court has held that "a mere lack of proportionality in results in one election" cannot prove an unconstitutional gerrymander; however, the Court said that it might intervene when there is "a history of disproportionate result."[55] It is important to remember that the United States does *not* employ proportional representation as do many European democracies. Hence we cannot expect proportionality in the seats–votes relationship. However, extreme and persistent differences in this relationship may signal the existence of partisan gerrymandering.

Affirmative Racial Gerrymandering

Gerrymandering designed to *dis*advantage blacks and language minorities is a violation of the Equal Protection Clause of the Fourteenth Amendment of the U.S. Constitution, and it is a violation of the federal Voting Rights Act of 1965.[56] In 1982 Congress strengthened the Voting Rights Act by outlawing any electoral arrangements that had the *effect* of weakening minority voting power (see "Securing the Right to Vote" in Chapter 4). The U.S. Supreme Court obliged the states whenever possible to maximize opportunities for blacks and minority candidates to win election.[57] This apparent mandate for **affirmative racial gerrymandering** governed redistricting following the 1990 census and resulted in a significant increase in black and minority representation in many state legislatures. However, the creation of some bizarre-shaped "**majority-minority**" congressional districts (see Figure 4–4 in Chapter 4) led the U.S. Supreme Court to express constitutional doubts about districts that appear designed exclusively to separate the races. In 2001, in *Hunt* v. *Cromartie*,[58] the Court ruled that while state legislatures can take racial considerations into account when redistricting, they cannot use race as the predominant factor. To do so violates the equal protection clause of the Fourteenth Amendment to the U.S. Constitution.

A new "one person, one vote" issue has been raised in the context of the redistricting process by prisoner advocacy groups. Looking ahead to the 2010 census, they are pushing for prisoners to be counted where they are from, not in the town in which they are incarcerated. They believe the current method shortchanges urban areas in population counts and in the amount of federal funding, especially for programs for poor and minorities, that they would otherwise get.[59]

Multimember Districts

Multimember legislative districts (those that elect two or more members to a legislative body) were once very common. (Seventeen states had multimember districts in at least one of their legislative chambers before 1990.) But court challenges and complaints by minority parties and racial minorities have restricted their use. The U.S. Supreme Court has never held multimember districts to be unconstitutional per se, as long as the population representation is equal.[60] (A two-member district, for example, should have twice the **ideal district population,** calculated by dividing the total state population by the total number of districts in each legislative chamber.) However, multimember district plans that discriminate against racial minorities are unconstitutional.[61] Single-member districts are strongly preferred by minorities—minority political parties as well as racial minorities.

District Size

State legislative districts, in both upper and lower chambers, are much smaller than congressional districts. Each of the 435 members of the U.S. House of Representatives serves about 654,506 constituents. (The only state legislative chambers in which members serve so many constituents are the California Senate, where 40 senators each serve 846,791 constituents, and the Texas Senate, where 31 senators each serve 672,639 constituents.) Some house districts in rural states have fewer than 10,000 constituents, while house districts in large urban states (California, Florida, Illinois, New York, Ohio, and Texas) have more than 100,000 constituents. (New Hampshire, with 400 house members serving a total population of only 1.2 million, has the nation's smallest legislative constituencies—3,089 persons.) Senate districts across the nation regularly exceed 100,000 constituents.

Who Draws the Lines?

Traditionally, legislatures drew up their own district lines. In most states this continues to be the case. Many legislatures employ private consultants to assist in the task, and computer mapping is now common. Legislatures generally try to protect incumbents, and the majority party frequently tries to maximize its advantages over the minority

AFFIRMATIVE RACIAL GERRYMANDERING

Drawing legislative district lines in order to maximize opportunities for minority candidates to win elections.

MAJORITY-MINORITY DISTRICTS

Districts in which minorities make up the majority of the population.

MULTIMEMBER LEGISLATIVE DISTRICTS

Districts from which two or more members are elected to a legislative body, must meet equal population size criteria

IDEAL DISTRICT POPULATION

The ideal population within a district, calculated by dividing the total state population by the total number of districts in each legislative chamber.

party. But in recent years, because of court challenges over apportionment (equality of population in districts) and racial gerrymandering, most legislative districting plans must be approved by courts. Reformers (Common Cause, National Municipal League, League of Women Voters) have urged state legislatures to turn over redistricting to **independent nonpartisan commissions**, and some states have done so (notably Hawaii, Idaho, Montana, New Jersey, and Washington).

Reformers argue that partisan gerrymandering devalues voter participation, reduces competition for legislative seats, and reduces the responsiveness of legislators by creating "safe" seats. There is some evidence that independent commissions go about their task of redistricting without much regard for incumbent protection or party advantage.[62] But one political scientist's study of state redistricting efforts by nonpartisan commissions from 2000 to 2002 concluded that the results are virtually the same as when legislators themselves "pick" their constituents. "The assumption that shifting control of redistricting from partisan state legislatures to nonpartisan commissions will dramatically increase the number of competitive districts is not supported by the record of such commissions," he concluded.[63]

Would having retired judges draw the lines make things any fairer? Some Californians, including Republican Governor Arnold Schwarzenegger, think so. If enough citizens sign a petition calling for an election to vote such a proposal into law, it could come to pass. However, some research suggests it might not alter the current geographical distribution of political power as much as reformers—and Republicans—would like. (California's legislature is predominantly controlled by Democrats.)

How Often to Redistrict?

Historically, most states have redrawn their legislative and congressional districts just once every ten years—right after the release of new census figures. That pattern has been disrupted in the 2000s. Several state legislatures attempted to redraw districts created for the 2002 election cycle in time for the 2004 cycle. In each instance, litigation ensued. In Colorado, the State Supreme Court threw out the new legislative plan. In New Hampshire, the state Supreme Court upheld the plan legislative. And in Texas, after much litigation, the new congressional districts were upheld by the federal courts, which rejected plaintiffs' claims that the plan was both a racial and partisan gerrymander and was a violation of the federal Voting Rights Act.[64]

LEGISLATIVE ORGANIZATION AND PROCEDURE

The formal rules and procedures by which state legislatures operate are primarily designed to make the legislative process fair and orderly. Without established customs, rules, and procedures, it would be impossible for 50, 100, or 200 people to arrive at a collective decision about the thousands of items submitted to them at a legislative session. State legislatures follow a fairly standard pattern in the formal process of making laws. Figure 6–4 provides a brief description of some of the more important procedural steps in lawmaking.

Procedures Have Consequences

What are the political consequences of the legislative procedures described in Figure 6–4? Obviously, it is a very difficult process for a bill to become a law—legislative procedures offer many opportunities to defeat legislation. Formal rules and procedures of state legislatures lend themselves easily to those who would delay or obstruct legislation. Figure 6–4 illustrates the deliberative function of legislatures and the consequent procedural advantages

THE FLORIDA SENATE -- *HOW AN IDEA BECOMES A LAW*

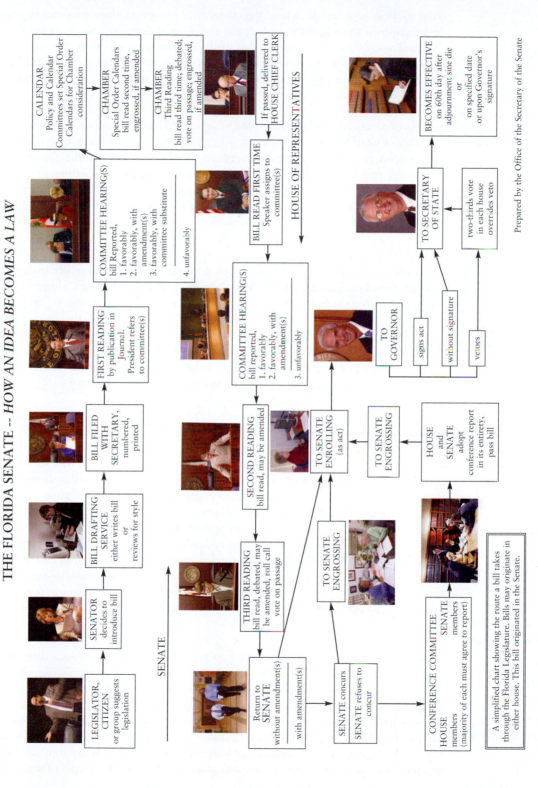

Prepared by the Office of the Secretary of the Senate

Available at http://www.flsenate.gov/data/civics/idea_to_law_chart.pdf

given to those who would defend the status quo. Moreover, these procedures imply that the legislature is structured for deliberation and delay in decision making, rather than speed and innovation. This suggests that the legislature functions as an arbiter, rather than an initiator, of public policy, since its procedures are designed to maximize deliberation, even at the expense of granting advantage to those who oppose change.

Disorderliness

As experienced legislators are fond of saying, "There are two things in the world you do not want to watch being made—sausages and laws." Lawmaking is a disorderly process, in spite of the formal procedures listed in Figure 6–4. Students often express shock and dismay when they spend some time watching or working in their legislature. After studying the formal rules, they may be unprepared for the "actual" haste, disorganization, logrolling, informality, infighting, petty jealousies, vote trading, ignorance, and ineptitude that they encounter. (See "*Up Close:* Informal Rules of the Game.")

Workload

Less than one in four bills introduced in a legislative session actually makes its way through the whole process and becomes law. In large states such as California and New York, nearly 10,000 bills may be introduced in a single legislative session, and 2,000 to 3,000 may be enacted into law. In smaller states, a typical legislative session may produce 300 to 500 laws. Most bills die in committee. Many bills are introduced with no real expectation they will pass; legislators simply seek to "go on record" as working for a particular goal or to get discussion of an issue started, knowing full well it might take several sessions for it to capture the full attention of other legislators.

Logjams

The end-of-session logjam is typically the most disorderly phase of lawmaking. In the closing days of a legislative session, hasty efforts are made to win approval for many bills and amendments that are still languishing somewhere in the legislative process. Legislative chambers sometimes become scenes of noisy confusion, with legislators voting blindly on bills described only by number, often resembling a "**train,**" because so many bills have been hooked together into one large omnibus bill. Most reformers condemn the end-of-session logjam as a source of inferior quality legislation. Other observers consider it an inevitable product of workload. For still others, the logjam is a strategy to enhance the power of legislative leaders. These leaders control the daily agenda and grant recognition to members seeking the floor; these decisions in a confused end-of-session logjam can determine whose bills get passed and whose do not. In some states in some sessions, over half of all the bills passed will be pushed through in the last few days of the session.[65]

Sessions

Traditionally, state constitutions limited legislative sessions to thirty or sixty days once every two years. These limits reflected the "citizen" nature of state legislatures, in contrast to the "professional" full-time congressional model of a legislature. Many observers still argue that the predominant occupation of members should *not* be "legislator," and that legislative sessions should be kept short so that citizens with other occupations can serve in the legislature. But the growing demands of legislative business have led to longer **regular sessions**.

Most states now hold **annual legislative sessions**; only a few are limited to **biennial sessions** (see Table 6–1). Fourteen states place no limit on the length of sessions while

up CLOSE Informal Rules of the Game

Partly to counteract the impact of formal rules and procedures, legislatures have developed a number of informal "rules of the game." These unwritten rules are not merely quaint and curious folkways. They support the purposes and functions of the legislature by helping to maintain the working consensus among legislators so essential to legislative output. Some rules contribute to the legislative task by promoting group cohesion and solidarity. In the words of legislators themselves, "Support another member's local bill if it doesn't affect you or your district"; "Don't steal another's bill"; "Accept the author's amendments to a bill"; "Don't make personal attacks on other members." Other informal rules promote predictability of behavior: "Keep your word"; "Don't conceal the real purpose of bills or amendments"; "Notify in advance if you cannot keep a commitment." Other rules try to put limits on interpersonal conflict: "Be willing to compromise"; "Accept half a loaf"; "Respect the seniority system"; "Respect committee jurisdiction." Finally, other rules are designed to expedite legislative business: "Don't talk too much"; "Don't fight unnecessarily"; "Don't introduce too many bills and amendments"; "Don't point out the absence of a quorum"; "Don't be too political."[a]

"Highly Undesirable" Legislative Behaviors[b]

- Concealing the real purpose(s) of a bill or purposely overlooking some portion of it in order to ensure its passage
- Dealing in personalities in debate or in other remarks made on the floor of the chamber
- Being a thorn to the majority by refusing unanimous consent, etc.
- Talking about decisions that have been reached in private to the press or anyone else

- Seeking as much publicity as possible from the press back home
- Being generally known as a spokesperson for some special interest group
- Introducing as many bills and amendments as possible during any legislative session
- Talking on a subject coming before the legislature about which you are not completely informed
- Giving first priority to your reelection in all of your actions as a legislator

A very important informal device is unanimous consent for the suspension of formal rules; this permits a legislature to consider bills not on the calendar, pass bills immediately without the necessary three readings, dispense with time-consuming formalities, permit nonmembers to speak, and otherwise alter procedure. Another informal rule is the practice in many states of passing "local bills" that would affect only one area of a state without debate or opposition when the delegation in that area unanimously supports the bill.

Most of these rules are enforced by **informal sanctions**. The most frequently mentioned sanction involves obstructing the bills of errant legislators by abstaining or voting against them, keeping their bills in committee, and amending their bills; more personal sanctions are using the "silent treatment," not trusting the legislator, and removing patronage and good committee assignments. Other sanctions include denial of legislative courtesies and occasionally even overt demonstrations of displeasure, such as ridicule, hissing, or laughing. The observance of rules, however, is not obtained primarily through fear of sanction so much as the positive recognition by legislators of the usefulness of rules in helping the legislature perform its chores.

[a]Quotations from state legislators interviewed by John C. Wahlke et al., *The Legislative System* (New York: John Wiley, 1962), 146–161.
[b]Items which at least 40 percent of Iowa House and Senate members checked as "highly undesirable." See F. Ted Hebert and Lelan E. McLemore, "Character and Structure of Legislative Norms," *American Journal of Political Science*, 17 (August 1973): 506–527.

SPECIAL SESSION

Legislative sessions that may be called by the governor, or in some states by the legislative leadership, to consider special topics.

INSTITUTIONAL-IZATION

The development of rules and procedures, organizational structures, and standard patterns of behavior in political bodies.

PROFESSION-ALISM

The extent to which members are devoted full time to their legislative jobs and have the assistance of staffs and other legislative support services.

STAFF

Aides employed to assist individual members or committees in their work.

State legislatures have gradually become more institutionalized.

the rest have either constitutional limits (the most common) or statutory limits. The most common limit is sixty days; most legislatures convene in January and adjourn in March.

Frequently legislatures convene in "**special sessions**" in addition to those regularly scheduled. Special sessions may be called by the governor, or in some states by the legislative leadership, to consider special topics, for example, projected budget deficits, reapportionment, or a lawsuit facing the state unless preemptive action is taken. Usually these sessions are limited to the topic for which they were called.

We should remember that legislators have many duties between sessions; their work does not end when the session adjourns. Often legislative committees meet between sessions, and constituents continue to contact legislators for services.

LEGISLATIVE INSTITUTIONALIZATION

Over time political bodies develop their own rules, organizational structures, and patterns of behavior. Social scientists refer to this process as "institutionalization." In legislative bodies, institutionalization is said to occur when (1) membership stabilizes and legislators come to look upon their service as a career; (2) staffs are added, salaries increased, and internal operations expanded; and (3) rules of procedure become more complex.[66]

State legislatures have gradually become more institutionalized. Overall, membership turnover has diminished over time (except where there are legislative term limits; see Table 2–6 in Chapter 2), legislative salaries and perks have risen, and incumbents have enjoyed a heavy advantage in seeking reelection. More legislators are coming to see their jobs as full-time occupations. (Review Figure 6–1.)

Professionalism

Some state legislatures are highly professional, while others are not. By professional we mean that in some legislatures the members are well paid and tend to think of their jobs as full-time ones; members and committees are well staffed and have good informational services available to them; and a variety of legislative services, such as bill drafting and statutory revision, are well supported and maintained. In other legislatures, members are poorly paid and regard their legislative work as part time; there is little in the way of staff for legislators or committees; and little is provided in the way of legislative assistance and services. Figure 6–5 groups the states by the professionalism of their legislatures.

Effects of Professionalization

Professionalization of state legislatures includes the development of large **staffs** for the leadership and for committees, as well as the provision of aides and assistants to individual members; the provision of offices, expense accounts, travel budgets, and other perks; assistance in communication with constituents, including printing and mailing of newsletters, press rooms and

TABLE 6–1 **The State Legislatures**

State	Official Name	Senate		House		Salaries	Regular Sessions
		Number	Term	Number	Term		
Alabama	Legislature	35	4	105	4	Per Diem	Annual
Alaska	Legislature	20	4	40	2	24,012+	Annual
Arizona	Legislature	30	2	60	2	24,000+	Annual
Arkansas	General Assembly	35	4	100	2	14,765+	Biennial—odd year
California	Legislature	40	4	80	2	113,098+	Annual*
Colorado	General Assembly	35	4	65	2	30,000+	Annual
Connecticut	General Assembly	36	2	151	2	28,000	Annual
Delaware	General Assembly	21	4	41	2	42,000	Annual
Florida	Legislature	40	4	120	2	30,996+	Annual
Georgia	General Assembly	56	2	180	2	17,342+	Annual
Hawaii	Legislature	25	4	51	2	35,900+	Annual
Idaho	Legislature	35	2	70	2	16,116+	Annual
Illinois	General Assembly	59	a	118	2	57,619+	Annual
Indiana	General Assembly	50	4	100	2	11,600+	Annual
Iowa	General Assembly	50	4	100	2	25,000+	Annual
Kansas	Legislature	40	4	125	2	Per Diem+	Annual
Kentucky	General Assembly	38	4	100	2	Per Diem+	Annual
Louisiana	Legislature	39	4	105	4	16,800+	Annual
Maine	Legislature	35	2	151	2	12,713+	Annual*
Maryland	General Assembly	47	4	141	4	43,500+	Annual
Massachusetts	General Court	40	2	160	2	58,237+	Biennial
Michigan	Legislature	38	4	110	2	79,650+	Annual
Minnesota	Legislature	67	4	134	2	31,141+	Biennial
Mississippi	Legislature	52	4	122	4	10,000+	Annual
Missouri	General Assembly	34	4	163	2	31,351+	Annual
Montana	Legislature	50	4	100	2	Per Diem+	Biennial—odd year
Nebraska	Legislature	49	4	N/A	N/A	12,000+	Annual
Nevada	Legislature	21	4	42	2	Per Diem+	Biennial—odd year
New Hampshire	General Court	24	2	400	2	200	Annual
New Jersey	Legislature	40	4(a)	80	2	49,000	Biennial
New Mexico	Legislature	42	4	70	2	no salary+	Annual
New York	Legislature	62	2	150	2	79,500+	Annual
North Carolina	General Assembly	50	2	120	2	13,951+	Annual*

(*continued*)

TABLE 6–1   (Continued)

State	Official Name	Senate Number	Senate Term	House Number	House Term	Salaries	Regular Sessions
North Dakota	Legislature Assembly	47	4	94	4	Per Diem+	Biennial—odd year
Ohio	General Assembly	33	4	99	2	58,934	Biennial
Oklahoma	Legislature	48	4	101	2	38,400+	Annual
Oregon	Legislature Assembly	30	4	60	2	18,408+	Biennial—odd year
Pennsylvania	General Assembly	50	4	203	2	73,613+	Biennial—odd year
Rhode Island	General Assembly	38	2	75	2	13,089	Annual
South Carolina	General Assembly	46	4	124	2	10,400+	Biennial
South Dakota	Legislature	35	2	70	2	12,000+	Annual
Tennessee	General Assembly	33	4	99	2	18,123+	Biennial
Texas	Legislature	31	4	150	2	7,200+	Biennial—odd year
Utah	Legislature	29	4	75	2	Per Diem+	Annual
Vermont	General Assembly	30	2	150	2	601/week+	Annual
Virginia	General Assembly	40	4	100	2	18,000+b	Annual
Washington	Legislature	49	4	98	2	36,311+	Annual
West Virginia	Legislature	34	4	100	2	15,000+	Annual
Wisconsin	Legislature	33	4	99	2	47,413+	Biennial
Wyoming	Legislature	30	4	60	2	Per Diem+	Biennial

Note: + means legislator gets per diem living expenses in addition to his or her legislative salary.
* means that session length varies.
a Term length varies by year.
b Virginia House and Senate are paid differently. The House only makes $17,640 (plus per diem living expenses).
Source: Book of States, 2007, Vol. 39, various tables pp. 75–82, 92–94.

television studios, and Web site development and maintenance; and, of course, higher salaries that allow legislators to spend more time both legislating and politicking.[67] All of these elements of professionalization combine to allow legislators to do more individual "casework" for constituents (often by contacting state agencies[68]), to devote more time pursuing their districts' interests, and, in effect, aiding them in campaign-type activities during their tenure in office. Knowing this, the press often focuses on the expense reimbursement requests filed by legislators, especially during an election year.

As the level of professionalism in a legislature increases, its members' probability of winning re-election rises. Legislative tenure increases. State legislative elections

FIGURE 6–5 Professionalism in State Legislatures

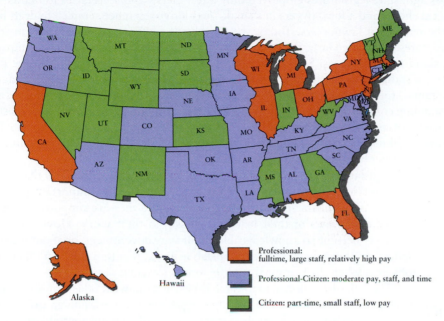

Professional:
fulltime, large staff, relatively high pay

Professional-Citizen: moderate pay, staff, and time

Citizen: part-time, small staff, low pay

Note: Data are for 2007.
Source: National Center for State Legislatures; NCSL Backgrounder Full and Part-Time Legislatures; January 2007; available at http://www.ncsl.org/programs/press/2004/backgrounder_fullandpart.htm

become less affected by political and economic developments in the nation and interstate. In other words, political and economic changes in the nation or in a state have their strongest effects on the probability that incumbents will win reelection when professionalism is low. **"Coattail" effects**—legislators gaining electoral support when running with a popular gubernatorial, U.S. senatorial, or presidential candidate of the same party—are diminished by professionalism. That is to say, professionalism tends to "insulate" legislative elections.[69]

Professionalism and Public Policy

Does it make any difference in public policy whether a legislature is "professional" or not? Reformers often *assume* that "professionalism" will result in legislatures that are "generally innovative in many different areas of public policy, generous in welfare and educational spending and services, and 'interventionist' in the sense of having powers and responsibilities of broad scope."[70] Does legislative reform, however, *really* have any policy consequences? Unfortunately, there is little systematic evidence that legislative professionalism has any *direct* effect on public policy. A state's income, urbanization, and education better explain policy outcomes than legislative professionalism.

"COATTAIL" EFFECTS

Legislators gaining electoral support when running with a popular gubernatorial, U.S. senatorial, or presidential candidate of the same party.

Legislative Staffing

Years ago, state legislatures employed only a few clerks and secretaries to handle the clerical chores and a few lawyers in a small "legislative reference service" to draft bills at the request of lawmakers. Today, the movement toward professionalism in state legislatures has created large professional staffs to serve the needs of the leadership and the standing committees. Some more "professional" legislatures have full-time professional staffs—lawyers, researchers, speechwriters, press liaisons, as well as secretarial assistants—for the house speaker, senate president, majority and minority leaders, and all standing committees; and many states now even provide full-time, year-round staff for each house and senate member. Only the less "professional" rural, small-state legislatures still depend on a small legislative reference service to serve all legislators in drafting bills and doing research.

Legislative staffs have grown rapidly over the last decade, so that today this new "legislative bureaucracy" is itself becoming an important political force.

Legislative staffs have grown rapidly over the last decade, so that today this new "legislative bureaucracy" is itself becoming an important political force. Staff members are political appointees, and they are supposed to reflect the political views of their legislator-bosses in their work. However, some "staffers" become so knowledgeable about state government, or about the state budget, or about their aspects of legislative work, that they are kept on in their jobs even when their original sponsor leaves the capital.

The staffs are expected to research issues, find out what other states are doing, assist in analyzing the budget, schedule legislative hearings, line up experts and interest groups to testify, keep abreast of the status of bills and appropriation items as they move through the legislature, maintain contact with state agencies and the governor's staff, make coffee and fetch doughnuts, write and rewrite bills, and perform other assorted chores and errands. As legislators come to rely on trusted "staffers," the "staffers" themselves become more powerful.[71] Their advice may kill a bill or an appropriation item, or their work may amend a bill or alter an appropriation, without the legislator becoming directly involved. Often "staffers" are young, and they exercise a great deal of influence in policymaking.[72] Staffers also have a good vantage point from which to assess who is most effective at influencing public policy outcomes. Majority party leaders are rated highest, minority party leaders the lowest. But the senate, the house, the governor, and committee chairs are ranked so closely they can almost be considered to be equal. (See Table 6–2.)

Turnover

TURNOVER RATE

In legislatures, the percentage of members replaced in each legislative session.

"INSTITUTIONAL MEMORY"

The knowledge of veteran legislators about how issues were handled in the past.

In states *without* term limits, the overall turnover rate (the percentage of legislators replaced each session) is roughly 25 percent. This means that about one-quarter of all state legislators are newcomers at any legislative session. They have taken the seats of members who do not return to the state house because of a career change, a run for higher office, retirement, illness or death, or, in relatively rare instances, defeat in their bid for reelection. Turnover rates vary by state, ranging from below 5 percent to above 40 percent. Interestingly, it is *not* party competition that increases turnover; far more legislators voluntarily quit than are defeated for reelection. There is *less* turnover in the larger states, which have longer legislative sessions and pay their legislators more money. In other words, more "professional" legislatures have lower turnover rates than the "amateur" legislatures. In general, high turnover rates cause some to worry about the loss of some "**institutional memory**"—the observations and insights of veteran legislators about how issues were handled in the past.

TABLE 6–2　Who Has the Most Influence in State Legislatures? The Staff's Perspective

[Scale of 1 (No Influence) to 7 (Dictates Policy)]

Player	All Staff	Nonpartisan Staff	Partisan Staff
Majority party leaders	5.9	6.0	6.2
The Senate	5.2	5.2	5.1
The House	5.1	5.0	5.2
Governor	5.0	5.0	5.0
Committee chairs	5.0	5.2	5.1
Interest groups/lobbyists	4.8	4.8	4.7
Executive agency staff	4.0	3.9	4.0
Partisan staff	3.6	3.3	4.3
Mass media	3.6	3.5	3.7
Nonpartisan staff	3.3	3.3	3.1
Minority party leaders	3.0	3.0	3.0

Source: "Who's the Boss", p. 7 from *State Legislatures*, January 2007. Copyright © 2007 by National Conference on State Legislatures. Reprinted by permission of National Conference on State Legislatures.

LEGISLATIVE COMMITTEES

While it is most convenient to study legislative decision making by observing floor actions, particularly the division of ayes and nays, the floor is not the only locus of important legislative decisions.[73] Committee work is essential to the legislative process. It is here that public hearings are held, lobbyists plead their case, policies are debated, legislation amended and compromised, and bills rushed to the floor or **pigeonholed** (ignored). The function of the committee system is to reduce legislative work to manageable proportions by providing for a division of labor among legislators. However, by so doing the committees themselves often come to exercise considerable influence over the outcome of legislation. Another opportunity is provided for delay and obstruction by less than the majority of legislators, sometimes by a single committee chairperson.

Committee work is essential to the legislative process.

Functions

A typical legislative chamber will have between twenty and thirty **standing committees** that consider all bills in a particular area, such as revenue (often referred to as "ways and means"), appropriations, highways, welfare, education, labor, judiciary, or local government. Typically, a legislator will serve on three, four, or five committees. In most state legislatures, committee assignments, including the assignment of chairpersons, are made by the speaker of the house and the president of the senate in their respective bodies. This power of appointment gives these leaders some control over the actions of committees.

Committees may decide to hold early hearings on a bill, send it to the floor with little or no revision, and recommend it favorably. Or committees may simply ignore a bill ("pigeonholing"), fail to schedule hearings on it, allow hostile witnesses to testify against it, write extensive revisions and amendments into it, and so forth. Some states reduce the power of committees by allowing bills to be considered on the floor even though they have not been reported out of committee, or by requiring that all bills be reported out either favorably or unfavorably.

"PIGEONHOLED"

A bill is ignored, never reported out of committee.

STANDING COMMITTEES

Regular committees of a legislature that deal with bills within specified subject areas.

BILL REFERRALS

The assignment of bills to specific committees, usually by the Speaker of the House and the Senate President.

Personnel

Committee assignments in most legislatures are made by the leadership. Occupational background frequently determines a legislator's initial committee assignments. Thus, lawyers are frequently assigned to committees on the judiciary and civil and criminal law, educators to education committees, farmers to agricultural committees, bankers to banking committees, and so on. The effect of these assignments is to further strengthen the power of special interests in the legislative process. Legislators with occupational ties to various interests dominate the committees that consider legislation dealing with those same interests.

Committee Preferences

How often do committees frustrate the preferences of their parent legislative chamber? Overall, committees generally reflect the preferences of the legislative chambers from which they are drawn. This is especially true where the speaker of the House and the president of the Senate control **bill referrals**—the assignment of bills to specific committees. One study reports that only about 5 percent of committees can be labeled as "outliers"—committees likely to defy the preferences of their parent chambers. And these are usually issue-specific committees, such as water resources, oil and gas, labor relations, and so on, or rather than key committees such as appropriations, ways and means, and rules.[74] Party leadership in most state legislative chambers prevents committees from becoming independent "fiefdoms," although some states have more powerful committee systems than others.

Committee System Power

States differ in how they structure their legislative committee system. The power of a state's committee system is measured using six criteria:[75]

- *Openness to the public.* Regularly scheduled meetings; advance notice of committee meetings and agendas; required open hearings and deliberations.
- *Independence in the legislative process.* No requirement that committees consider and report all legislation referred to them; no deadlines on committee action.
- *Ability to gather information.* The ability to subpoena people and documents and to conduct investigations; to hire staff; to meet before and between sessions.
- *Power to initiate legislation.* Committees can introduce bills and offer substitute bills; restrictions against referral of bills to multiple committees.
- *Ability to protect the Committee's positions on the floor.* Automatic incorporation of committee amendments; provisions that make it difficult for the floor to overturn adverse reports and amend legislation out of committee.
- *Protection from the floor controlling committee actions.* Provisions to make it difficult for the floor to request bills to be considered and to withdraw bills from committee; requiring bills to be placed on the final action calendar in the order reported out of committee.

LEADERSHIP AND ROLE-PLAYING IN LEGISLATURES

Roles are expectations about the kind of behavior people ought to exhibit. Expectations are placed upon a legislator by fellow legislators, the legislator's party, the opposition party, the governor, constituents, interest groups, and by friends, as well as by the legislators themselves.

Leadership Roles

Perhaps the most distinctive roles in the legislative process are those of the leadership. A typical legislative chamber has a **presiding officer** (usually a **house "speaker"** and a **senate "president"**), a majority and a minority floor leader, a number of committee chairpersons, and a steering committee. These leaders perform functions similar to the functions of rules. First, leaders are expected to help make the legislative system stable and manageable. They are expected to maintain order, to know the rules and procedures, to follow the rules, and to show fairness and impartiality. Leaders are also expected to help focus the issues and resolve conflict by presenting issues clearly, narrowing the alternatives, organizing public hearings, and promoting the party or administrative point of view on bills. The **majority leader** is supposed to "get the administrative program through," while the **minority leader** develops a "constructive opposition."

Leaders are also expected to administer the legislature and expedite business. This includes "promoting teamwork," "being accessible," starting the sessions on time, keeping them on schedule, and distributing the workload. It involves communication, coordination, and liaison with the governor, the administrative departments, and the other chamber.

Members' Expectations of Leaders

From the members' perspective, successful leaders are those who assist them in achieving their personal political goals. Most legislators possess a desire for reelection, as well as power and policy influence within the legislature. The relative importance of these goals will vary for each individual member. A freshman lawmaker who feels electorally insecure will have different priorities than a senior legislator from a safe district. The key to effective leadership is to understand the particular needs and goals of individual members and to respond as necessary.[76]

Leaders' Legislative Priorities

Leaders face a difficult challenge in balancing competing priorities with limited resources. In recent years the top priorities identified by state legislative leaders across the country have been in the areas of crime and homeland security, tax reform, job creation and expansion, education, health care, Medicaid, and child protective services.[77] And, of course, they want fewer unfunded federal mandates to the states and greater control over federal programs in their state (see Chapter 3).

Expert Roles

Another set of legislative roles that are commonly encountered and make important contributions to the legislative process are the **"subject-matter experts."** Unlike leadership roles, the roles of subject-matter experts are not embodied in formal offices. The committee system introduces specialization into the legislature, and the seniority system places at the head of the committee those persons longest exposed to the information about the committee's subject matter. Thus, subject-matter experts emerge among legislators in the fields of law, finance, education, agriculture, natural resources, local government, labor, transportation, and so on.

Trustees, Delegates, and Politicos

Another way of describing roles in a legislature is to discover the legislators' orientations toward the expectations of constituents. Legislators can be classified as

PRESIDING OFFICER

Leader of a legislative chamber selected from the majority party.

SPEAKER OF THE HOUSE

The presiding officer of the lower house of a legislature.

PRESIDENT OF THE SENATE

The presiding officer of the upper house of a legislature.

MAJORITY LEADER

A leader in the controlling party who is supposed to "get the administrative program through."

MINORITY LEADER

The leader of the minority party who is supposed to develop a "constructive opposition" against the policies of the controlling party.

SUBJECT-MATTER EXPERTS

Legislators who gain a reputation for having in-depth knowledge of a particular issue.

People in POLITICS

Leaders Assess The Changing Role of State Legislatures . . . and Legislators

The magazine *State Legislatures* interviewed four state legislative leaders and asked each the question: "How do you see the role of the legislature—and the legislator—changing in twenty-first-century America?"

"The challenge for legislatures is to continue to work through a declining ability by the federal government to help the states. . . . I think that has been most clearly demonstrated with Medicaid. We do not feel that we're getting the help from the federal government that we need so we are addressing it ourselves."

"In North Dakota we are trying to approach our role in the legislature as a board of directors—not to get into micro managing—but to act like a big company board of directors and ask, Where are we going? Where do we want to end up? And what are the results we want?"

Rep. Kim McMillan (D)
House Minority Leader, TN

"The legislative role in Colorado has changed quite a bit over the last several years and term limits have been a big part of that. I think we will see fewer legislators who serve long enough to develop any real expertise in more than one area. . . . We rely more and more on our Legislative Council for research. . . . We depend on others for lots of information. When advocates or special interests supply more and more information, it could easily increase their influence."

Rep. Alice Madden (D)
House Majority Leader, CO

"Running for the legislature is harder to do because it's still part-time pay and approaching full-time work. Businesses don't want to give the release time anymore. And so we're having trouble getting people to serve. Yet most of us think the idea of being part-time, being able to be at a youth ball game, working at another job, and getting that closeness to people is good. But it's a serious challenge for us."

Rep. Rick Berg (R) House
Majority Leader, ND

Rep. Bob Ward (R) House
Minority Leader (CT)

Source: "Leaders: What Matters Now," *State Legislatures*, January 2006, p. 18.

TRUSTEE

A role that representatives adopt when they decide to vote their conscience and use their best personal judgment rather than catering to the narrow interests of their constituents.

trustees (those who are guided in legislative affairs solely by their personal conscience) and **delegates** (those who are guided by the instructions or wishes of their constituents). One study has found that more legislators see themselves as trustees than delegates, especially where there are term limits in place or multimember legislative districts.[78] Should legislators represent their constituency or their own conscience?

A classic dilemma of representative government is whether the legislator should vote his or her own conscience—"the trustee"—or vote the constituency's wishes— "the delegate." Good philosophical arguments can be found to support either of these guiding principles. Nearly 200 years ago the English political philosopher Edmund

Burke confronted this question directly and urged representatives to vote their own conscience about what is right for society. Burke believed that the voters should elect wise and virtuous representatives to govern *for* them—to use their own judgment in deciding issues regardless of popular demands. Even today the term **Burkean representation** refers to the willingness of a representative to ignore public opinion and decide public issues on the basis of one's own best judgment about what is right for society.

Other political philosophers stress responsiveness of representatives to the views of their constituents. Consider, for example, philosopher Hanna Pitkin's definition of representation: "Representation means acting in the interest of the represented, in a manner responsive to them."[79] **Responsiveness** connotes a deliberate effort by legislators to match their votes on public policy issues to their constituency's preferences. However, to be "responsive" to one's constituents, two conditions must be met: (1) The legislator must correctly perceive the constituents' views on the issues, and (2) the legislator must act in accord with these views.

Do legislators know the views of their constituents on public issues and how often do they vote on bills before them accordingly? Unfortunately, the evidence is mixed. When Iowa legislators were asked to predict whether their own district would vote for or against some proposed constitutional amendments, the resulting predictions were good on some issues but poor on others.[80] Interestingly, the poorest predictions came from legislators from poor districts, suggesting that legislators have less understanding of the views of poor constituents than affluent ones. In contrast, when Florida legislators were asked to predict how both their state and district would vote on referenda on school busing and school prayer, nearly all of them made accurate predictions for both their district and the state.[81]

Perhaps one explanation for these apparently conflicting findings is that legislators know their constituents' views on well-publicized, controversial, emotionally charged issues, but that legislators are poor predictors of constituent opinion on other kinds of issues. This scenario has generated a third legislative orientation—that of the "**politico,**" which refers to a legislator who plays both the delegate and trustee roles, but at different times. Legislators in this category vote as a delegate on hot-button issues that are high priorities back home in the district but as a trustee on other low-key issues.

Term Limits

Legislative behavior is affected by the imposition of term limits. Studies show that in states with term limits

- The power of the governor over legislation increases; the influence of majority party leaders and committee chairs is weakened.[82]
- Power is shifted to the upper chamber; the power of party caucus leaders is reduced; contributions to incumbents decline somewhat.[83]
- Bipartisanship and consensus building are more difficult.[84]
- Overall legislative policy knowledge is reduced, especially in part-time legislatures with small staffs.[85]
- Term-limited legislators are more likely to be motivated by issues than non-term-limited legislators and are also more likely to possess progressive ambition—to run for higher offices.[86]
- The power of lobbyists is increased, especially in less professional legislatures.

DELEGATE

A legislator votes on bills based on the priorities of the constituents back home rather than on his/her personal views.

BURKEAN REPRESENTATION

The belief that legislators should use their own best judgment about what is good for their state or nation, rather than conforming to their constituents' narrow interests.

RESPONSIVENESS

The extent to which legislators appear to reflect the views of their constituents in their lawmaking.

"POLITICO"

A legislator who plays both the delegate and trustee roles, but at different times, depending on how "hot" the issue is back home in the district.

- Some ambitious legislators resign before their term is up to run for another legislative post when there is an open seat—the "anticipatory effect."[87]
- Some "careerist" termed-out legislators run for offices once seen as "less valuable" than the one they hold (e.g., a senator running for the house or for a local office).[88]

There is also little evidence that adopting term limits has increased the representation of women and minorities in the legislature.[89]

Ethical Behavior

Legislators must establish the rules spelling out what is ethical behavior on their part and what is not. The National Conference of State Legislatures Ethics Center has identified seven major categories of ethics-related activities or situations that are regulated by various states:[90] gift giving and receiving, honorariums (payments for speeches, articles, or personal appearances), nepotism (hiring relatives), legislators lobbying government after they leave office (revolving door scenarios), conflict of interest (representing others before government, contracting with government, voting on an issue in which one has some formal role), personal financial disclosures, and legislative interaction with lobbyists. In thirty-nine states, there are state ethics commissions, which watch over legislators and state staff as well. And there is always the capitol press corps whose job it is to play a watchdog role. The rules in place can affect the occupational composition of state legislators. For example, strict financial disclosure laws reduce the number of business owners who run for the legislature.[91]

PARTY POLITICS IN STATE LEGISLATURES

While the influence of parties varies from state to state, overall, parties are perhaps the single most important influence over legislative behavior.

Traditional One-Party States

Traditionally the party in one-party (Democratic) states did not exercise tight party discipline over the voting of legislators. Being a Democrat in the legislature of a one-party southern Democratic state did not influence roll-call voting behavior very much. Democratic governors in these states could not depend on party loyalty to win legislative support for their programs. However, the *minority* Republicans in these states tended to stick together.

Emerging Legislative Party Conflict

As Republicans won more seats in the southern and border state legislatures, party organizations and party voting within the legislatures increased. Republican legislators became more likely to organize themselves into a party caucus, to develop a party legislative program, and to vote cohesively. The emerging "threat" of a Republican opposition usually spurred the Democrats to do the same.[92]

Increasing Party Competition

Traditionally the Democrats have controlled more state legislatures than the Republicans. But Republican victories in the 1994 elections extended from Congress (where Republicans won control of the U.S. House of Representatives for the first time in forty years) to the nation's state legislatures. For the first time in more than thirty years, the

GOP won control of more state legislatures than the Democrats. Over time, the Republicans have gained near parity in the total number of legislative seats they occupy throughout the nation, but in the mid-2000s, Democrats began to widen the gap again. (see Figure 5–2 in Chapter 5).

Two-Party States

As the parties have become more competitive in the states, party divisions on legislative roll-call votes have become more frequent than any other divisions, including rural–urban divisions. One common measure of party influence on voting is the percentage of nonunanimous roll-call votes on which a majority of Democrats voted against the majority of Republicans. Compilations by the *Congressional Quarterly* show that the proportion of roll calls in Congress in which the two parties have been in opposition has ranged from 35 to 50 percent over the years. Party voting in competitive state legislatures such as New York, Pennsylvania, Ohio, Delaware, Rhode Island, Massachusetts, and Michigan may be even higher than it is in Congress.

Leadership Votes

Voting along strict party lines is the norm for legislative leadership posts, notably for speaker of the house and president of the senate. Leaders are initially selected in the majority party's caucus; all party members are then expected to support their party's choice in the official house vote that follows. Indeed, real difficulties have emerged where parties have evenly divided legislative seats in a state house. (The Indiana house once resolved the issue by agreeing to "co-speakers" who would preside on alternate days; the Florida senate once resolved the issue by agreeing to switch presidents each year of the session.) Rarely do legislators break party lines in voting on leadership posts, although considerable pressure may be placed upon some to do so where the parties are evenly or almost evenly divided. One side effect of term limits has been to speed up legislators' campaigns for leadership posts in each chamber. Some freshmen start campaigning among their peers to become president of the senate or speaker of the house almost as soon as they take the oath of office.

Party Issues

On what types of issues do the parties exercise their greatest influence? Parties usually display the greatest cohesion on issues involving taxation and appropriations, welfare, and regulation of business and labor—in short, the major social and economic controversies that divide the national parties. Minor bills involving the licensing of water well drillers, cosmotologists, or barbers do not usually become the subject matter of party votes, and only infrequently will the parties divide over such matters as the designation of an official state bird. Party influence in budgetary matters is particularly apparent, since the budget often involves issues of social welfare and class interest on which parties in many states are split. In addition, the budget is clearly identified as the product of the governor and carries the label of the party of the governor. Another type of bill that is often the subject of party voting is one involving the party as an interest group. Parties often exhibit an interest in bills proposing to transfer powers from an office controlled by one party to an office controlled by the other, or bills proposing to create or abolish non–civil service jobs. Parties display considerable interest in bills affecting the organization of local government, state administration, the civil service, registration and election laws, and legislative procedure. And during an election year session, both parties are intent on establishing voting records that legislators can take with them on the campaign trail back home.

PARTY VOTING

In legislatures, voting in which a majority of one party's members vote in opposition to a majority of the other party's members.

Sources of Party Voting

What factors distinguish those states in which the party substantially influences legislative decision making from those states in which it does not?

Party cohesion is strongest in those urban industrial states in which the parties represent separate socioeconomic constituencies. Party voting occurs in those competitive states in which Democratic legislators represent central-city, low-income, ethnic, and racial constituencies, and Republican legislators represent middle-class, suburban, small-town, and rural constituencies. Party cohesion is weak in states where party alignments do not coincide with socioeconomic divisions of constituencies.

It is this division of constituencies that is the basis of party cohesion and influence in the legislature. Even within each party, members from districts typical of their party in socioeconomic attributes support the party position more often than members from districts atypical of the party. Constituency characteristics, then, help to explain not only the outcome of elections but also the behavior of the elected.

THE GROWING ROLE OF THE MEDIA IN THE LEGISLATIVE PROCESS

Constituents learn about their legislators via the media, and the legislators know it! Some have become quite adept at getting good media coverage—writing clever press releases, staging a press conference at a time virtually guaranteeing that it will be covered on the evening news, appearing on popular radio and television news magazine shows, and so forth. But a legislator's use of the media is not just to influence the voters back home. It is often aimed at fellow legislators or even the governor, the motive being to improve the odds that the legislator's bills may pass.

The capitol press corps is comprised of reporters from various news outlets across a state who are assigned to cover state government full time. The media and state legislators are a bit wary of each other, but generally each acknowledges they need the other to get their own job done.

The growing media savvy of state legislators has prompted scholars to ask whether legislators now regard use of the media as a more common, and effective, way of accomplishing policy successes than the traditional tactics (such as personally contacting other legislators, the governor, or executive agency officials; meeting with lobbyists). One study of state legislators from California, Georgia, and Iowa found that while legislators still use traditional legislative tactics more often, they generally believe that media tactics are more effective.[93] (See Table 6–3.)

At the same time legislators acknowledge the media can be helpful to them, they are somewhat wary of members of the **capitol, or statehouse, press corps**. (These are reporters from various news outlets across the state who are assigned to cover state government full time. The capitol press corps usually expands while the legislature is in session.) The "wariness" feeling is mutual. The reporters are on guard for legislators trying to "spin" them.

A Web-based survey designed to compare the views of legislators and capitol reporters found that "reporters question legislators' honesty and understanding of how the media operates. And legislators question reporters' coverage choices and objectivity."[94] (See Table 6–4.) However, both acknowledge they need each other. In the words of one Pennsylvania state representative who is a former reporter: "It's a parasitic relationship. Each person in the relationship has a need that the other person can fill. For the reporter, the need is information. And for the legislator, the need is free publicity. . . . We each have a job to do."[95]

CAPITOL, OR STATEHOUSE, PRESS CORPS

Reporters from various news outlets who are assigned to cover state government full time. The capitol press corps usually expands while the legislature is in session.

TABLE 6–3 Legislators Compare Use and Effectiveness of Traditional and Media Tactics

Tactics	Frequency Mean[a]	Effectiveness Mean[b]
Traditional Tactics		
Contacting other legislators directly	3.7	2.5
Proposing legislation	3.4	2.9
Contacting government agencies	3.2	3.2
Contacting the governor's office	2.9	3.3
Speaking on the floor	3.1	3.3
Meeting with lobbyists	3.5	3
Meeting with party caucus	3.5	3
Average for traditional tactics	3.3	3
Media Tactics		
Appearing on TV news	2.3	3.2
Writing OP-ED articles	2.7	3.4
Issuing press releases	3.2	3.3
Appearing on public access TV	2.2	3.4
Average for media tactics	2.6	3.3

[a]4 = Frequently, 3 = Occasionally, 2 = Rarely, 1 = Never.
[b]4 = Very Effective, 3 = Effective, 2 = Somewhat Effective, 1 = Not Effective.
Study based on responses of state legislators in California, Georgia, and Iowa.

Source: Christopher A. Cooper, "Media Tactics in the State Legislature," *State Politics and Policy Quarterly* 2 (4) (Winter 2002): 353–371. Reprinted by permission of the publisher.

TABLE 6–4 State Legislators and Reporters Have Very Different Views of Their Respective Professions

View	Legislators (% Agree)	Reporters (% Agree)
Legislators generally understand what qualifies as a news story.	53	30
Members of my profession are ethical.	78	78
Members of the *other* profession are ethical.	54	57
Generally, legislators are honest when responding to media inquiries.	83	47
Most news segments are neutral, unbiased accounts.	17	71
Generally, the media in my state adequately provides citizens with the information they need to know about policy decisions in the state legislature.	29	56

Source: Nicole Casal Moore, "Adversaries Always: Legislators and Reporters See Their Own as Ethical but Neither Profession Thinks Too Highly of the Other," *State Legislatures* 31 (May 2005): 21–23. Copyright © 2005 by National Conference on State Legislatures. Reprinted by permission of National Conference on State Legislatures.

LOBBYING IN STATE LEGISLATURES

The influence of organized interest groups in the legislative process varies from state to state. In Chapter 5 we discussed interest groups in the fifty states and their involvement in public relations, campaign financing, and lobbying. We defined lobbying as any communication by someone acting on behalf of a group directed at a government decision maker with the hope of influencing decisions. Lobbying is done by professionals but it is also done by average constituents. In fact, many interest groups encourage their members to lobby legislators via email, personal visits to their district or state capitol offices, letters, or phone calls because they know that "The best lobbyist is a constituent residing—and voting—in a representative's district."[96] Association leaders are quick to point out the advantages of lobbying at the state level (rather than the federal) to encourage more individual citizens to let their representatives know how they feel about key issues before the legislature.

"**Constituent lobbying**" of state legislators is easier than citizen lobbying of U.S. Congress members because (1) there are fewer members in a state legislature than in the U.S. Congress; (2) members of a state legislature are, in most cases, more accessible—they spend more time in their home district, making it easier for citizens to have personal contact with them; (3) there is less interference from state legislative staffs than from congressional staffs; and (4) there is less emphasis placed on campaign contributions as a means of accessing the state legislator.[97]

Lobbying groups often honor state legislators. The Washington Indian Gaming Association and the Tulalip Tribes sponsored an event at Evergreen State College celebrating the largest number of Washington lawmakers ever claiming American Indian or Alaska Native heritage. The four lawmakers are from the Ottawa Nation of Oklahoma and the Nez Perce, Tulalip, and Tsimsian Tribes.
Source: "Washington Native American Lawmakers Honored," Washington Indian Gaming Association, January 9, 2007. Available at www.washingtonindiangaming .org/Washington-Native-American-Lawmerks-Honored.asp

Narrow Issues

On what kinds of decisions are interest groups more likely to exercise influence? Party and constituency interests are most apparent on broad social and economic issues. On narrower issues voters are less likely to have either an interest or an opinion. The legislator is, therefore, freer to respond to the pleas of organized groups on highly specialized topics than on major issues of public interest. Economic interests seeking to use the law to improve their competitive position are a major source of group pressure on these specialized topics. Particularly active in lobbying are the businesses subject to extensive government regulation. The truckers, railroads, insurance companies, and gaming, tobacco, liquor, and restaurant interests are consistently found to be among the most highly organized and active lobbyists in state capitals. Organized pressure comes from associations of governments and associations of government employees. State chapters of the National Education Association are persistent in presenting the demands of educational administrators and occasionally the demands of the dues-paying teachers as well.

Information Exchange

Legislators depend on lobbyists for much of their information on public issues. Legislators are aware of the potential bias in information given them by lobbyists. But the constant proximity of lobbyists to legislators facilitates information exchange.[98] Legislators *use* lobbyists, just as lobbyists use legislators:

> Typically, legislators utilize lobbyists as sources of influence in three ways: by calling upon lobbyists to influence other legislators, by calling upon lobbyists to help amass public opinion in favor of the legislator's position, and by including lobbyists in planning strategy in an effort to negotiate a bill through the legislature.[99]

Threats and Unsolicited Campaign Contributions

It is unwise for lobbyists to threaten legislators, for example, by vowing to defeat them in the next election. This is the tactic of an amateur lobbyist, not a professional. It usually produces a defensive response by the legislator. As one lobbyist put it, "Once you have closed the door you have no further access to the individual. Once you've threatened an individual, there is no possibility of winning in the future."[100] Legislators also do not appreciate unsolicited campaign contributions from lobbyists. "Even if you don't ask for it, they'll send you money—if they think you're going to win," complained one legislator who intentionally funded his own campaign to avoid being painted by the media as dependent on special interest money.[101]

Getting the Message

Testimony at legislative committee hearings is a common form of information exchange between lobbyists and legislators. Often this testimony is the legislators' primary source of information about legislation. Direct meetings in legislators' offices are also frequent and effective. Social gatherings (where the liquor is usually furnished by the lobbyist) are more important in establishing friendships; professional lobbyists seldom bring up "business" on such occasions. Legislators are wined and dined so much during legislative sessions that attendance at social functions is sometimes viewed as a chore. The least effective method of lobbying is the submission of long letters or reports.

CONSTITUENT LOBBYING
Individual citizens letting their representatives know how they feel about key issues before the legislature, these constituents are therefore lobbying their representatives.

Lobbying the Staff

One form of lobbying that is growing rapidly in importance is communication with legislative *staff* personnel. As state legislatures acquire more full-time staff for their standing committees, house and senate leaders, and majority and minority party caucuses, professional lobbyists are coming to recognize that these staff people can have as much or more to do with the specific content of bills as legislators themselves. Many of the more "modernized," "professional" state legislatures rely heavily on the advice of professional staffs. The wise lobbyist in these states cultivates friendships among staff personnel.

Regulation of Lobbying

The U.S. Constitution guarantees the right "to petition the government for redress of grievances." This First Amendment right protects individuals and groups in their attempts to communicate with and influence their lawmakers. Nonetheless, lobbying is regulated in some fashion in all of the states. Most state laws require lobbyists ("anyone receiving compensation to influence legislative action") to (1) register with the clerk or secretary of the house or senate, and (2) file periodic reports of direct expenditures for lobbying activity. (Figure 6–6 lists the states where spending on lobbyists is the greatest and the states with the most registered lobbyists.) These regulations have relatively little impact on lobbying activity; many organizations claim that they are educational or religious in nature and not really lobbies, and they do not register. Many lobbies do not report all of their educational and public relations expenditures, but only a small portion, which they attribute directly to lobbying. Campaign contributions usually must be reported under state election laws. Of course, bribery and conspiracy may be prosecuted under criminal laws.

State legislatures and agencies charged with enforcement of lobbying regulations have traditionally been notorious for their neglect of their responsibilities. An analysis of state lobbyist disclosure laws by the Center for Public Integrity gave just nine states a satisfactory score; twenty-seven failed outright.[102] However, increasing professionalization of state legislatures appears to increase both their capacity and willingness to regulate lobbying.[103]

FIGURE 6–6 Lobbyist Spending: Top Ten States

Top Ten States: *Lobbyist Spending and Registered Lobbyists*

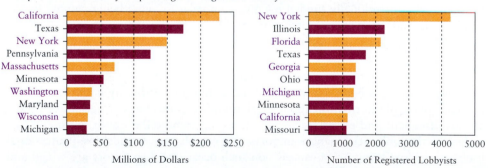

Notes: Data are for 2005. *Total does not include lobbyist salaries/compensation.
Source: Center for Public Integrity, http://www.publicintegrity.org/hiredguns/chart.aspx?act=lobbyspending/ &sort=2. Copyright © 2005. Reprinted by permission of Center for Public Integrity.

Ex-Legislators as Lobbyists

Some legislators choose to become lobbyists after they leave office. Special interests (public, private, nonprofit) hire them for their knowledge of the legislative process, personal connections with legislators, and their subject matter expertise. One study found that former legislators often turn out to be powerful, well-connected lobbyists.[104]

STATE LEGISLATURES: A CRITICAL ASSESSMENT

State legislatures are not very popular with the American people. Over thirty years ago, politial scientist William Keefe wrote, "It is very possibly true that no American political institution has ever had so many detractors, so few defenders, or such a wide array of charges levied against it. . . . Legislatures are located on the outskirts of public esteem and affection."[105] And despite institutional reforms of the past decades—higher salaries, more professional legislators, longer sessions, increased staff, better resources—it does not appear that state legislatures have improved their standing with the American people. Indeed, the strong support of term limits wherever they have appeared on the ballot suggests that Americans continue to hold state legislatures in low esteem. In a well-titled book, *The Decline of Representative Democracy*, political scientist Alan Rosenthal describes the general public's growing preference for direct democracy—voting on referendum issues themselves—over representative democracy.[106]

It is likely that the public's disdain of state legislatures is part of the popular cynicism for politics generally. About two-thirds of the American public says that government "is pretty much run by a few big interests looking out for themselves" rather than "run for the benefit of all people." But political scientists argue that state legislatures themselves have contributed to their own unpopularity. They hurt themselves by

- Legislating on matters of self-interest, including setting of their own salaries, drawing of their own legislative district lines, deciding on their own staff and office resources, regulating their own election campaign financing, regulating their own interactions with interest groups, and even determining what is or is not ethical behavior for themselves.

- Spending too much money on themselves, including expenditures for state legislative operations, which cost taxpayers nationwide about $2 billion a year. In most states lawmaking expenditures *per legislator* run in excess of $100,000; in larger states these expenditures run in excess of $500,000 (and the California legislature spends $1.5 million for each of its members).

- Providing themselves with excessive perks of office, including per diem allowances, travel expenses, office staff, and retirement and insurance benefits. The media focus on salaries, but what they fail to report are the fringe benefits legislators provide themselves. These may double or triple overall compensation.

- Dramatically increasing their spending on legislative campaigns, and the heavy advantage that incumbents have over challengers in raising money.

- Generally failing to pass or enforce stringent campaign financing laws, including reporting requirements, which seldom result in any media coverage prior to the election. Even where campaign finance laws are reasonably written, the typical state enforcement agency has little funding, staffing, or authority for enforcement.

- Generally failing to pass or enforce laws regulating ethics and financial disclosure of personal assets. (Legislators themselves generally believe that detailed personal financial disclosure laws are an invasion of privacy, and that strengthening such laws will drive quality people away from serving in the legislature.) Although lobbying activities are more or less regulated in all fifty states (including registration of lobbyists and reporting of their direct lobbying expenditures), states are generally lax about enforcing these requirements of placing limits on lobbying activity.[107]

But it is not certain that handing over these responsibilities to neutral and independent commissions—redistricting commissions, ethics commissions, compensation commissions, campaign finance commissions, lobby regulation commissions, and so on—would resolve all of these problems or restore public confidence in state legislatures. After all, state legislators often play a key role in appointing members to these commissions. But the desire to improve the representativeness and responsiveness of state legislatures is motivation enough for the ever-vigilant reformers.

Each state's governmental home page provides a direct link to the state legislature. (See "On the Web," Chapter 3.) These state legislative pages usually include information on the current legislative session, access to bill monitoring, and biographical information on each member of the legislature.

Here are some other very useful sites:

www.ncsl.org

The National Conference of State Legislatures is the best source of comparative information on state legislatures. The site includes schedules of all state legislative sessions in the nation, the partisan composition of each state's House and Senate, and a brief overview of key issues currently confronting state legislatures.

www.rci.rutgers.edu/~cawp

The Center for the Study of Women in Politics at Rutgers University is an important source of information on women in both legislative and executive offices in the states. Included in the information found at this site is a count of women in each state's legislature, along with information on the number of women in state legislative leadership posts.

www.nbcsl.com

The official site of the National Black Caucus of State Legislators; includes access to NBCSL magazine, *The Legislator*.

www.nhcsl.org

The official site of the National Hispanic Caucus of State Legislators; provides excellent links to major Hispanic organizations; highlights policy position papers.

www.ncsl.org/wln

The Women's Legislative Network of NCSL site provides information on women in state legislatures—totals, women legislative leaders, women legislators in the news, along with policy updates and publications aimed at improving women's legislative skills.

www.alldc.org

Home site of the American League of Lobbyists, established in 1979; provides access to the League's Lobbyists' Code of Ethics, and provides general information on lobbying registration, hiring a lobbyist, and lobbying as a career.

www.publicintegrity.org/hiredguns

Reports total amount of spending by lobbyists in each state; ranks states by their lobby spending, identifies state loopholes, and provides access to reports by the Center for Public Integrity.

www.redistrictinggame.com:80/

Redistricting game that calls for users to draw districts with challenges like bipartisan districts, those consistent with the Voting Rights Act, and more.

GOVERNORS IN STATE POLITICS

7

THE MANY ROLES OF A GOVERNOR

Governors are central figures in American state politics. People are more likely to be able to recall their governor's name than the name of any public official other than the president and vice president of the United States. In the eyes of many citizens, governors are responsible for everything that happens in their states during their terms of office, whether or not they have the authority or the capacity to do anything about it. Governors are expected to bring industry and jobs into their states, prevent prison riots, raise teachers' salaries, keep taxes low, see that the state gets its fair share of grant money from Washington, provide disaster relief, and bring tourists into the state. Governors offer reassurance to citizens during crises and disasters—everything from floods, hurricanes, fires, and droughts, to toxic waste spills, nuclear plant accidents, and acts of terrorism. These public expectations far exceed the **formal powers** of governors spelled out in the state constitution or in state statutes.

Formal powers are just one-half of the formula to gauge gubernatorial power. **Informal powers** are the other half. They are a bit more difficult to measure because they are more intangible and are uniquely personal. A governor's popularity, charisma, ability to generate positive media attention, path-breaker status (gender, race/ethnicity, age, party), unusual occupation, atypical political career progression, famous relatives, designation as a potential presidential candidate, or the crisis situation under which he or she took office are but a few sources of power. And of course, what voters in one state find appealing and enduring may have the opposite effect in another because the states are so different in their makeup and politics. For example, South Carolinians could identify with *their* governor when he "carried two squealing piglets into the Statehouse to make a point against pork" . . . and "brought a horse and buggy to the Statehouse entrance to argue against South Carolina's outmoded system of governance."[1] But it is doubtful that New Yorkers would have reacted the same way if *their* governor had used similar tactics. Political scientists agree that "the dynamics of gubernatorial approval are highly idiosyncratic."[2]

In many ways the expectations placed upon the governor resemble those placed upon the president, which isn't all that surprising since both are elected chief executives. Like the president, governors are expected to be their state's chief administrator, chief legislator, leader of their party, ceremonial head of their government, chief ambassador to other governments, leader of public opinion, and chief crisis manager.

> *People are more likely to be able to recall their governor's name than the name of any public official other than the president and vice president of the United States.*

Chief Administrator

As *chief administrator*, the governor must try to coordinate the state's bureaucracy, oversee the preparation of the state's budget, and supervise major state programs. Governors must resolve conflicts within their administrations and troubleshoot where difficulties arise. They must be concerned with scandal and endeavor to prevent it from becoming public, or act decisively to eliminate it if it does. The public will hold them responsible for any scandal in their administration, whether they were a party to it or not. The public will hold them responsible for the financial structure of the state, whether it was they or their predecessors who were responsible for the state's fiscal troubles. And the voters will blame the governor if an appointee has to be removed as head of an agency for incompetence or corruption.

Yet, as we shall see in this chapter, the formal administrative powers of a governor are severely restricted. Many of the governor's administrative agencies are headed by

FORMAL POWERS
Gubernatorial authority established in state statutes or a state constitution; a governor's tenure potential, appointment, budget and veto powers, and party control.

INFORMAL POWERS
A governor's strength stemming from personal attributes or unusual circumstances.

elected officials or independent boards or commissions, over which the governor has little or no control. Governors' powers of appointment and removal are severely restricted by state constitutions. Governors do not have control over their administration that is commensurate with their responsibility for it.

Chief Legislator

As *chief legislator*, the governor is responsible for initiating major statewide legislative programs. There is a general public expectation that every governor will put forward some sort of legislative program. By sending bills to the legislature, governors are cast in the role of the "initiator" of public policy decisions. If they want to see their legislative proposals enacted into law, they must also persuade legislators to support them. In other words, they must involve themselves directly in legislative decisions.

The **veto power** gives the governor bargaining power with the legislature. Few vetoes are overridden; in most states a two-thirds majority vote in both houses is required to override a veto. This means a governor needs only one-third plus one in either house to sustain his or her veto. So even the *threat* of a veto can force changes in a bill under consideration in the legislature. Moreover, in most states, the governor possesses the **line item veto,** allowing the governor to veto specific items in an appropriations bill, including legislators' home district **"pork" or "turkeys."** The threat of vetoing these vote-winning projects gives the governor additional bargaining power with legislators. A governor can also call special sessions of the legislature, allowing the governor to spotlight specific issues and pressure the legislature to do something about them.

Party Leader

Traditionally governors were regarded as the head of their party in the state.[3] But governors do not have the power to deny party nominations to recalcitrant legislators of their own party. Party nominations are won independently by legislators in primary elections held in their own districts. Governors have no formal disciplinary powers over members of their own party. And governors may choose to emphasize their own independence from their national party to further their own electoral ambitions.

However, within the legislature, parties still count. The governor usually receives greater support for his or her program from members of his or her own party. Legislators who run for office under the same party label as the governor have a stake in his or her success. Since all who run under the party's label share its common fortunes, and since its fortunes are often governed by the strength of its gubernatorial candidate, there will always be a tendency for loyal party members to support their governor. The organization of the legislature along party lines reinforces the party role of the governor. Legislative leaders of the governor's party—whether in the majority or minority— are expected to support the governor's program. (When they don't, it makes big news and the governor is cast as "weak," even though these leaders may have their eyes on the governor's chair. This happens most when governors are lame ducks.)

Ceremonial Head

Ceremonial duties occupy a great deal of a governor's time—signing bills, welcoming delegates attending professional association conventions held in their state, meeting with school children visiting the state capitol, and, of course, representing their state at important events held nationally and internationally. A governor may not be able to mobilize the symbolic and ceremonial power of the office on behalf of state goals in the

VETO POWER

Rejection of proposed legislation by the chief executive (governor), usually subject to legislative override by a two-thirds vote of both houses.

LINE ITEM VETO

The power of a governor to reject certain portions of a legislative appropriations bill without killing the entire bill.

"PORK" OR "TURKEYS"

Pet projects in the budget that will benefit an individual legislator's district but not any others; often vetoed by a governor.

same way that the president can mobilize the power of that office on behalf of national goals. Nonetheless, the skillful use of symbols and ceremonies can add to a governor's prestige and popularity. These assets can in turn contribute to political power.

Chief Negotiator

The governor is the *chief negotiator* with other governments in the American federal system, a variation of the diplomatic role of the president. Governors must negotiate with their local governments on the division of state and local responsibilities for public programs, and with other state governments over coordinating highway development, water pollution, resource conservation, and reciprocity in state laws. Governors must undertake responsibility for negotiation with the national government as well. The governor shares responsibility with the state's United States senators in seeing to it that the state receives a "fair share" of federal contracts, highway monies, educational monies, poverty funds, doesn't lose key military bases when the Pentagon proposes to close bases, and so on.

Opinion Leader

Governors are *leaders of public opinion* in their states. They are the most visible of state officials. Their comments on public affairs make news, and they are sought after for television, radio, and public appearances. They are able to focus public opinion on issues they deem important. They may not always be able to win public opinion to their side, but at least they will be seen and heard.

A governor's performance in a crisis may determine his or her standing with the public.

Crisis Manager

Finally, governors may be called upon to *manage crises* in their states—hurricanes, floods, droughts, mudslides, tornadoes, blizzards, civil disorders, collapsing infrastructure, and other disasters. Indeed, a governor's performance in a crisis may determine his or her standing with the public.

THE MAKING OF A GOVERNOR

As the central position in American state politics, the governorship is a much sought-after office. The prestige of being called "governor" for the rest of one's life, and the opportunity to use the office as a stepping-stone to the United States Senate, or even the presidency or vice presidency of the United States, is extremely attractive to people of ambition in American politics.

Varieties of Background

Historically, many governors were the sons of families of great wealth, who chose public service as an outlet for their energies—the Roosevelts, the Harrimans, the Rockefellers, the Scrantons, and, more recently, the Bushes. Others, particularly the old-time southern governors, were men who emphasized, or exaggerated, their humble beginnings—Huey Long of Louisiana, "Big Jim" Folsom of Alabama, "Pitchfork Ben" Tillman of South Carolina, "Old Gene" Talmadge of Georgia. The southern "populist" governors, however, were gradually replaced by more moderate and better-educated men—Bob Graham of Florida, Bill Clinton of Arkansas, and Jimmy Carter of Georgia. George C. Wallace of Alabama may have been the last governor in the true populist tradition.

Deval L. Patrick: From Tenement House to Governor

In 2006, Deval Patrick became the first African American elected governor of Massachusetts and the second African American ever elected governor in U.S. history. (The first was Virginia Governor Douglas Wilder, who was elected in 1989.) Patrick won in a state which is only 6 percent black and has a history of racial problems. His background and message appealed to white liberals (a sizable portion of the Massachusetts electorate). Voting for him also gave many the feeling that they were making history in the process.

Patrick's story began on the South Side of Chicago in a welfare family (headed by a single mother), living in a two-bedroom tenement. While only 14 and still in middle school, Patrick was identified by A Better Chance, a national nonprofit organization that identifies and develops leaders among academically gifted African American students. He received a full scholarship to the private prestigious prep school, Milton Academy, in Massachusetts. He graduated from Milton in 1974 and from Harvard College in 1978 with a major in English literature. He spent a year working with the United Nations in Africa and then went on to Harvard Law School.

Following law school, Patrick worked briefly with the NAACP Legal Defense and later joined a Boston law firm. In 1994, President Bill Clinton appointed Patrick Assistant Attorney General for Civil Rights, the nation's top civil rights post. In that post, Patrick cites his work on hate crimes and abortion clinic violence, employment discrimination, the enforcement of fair lending laws, and the investigation of church bombings in the South. In 1997, he left his post in the Justice Department to return to private practice. He subsequently joined the Board of Directors of Texaco and became vice president and general counsel for the Coca-Cola Company.

The battle to replace Republican Mitt Romney as Massachusetts governor was fierce. Patrick began his quest for office in the quarrelsome Democratic primary in late 2005, where he faced two veteran Massachusetts politicians. Patrick won 49 percent of the vote and became his party's nominee in a four-way race in the general election in 2006. Patrick went on to defeat the Republican, Independent, and Green party candidates, winning 56 percent of the vote.

As governor, Patrick has led the fight for the recognition of same-sex marriage, opposed reinstating the death penalty, supported the expansion of the state's health care system, supported state investment in stem cell research, and favored the provision of state services for illegal immigrants. He acknowledged an early mistake in contacting Citigroup chairman and former Treasury Secretary Robert Rubin on behalf of a mortgage company of which Patrick had been a board member. "I appreciate that I should not have made the call. I regret the mistake." And some of his supporters became critical when he submitted his first state budget and it failed to live up to his many promises to aid communities and lower income residents. But Patrick pledges his governorship to his "grassroots message of hope, community, and hard work."

Many see Patrick as exemplary of the new generation of successful black politicians. "Raised in the post-civil rights era, they attended elite schools, built coalitions of white and black supporters, and cast themselves as agents of change."[a]

[a]Based on Alec MacGillis and Perry Bacon, Jr. "Obama Rises in New Era of Black Politicians," *Washington Post*, July 28, 2007, p. A01.

Governors have been movie actors (Ronald Reagan of California), restaurant owners (Lester Maddox of Georgia), truck drivers (Harold Hughes of Iowa), country music singers (Jimmie Davis of Louisiana, who wrote "You Are My Sunshine"), and wrestlers (Jesse "The Body" Ventura of Minnesota). However, the majority of governors have been *lawyers* by profession.

The occupations of twenty-first-century women governors, while equally diverse, are not as colorful: law (Janet Napolitano—Arizona, Jennifer Granholm—Michigan; Christine Gregoire—Washington), small business owners (Ruth Ann Minner—Delaware, a towing business; Judy Martz—Montana, a garbage disposal service), journalism (Linda Lingle—Hawaii), public school teacher (Kathleen Babineaux Blanco—Louisiana; Jeanne Shaheen—New Hampshire); campaign professional (Christine Todd Whitman), and homemakers (Jodi Rell—Connecticut; Kathleen Sibelius—Kansas). However, for women, their occupations are far less interesting or unique than their "*path-breaker*" status: first woman to be elected governor in their state.

The first independent candidate to win a governorship in modern history was James B. Longley of Maine; he has been followed by independent mavericks Walter Hickel of Alaska, Lowell Weicker of Connecticut, Angus King of Maine, and Jesse Ventura of Minnesota. Independent and third party candidates are most likely to enter a governor's race when they perceive there is little difference ideologically or on issues between the major party candidates.[4]

Age

Television has accented youth and good looks among state governors. It helps "image-wise" to be tall, slim, attractive, fashionable, and smiling. The median beginning age of governors has declined over the last few decades to a youngish forty-seven. Bill Clinton became the nation's youngest governor when he won that post in Arkansas in 1978 at age thirty-two. Most current governors, on average, are in their mid-fifties.

Governors are getting younger. Alaska Governor Sarah Palin (R), the state's first female governor, was 42 when first elected. In college, she majored in communications-journalism which undoubtedly gave her a clear understanding of how to effectively use television as a campaign tool.

Race/Ethnicity

Until Democrat Douglas Wilder's successful run for the Virginia statehouse in 1989, no state had ever elected a black governor. Democrat Deval Patrick became the nation's second African-American governor when elected by Massachusetts voters in 2006. Several Hispanics have been elected governor: Democrat Jerry Abodaca of New Mexico, Democrat Raul Castro of Arizona, Demo-crat Toney Anaya of New Mexico, Republican Bob Martinez of Florida, and, more recently, Democrat Bill Richardson of New Mexico. Asian-American Democrat Gary Locke served as Washington State's governor from 1997 to 2005. (For a list of African Americans, Hispanics, and Asian Americans elected governor, see Table 7–1.)

TABLE 7–1 Minority and Women Governors

Governor	State	Served as Governor
Asian American Governors		
George Ariyoshi (D)	Hawaii	1974–1986
John Waihee (D)	Hawaii	1986–1995
Benjamin Cayetano (D)	Hawaii	Jan. 1995–Dec. 2002
Gary Locke (D)	Washington	Jan. 1997–Jan. 2005
African American Governors		
Pinckney Benton Stewart Pinchback (R)	Louisiana	Dec. 1872–Jan. 1873
L. Douglas Wilder (D)	Virginia	Jan. 1990–Jan. 1994
Deval Patrick (D)	Massachusetts	Jan. 2007–present
Hispanic Governors		
Raul H. Castro (D)	Arizona	Jan. 1975–Jan. 1977
Toney Anaya (D)	New Mexico	Jan. 1983–Jan. 1987
Robert Martinez (R)	Florida	Jan. 1987–Jan. 1991
Bill Richardson (D)	New Mexico	Jan. 2003–present
Female Governors		
Nellie Tayloe Ross (D)[a]	Wyoming	Jan. 1925–1927
Miriam Amanda Ferguson (D)[b]	Texas	Jan. 1925–1927; Jan. 1933–1935
Lurleen Burns Wallace (D)[c]	Alabama	Jan. 1967–1968
Ella Grasso (D)[d]	Connecticut	Jan. 1975–1980
Dixy Lee Ray (D)	Washington	Jan. 1977–1981
Vesta M. Roy (R)[e]	New Hampshire	Dec. 1982–Jan. 1983
Martha Layne Collins (D)	Kentucky	Dec. 1983–1987
Madeleine M. Kunin (D)	Vermont	Jan. 1985–1991
Kay A. Orr (R)	Nebraska	Jan. 1987–Jan. 1991
Rose Mofford (D)[f]	Arizona	April 1988–Jan. 1991
Joan Finney (D)	Kansas	Jan. 1991–Jan. 1995
Barbara Roberts (D)	Oregon	Jan. 1991–Jan. 1995
Ann W. Richards (D)	Texas	Jan. 1991–Jan. 1995
Christine T. Whitman (R)	New Jersey	Jan. 1994–Jan. 2001
Nancy P. Hollister (R)[g]	Ohio	Dec. 31, 1998–Jan. 11, 1999
Jane Dee Hull (R)[h]	Arizona	Sep. 1997–Jan. 2003
Jeanne Shaheen (D)	New Hampshire	Jan. 1997–Jan. 2003
Jane Swift (R)[i]	Massachusetts	April 2001–Jan. 2003
Ruth Ann Minner (D)	Delaware	Jan. 2001–present
Judy Martz (R)	Montana	Jan. 2001–Jan. 2005
Sila M. Calderón (D)	Puerto Rico	Jan. 2001–Jan. 2005
Linda Lingle (R)	Hawaii	Dec. 2002–present

(*continued*)

TABLE 7–1 (Continued)

Governor	State	Served as Governor
Janet Napolitano (D)	Arizona	Jan. 2003–present
Kathleen Sebelius (D)	Kansas	Jan. 2003–present
Jennifer Granholm (D)	Michigan	Jan. 2003–present
Olene S. Walker (R)[j]	Utah	Nov. 2003–Jan. 2005
Kathleen Blanco (D)	Louisiana	Jan. 2004–Jan. 2008
M. Jodi Rell (R)[k]	Connecticut	July 2004–present
Christine Gregoire (D)	Washington	Jan. 2005–present
Sarah Palin (R)	Alaska	Dec. 2006–present

Asian-American Notes: Gov. Waihee was the first elected governor of Hawaiian ancestry. Gov. Gary Locke (D) of Washington, who was inaugurated in January 1997, was the first Asian American to be elected governor of a state in the forty-eight contiguous states. Hawaii Gov. Benjamin Cayetano (D) was elected in November 1994, becoming the first governor of Filipino ancestry in the United States.

African-American Notes: Gov. Pinchback served as governor for about one month, from December 1872 to January 1873. He was elected to the state senate in 1868 and served as president pro tempore and acting lieutenant governor from 1871 to 1872. He completed the term of Gov. Henry Clay Warmoth after Warmoth was impeached in December 1872. Pinchback was born May 10, 1837, and died in 1921. Gov. L. Douglas Wilder of Virginia (D) was the first elected black governor in the United States (excluding the commonwealths and territories).

Female Notes: [a]Gov. Ross succeeded her husband, who died in office.

[b]Gov. Ferguson succeeded her husband who died in office.

[c]Gov. Wallace succeeded her husband, who was not eligible to seek re-election.

[d]Gov. Grasso was the first woman elected in her own right.

[e]Vesta M. Roy, as State Senate President, succeeded to office after Gov. Hugh J. Gallen passed away.

[f]Gov. Mofford, as secretary of state, became acting governor on February 8, 1988, and became governor on April 5, 1988. She did not run for re-election in 1990.

[g]Gov. Hollister, as lieutenant governor, became governor on Dec. 31, 1998, when Gov. George V. Voinovich stepped down to serve in the U.S. Congress. She served the remainder of Gov. Voinovich's term until Jan. 11, when Gov. Bob Taft was sworn in.

[h]Gov. Hull, as secretary of state, became governor in September 1997 after Gov. Fife Symington resigned.

[i]Lieutenant Gov. Jane Swift succeeded Gov. Argeo Paul Celluci, who was appointed as an ambassador to Canada. Swift is also the first governor to give birth while serving her term of office.

[j]Gov. Walker, as lieutenant governor, became Utah's first female governor on November 5, 2003, after Gov. Michael Leavitt was appointed as Administrator of the Environmental Protection Agency.

[k]Gov. Rell, as lieutenant governor, became governor on July 1, 2004, following the resignation of Gov. John Rowland.

Sources: Available at: http://www.nga.org/governors/1,1169,C_TRIVIA^D_2119,00.html,

http://www.nga.org/governors/1,1169,C_TRIVIA^D_2118,00.html,

http://www.nga.org/governors/1,1169,C_SEARCH_GOV,00.html,

http://www.nga.org/governors/1,1169,C_TRIVIA^D_2117,00.html.

http://www.cawp.rutgers.edu/Facts/Officeholders/govhistory.pdf

Gender

Over thirty women have served as governor or acting governor in U.S. history. (See Table 7–1.) Prior to 1974, only three women had *ever* served as governor of a U.S. state, and all three succeeded their husbands in office—Nellie Ross of Wyoming and Miriam "Ma" Ferguson of Texas in the 1920s, and Lurleen Wallace of Alabama in the 1960s. In 1974, Ella T. Grasso of Connecticut became the first woman governor whose husband had not previously held the office. Later that same year, Dixy Lee Ray of Washington accomplished the same feat. Martha Collins was elected governor of Kentucky in 1983; Kay Orr won the governorship of Nebraska in 1986; and Madeleine Kunin won the office in Vermont that same year. Democrat Ann Richards's hard-fought victory in the Texas governor's race in 1990 demonstrated that women can triumph in rough, bitter personal campaigns. (Richards then lost to George W. Bush, the former president's son, in 1994.) Christine Whitman (R-New Jersey) served two terms as governor of her state before being named by President George W. Bush to head the U.S. Environmental Protection Agency.

Since then, the number of women running for and winning the state's top executive post has been climbing as more women hold positions that are seen as excellent training grounds. Political scientists have found that the public is impressed with governors who have experience in local elective offices, statewide executive posts, agency administration, and law enforcement.[5] A sizeable number of the current women governors have been mayors or county commissioners, state agency directors, lieutenant governors, attorneys general, and/or chairs of statewide boards and commissions.

Arizona governor Janet Napolitano (D), a lawyer, is the first female governor to succeed a woman governor. Napolitano succeeded Republican Governor Jane Hull. Here Governor Napolitano meets with young Apache constituents while attending the White Mountain Apache Rodeo and Fair at Whiteriver.

Political Experience

Governors usually come to their office with considerable experience in public affairs. Only about 14 percent come into the governor's chair without prior officeholding. The number has escalated as more independently wealthy candidates make a run, often promising to make government run more like a business and to wrest state government from the hands of the "professional politicians." But the more common, well-worn paths are from a statewide elective office—lieutenant governor and attorney general, especially—or from a state legislative office. More Congress members (U.S. Senators and U.S. Representatives) are choosing to come back home to run for governor, especially those from the South and Northeast.[6] Many interviews with current and past governors all seem to come to the same conclusion: They believe the governor's job is the best one in politics—an indication of the power and prestige of the office of governor more than the salary. Some, like Arnold Schwarzenegger, donate their salaries back to the state while others fight a pay raise if one is proposed. (California's governor is the highest paid at $206,500; the lowest is Maine's at $70,000. But it often takes millions to win the office.)

GUBERNATORIAL POLITICS

State governors appear to be gaining political strength within their states and in national politics. Governors are receiving more media attention, undertaking more initiatives in policies and programs, winning more legislative battles, and even acquiring more national political clout. More governors have ascended to the presidency than U.S. senators (see "*Did You Know? How Many Governors Later Became President?*" at the end of this chapter). Consequently, the national media are always interested in covering "governors who might become president."

Competition

Competition is usually strong, both in primary and general elections, for the governorship. Indeed, competition for the job has been increasing over time, especially in the southern states where Republican candidates now have an equal chance of winning governorships. Yet traditionally the Democratic party has dominated state gubernatorial politics. In 1994, for the first time in thirty years Republican governors (thirty) outnumbered Democratic governors (nineteen), and Republican governors continued to outnumber Democratic governors until 2006. (See Figure 5–1 in Chapter 5.)

Getting Elected

What forces influence the outcome of gubernatorial elections? Are gubernatorial elections affected by national voting trends—"**coattails**"? Or are they more affected by conditions within the states, especially the performance of the state's economy? Or are gubernatorial elections primarily "**candidate centered**"—influenced mostly by the personal qualities of the candidates, their handling of state issues, the strength of their own political organizations, and their success in fundraising and campaigning?

Gubernatorial Vote Choice

If voters are asked "What mattered most in voting for governor?," they cite personal leadership qualities of the candidate more often than anything else. Party affiliation and agreement on issues follow in importance. Negative voting—dislike of the opponent—also plays a significant role in gubernatorial voting.

Governors are better known to the voters than any other state officials or even U.S. senators and House members. Governors receive more media attention than any other state official. However, this does not always guarantee that governors will be liked better than other elected officeholders.

Voters do not usually hold a governor solely responsible for economic problems confronting the state, unless they perceive the problems were caused by specific taxing or spending decisions recommended by the governor. Most voters recognize that state economic conditions depend more on national market factors, or on the actions of the national government, including the president, than on the governor.[7] State (or local) officials may be held responsible for actions that make an already weak economy worse; voters may expect a governor to do all that he or she can to ameliorate hard times. And there is some evidence that the popularity of governors is linked to unemployment rates in their states, even though there is little that governors can do to reduce unemployment.[8] It is true that governors emphasize economic, or "**pocketbook," issues** more than twice as much as social issues in their annual state-of-the-state addresses to their citizens.[9]

While presidential and congressional elections are influenced by national economic conditions (recessions adversely affect the vote for candidates of the party in power, while prosperity generally helps), the national economy is less influential in state legislative or gubernatorial elections. "Voters in state elections appear to hold politicians outside of the state, specifically the president and the president's party, responsible for economic conditions, and if conditions in a state should differ from those in neighboring states, to hold the governor only minimally responsible."[10]

COATTAILS

In politics, a reference to the effect that a party's leader may have on voting for that party's candidates for other offices.

CANDIDATE-CENTERED ELECTION

Refers to an election primarily focusing on the personal qualities of the candidates.

POCKETBOOK ISSUES

Those affecting a voter's wallet; economic issues.

Coattail Effects

There are some coattail effects in state gubernatorial and legislative elections. Gubernatorial candidates running on the same party ticket as popular presidential candidates enjoy a significant advantage. But most gubernatorial elections are held in "**off years**"—years in which the nation is not electing a president. Off-year elections are deliberately designed to minimize the effects of presidential voting trends on state governors' elections. Nonetheless, there is some evidence that the electoral fate of gubernatorial candidates is affected by the popularity of the president. Gubernatorial candidates of the president's party attract more votes when the president's popularity in opinion polls is high. This is true whether the candidates are incumbents or aspirants.[11] Conversely, gubernatorial candidates of the president's party suffer when the president's popularity is low. Insofar as a president's popularity is affected by national economic trends, gubernatorial candidates of the president's party can suffer from national recessions and benefit from national prosperity.

OFF-YEAR ELECTIONS
Usually refers to an election not in the same year as a presidential election.

Candidate Effects

Despite these coattail effects, gubernatorial elections are mostly candidate centered. Governors are less closely tied to national policy issues than members of Congress; governors are seldom called upon by the media to explain their votes in support or opposition to the president's policy positions. The outcome of gubernatorial elections depends mostly on the personal qualities of the candidates, their ability to associate themselves with popular issues, the strength of their personal political organizations, their ability to raise campaign funds, and their skills in campaigning.

The popularity of the incumbent governor has a significant effect on voters' decisions, not only with respect to reelecting the incumbent but also electing the candidate of the incumbent's party when the incumbent is not running for reelection.[12] Unpopular lame duck governors often spell trouble for his or her party's gubernatorial candidate in the general election. Nothing makes a governor more unpopular than people out of jobs. Some scholars have found that a state's unemployment rate is a better gauge of gubernatorial popularity than more political matters.[13]

Campaign Issues

Even though most gubernatorial elections are candidate centered, the candidates are obliged to talk about issues. The cynical stereotype is a candidate who polls the state and then proclaims the most popular positions as his own. But the selection of issues on which to campaign is a little more complicated than that. Candidates who change their positions based on polls can be accused of "flip-flopping" and some candidates prefer to remain true to their beliefs. So instead, candidates focus on issues on which they are in a favorable position vis-à-vis the electorate. They ignore those on which they are in disagreement with poll results. Campaigns consciously seek to highlight issues on which the candidate is well positioned (or the opponent is poorly positioned) relative to the voters' preferences. Setting the campaign issue agenda is often the key to victory.[14] Debates and candidate forums play a big part in forcing the candidates to constantly fine-tune their positions or reprioritize their issues.

In recent years the overall success rate for incumbent governors seeking re-election has averaged about 75 percent.

Re-election

Incumbent governors who seek reelection are usually successful. In primary elections, incumbent governors usually face *little* serious opposition.[15] In recent years the overall success rate for incumbent governors seeking re-election has averaged about 75 percent. However, governors are somewhat more vulnerable to defeat than U.S. senators (whose re-election rate is 85 percent) or House members (whose re-election rate is over 90 percent).[16] Occasionally governors are defeated, more often in the general election than in their own party primary, and it is interesting to try to understand these failures.

Political folklore includes the belief that any governor who raises taxes during his or her term will be defeated for re-election. But a careful study of this notion shows only a weak connection between tax increases and electoral defeat for governors.[17] Most governors who raise taxes and then seek re-election are successful, especially if the taxes are on tobacco products. Frequently, however, those who are defeated *blame* their loss on raising taxes. But more often than not, when taxes are the key issue bringing down an incumbent, it is because of the governor's refusal to get rid of an unpopular fee or tax, like a car tag tax.

Campaigning

Modern gubernatorial campaigns are quite professional: They usually involve high-powered public relations organizations, experienced mass media and television advertising firms, professional polling and political consultants, and sophisticated direct mail and fundraising techniques. (See "Professional Media Campaigns" in Chapter 5.) Until recently, party organizations and amateur volunteers have played a very limited role in most gubernatorial campaigns in the states. Now state-level campaigns are patterned after presidential campaigns. Both political parties rely upon thousands of citizen volunteers to mobilize voters and virtually act as "hometown" surrogates for the candidates who simply cannot physically visit every community. Candidates for governor still do the traditional barnstorming, stump-speaking, hand-shaking, and door-to-door canvassing campaigns, but by necessity they must rely more on media-based campaigns than on in-person interactions with voters. And media-based campaigns aren't cheap. Of course, campaign themes and candidate "images" must be tailored to a state's political culture and tradition.

Money

Modern mass media campaigns—with professional media advertising, opinion polls, direct mail persuasion, and political consultants—are very costly. Today a typical gubernatorial campaign costs $5 million to $10 million in small states and $25 million to $50 million or more in the larger states. But it can be over $100 million in big states with lots of expensive media markets. Television advertising, polling, and precisely targeted direct mail are the major reasons for increased costs, not to mention population growth. But so is greater competition at both the primary and general election stages. Candidates for governor have spent anywhere from $3 to nearly $50 *per vote*. Costs per vote seem to be highest when there is an open seat (no incumbent running) or when an unpopular incumbent is running for reelection (and loses)—high turnout scenarios. "Hotly contested, high-spending" gubernatorial campaigns can increase voter turnout.[18]

Although money cannot buy a governorship, it is important to realize that (1) no one can mount a serious gubernatorial campaign without either personal wealth or strong financial backing by others, and (2) the heavier-spending candidate wins in two out of three elections. Most states require public reporting of campaign contributions and expenditures, and most states place limits on contributions by individuals and groups (although research shows these limits do not hold down overall spending).[19]

Nonetheless, individuals and independent advocacy groups ("527s") can spend what they wish in order to express their personal political preferences separate from official campaigns; fundraising political action committees (PACs) can multiply in number; and wealthy candidates can spend as much of their own money as they wish on their own campaigns. (See Chapter 5.)

Political Ambitions

About one-third of the nation's presidents have been chosen from among the ranks of America's state governors, particularly the governors of the larger states. (See *Did You Know?* How Many Governors Later Became President?) During the Cold War, the importance of international affairs in American politics detracted somewhat from the popular image of the governorship as the stepping-stone to the presidency. Governors tend to be associated with domestic rather than foreign policy questions. Men such as Truman, Nixon, McGovern, Humphrey, Kennedy, Goldwater, and Johnson found the United States Senate a good place to promote their campaigns for vice-presidential and presidential nominations. For a while, scholars attributed the decline in the number of governors selected as presidential candidates to a general decline in the popularity of governors. But in recent years, distrust of "the government in Washington" and the low esteem of Congress in the eyes of the general public have improved the presidential fortunes of governors.

EXECUTIVE POWER IN STATE GOVERNMENT

Frequently we speak of "strong" and "weak" governors. Yet it is difficult to compare the power of one governor with that of another. To do so, we must examine their *formal, or institutional powers*—the constitutional position of governors relative to others, their powers of appointment and removal over state officials, their ability or inability to succeed themselves, their powers over the state budget, their veto powers, and their position in their own party and its position in state politics. But we must also measure their personal, or informal, powers—their margin of victory over their opponent, political career progression, personal ambitions, and influence over public opinion in the state.[20]

Governors, Weak and Strong

In many ways the organization of American state government resembles political thinking of earlier historical eras. Jacksonian "popular democracy" brought with it the idea that the way to ensure popular control of state government was to elect separately as many state officials as possible. The Reform movement of the late nineteenth and early twentieth centuries led to merit systems and civil service boards, which further curtailed the governor's power of appointment. Many important state offices are governed by boards or commissions whose members may be appointed by the governor with the consent of the state senate but for long overlapping terms, which reduces the governor's influence over members of these boards and commissions. Not all of these trends were experienced uniformly by all fifty states, and there are considerable variations from state to state in the powers that governors have over the state executive branch. Today there are over 300 separately elected executive branch officials in the fifty states. Ten states also elect members of various other multimember boards, commissions, or councils.[21] Only Maine, New Hampshire, New Jersey, and Tennessee have a single statewide elected official, the

TABLE 7–2 Elected Executive Officials in the States

Office	Number of States Electing
Governor	50
Lieutenant governor	47*
Attorney general	43
Treasurer	37
Secretary of state	35
Auditor	23
Comptroller	14
Education (superintendent or board)	13
Secretary of agriculture	13
Insurance commissioner	10
Public utilities commissioner	7
Labor commissioner	4
Adjutant general (National Guard)	2

Note: Data are for 2007.

*Includes New Jersey Lieutenant governor elections, which begin in 2009.

Source: *The Book of the States*, 2007, Vol. 39, various tables pp. 181–186, 196, 207, 217, 227, 242–243.

governor. The others must share at least some executive authority with other elected officials, effectively diluting some of their executive authority. (See Tables 7–2 and 7–3.)

Executive Reorganization

Modern public administration generally recommends a stronger governor and a more centralized state executive branch. Reform and reorganization proposals usually call for: (1) four-year terms for governors with the ability to succeed themselves; (2) the elimination of many separately elected state executive officials and limiting the statewide ballot to governor, lieutenant governor, and attorney general; (3) elimination of boards and commissions as heads of agencies and their replacement by single, removable gubernatorial appointees; and (4) the consolidation of many state agencies into larger departments reporting directly to the governor. However, states have been slow to adopt these reforms.

Political Opposition to Reorganization

Separately elected officials and independent boards and officials will be around for a long time. Political parties and public officials develop a stake in the continued existence of these elected offices. Moreover, many interest groups prefer to be governed by boards and commissions or separately elected officials. They feel they have more influence over these independent offices than those that come directly under a governor's authority. Interest groups, from educational administrators and teachers' unions, to the agriculture, insurance, real estate, and public utility industries, prefer to have direct access to executive officials. Incumbent officeholders are usually able to rally their client groups to defeat reorganization proposals that threaten their office.

(continued)

TABLE 7-3 Formal Powers of Governors

Governors' Institutional (Formal) Powers (Rankings for each power are reported in descending order; the party control rankings may change when new legislators are elected)

Separately Elected Executive Branch Officials		Tenure Potential		Appointment Powers		Budgetary Powers		Veto Powers		Party Control	
New Hampshire	5	Connecticut	5	Arizona	5	Maryland	4	Virginia	5	Montana	5
Alaska	5	Illinois	5	California	5	West Virginia	4	Alaska	5	Idaho	5
Hawaii	5	Iowa	5	Kentucky	5	Nebraska	4	Arizona	4	Alaska	5
Maine	5	Massachusetts	5	Pennsylvania	5	New York	4	California	4	Florida	5
New Jersey	5	Minnesota	5	Tennessee	5	New Hampshire	4	Colorado	3	Georgia	5
Tennessee	4.5	New York	4.5	West Virginia	5	Vermont	4	Delaware	3	Indiana	5
Colorado	4	North Dakota	4	Vermont	5	Virginia	3.5	Florida	3	Louisiana	5
Maryland	4	Texas	4	Virginia	5	Alabama	3.5	Georgia	3	Maine	5
Michigan	4	Utah	4	Alaska	5	Alaska	3.5	Hawaii	3	Missouri	5
Nebraska	4	Washington	4	Colorado	5	Arizona	3.5	Idaho	3	New Jersey	5
Ohio	4	Wisconsin	4	Delaware	5	Arkansas	3.5	Kansas	3	New Mexico	5
Pennsylvania	4	Alabama	4	Louisiana	4	California	3.5	Louisiana	3	North Carolina	5
Connecticut	4	Alaska	4	Maine	4	Colorado	3.5	Maryland	3	Ohio	5
Massachusetts	4	Arizona	4	Michigan	4	Delaware	3.5	Michigan	3	South Carolina	5
Minnesota	4	Arkansas	4	Nevada	4	Florida	3.5	Mississippi	3	South Dakota	5
New York	4	California	4	New Jersey	4	Georgia	3.5	Missouri	3	West Virginia	5
Utah	4	Colorado	4	North Carolina	4	Hawaii	3.5	Montana	3	Illinois	5
Florida	3	Delaware	3	Ohio	4	Idaho	3.5	Nebraska	3	North Dakota	5
Indiana	3	Florida	3	South Dakota	4	Indiana	3.5	New Jersey	3	Texas	5
Kansas	3	Georgia	3	Wyoming	4	Kansas	3.5	New Mexico	3	Utah	5
Kentucky	3	Hawaii	3	Massachusetts	4	Kentucky	3.5	Ohio	3	Washington	5
Montana	3	Idaho	3	New York	4	Louisiana	3.5	Oklahoma	3	Delaware	5
New Mexico	3	Indiana	3	North Dakota	4	Maine	3.5	Oregon	3	Kentucky	5
South Dakota	3	Kansas	3	Washington	4	Michigan	3.5	Pennsylvania	3	Nebraska	5
Illinois	3	Kentucky	3	New Hampshire	4	Mississippi	3	South Carolina	3	Nevada	5
Iowa	3	Louisiana	3	Alabama	4	Missouri	3	South Dakota	3	Oklahoma	5
Louisiana	3										

3.5(i)

TABLE 7-3 (Continued)

Governors' Institutional (Formal) Powers (Rankings for each power are reported in descending order; the party control rankings may change when new legislators are elected)

Separately Elected Executive Branch Officials	Tenure Potential	Appointment Powers	Budgetary Powers	Veto Powers	Party Control
North Dakota 3	Maine 4	Arkansas 4	Montana 3	West Virginia 3	Oregon 5
Wisconsin 3	Maryland 4	Kansas 4	Nevada 3	Wyoming 3	Tennessee 5
Vermont 2.5	Michigan 4	Missouri 4	New Jersey 3	Connecticut 3	Iowa 5
Virginia 2.5	Mississippi 4	Montana 4	New Mexico 3	Illinois 3	Minnesota 5
Arizona 2.5	Missouri 4	Nebraska 4	North Carolina 3	Iowa 3	New York 5
Arkansas 2.5	Montana 4	New Mexico 4	Ohio 3	Massachusetts 3	New Hampshire 2
Delaware 2.5	Nebraska 4	Oregon 4	Oklahoma 3	Minnesota 3	Vermont 2
Missouri 2.5	Nevada 4	Rhode Island 4	Oregon 3	New York 3	Virginia 2
Nevada 2.5	New Jersey 4	Illinois 4	Pennsylvania 3	North Dakota 3	Alabama 2
Rhode Island 2.5	New Mexico 4	Iowa 4	Rhode Island 3	Texas 3	Arizona 2
West Virginia 2.5	North Carolina 4	Utah 4	South Dakota 3	Utah 3	Arkansas 2
Idaho 2	Ohio 4	Florida 4	Tennessee 2.5	Washington 3	California 2
Oregon 2	Oklahoma 4	Hawaii 4	Wyoming 2.5	Wisconsin 3	Colorado 2
Wyoming 2	Oregon 4	Indiana 4	Connecticut 2.5	Alabama 3	Kansas 2
Texas 2	Wyoming 4	Maryland 4	Illinois 2.5	Arkansas 3	Maryland 2
Mississippi 1.5	Texas 4	Connecticut 4	Iowa 2.5	Kentucky 3	Michigan 2
Alabama 1	Pennsylvania 4	Minnesota 4	Massachusetts 2.5	Tennessee 3	Mississippi 2
California 1	Rhode Island 4	Georgia 4	Minnesota 2	New Hampshire 3	Pennsylvania 2
Georgia 1	South Carolina[a] 4	Idaho 4	North Dakota 2	Vermont 3	Connecticut 2
Louisiana 1	South Dakota 4	Mississippi 4	Utah 2	Indiana 3	Wisconsin 2
North Carolina 1	Tennessee 4	South Carolina 4	Washington 2	Maine 3	Hawaii 1
Oklahoma 1	West Virginia 4	Wisconsin 4	Wisconsin 2	Nevada 3	Rhode Island 1
South Carolina 1	Virginia 3	Oklahoma 2	South Carolina 1	North Carolina 2	Wyoming 1
Washington 1	New Hampshire 2	Texas 2	Texas 1	Rhode Island 2	Massachusetts 1
	Vermont 1				
50 = state average 2.9	50 = state average 4.1	50 = state average 4.1	50 = state average 3.1	50 = state average 3.1	50 = state average 4.5

TABLE 7-3 (Continued)

SEP—Separately elected executive branch officials: 5 = only governor or governor/lieutenant governor team elected; 4.5 = governor or governor/lieutenant governor team, with one other elected official; 4 = governor/lieutenant governor team with some process officials (attorney general, secretary of state, treasurer, auditor) elected; 3 = governor/lieutenant governor team with process officials, and some major and minor policy officials elected; 2.5 = governor (no team) with six or fewer officials elected, but none are major policy officials; 2 = governor (no team) with six or fewer officials elected, including one major policy official; 1.5 = governor (no team) with six or fewer officials elected, but two are major policy officials; 1 = governor (no team) with seven or more process and several major policy officials elected.

[*Source:* Council of State Governments CSG, *The Book of the States, 2003* (2003): 201–206].

TP—Tenure potential of governors; 5 = 4-year term, no restraint on re-election; 4.5 = 4-year term, only three terms permitted; 4 = 4-year term, only two terms permitted; 3 = 4-year term, no consecutive election permitted; 2 = 2-year term, no restraint on re-election; 1 = 2-year term, only two terms permitted.

[*Source:* CSG, *The Book of the States, 2003* (2003): 183–184].

AP—Governor's appointment powers in six major functional areas: corrections, K–12 education, health, highways/transportation, public utilities regulation, and welfare. The six individual office scores are totaled and then averaged and rounded to the nearest 0.5 for the state score. 5 = governor appoints, no other approval needed; 4 = governor appoints, a board, council or legislature approves; 3 = someone else appoints, governor approves or shares appointment; 2 = someone else appoints, governor and others approve; 1 = someone else appoints, no approval or confirmation needed.

[*Source:* CSG, *The Book of the States, 2003* (2003): 201–206].

BP—Governor's budget power: 5 = governor has full responsibility, legislature may not increase executive budget; 4 = governor has full responsibility, legislature can increase by special majority vote or subject to item veto; 3 = governor has full responsibility, legislature has unlimited power to change executive budget; 2 = governor shares responsibility, legislature has unlimited power to change executive budget; 1 = governor shares responsibility with other elected official, legislature has unlimited power to change executive budget.

[*Sources:* CSG, *The Book of the States, 2003* (2003): 188–189, 392–393, and NCSL, "Limits on Authority of Legislature to Change Budget" (1998).]

VP—Governor's veto power: 5 = governor has item veto and a special majority vote of the legislature is needed to override a veto (3/5's of legislators elected or two-thirds of legislators present); 4 = has item veto with a majority of the legislators elected needed to override; 3 = has item veto with only a majority of the legislators present needed to override; 2 = no item veto, with a special legislative majority needed to override a regular veto; 1 = no item veto, only a simple legislative majority needed to override a regular veto.

[*Source:* CSG, *The Book of the States 2003* (2003): 145–147, 188–189].

PC—Gubernatorial party control: The governor's party—5 = has a substantial majority (75% or more) in both houses of the legislature; 4 = has a simple majority in both houses (under 75%), or a substantial majority in one house and a simple majority in the other; 3 = split control in the legislature or a non-partisan legislature; 2 = has a simple minority (25% or more) in both houses, or a simple minority in one and a substantial minority (under 25%) in the other; 1 = has a substantial minority in both houses.

[*Source:* NCSL Web page and report on the 2003 legislative elections].

Total—sum of the scores on the six individual indices. Score—total divided by six to keep 5-point scale. [j] In December 2004, the Montana Supreme Court made a decision that evicted one State House member who was a Constitutionalist and then replaced that representative with a Democrat. That split the State House into a partisan tie with 50 Democrats and 50 Republicans. However, since the newly elected governor was a Democrat, the Democrats received the ability to organize the State House and were placed in the leadership positions. Hence the 3.5 rating on this index.

Note: Data are from 2005.

Source: Available at http://www.unc.edu/~beyle/tab7.5–InstPowers05.doc

Tenure Power

Another component of a governor's influence is the ability or inability to succeed him- or herself in office. Governors with the highest "tenure power" are those who are elected for a four-year term and are permitted to succeed themselves indefinitely—no term limits. (See Table 7–3.) Governors with the lowest "tenure power" are those who have only two-year terms. The Twenty-Second Amendment to the U.S. Constitution restricts executive tenure at the presidential level to two terms, and most states now have similar restrictions on their governors.

Managerial Powers

Governors are chief executives; they are supposed to manage state governmental bureaucracies. But aside from intervening occasionally in response to a crisis, governors generally turn over their management chores to others. Governors downplay their managerial role and avoid expending energy and power on management because "greater rewards derive from the pursuit of other functions—formulating policy, building popularity and support among the public, helping develop the state economy."[22]

Executive Orders

Managing in the state bureaucracy is generally left to the governor's staff and department heads (see Chapter 8). But from time to time governors directly intervene in well-publicized, politically sensitive executive decisions. Governors may do so by executive order—a special directive issued by the governor to one or more executive agencies. Executive orders must be based on state constitutional powers given governors or on powers delegated to them by state laws. Executive orders are often issued to deal with public emergencies or disasters, or political messes that require the suspension or removal of a public official.

Appointment Powers

Perhaps the most important managerial power is the power to appoint subordinate officials. Appointment of subordinates does not guarantee their responsibility, but there is a greater likelihood that an official appointed by a governor will be someone whose values coincide with those of the governor. If an agency head is separately elected by the people (as are most attorneys general, treasurers, and secretaries of state), then the governor has little direct control over them. If the governor can appoint an agency head *without* the need for legislative approval, we can say that the governor has stronger appointive powers than if legislative confirmation of appointment is required. Indeed, agency heads themselves tend to evaluate the governor's influence largely in terms of his or her ability to appoint them to office.[23] (There is an old saying that to understand who has power or influence over someone, just identify who can hire and fire that person.)

States that have had major constitutional revisions in recent decades, such as New York and Illinois, tend to give their governor strong appointive powers. (See Table 7–3.) This is a reflection of the extent of management reform in these states.[24] But even in states where many appointments are made by boards, commissioners, or agency heads, "a politically shrewd governor with an efficient political operation in the governor's office can probably orchestrate many of the selections," making them less powerless than their formal appointment powers would suggest.[25]

State Cabinets

State cabinets, composed of the heads of the major executive departments, advise the governors in most of the states. Indeed, in a few states the cabinet is recognized in the state constitution and given more than just advisory powers. Cabinets range in size from less than ten members to more than twenty-five. Most cabinets meet at the governor's discretion and function more or less in the fashion of the president's cabinet in the national government. In a few states they function as a body of equals on certain issues, such as granting pardons, purchasing environmentally sensitive land, and so forth, but that is not the norm.

Removal Powers

Restrictions on governors' powers of appointment are further complicated by restrictions on their powers of removal. A common statutory or constitutional provision dealing with governors' removal powers states that removal must be **"for cause only"**; that is, governors must provide a clear-cut statement of charges and an opportunity for an open hearing to the employee they are trying to oust. This process is often unpleasant, and governors seek to avoid it unless they have strong evidence of incompetence, fraud, or mismanagement. It is especially painful and politically embarrassing when the person to be removed is one of the governor's appointees. Such a situation is guaranteed to generate big headlines. That is why governors have become more careful in checking the credentials of a potential appointee.

When a governor's removal powers are limited "for cause only," it is next to impossible to remove a subordinate for policy differences. A governor may request an officeholder to resign, even when the governor's removal power is limited, and such a request may be honored by the officeholder in preference to continued unhappy relationships with the governor's office or in fear of the governor's ability to mobilize public opinion against him or her. As a final resort, a determined governor with influence in the legislature can always oust an official by a legislative act, which abolishes the office or agency the official heads and replaces it with another; this device is sometimes called a **"ripper bill."**

Fiscal Power

Governors are generally responsible for preparing the state budget for consideration by the legislature. The state budget is the single most important policy document in state government. Although the legislature must enact the state budget into law, and no state monies may be spent without the passage of an appropriations act by the legislature, in practice the governor exercises considerable influence over state spending in the preparation of the state budget. Research shows that governors with greater power over the budget process are more effective at influencing public policy.[26] It is always a big media day when a governor formally announces his or her proposed budget and sends it to the legislature. Governors are aided by their budget offices in preparation of each fiscal year's "Budget Recommendations" to the legislature (see Chapter 8).

THE GOVERNOR'S LEGISLATIVE POWERS

The responsibility for initiating major statewide legislative programs falls upon the governor. The governor's programs are presented to the legislature in various speeches, reports, and in the budget. While these instruments are only recommendations, the governor can

CABINET
The heads of major executive departments of a government.

REMOVAL POWER
Authority to force an official to step down from his or her position.

"FOR CAUSE ONLY"
Governors must provide a clear-cut statement of charges and an opportunity for an open hearing to the employee they are trying to oust.

"RIPPER BILL"
Removing an official by a legislative act, which abolishes the office or agency the official heads and replaces it with another.

The state budget is the single most important policy document in state government.

set the agenda for policy debate with them. "**Agenda setting**" is an important power. Much of the governor's power over the legislature stems from his or her power to set the policy agenda. Increasingly this is being done through televised State of the State addresses, often given the opening day of the annual legislative session.

Setting Priorities

Governors are well advised to limit their policy agenda to a few priority issues each year, rather than sending the legislature a smorgasbord of items without any unifying goal or theme. (They usually unveil these issues in their annual "State of the State" speeches.[27]) A governor wants to develop a **strong "batting average"**—a reputation for getting a high percentage of his or her recommendations enacted by the legislature. Submitting multiple proposals increases the chances for defeat. Submitting only a few high-visibility proposals, and concentrating energy and power on securing their passage, usually increases the ratio of bills passed to bills submitted. But it is often difficult for governors to select their priority issues from the host of recommendations that come to them from interest groups and executive agencies. Governors can expand their policy agenda in good economic times when there are more revenues to pay for new initiatives. But in recessionary times, governors are constrained to few if any new initiatives. It is in such situations that being governor is the least rewarding.

Providing Leadership

"What does the governor want?" is a frequent question heard in legislative debate. Leadership requires the governor to do more than simply propose legislation. The governor must also "make it happen." Governors must rally public support, packaging their proposals in a way that people will understand and support. They must make speeches and public appearances and prepare news releases highlighting their proposals. This "outside" strategy must be integrated with an "inside" strategy to persuade legislators to support the program. Governors must carefully steer their proposals through the legislative process—the committee system, floor proceedings, votes on amendments, conference committees, and final passage. They must develop good working relationships with the legislative leadership and with as many rank-and-file members as possible. They must mobilize the support of interest groups behind their proposals. Finally, governors must be willing to compromise—to take "half a loaf" and declare victory. Governors must be flexible, accepting legislative amendments when necessary to preserve the major thrust of their program.

Special Sessions

Governors can increase pressure on legislatures to act on particular recommendations by calling special sessions. The governor can specify the topics that should be considered in the special session. This device can be particularly effective if the legislature has buried one of the governor's favorite programs in the regular session. Legislators do not like to be called back from their businesses to the state capital for a special session, so even the threat of one may force them to pass the governor's program in the regular session. Of course, legislatures can defeat a governor's program even in special session, but their actions will be spotlighted.

AGENDA SETTING

Initiating major statewide legislative programs; prioritizing the issues to be discussed.

STRONG BATTING AVERAGE

A reputation for getting a high percentage of a governor's recommendations enacted by the legislature.

Vetoes

The **governor's veto** power is a major source of power within the legislature. Only in North Carolina does the governor have no veto power at all. In some states, the veto power is restricted by giving the governor only a short time to consider a bill after it has passed the legislature, by permitting a simple majority of legislative members to **override the veto,** or by requiring vetoed bills to reappear at the next legislative session. In other states, governors are given longer periods of time to consider a bill, and a two-thirds vote of both houses of the legislature is required to override a veto, rather than a simple majority. (See Table 7–3.)

The veto is often the governor's principal source of bargaining power in the legislature. Veto overrides by legislatures are rare. While the possibility of override gives the legislature "the last word" in theory, in practice few governors are so weak that they cannot garner at least one-third plus one of either house to sustain a veto. Only about 5 percent of bills passed by state legislatures are vetoed by governors, and governors are overridden on less than 10 percent of their vetoes. Of course vetoes are more common when a governor faces a legislature controlled by the opposition party.[28] (See "*Up Close: Governors Tell It Like It Is (In Their State)*.")

The *threat* of a veto may be a more important bargaining tool than the actual exercise of the veto. A governor can threaten to veto a bill with objectionable provisions before it reaches a floor vote. Governors can negotiate from a position of strength throughout the legislative process, shaping the bill to their preferences.

Occasionally legislatures may challenge governors to veto bills. This is more likely to occur with divided party control of state government—one party controls the legislature with a governor from the opposition party. The legislature can pass a popular bill opposed by the governor and then dare the governor to veto it. Even if the governor's veto is sustained, the majority party leaders in the legislature may feel they have created an issue for the next gubernatorial election. But this strategy usually guarantees a failure to get the bill enacted into law. Legislative leaders must decide whether they want the bill passed (for which they must bargain with the governor for his or her signature) or whether they want an issue for the next election.

Line Item Veto

Most governors also have the power to veto particular items in larger appropriations bills. This allows them to pick out particular legislative spending proposals (frequently labeled "turkeys" by unsympathetic governors) and veto those proposals without jeopardizing the entire budget. In states *without* the line item veto, governors may be forced to accept many legislative spending proposals in order to get a budget passed.

The **line item veto** can be a powerful weapon in the governor's arsenal. The line item veto allows the governor to take legislators' pet budget items as hostage for their support on other unrelated legislation favored by the governor. Legislators who fail to support the governor risk losing their "turkeys." Trade-offs need not be explicit. Legislators who consistently oppose the governor's programs throughout the legislative session risk losing pork for their district when the governor goes through the appropriations acts line by line.

GOVERNOR'S VETO

Formal rejection of proposed legislation by governors.

VETO OVERRIDE

Legislative power to enact a law over a veto by the governor, usually requiring a two-thirds vote of both houses.

For most governors, working with the legislature is considered the most difficult and demanding part of their job.

LINE ITEM VETO

The power of a governor to reject certain portions of a legislative appropriations bill without killing the entire bill.

**DIVIDED
GOVERNMENT
(POWER SPLIT)**

A government in
which one party
controls the gover-
nor's office while
another party controls
one or both houses of
the legislature.

Governor–Legislature Relations

For most governors, working with the legislature is considered the most difficult and demanding part of their job. "Practically all governors regard their legislature as a problem and are happy when the legislature leaves town."[29] About half of all governors have had some legislative experience before becoming governor. They may have some friends and acquaintances left over from their legislature days. And they may have greater respect for the legislative branch and greater empathy with the concerns of legislators. But many governors have little sympathy or patience with the slow and complicated legislative process.

Frequently legislators resent the exalted role of the governor. As a New York legislator remarked about former Governor Mario Cuomo, "Relating to the governor is like relating to the Pope, except that the only thing you have to kiss on the Pope is his ring."[30] Legislatures do not want to appear to be pushed around by governors. Many legislators develop a loyalty to the institution itself; they wish to preserve the independence of the legislature.

What works with the legislature? Governors should

Stand tall.   This entails not only the appearance of strength and decisiveness but a willingness to punish one's enemies.

Consult members.   Inform legislators of plans and programs and listen to their concerns.

Talk turkey.   Communicate in legislators' language of patronage and deals, give and take, reciprocity.

Rub elbows.   Stay in personal contact with legislators on a regular basis.

Massage egos.   Legislators like to share center stage with the governor, to be seen at bill signings, to be invited to dinner at the governor's mansion, to have the governor praise them in public.[31]

When partisan differences are added to institutional rivalry, conflict rather than cooperation is more likely to characterize relations between the governor and the legislature.

DIVIDED GOVERNMENT: GOVERNOR VERSUS THE LEGISLATURE

Divided government, where one party controls one or both houses of the legislature and the other party controls the governorship, is increasingly frequent in American state politics. (It is also referred to as a **"power split."**) In recent years over half of the states have experienced divided party control. The election of Republican governors in southern states with heavily Democratic legislatures helps to explain the increased occurrence of divided government in the states, as well as an increased tendency of voters everywhere to split their tickets. Republican governors are more likely to face Democratic-controlled legislatures than the reverse. But divided government itself has a major impact on executive–legislature relations.

Partisanship Cuts Both Ways

Party works to the advantage of governors when their party has a majority in the legislature. The governor and a legislature controlled by the same party have an incentive to produce results. There is still institutional rivalry, wherein governors contend with legislatures for policy leadership. But both have an interest in

up CLOSE Governors Tell It Like It Is (In Their State)

Governor M. Jodi Rell, R, Connecticut

(On Taking Office after a Corrupt Governor Is Tossed Out)

Upon taking office, she immediately fired key players on the former governor's staff and accepted the resignations of others. Gov. Rowland was convicted of corruption and went to jail. From her inaugural address:

"*Let the message be clear: From this day forward, if you are entrusted with public office, you will uphold the highest standards of public integrity and ethical principles.*"[a]

Governor Eliot Spitzer, D, New York

(On Being Accused of Calling the Republican Senate Majority Leader "Senile" and Some Other Things)

Gov. Spitzer and Sen. Joe Bruno were at odds over several pieces of major legislation that were caught up in gridlock. It was alleged that Spitzer had referred to the 78-year-old Republican as "an old, senile, piece of s—t" during a conversation with another GOP legislator. Spitzer denied using specific words but expressed remorse over the conflict with a key legislator.

"*I am never going to say I don't regret anything that I have ever said. There are moments when he is frustrated*

with me and I am frustrated with him. It's the type of relationship that has bumps in it."[b]

Governor Nancy Sibelius, D, Kansas

(On What "Red" & "Blue" Mean)

Her statement to a reporter, reflecting her belief that Kansas voters and the legislators who represent them are more pragmatists than staunch partisans.

"*Our Legislature is here for 90 days, and we don't hear them saying 'I'm blue, I'm red' unless they're talking about the Jayhawks*" [mascot of the University of Kansas whose colors are red and blue].[c]

Governor C.L. "Butch" Otter, R, Idaho)

(On Being the "New Horse" in the Pasture With Legislators)

The newly elected governor (a former Congressman) warned state legislators in a humorous sort of way that his power vis-à-vis them would increase as he got a little experience being governor under his belt.

"*It's kind of like getting a new colt . . . [The older horses] have to establish a pecking order, but they forget that the new colt's going to grow up. Once he gets his feet and his stride, the game can change.*"[d]

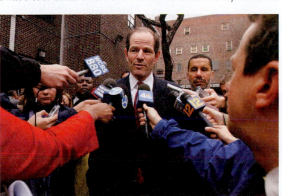

(continued)

[a]Mark Davis, "Rell Sworn in as 87th Connecticut Governor," accessed at www.wtnh.com/globalstory.asp?s=1982532& Client Type=Printable, June 2, 2005.
[b]Joe Mahoney, "Bruno Still My Pal," *New York Daily News, July 8, 2007; accessed at www.nydailynews.com/news/2007/07/ 08/2007-07-08_bruno_still_my_pal.html, July 27, 2007.*
[c]Susan Page, "What's a Governor Like You Doing in a State Like This?" *USA Today*, May 23, 2005, p. 1D.
[d]Idaho Public Television, "Idaho Reports: Quotes From the 2007 Session." Accessed at http://idahoptv.org/idreports/ QuotesArchive.cfm, July 27, 2007.

compiling a record of success that the voters can attribute to everyone running under the party label in the next election.[32] But when partisan differences are added to institutional rivalry, conflict rather than cooperation is more likely to characterize relations between governor and legislature.

Confronting Gridlock

A governor confronting opposition party control of the legislature must spend a great deal of time bargaining and compromising with legislative leaders of the opposition party. Governors must ensure that they keep their own party's legislators behind their proposals and then either work out accommodations with the opposition leadership or try to chip off enough votes from less loyal opposition members to win passage of their proposals.[33] Neither is an easy task. Party activists, including legislators, differ on ideological grounds and policy issues. Moreover, the opposing party looks forward to defeating the governor in the next election. Often one or more opposition party aspirants for the governorship are sitting in the legislature. They seek to discredit the governor, not only during the election campaign, but during his or her entire term of office. Often the opposition party in the legislature will prefer that a needed bill go down to defeat just to hurt the governor's reputation. Only a very able governor can avoid gridlock with divided party control of state government. Sometimes it just boils down to the interpersonal skills of the governor.

> *Impeachment is a political process, not a legal process.*

IMPEACHMENTS, INVESTIGATIONS, AND RECALLS

Impeachment is a political process, not a legal process. While state constitutions, like the U.S. Constitution, usually define an impeachable offense as "treason, bribery, or other high crimes and misdemeanors," the political errors of impeached officials are usually more important than their legal offenses.

Impeachment, Trial, and Removal

IMPEACHMENT
The power of legislatures to remove executive and judicial officers from office for good cause; generally the lower house must first vote for impeachment, then the upper house must hold a trial and vote for removal.

All state constitutions, except Oregon's, provide for the impeachment of elected state officials by the legislature. Impeachment proceedings are initiated in the lower houses of forty-seven states, in the unicameral legislature of Nebraska, and in the upper house in Alaska. Impeachment trials are held in the upper houses in forty-five states, in a special court of impeachment in Nebraska, in the lower house in Alaska, in a special commission in Missouri, and in the senate and court of appeals in New York. Most states require a two-thirds vote to convict and remove an official.

These impeachment provisions are rarely used. There appear to have been only seventeen gubernatorial impeachments since the nation's birth and seven trial convictions.

When Arizona Governor Evan Mecham (R) was impeached and convicted by the state legislature in 1988 for fiscal improprieties, it was the first such event in nearly sixty years. Several other governors have resigned when threatened with impeachment. Connecticut Governor John Rowland (R) did so in 2004, following an investigation by the legislature for taking gifts from contractors doing business with the state. He was then prosecuted, convicted, and sent to federal prison in 2005.

Criminal Investigations

Criminal investigations have led to the demise of a number of other governors over the years. Some were convicted, while others were acquitted of criminal charges, but all were finished politically; no miraculous comebacks were possible. For example, former Illinois Governor George Ryan (R) was convicted of racketeering, fraud, obstructing the Internal Revenue Service, and lying to the FBI. The corruption scandal ended his political career. The same year, former Alabama Governor Don Siegelman (D) was convicted of a "pay-to-play" scheme—trading government favors for campaign donations when he was governor and, before that, lieutenant governor. At the time he was attempting to make a comeback by running for the Democratic nomination for governor. The voters said "No" loud and clear.

Recall

Eighteen states allow citizens to recall the governor. (The **recall process**, initiated by a citizen petition, allows a vote on whether to remove an elected official from office before his or her term is completed.) The most famous recall took place in 2003 when California voters tossed out California Governor Gray Davis (D) and voted in Governor Arnold Schwarzenegger (R). (See Chapter 2.) Prior to that, North Dakota Governor Lynn Frazier (R) was recalled in 1921 during his third term. Several other governors had recall petitions certified during their tenure but left office before the recall election could be held.

RECALL PROCESS Initiated by a citizen petition, it allows a vote on whether to remove an elected official from office before his or her term is completed.

THE GOVERNOR AS POLITICAL LEADER

The formal powers of governors can only take them so far. Their personal (informal) powers, or "political clout," are often essential to helping them gain control of public policy, legislative output, and bureaucratic performance. A landslide election that carries the governor's party into control of both houses of the legislature can overcome many formal weaknesses in a governor's powers. A politically resourceful governor enjoying widespread public popularity who can skillfully employ the media to his or her advantage can overcome many constitutional weaknesses in the office. A young, up-and-coming governor from a big state with lots of Electoral College votes can gain a spot on the national stage, which catches people's attention at home.

Governors spend more time meeting the general public, attending ceremonial functions, and working with the press and television than they do managing state government and working with the legislature. They focus on these public relations tasks not only to improve their chances for re-election, but also to give themselves the political clout to achieve their goals for state government. All fifty governors have press secretaries or public information offices,

Governors spend more time meeting the general public, attending ceremonial functions, and working with the press and television than they do managing state government and working with the legislature.

some with large staffs. Press conferences, policy announcements, and other media events are carefully orchestrated for maximum coverage in the nightly news and morning papers. Increasingly, state legislatures are creating their own media offices, but media coverage of state legislatures has traditionally been very sparse, mostly because many do not meet year-round, like Congress does.

Media Access

Governors are the most visible figures in state politics. An attractive governor who is skillful in public relations can command support from administrators, legislators, local officials, and party leaders through public appeals to their constituents. Politicians must respect the governor's greater access to the communications media and hence to the minds of their constituents. Effective governors not only understand the broad range of issues facing their states but also are able to speak clearly and persuasively about them. Many have their press conferences video-streamed on the Web.

State Media Coverage

Press and television coverage of state government generally suffers a great deal of neglect. Governors are far more visible in the media than state legislators, but the focus of the media—even local television news broadcasts—is on national events. In many states a majority of even *daily* newspapers do not have full-time reporters assigned to the state capital.

Overall, reporters lean more heavily Democratic than Republican in their own politics. A survey of 1,149 print, radio, and television journalists found that in American newsrooms, Democrats outnumber Republicans by two-to-one (37 percent to 18 percent), with one-third saying they are independents.[34] This is nothing new. Similar patterns have been observed since the 1980s, when a path-breaking study by S. Robert Lichter first observed the partisan leanings of the press.[35] Thus, it is not surprising that there is a general perception among political analysts that Democratic governors tend to get more positive coverage than Republican governors. But **"media savvy"**—skill in working with the media—is more important than partisan affiliation in winning good media coverage. A governor who "knows what's newsworthy," puts ideas across in brief "sound bites," makes timely use of widely reported events to get into the news, "hangs around the press area in the state capitol building," and cultivates good relationships with reporters is far more likely to garner favorable media stories than a governor who is "media shy," "tongue-tied," "standoffish," self-conscious, or who "hates the press," "blames the media," and thereby encourages an adversarial relationship with them.[36]

MEDIA SAVVY
Knowledge of how to use the press to get one's message across to the public.

Popularity

Media access and the visibility it produces provide governors with the opportunity to promote their personal popularity with the citizens of the state. The legislature is seldom as popular as the governor. Even if individual legislators are popular in their districts, the legislature as an institution is rarely very popular. (See Figure 7–1.) Statewide opinion polls do not track governors' popularity as closely as national polls track the president of the United States. But opinion in most large states is regularly surveyed by private, university, and newspaper polls. All governors have press secretaries whose responsibility it is to develop and maintain a favorable media image for the governor. Many governors devote a great deal of their personal attention to this task—massaging the capital press, organizing media events, holding town meetings or "virtual" town meetings, personally answering their email or going into

The legislature is seldom as popular as the governor.

FIGURE 7–1 **Governor and Legislature: Popularity Ratings in Florida**

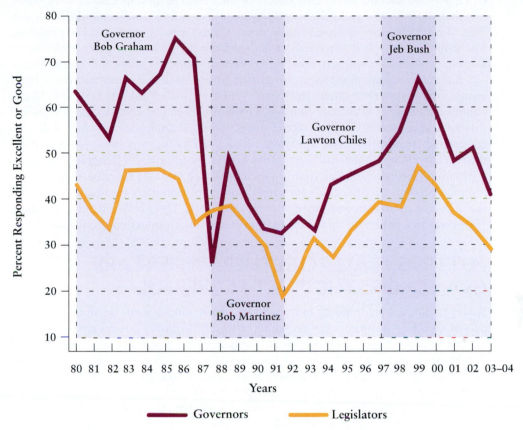

Q: "How would you rate the job [governor] [the Florida legislature] is doing?" Percent saying excellent or good, versus fair or poor or don't know.
Source: Florida Annual Policy Survey. Florida State University. Various years.

official chat rooms, traveling about the state, and so on. There may be some tendency for legislators and interest groups to avoid direct confrontations with a popular governor. Certainly a popular governor is in a better position to advance his or her program than an *un*popular governor. But the real problem is turning personal popularity into political power.

Leadership

Governors' reputations as leaders stem not only from what they say but also from what they do. Their reputations must include a capacity to decide issues and to persist in the decision once it is made. A reputation for backing down, for avoiding situations that involve them in public conflict, or for wavering in the face of momentary pressures invites the governors' adversaries to ignore or oppose them. A sense of insecurity or weakness can damage a governor's power more than any constitutional limitation. Governors can also increase their influence by developing a reputation for punishing their adversaries and rewarding their supporters. Once the reputation as an effective leader is established, cooperation is often forthcoming in anticipation of the governor's reaction.

Party

Governors are also the recognized leaders of their state parties. In a majority of states, it is the governor who picks the state party chairperson and who is consulted on questions of party platform, campaign tactics, nominations for party office, and party finances. The amount of power that a governor derives from the position of party leader varies from state to state according to the strength, cohesion, and discipline of the state parties.

But there are limitations to the power that governors derive from their role as party leader. First, a governor cannot deny party renomination to disloyal members. Nominations are acquired in primary elections. Legislators must first consider the demands of their own constituents, not the voice of the governor. Second, the frequency of divided control, where governors face legislatures dominated by the opposition party, requires them to bargain with individuals and groups in the opposition party. If they have acquired a reputation for being too "partisan" in their approach to state programs, they will find it difficult to win over the necessary support of opposition party members. Finally, the use of patronage may make as many enemies as friends. There is an old political saying: "For every one patronage appointment, you make nine enemies and one ingrate."

PUTTING IT ALL TOGETHER: WHERE ARE GOVERNORS THE MOST POWERFUL?

Power rankings are constantly in flux. State constitutions are amended, new laws are passed, and new governors get elected to office. Institutional powers change less frequently than do the governors who wield them. Personal power rankings shift the most because they are calculated solely on the attributes of the governors in office at a single point in time. As newly elected governors replace outgoing chief executives, the personal power rankings of individual states' governors change.

Political scientist Thad Beyle, who regularly calculates these power rankings, found that since the 1960s, the overall institutional powers of the nation's governors have increased.[37] The greatest gains have been in their veto and appointment powers and their tenure potential. As a group, they have actually lost some of their budgetary powers and experienced a drop in gubernatorial party control as the South has became a more competitive two-party region. By the mid-2000s, the states whose governors had the most institutional power were located all over the country; there was no clear regional pattern. However, governors with the weakest formal powers tend to be in the South and in the smallest New England states. Governors in these latter states are weakened most by having to share power with other statewide separately elected officials, and by their weaker appointment and veto powers.

Governors also possess personal informal power. States whose governors have more personal powers tend to be located in the Northeast and upper Midwest. These governors are more likely to have steadily climbed up the political career ladder and to have strong job performance ratings—in line with research showing the two to be strongly linked.[38]

When the two sets of rankings are combined to create an overall ranking of gubernatorial power across the states (see "*Rankings of the States:* Combined Powers"), it shows that among the five most powerful, three are in the Midwest, one in the West, and one in the East. Four of the five most powerful governors head states where there is divided control. But as Beyle cautions, "These ratings change as incumbents are replaced with a new group of men and women carrying with them their own personal styles and strengths or weaknesses."[39]

RANKINGS of the STATES

Combined Powers: Formal (Institutional) + Informal (Personal) Powers

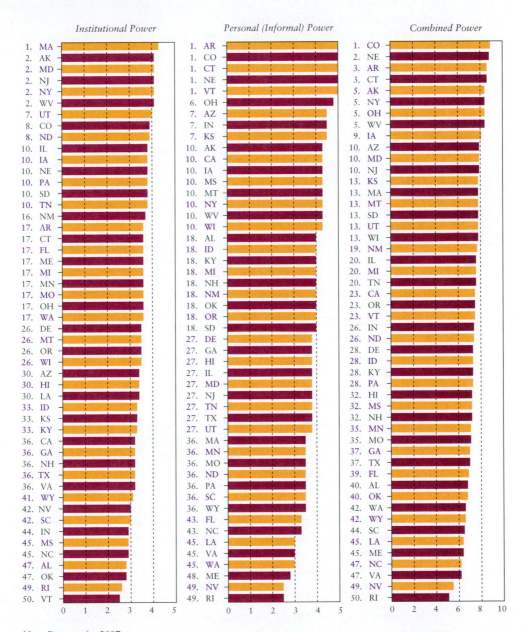

Institutional Power	Personal (Informal) Power	Combined Power
1. MA	1. AR	1. CO
2. AK	1. CO	2. NE
2. MD	1. CT	3. AR
2. NJ	1. NE	3. CT
2. NY	1. VT	5. AK
2. WV	6. OH	5. NY
7. UT	7. AZ	5. OH
8. CO	7. IN	5. WV
8. ND	7. KS	9. IA
10. IL	10. AK	10. AZ
10. IA	10. CA	10. MD
10. NE	10. IA	10. NJ
10. PA	10. MS	13. KS
10. SD	10. MT	13. MA
10. TN	10. NY	13. MT
16. NM	10. WV	13. SD
17. AR	10. WI	13. UT
17. CT	18. AL	13. WI
17. FL	18. ID	19. NM
17. ME	18. KY	20. IL
17. MI	18. MI	20. MI
17. MN	18. NH	20. TN
17. MO	18. NM	23. CA
17. OH	18. OK	23. OR
17. WA	18. OR	23. VT
26. DE	18. SD	26. IN
26. MT	27. DE	26. ND
26. OR	27. GA	28. DE
26. WI	27. HI	28. ID
30. AZ	27. IL	28. KY
30. HI	27. MD	28. PA
30. LA	27. NJ	32. HI
33. ID	27. TN	32. MS
33. KS	27. TX	32. NH
33. KY	27. UT	35. MN
36. CA	36. MA	35. MO
36. GA	36. MN	37. GA
36. NH	36. MO	37. TX
36. TX	36. ND	39. FL
36. VA	36. PA	40. AL
41. WY	36. SC	40. OK
42. NV	36. WY	42. WA
42. SC	43. FL	42. WY
44. IN	43. NC	44. SC
45. MS	45. LA	45. LA
45. NC	45. VA	45. ME
47. AL	45. WA	47. NC
47. OK	48. ME	47. VA
49. RI	49. NV	49. NV
50. VT	49. RI	50. RI

Note: Data are for 2007.
Source: Update provided to the authors by Dr. Thad Beyle. May 2007. Courtesy of Dr. Thad Beyle. Available at http://www.unc.edu/~beyle/gubnewpwr.html

OTHER EXECUTIVE OFFICES

Lieutenant Governor

In some states, the governor and the lieutenant governor run on the same ticket, much as the president and vice president. In others, the lieutenant governor position is separately elected. When gubernatorial candidates have to choose a running mate, one question that often surfaces is whether putting a woman on the ticket will help. One study has found that it often does.[40] (Currently, there are seven female lieutenant governors who were selected as running mates.)

The lieutenant governor's office in many states is looked upon as a campaign platform for the governorship. In fact, a study by the National Lieutenant Governors Association found that lieutenant governors are more successful at being elected governor than any other local, state, or congressional office. Lieutenant governors are said to have a head start for the top job. The lieutenant governor's formal duties are comparable to those of the vice-president of the United States; in other words, lieutenant governors have relatively few formal powers. The two basic functions of the office are to serve in direct line of succession to the governor and replace him or her in the event of a vacancy in that office, and to be the presiding officer of the state senate, or secretary of state in a handful of states. The issue of succession has gained more attention. Within the span of eighteen months in the early 2000s, four lieutenant governors succeeded to the office of governor following the death, resignation, or criminal conviction of a sitting governor.

Since lieutenant governors generally have political ambitions of their own, they seldom make good "assistant governors" who will submerge their own interests for the success of the governor's administration. Unlike the vice president, lieutenant governors are separately elected in eighteen states and are sometimes members of the governor's opposition party. (In twenty-four states they run on the same ticket as the governor; eight states don't elect a lieutenant governor.)

Some efforts have been made to reduce the boredom of the lieutenant governor's office by assigning them membership on various boards and commissions and tasking them with a wider range of policy functions.

Attorney General

The office of attorney general has more real powers and responsibilities than that of the lieutenant governor. Attorneys general are elected in forty-three states, and appointed in the other states, usually by the governor. Attorneys general (AGs) are the chief legal counsel for their states. They represent the state in any suits to which it is a party. They act as legal counsel for the governor and for other state officials. The legal business of state agencies is subject to their supervision. The source of the attorney general's power comes from the quasi-judicial duty of rendering formal written opinions in response to requests from the governor, state agencies, or other public officials regarding the legality and constitutionality of their acts. These opinions have the power of law in state affairs unless they are successfully challenged in court. The governor and other officials are generally obliged to conform to the attorney general's legal opinion until a court specifies otherwise. Attorneys general render authoritative interpretations of state constitutions, laws, city ordinances, and administrative rulings.

The attorney general also has substantial law enforcement powers. Most states allow attorneys general to initiate criminal proceedings on their own motion, and nearly all states assign them responsibility for handling criminal cases on appeal to higher state courts or to federal courts. In some states the attorney general has supervisory powers over law enforcement throughout the state.

The state AGs, through the National Association of Attorneys General, have become more powerful politically by jointly suing companies for consumer fraud and using the settlement monies (in the billions) to fund important consumer protection–related activities in their respective states. The Association routinely monitors issues such as antitrust, bankruptcy, civil rights, cyber crime, end-of-life health care, the environment, Medicaid fraud, and violence against women. The growing clout and visibility of state attorneys general have led some to conclude that of all the statewide elected offices, it is the one that has undergone the most change in recent years.

Treasurers, Auditors, and Comptrollers

Most states have elected *treasurers*, and treasurers in other states are appointed by either the governor or the legislature. Treasurers are the trustees of the public purse. They are the state "*money managers*," custodians of state funds: collecting taxes, acting as paymaster for the state, managing trust funds (like the tobacco settlement monies in twenty-four states), and administering the investment of state funds. (States invest billions of dollars annually.) The principal job of the treasurer is to make payments on departmental requisitions for payrolls and for checks to be issued to those who have furnished the state with goods and services. Generally, the department's requests for checks must be accompanied by a voucher showing the proper legislative authority for such payment. Requests for payment usually are accompanied by a statement from the auditor's or the comptroller's office that legislative appropriations are available for such payment. Thus, the treasurer's office works in close relation to another executive office of importance: that of auditor or comptroller.

The principal duty of the office of state *auditor* is that of assuring the legislature that expenditures and investment of state funds have been made in accordance with the law. This function is known as a **"post-audit"** and occurs after state expenditures have been made.

The primary duty of the office of the state *comptroller* is to ensure that a prospective departmental expenditure is in accordance with the law and does not exceed the appropriations made by the legislature. This **"pre-audit"** occurs before any expenditure is made by the treasurer. Public administration experts consider the comptroller's job of pre-audit to be an executive function, and they urge that the comptroller be appointed by the governor. On the other hand, the job of post-audit is essentially a legislative check on the executive, and students of public administration generally feel that the auditor should be elected or appointed by the legislature. However, there is still some confusion in state organizations about the separate functions of auditors and comptrollers— some auditors do "pre-auditing" and some comptrollers do "post-auditing."

The National Association of State Treasurers has become more active of late, bringing state financial officers together to tackle such big issues as the financial soundness of state retirement systems and prepaid college savings plans, the security of the state's financial system in the event of natural disasters or terrorist attacks, investment fraud, and identity theft.

POST-AUDIT
An auditor's duty, it involves making sure that expenditures and investment of state funds have been made in accordance with the law; done after expenditure is made.

PRE-AUDIT
The state comptroller's duty; it involves making sure that a prospective departmental expenditure is in accordance with the law and does not exceed the appropriations made by the legislature before any expenditure is made by the treasurer.

How Many Governors Later Became President?

President	State	Served as Governor
Thomas Jefferson	Virginia	1779–1781
James Monroe	Virginia	1799–1802
Martin Van Buren	New York	1828–1829
John Tyler	Virginia	1825–1827
James Polk	Tennessee	1839–1841
Andrew Johnson	Tennessee	1853–1857
Rutherford B. Hayes	Ohio	1867–1871, 1875–1877
Grover Cleveland	New York	1882–1884
William McKinley	Ohio	1892–1896
Theodore Roosevelt	New York	1898–1900
Woodrow Wilson	New Jersey	1911–1912
Calvin Coolidge	Massachusetts	1918–1920
Franklin D. Roosevelt	New York	1929–1933
Jimmy Carter	Georgia	1971–1975
Ronald Reagan	California	1967–1975
Bill Clinton	Arkansas	1979–1981, 1983–1992
George W. Bush	Texas	1994–2000

Secretary of State

Another interesting state office is that of secretary of state. Thirty-five states elect secretaries of state. These officials are the chief custodians of state records and, in the case of several states, "keepers of the great seal of the commonwealth." They are also the state's chief elections officer. It is this function, more than the record-keeping function, which puts secretaries of state in the news. When there are close, contested elections (Florida, 2000; Ohio, 2004; Washington State, 2004), secretaries of state become the focal point of massive media attention and lawsuits. Secretaries of state are responsible for supervising the preparation of ballots and certifying election results for the state. Their Web sites typically report historical and current voter registration and turnout data, candidate filings, campaign contributions and spending, and include links to local election officials. Secretaries of state, who belong to the National Association of Secretaries of State, have been given more important roles in election administration by the Help America Vote Act of 2002. In their less visible record-keeping function, they register corporations, trademarks, and trade names, publish state administrative codes and registers, handle business and occupational licensing, and administer the uniform commercial code. They also register lobbyists, record all laws, and publish the state constitution.

Personal Staff

All governors are permitted to maintain a small group of loyal, dedicated personal aides—the governor's staff. Many staff members previously worked in the governor's political campaign. Most work long hours in small offices for relatively low pay. Most are young. Most envision some sort of political career for themselves in the future; they believe the experience they are acquiring in the governor's office, and the contacts they are making, will help in their careers. The governor may have a chief of staff, an appointments secretary, a press secretary, a legal counsel, several speechwriters, one or more legislative aides, and advisors in key policy areas—education, welfare, highways, health, homeland security. As the policymaking role of governors has expanded and policies have become more complex, governors have added more policy analyst positions to their staffs and hired more professionals to fill them. No one on the governor's staff is a civil service employee; their job depends directly on their value to the governor. Without a doubt, the smooth operation of a governor's office is heavily dependent upon the staff.

It's no wonder that many governors who have held other elected offices describe being governor as "the best job they ever had."

ON THE WEB

The Office of the Governor in each state maintains its own Web site. These sites can be accessed through each state's governmental home page (see "On the Web" in Chapter 3). Usually the governor's Web site includes a flattering biography of the governor, statements and policy positions of the governor, and links to state executive departments and agencies.

The best source of comparative information on governors in all fifty states is the National Governors Association Web site: www.nga.org. This site includes the latest news releases and policy positions of the National Governors Association. Perhaps more important, it provides biographical information on each governor in a comparative format, and it also offers complete texts of the latest inaugural addresses and/or state-of-the-state addresses of each governor.

Other very informative association sites, which discuss the roles and responsibilities of other major statewide executive officials, spell out the issues facing them, identify the current officeholders, and allow access to major position papers and reports are as follows:

www.nlga.us

The official site of the National Lieutenant Governors Association

www.naag.org

The official site of the National Association of Attorneys General

www.nast.net

The official site of the National Association of State Treasurers

www.nass.org

The official site of the National Association of Secretaries of State

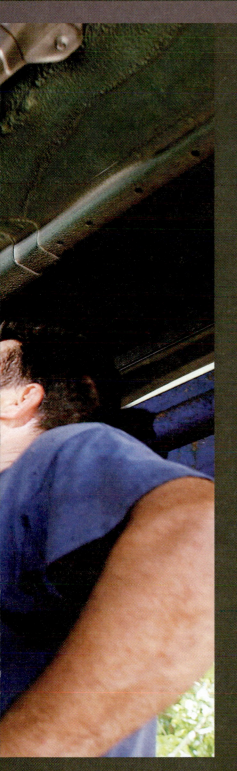

CHAPTER EIGHT

BUREAUCRATIC POLITICS IN STATES AND COMMUNITIES

8

QUESTIONS TO CONSIDER

Do you think of government workers as bureaucrats or public servants?
- ■ Bureaucrats
- ■ Public servants

Should laws be written to limit bureaucratic discretion or should laws allow bureaucratic flexibility in implementation?
- ■ Laws should limit bureaucratic discretion.
- ■ Laws should allow bureaucratic flexibility.

Do you believe that most bureaucrats seek to expand their power and authority and increase their budgets?
- ■ Yes   ■ No

Should governments be run more like private businesses, treating citizens like customers and charging for as many services as practicable?
- ■ Yes   ■ No

Have you considered a career in state or local government?
- ■ Yes   ■ No

GOVERNMENT AND BUREAUCRACY

Political conflict does not necessarily end after the state legislature passes a law or the city council enacts an ordinance.

Over time, bureaucrats themselves come to exercise considerable power in state and local politics.

Political conflict does not necessarily end after the state legislature passes a law or the city council enacts an ordinance. Eighty-seven percent of all government employees work for state and local governments. These workers come under a lot of scrutiny from citizens, interest groups, the press, and politicians primarily because they are responsible for implementing laws passed by state and local legislative bodies. Dedicated opponents of a law not only regroup to fight for repeal by the legislative body, but they also turn their attention to the bureaucracy, hoping to delay, modify, or even cripple the implementation of the law. Dedicated supporters of the law must also turn to the bureaucracy to ensure the law's prompt implementation and strict enforcement. State and local government employees are pressured from all sides. Over time, bureaucrats themselves come to exercise considerable power in state and local politics.

In popular conversation, **"bureaucracy"** has come to mean red tape, needless paperwork, waste and inefficiency, senseless regulations, impersonality, and unresponsiveness to the needs of people. And indeed bureaucracy is all of that (although certainly not all government employees act in such a manner). But the true meaning of bureaucracy is simply a "rational" way for an organization to go about carrying out its tasks. Bureaucracies may be governmental or corporate or military. They are the administrative structures of any organization, public or private. All that is required for an organization to be a bureaucracy is

BUREAUCRACY
Departments, agencies, bureaus, and offices that perform the functions of government.

- A chain of command in which authority flows downward;
- A division of labor in which workers specialize in their tasks;
- Clear lines of responsibility;
- Specific organizational goals; and
- Impersonal treatment of all persons equally and according to rules.

In the public sector, a "bureaucrat" is someone working in a bureaucracy—a non-elected person who is employed by government.

Despite pledges of many elected officials, especially Republicans, to "freeze," "shrink," or "downsize" government, state and local government employment continues to grow throughout the nation. Overall, there are approximately 20 million employees of state and local governments. Even states operating under employment "caps" and "freezes" have expanded their workforces. "What you're seeing is that some rational fundamentals—including growth in economics and growth in population—really win out over conservative ideology."[1] But even slow-growing states are expanding public employment. Moreover, this employment growth has occurred during a period in which privatizing public services has been politically popular, although that trend has stabilized somewhat (see "Reform, Privatization, and Reinventing Government" later in this chapter). If all of the people employed under state contracts to outside organizations were counted as public employees, the numbers of "public" employees would be much higher.

If all of the people employed under state contracts to outside organizations were counted as public employees, the numbers of "public" employees would be much higher.

SOURCES OF BUREAUCRATIC POWER

In theory, government bureaucracies, whether at the federal, state, or local level, do *not* make policy. Rather, they are created to *implement* policies passed by legislative bodies. But in practice, government bureaucracies do engage in policymaking as they go about their tasks. How do bureaucrats exercise power and why has their power grown over the years?

Implementation

Implementation is the development of procedures and activities to carry out policies enacted by the legislative body. It may involve creating new agencies or bureaus or assigning new responsibilities to old agencies. It often requires bureaucracies to translate laws into operational rules and regulations and usually to allocate resources—money, personnel, offices, supplies—to the new function. All of these tasks involve decisions by bureaucrats—decisions that drive how the law will actually affect society.

Implementation is the continuation of policymaking. For example, bureaucrats may delay the development of regulations based on a new law, assign enforcement responsibility to existing offices with other higher-priority tasks, and allocate few people with limited resources to the task. Or, alternatively, bureaucrats may act promptly in making new regulations, insist on strict enforcement, assign responsibilities to newly created aggressive offices with no other assignments, and allocate a great deal of staff time and agency resources to the task. Interested groups have a strong stake in these decisions, and they actively seek to influence the bureaucracy.

Regulation

Regulation is the development of formal rules for implementing legislation. State agencies charged with the task of regulating various activities—for example, environmental protection, business and professional codes, banking and insurance regulations, consumer affairs, public utilities, and so forth—must develop and publish very specific (and sometimes very lengthy) sets of rules. Most states require that proposed new regulations be published in advance of any action, that hearings be held to allow individuals and groups to comment on the proposed new regulations, and that new regulations be formally published prior to implementation. This process is designed to allow all interested parties the chance to help shape the actual rules that set policy.

Adjudication

Adjudication is bureaucratic decision making about individual cases. While regulation resembles the legislative process, adjudication resembles the judicial process. In adjudication, bureaucrats must decide whether an individual or firm is failing to comply with laws or regulations and, if so, what penalties or corrective actions are to be applied. Bureaucrats can decide to hold individuals strictly accountable to rules, to impose heavy penalties, or to mandate expensive corrective actions. Alternatively, they can interpret the rules loosely and allow individuals or firms that violate rules to get off lightly.

Discretion

Bureaucrats almost always have some discretion in performing even the most routine tasks. Discretion is greatest in cases that do not exactly fit established rules, or when more than one rule might be applied to the same case, resulting in different outcomes.

IMPLEMENTATION
The development by executive bureaucracies of procedures and activities to carry out policies enacted by the legislature.

REGULATION
The development by the bureaucracy of formal rules for implementing legislation.

ADJUDICATION
Decision making by bureaucracies as to whether or not an individual or organization has complied with or violated government laws and/or regulations.

DISCRETION
The ability of public agencies and employees to make decisions based on their own judgment so long as the decision is reasonable and lawful.

Bureaucrats may be courteous, helpful, and accommodating to citizens; or, alternatively, impersonal, unhelpful, and even downright frustrating. Increasingly governments are conducting citizen surveys to determine how well citizens believe employees of a particular agency treat them.

Bureaucratic Goals

Bureaucrats generally believe strongly in the value of their programs and the importance of their tasks. But beyond these public-spirited motives, bureaucrats, like everyone else, seek added power and prestige for themselves. These public and private motives converge to inspire them to seek to expand their authority, functions, and budgets. (Rarely do bureaucrats request a reduction in their authority, the elimination of the program under their direction, or a decrease in their agency's budget.) Rather, over time, bureaucrats help to expand governmental functions and increase governmental spending.

THE GROWTH OF BUREAUCRATIC POWER

Bureaucracies at all levels of government—federal, state, and local—have grown over time. Several explanations have been offered for this growth.

Societal Complexity

One standard explanation for the growth of bureaucratic power cites advances in technology and increases in the size and complexity of society. Governors and legislators must delegate more and more authority to experts who have the time, energy, and knowledge to handle the details of policymaking. Elected officials cannot be expected to deal with the myriad details of environmental protection, insurance and banking regulations, law enforcement, highway planning and construction, university governance, school curriculum, and so forth. They must, therefore, create bureaucracies, appropriate money to run them, and authorize them to draw the rules and regulations that actually govern us. Increasingly they are hiring better-educated employees with expertise in specific policy areas and with advanced technical skills. However, some governors and legislators still get heavily involved in trying to shape policy outputs in state agencies. Where they do so, they are usually successful.[2]

Political Advantage

It is not uncommon for elected officials to deliberately pass vague and ambiguous laws, allowing them to demonstrate their concern for problems confronting their states or communities, but without actually deciding how to solve the problems. Legislators can express lofty goals in legislation yet avoid controversies surrounding the actual attainment of these goals. Bureaucrats must give practical meaning to the symbolic measures passed by politicians. If bureaucratic implementation to enforce laws proves unpopular, elected politicians can blame the bureaucrats and avoid direct responsibility themselves for the failure of legislation.

Bureaucratic Expansionism

As noted earlier, bureaucrats themselves have both public and personal motives to expand their own authority, increase the amount of money they can spend, and augment the number of employees under their supervision.

Incrementalism

Bureaucracies expand because governmental decision making is incremental. By that we mean that each year bureaucrats and elected officials focus on proposed *new* programs and policies and *increases* in budgets and personnel. Existing policies, programs, agencies, or expenditures are seldom reviewed as a whole each year. Doing so would require far too much time and energy, simply to confirm decisions that had been made in previous years. But over time the effect of incremental decision making is to expand the size of bureaucracies, as new programs and new spending are authorized while old programs and previous spending levels are seldom reconsidered.

STATE BUREAUCRACIES

State governments in America spend most of their money on education, welfare, health and hospitals—combined, highways, corrections, and government administration. (See Figure 8–1.) State departments and agencies responsible for these functions are usually the largest bureaucracies at the state capital. However, the authoritative *Book of the States* lists forty-six separate bureaucratic functions in state governments:

Adjutant general	Community affairs	Elections administration
Administration	Comptroller	Emergency management
Agriculture	Consumer affairs	Employment services
Banking	Corrections	Energy
Budget	Economic development	Environmental protection
Civil rights	Education, higher	Finance
Commerce	Education, public schools	Fish and wildlife
General services	Natural resources	Purchasing
Health	Parks and recreation	Revenue
Highways	Personnel	Social services
Historic preservation	Planning	Solid waste management
Information systems	Post audit	State police
Insurance	Preaudit	Tourism
Labor relations	Public library development	Transportation
Licensing	Public utility regulation	Welfare
Mental health		

Not all states have separate agencies for each of these functions; on the contrary, many functions are combined in larger departments.

Organizational Disarray

The executive branches of virtually all state governments in the United States are fragmented, complex, and unwieldy. These organizational problems arise, first of all, as a result of the separate election of many statewide officials—for example, attorney general, secretary of state, treasurer, comptroller, superintendent of education, and others (see Table 7–2 in Chapter 7). There are more than 300 separately elected executive-branch officials in all the states. Only four states—Maine, New Hampshire, New Jersey, and Tennessee—have a single statewide elected executive, the governor, who heads the executive branch of government.

FIGURE 8–1 State Government Expenditures by Function

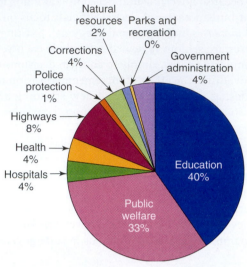

Note: Data are from 2005.
Source: U.S. Census Bureau. Available at http://www.census.gov/govs/state/0500usst.html

Organizational problems also arise as a result of the extensive use of boards and commissions throughout the states to head executive departments. Appointments to these boards and commissions are often for long terms and members cannot be removed except for "cause"—proven misconduct in office. Governors can rarely remove the members of these independent entities for their policy decisions, no matter how at odds these decisions may be with the governors' preferences.

The proliferation of separately elected executive officers in the states as well as independent boards and commissions creates very messy organizational charts for state governments. To see this clearly, contrast the organizational chart for Mississippi's Executive Branch—which is composed of the *governor* heading twelve departments, nine *separately elected executive officials*, and sixteen *independent agencies and institutions*—with that of Michigan whose governor is shown at the top of the chain of command for nineteen departments (including the State Department headed by a separately elected Secretary of State and the Attorney General Department headed by a separately elected Attorney General). There are no separate independent boards or commissions on the chart. (See Figure 8–2, Mississippi, and Figure 8–3, Michigan.)

Executive Reorganization

Modern public administration generally recommends a stronger governor and a more centralized state executive branch. Reform and reorganization proposals usually call for (1) the elimination of many separately elected state executive officials and limiting the statewide ballot to governor, lieutenant governor, and attorney general; (2) elimination of boards and commissions as heads of agencies and their replacement by single, removable gubernatorial appointees; and (3) the consolidation of many state agencies into larger departments reporting directly to the governor. While states have been slow to adopt these reforms, there has been some movement in this direction, but only marginally, as noted in Chapter 7.

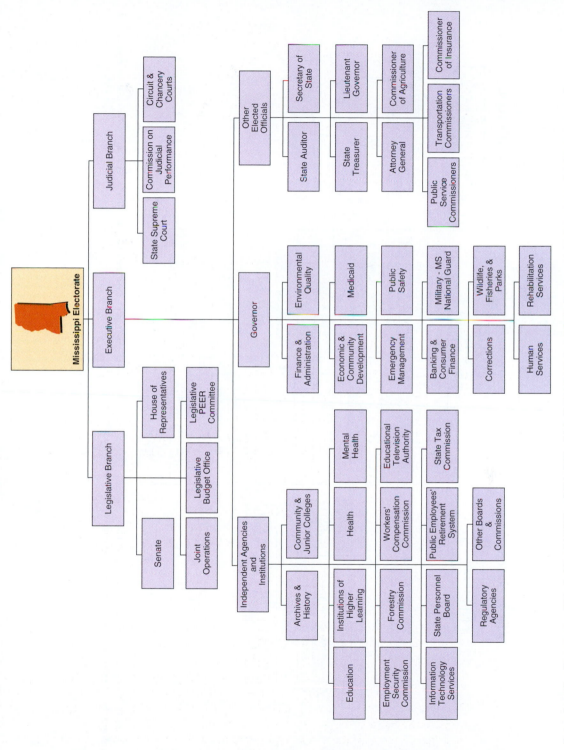

Source: https://merlin.state.ms.us/Web_Archives/SAASWA.nsf/626e6035eadbb4cd852564990061b5a6/29d05b0c1b1c12bd8625e53004c596f/$FILE/orgchart.pdf

FIGURE 8–3 State of Michigan Organization Chart (Less Fragmented Executive Branch)

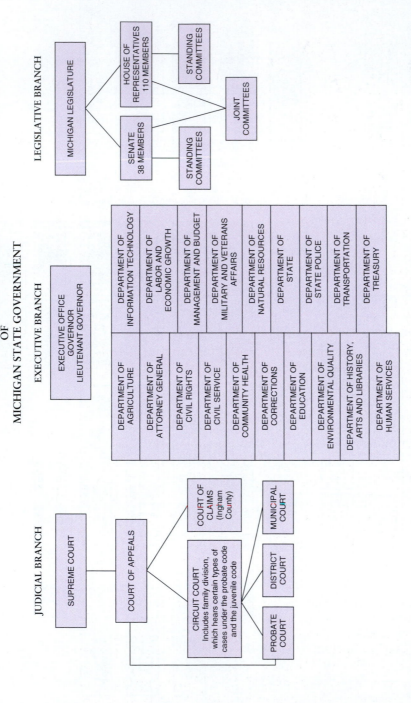

Note: The Michigan Department of State is headed by a separately elected Secretary of State; the Department of Attorney General is headed by a separately elected Attorney General.
Source: http://www.legislature.mi.gov/documents/publications/citizensguide.pdf

Political Opposition to Reorganization

Separately elected officials and independent boards and officials will be around for a long time. Political parties and public officials develop a stake in the continued existence of these elected offices. Moreover, many interest groups prefer to be governed by boards and commissions or separately elected officials. They feel they have more influence over these independent offices than those that come directly under a governor's authority. Interest groups, from educational administrators and teachers' unions, to the agriculture, insurance, real estate, and public utility industries, prefer to have direct access to executive officials. Incumbent officeholders are usually able to rally their client groups to defeat reorganization proposals that threaten their office.

BUREAU-CRATIZATION
A general reference to the size of government, often measured by spending per capita and public employment per 10,000 population.

Variations in Bureaucracy among the States

Bureaucracies are frequently measured by how much money they spend and how many people they employ. As we would expect, states with larger populations spend more money and employ more people than states with smaller populations. Perhaps **"bureaucratization"** might be better measured by state and local spending per capita and state and local employment per 10,000 population. These measures control for population size and tell us how large a part state and local government spending and employment play relative to the population of each state (see "*Rankings of the States*: Government Spending and Employment").

Populous states require big bureaucracies. It is no surprise that California, New York, Texas, and Florida, the nation's four largest states in terms of population, employ more people and spend more money than other states. However, when population size is controlled, it turns out that the largest states are not necessarily the biggest spenders. In terms of per capita (per person) spending, New York ranks second, California ranks sixth, while Florida is thirty-sixth, and Texas forty-second.

Nor are these states necessarily the most "bureaucratized" in terms of government employment in relation to their populations (employees per 10,000 population). Using this measure, Pennsylvania and Nevada rank as the least bureaucratized states in terms of state and local government employees combined, while California and Florida rank as the least bureaucratized in terms of state employees only and Delaware and Hawaii in terms of local government employees only.

BUREAUCRACY, DEMOCRACY, REPRESENTATIVENESS, AND RESPONSIVENESS

There are certain questions that repeatedly get asked about government bureaucracies and their employees. They are raised by both citizens and politicians who want government to operate differently in a representative democracy. How can we overcome the "bankruptcy of bureaucracy"—the waste, inefficiency, impersonality, and unresponsiveness of large government organizations? How can democratic governments overcome the "routine tendency to protect turf, to resist change, to build empires, to enlarge one's spheres of control, to protect programs regardless of whether or not they are any longer needed?"[3] Should governments be staffed by people politically loyal and responsive to elected officials? Or should governments be staffed by nonpartisan people selected on the basis of merit and protected from political influence?

RANKINGS of the STATES

Government Spending and Employment

Total State and Local Expenditures per Capital (in dollars)

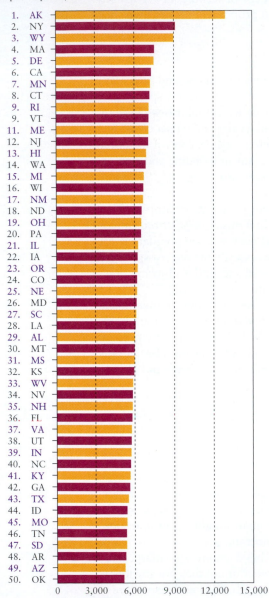

1. AK
2. NY
3. WY
4. MA
5. DE
6. CA
7. MN
8. CT
9. RI
9. VT
11. ME
12. NJ
13. HI
14. WA
15. MI
16. WI
17. NM
18. ND
19. OH
20. PA
21. IL
22. IA
23. OR
24. CO
25. NE
26. MD
27. SC
28. LA
29. AL
30. MT
31. MS
32. KS
33. WV
34. NV
35. NH
36. FL
37. VA
38. UT
39. IN
40. NC
41. KY
42. GA
43. TX
44. ID
45. MO
46. TN
47. SD
48. AR
49. AZ
50. OK

(x-axis: 0, 3,000, 6,000, 9,000, 12,000, 15,000)

Note: Data are for 2004.
Source: U.S. Bureau of the Census. "State and Local Government Finances: 2003–2004" (http://www.census.gov/govs/www/estimate04.html)

State and Local Employees per 10,000 Population

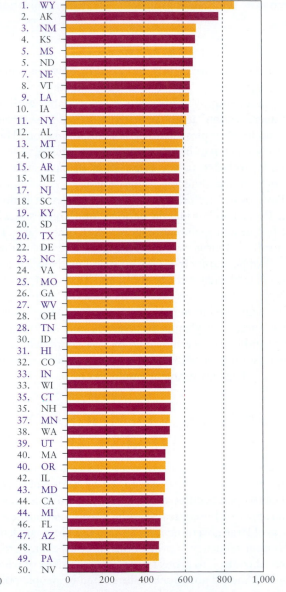

1. WY
2. AK
3. NM
4. KS
5. MS
5. ND
7. NE
8. VT
9. LA
10. IA
11. NY
12. AL
13. MT
14. OK
15. AR
15. ME
17. NJ
18. SC
19. KY
20. SD
20. TX
22. DE
23. NC
24. VA
25. MO
26. GA
27. WV
28. OH
28. TN
30. ID
31. HI
32. CO
33. IN
33. WI
35. CT
35. NH
37. MN
38. WA
39. UT
40. MA
40. OR
42. IL
43. MD
44. CA
44. MI
46. FL
47. AZ
48. RI
49. PA
50. NV

(x-axis: 0, 200, 400, 600, 800, 1,000)

Note: Data are for 2005
Source: U.S. Bureau of the Census. "State and Local Employment and Payroll—March 2005," (http://www.census.gov/)

The Patronage System

Historically, government employment in states, counties, and cities was allocated by the patronage system. Jobs were handed out on the basis of party loyalty, electoral support, political influence, personal friendships, family ties, and financial contributions, rather than on the basis of job-related qualifications.

Although widely condemned by reformers, the traditional patronage system helped to strengthen political parties. It helped organize voters and motivated them to go to the polls. It maintained discipline within a party's ranks. Patronage was a central component of political "machines" and a source of power for political "bosses" (see "Old Style Machine Politics" in Chapter 11).

Patronage was also a major source of power for state governors. As late as the 1960s, almost half of all state jobs were filled by the governor or the governor's patronage advisors from the ranks of "deserving" party workers. Party organizations were sustained with jobs in tax collection, licensing, parks, commerce, agriculture, welfare, and especially highways. The governor's office would "clear" appointments with party county chairpersons throughout the state, and patronage appointees were expected to work for the party organization at election time. Often state patronage employees held party posts themselves. Patronage was especially widespread in the older, two-party states of the East and Midwest.

The Merit System

The merit system—government employment based on competence, neutrality, and protection from partisanship—was introduced at the federal level in the Pendleton Act of 1883. This Act created the federal Civil Service Commission (now called the Office of Personnel Management), which selects government personnel based on merit. That same year New York became the first state to enact a merit system. Yet for many years only a few states adopted merit systems, and even in those states only a small proportion of government employees came under civil service protection.

But over time the merit system came to replace patronage as the principal means of staffing state and local government. In 1939 Congress amended the Social Security Act of 1935 to require states to set up merit systems in welfare and unemployment compensation agencies that received federal grants-in-aid. Gradually the states expanded their merit systems to encompass most of their employees.

In some states nearly all state workers are covered by civil service, and patronage is limited to boards, commissioners, policymaking offices, university trusteeships, and judicial posts. The patronage system was always awkward to administer; many lower-paid menial jobs were unattractive to party workers. As the influence of parties declined in electoral politics (see "American Political Parties" in Chapter 5), governors themselves came to view patronage systems as more of a burden than a benefit to their administrations. Reform governors capitalized on the public's image of patronage as corrupt, and they gradually expanded civil service coverage. Finally, the federal courts began to strike at patronage systems with decisions preventing governments from firing their employees for partisan political reasons.[4]

Bureaucratic "Cultures"

Bureaucracies often develop their own "cultures," usually in strong support of the function they serve, their client interest group, and, of course, their own pay, perks, and job security.

PATRONAGE SYSTEM

Selection of employees for government agencies on the basis of political loyalty and electoral support.

MERIT SYSTEM

Selection of employees for government agencies on the basis of competence, with no consideration of an individual's political loyalties or support.

Government agencies become dominated by people who have worked there for most of their lives. They believe that their work is important, and they resist efforts by governors, legislators, mayors, and council members to reduce the authority, size, or budget of their agency. Change comes hard. Even when organizational charts are redrawn, new management philosophies are put in place, and new leaders get installed at the top, change will not be automatic. Success is often dependent on the degree to which persons at the lower levels of the organization are involved and can see potential personal benefits from shaking up business as usual.

The Problem of Productivity

Another troublesome problem in federal, state, and local bureaucracies is that of ensuring productivity—producing desired results at the least possible cost to taxpayers. Civil service employees suffer a popular reputation for inefficiency. Government executives often find it difficult to improve job performance because of the obstacles to rewarding or punishing public employees. Seldom can good performance be rewarded with raises or bonuses as in private employment. And, at the same time, poor performance often goes unpunished. It is very difficult to fire a public employee (see "*Up Close:* Firing a Public Employee"). Often a state executive confronting a poorly performing employee must spend more than a year in extended proceedings to secure a dismissal. As a result, sometimes costly substitute strategies are devised, for example, transferring nonperforming employees to other agencies or taking away their responsibilities while letting them keep their jobs. Of course the latter approach only alienates and angers fellow coworkers who have to pick up the additional slack.

Centralized Personnel Management

Most bureaucratic hiring actually comes about through "networks" of personal friends and professional associates.

Today virtually all states (Texas is a notable exception) have centralized personnel management systems that purport to function under the merit principle. State personnel offices are generally responsible for recruitment and testing of prospective employees. The personnel offices classify jobs in state government and determine the qualifications needed to perform them. They establish uniform pay and compensation systems, oversee performance evaluations, assist and counsel employees, and hear complaints and appeals from employees who have been disciplined.

But the merit system is frequently circumvented in states and cities across the nation. Very few people ever get hired by taking a state or city civil service examination and then waiting to be called for an interview by an agency. Most bureaucratic hiring actually comes about through "networks" of personal friends and professional associates. Agency insiders contact their friends, associates, and the professional associations to which they belong when they know a position will become vacant. Thus, some candidates know about openings well before they appear on any list of vacant positions published by the central personnel office. They can apply early and tailor their applications to the official job description. Personnel offices usually send three or more names of qualified people to an agency with a vacancy; the agency itself usually makes the final employment decision. Network recruiting generally ensures that new people entering a bureaucracy will share the same values and attitudes of people already there.

Moreover, civil service systems, particularly those administered by independent civil service commissions, significantly reduce executive control over program administration.

up CLOSE   Firing a Public Employee

I t is not impossible to fire the poorly performing state employee. But it takes a lot of managerial skill and tenacity.

It is a common perception that public employees cannot be fired for incompetence, that civil service protections, union contracts, court decisions, and smart lawyers can keep even the worst state and city employee on the public payroll. And, indeed, it is true that the involuntary discharge rate for public employees is estimated to be well below 1 percent, compared to 10 percent for privately employed service workers. But if government executives follow specific processes for firing a truly poorly performing employee, they can do so. This means successfully negotiating a myriad of legal constraints, contract provisions, published regulations, appeals, and other assorted hoops and hurdles. For example, typically the following steps are required to fire a state or city employee:

1. The employee is given a notice of disciplinary termination.
2. The employee has fifteen to thirty days to respond.

3. If the employee responds, the agency must schedule a hearing before an uninterested officer.
4. The decision of the hearing officer following the hearing may be appealed by the employee to the personnel or civil service board.
5. The employee is entitled to legal counsel during all phases of the process. Unionized employees are often provided free counsel by their union.
6. Personnel boards frequently have lengthy backlogs. They review written appeals, hold hearings, listen to testimony, and often delay their final decisions for many months. Normally the employee remains on the public payroll during this time.
7. The decisions of the personnel board may be appealed to state or federal courts, which may under some circumstances issue an injunction against firing the employee until after the case is fully resolved.

A common problem in firing a public employee is the manager's failure to maintain a written record of poor performance. Or, worse yet, the manager may have previously provided regular satisfactory job evaluations. Having checked "satisfactory" on previous standardized forms, perhaps in haste or to avoid conflict, the manager is in a poor position to later fire an employee for unsatisfactory performance. Government managers must carefully document poor job performance over time, logging in absences, tardiness, insubordination, incompetence, and so forth each time these offenses occur. Managers must communicate with errant employees after each and every offense and give them some opportunity to improve their performance. Most important, managers must carefully follow all procedural rules and regulations set forth in state laws, city ordinances, personnel manuals, and union contracts.

There is a persistent tendency for civil service systems to be routine, mechanical, and unimaginative. Job classification schemes, to which recruitment, qualifications, and pay scales are closely tied, become so rigid with time that executives have little flexibility in recruiting really talented people to state government. Executives whose authority to promote, hire, and fire their employees is severely curtailed can hardly be expected to obtain maximum effort and cooperation from their employees. On a more positive note, state and local governments are being forced to revamp their job classification systems, and their personnel recruitment and retention policies in response to vacancies being created by retiring Baby Boomers (those born between 1946 and 1964). At least ten states are projected to suffer severe government worker shortages within the next ten years.[5]

REPRESEN-
TATIVENESS

As applied to public bureaucracies, the extent to which their workforces generally reflect the social characteristics of the citizens they serve.

AFFIRMATIVE
ACTION
PROGRAMS

In government agencies, efforts to achieve minority and gender representativeness in the workforce through preferential hiring and promotion.

The Problem of Representativeness

Democratic governments generally seek to ensure a representative bureaucracy. This means the recruitment and employment of a workforce that generally reflects the social composition of the population being served. It is believed that a representative workforce will reflect the values and interests of the people it serves and will be responsive to their problems and concerns. Moreover, a representative workforce provides symbolic evidence of a government "of the people, by the people, and for the people."

Protection against discrimination based on race, gender, age, physical handicap, and other factors unrelated to job performance is embodied in the Civil Rights Act of 1964, the Age Discrimination Act of 1973, and the Americans with Disabilities Act of 1990, as well as the Fourteenth Amendment to the U.S. Constitution.

But how can state and local governments go about ensuring representativeness of their workforces without compromising the merit principle? Should state and local governments extend preferential treatment to minority job applicants in order to achieve a representative workforce?

Affirmative action programs were initially developed in the federal bureaucracy. **Affirmative action programs** seek to achieve minority and gender representativeness in the workforce through preferential hiring and promotion schemes designed to redress perceived imbalances. Virtually all state and local governments in the United States today have affirmative action programs.

The constitutional question posed by affirmative action programs is whether or not they discriminate against nonminorities in violation of the Equal Protection Clause of the Fourteenth Amendment. (We shall explore this topic in more detail in Chapter 15, "Politics and Civil Rights.") The Supreme Court has generally approved of affirmative action programs when there is evidence of past discriminatory employment practices. However, the Court has also held that race-based actions by government—any differences in treatment of the races by public agencies—must be found necessary to remedy past proven discrimination, or to further clearly identified, compelling, and legitimate government objectives. Moreover, race-based actions must be "narrowly tailored" so as not to adversely affect the rights of nonminority individuals.

Overall, state and local government employment in the United States is fairly representative of the general population. About 45 percent of the public workforce is female (compared to 51 percent of the population), about 19 percent of the public workforce is African American (compared to 12 percent of the population), and 8 percent is Hispanic (compared to 13 percent of the population). But these figures vary widely by occupational category (see Table 8–1). Today, African Americans and Hispanics are fairly well represented nationwide among firefighters, police officers, correctional guards, and technicians, and among support, service, and maintenance jobs.

Women and minorities are still underrepresented among top-ranked policymaking administrators at the state level (heads of departments, agencies, boards, commissions, and authorities; top staff advisors with policy-influencing responsibility in governor's offices).[6] A study of gubernatorial-appointed agency heads across the country found that about 32 percent were women, 8 percent were African Americans, 3 percent were Hispanic, 2 percent were Asian American/Pacific Islander, and less than 1 percent were American Indians/Native Alaskans.[7] Only five states (Massachusetts, Oregon, Florida, Iowa, and Missouri) are close to gender parity in top policy positions. African American women have made the greatest strides in gaining these top policy positions. Nevertheless, women

TABLE 8–1   State and Local Government Employment

Categories	Total	Male (%)	Female (%)	White (%)	African American (%)	Hispanics (%)
Officials/Administrators	341,000	63.1	36.9	80.6	11.4	5.0
Professional	1,473,000	44.4	55.6	72.2	15.5	6.5
Technicians	477,000	57.2	42.8	71.3	15.7	8.4
Protective Service	1,132,000	81.5	18.5	70.2	18.1	9.5
Paraprofessionals	410,000	26.6	73.4	58.0	29.0	9.5
Administrative Support	917,000	13.3	86.7	64.7	20.5	11.1
Skilled Craft	424,000	94.6	5.4	72.6	15.8	8.7
Service/Maintenance	570,000	76.6	23.3	53.7	31.1	12.5

Note: Data are from 2003.

Source: U.S. Census Bureau, *Statistical Abstract of the United States* 2007. Available at http://www.census.gov/prod/2006pubs/07statab/stlocgov.pdf, No. 453.

and minority employment at all levels of state and local *government* exceeds that in the *private-sector* workforce.

Government workers are "substantially better educated and older, on average, as well as more likely to be female and black" than private sector employees.[8] Public employees cite helping others, being useful to society, and doing interesting work as important factors in choosing a job whereas private-sector employees are more likely to say they value high income and advancement opportunities. Both groups agree that job security is a very important consideration.[9]

COLLECTIVE BARGAINING

The determination of wages, benefits, and working conditions through bargaining with unions that represent employees.

THE POWER OF PUBLIC EMPLOYEE UNIONS

Unions among public employees further complicate executive control of the bureaucracy. Today, over one-third of all state and local government employees are unionized. The largest public employee union in the states is the American Federation of State, County, and Municipal Employees (AFSCME). **Collective bargaining agreements** between state and local governments and public employee unions usually stipulate salaries and wages, pensions and benefits, grievance procedures, and seniority. These restrict executive authority over dismissals, layoffs,

The largest *public* employee union in the states is the American Federation of State, County, and Municipal Employees (AFSCME). Government employee unions fight vigorously against any sort of privatization because it means lost jobs for their members. The nation's largest *private* sector union is the Teamsters.

PEOPLE in POLITICS

What Makes a State Employee Outstanding?

Virginian John Marshall,[a] Iowan Reyna Taylor,[b] and a team of feed mill inspectors from North Carolina[c] all have one thing in common—they have been recognized as outstanding state employees. Awards programs are growing in popularity. They are morale boosters for the winning individuals or teams of employees who deserve to be called "public servants" rather than labeled as "bean counters," "red-tape tanglers," or "bureaucrats." Recipients come from all levels of an organization, from agency head, to mid-level professionals, to those on the "front line"—the ones with whom the public interacts the most. The growing number of team awards across the states has paralleled the adoption of organizational reforms such as TQM (Total Quality Management), Reinventing Government (REGO), and performance-based employee reward and budgeting systems.

John W. Marshall
Secretary of Public Safety, Virginia

Each state develops its own standards for measuring outstanding performance. The state of Utah, for example, considers five criteria: (1) extraordinary competence in work performance (quality work, work ethics, special achievements); (2) creativity in identifying problems and devising workable, cost-effective solutions; (3) excellent relationships with the public and other employees (includes attitude at work); (4) commitment to serving the public as the client; and (5) commitment to economy and efficiency in state government.[d]

Sources: [a]National Forum for Black Public Administrators, "Congratulations to the 2004 Awards Recipients," www.nfbspa.org, accessed June 4, 2005; "Secretary of Public Safety John William Marshall," www.publicsafety.virginia.gov/SecInfo/SecBio.cfm, accessed June 4, 2005. Michael D. Shear. "Va. Safety Chief May Run for Lt. Governor," *Washington Post,* June 11, 2004, p. B03.
[b]Iowa Workforce Development, "Golden Dome Recipients and Nominees Honored," *Workforce Wednesday,* May 2002 issue, accessed June 5, 2005.
[c]North Carolina Department of Agriculture & Consumer Affairs, "NCDA&CS Employees Recognized for Service; Employee of the Year Named," May 19, 2005; www.ncagr.com/paffairs/release/2005/5-05eoy.htm, accessed June 5,2005.
[d]Utah Department of Human Resource Management, "2005 Outstanding State Employee Award Criteria," www.dhrm,utah.gov/er/printety.html, accessed June 5, 2005.
(Pictures available at: http://www.ncagr.com/paffairs/release/2005/5-05eoy.htm; www.publicsafety.virginia.gov/SecInfo/SecBio.cfm; www.iowaworkforce.org/iwdstaff/2002/0502.htm)

reorganization, elimination of positions, merit and incentive pay plans, and other actions affecting public employees.

Indeed, while unions in the public sector have shrunk, membership in public sector unions has remained fairly stable in the 2000s. (See Figure 8–4.)

Collective Bargaining

Most state laws today recognize the right of public employees to organize unions and bargain collectively with state and local governments over wages, hours, and conditions of work. However, only a handful of states continue to resist collective bargaining with public employees (including Arizona, Colorado, Utah, Arkansas, Louisiana, Mississippi,

FIGURE 8–4 Unionization of Public versus Private Employees

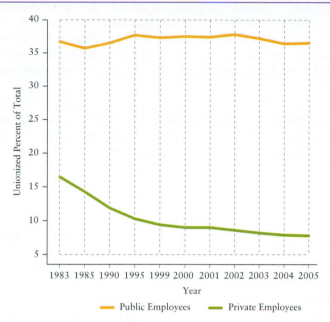

Source: U.S. Census Bureau *Statistical Abstract of the United States 2007.* Available at http://www.census.gov/
prod/2006pubs/07statab/labor.pdf

North Carolina, South Carolina, and Virginia). Public employees everywhere have a
constitutional right to *join* a union, but governments are not required by federal laws or
the U.S. Constitution to *bargain* with them. Nevertheless, over 40 percent of all state and
local government employees are covered by collective bargaining agreements.

Strikes

In contrast to *private* employees, *public* employees are generally prohibited by law from
striking. Instead, most state laws stipulate that public employee labor disputes are to
go to **arbitration**—that is, be submitted to neutral third parties for decision. Decisions
of arbitrators (or arbitration boards consisting of equal representation from employees
and employers, together with neutral members) may or may not be binding on both the
city and union, depending on specific provisions of each state's laws. However, many
public employee unions throughout the country have rendered "no-strike" laws practically useless in a heated labor dispute. Police, firefighters, teachers, sanitation workers, and others have struck in many large cities, and there have been statewide strikes
as well. Unions can nullify no-strike laws by simply adding another demand—no legal
prosecution of strikers or union leaders—as a condition of going back to work.

Wages and Benefits

State and local employees, who for generations were paid wages below those for comparable jobs in private enterprise, now at least match private employees in salaries,
benefits, pensions, and so on for many government jobs. Theoretically, public employee
unions should be very effective in raising wages. It might be reasoned that (1) elected
government officials are less constrained than private employers by profit and loss

ARBITRATION
Disputes between
parties are submitted
and decided by a
neutral third party.

CLOUT

Informal power in the world of politics; usually infers someone who can get things done in the political process.

considerations and more likely to grant union demands; and (2) unlike employees in the private sector, public employees participate in electing their own bosses, placing additional pressure on them to succumb to union demands. Empirical research does suggest that unionized municipal workers earn more than nonunionized municipal workers.[10] But unions may have even greater impact on raising fringe benefits (retirement, health benefits, vacations, etc.) and ensuring job security of government employees.

Political Clout

Unions in the *private* sector of the American economy have been in steep decline in recent decades; today only about 10 percent of the private workforce is unionized. But unions in the *public* sector have grown dramatically, although lately they, too, have experienced a slight decline in membership. (See Figure 8–4.) AFSCME is the nation's second largest union, after the Teamsters, and it adds members each year. Most of its membership is concentrated in ten states—New York, Ohio, Pennsylvania, Michigan, Illinois, Wisconsin, Massachusetts, Minnesota, Connecticut, and Hawaii.

Government employee unions can usually be counted on to lend strong support for tax increases at all levels of government. They are also vigorous opponents of privatization (see later discussion). AFSCME objects strongly to the idea that private contractors can provide services more efficiently than municipal bureaucracies. Moreover, the union claims that privatization "diminishes government accountability to citizens."

Public-sector unions, notably AFSCME and state chapters of the National Education Association (NEA) and the American Federation of Teachers (AFT), are regularly ranked among the most effective lobbying groups in state capitals. And public employee union PACs regularly rank among the largest campaign contributors in state gubernatorial and legislative elections. Public employees and their families turn out on Election Day far more frequently than the average voter.

Public Employee Views of Unions

The vast majority of public service employees trust labor *unions* more than the governments they work for to provide good wages and benefits (72 percent), provide accurate information about workplace issues (72 percent), provide safe working conditions (65 percent), and provide steady employment (61 percent). But 67 percent say they trust *government* to increase employee productivity, not unions, and 44 percent believe that unions tend to oppose management when it comes to improving production goals and work rules.[11]

STATE REGULATORY POLICY

The emergence of new regulations often tracks closely with intense media coverage of a problem—an outbreak of food poisoning, child pornography on a teacher's computer at work, the death of an infant in a day care facility, a faulty roof job on an elderly person's home following a hurricane, or an identity theft scam that led to ruined lives. Other times regulations get put in place when one level of government is attempting to "control" another or when interest groups seek to maintain or expand control over a process, profession, or product. The evolution of regulatory policy closely parallels the evolution of federal–state–local relations. However, most Americans see the regulatory maze as federalism at its worst, rather than federalism at its finest.

Regulatory power in the United States has accumulated over time at the federal level. The Federal Reserve Board exercises great power over the banking industry;

the National Labor Relations Board protects unions and prohibits "unfair labor practices"; the National Transportation Safety Board oversees safety in automobiles, trucks, and buses; the Federal Trade Commission oversees product labeling; the Equal Employment Opportunity Commission investigates complaints about racial and sexual discrimination in jobs; the Consumer Product Safety Commission reviews the safety of marketed products; the Federal Communications Commission regulates radio and television broadcasting; the Food and Drug Administration determines when drugs are "safe and effective"; the Department of Agriculture inspects agricultural products; the Occupational Safety

Federal-state battles over regulatory authority, particularly with regard to energy policy, are often intense. The federal Environmental Protection Agency is concerned about the environmental impacts of wind power while state economic development agencies see the new energy source as important to the state's economic growth and competitiveness.

and Health Administration inspects the workplace; and the Environmental Protection Agency has broad powers over virtually every aspect of American life. It is difficult to find an activity in public or private life that is *not* regulated at the federal level.

However, states exercise considerable regulatory power and authority in fields *not preempted* by federal law and regulation. For example, *state* regulatory agencies exercise principal powers over public utilities, including electric and gas, corporate chartering, insurance, alcoholic beverages, occupational licensing, health and hospitals, the real estate industry, and motor vehicles (see Table 8–2). Moreover, many federal regulatory

---

TABLE 8–2   Selected State Regulatory Functions

Public utilities, including electric and gas wholesale and retail rate regulation.

Corporate chartering, including registration of all corporations, their officers, and businesses.

Insurance, including licensing of insurance companies, rate regulation, and liability laws.

Alcoholic beverages, including regulation of sales to minors and licensing of wholesale and retail distributors and places serving alcoholic beverages.

Occupational licensing, from certified public accountants, barbers, cosmetologists, architects, plumbers, electricians, massage therapists, and chiropractors; to physicians, nurses, dentists, and pharmacists.

Health and hospitals, including public health regulations, regulation and licensing of hospitals and nursing homes.

Motor vehicles, including registration, driver's licensing, insurance requirements, speed limits, traffic regulations, seat belt laws, and child restraints.

Gaming, including regulation of horse and dog racetracks, off-track betting, casinos, and lotteries.

PARTIAL PRE-EMPTION

State laws on the same subject are valid as long as they do not conflict with federal law on that subject.

PRINCIPAL–AGENT PROBLEM

In government, the problem of ensuring that bureaucrats (agents) carry out the intentions of elected officials (principals), that the self-interests of bureaucrats do not conflict with these intentions.

CAPTURE THEORY

The theory that over time regulatory agencies come under the influence of the industries they are supposed to regulate.

agencies exercise *partial preemption* (where state laws on the same subject are valid as long as they do not conflict with federal law on that subject). (See "Coercive Federalism: Preemptions and Mandates" in Chapter 3.) And the current rhetoric in Washington about "devolution" of responsibilities from federal government to the states has resulted in increased regulatory authority for state agencies, especially in welfare and work training.[12]

Understanding Regulatory Policy

Regulations usually do not involve large amounts of direct government expenditures. Instead, regulatory policy allows governments to shift costs to private firms and individuals by directing them to spend money and resources to comply with regulations. Indeed, often a regulatory approach to public problems is preferred by politicians precisely *because* it does not involve the direct expenditure of tax monies. For example, state governments do not appropriate money for power plants but their regulatory agencies can impose costs on private electric utilities by mandating safety regulations, employment rules, and even the rates they are permitted to charge customers. However, if a state's regulatory environment becomes too burdensome, it may become more difficult to attract new jobs and industries. Economic development–oriented groups routinely publish rankings of state business climates; regulations are one of the key factors used to calculate those rankings.

Principal–Agent Theory

Regulatory policy is often highly technical, requiring significant bureaucratic expertise and consequently the delegation of considerable policymaking power *from* the legislature and the governor *to* agencies, boards, and commissions. This delegation of authority raises what economists refer to as the "principal–agent problem"— how the governor and legislature (the "principal") can ensure that their true intentions and interests are being pursued by bureaucratic agencies (the "agent") especially when bureaucrats may have their own interests to pursue. The principal–agent problem in government is complicated by the fact that *two* principals are involved—the governor and the legislature. Both are supposed to oversee regulatory activity—legislatures through direct legislative oversight committees and annual appropriations, and governors through appointments, executive orders, and gubernatorial budgeting.[13] (It is generally believed that governors exercise less influence over regulatory agencies, boards, and commissions than legislatures simply because they are less interested in routine governmental functions.)

Capture Theory

Interest groups, especially those directly subject to regulation, may exercise even more influence over a bureaucracy than the governor or legislature. These groups—electric and gas utilities, banks, insurance companies, the alcoholic beverage industry, the gaming industry, nursing home operators, day care providers, the medical association, the Bar Association, and so on—focus their attention on the day-to-day activities of the regulators. They have the greatest stake in regulation. A "capture theory" suggests that over time, because of the close interaction between the regulators and the regulated, regulatory agencies gradually come under the influence of the industries, occupations, and professions that they are supposed to regulate and become "neglectful of the interests of the broader public that is supposed to benefit from regulation."[14]

Bureaucratic Self-Interest

Bureaucrats themselves often come to exercise considerable power, independent of the governor, the legislature, or interest groups. Bureaucrats often believe strongly in the importance of their activities. In addition to public-spirited motives, bureaucrats, like everyone else, seek to expand their own authority. They can be expected to recommend expansion of their own powers and functions and continuing increases in their budgets. This **"budget maximization"**—effort by bureaucrats to expand their own power, functions, staff, and budgets—is one of the reasons that government grows over time. The fact that so many state agencies, boards, and commissions are independent of the governor, their members are appointed for long terms, and their status is protected in the state's constitution adds to their own power.

REFORM, PRIVATIZATION, AND "REINVENTING GOVERNMENT"

Polls repeatedly show that people believe governments are spending more but delivering less; they are frustrated with bureaucracies over which they have little control and tired of politicians who raise taxes and cut services. Specifically, a majority believes that elected officials do not care what the average citizen thinks and that government bureaucracies have become "too powerful." Less than half of the populace believes that government is run for the benefit of all people. A sizable majority believe that when government does something, it is usually inefficient and wasteful. They also are convinced that government regulation of business usually does more harm than good. (See Table 8–3.) But they would rather have governments closer to home in charge than the federal government.

BUDGET MAXI-MIZATION
The tendency of bureaucrats to expand their own hours, functions, staff, and budgets.

The fact that so many state agencies, boards, and commissions are independent of the governor, their members are appointed for long terms, and their status is protected in the state's constitution adds to their own power.

TABLE 8–3	Citizen Views on Government Responsiveness, Effectiveness, and Efficiency		
View	**Agree (%)**	**Disagree (%)**	**Don't Know (%)**
Most elected officials care what people like me think	34	62	4
People like me don't have any say about what the government does	48	50	2
Government regulation of business usually does more harm than good	57	35	8
The federal government should run ONLY those things that cannot be run at the local level	74	20	6
When something is run by the government, it is usually inefficient and wasteful	62	34	4
The government is really run for the benefit of all the people	45	52	3

Source: Trends in Political Values and Core Attitudes: 1987–2007; Pew Research Center (March, 2007). Copyright © 2007. Reprinted by permission of The Pew Research Center for the People and the Press. Available at http://people-press.org/reports/pdf/312.pdf

PRIVATIZATION

Shifting the production of government services from public bureaucracies to private firms.

"LOAD SHEDDING"

Government selling off many of its enterprises—for example, housing projects, airports, stadiums—to private individuals or firms who would operate them more efficiently and effectively.

Today, bureaucratic regulations of all kinds—environmental controls, workplace safety rules, municipal building codes, government contracting guidelines—have become so numerous, detailed, and complex that they are stifling initiative, curtailing economic growth, wasting billions of dollars, and breeding popular contempt for law and government. One critic summarizes the problem as follows:

> Our regulatory system has become an instructional manual. It tells us and the bureaucrats exactly what to do and how to do it. Detailed rule after detailed rule addresses every eventuality or at least every situation that lawmakers and bureaucrats can think of. Is it a coincidence that almost every encounter with government is an exercise in frustration? . . . We have constructed a system of regulatory law that basically outlaws common sense.[15]

The result is that we direct our energy and wealth into defensive measures, designed not to improve our lives but to avoid tripping over senseless rules. People come to see government as their adversary and government regulations as obstacles in their lives.

Bureaucrats become more concerned with following rules than with promoting sensible outcomes. They seek to protect themselves by following detailed rules and by focusing on time-consuming and costly procedures (paperwork, forms, hearings, appeals, and delays) rather than the actual effect of their decisions. Following procedures substitutes for personal responsibility. Ironically, when employees are rewarded for being outstanding, it is often because they "think outside the box." (See *People in Politics:* "What Makes a State Employee Outstanding?")

Privatization as Reform

Political conservatives have mounted a reform movement in state and local government, centering on the notion of the "privatization" of public services. Traditionally, conservatives have sought to restrain the growth of government:

> The bigger the government the greater the force for even bigger government. Budgets will expand, resulting in the appointment of more officials and the hiring of more workers. These will go to work at once to enlarge their budgets, do less work, hire still more workers, obtain better-than-average raises, and vote for more spending programs, while encouraging their constituents and beneficiaries to do the same. The forecast seems ominous: Sooner or later everyone will be working for government.[16]

Occasionally citizens revolt against the trend toward ever larger governments by voting for tax limitation proposals or threatening to move to lower tax jurisdictions. But according to the proponents of privatization, "a more educated, critical, and sophisticated" approach to controlling the growth of government is needed, namely the privatization of government services wherever and whenever possible.

Privatization

In the broadest sense, privatization includes the shifting of many responsibilities *from* government *to* the private marketplace. **"Load shedding"** implies that government should sell off many of its enterprises—for example, housing projects, airports, stadiums—to private individuals or firms who would operate them more efficiently and effectively. But privatization has also generally come to mean greater reliance on private and not-for-profit providers of governmental services functioning in a competitive marketplace and giving individuals greater choice in services.

Privatization recognizes a distinction between government provision of a service and government production of a service. Governments may decide to *provide* citizens with certain goods and services—for example, schools, police and fire protection, garbage collection, bus transportation, street maintenance, and so on—but not necessarily *produce* these services directly through government bureaucracies—public schools, municipal police and fire departments, municipal garbage collection, city-owned buses, city street maintenance departments, and so on. Rather, a variety of other methods of "service delivery" are available that rely more on private or not-for-profit, competitive producers, and individual choice.

How to Privatize

The following are among the most common methods of privatizing the provision of government services:

- *Contracting:* Governments contract with private or not-for-profit organizations to provide a publicly funded service. These firms compete to win and keep the contracts by providing quality services at low costs.
- *Franchising:* Governments grant exclusive contracts for a certain period of time to a private firm to provide a monopoly service—for example, cable television or garbage collection. The private firm collects fees directly from citizens under contractual terms agreed to by the government. The franchise firm may pay a fee to the government for the privilege. Government may terminate the franchise for poor performance or excessive fees charged to citizens.
- *Grants:* Governments provide direct grants of money to private firms or nonprofit organizations conditioned on their providing low-cost services to citizens. Grants are typically made to hospitals and health facilities, libraries and cultural centers, and low-cost housing projects, among others.
- *Vouchers:* Vouchers are given directly to citizens who qualify for them, allowing these citizens to exercise free choice in selecting the producers of the service. Unlike grants, in which the government chooses the producers of the service, vouchers give citizens the power to choose the producer. Producers compete to attract citizens who have vouchers; the vouchers are later turned in to the government by producers for cash. For example, rent vouchers to the poor or homeless allow them to select housing of their choice; grants to public housing organizations oblige the poor and homeless to seek shelter in specific projects. Education vouchers (see Chapter 16) would allow parents to choose any school, public or private, for their children. Schools would compete to attract pupils, cashing in their accumulated vouchers.

Surveys show that at the state level, the most commonly privatized (contracted out) programs and services are in the corrections, education, health and human services, transportation, and personnel areas. (See Table 8–4.) At the local level, they are (in descending order)[17]: vehicle towing and storage; commercial and residential solid waste disposal; day care facilities; street light operation; traffic signal installation/maintenance; street repairs; bus system operation; ambulance service; airport operation; and hospital operations/management. A few cities and counties have even privatized jail operations, building and grounds maintenance, data processing, tax billing, delinquency tax collection, and other functions traditionally performed by government employees.

The Politics of Privatization

Privatization is usually defended as a cost-saving measure—a way of reducing the waste, inefficiency, and unresponsiveness of "bloated bureaucracies." It is argued

TABLE 8–4   State Privatization

Most Popular Privatized Services

Corrections Programs and Services

Service	Number of States
Medical/Health Services	26
Food Services	16
Substance Abuse Treatment	8
Mental Health Services	7
Private Prisons	7
Inmate Housing	7

Education Programs and Services

Service	Number of States
Information Technology	16
Professional Development/Training	7
Statewide Student Assessment	5
Product/Program Development	5
Special Education	5

Health and Human Services Programs and Services

Service	Number of States
Mental Health Services	10
Child Welfare Services	8
Substance Abuse Treatment/Prevention	6
Child Support Administration	6
Medical Services/Staff	5

Personnel Programs and Services

Service	Number of States
Training Program Staff/Development	10
Information Technology	6
Workers' Compensation Claims Processing	3
Health Insurance Claims Processing	2
General Program Administration/Support	2
Consultants	2

Transportation Programs and Services

Service	Number of States
Collective Bargaining Negotiations	2
General Project Design/Engineering	19
General Construction/Maintenance	16
Information Technology	9

Service	Number of States
Inspections	8
Grass Mowing	7
Rest Area Operation/Maintenance	7
Highway Construction/Maintenance	7

Source: The Book of the States, 2004, p. 477.

that private contractors, operating in a competitive marketplace, can provide the same services at much lower costs than government bureaucracies. Privatization advocates also believe that businesses and nonprofits have a greater propensity to be innovative and more "resources in computer technology, high volume processing equipment, and specialized personnel, plus the flexibility to assign [workers] wherever they are needed most."[18] At the same time, privatization is seen as strengthening private enterprise.

But privatization is usually opposed by powerful political groups—especially municipal employees and their unions and teachers' unions and public school administrators. They argue that the cost savings of privatization are often exaggerated and that the savings come at the price of reduced quality and/or a failure to serve all of the people. From the government employees' perspective, they argue that "privatization threatens job security, pay and benefits, working conditions, and career opportunities."[19] There is also concern about the loss of public control of services through privatization and a belief that government contractors and franchises can become at least as arrogant and unresponsive as government bureaucracies. These latter problems, the loss of accountability and the rise of unresponsiveness, become big concerns when governments do not properly audit the contractors and subcontractors.

Conditions for Success

Successful privatization efforts do not just happen. A study of state and local government privatizations by the U.S. General Accounting Office identified six keys to success[20]: (1) a committed political leader who supports it; (2) an organizational structure that can effectively implement it; (3) a legislature's cuts in funding to an agency to give it an incentive to privatize a service or program; (4) the availability of reliable cost data; (5) an effective plan to help government employees affected by the privatization find another job; and (6) effective monitoring of the results.

Some reformers acknowledge that privatization is not a cure-all. Reformer David Osborne writes that "privatization is one answer, but not *the* answer."[21] Government's job, according to Osborne, is to determine whether a particular function can best be produced by government employees; private contractors; or nonprofit, voluntary organizations. Governments cannot hand over the responsibility of *governance* to others; governments still make the policy decisions and provide the financing. Reformers also warn state and local policymakers against viewing all privatization efforts as the same. Some have saved money, others have not. Some have made government programs and services work more efficiently, effectively, or fairly; others have produced little or no change in program operations.

"REINVENTING GOVERNMENT"

A reform movement that encourages government bureaucracies to be more entrepreneurial, mission driven, results oriented, decentralized, and responsive to citizens' needs.

"Reinventing Government"

Reformers have also argued that "Our fundamental problem today is not too much government or too little government . . . [but] the wrong kind of government." Rather than rely exclusively on either bureaucratization or privatization, they call for an "entrepreneurial" government that "searches for efficient and effective ways of managing."

How is the "entrepreneurial spirit" to be encouraged in government? A widely read and cited book, *Reinventing Government*, sets out ten principles of government entrepreneurialship:

- *Steer rather than row.* Separate policy decisions (steering) from service delivery (rowing). Government should focus on steering while relying more on private firms to deliver services. Government should be a catalyst.

- *Empower people rather than simply deliver services.* Governments should encourage communities and neighborhoods to undertake ownership and control of public services. Government should be community owned.

- *Inject competition into service delivery.* Competition between public and private agencies, among private contractors, or between different governments encourages efficiency, innovation, and responsiveness. Government should be competitive.

- *Make government organizations mission driven rather than rule driven.* Do not prescribe how government organizations should go about doing things by prescribing rules, procedures, and regulations but, rather, set goals and encourage government organizations to find the best ways to achieve them. Government should be mission driven.

- *Encourage governments to be results oriented.* Government bureaucracies should be measured in terms of their results, not their size, numbers, or services. Government should fund outcomes, not inputs.

- *Focus on the needs of customers, not the bureaucracy.* Governments should treat citizens as if they were customers, responding to their needs, "putting them in the driver's seat." Government should be customer-driven. (See "*Did You Know?* Bureaucrats Challenged to 'Write It Simple!'")

- *Encourage governments to earn money through user charges.* Charging the users of government services, whenever possible, is fair; it raises revenues and balances demands for services. Governments should be enterprising.

- *Practice prevention rather than cure.* Problems from fires to ill health are cheaper to address through prevention than services. Government should be anticipatory.

- *Decentralize government organizations.* Decentralization increases flexibility, effectiveness, innovation, morale, and commitment. Government should be decentralized.

- *Use market incentives to bring about change rather than command and control.* Market mechanisms are preferred over regulations. Government should be market oriented.[22]

Note that these are guiding principles, rather than recommendations for changes in the structure of state or local government. Unlike earlier reformers who focused on structural changes, today's reformers are more concerned about *how* governments go about their tasks.

Politics of Reinvention

The principles of "reinvention" are identified with the "neoliberal" ("new" liberals) and Democrats who acquired influence in state and local politics in the 1980s. A recognized

did YOU know? Bureaucrats Challenged to "Write It Simple!"

Citizens constantly complain that there is too much jargon in government documents. Florida's Agency for Health Care Administration (AHCA) has implemented a "Plain Language Program." When employees log on to their computers, they see a big "splash screen" that pulls a wordy policy statement from an agency document and challenges the worker to rewrite it. The following day, the workers receive another e-mail showing the statement rewritten in plain language. Here are some examples:

First day: the challenge

Plain Language
The art of clear and concise communication

Change the words below to plain language.

Pursuant to Section 409.913(3), Florida Statutes, the Agency for Health Care Administration has determined that a prepayment review be conducted on your Medicaid claims. This action is effective for those claims currently in the system for processing as well as claims submitted after this date. These claims will be suspended by the Agency for review prior to processing.

AHCA
American Health Care Association

question: Pursuant to Section 409.913(3), Florida Statutes, the Agency for Health Care Administration has determined that a prepayment review be conducted on your Medicaid claims. This action is effective for those claims currently in the system for processing as well as claims submitted after this date. These claims will be suspended by the Agency for review prior to processing.

answer: Under Section 409.913(3), Florida Statutes, the Agency for Health Care Administration will conduct a review of your Medicaid claims prior to processing them. This action affects claims currently in the system as well as future claims.

Following day: the challenge and the answer

Other examples

Source: Palm Beach Post, available at http://www.palmbeachpost.com/politics/content/local_news/slideshows/plain_language/

leader of the movement was Arkansas Governor Bill Clinton, who was widely praised for his innovative efforts in education and economic development in that state.[23] Clinton served for several years as chair of the Democratic Leadership Conference (DLC), designed to move the national Democratic party toward a more moderate, centrist position that could win back the support of white middle-class voters in presidential elections. Upon entering the Oval Office, Clinton commissioned Vice President Al Gore to head a National Performance Review specifically committed to "reinventing" the federal government.[24]

But political opposition to the new reform arises from many of the core constituency groups of the Democratic party—government employees, teachers' unions, environmental groups, and black leaders and organizations. Jesse Jackson once described the DLC derisively as "Democrats for the Leisure Class." Government employees and their unions are concerned about the antibureaucratic thrust of many of the new reforms; they fear a loss of the government-sector jobs to private contractors. Likewise, teachers' unions have been concerned with the reformers' focus on government performance, fearing that it means competence testing of students *and* teachers (see Chapter 16). Blacks and other minority groups fear that the focus on efficiency and productivity will overshadow concerns about equity. User fees and charges often place heavy burdens on the poor.

Support for "reinvention" is strong in the business community. Business interests have long bemoaned bloated government bureaucracies and senseless rules and regulations. High-tech companies have an added interest in selling governments computer hardware and software designed to make governmental operations more efficient. Major management consulting firms, like Peat Marwick and Price Waterhouse, are anxious to win contracts from state and local governments to proceed with reinvention. And many elected state and local officials understand the political appeal to taxpayers of efforts to reinvent government. Various "cookbooks" are now available to assist them in these efforts.[25]

The search for new ways of doing things is ongoing. Pick up any public administration text and you can read about a multitude of past efforts, including management by objectives (MBOs), **zero-based budgeting** (ZBB), total quality management (TQM), performance-based management (PBM), **balanced scorecard** (BSC), and best practices (BP), to name a few. Some long-time public employees are very frustrated with "this constant cycle of reform by acronymn."[26] But it's no different in government than in the business world, where new books on "how to be a success in corporate America" are constantly being released in the wake of new technologies or on the heels of management scandals.

New Emphasis on Ethics and Codes of Conduct

Many governments have established ethics commissions or committees and require all employees to engage in some form of ethical conduct training as a condition of employment. Most often ethics codes prohibit employees from engaging in political activities at work, soliciting or accepting gifts from certain types of persons (e.g., contractors doing business with the government, lobbyists, someone seeking an official action from the employee or their agency), asking for or taking bribes, using their position to get special favors for a family member or business associate, or revealing confidential information to an unauthorized person for personal gain or benefit. Some state and local governments have ethics specialists in their personnel and legal offices to develop training materials, conduct training, and advise employees on ethics matters.

According to the National Conference of State Legislatures' Center for Ethics in Government, more than forty states include ethics training in their new member orientation programs. All fifty states have constitutional provisions that spell out penalties and enforcement procedures for those who violate conflict of interest laws. And all fifty states have whistle-blower protection laws protecting an employee from retaliation when he or she reports someone for illegal or unethical conduct.[27] Many employees belong to professional associations, such as the American Society for Public Administration, that have developed their own ethics codes of conduct.

The Quality of State Bureaucracies

Despite the many criticisms heaped upon state government agencies, there is some evidence that they are performing reasonably well and certainly better than in years past. An extensive evaluation of state government administrative performance by a team of *Governing* magazine analysts and university professors graded states in four areas: money, people, infrastructure, and information. Most states got B's and C's. There were also a handful of A's but no F's. The study found considerable variation among the states in each of the areas being graded and concluded that overall the management of state government had improved in virtually all of them.[28]

> Some long-time public employees are very frustrated with "this constant cycle of reform by acronymn."

ZERO-BASED BUDGETING

A method of budgeting that demands justification for the entire budget request of an agency, not just its requested increase in funding.

BALANCED SCORECARD

A management decision making system that considers both human capital and financial capital costs in making decisions.

BENCHMARKING

Comparing and measuring policies, practices, philosophies, and performance measures against those of other high-performing state or local governments.

THE BUDGETARY PROCESS

Too often we think of budgeting as the dull province of clerks and statisticians. Nothing could be more wrong. **Budgets** are political documents that record the struggles over "who gets what." The budget is the single most important policy statement of any government. It is prepared by the executive branch but must be approved by the legislative body. There are very few government activities or programs that do not require an expenditure of funds, and no public funds may be spent without budgetary authorization. The budget sets forth government programs, with price tags attached. The size and shape of the budget is a matter of serious contention in the political life of any state or community. Governors, mayors, administrators, legislators, interest groups, and citizens all compete to have their policy preferences recorded in the budget. The budget lies at the heart of the political process. (See Figure 8–5.)

The Executive Budget

The budgetary process begins with the governor or mayor's budget office sending to each governmental agency and department a budget request form, accompanied by broad policy directives to agency and department heads about the size and shape of their requests. Very often these budget requests must be made six to twelve months prior to the beginning of the **fiscal year** for which the requests are made; state and local governmental fiscal years usually run from July 1 to June 30.[29] After all requests have been submitted to the budget office, the serious task of consolidating these many requests begins. Individual department requests are reviewed, revised, and generally scaled down; often departments are given more or less formal hearings on their budget request by the budget director. The budget agency must also make revenue estimates based on information it obtains from the tax department.

Governors or mayors must decide the overall size and scope of their budget; whether particular departmental requests should be increased or reduced, in view of the programs and promises important to their administrations; whether economies should involve

BUDGET

A document prepared by the executive branch of government that estimates next year's revenue and proposes programs and the objects of expenditures; must be approved by the legislature.

FISCAL YEAR

The yearly government accounting period, not necessarily the same as the calendar year; most state and local government's fiscal years begin July 1 and end June 30.

FIGURE 8–5 The Budgetary Process

GOVERNOR/ BUDGET OFFICE	DEPARTMENTS AGENCIES	GOVERNOR/ BUDGET OFFICE	LEGISLATURE	GOVERNOR
■ Provide Budget Instruction to Departments ■ Estimate Revenue	■ Prepare Strategic Plans ■ Prepare Legislative Budget Request ■ Prepare Capital Improvement Plan	■ Review/Analyze Agency Legislative Request, Strategic Plan, Capital Improvement Plan, Information Resource Plan ■ Hold Public Hearings ■ Develop Recommendations Based on Governor's Priorities and Available Revenues	■ Prepare Appropriations Act Review Governor's Recommendations Review/Analyze/ Revise Budget ■ Appropriations Act Passed by Both Houses	■ Review/Analyze Changes Governor May Line-Item Veto Specific Appropriations ■ Governor Signs into Law

APPROPRIATION

An act of the legislature that authorizes executive agencies to spend a specific amount of money.

Requesting an increase in funds affirms the significance and protects the status of agency employees, and it assures clientele groups that new and higher standards of service are being pursued aggressively.

overall "belt tightening" by every agency or merely the elimination of particular programs; or, finally, whether they should recommend the raising of new taxes or the incurring of additional debt. These decisions may be the most important that mayors or governors make in their terms of office, and they generally consult both political and financial advisors—budget and tax experts, party officials, interest group representatives, and legislative leaders. Ordinarily, these difficult decisions must be made before governors or mayors present their budget message to the legislature. This budget message explains and defends the final budget presented by the chief executive to his legislative branch.

Budget Making

Budget making involves bringing together the requests of all existing state agencies, calculating the costs of new state programs, estimating the probable income of the state, and evaluating these costs and income estimates in light of program and policy objectives. The final budget document is submitted to the legislature for its adoption as an appropriations bill. No state monies can be spent without a legislative **appropriation**, and the legislature can make any alterations in the state budget that it sees fit. Potentially, then, a legislature can control any activity of the state government through its power over appropriations, but as a practical matter, the legislature seldom reviews every item of the governor's budget. In practice, budgets tend to reflect the views of those responsible for their preparation, namely the governor.

The most common budgetary behaviors in the states are as follows:

- Agency heads consistently request higher funds.
- Governors' budget staffers consistently reduce agency requests.
- The governor consistently pursues a balanced budget at higher expenditure levels than the previous year.
- Legislatures approve higher appropriations but try to blame the governor if higher taxes are required.

Illinois Corrections workers protest against proposed budget cutbacks that they see as affecting their own safety on the job: "Our lives are worth more than pennies."

Agency Pressure

The pressure for budget increases comes from the requests of agency officials. Most agency officials feel compelled to ask for more money each year. Requesting an increase in funds affirms the significance and protects the status of agency employees, and it assures clientele groups that new and higher standards of service are being pursued aggressively. Requested increases also give the governor's office and the legislature something to cut that will not affect existing programs. The governor's budget staff generally recognizes the built-in pressure to expand budgets. The budget staff sees themselves as "cutters." Agencies press for budgetary expansion with better programs in mind, while the governor's budget staff tries to reduce expenditures with cost cutting in mind (see "*Up Close:* How to Win at the Budget Game").

up CLOSE   How to Win at the Budget Game

Experienced bureaucrats have learned a number of strategies that help them "maximize" their budgets.

Spend it all. Spend all of your current year's appropriation. A failure to use up an appropriation indicates that the full amount was unnecessary in the first place, which in turn implies that your budget should be cut next year.

Ask for more, not less. Never request a sum less than your current appropriation. It is easier to find ways to spend up to current appropriation levels than it is to explain why you want a reduction. Besides, a reduction indicates your program is not growing and this is an embarrassing admission to most government administrators.

Hide new programs in the base. Put top-priority programs into the base, that is, that part of the budget that is within current appropriation levels. Budget offices, governors and mayors, and legislative bodies will seldom challenge programs that appear to be part of existing operations.

Make changes appear incremental. Increases that are desired should be made to appear small and should appear to grow out of existing operations. The appearance of a fundamental change in a budget should be avoided.

Give them something to cut. Give the budget office, chief executive, and the legislature something to cut. Normally it is desirable to submit requests for substantial increases in existing programs and many requests for new programs, in order to give higher political authorities something to cut. This enables them to "save" the public untold millions of dollars and justify their claim to promoting "economy" in government. Giving them something to cut also diverts attention away from the basic budget with its vital programs.

Make cuts hurt. If confronted with a real budget cut—that is, a reduction from last year's appropriation—announce reductions in, or elimination of, your agency's most popular program. Never acknowledge that cuts might be accommodated without reducing needed services.

The Legislative Appropriation

The governor's budget generally appears in the legislature as an appropriations bill, and it follows the normal path of any bill. It is assigned to an appropriations committee, which often holds hearings on the bill and occasionally reshapes and revises the executive budget. The fate of the governor's budget in the legislature generally depends on his or her general political power, public reactions to recommendations, the degree of support he or she receives from department heads (who are often called to testify at legislative budget hearings), his or her relationships with key legislative leaders, and the effectiveness of interest groups that favor or oppose particular expenditures.

After it is passed in identical form by both houses, the final appropriations measure is sent to the governor for signature. If the governor has an item veto, he or she can still make significant changes in the budget at that time.

ZERO SUM GAME

The theory that for someone to win, someone must lose.

THE POLITICS OF BUDGETING

Budgeting is very *political.* It is often described as a **zero sum game**—"for every dollar spent on *x*, there is one less dollar to spend on *y*." Being a good politician involves (1) the cultivation of a good base of support for one's requests among the public at large and among people served by the agency; (2) the development of interest, enthusiasm, and support for one's program among top political figures and legislative leaders; and

EARMARKING

In government budgeting, the practice of allocating specific revenue sources to specific programs, such as gasoline taxes to highways.

(3) skill in following strategies that exploit one's opportunities to the maximum. Informing the public and one's clientele of the full benefit of the services they receive from the agency may increase the intensity with which they will support the agency's request. If possible, the agency should inspire its clientele to contact governors, mayors, legislators, and council members and help work for the agency's request. This is much more effective than the agency trying to promote its own requests. However, a mistake that many citizen groups who want to influence the budget process make is to wait to get involved until the budget is being considered for *approval* by the legislative body. Often, a more effective strategy is to become proactive during the budget *formation* stage—in agency deliberations or when it is still in the hands of the governor or mayor.

"Incrementalism" in Budgeting

What forces are actually involved in the budget-making process? Invariably, the forms provided by the budget office require departments to prepare budget requests alongside the previous year's expenditures. Decision makers generally consider the last year's expenditures as a base (a starting point). Consequently, active consideration of budget proposals is generally narrowed to new items or requested increases over the last year's base. The attention of governors and legislators, and mayors and councils, is focused on a narrow range of increases or decreases in a budget. A budget is almost never reviewed as a whole every year, in the sense of reconsidering the value of existing programs. Departments are seldom required to defend or explain budget requests that do *not* exceed current appropriations; but requested increases in appropriations require extensive explanation, and they are most subject to downward revision by higher political officials. Consequently, "padding" in existing budget lines is far less obvious than in proposed new lines of spending or in lines featuring big increases over the previous budget year. A sizable portion of the proposed spending is "untouchable" due to earmarking and other uncontrollable expenses.

"Earmarking"

Chief executives have little influence over many items of state and local government spending. Over 50 percent of state finances come from specially earmarked (dedicated) funds. It is quite common to earmark in state constitutions and laws certain funds for particular purposes, such as gasoline taxes for highways or lottery funds for education. The earmarking device provides certain agencies with an independent source of income, thus reducing the chief executive's control over operations. What is left, "general fund expenditures," is also largely committed to existing state programs, particularly welfare and education.

"UNCONTROL-LABLES"

In government spending, increases that cannot be easily limited because of prior commitments to existing programs or legal mandates.

"Uncontrollables"

Politicians typically campaign on platforms stressing both increased service and lower taxes. Once in office, however, they typically find it impossible to accomplish both and very difficult to accomplish either one. Often new programs planned by a governor must be put aside, because of "uncontrollable" growth in existing programs. For example, additional money may be required to educate more students who are entitled to an education under existing programs; or money must be found to pay the welfare benefits of additional clients or the Medicaid costs of additional patients "entitled" to care under existing laws. These *entitlement programs* constitute over three-quarters of state general fund appropriations. Another uncontrollable expense occurs when the federal government issues "*mandates*" requiring state and local governments to spend money to meet certain legislatively dictated criteria. Lawsuits and *litigation* are a third, and growing, uncontrollable expense.

Nonprogrammatic Budgeting

Finally, in some jurisdictions—usually smaller ones—the budget format is primarily *nonprogrammatic*. Specific expenditure items, or "lines," are listed under broad categories such as "personnel services," "contractual services," "travel," "supplies," or "equipment." (This is known as a line item, object-of-expenditure format.) Needless to say, it is impossible to tell from such a listing exactly what programs the agency is spending its money on, which is why many governments no longer exclusively use this budget format. Even if these categories are broken down into line items (e.g., under "personnel services," the line item budget might say, "John Doaks, Assistant Administrator, $35,000"), it is still next to impossible to identify the costs of various programs. It is also impossible to determine whether the program efficiently, effectively, or equitably achieved what lawmakers had in mind when they funded it.

Program and Performance-Oriented Budget Reforms

Over the years, reform-oriented administrators have favored expanding the amount of information included in budgets—making them more useful as management tools, not just as accounting tools, although financial control is still a major function of budgets. Reforms over the years have attempted to tie inputs (spending) with outcomes (results). Since many governments are in a "perpetual fiscal crisis," they are always in search of ways to "do more with less" . . . and, at the same time, to do it better.[30] Reformers have also emphasized putting budgetary information in more "citizen-friendly" or "customer-friendly" formats and making the process more accessible to citizen input in response to growing taxpayer demands for more accountability.

That doesn't mean that all agency heads or public employees automatically or enthusiastically buy in to the latest budget reform. Often it's not that they are resisting change as much as it is that their staff is already stretched thin. New budgeting systems, like new technology, are often perceived by managers as having pretty steep start-up costs whether they are in the form of staff training, new data entry requirements, or organizational restructuring. If the latest reform ends up requiring too much effort in justifying already accepted programs, produces massive amounts of information that cannot be absorbed by decision makers, or doesn't result in improved program operations, the budget process reverts back to incrementalism. Overall, however, experts agree that the *cumulative* effect of these reform efforts over the years has been to make government more accountable for its spending.

In summary, the "incremental" nature of budgetary politics—and reforms—helps reduce political conflict and maintains stability in governmental programs. As bruising as budgetary battles may be in state capitols and city halls, they would be much worse if governments tried to review the value of *all* existing expenditures and programs each year. Comprehensive budgetary review would "overload the system" with political conflict by refighting every policy battle every year.

PERFORMANCE BUDGETING

Instead of focusing on an organizational unit, a budget is done by program or activity and includes performance to tie expenditures for each program to specific goals established for that program.

SHORTFALLS

Revenues that fall below those estimated in the budget and force spending cuts during a fiscal year.

Balancing the Budget

Unlike the federal government, most state budgets must be balanced. The same is true for most cities, counties, and school districts. This means that chief executives must submit to the legislature a budget in which projected revenues are equal to recommended expenditures. And the legislature must not appropriate funds in excess of projected revenues. There are, of course, many accounting devices that allow governors and mayors and legislatures and councils to get around the balanced budget limitation—devices known as "blue smoke and mirrors." These include "off-budget" special funds, separate state authorities, capital budgets, and so on (see Chapter 14).

Nonetheless, balanced budget requirements are a major restraint on state and local government spending. Indeed, often revenue **"shortfalls"**—revenues that fall below those estimated for the year in the budget—force painful mid-year spending cuts. Only a few states allow deficits to be carried over into the next fiscal year. And these carry-over deficits force governors and legislatures to be more conservative in their spending plans for the following year.[31]

State and local government agencies and employees are constantly reacting to changes in the political and economic climate—and often catching flak for their responses from some citizens, but praise from others. Such is life in the bureaucracy.

The American Society for Public Administration is the largest association in the field of public administration. It includes both "practitioners" and faculty who teach public administration in colleges and universities; it also welcomes student members. It maintains a Web site at

www.aspanet.org

This site contains general information on governmental administration, links to the association's publications, including the monthly *PA Times* and the quarterly *Public Administration Review*, and it even offers a listing of current job openings in public administration across the nation.

Major state executive departments and agencies often form national associations to exchange information, assist in bureaucratic networking, and lobby in Washington to expand federal aid to their particular function. The following associations all maintain interesting Web sites:

National Association of State Budget Officers: **www.nasbo.org**

National Association of State Purchasing Officials: **www.naspo.org**

National Association of Medicaid Directors: **www.nasmd.org**

Council of Chief State School Officials: **www.ccsso.org**

American Association of State Highway and Transportation Officials: **www.aashto.org**

A Web site devoted to listing links to Ethics Resources on the Web is

www.defenselink.mil/dodgc/defense_ethics/resource_library/resourcesindex.html

For profiles of *Governing* magazine's annual Public Officials of the Year winners, go to

http://governing.com/poy/poy.htm

CHAPTER NINE

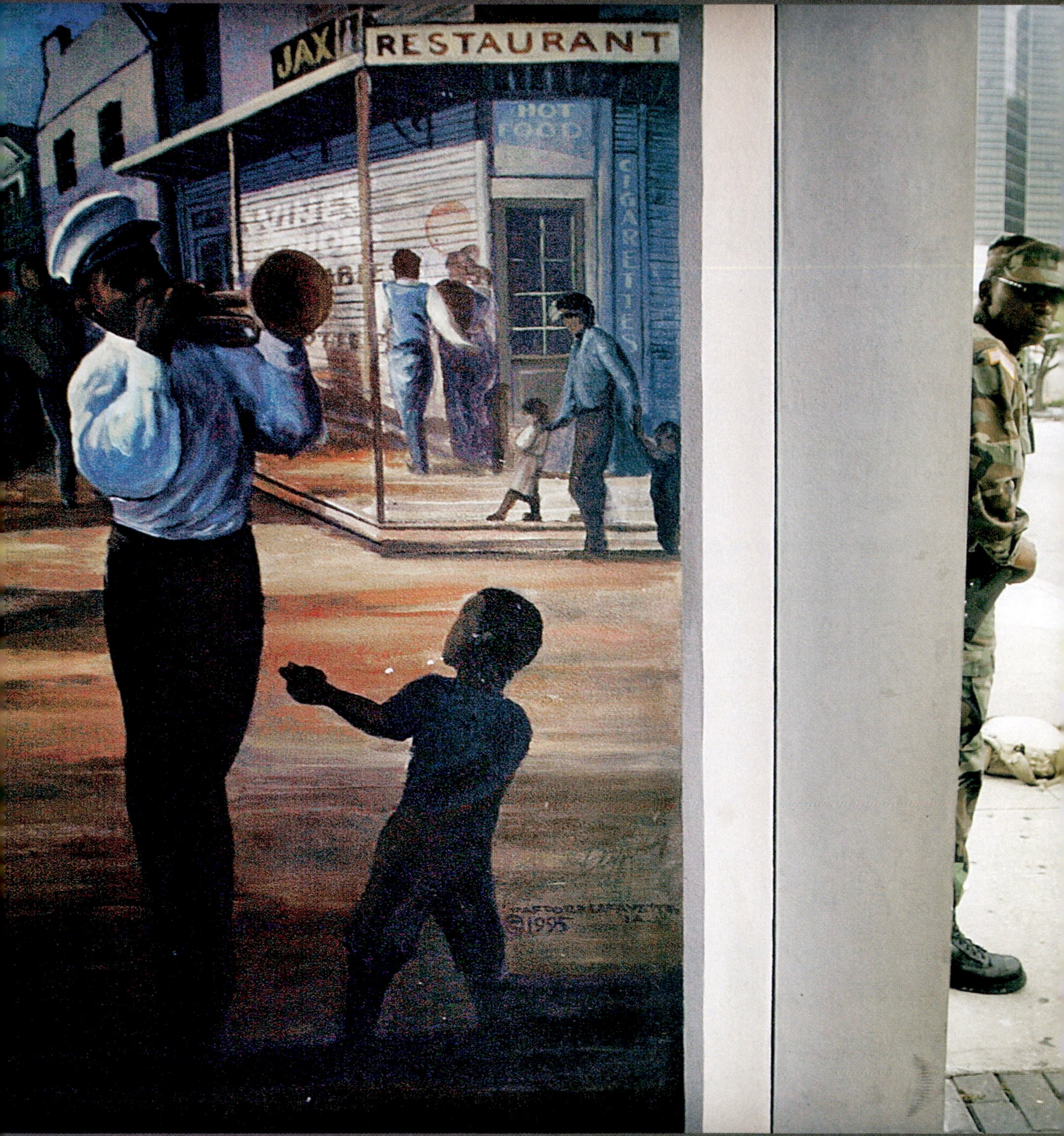

COURTS, CRIME, AND CORRECTIONAL POLICY

9

QUESTIONS TO CONSIDER

Can state courts expand on the personal liberties guaranteed by the U.S. Constitution?
- ☐ Yes
- ☐ No

How should states go about selecting judges?
- ☐ Appointment by the governor
- ☐ Voter choice in elections
- ☐ Appointment followed by retention vote

Can certain, swift, and severe punishment really deter crime?
- ☐ Yes
- ☐ No

Does serving on a jury make Americans more or less supportive of the court system?
- ☐ More
- ☐ Less

Is the death penalty a deterrent to murder?
- ☐ Yes
- ☐ No

POLITICS AND THE JUDICIAL PROCESS

Large television audiences watch prime-time courtroom, crime-scene investigation, and law and order–related programs, ranging from the "light" *Judge Judy* and "pet courts" to the more serious dramas that focus on children murdering parents, terrorists infiltrating the criminal justice system, or family members "helping" loved ones die. Millions of Americans are fascinated with the four C's—courts, crime, criminals, and convictions. But for most of the millions of cases filed every year in state and local courts, there is no such media feeding frenzy. They involve everyday citizens caught up in disagreements with each other, with corporations, or with government over money, children, property, products, and individual rights (such as privacy, religion, speech, and gun ownership).

Several questions loom large in legal conflicts: Which is more important—individual rights or the rights of society? The rights of the convicted or the rights of the victim? Is justice different for the rich and the poor? The young and the old? The well-connected and the not-so-plugged-in persons? Is justice color blind? Gender neutral? And nonpartisan?

Overall, public opinion polls show that a plurality of Americans believe that courts have about the right amount of power, although more believe the courts have too much power than think they have too little power. Citizens are more evenly divided in their opinions about the objectivity of judges in making decisions. (See Table 9–1.)

Courts are "political" institutions because they attempt to resolve conflicts in society. Like legislative and executive institutions, courts make public policy in the process of resolving conflict. Some of the nation's most important policy decisions have been made by courts rather than legislative or executive bodies. Federal courts have taken the lead in eliminating racial segregation, ensuring the separation of church and state, defining the rights of criminal defendants, guaranteeing individual voters an equal voice in government, and establishing the right of women to obtain abortions. These are just a few of the important policy decisions made by courts—policy decisions that are just as significant to all Americans as those made by Congress or the president. Courts, then, are deeply involved in policymaking, and they are an important part of the political system in America. Sooner or later in American politics, most important policy questions reach the courts.

The Judicial Style of Decision Making

In resolving conflict and deciding about public policy, courts function very much like other government agencies. However, the *style* of judicial decision making differs significantly from legislative or executive decision making. Let us try to distinguish between courts as policymaking institutions and other legislative and executive agencies.

- *A passive appearance:* First, courts rarely initiate policy decisions. Rather, they wait until a case involving a policy question they must decide is brought to them. The vast majority of cases brought before courts do not involve important policy issues. Much court activity involves the enforcement of existing public policy. Courts punish criminals, enforce contracts, and award damages to the victims of injuries. Most of these decisions are based on established law. Only occasionally are important policy questions brought to the court.

- *Special rules of access:* Access to courts is through cases. (Only rarely do state courts render advisory opinions to governors or legislatures.) A **case** requires two disputing parties, one of which must have suffered some damages or faces some penalties as a result of the action or inaction of the other. The accused party is the **defendant**; the accusing party is the **plaintiff** or **prosecutor**.

CASE

A court matter involving two disputing parties.

DEFENDANT

The accused party in court.

PLAINTIFF

The accusing party in court.

PROSECUTOR

The attorney acting on behalf of the government in a criminal case.

TABLE 9–1   The Public's View of Courts and Judges

Courts

Do you think the courts in this country have too much power, too little power, or about the right amount?[a]

Too Much	Too Little	About Right	Unsure
39	11	45	6

Do you think judges today are generally too liberal in their decisions, too conservative, or about right in their decisions?[a]

Too Liberal	Too Conservative	About Right	Unsure
32	19	38	11

Do you think the U.S. Supreme Court is too powerful, not powerful enough, or does it have about the right amount of power?[b]

Too Powerful	Not Enough Power	About Right	Unsure
23	10	62	5

As you may know, U.S. Supreme Court justices are appointed for their lifetimes, and they do not have to retire at a certain age. Do you think there should be a mandatory retirement age for U.S. Supreme Court justices, or not?

Should	Should Not	Unsure	Unsure
60	39	1	3

[a] Time Poll conducted by Schulman, Ronca & Bucuvalas (SRBI) Public Affairs. May 10–12, 2005. N = 1,011 adults nationwide. Margin of error: ± 3.

[b] Associated Press–Ipsos poll conducted by Ipsos–Public Affairs. Nov. 19–21, 2004. N = 1,000 adults nationwide. Margin of error: ± 3.

■ *Legal procedures:* The procedures under which judges and other participants in the judicial process operate are also quite different from procedures in legislative or executive branches of government. Facts and arguments must be presented to the courts in specified forms—writs, motions, written briefs, and oral arguments that meet the technical specifications of the courts. While an interest group may hire lobbyists to pressure a legislature, they must hire a law firm to put their arguments into a legal context.

■ *Decisions in specific cases:* Courts must limit their decisions to specific cases. Rarely do the courts announce a comprehensive policy in the way the legislature does when it enacts a law. Of course, the implication of a court's decision in a particular case is that future cases of the same nature will be decided the same way. This implication amounts to a policy statement; however, it is not as comprehensive as a legislative policy pronouncement, because future cases with only slightly different circumstances might be decided differently. (It is true that higher appeals courts, like state supreme courts, may decide to hear a case knowing that the decision will have a far-reaching impact beyond just the case at hand.)

■ *Appearance of objectivity:* Perhaps the most important distinction between judicial decision making and decision making in other branches of government is that judges must not appear to permit political considerations to affect their decisions. Judges must not appear to base their decisions on partisan considerations, to bargain, or to compromise in decision making. The *appearance of objectivity* in judicial decision making gives courts a measure of prestige that other governmental institutions lack. Court decisions appear more legitimate to the public if they believe that the courts have dispensed unbiased justice. Unfortunately, the highly partisan battle over the confirmation of *federal* court judges has made Americans somewhat less confident about the objectivity of judges at all levels.

The United States is the most litigious society in the world. We are threatening to drown ourselves in a sea of lawsuits.

Foundation of Common Law

Legal traditions are influential in court decisions. English common law has affected the law of all of our states except Louisiana, which was influenced by the French Napoleonic Code. English common law developed in the thirteenth century through the decisions of judges who applied their notions of justice to specific cases. This body of judge-made law grew over the centuries and is still the foundation of our legal system today. However, **statutory law**—laws passed by legislatures—take precedence over common law. The **common law** is only applied by the courts when no statutory provisions are relevant or when statutory law must be interpreted. The degree to which statutory law has replaced common law varies among the states according to the comprehensiveness of state statutes and codes.

Common law covers both criminal and civil law, although the common law of crimes has been replaced by comprehensive criminal codes in the states.

THE LAWYERING OF AMERICA

The United States is the most litigious society in the world. We are threatening to drown ourselves in a sea of lawsuits. The rise in the number of lawsuits in the United States corresponds to a rise in the number of lawyers. There were 285,000 practicing lawyers in the nation in 1960; by the mid-2000s, this figure had grown to over 1.1 million (compared to 650,000 licensed physicians). The continuing search for legal fees by these bright professional people has brought an avalanche of **civil cases** in federal and state courts—about 15 million per year. An analysis by the Bureau of Justice Statistics finds that cases involving the highest estimated median damage awards are medical malpractice ($600,000) and product liability ($350,000) lawsuits.

- *Expanded liability.* Virtually any accident involving a commercial product can inspire a product **liability** suit. An individual who gets cut opening a can of peas can sue the canning company. Manufacturers must pay large insurance premiums to insure themselves against such suits and pass on the costs of the insurance in the price of the product. Municipal and state governments, once generally protected from lawsuits by citizens, have now lost most of their "immunity" and must purchase liability insurance for activities as diverse as recreation, street maintenance, waste collection, and police and fire protection. Real estate brokers may be sued by unhappy buyers and sellers. Homeowners and bar owners may be sued by persons injured by their guests. Hotels have paid damages to persons raped in their rooms. Coastal cities with beaches have been successfully sued by relatives of persons who drowned themselves in the ocean.

- *Contingency fees.* Many of these lawsuits are initiated by lawyers who charge fees on a **contingency** basis; the plaintiff pays nothing unless the attorney wins an award. Up to half of that award may go to the attorney in expenses and fees. Trial attorneys argue that many people could not afford to bring civil cases to court without a contingency fee contract.

- *Third-party suits.* Defendants in civil cases are not necessarily the parties directly responsible for damages to the plaintiff. Instead, wealthier third parties with "**deep pockets**," who may indirectly contribute to an accident, are favorite targets of lawsuits. For example, if a drunk driver injures a pedestrian, but the driver has only limited insurance and small personal wealth, a shrewd attorney will sue the bar that sold the driver the drinks instead of the driver. Insurance premiums have risen sharply for physicians seeking malpractice insurance, as have premiums for recreation facilities, nurseries and day care centers, nursing homes, motels, and restaurants.

- *Pain and suffering and punitive awards.* Awards in liability cases, sometimes running into tens of millions of dollars, cover much more than the doctor bills, lost wages, and cost of future care for injured parties. Most large damage awards are for **pain and suffering**. Pain and suffering awards are *added* compensation for the victim, beyond actual costs for medical care and lost wages. So also are **punitive damage awards,** multiples of the actual damages designed to deter and punish persons or firms found to be at fault.

- *Joint and several liability.* Moreover, a legal rule known as **joint and several liability** allows a plaintiff to collect the entire award from any party that contributed in any way to the accident, if other defendants cannot pay. So if a drunk driver crosses a median strip and crashes into another car leaving its driver disabled, the victim may sue the city for not placing a guard railing in the median strip. The rule encourages trial lawyers to sue the party "with the deepest pockets," that is, the wealthiest party rather than the party most responsible for the accident. Unsophisticated juries can be emotionally manipulated into granting huge damage awards, especially against businesses, municipalities, and insurance companies.

- *Alternative dispute resolution.* A less controversial reform, and one that is now found in most states, is alternative dispute resolution, that is, the use of mediation or arbitration in order to settle civil suits without a formal trial. Over 60 percent of the conflicts that end up in arbitration are contract and personal injury disputes.[1] Often third-party mediators are retired judges or attorneys who try to get the parties to voluntarily agree to a binding resolution of their case. The parties get a quick settlement, usually some compromise, and the courts reduce their backlogs. Most are very satisfied with the arbitrator's performance, the confidentiality of the process, and its length. Persons who have used the arbitration process rate it as faster (74 percent), simpler (63 percent), and cheaper (51 percent) than going to court. Two-thirds said they would be likely to use arbitration again.[2]

Tort Reform

A **tort** is a civil wrong or injury case involving private parties. The role of the court in such cases is to provide a remedy in the form of damages. Reforming the nation's liability laws is a major challenge confronting the nation's state governments. The most common reform proposals are capping the award for pain and suffering at $250,000 or $500,000; eliminating punitive damage awards; restricting the fees that lawyers can subtract from a victim's award; and ending the rule of joint and several liability. Perhaps the simplest reform is a **"loser pays" law**— a requirement that the losing party in a civil suit pay the legal fees of the winner. This would discourage frivolous suits that are often designed to force innocent parties to pay damages rather than incur even higher costs of defending themselves. The reform movement has been heavily supported by some traditionally powerful groups—the insurance companies, product manufacturers, physicians and hospitals, and even municipal governments.

On the other side are the trial lawyers, who are disproportionately represented in state legislatures and very willing to continue to fund fights against tort reform (see Chapter 6). The American Trial Lawyers Association is bitterly opposed to tort reform, believing that such initiatives will limit the average citizen's access to the courts and stop people from suing who have been harmed.

JUDICIAL FEDERALISM

The Supremacy Clause of the U.S. Constitution (Article VI) ensures that the federal constitution supersedes state constitutions and binds the judges in every state. State constitutions cannot deny rights granted by the U.S. Constitution, and state courts may

PAIN AND SUFFERING AWARDS

Added compensation for the victim of a crime, beyond actual costs for medical care and lost wages.

PUNITIVE DAMAGE AWARDS

Multiples of the actual damages found; designed to deter and punish persons or firms found to be at fault.

JOINT AND SEVERAL LIABILITY

Legal responsibility for full damages regardless of the degree of contribution to harm.

TORT

A legal harm caused by civil wrongdoing.

LOSER PAYS LAW

Requirement that the losing party in a civil suit pay the legal fees of the winning party.

JUDICIAL
FEDERALISM

State courts' authority
to interpret their own
state's constitutional
guarantees beyond
those in the U.S.
Constitution.

*"Court shopping" is
a common strategy
of lawyers; it in-
volves the search
for a court that will
be most favorably
disposed to one's
argument.*

not limit federal constitutional guarantees. But state constitutions cover many topics that are not addressed in the U.S. Constitution. More importantly, state constitutions may add individual rights that are not found in the U.S. Constitution, and state courts may interpret state constitutional language to expand individual rights beyond federal constitutional guarantees. We might think of the U.S. Constitution as a floor, providing minimum protection of individual rights for all persons in the nation. But state constitutions can build on that floor, adding individual protections for persons within their state.

Judicial Federalism

Judicial federalism refers to state courts' exercise of their authority to interpret their own state constitutions to guarantee protections to individual rights beyond those protected by the U.S. Constitution. While this authority has always existed under the American federal system, it was seldom exercised in the past. Historically, the remedy to civil rights violations was to be found in federal court if it was to be found at all. Civil rights attorneys almost always turned to federal courts and the U.S. Constitution to seek protection for their clients. But the new activism of state courts in interpreting their own states' constitutional guarantees has begun to change this pattern. **"Court shopping"** is a common strategy of lawyers; it involves the search for a court that will be most favorably disposed to one's argument. In the past, federal courts were almost always the forum of choice for civil rights claims. But recently state courts have become the forums of choice for some claims.

Probably the highest-profile case that ended up being tossed between the state and federal courts for years was the Terri Schiavo case, which pitted her husband against her parents in a heart-wrenching right-to-live versus right-to-die battle that was only resolved by her death.

Many state constitutions contain rights not explicitly found in the U.S. Constitution. For example, various state constitutions guarantee rights to privacy, rights of political participation, rights of victims of crime, rights to public information, rights to work, rights to free public education, and equal gender rights (state ERAs).

Nationalizing the Bill of Rights

The Bill of Rights in the U.S. Constitution begins with the words "*Congress* shall make no law . . . ," indicating that it was originally intended to limit only the powers of the federal government. The Bill of Rights was added to the Constitution because of fear that the *federal* government might become too powerful and encroach on individual liberty. But what about encroachments by state and local governments and their officials? The Fourteenth Amendment to the U.S. Constitution includes the words "No State shall . . ."; its provisions are directed specifically at states. Initially, the U.S. Supreme Court rejected the argument that the Fourteenth Amendment's Privileges or Immunities Clause and the Due Process Clause incorporated the Bill of Rights. But beginning in the 1920s, the Court handed down a long series of decisions that gradually brought about the "*incorporation*" of almost all of the protections of the Bill of Rights into the "liberty" guaranteed against state actions by the Due Process Clause of the Fourteenth Amendment. In *Gitlow v. New York* (1925), the Court ruled that "freedom of speech and of the press—which are protected by the First Amendment from abridgment by Congress—are among the fundamental personal rights and liberties protected by the due

FORUM, VENUE,
COURT
SHOPPING

Common strategy of
lawyers; it involves the
search for a court that
will be most favorably
disposed to one's
argument.

process clause of the Fourteenth Amendment from impairment by the states."[3] Over time, the Court applied the same reasoning in incorporating almost all provisions of the Bill of Rights into the Fourteenth Amendment's Due Process Clause. (See Table 9–2.) States and all of their subdivisions—cities, counties, townships, school districts, and so on—are bound by the Bill of Rights.

Extending Personal Liberties

Several state supreme courts have taken the lead in extending personal liberties under their own state constitutions, even when the U.S. Supreme Court has declined to incorporate these same liberties within the U.S. Constitution. Examples include the following:

- The Florida Supreme Court decided that the state constitutional guarantee of the right of privacy struck down laws restricting abortion, although the U.S. Supreme Court had earlier upheld similar restrictions as permissible under the U.S. Constitution (*Webster* v. *Reproduction Health Services*, 1989).

- The Texas Supreme Court (and several other states' high courts) held that the state's constitutional guarantee of equality in public education required the system of local school finance to be replaced with statewide financing that equalized educational spending throughout the state. Years earlier, the U.S. Supreme Court had decided that the U.S. Constitution did *not* include a right to equal educational funding across school districts (*San Antonio Independent School District* v. *Rodriguez*, 1973).

- New York and Pennsylvania Supreme Courts were the first to strike down state sodomy laws (anal sexual penetration) under privacy provisions of their state constitution, although

TABLE 9–2	Incorporating the U.S. Constitution's Bill of Rights into the Fourteenth Amendment		
Year	**Issue**	**Amendment Involved**	**Court Case**
1925	Freedom of speech	I	*Gitlow* v. *New York*, 268 U.S. 652
1931	Freedom of the press	I	*Near* v. *Minnesota*, 283 U.S. 697
1932	Right to a lawyer in capital punishment cases	VI	*Powell* v. *Alabama*, 287 U.S. 45
1937	Freedom of assembly and right to petition	I	*De Jonge* v. *Oregon*, 299 U.S. 353
1940	Freedom of religion	I	*Cantwell* v. *Connecticut*, 310 U.S. 296
1947	Separation of church and state	I	*Everson* v. *Board of Education*, 330 U.S. 1
1948	Right to public trial	VI	*In re Oliver*, 333 U.S. 257
1949	No unreasonable searches and seizures	IV	*Wolf* v. *Colorado*, 338 U.S. 25
1961	Exclusionary rule	IV	*Mapp* v. *Ohio*, 367 U.S. 643
1962	No cruel and unusual punishment	VIII	*Robinson* v. *California* 370 U.S. 660
1963	Right to a lawyer in all criminal felony cases	VI	*Gideon* v. *Wainwright*, 372 U.S. 335
1964	No compulsory self-incrimination	V	*Malloy* v. *Hogan*, 378 U.S. 335
1965	Right to privacy	I, III, IV, V, IX	*Griswold* v. *Connecticut*, 381 U.S. 363
1966	Right to an impartial jury	VI	*Parker* v. *Gladden*, 385 U.S. 363
1967	Right to speedy trial	VI	*Klopfer* v. *North Carolina*, 386 U.S. 213
1969	No double jeopardy	V	*Benton* v. *Maryland*, 395 U.S. 789

the U.S. Supreme Court had upheld a Georgia sodomy statute ruling that "there is no constitutional right to commit sodomy" (*Bowers* v. *Hardwick*, 1986).

- California's Supreme Court ruled that the state's constitution compelled the state to pay for abortions for poor women, although the U.S. Supreme Court ruled that there was no requirement in the U.S. Constitution that states fund abortions (*Harris* v. *McRae*, 1980).
- The Massachusetts Supreme Court ruled that nude go-go dancing is a protected form of free expression under the state's constitution, even though the U.S. Supreme Court had ruled that it is *not* protected by the First Amendment (*Barnes* v. *Glen Theatre Inc.*, 1991).

Judicial activism by state supreme courts encourages interest groups to bring cases and **amici curiae briefs** (written arguments submitted by "friends of the court") to state "forums." Of course, the state strategy has significant drawbacks compared to winning at the U.S. Supreme Court level; interest groups must proceed from state to state instead of dealing with the issue once and for all in the nation's highest court.[4]

Judicial Policy Divergence

While civil rights organizations generally applaud the new judicial federalism, others have expressed concern over increased divergence between U.S. Supreme Court policy and the policies of state courts. A stable and predictable system of law is essential for democracy. Judicial federalism seems to open the law to diversity between federal and state law as well as to the balkanization of law from state to state. Judicial policy diversity opens the nation's court system to intensified interest group activity and perhaps greater partisan political influence.[5] The good news is that in some states, their supreme courts often make decisions with an eye as to what the U.S. Supreme Court might do in a pending case.[6]

THE STRUCTURE OF COURT SYSTEMS

State courts are generally organized into a hierarchy similar to that shown in Figure 9–1. The courts of a state constitute a single, integrated judicial system; even city courts, traffic courts, and justices of the peace are part of the state judicial system. Ten states have **unified court systems** (Connecticut, California, Iowa, Missouri, Kansas, North Dakota, South Dakota, Minnesota, Michigan, and Illinois). Unified court systems are more streamlined; they treat the courts in a state as a single administrative unit. The administrative tasks of the court are handled by professional court administrators who are trained in management. Sophisticated and integrated data management and budgeting systems are in place in unified systems and each court's jurisdictional authority is clearly spelled out. States whose courts are not unified may have as many as nine different trial courts combined with many appellate courts (e.g., Georgia, Indiana).[7]

Minor Trial Courts

At the lowest level are minor trial courts, often referred to as **courts of limited jurisdiction**. These may be municipal courts, magistrate courts, police courts, traffic courts, family courts, and small claims courts. They are presided over by justices of the peace, magistrates, or police judges, not all of whom are trained in the law. These courts are concerned principally with traffic cases, small claims, divorces and child custody, juvenile offenses, and misdemeanors, although they may hold preliminary hearings to determine whether a person accused of a felony shall be held in jail or placed under bond. (A **felony** is a crime punishable by at least a year's imprisonment; a **misdemeanor** is a

---

AMICUS CURIAE

"Friend of the court"—a person or group not directly involved in a case who submits written arguments to the case.

UNIFIED COURT SYSTEM

All courts in a state are part of a single administrative unit.

COURTS OF LIMITED JURISDICTION

Courts that are concerned principally with traffic cases, small claims, divorces and child custody, juvenile offenses, and misdemeanors.

FELONY

A serious violation of criminal law that can bring a penalty of one year or more in prison.

MISDEMEANOR

A crime that is punishable by a fine or less than one year in jail.

FIGURE 9–1 **The Structure of State and Local Courts**

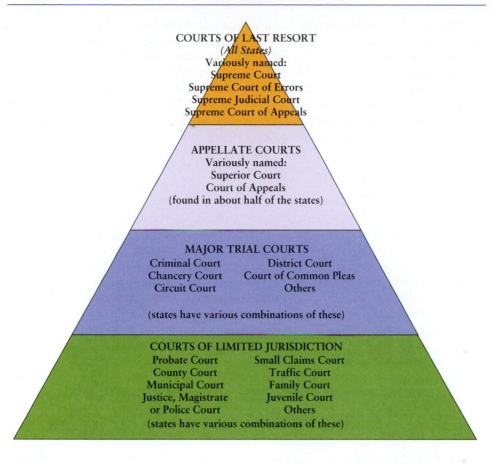

COURTS OF LAST RESORT
(All States)
Variously named:
Supreme Court
Supreme Court of Errors
Supreme Judicial Court
Supreme Court of Appeals

APPELLATE COURTS
Variously named:
Superior Court
Court of Appeals
(found in about half of the states)

MAJOR TRIAL COURTS
Criminal Court District Court
Chancery Court Court of Common Pleas
Circuit Court Others

(states have various combinations of these)

COURTS OF LIMITED JURISDICTION
Probate Court Small Claims Court
County Court Traffic Court
Municipal Court Family Court
Justice, Magistrate Juvenile Court
or Police Court Others
(states have various combinations of these)

BENCH TRIAL

Cases that are handled informally at the bench in discussions with the judge.

crime punishable by a fine or less than a year's imprisonment.) Rarely are these cases heard by juries; mostly the judge decides guilt or innocence and the sentence.

In many cities, municipal courts dispense justice in a "production line" style. Courtrooms are old, crowded, noisy, and confusing; witnesses, defendants, friends, and relatives all wait for hours for their cases to be called. Most cases are handled informally at the bench in discussions with the judge (a **bench trial**). Leniency is the rule with most judges, unless the face of the defendant is very familiar to the judge; then thirty-, sixty-, or ninety-day sentences may be imposed very quickly. Rarely are juries involved in misdemeanor, or minor, court cases. Usually

Problem-solving courts, like drug courts, emphasize probation and rehabilitation over incarceration for first-time offenders. They often have "graduation ceremonies" that friends and family members are invited to attend in hopes of creating a strong supportive network.

JURY TRIAL

A case where a jury decides guilt or innocence and the judge determines the sentence.

SMALL CLAIMS COURT

Court in which two parties simply "tell it to the judge", without the need for lawyers.

PROBLEM-SOLVING COURTS

Specialty courts that deal with defendants facing minor charges, like county drug courts and domestic violence courts.

TRIAL COURTS OF GENERAL JURISDICTION

Courts that handle major civil and criminal cases arising out of statutes, common law, and state constitutions.

PETIT JURIES

A jury that determines the guilt or innocence of criminal defendants.

GRAND JURIES

Juries that have two primary functions—investigation and indictment.

when a **jury trial** is used, the jury decides guilt or innocence and the judge determines the sentences.

The trend is toward specialized courts, particularly in large, diverse metropolitan areas with heavy caseloads. The growth of **small claims courts** throughout the country has helped millions of people who could not afford an attorney to bring a civil claim into the court with simplicity and low cost. Television shows, including *The People's Court*, have popularized the functioning of small claims courts. Proceedings in these courts are very informal: Both sides simply "tell it to the judge." Buyers and sellers, landlords and tenants, creditors and debtors can get a resolution to their case quickly and easily. Plaintiffs usually prevail in small claims courts, often because the defendant never shows. The biggest problem for the winner, however, is actually collecting the money the court has ruled they are owed.

The newer specialty ("boutique") courts that have sprung up in some states are often called "**problem-solving courts**": drug courts (adult, juvenile, family), mental health courts, community courts, domestic violence courts, dependency courts (substance abuse treatment services for parents charged with child abuse and neglect), and reentry courts (overseeing the release of prisoners back into society). In general, problem-solving courts "impose probation and rehabilitation rather than incarceration on defendants facing minor charges and with few or no previous convictions."[8] Miami-Dade County was the first to create a County Drug Court. Now there are some 1,100 across the United States, along with 20 community courts, 70 mental health courts, and some 200 domestic violence courts.[9]

Major Trial Courts

Major **trial courts of general jurisdiction**—sometimes called district courts, circuit courts, superior courts, chancery courts, county courts, criminal courts, or common pleas courts—handle major civil and criminal cases arising out of statutes, common law, and state constitutions. The geographic jurisdiction of these courts is usually the county or city; there are about 1,500 major trial courts in the United States and some 30,000 trial court judges. On average, state court systems employ just fewer than four general jurisdiction trial judges per 100,000 population. The average caseload is over 1,000 cases per judge.[10] These courts handle criminal cases involving felonies and important civil suits. Criminal cases are more likely than civil cases to be heard by a jury; just one-fifth of the civil cases heard in general trial courts are jury trials and there are more civil than criminal cases.[11] In **criminal cases**, the prosecutor is the state attorney or district attorney—an elected official. Almost all cases decided by state courts originate in these major trial courts; trial courts make the initial decisions in cases carried to appellate and supreme courts and may also handle some appeals from minor courts.

Juries: Trial (Petit) and Grand

There are two types of juries: trial (petit) and grand. **Petit juries** seated to hear cases in trial courts determine the guilt or innocence of the accused. **Grand juries**, ranging in size from twelve to twenty-three jurors, have two primary functions—investigation and indictment. While grand jury investigations usually involve crimes, in some states, the focus may be on the misconduct of public officials, corruption, prisons, public records, public offices, or public facilities. The proceedings are secret to protect the accused.[12] Historically, *petit juries* have been composed of twelve citizens, plus a couple of alternate jurors ready to step in should a regular juror become unable to serve.

However, several states allow smaller juries (six or eight members) in non–capital felony criminal cases while most states permit smaller juries in civil cases. Smaller juries are seen as saving time and money, although some have criticized them for their lack of diversity. Some states do not require unanimous verdicts if the jury is large (twelve members) or for civil cases. But unanimous verdicts are mandatory in a death penalty case.

The racial/ethnic makeup of juries assigned to hear death penalty cases has gotten the attention of the U.S. Supreme Court. In 2005, it instructed lower courts and prosecutors against removing potential jurors on the basis of their race thereby creating racial bias in jury selection. The Court ordered new trials for two black murder defendants (one in Texas, one in California) after hearing their appeals claiming that they faced juries made up of white jurors unfairly selected.[13] The 2005 ruling strengthened the court's 1986 decision in *Batson* v. *Kentucky*,[14] which set standards for proving claims of prosecutorial bias in the use of **"peremptory strikes,"** or automatic objections to potential jurors for which no reason must be given.[15]

States differ in how they select potential jurors. Many randomly select jurors from sources like driver's license lists, motor vehicle registration lists, or voter registration rolls. Usually jurors must be residents and age eighteen or older, although the age requirement is higher in two states (Mississippi and Missouri). States also differ in the maximum time they expect a juror to serve. (See Table 9–3.) Most states allow some persons to be exempt from jury duty—the sick, the mentally handicapped, teachers, doctors, and other professionals. But with the growing technical complexity of issues and evidence, states are beginning to eliminate some of these exemptions. While some Americans try to avoid jury duty, studies show that those who serve end up feeling more positive about the court system than their fellow citizens who do not serve.[16]

The Public Defender

If arrested, people who cannot afford an attorney must be provided one by the state. So ruled the U.S. Supreme Court in *Gideon* v. *Wainwright* (1963)[17] and *Argersinger* v. *Hamlin* (1972).[18] The right to legal counsel stems from the Sixth Amendment to the U.S. Constitution: "In all criminal prosecutions, the accused shall enjoy the right . . . to have the assistance of counsel for his defense." States vary on how lawyers defending the indigent are selected. (Even in the same state, the method may differ across counties.) They may rely on public defenders, who are usually county elected officials. They may turn to nonprofit agencies that specialize in public defense cases. The state may contract with individual attorneys or law firms to handle court-appointed cases. Or the state may rely on an assigned-counsel system in which an attorney is appointed off of a list and paid by the case or by the hour.[19] Groups like the American Bar Association, the National Association of Criminal Defense Lawyers, and the National Legal Aid and Defenders Association constantly monitor the quality of lawyers assigned to represent the poor and the fairness of the assignment process. Inadequate representation can be grounds for an appeal.

CRIMINAL CASES
Cases brought by government prosecutors against persons or organizations charged with law-breaking.

PEREMPTORY STRIKE
Lawyer rejects a potential juror without having to give cause.

PUBLIC DEFENDER
Attorneys provided by the state to those who could not otherwise afford an attorney.

OUR MISSION:
"To protect the rights, liberties, and dignity of all persons in San Diego County and maintain the integrity and fairness of the American Justice System by providing the finest legal representation in the cases entrusted to us."

Public defenders provide legal representation for persons who cannot afford an attorney and are usually county elected officials. Many law students intern in these offices and/or begin their legal careers there.

TABLE 9–3 State Laws: Jury Duty Service and Exemptions

State-Established Maximum Terms of Service

Terms of Service	States
One day or one trial	AZ, CA, CO, CT, DC, FL, HI, IN, MA, OK
Two to five days (one week)	NY, SC
Six days to 1 month	GA, KY, ME, NH, ND, OH, RI
Greater than 1 month to 6 months	NM
Longer than 6 months	MT, UT, VT, WV
No established limits	All other states

Statutory Exemption Categories

Exemption	# States
Previous jury service	47
Age	27
Political officeholder	16
Law enforcement	12
Other exemptions	12
Judicial officers	9
Healthcare professionals	7
Sole caregiver	7
Licensed attorneys	6
Active military	5

Number of Exemption Categories by State

Total Exemptions	States
0	LA
1	AL, AR, CO, DC, ID, IA, MT, NM, NY, UT, VT, WA, WI
2	CA, IL, IN, KS, KY, MD, NV, NH, ND, PA, SD
3	AZ, DE, MI, NC, OR, SC, WY
4	AK, MA, MN, MO, NJ, OH, TX, WV
5	CT, GA, ME, MS, NE
6	HI, RI
7	OK, TN, VA
8	
9	FL

Source: Center for Jury Studies of the National Center for State Courts, April 2007. Gregory E. Mize, Paula Hannaford Agor, and Nicole L. Waters, "The State-of-the-State Survey of Jury Improvement Efforts: A Compendium Report."

Appellate Courts: District Courts and State Supreme Courts

Every state has a court of last resort, which is generally called the supreme court. These courts consist of three to nine judges, and most of their work is devoted to cases on appeal from major trial courts, although some states grant original jurisdiction to supreme courts in special types of cases. Since they consider questions of law rather than questions of fact, they sit without a jury. **State supreme courts** are the most important and visible judicial bodies in the states. Their decisions are written, published, and distributed like the decisions of the U.S. Supreme Court. Judges can express their views in majority opinions, dissenting opinions, or concurring opinions. These courts get the most controversial cases and those with the most at stake, since these cases are most likely to be appealed all the way to the state's highest court.

To relieve state supreme courts of heavy case burdens, many of the more populous states maintain intermediate courts of appeal between trial courts and courts of last resort. (Only eleven states do not have an intermediate appellate court.) Intermediate appellate courts range in size from three judges (Alaska, Alabama, Hawaii, and Idaho) to ninety-three judges (California). Often appellate courts are divided into regions or districts. To help move the caseload along, several appellate judges (a **panel**) in a district may be assigned to hear a case rather than the entire body of appellate court judges (**en banc**) in that district. State appellate courts also differ in the type of jurisdiction they have: discretionary or mandatory. (**Discretionary jurisdiction** means that they pick which trial court cases they will hear on appeal; **mandatory jurisdiction** means that state law dictates which cases they must hear on appeal from the lower trial court.) Appeals court judges hear arguments of law rather than arguments about the facts of a case. There are no juries in appellate courts.

All state supreme courts stand atop their own state's judicial system. In thirty-nine states, the state supreme court has considerable discretionary jurisdiction, typically turning down some 90 percent of the appeals.[20] Some have mandatory jurisdiction over certain types of cases—death penalty appeals, interjurisdictional disputes among state agencies and branches or between local governments, the constitutionality of a state law, or complaints involving judges. Some state supreme courts enjoy national reputations. Their decisions on points of law are often cited by other state supreme courts as well as by federal courts. Indeed, it is possible to identify judicial leadership among state courts by examining the number of times they are cited by other courts.[21] Supreme courts in California, New York, New Jersey, Massachusetts, and Pennsylvania enjoy superior reputations, followed by those in Illinois, Wisconsin, Washington, Michigan, Iowa, Colorado, and Minnesota.

Appeals to the U.S. Supreme Court

Appeals from the state supreme courts may go directly to the U.S. Supreme Court on federal constitutional grounds. State supreme courts have the final word in the interpretation of *state* constitutions and laws. But many cases also raise federal constitutional questions, especially under the broad meaning of the "due process" clause and "equal protection" clause of the Fourteenth Amendment. So while most judicial appeals will end in state courts, the U.S. Supreme Court exercises general oversight through its power to accept appeals based on federal questions.

THE MAKING OF A JUDGE

Political debate over methods of selecting judges in the states has been going on for many years. In writing the federal Constitution, the Founders reflected conservative views in establishing an independent federal judiciary, whose members were appointed by the president for life terms and were not subject to direct popular control. Jacksonian views

Every state has a court of last resort, which is generally called the Supreme Court.

STATE SUPREME COURTS
The highest courts of appeal in the states.

PANEL
A few judges assigned to a particular court hear and decide a case.

EN BANC
All judges assigned to a particular court hear and decide a case.

DISCRETIONARY JURISDICTION
An appellate court chooses which cases they will hear on appeal.

MANDATORY JURISDICTION
State law dictates types of cases appellate courts must hear on appeal.

of popular election were strong in the states, however, and today a majority of state judges are directly elected by the people on partisan or nonpartisan ballots.

Five different methods of selecting judges are found in the fifty states: *partisan election, nonpartisan election, appointment by the governor, legislative selection*, and the *appointment–retention election plan*. Many states use more than one method. (See Table 9–4 for the method used to select state supreme court justices.) Twenty-two states elect their supreme court justices, either in partisan elections (nine) or in non-partisan elections (thirteen) in which candidates for the bench do not carry party labels. In two states, judges are chosen by their legislatures, and in four states, they are appointed by the governor. Twenty-two states have adopted the **appointment–retention election plan** (initially called the Missouri Plan), in which governors appoint judges on the recommendation of a select committee, and after the judge has been in office for a year or more, the voters are given the opportunity to retain or oust the appointed judge.

Appointment

The argument for selecting judges by appointment rests upon the value of judicial independence and isolation from direct political involvement. Critics of the elective method feel that it forces judges into political relationships and compromises their independence on the bench. This is particularly true if judicial elections are held on a partisan rather than a nonpartisan ballot, where judges must secure nomination with the support of party leaders. Moreover, it is argued that voters are not able to evalu-ate "legal" qualifications—knowledge of the law, judicial temperament, skill in the courtroom, and so on. Hence, judges should be appointed, rather than elected by vot-ers. Attorneys, bar associations, and judges themselves prefer an appointive method in which they are given the opportunity to screen candidates and evaluate legal qualifi-cations prior to appointment.

Actually it is not possible to "take judges out of politics." Selection by appoint-ment removes the selection of judges from *party* politics but simply places the selection in different political hands. Instead of party leaders, the governor or the bar association become the principal actors in judicial selection. It is not clear which system leads to "better" judges, or whether "better" judges are those more sensitive to community values or more trained in legal procedures.

Actually it is not possible to "take judges out of politics."

Interim Appointment

In practice many judges come to the bench in elective states through the appoint-ment procedure. The apparent paradox comes about because even in elective states, governors generally have the power to make interim appointments when a judgeship is vacant because of the retirement or death of a judge between elections. Interim-appointed judges must seek election at the next regular election, but by that time they have acquired the prestige and status of a judge, and they are unlikely to be defeated by an outsider. Many members of the judiciary in elective states deliberately resign before the end of their term, if they are not seeking reelection, in order to give the governor the opportunity to fill the post by appointment. It is interesting to note that over half of the supreme court judges in states that elect their judiciary come to the bench initially by means of appointment. In practice, then, the elective system of judicial selection is greatly compromised by the appointment of judges to fill unex-pired terms.

TABLE 9–4 Methods of Selecting State Supreme Court Justices[a]

Election		Appointment		Combination
Partisan Election (Run with a Political Party Label)	**Nonpartisan Election (Do Not Run with a Political Party Label)**	**Selection by Legislature**	**Governor Appointment**	**Appointment–Retention Election**
Alabama	Arkansas	South Carolina	California	Alaska
Illinois	Georgia	Virginia	Maine	Arizona
Louisiana	Idaho		New Hampshire	Colorado
Michigan	Kentucky		New Jersey	Connecticut
New York	Minnesota			Delaware
Ohio	Mississippi			Florida
Pennsylvania	Montana			Hawaii
Texas	Nevada			Indiana
West Virginia	North Carolina			Iowa
	North Dakota			Kansas
	Oregon			Maryland
	Washington			Massachusetts
	Wisconsin			Missouri
				Nebraska
				New Mexico
				Oklahoma
				Rhode Island
				South Dakota
				Tennessee
				Utah
				Vermont
				Wyoming

[a]In some states different methods of selection are used for different courts.

Source: Book of the States, 2004, pp. 250–253.

Election

Few incumbent judges are ever defeated in running for reelection. The majority of judges seeking reelection are unopposed by anyone on the ballot, and very few judges seeking reelection are ever defeated. Voter interest in judicial elections is quite low.[22] Given a lack of information and interest in these elections, incumbent judges have an enormous advantage. They have the prestigious title "Judge" in front of their names and some name recognition. In states with partisan elections, judges are occasionally defeated if their party loses badly.[23] But even in these partisan elections judges enjoy more stability and independence from popular control than do legislators or governors, although judicial elections can be very expensive and contentious.

Very few voters know anything about judicial candidates, although that may be changing. One study suggests that fewer than 15 percent of voters *coming from the*

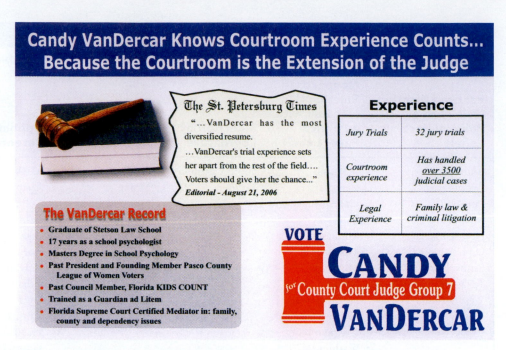

Judicial candidates' ads stress experience, law school credentials, and community involvement but do not include information on how candidates would rule from the bench once elected. But citizens often want to know whether the person would be tough on criminals or would be more inclined to rule for rehabilitation or probation. Consequently, citizens complain they cannot get the type of information they would really like to have about judicial candidates. However, laws limiting such information are designed to maintain the perception that once judges are elected, they will be objective, rather than partisan, in their rulings.

polls remembered the name of one candidate for the state supreme court, and fewer than 5 percent could remember the name of one candidate for county court.[24] An estimated 10 to 15 percent of the voters just skip over the judicial contests. Part of the problem is that historically many states have greatly restricted how judicial candidates may campaign in order to maintain the perception of objectivity in the judiciary. Consequently, candidates for judicial posts are often limited in the kind of statements they may make in their ads and campaign literature. But in 2002, a 5–4 U.S. Supreme Court ruling (*Republican Party of Minnesota* v. *White*) based on the First Amendment (freedom of speech) prevented government from prohibiting candidates from communicating relevant information to voters during an election.[25] Consequently, judicial elections are beginning to look like other political campaigns. Some see the politicization of judicial elections, particularly the infusion of out-of-state money into trial court races, as one of the biggest threats to the state judiciary. In the words of California's chief justice, "if the judiciary becomes politicized, then the rule of law is in jeopardy."

Appointment–Retention Election Plan

Appointment by the governor followed by a retention election combines the elective and appointive systems of selection. Under this Missouri plan, a select committee of judges, attorneys, and laypeople make nominations for judicial vacancies. (In various states these nominating committees are called the Judicial Nominating Commission, or

RETENTION ELECTION

A judicial election in which voters choose between keeping or ousting an incumbent judge.

the Judicial Council, or the Commission on Court Appointments, etc.) The governor appoints one of the committee's nominees to office. (*See Up Close:* "Florida Supreme Court Justice Peggy Quince.") After the judge has served a specified time period (usually one year), the judge's name is placed on a nonpartisan ballot without any other name in opposition. "Shall judge (the name of the judge is inserted) of the (the name of the court is inserted) be retained in office? Yes_____No_____." If voters vote yes, the judge is then entitled to a full term of office. If the voters vote no, the governor must select another name from those submitted by the nominating committee and repeat the whole process. In practice, a judge is hardly ever defeated in a retention election, in part for the same reasons that make it difficult to defeat an incumbent judge (see preceding discussion). Moreover, since "you can't beat somebody with nobody," running in a judicial retention election is the equivalent of being unopposed. Less than 2 percent of judges are voted out of office in retention elections.[26] The effect is to place judicial selection in the hands of the judges or attorneys who compose the nominating committee and the governor, with only a semblance of voter participation. Reformers argue that the plan removes judges from politics and spares the electorate the problem of voting on judicial candidates when they know little about their professional qualifications.

Status

Judges are rarely recruited from among the most prestigious high-paying law firms. Judges at the trial level may earn $94,000 to over $168,000 per year, and appellate and supreme court judges up to $200,000 or more (chief justice). These incomes exceed those of the average attorney, but they are lower than salaries of senior partners at elite law firms. Moreover, judges are restricted in investments and opportunities for outside income by judicial ethics codes. While a judge enjoys status in his or her courtroom, much of the work at the trial court level is tedious and repetitious. Finally, many elite lawyers do not relish the political tasks required to secure a judgeship—garnering the support of the bar association's judicial selection panel, or attracting the nod of the governor, or, worse, campaigning for the office in an election.

Party Affiliation

Traditionally, Republicans fared better in capturing judgeships than in winning legislative seats or governors' chair. Republicans did proportionately better in winning judgeships than in winning legislative seats or governorships when they were the minority party. Most of the judges selected in nonpartisan elections refuse to identify themselves with a political party, as do nearly all the judges selected under the appointment–retention election plans, although the media and challengers may try their best to "paint" a judge as a Democrat or Republican based on his or her past voter registration information, which is public information. Judges selected in partisan elections, of course, usually do not hesitate to identify themselves as Republicans or Democrats.

The Psychology of Judges

While most judges share a common background before coming to the bench—law school, practicing attorney, prosecutor—they are not always well prepared to assume judicial robes. The high esteem and prestige of the judiciary tend to obscure the negative aspects of the job: the requirement to remain aloof from courtroom battles, to isolate oneself, and to deal with the routines of judging.

PEOPLE in POLITICS

Florida Supreme Court Justice Peggy Quince

Florida Supreme Court Justice Peggy Quince was appointed to that state's high court by both Democratic Governor Lawton Chiles and Republican Governor Jeb Bush. The unprecedented double appointment occurred when Governor Chiles died in office before the state Senate confirmed Justice Quince, and she was later reappointed by Governor Bush.

Peggy Quince is a 1970 graduate of Howard University and later earned a law degree from Catholic University of America in Washington, DC. She returned briefly to her hometown of Norfolk, Virginia, before moving permanently to Florida, initially to practice general civil law. But in 1980 her legal career took a dramatic turn when she joined the Criminal Division of the Florida Attorney General's office. She was given principal responsibility for handling death penalty cases on behalf of the State of Florida. She served in this post for nearly fourteen years. In 1993 Governor Chiles appointed her to Florida's District Court of Appeals. She easily won a retention election to this appellate post in 1996. Then in 1998–1999 she was appointed and

(Justice Quince)

reappointed by governors Chiles and Bush to the Florida Supreme Court.

While on the Florida Supreme Court she participated in the historic dispute over the state's electoral votes in the 2000 presidential election between Republican George Bush and Democrat Al Gore. In *Gore v. Harris* the Florida Supreme Court ordered the state's Secretary of State, Katherine Harris, to extend the deadline for the vote recounts and specifying that "the intent of the voter" should be the criterion for deciding how to count a ballot.[a] But the Florida Supreme Court decision was overturned by the U.S. Supreme Court in *Bush v. Gore*. The nation's High Court ruled that "the use of standardless manual recounts violates the Equal Protection and Due Process Clauses [of the U.S. Constitution] . . ." and that the Florida Supreme Court's decision to set aside the deadline for recounts "plainly departed from the legislative scheme."[b] The effect of the decision was to give the Electoral College vote to George Bush, although Al Gore had won the nationwide popular vote.

[a]*Gore v. Harris*, Florida Supreme Court, December 8, 2000.
[b]*Bush v. Gore*, 531 U.S. 98 (2000).

Danger: The Personal Safety of Judges in Courthouses and at Home

Attacks on judges are on the upswing. Between 1974 and 2005, three federal judges and six state judges were murdered. Hundreds of threats are made annually against judges at all levels—via telephone, letter, e-mail, or in person. Many state and local officials are grappling with the question of how to protect judges, court employees, and citizens without denying the public access to the courthouse. Some judges have even asked that their photographs and other personal information be removed from public directories.

Disciplining and Removing Judges

Usually state constitutions spell out the methods to be used to remove state judges. The most common method of removal is by **judicial conduct commissions**, in combination with state supreme courts. All states have some type of judicial disciplinary body, often made up of judges, lawyers, and citizens, with the authority to hold hearings and make recommendations regarding members of the judiciary. They may recommend a judge be suspended, fined, censured, involuntarily retired, or removed, but the supreme court makes the final determination.[27] In one year alone, twelve judges were removed from office, twenty-two resigned or retired, and eighty-two were publicly sanctioned.

Almost all states have constitutional provisions for removing state judges by impeachment. The decision about whether to formally charge or indict a judge is made by the House of Representatives; the actual trial takes place in the state Senate. The Senate determines guilt or innocence. Grounds for impeachment include "malfeasance," "misfeasance," "gross misconduct," "gross immorality," "high crimes," "habitual intemperance," and "maladministration."[28] Of course, state laws define what each of those terms means. Impeachment rarely happens. In the past fifteen years, only two state judges have been impeached (formally charged) and only one convicted.

Sixteen states have a provision for **legislative address**—a procedure that allows the state legislature, often with the governor's consent, to vote to remove a judge from the bench. But it has rarely been used. The **recall procedure** has not been used very often either, primarily because only a few states allow recall elections for judges. Even where judges are elected, few are ever tossed out of office by voters.

THE JUDICIAL SELECTION CONTROVERSY

What is the "best" method of selecting judges—by appointment, in partisan elections, in nonpartisan elections, or in appointment–retention elections? Reformers argue that partisan elections result in political "contamination" of the judiciary. They contend that judicial elections generally are characterized by lackluster campaigns, devoid of issues, and disconnected from any real evaluation of the candidates. Reformers' first preference is the Missouri Plan, with appointments followed by periodic retention elections; if competitive elections are held, reformers prefer nonpartisan elections. Reformers generally stress the value of independence of the judiciary. In contrast, defenders of judicial elections stress accountability, the ability of the voters to choose among competing candidates and thereby exercise some democratic control over the judiciary.

Competition in Judicial Elections

Historically, judicial elections have produced very little competition. Only about 25 percent of state supreme court justices running for reelection in *nonpartisan* elections face any challengers at all. About 35 percent of incumbent justices in *partisan* elections face any challengers. (In *retention* elections judges can only be challenged by a "No" vote.)[29]

Incumbent state supreme court justices running for retention or reelection are seldom defeated. A careful study of judicial elections in the states over a fifteen-year period revealed that only 1.7 percent of all state supreme court justices voted upon for retention were defeated (see Table 9–5). In nonpartisan elections 8.6 percent of incumbent justices were defeated, and in partisan elections 18.8 percent of incumbent justices were ousted.

Even when incumbent justices are challenged, they usually win by overwhelming margins—an average of 80 percent in nonpartisan elections and 72 percent in partisan

TABLE 9–5   The Electoral Fortunes of State Supreme Court Justices

	Retention Elections (%)	Nonpartisan Elections (%)	Partisan Elections (%)
Incumbents challenged	—	25.4	35.6
Incumbents defeated	1.7	8.6	18.8
Incumbent average vote	71.2	80.2	72.3
Incumbent close races (won by 55% or less)	2.6	17.2	34.7

Source: Various tables found in Melinda Gann Hall, "State Supreme Courts in American Democracy," *American Political Science Review* 95 (June 2002): 315–333. Copyright © 2002. Reprinted with permission of Cambridge University Press.

elections. Very few of these elections are close, that is, won by less than 58 percent of the vote. This may change now that judicial candidates are less restricted in how they may campaign and as judicial elections become more politicized. New studies of state judicial elections are finding just that—judicial campaigns looking like campaigns for any other office, filled with fundraising and television advertising by both the candidates and 527s. Judicial elections are more competitive: where there are lots of lawyers or a new judge; when they are partisan, involve an open seat, and are held in a presidential election year; and in a state where justices have longer terms, can determine whether citizen initiatives get on the ballot, and decide a high number of tort cases.[30]

Murder as the Issue

One issue stands out in judicial elections—murder.

One issue stands out in judicial elections—murder. Voter support for incumbent state supreme court justices varies with state murder rates. Overall, a 10 percent increase in the murder rate reduces the incumbent justices' vote share by about 11 percent.

In states with partisan competitive judicial elections, justices are more likely to support the death penalty. And judges selected in partisan elections are more amenable to using political rather than legal rationales in decision-making. But state supreme courts chosen by different methods showed no clear or consistent trends in deciding for the state when it is a party to the case, or for criminal defendants, or for corporations against individuals.

Quality of Justices

There seems to be very little difference in the kinds of people (educational qualifications, experiences, social background) elevated to judgeships by different judicial selection methods (except that judges selected by state legislatures are more likely to have been state legislators).

JUDICIAL DECISION MAKING

Social scientists know more about the behavior of U.S. Supreme Court justices and federal court judges than they know about the thousands of state and local judges throughout the nation. This is largely because the decisions of federal courts are very visible and closely watched by lawyers and scholars.

Trial Courts

The actions of trial judges do not appear, at first glance, to have broad political impact. Nevertheless, trial court judges have enormous discretion in both civil and criminal cases. Perhaps the most dramatic and visible area of trial judge discretion is **sentencing**. Trial court judges display great disparities in the sentences they give out in identical cases. As most good attorneys know, as well as many defendants with long criminal records, it matters a great deal who sits as the judge in your case. The outcome of *most* criminal cases is decided in "**plea bargaining**" between prosecuting attorneys and defense attorneys, where defendants agree to plead guilty to a lesser offense and the prosecution agrees not to press more serious charges or ask for stiffer penalties. However, the bargain must be approved by the judge. Wise attorneys know in advance what kinds of bargains different judges are likely to accept. It is *not* the determination of guilt or innocence that concerns judges, so much as the processing of cases, the acceptance of pleas, and sentencing. One study presented forty-eight trial judges in Wisconsin with the same hypothetical case: breaking and entering, one count, in which the defendant was a twenty-five-year-old, employed, white male without any previous record. The sentences ranged from eleven months in jail to thirty days of unsupervised probation.[31]

Supreme Courts

Criminal appeals account for less than one-third of the workload of state supreme courts. The largest proportion of state supreme court decision making involves economic interests. A large number of cases involving economic interests result from the important role of the states in the allocation of economic resources. All states regulate public utilities, including water, electric companies, gas companies, and public transportation companies. The insurance industry is state regulated. Labor relations and worker's compensation cases are frequently found in state courts. Litigation over natural resources, real estate, small-business regulations, gas, oil, lumber and mining, alcoholic beverage control, racing, and gambling reflects the importance of state regulation in these fields. There is a correlation between the kinds of economic litigation decided by state supreme courts and the socioeconomic environment of the state. Supreme courts in poorer, rural states spend more time on private economic litigation (wills, trusts, estates, contracts, titles, and so on), while courts in urban industrial states wrestle with corporate law and governmental regulation of large economic interests. Judges are also called upon to make decisions in political controversies—disputes over elections, appointments to government positions, and jurisdictional squabbles between governments.

Partisanship in State Courts

What is the impact of the party affiliation of the judges in court decision making? Party affiliation probably has little impact on decisions in lower trial courts, where much of the litigation has little to do with policymaking. However, several early studies showed that party affiliation tended to correlate with state supreme court decision making.[32] Democratic judges tended to decide more frequently (1) for the administrative agency in business regulation cases; (2) for the claimant in unemployment compensation; (3) for the government in tax cases; (4) for the tenant in landlord–tenant cases; (5) for the consumer in sale-of-goods cases; and (6) for the employee in employee injury cases. Another study showed that Democratic judges, especially those appointed

An agreement by a criminal defendant to plead guilty to lesser charges with lighter penalties in order to avoid a jury trial.

SENTENCING

A decision as to the penalty to be imposed following a verdict of guilty.

JUDICIAL ACTIVISM

The making of new laws through judicial interpretation of laws and constitutions.

JUDICIAL RESTRAINT

Self-imposed limits on courts to defer to legislative intent or to previous court decisions.

CRIME RATE

The number of serious offenses reported to police per 100,000 population, as tabulated by the FBI.

VIOLENT CRIME

Crimes against persons, including murder and non-negligent manslaughter, forcible rape, robbery, and aggravated assault.

rather than elected and those serving for long terms, were more likely to oppose the death penalty than Republican judges.[33] Even among the lawyer ranks, there is a general partisan divide: "plantiff's lawyers (often Democrats) represent individuals who sue insurance companies, hospitals, and other businesses and organizations for injuries or other damages, and defendants' lawyers (often Republicans) defend these organizations from lawsuits."[34]

Judicial Activism versus Restraint

Great legal scholars have argued the merits of activism versus self-restraint in judicial decision making for more than a century.[35] The traditional restraint of state courts has been increasingly challenged in recent years by activism on the part of some state courts. As noted earlier, some state supreme courts have decided to go beyond the U.S. Supreme Court in finding new constitutional rights for citizens. And several state supreme courts have insisted on protections for criminal defendants that go beyond those provided by the U.S. Supreme Court.[36]

Liberals, Conservatives, and Judicial Activism

Theoretically, activist and the more restrained views of the judicial role are independent of liberal or conservative ideology. That is, **judicial activism** could be used in support of either liberal or conservative goals; or, alternatively, **judicial restraint** could limit the lawmaking of judges disposed to either liberal or conservative ideas. However, there appears to be a tendency for liberal judges to be more activist than conservative judges. But the major impact of ideology is *through* the role orientation of judges. Self-restraint reduces the impact of ideology on judges' decisions. Activism greatly increases the impact of judges' ideologies. Activist judges are overtly ideological in reactions to criminal appeals—activist liberal judges vote for the defendant far more frequently than activist conservative judges who tend to support the prosecution.[37] Although modified by role orientation, liberal and conservative ideology can be influential in state supreme court decision making.

A careful study of the ideological predispositions of supreme courts in the fifty states produced a ranking from liberal to conservative. Among the most liberal state supreme courts are Hawaii, Rhode Island, Maryland, Massachusetts, New York, Connecticut, and California. Among the most conservative are Arizona, Mississippi, New Hampshire, Iowa, Kansas, Nebraska, Idaho, Indiana, Nevada, and Texas.[38] And another study of state supreme court justices concluded that their religious affiliation also affected their decision making: evangelical justices were found to be significantly more conservative than mainline Protestant, Catholic, and Jewish justices in death penalty, gender discrimination, and obscenity cases.[39]

CRIME IN THE STATES

Crime rates are the subject of a great deal of popular discussion. Crime rates are based on the Federal Bureau of Investigation's *Uniform Crime Reports*, but the FBI reports are compiled from figures supplied by state and local police agencies. (See Table 9–6.) The FBI has established a uniform classification of the number of serious crimes per 100,000 people that are known to the police: **violent crimes** (crimes committed against persons)— murder and non-negligent manslaughter, forcible rape, robbery, and aggravated assault;

TABLE 9–6	Crime Rates in the United States					
Rate Offenses Reported to Police per 100,000 Population						
	1960	**1970**	**1980**	**1990**	**2000**	**2005**
Violent Crimes	160	360	581	729.6	506.5	469.2
Murder	5	8	10	9.4	5.5	5.6
Forcible Rape	9	18	36	41.1	32.0	31.7
Robbery	60	172	244	256.3	145	140.7
Aggravated Assault	85	162	291	422.9	324	291.1
Property Crimes	1716	3599	5319	5073.1	3618.3	3429.8

Source: Federal Crime Bureau of Investigation, Crime in the United States, Uniform Crime Reports 2005. Available at http://www.fbi.gov/ucr/05cius/data/table_01.html

PROPERTY CRIMES

Crimes against property, including burglary, larceny, arson, and theft.

property crimes. (crimes committed against property)—burglary, larceny, arson, and theft, including auto theft. However, one should be cautious in interpreting official crime rates. They are really a function of several factors: the tendencies of victims to report crimes to police, the adequacy of police departments in tabulating crime, and the amount of crime itself.

Perhaps as many as one-half of all crimes today are drug related.

Trends in Crime Rates

From 1960 to 1980, the national crime rate rose dramatically, and "law and order" became an important political issue. But in the early 1980s crime rates leveled off and even declined slightly from their record years. It was widely believed that the early rapid increase and later moderation was a product of age group changes in the population: The early baby boom had expanded the size of the "crime-prone" age group in the population, people age fifteen to twenty-four; later, crime rates leveled off when this age group was no longer increasing as a percentage of the population. In the early 1980s, many analysts were looking forward to gradual decreases in crime rates based on smaller crime-prone age groups. But by 1990 crime rates had soared upward again. The new factor in the crime rate equation appeared to be the introduction of relatively cheap "crack" cocaine and later methamphetamine ("meth"). Perhaps as many as one-half of all crimes today are drug related.

Since peaking in the early 1990s, crime rates have actually declined in the 2000s. Law

Nearly one-half of all crimes committed today are drug related.

enforcement officials attribute recent successes in crime-fighting to police "crackdowns," more aggressive "community policing," and longer prison sentences for repeat offenders, including "three strikes you're out" laws. (All are discussed later in this chapter.) In support of this claim, they observe that the greatest reductions in crime have occurred in the nation's largest cities, especially those such as New York, which have adopted tougher law enforcement practices.

Variations among the States

Crime rates in some states (e.g., Arizona, Washington) are nearly three times greater than in other states (e.g., New Hampshire, South Dakota). (See *Rankings of the States:* Crime and Law Enforcement.") Crime rates in the states appear related to population growth, urbanization, and economic development. Generally the urban states with more mobile populations have higher crime rates than rural states with more stable populations. Variations in crime rates among cities are even greater. Each year Miami, Atlanta, New Orleans, Detroit, and Washington, DC, struggle to avoid the designation "crime capital of America." All rank high nearly every year in crime rates, most notably murder.

Juvenile Crime

The juvenile system is not designed for deterrence. Children are not held personally responsible for their actions, in the belief that they do not possess the ability to understand the nature or consequences of their behavior or its rightness or wrongness. Yet juvenile crime, most of which is committed by fifteen- to seventeen-year-olds, accounts for about 16 percent of the nation's overall crime rate. Research shows that juvenile crime, including violent offenses, peaks between 3 P.M. and 6 P.M., generally right after school lets out. But some occurs at school. During the average school year, there are hundreds of school crimes, violence, and crisis incidents reported. [40]

Offenders under eighteen years of age are usually processed in a separate juvenile court system, regardless of the seriousness of their crime. Only about 5 percent of all young violent offenders are tried as adults. Very few juveniles are sentenced to detention facilities for very long. Their names are withheld from publication, eliminating the social stigma associated with their crimes. Their juvenile criminal records are expunged when they become adults, so that they can begin adulthood with "clean" records.

States differ in their approach to reforming the juvenile criminal justice system. Some have taken "get tougher" steps: more detention facilities, "boot camps" with intensive disciplinary training, and transfers of older youths who commit violent crimes to the adult justice system. Other states have moved more in the direction of rehabilitation and community-based intervention programs, especially with the overcrowding of detention facilities. Whatever the merits of the juvenile system in the treatment of young children, it is clear that the absence of deterrence contributes to criminal behavior among *older* youths—fifteen-, sixteen-, and seventeen-year-olds. Indeed these years are among the most crime-prone ages.

HATE CRIME

Offense committed against individuals on the basis of their race/ethnicity, religion, and sexual orientation.

Hate Crimes

In 1990, Congress mandated that the FBI compile and publish annual statistics on hate crimes—offense committed against individuals on the basis of their race/ethnicity, religion, and sexual orientation. The reports are based on information submitted by more than 11,900 law enforcement agencies around the country. Only about 16 percent of

RANKINGS of the STATES

Crime and Law Enforcement (Three Rankings): Crime Rate; Police Protection; Incarceration Rate

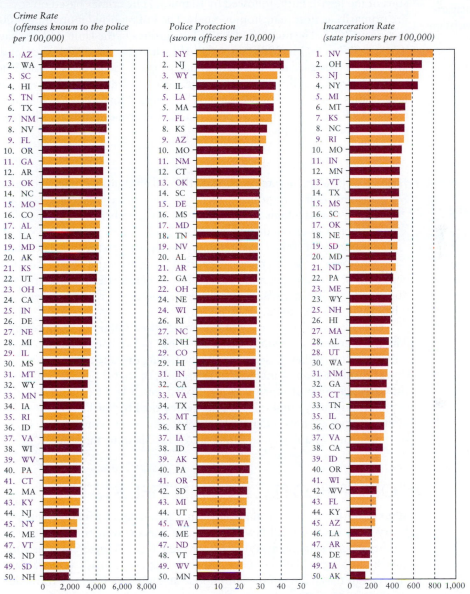

Crime Rate
(offenses known to the police per 100,000)

1.	AZ
2.	WA
3.	SC
4.	HI
5.	TN
6.	TX
7.	NM
8.	NV
9.	FL
10.	OR
11.	GA
12.	AR
13.	OK
14.	NC
15.	MO
16.	CO
17.	AL
18.	LA
19.	MD
20.	AK
21.	KS
22.	UT
23.	OH
24.	CA
25.	IN
26.	DE
27.	NE
28.	MI
29.	IL
30.	MS
31.	MT
32.	WY
33.	MN
34.	IA
35.	RI
36.	ID
37.	VA
38.	WI
39.	WV
40.	PA
41.	CT
42.	MA
43.	KY
44.	NJ
45.	NY
46.	ME
47.	VT
48.	ND
49.	SD
50.	NH

0   2,000   4,000   6,000   8,000

Source: Federal Bureau of Investigation, *Crime in the United States, 2005*, www.fbi.gov

Note: Data are for 2005.

Police Protection
(sworn officers per 10,000)

1.	NY
2.	NJ
3.	WY
4.	IL
5.	LA
5.	MA
7.	FL
8.	KS
9.	AZ
10.	MO
11.	NM
12.	CT
13.	OK
14.	SC
15.	DE
16.	MS
17.	MD
18.	TN
19.	NV
20.	AL
21.	AR
22.	GA
22.	OH
24.	NE
24.	WI
26.	RI
27.	NC
28.	NH
29.	CO
29.	HI
31.	IN
32.	CA
33.	VA
34.	TX
35.	MT
36.	KY
37.	IA
38.	ID
39.	AK
40.	PA
41.	OR
42.	SD
43.	MI
44.	UT
45.	WA
46.	ME
47.	ND
48.	VT
49.	WV
50.	MN

0   10   20   30   40   50

Source: U.S. Census Bureau, *Public Employment in 2005*, www.census.gov

Incarceration Rate
(state prisoners per 100,000)

1.	NV
2.	OH
3.	NJ
4.	NY
5.	MI
6.	MT
7.	KS
8.	NC
9.	RI
10.	MO
11.	IN
12.	MN
13.	VT
14.	TX
15.	MS
16.	SC
17.	OK
18.	NE
19.	SD
20.	MD
21.	ND
22.	PA
23.	ME
23.	WY
25.	NH
26.	HI
27.	MA
28.	AL
28.	UT
30.	WA
31.	NM
32.	GA
33.	CT
33.	TN
35.	IL
36.	CO
37.	VA
38.	CA
39.	ID
40.	OR
41.	WI
42.	WV
43.	FL
44.	KY
45.	AZ
46.	LA
47.	AR
48.	DE
49.	IA
50.	AK

0   200   400   600   800   1,000

Source: Department of Justice, www.ojp.usdoj.gov

those agencies report any hate crimes in their jurisdictions.[41] But where such crimes take place, FBI reports show that more than half are motivated by racial prejudice, most often against blacks. Nearly two-thirds of the crimes involved in such cases are intimidation, vandalism, or property destruction, but some incidents involve murder. Increasingly racially-based hate crimes involve minorities against one another, most often blacks and Latinos.[42] Hate crimes based on religion are most prevalent against persons of the Jewish faith, followed by Islamics. Hate crimes based on sexual orientation are primarily against male homosexuals. The FBI reported more than 8,000 hate-crime victims in 2005. The number of active hate groups in the United States has grown from 474 in 1997 to 803 in 2005, often fueled by hate-centered Web sites, and racist music and concerts designed to attract new young people.[43] Congress is considering adding protection based on gender identity (transgender), gender, and disability to existing federal hate-crimes legislation addressing violent crimes. However, eleven states and the District of Columbia already have laws that define crimes motivated by the victim's gender identity as hate crimes.[44]

Victimization

Official crime rates understate the real amount of crime.

Official crime rates understate the real amount of crime. Citizens do not report many crimes to police. "Victimization" surveys regularly ask a national sample of individuals whether they or any member of their household has been a victim of crime during the past year.[45] These surveys reveal that the actual amount of crime is greater than that reported to the FBI. The number of forcible rapes is twice the number reported, burglaries and aggravated assaults and larcenies more than double, and robbery 50 percent greater than the reported rate. Only auto theft statistics are reasonably accurate, indicating that most people call the police when their cars are stolen.

Interviewees give a variety of reasons for their failure to report crime to the police. The most common reason is the feeling that police could not be effective in dealing with the crime. Other reasons include the feeling that the crime was a "private matter," that the offender was a member of the family, or that the victim did not want to harm the offender. Fear of reprisal is mentioned much less frequently, usually in cases of assaults and family crimes. Data collected by the FBI routinely show that the victims of violent crimes are most likely to be disproportionately young, male (except in the case of rape/sexual assault), poor, single, and a racial/ethnic minority.

POLICE PROTECTION IN THE STATES

State, county, and municipal governments are all directly involved in law enforcement. Every state has a central law enforcement agency, sometimes called the state police, state troopers, state highway patrol, or even Texas Rangers. At one time, state governors had only the National Guard at their disposal to back up local law enforcement efforts, but the coming of the automobile and intercity highway traffic led to the establishment in every state of a centralized police system. In addition to patrolling the state's highways, these centralized agencies now provide expert aid and service for local police officers and strengthen law enforcement in sparsely populated regions.

Most of the states have given their central police agencies full law enforcement authority in addition to highway duties. They may cooperate with local authorities in the apprehension of criminals, or even intervene when local authorities are unable or unwilling to enforce the law. The size and influence of these agencies vary from state to state. On the whole, however, state police forces constitute a very small proportion of the total law enforcement effort in America. About 9 percent of all state and local law enforcement officers are state police, 31 percent are county officers (sheriffs and deputies), and 60 percent are city police officers. Law enforcement in the nation is principally a local responsibility. The size of a local police force is often best explained by the extent to which there have been racial disorders in the community in the past and to a lesser extent by the violent crime rate and the size of the minority population.[46] However, attitudes toward the police are not the sole function of race or class; they are also affected by a resident's perceptions of the community's social capital.[47]

The County Sheriff

There are 3,067 elected sheriffs in the United States. Historically, the county sheriff has been the keystone of law enforcement in the United States. Sheriffs and their deputies are still the principal enforcement and arresting officers in the rural counties and in the unincorporated fringe areas of many urban counties. In addition, the sheriff serves as an executive agent for county and state courts in both civil and criminal matters, and maintains the county jail for the retention of persons whose trials or sentences are pending or who are serving short sentences. The sheriff's office is a political one; in every state except Rhode Island the sheriff is an elected official. Prior to 9/11, heavier reliance upon the sheriff's office for law enforcement was more characteristic of rural states. In the more urbanized states, city police forces played the larger role. However, since 9/11, federal and state laws dictate that sheriffs must play a major role in homeland security preparedness, regardless of whether the county is rural or urban. That mandate plus the growing number of drug-related incidents, street gangs, identify theft rings, and hate crimes have thrust urban sheriffs into more active roles, often working in partnership with city police chiefs.

City Police

Urban police departments are the most important instruments of law enforcement and public safety in the nation today. Nationwide, there are around 13,000 local police departments. City police officers vastly outnumber all other state and county law enforcement officers combined. The urban police department does more than merely enforce the law; it engages in a wide range of activities for social control. In large police departments, officers usually are assigned to a specific type of duty. Some are uniformed patrol officers who are assigned to patrol a specific geographic area. During their shift, they may identify, pursue, and arrest suspected criminals, resolve problems within the community, and enforce traffic laws. Other police officers specialize in such diverse fields as chemical and microscopic analysis, training and firearms instruction, or handwriting and fingerprint identification. Some cities may have special police units such as horseback, bicycle, motorcycle, or harbor patrol; canine corps; or special weapons and tactics (SWAT) or emergency response teams. A few local and special law enforcement officers primarily perform jail-related duties or work in courts.[48]

Police and Crime

The total number of full-time sworn police officers nationwide has grown to more than 800,000. This figure includes all city, county, state, federal, and specialized law enforcement agencies. But police protection varies considerably among the fifty states, with some states having more than 40 law enforcement personnel per 10,000 population, and other states with fewer than 25 (see "Law Enforcement Employees" in *Rankings of the States:* Crime and Law Enforcement"). But the number of officers has *not* kept abreast of crime. On the contrary, the number of police officers relative to the number of reported crimes has declined steadily. This decline is unique to police personnel, as growth in the number of other state and local employees has generally exceeded the growth of their workload.

POLICE AND LAW ENFORCEMENT

Police perform at least three important functions in urban society—enforcing laws, keeping the peace, and furnishing services. Actually, law enforcement may take up only a small portion of a police officer's daily activity, perhaps only 10 percent. The service function is far more common—attending accidents, directing traffic, escorting crowds, assisting stranded motorists, and so on. The function of peacekeeping is also very common—breaking up fights, quieting noisy parties, handling domestic or neighborhood quarrels, and the like. It is in this function that police exercise the greatest discretion in the application of the law. In most of these incidents blame is difficult to determine, participants are reluctant to file charges, and police must use personal discretion in handling each case.

Police are on the front line of society's efforts to resolve conflict. Indeed, instead of a legal or law enforcement role, the police are more likely to adopt a peacekeeping role. Police are usually lenient in their arrest practices; that is, they use their arrest power less often than the law allows. Rather than arresting people, the police prefer first to reestablish order. Of course, the decision to be more or less lenient in enforcing the law gives the police a great deal of discretion. But the growing tendency of Americans to sue police officers makes them more prone to "go by the book" in arresting individuals.

Police "Culture"

What factors influence police decision making? Probably the first factor to influence police behavior is the attitude of the other people involved in police encounters. If people adopt a cooperative attitude, display deference and respect for the officers, and conform to police expectations, they are much less likely to be arrested than those who show disrespect or use abusive language toward police. Formal police training emphasizes self-control and caution in dealing with the public, but on-the-job experiences probably reinforce predispositions toward distrust of others. The element of danger in police work makes police officers naturally suspicious of others. They see many of the "worst kind" of people, and they see even the "best kind" at their worst.

Police and Crime Reduction

Does increased police protection significantly reduce crime? The common assumption is that increased numbers of police officers and increased police expenditures can significantly reduce crime in cities. However, unfortunately, it is very difficult to produce firm evidence to support this assumption. So many other factors may affect crime rates in cities—size, density, youth, unemployment, race, poverty, and so on—that police activity appears insignificant.

Community Policing

Most police activity is "reactive": typically two officers in a patrol car responding to a radio dispatcher who is forwarding reports of incidents. Police agencies frequently evaluate themselves in terms of the number and frequency of patrols, the number of calls responded to, and the elapsed time between the call and the arrival of officers on the scene. But there is little evidence that any of these measures affect crime rates or even citizens' fear of crime or satisfaction with the police.

An alternative strategy is for police to become more "proactive": typically becoming more visible in the community by walking or bicycling the sidewalks of high crime areas; learning to recognize individuals on the streets and winning their confidence and

Cops on bikes are examples of special police units, which are more common in urban than rural areas. Their purpose is to permit police officers to become more familiar with the people and the neighborhoods they are responsible for protecting and to develop a better rapport with the residents.

respect; deterring or scaring away drug dealers, prostitutes, and their customers by a police presence. But this **"community policing"** is often expensive and potentially more dangerous for police officers.

Police Crackdowns

Police crackdowns—beefed-up police actions against juvenile gangs, prostitutes, and drug traffickers; the frisking of likely suspects on the street for guns and drugs; and arrests for (often ignored) public drinking, graffiti, and vandalism—can reduce crime only if supported by the community as well as prosecutors and judges. Crime rates, even murder rates, have been significantly reduced during periods of police crackdowns in major cities.[49] But these efforts are often sporadic; enthusiasm ebbs as jails fill up and the workload of prosecutors and courts multiplies.

"Broken Windows"

New York City once ranked among the most crime-ridden of the nation's cities. It is no longer. (See *Did You Know? America's Most Crime-Ridden Big Cities.*) In 1993 the city's newly elected mayor Rudolph Giuliani began to implement what became known as the **"broken windows" strategy** in law enforcement. The strategy is based on the notion that one neglected broken window in a building will soon lead to many other broken windows. In crime-fighting, this theory translates into more arrests for petty offenses (e.g., subway turnstile jumping, graffiti, vandalism, and aggressive panhandling, including unwanted automobile window washing) in order not only to improve the quality of life in the city but also to lead to the capture of suspects wanted for more serious crimes. This strategy was coupled with the use of the latest computer mapping technology to track crime statistics and pinpoint unusual activity in specific neighborhoods. Each police precinct was regularly evaluated on the number and types of crimes occurring in it.

The introduction of these hard-line tactics created more than a little controversy. Civil libertarians, as well as many minority-group leaders, complained that these police

COMMUNITY POLICING

More active involvement of police with individuals and groups on streets and sidewalks.

"BROKEN WINDOWS"

The theory that overall crime rates can be reduced by strictly enforcing laws against petty offenses.

tactics fall disproportionately on minorities and the poor. It was alleged that Mayor Guiliani's hard-nosed attitude toward crime created an atmosphere that led to increased police brutality.

But the "broken windows" strategy appears to have made New York City a safer city. Over a five-year period following the introduction of Mayor Giuliani's tough policies, the city's overall crime rate fell by an unprecedented 50 percent, and murders fell by 70 percent. After decades of social malaise, New York City was no longer seen as "ungovernable," but rather as one of the nation's leading tourist destinations and the self-proclaimed "Capital of the World." It has remained so even after the 9/11 attacks.

Citizen Action

Anticrime efforts by private citizens have risen dramatically over the last decade. Today there are over one million private security guards, overseeing businesses, banks, ports, airports, stores, hotels, and residential communities. (In effect, this force doubles the size of the nation's police force.) Improved security devices are now found in virtually all commercial establishments—from gas stations and neighborhood convenience stores to banks and schools. Millions of Americans live in communities with security gates and guards and millions more have installed security systems in their houses. Citizen patrol groups and "town watch" associations have multiplied.

Police Efficiency

Most crimes are never solved. This is particularly true of property crimes like burglary; these crimes seldom produce eyewitnesses or other useful information. On average across the nation, police claim to solve about 13 percent of burglaries; this is their official "clearance rate." Police "clear" only about 46 percent of all violent crimes, and 62 percent of murders. (See Table 9–7.) Most clearances occur in cases in which the victim and perpetrators know each other.

More than 14 million people are arrested each year, and many more millions of traffic citations are issued. But even this huge number is less than the actual crime rate. Just 47 percent of all violent crimes (rape/sexual assault, robbery, aggravated and simple assault) and 40 percent of all property crimes (household burglary, theft, and motor vehicle theft) are reported to the police.[50]

THE POLITICS OF PROSECUTION

Prosecution is also part of the political process. Legislatures and governors enact policy, but its enforcement depends on the decisions of prosecutors as well as judges. Political pressures are most obvious in the enforcement of controversial policies—gambling laws, Sunday closing laws, liquor rules, laws against prostitution, and other laws that are contrary to the interests of significant segments of the population. Prosecution also involves decision making about the allocation of law enforcement resources to different types of offenses—traffic violations, juvenile delinquency, auto theft, assault, burglary, larceny, and robbery. Decisions must be made about what sections of the city should be most vigorously protected and what segments of the population will be most closely watched. The public **prosecutor,** sometimes called the district attorney (D.A.) or state's attorney, is at the center of diverse pressures concerning law enforcement. Over 95 percent of all chief prosecutors are elected.[51]

PROSECUTOR

The attorney acting on behalf of the government in a criminal case.

TABLE 9–7   Crime Clearance Rate

Crime	Clearance Rate (Arrest Rate) (%)
Violent Crimes	**45.5**
Murder	62.1
Aggravated Assault	55.2
Forcible Rape	41.3
Robbery	25.4
Property Crimes	**16.3**
Larceny/Theft	18.0
Arson	17.9
Motor Vehicle Theft	13.0
Burglary	12.7

Note: Data are for 2005.

Source: Federal Bureau of Investigation, Crime in the United States, 2005. Available at www.fbi.gov/ucr/05cius/data/table_25.html

The political nature of the prosecutor's job is suggested by the frequency with which this job leads to higher political office. Prosecuting attorney is often a stepping-stone to state and federal judgeships, congressional seats, and even the governorship. Ambitious D.A.s, concerned with their political future, may seek to build a reputation as a crusader against crime and vice, while at the same time maintaining the support and friendship of important interests in the community.

Prosecutor's Discretion

The political power of prosecutors stems from their discretion in deciding (1) whether or not to prosecute in criminal cases, and (2) whether prosecution will be on more serious or less serious charges. Prosecutors may decide simply to drop charges ("**nol-pros**") when they feel adequate proof is lacking, or when they feel that police have committed a procedural error that infringed on the defendant's rights, or when they feel that the resources of their office would be better allocated by pursuing other cases. About half of all felony arrests result in dismissal of charges against the defendant. Prosecutors may also engage in plea bargaining—reducing the charges from more serious to less serious crimes in exchange for defendants' promises to plead guilty. Or prosecutors may reduce charges because they believe it will be easier in court to obtain a guilty verdict on the lesser charge.

NOL-PROS
A prosecutor's decision to simply to drop charges.

The Role of Grand Juries

Are there any checks on the power of prosecutors? In principle, the grand jury is supposed to determine whether evidence presented to it by the prosecutor is sufficient to warrant the placing of a person on trial in a felony case. Ideally, the grand jury serves as a check against the overzealous district attorney, and as a protection for the citizen against unwarranted harassment. However, in practice, grand juries spend very little time deliberating on the vast majority of the cases.[52] A typical grand jury spends only five to ten minutes per case, primarily listening to the prosecutor's recommendation as to

GRAND JURY
A jury that decides whether sufficient evidence exists to indict and try a defendant.

how the case should be decided. Over 80 percent of the cases may be decided on an immediate vote, without discussion among jurors, and almost always with unanimous votes. Finally, and most importantly, grand juries follow the recommendations of prosecutors in over 98 percent of the cases presented to them. The prosecutor controls the information submitted to grand juries, instructs them in their duties, and is usually perceived by jurors as an expert and relied on for guidance. In short, there is no evidence that grand juries provide much of a check on the power of prosecutors.

Plea Bargaining

Most convictions are obtained by guilty pleas. Indeed, about 90 percent of the criminal cases brought to trial are disposed of by guilty pleas before a judge, not trial by jury. The Constitution guarantees defendants a trial by jury (Sixth Amendment), but guilty pleas outnumber jury trials by ten to one.

Plea bargaining, in which the prosecution either reduces the seriousness of the charges, drops some but not all charges, or agrees to recommend lighter penalties in exchange for a guilty plea by the defendant, is very common. Some critics of plea bargaining view it as another form of leniency in the criminal justice system that reduces its deterrent effects. Other critics view plea bargaining as a violation of the Constitution's protection against self-incrimination and guarantee of a fair jury trial. Prosecutors, they say, threaten defendants with serious charges and stiff penalties to force a guilty plea. Still other critics see plea bargaining as an under-the-table process that undermines respect for the criminal justice system and leads to different sentences for the same crime.

It is very fortunate for the nation's court system that most defendants plead guilty. The court system would quickly break down from overload if any substantial proportion of defendants insisted on jury trials

STATE PRISONS AND CORRECTIONAL POLICIES

The United States has experienced an explosive growth in its prison population in recent years. Millions of Americans each year are brought to a jail, police station, or juvenile home or prison. The vast majority are released within hours or days. Around 5 million adult men and women are under federal, state, or local probation or parole jurisdiction. Most (85 percent) are on **probation**, court-ordered community supervision of convicted offenders by a probation agency. Others (15 percent) are on **parole** supervision following a conditional release from prison. There are, however, over 2.2 million inmates in state and federal prisons in the United States, amounting to almost 500 for every 100,000 population. (See Figure 9–2.) These prisoners are serving time for serious offenses, with sentences of more than one year. Ninety percent had a record of crime before they committed the act that led to their current imprisonment. An additional 766,000 persons are temporarily residing in city or county jails at any one time across the country.

The jail population includes persons confined to a local jail awaiting trial or awaiting sentencing, as well as persons serving sentences of less than one year. Many counties have been forced to build new jails or jointly build larger regional jails, subcontract with another local jurisdiction with more jail space capacity, or even turn to privately operated prison facilities to house the growing number of inmates. (Over 7 percent of all prisoners are housed in private correctional facilities.)[53] Overcrowding

PROBATION
Court-ordered community supervision of convicted offenders by a probation agency.

PAROLE
Conditional release from prison.

FIGURE 9–2 Growth in Prison Population

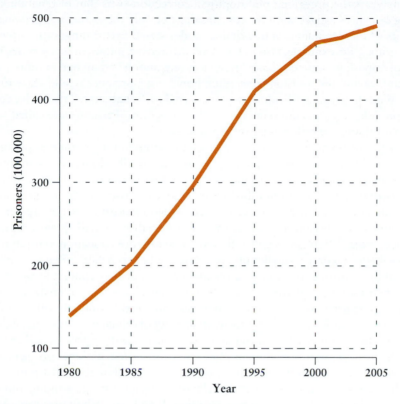

Note: Rate per 100,000 estimated population. Federal and state prisoners.
Source: Bureau of Justice Statistics, Correctional Populations in the United States and Prisoners 2005. www.ojp.usdoj.gov/bjs

has created other problems such as prison riots, viral outbreaks, and strained budgets stemming from the need to hire more corrections officers and pay more overtime.

Prisoners in the States

States differ a great deal in the number of prisoners and the proportion of their populations behind bars. (See "Incarceration Rate" in "*Rankings of the States:* Crime and Law Enforcement.") As might be expected, prisoner populations generally reflect the crime rate in the states; higher crime rate states have larger proportions of their population in prison. In recent years, the growing number of violent offenders and drug offenders have swelled state prison populations. Another cause of increased prison populations in the states is an increase in the length of criminal sentences. In recent years many states have attempted to "get tough on crime" by legislating longer sentences for particular crimes, specifying **mandatory minimum sentences** for crimes, eliminating judicial variation in sentences, adding years to the sentences given repeat or "habitual" criminals, and abolishing parole. Some judges resent the loss of their discretion and have begun to pressure state legislators to restore some of their flexibility in sentencing. But flexibility in sentencing sometimes leads to claims of injustice, particularly when statistics show differences by race and gender.[54]

MANDATORY MINIMUM SENTENCES

Minimum sentences for various crimes enacted into law by state legislatures.

RECIDIVISM

The percent of former convicts who return to prison for new crimes.

The Failure of Rehabilitation

For many years the prevailing philosophy in corrections was that of rehabilitation. In deciding sentences judges were free to consider not only the crime, but personal characteristics of the defendant. State criminal codes stated broad ranges of sentences for various crimes, for example, two to ten years. Moreover, judges in many states had the option of imposing "indeterminate" sentences (e.g., not less than one or more than five years) and leaving the decision concerning how long a prisoner would serve to parole boards. While in prison, individuals were expected to "rehabilitate" themselves through education, job training, counseling, and other programs. Prisons were called "correctional institutions" to reflect their therapeutic value.

Over time it became increasingly difficult to maintain the fiction that prisons were designed to rehabilitate people. Over 80 percent of all felonies are committed by repeaters—individuals who have had prior contact with the criminal justice system and were not corrected by it. Within three years of release from prison, 67 percent of the released are rearrested and 52 percent are returned to prison. Of the "recidivists"— people returned to prison for new crimes, almost half have had three or more prior prison sentences.[55] Reformers generally recommend more education and job training, more and better facilities, smaller prisons, halfway houses where offenders can adjust to civilian life before parole, more parole officers, and greater contact between prisoners and their families and friends. But there has never been any convincing evidence that these investments reduce what criminologists call "**recidivism**," the offenders' return to crime. There is little evidence that the vast majority of criminals *can* be "rehabilitated," no matter what is done. Even the maintenance of order *within* prisons and the protection of the lives of guards and inmates have become serious national problems.

Prison life does little to encourage good behavior. For the most part, inmates spend their days in idleness—watching television, weightlifting, walking and talking in the yard. "Meaningful educational, vocational, and counseling programs are rare. Strong inmates are permitted to pressure weaker prisoners for sex, drugs, and money. Gangs organized along racial and ethnic lines are often the real 'sovereign of the cellblocks.'"[56] Most state prison systems, like the Federal Bureau of Prisons, operate **maximum-security institutions** for high-risk inmates who have proven too violent to mix with the general prison population.

MAXIMUM-SECURITY INSTITUTION

Prison facility housing high-risk inmates who have proven too violent to mix with the general prison population.

Sentencing

Clearly, indeterminate sentencing and discretion given parole boards do *not* serve the goal of deterrence. Rather, deterrence is served by making prison sentences predictable (certain) and long (severe). Potential lawbreakers are supposed to say to themselves, "If you can't serve the time, don't do the crime." Throughout the 1980s states enacted amendments to their criminal codes specifying **determinate sentences** for various crimes. The discretion of judges was restricted. Variation in sentencing was reduced (although not eliminated); judges were obliged by law to mete out sentences based on the crime and the number of previous convictions amassed by the defendant. Greater uniformity of sentencing also served the goal of reducing arbitrary, unfair, and discriminatory sentencing. For many crimes, deterrence was also strengthened by long mandatory minimum sentences. For example, many states enacted mandatory one-, two-, or three-year prison terms for the use of a gun in the commission of a felony. Some states are rethinking strict mandatory sentencing laws, particularly for drug offenders and non-violent offenders, due to prison overcrowding.

DETERMINATE SENTENCES

Sentences for various crimes enacted into law and limiting the discretion of judges.

Prison Overcrowding

The effect of longer sentences, combined with higher crime rates and more prisoners, has been to create mammoth prison overcrowding. Overcrowding contributes directly to unsanitary and dangerous prison living conditions; overcrowding is associated with assaults, rapes, homicides, suicides, and riots. Prison staff are also placed at risk by overcrowding and the violence it produces. Lawsuits against the prison system are brought by inmates and prison personnel alike.

Federal courts have determined that prison overcrowding is a violation of the U.S. Constitution's Eighth Amendment prohibition against "cruel and unusual punishments." (Simple crowding per se is not unconstitutional; federal courts must also find evidence of adverse effects of overcrowding.) Virtually all of the states confront federal court orders to reduce prison overcrowding at one or more of their prisons or their entire prison system. Most state prison systems are near, at, or over their capacity to house prisoners.

Early Releases

As a result of overcrowding, most states have had to resort to **early release programs**. Sentences of prisoners are automatically reduced and those near the end of their terms are let go first. Some states deny early release to certain violent offenders. Nonetheless, violent criminals on the average serve less than half of their sentences, and nonviolent offenders less than one-third of their sentences. In some states, due to prison overcrowding, inmates serve only one-quarter of their sentences.[57] In many states, early release programs have become institutionalized. The national average prison time actually served by convicted murderers is eight years, eight months.

The 85 Percent Solution

Media reports of "**avertable crimes**"—crimes committed by persons who would still have been imprisoned based on earlier convictions if they had served their full sentence—has placed heavy pressure on state legislatures to end early releases. (It is estimated that 20 percent of all violent crimes and 30 percent of property crimes are committed by persons who would still be in prison if they had been forced to serve their full sentence.)[58] In order to stem the tide of early releases, many state legislatures initially turned to the "85 percent solution"—mandating that all convicted felons serve at least 85 percent of the length of their sentences. These "**truth in sentencing**" laws, adopted in some form by 39 states, have effectively lengthened the average time served by prisoners. (Courts have held that prisoners convicted prior to the passage of such laws cannot be held to the new standard.) In recent years, prosecutors have been pressing for longer sentences and judges have been imposing them. This trend, together with a mandated serving of 85 percent of sentences, added to the need for more prison space.

It is not just the need for more prison space that has prompted some states to reexamine their 85 percent laws. It is also the rising costs of providing health care for sick elderly inmates. At least sixteen states already provide special housing units for geriatric inmates; more than two dozen states operate hospice facilities inside prisons to provide end-of-life care. An Arizona study found that prison inmates age even faster than people on the outside. A lifetime of poor diets, drug and alcohol abuse and violence, coupled with the stress of prison, triggers the earlier onset of chronic and geriatric ailments. Often, an inmate's physiological age is 10 years older than his chronological age. As a result, 55 is considered elderly in prison.[59] This situation has

EARLY RELEASE PROGRAMS

In an effort to relieve overcrowding sentences of prisoners are automatically reduced and those near the end of their terms are let go first.

AVERTABLE CRIMES

Crimes committed by persons who would still have been imprisoned based on earlier convictions if they had served their full sentence.

85 PERCENT SOLUTION

Mandating that all convicted felons serve at least 85 percent of the length of their sentences.

TRUTH IN SENTENCING

Definitive punishments that leave judges no flexibility in assessing penalties.

caused some states to consider creating early release programs for elderly prisoners who are chronically or terminally ill. Spending on medical care for prisoners in general makes up 12 percent of prison operating expenditures.

Building More Prisons

States have been compelled to build more prisons in recent years. But taxpayers are understandably upset with the prospects of spending on average over $26,000 per prisoner each year to keep him or her behind bars.[60] But if the costs of incarceration are weighed against its benefits, taxpayers may feel better about prison construction and maintenance. A prisoner's "rap sheet" may list only three or four convictions and a dozen arrests. But interviews with offenders suggest the typical convict has committed hundreds of crimes. Various studies have attempted to estimate the dollars lost to society in the crimes committed by the typical convict in a year.[61] Estimates run from $200,000 to $400,000. This means that a year of crime may be ten to twenty times more costly to society than a year of incarceration.

"Three Strikes You're Out"

The "revolving door" syndrome, with its heavy toll in crimes committed by persons previously convicted of crimes, has led to a nationwide movement to impose minimum 25-years-to-life sentences on criminals convicted of a third felony or third violent felony crime. A California citizens' initiative in 1994, Three Strikes You're Out, illustrates the popularity of this crackdown with voters; it passed 72 to 28 percent. Twenty-four states have passed similar legislation. The California initiative was begun by a father whose eighteen-year-old daughter had been murdered by a parolee. Some of these initiatives are broadly written to include *all* felony convictions and therefore often encompass drug offenders, bad-check writers, and other nonviolent criminals. Other initiatives specify three *violent* felony convictions and thus target a smaller population of repeat criminals. In 1995, Congress mandated life sentences for federal defendants convicted of their third violent felony. But like the 85 percent rule, "three strikes and you're out" rules have increased the prison population and put pressure on state budgets causing several states to alter their rules. For example, the Indiana State Legislature repealed mandatory minimum sentences in many drug cases; Louisiana amended its "three strikes" law to read that the first two "strikes" refer only to violent crimes.[62] In general, however, states with tough sentencing laws are keeping them. Public opinion polls repeatedly show that a majority of Americans do not want criminals released early.

The Failure of Probation and Parole

Parole and probation have been just as ineffective as prison in reducing crime. Even though persons placed on probation are considered less dangerous to society than persons imprisoned, studies indicate that nearly two-thirds of probationers will be arrested and over one-half will be convicted for a serious crime committed while on probation.

The function of parole and post-release supervision is (1) to procure information on the parolee's post-prison conduct and (2) to facilitate and graduate the transition between prison and complete freedom. These functions are presumably oriented toward protecting the public and rehabilitating the offender. However, studies of recidivism indicate that up to two-thirds of persons paroled from prison will be rearrested for serious crimes. There is no difference in this high rate of recidivism between persons released under supervised parole and those released unconditionally. Thus, it does not appear that parole succeeds in its objectives. (See also "*Up Close:* Can Punishment Deter Crime?")

THE DEATH PENALTY

Perhaps the most heated debate in criminal justice today concerns **capital punishment.** While a majority of Americans still favor the death penalty, support has slipped in recent years. Opponents of the death penalty argue that it is "cruel and unusual punishment" in violation of the Eighth Amendment of the U.S. Constitution. They also argue that the death penalty is applied unequally. A large proportion of those executed have been poor, uneducated, and nonwhite. Recognizing that in the past many indigents facing the death penalty did not have the best lawyers, Congress passed the Innocence Protection Act (formally the Justice for All Act of 2004, Public Law No: 108–405). Besides creating a DNA testing program, the Act authorizes a grant program, to be administered by the United States Attorney General, to improve the quality of prosecution and defense representation in capital cases. The grants may not be used to pay for lawyers in specific cases, but instead are to be used to establish, implement, or improve an effective system for providing competent legal representation to indigents charged with capital offenses or sentenced to death and seeking appellate review in state court.[63]

In contrast, there is a strong sense of justice among many Americans that demands retribution for heinous crimes—a life for a life. The death penalty dramatically signifies that society does not excuse or condone the taking of innocent lives. It symbolizes the value that society places on innocent lives. A mere jail sentence for murder devalues the life of the innocent victim. In most cases, a life sentence means less than ten years in prison under the current parole and probation policies of most states. Convicted murderers have been set free, and some have killed again. Moreover, prison guards and other inmates are exposed to convicted murderers who have "a license to kill," because they are already serving life sentences and have nothing to lose by killing again.

Furman v. *Georgia* and Unfair Application

Prior to 1972, the death penalty was officially sanctioned by about one-half of the states. Federal law also retained the death penalty. However, no one had actually suffered the death penalty since 1967, because of numerous legal tangles and direct challenges to the constitutionality of capital punishment. In 1972, the Supreme Court ruled that capital punishment as it was then imposed violated the Eighth and Fourteenth Amendment prohibitions against cruel and unusual punishment and due process of law.[64] The decision was made by a narrow 5–4 vote of the justices, and the reasoning in the case is very complex. Only two justices—Brennan and Marshall—declared that capital punishment itself is cruel and unusual. The other three justices in the majority—Douglas, White, and Stewart—felt that death sentences had been applied unfairly: A few individuals were receiving the death penalty for crimes for which many others were receiving much lighter sentences. These justices left open the possibility that capital punishment would be constitutional if it were specific for certain kinds of crime and applied uniformly.

up CLOSE   Can Punishment Deter Crime?

Can punishment deter crime? This is a difficult question to answer. First, we must distinguish between *deterrence* and *incapacity*. *Incapacity* can be imposed by long terms of imprisonment, particularly for habitual offenders; the policy of "keeping criminals off the streets" does indeed protect the public for a period of time, although it is done at a considerable cost. The object of *deterrence* is to make the certainty and severity of punishment so great as to inhibit potential criminals from committing crimes.

In theory, deterrence is enhanced by

1. The *certainty* that a crime will be followed by costly punishment. Justice must be sure.
2. The *swiftness* of the punishment following the crime. Long delays between crime and punishment break the link in the mind of the criminal between the criminal act and its consequences. And a potential wrongdoer must believe that the costs of a crime will occur within a meaningful time frame, not in a distant, unknowable future. Justice must be swift.
3. The *severity* of the punishment. Punishment that is perceived as no more costly than the ordinary hazards of life on the streets that the potential criminal faces anyhow will not deter. Punishment must clearly outweigh whatever benefits might be derived from a life of crime in the minds of potential criminals. Punishment must be severe.

These criteria for an effective deterrent policy are ranked in the order of their probable importance. That is, it is most important that punishment for crime be certain. The severity of punishment is probably less important than its swiftness or certainty.

However, the best available estimates of the *certainty* of punishment for serious crime suggest that very few crimes actually result in jail sentences for the perpetrators. Far more serious crimes are reported to the police than are ever arrested for these crimes. Some of those arrested are charged with committing more than one crime, but it is estimated that police clear less than 20 percent of reported crimes by arresting the

offender. Prosecutors do not charge about half of the persons arrested for serious offenses. Some offenders are handled as juveniles; some are permitted to plead guilty to minor offenses; others are released because witnesses fail to appear or evidence is weak or inadmissible in court. Of the persons charged with serious offenses by prosecutors, only about 25 percent receive jail sentences for their crimes. Convicted felons are three times more likely to receive probation instead of a prison sentence. Thus, even if punishment could deter crime, our current criminal justice system does *not* ensure punishment for crime.

Of course, there are many other conflicting theories of crime in America. For example, it is sometimes argued that this nation's high crime rate is a product of its social heterogeneity—the multiethnic, multiracial character of the American population. Low levels of crime in European countries, Japan, and China are often attributed to their homogeneous populations and shared cultures. Blacks in the United States are both victims and perpetrators of crime far more frequently than whites. While blacks constitute only about 12 percent of the population, they account for almost one-third of all persons arrested for serious crimes. A larger segment of the black population is in the young crime-prone age (fifteen to twenty-four years), and these youths are more likely to live outside husband–wife families. It is argued that "the streets" of the nation's black inner cities produce a subculture that encourages crime.

It is also argued that crime is irrational, that is, the criminal does not weigh benefits against potential costs before committing the act. Many "crimes of passion" are committed by persons acting in blind rage—murders and aggravated assaults among family members, for example. Many rapes are acts of violence, inspired by hatred of women rather than efforts to obtain sexual pleasure. More murders occur in the heat of arguments than in the commission of other felonies. These are crimes of passion rather than calculated acts. Thus, it is argued, no rational policies can be devised to deter these irrational acts.

The Death Penalty Reinstated

After *Furman* v. *Georgia*, most states rewrote their death-penalty laws to try to ensure fairness and uniformity of application. Generally, these laws mandate the death penalty for murders committed during rape or robbery, hijacking or kidnapping; murders of prison guards; murder with torture; multiple murders; and so on. Two trials are held: one to determine guilt or innocence and another to determine the penalty. At the second trial, evidence of **"aggravating" and "mitigating" factors** are presented; if there are aggravating factors but no mitigating factors, the death penalty is mandatory. In 1976, in *Gregs* v. *Georgia*, the Supreme Court upheld state laws that were carefully written to ensure fairness and due process in the application of the death penalty.[65] The Court declared that capital punishment itself was not "cruel or unusual" within the meaning of the Eighth Amendment; that the authors of the Constitution did not consider it cruel or unusual; and that the reenactment of the death penalty by so many state legislators was evidence that the death penalty was not considered cruel or unusual by contemporary state lawmakers. Today, thirty-seven states have the death penalty. (See Figure 9–3.)

AGGRAVATING FACTORS

Factors and circumstances of a crime that would cause the harshest sentence available to be given.

MITIGATING FACTORS

Characteristics of a defendant and the circumstances of the crime that would cause a juror to favor imposing a lesser sentence.

FIGURE 9–3 Death Penalty Laws in the States

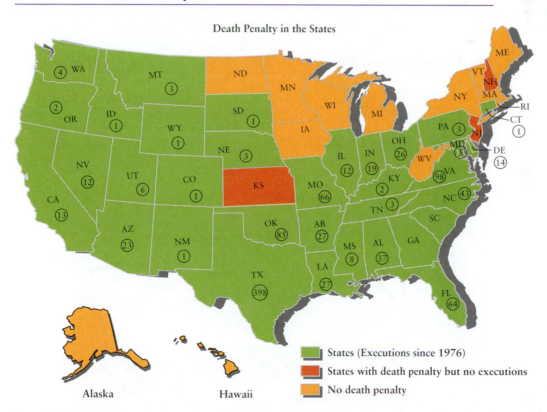

Death Penalty in the States

- States (Executions since 1976)
- States with death penalty but no executions
- No death penalty

Source: Death Penalty Information Center.

No Death Penalty for the Mentally Challenged or Juveniles

The U.S. Supreme Court has upheld the death penalty but ruled that it is unconstitutional when ordered for a mentally handicapped person or a juvenile (a person who was under the age of eighteen at the time they committed a crime punishable by death). In both instances, the court said that putting those persons to death would be "cruel and unusual punishment" in violation of the Eighth Amendment to the U.S. Constitution. In 2002, by a 6–3 vote in *Atkins* v. *Virginia*,[66] the court barred the execution of Daryl Renard Atkins, who was sentenced to death for the 1996 murder of a U.S. airman in Virginia for beer money. Atkins has an IQ of 59, a score classified by the American Association of Mental Retardation as mild retardation. In 2005, by a 5–4 vote, the U.S. Supreme Court, in *Roper* v. *Simmons*,[67] upheld a ruling by the Missouri State Supreme Court outlawing the death penalty for juveniles. "Comprehensive neuropsychiatric and psychosocial assessments of death-row inmates and imaging studies exploring brain maturation in adolescents" played a key role in the decision.[68]

Few Executions

In recent years, fewer executions have been carried out. Slightly over 3,300 prisoners are currently awaiting execution on "death row." In any single year, fifty to seventy will be executed. California has had the highest number of prisoners on **death row** (660 in 2007); it carried out only 13 executions between 1976 and 2007. Southern states generally lead the nation in executions; Texas has carried out more than three times as many executions as any other state since 1976. (Review Figure 9–4.)

DEATH ROW

Prison cells for inmates awaiting execution.

FIGURE 9–4 **Racial Differences in Attitudes towards the Death Penalty**

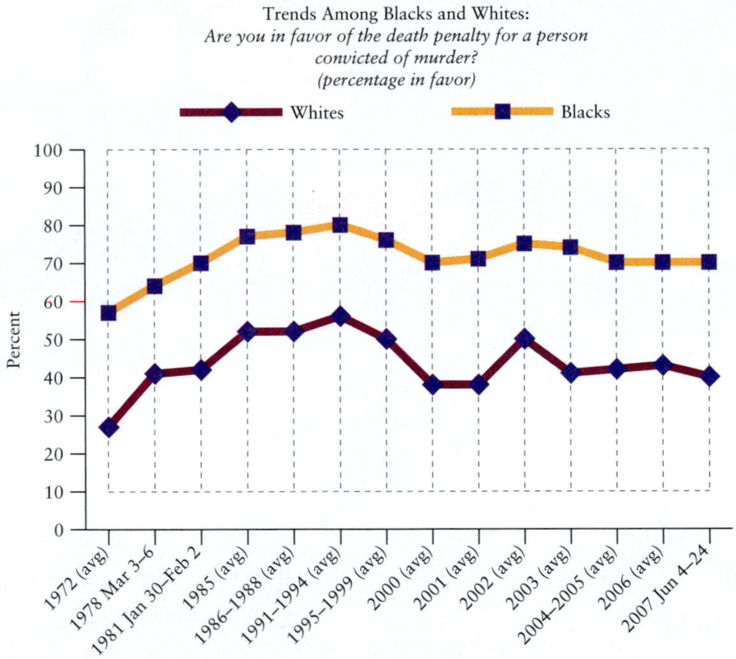

Trends Among Blacks and Whites:
Are you in favor of the death penalty for a person convicted of murder?
(percentage in favor)

Source: Lydia Saad, "Racial Disagreement Over Death Penalty Has Varied Historically," Gallup News Service, July 30, 2007. Copyright © 1972–2007 by The Gallup Organization. Reprinted by permission of The Gallup Organization.

With only about 2 percent of death sentences actually carried out over the past decade, the death penalty cannot possibly be a deterrent to murder. Respect for the court system is eroded when the decisions of juries and judges are frustrated by convicted murderers. As trial judges and juries continue to impose the death penalty, and appellate courts continue to grant stays of execution, the number of prisoners on death row grows. The few who have been executed have averaged ten years' delay between trial and execution. This frustrates many citizens, but they do want to make sure someone is absolutely guilty.

The racial make-up of those on death row has prompted many minority rights groups to protest against the death penalty.

Who's On Death Row?

Much more attention is given to the racial make-up of those on death row than the gender composition. Minority rights groups rigorously track such statistics and use them as evidence of racial inequality in the criminal justice system. And Gallup Polls over the years have shown a big racial divide in opinions about the death penalty. (See Figure 9–4.) As of 2007, 45 percent of those awaiting execution were white, 42 percent African American, 11 percent Hispanic, and 2 percent were other races. Women make up a very small percentage of those on death row (1.4 percent); however, the number of females in the criminal justice system is on the upswing.

Method of Execution

Although there are five methods of execution, all states but one (Nebraska) that have the death penalty use lethal injection as their primary method of execution. The other little-used methods are electrocution, gas chamber, hanging, and firing squad; where these methods still exist, the law generally gives a convicted person the right to choose them over lethal injection which rarely happens. Since 1976, 84 percent of all executions have been by lethal injection. (Nebraska is the only state to solely use electrocution). Recently, even the lethal injection method has been vigorously debated in state legislatures and in the courts. The tough questions are "about how much pain the condemned feel as they die and what role, if any, medical professionals should play in executions?"[69] Critics argue that medical practitioners are better able to administer the fatal dose than correctional officers who, in some instances, have not done the job properly, leading to legal claims of "cruel and unusual punishment."

Moratoriums, Abandonments, and Reinstatements

The potential for wrongful executions has always worried Americans. With the emergence of better evidence (DNA), proactive civil rights lawyers, and more cautious judges, convicted persons have been removed from death row because of trial errors, attorney incompetence, evidence withheld by the prosecution, new DNA evidence, and the like. (Since 1973, over 120 people have been released from death row based on new evidence of their innocence.) In 2000, the Illinois governor declared a moratorium on executions in

America's Most Crime-Ridden Big Cities

Crime rates in large cities are generally higher than those in suburbs, small towns, and rural areas. Indeed, overall crime rates in some of America's big cities are higher than the national rate. But even among the large cities, overall and specific crime rates vary tremendously. Note that New York, once regularly listed among America's most crime-ridden large cities, is now one of the safest.

Large U.S. Cities with Highest and Lowest Crime Rates

Cities with Highest Crime Rates		Cities with Lowest Crime Rates	
Crime Index Total			
Tucson, AZ	9,937	New York, NY	2,800
Memphis, TN	9,861	San Jose, CA	2,826
Atlanta, GA	9,558	Virginia Beach, VA	3,281
Oklahoma City, OK	9,506	Long Beach, CA	3,798
Kansas City, MO	9,295	El Paso, TX	4,056
Dallas, TX	8,972	San Diego, CA	4,075
Columbus, OH	8,659	Los Angeles, CA	4,347
Portland, OR	8,372	Louisville, KY	4,716
Charlotte-Mecklenburg, NC	8,189	Phoenix, AZ	4,767
Tulsa, OK	8,133	Honolulu, HI	5,144
Murder			
New Orleans, LA	56.0	El Paso, TX	1.9
Baltimore, MD	43.5	San Jose, CA	2.6
Detroit, MI	42.1	Honolulu, HI	2.9
Washington, DC	35.8	Virginia Beach, VA	3.4
Atlanta, GA	25.8	Colorado Springs, CO	3.7
Philadelphia, PA	22.2	Austin, TX	3.8
Dallas, TX	20.2	Arlington, TX	3.9
Kansas City, MO	19.9	Seattle, WA	4.2
Miami, FL	17.9	San Diego, CA	4.8
Cleveland, OH	17.1	Omaha, NE	4.9
Motor Vehicle Theft			
Detroit, MI	2,687	Virginia Beach, VA	172
Phoenix, AZ	1,740	New York, NY	260
Sacramento, CA	1,618	El Paso, TX	310
Seattle, WA	1,607	Austin, TX	386
Washington, DC	1,470	Arlington, TX	423
New Orleans, LA	1,387	San Antonio, TX	459
Atlanta, GA	1,338	Louisville, KY	484
Denver, CO	1,337	San Jose, CA	497
Las Vegas, NV	1,304	Wichita, KS	500
Dallas, TX	1,293	Colorado Springs, CO	554

Source: U.S. Census Bureau, *Statistical Abstract of the United States 2007*, "Law Enforcement, Courts, and Prison," Table 298. Available at http://www.census.gov/prod/2006pubs/07statab/law.pdf

that state, citing the many trial errors that were reported to him and the possibility that an innocent person might be put to death. He commuted the death sentences of all 167 inmates on death row, citing a state investigation that uncovered police corruption and racial bias in the state's capital punishment system. Several other states followed suit. In 2006, the U.S. Supreme Court ruled, in *House* v. *Bell*,[70] that a Tennessee death row inmate be given a new trial based on new DNA evidence, establishing that as precedent. In that same year, a number of states imposed temporary halts to executions because of questions over the administration of lethal injections.

In 2004, death penalty statutes in New York and Kansas were ruled unconstitutional by those states' high courts. (In 2006, the U.S. Supreme Court reinstated Kansas's death penalty law in *Kansas* v. *Marsh*.) In 2005, New York's State Assembly voted against reinstating it, making New York the first state to abandon the death penalty since the U.S. Supreme Court reinstated it in 1976 followed by New Jersey in 2007. Several other states have since considered removing the death penalty.

On the other hand, bills to reinstate the death penalty have been introduced in some of the states that do not have it. Prosecutors, victims' advocates, and a sizable portion of the public in those states believe it is an effective crime-fighting tool and righteous punishment for heinous crimes. Aware of the concerns of putting an innocent person to death, some of these states contemplating adopting the death penalty are looking at more stringent ways to safeguard against wrongful convictions. Being considered are stricter requirements for scientific evidence, such as DNA and fingerprints, and raising the bar for a death penalty sentence from the normal legal standard of guilt "beyond a reasonable doubt" to a finding of "no doubt about the defendant's guilt."[71]

Courts, crime, and correctional issues are well documented on the Internet. The Cornell University Law School maintains a free Web site with access to *all* U.S. Supreme Court decisions from 1990 to the present, together with 610 most important historical decisions of the Court. The decisions are indexed by topic as well as by name: **http://supct.law.cornell.edu/supct**

State court decisions usually must be researched in law school libraries. But the National Center for State Courts maintains a site at **www.ncsconline.org**

This organization is primarily concerned with court administration, the processing of cases, caseloads, and related issues. Its Web site contains links to the Conference of Chief Justices (of state courts) and the Conference of State Court Administrators.

The U.S. Bureau of Justice Statistics provides a goldmine of information on crime rates (total and by type of crime), victimization rates, arrests, prosecutions, and federal and state prison, parole, and probation populations. Both nationwide and state-by-state figures are provided. Moreover, most of the data are presented in trend lines for the past twenty to thirty years in both table and graphic form. This site can be accessed at

www.ojp.usdoj.gov/bjs

The Federal Bureau of Investigation maintains its own Web site at

www.fbi.gov

This is a frequently accessed site; it includes the FBI's Ten Most Wanted list. It also includes the semiannually updated *Uniform Crime Reports* (UCRs). UCRs are provided for all types of crime both nationwide and by city. (However, the latest figures are given as percentage increases or decrease from the previous year, requiring viewers to access the previous year and do the math themselves to obtain the latest actual crime rates.)

Other useful sites are as follows:

Death Penalty Information Center: A quarterly report by the Capital Punishment Project: **http://www.deathpenaltyinfo.org**

Human Rights Watch—Death Penalty: **www.hrw.org/campaigns/deathpenalty**

National Sheriff's Association: **www.sheriffs.org**

National Legal Aid and Defender Association: **www.nlada.org**

GOVERNING AMERICA'S COMMUNITIES

10

QUESTIONS TO CONSIDER

Where you currently live, which type of local government has the primary responsibility for law enforcement?
- ■ City
- ■ County
- ■ Township

What form of government does your county have?
- ■ Traditional county commission structure
- ■ Elected county executive/county mayor structure
- ■ County administrator structure

Do you believe that city council members should be elected at-large (each elected by all of the city voters), by districts (each elected by voters in separate districts), or by a combination of the two (some at-large, some by districts)?
- ■ At-large ■ By districts ■ By combination

Which of the following do you think would be the best measure of whether there is a "sense of community" where you live?
- ■ Neighbors regularly interact with each other.
- ■ Citizens say they are proud to live there.
- ■ Volunteerism is high.
- ■ Turnout in local elections is high.
- ■ Local governments cooperate.

What type of local government has the primary responsibility for governing local schools in your community?
- ■ County
- ■ City
- ■ School district

Could minority candidates in your community be elected more easily in at-large elections or in district elections?
- ■ At-large elections
- ■ District elections

SO MANY LOCAL GOVERNMENTS, SO MUCH CONFUSION

A bomb threat is called into a local television station. An explosion occurs at a nearby oil refinery. A neighborhood panics when its drinking water suddenly has a suspicious color and odor. Several gunmen go on a shooting rampage at a local pharmaceutical company's research lab. Dangerous microorganisms are missing. A stranger hops onto a school bus en route to the local high school and terrifies the students who use their cell phones to call their parents. In each instance, the first question that will be raised in the minds of many citizens is likely to be: "Are terrorists to blame?" followed by an even more critical question: "Whose responsibility is it to take charge of the situation?" Soon thereafter, the community's residents will begin asking whether the response of the local government(s) in charge has been efficient, effective, and conducted fairly. Initially, most citizens will not know whether it is the county, the city, a town, township, some special district government (the hospital district, school district), or some combination thereof that must react because most Americans do not have a clear idea of which local government does what even in noncrisis situations. If they do know which local government is responsible, they may not know which official within that government has the authority to act.

America's communities are incredibly diverse—in population size, square miles, and socioeconomic composition. Our communities are governed in vastly different ways. To put it simply—there is no "one size fits all" local governance structure. Even within the same state, there is likely to be considerable variation in what form of local government has been adopted, the powers and responsibilities of local officials, and the method of electing local officials.

The local government arena is incredibly complex, fragmented, and often confusing to Americans who tend to move around a lot.

Generalizing about community politics is perhaps even more difficult than generalizing about American state politics. There are nearly 88,000 local governments in the United States. These include cities, municipalities, townships, counties, and a host of other school districts and special districts. (See Table 10–1.) Nearly two-thirds of the American people live in urban units of local government known as "municipalities," including "cities," "boroughs," "villages," or "towns." Other Americans are served by county or township governments. Moreover, there are 371 metropolitan areas in the United States; these are clusterings of people and governments around a core city of 50,000 or more residents. These metropolitan areas range in size from the Lewiston, Idaho, area, population 57,961, up to the New York City area, which has 600 local governments and over 18 million people. In short, one may conceive of communities as counties, towns, and villages, and cities of all sizes, or even sprawling metropolitan areas.

Within the same geographical area, a multitude of local governments coexist to provide citizens with a wide array of services, activities, and infrastructure. These range from public safety, mosquito control, water, sewers, sports stadiums, and schools to ports, hospitals, and libraries, depending on where you live. The local government arena is incredibly complex, fragmented, and often confusing to Americans who tend to move around a lot. Local governments vary significantly in their

TABLE 10-1 Local Governments in the United States	
General Purpose	
Counties	3,034
Municipalities	19,431
Townships	16,506
Total	**38,971**
Special Purpose	
School Districts	13,522
Special Districts	35,356
Total	**48,878**
Total Local Governments	**87,849**

Note: Data are for 2002.

Source: U.S. Census Bureau. Available at http://ftp2.census.gov/govs/cog/2002COGprelim_report.pdf

functions, the titles and responsibilities they give to their elected officials, and in how and when they conduct local elections.

Creating a "Sense of Community"

One of the biggest challenges facing local governments in the twenty-first century, especially in light of America's highly mobile population, is how to define and create a "sense of community" among an area's residents. Community ties are stronger where friends and neighbors frequently interact with each other socially, volunteerism rates are high, communication channels between government and citizens are open, citizens are satisfied with local services, local governments cooperate with each other more than they conflict, and turnout in local elections is high.[1] In such places, a higher proportion of residents say they are proud to live there. Studies have found that "strong, engaged communities are desirable places to live because they offer residents a sense of belonging and a feeling of efficacy."[2] That doesn't necessarily mean that everyone agrees on what their local officials should do.

Providing Services and Managing Conflict

Community political systems serve two principal functions. One is that of supplying goods and services—for example, police protection or sewage disposal—that are not supplied by private enterprise. This is the *"service" function.*

SENSE OF COMMUNITY
Friends and neighbors frequently interact with each other socially, volunteerism rates are high, and communication channels between government and citizens are open.

People feel more of a sense of community when friends and neighbors interact with each other socially, often by volunteering to do something to improve their community.

Negative aspects within a community that can cause that community to be undesirable.

Positive aspects within a community that can cause that community to be desirable.

The other function is the *"political"* one, that of *managing conflict* over public policy. Of course, the "political" and the "service" functions of local governments are often indistinguishable in practice. A mayor who intervenes in a dispute about the location of a park is managing a local government service, namely recreation, at the same time that he or she is managing political conflict about whose neighborhood should get the most benefit from the new park.

Sources of Community Conflict

What are the sources of community conflicts? Human diversity is the source of all political conflict—differences among people in wealth, occupation, education, ethnicity, race, religion, and style of living. In the United States, there are many rural communities, small towns and cities, and compact suburbs with relatively homogeneous populations. In these communities, there are fewer differences among citizens and fewer permanent lines of cleavage. Some conflicts occur in these communities, of course, but groupings of forces are usually temporary. In contrast, in most large cities and metropolitan areas there are many different kinds of people living closely together, and there are more lasting cleavages, or "fault lines," which tend to open when controversial issues arise. These cleavages are readily recognized in disputes among upper-, middle-, and lower-income groups; ethnic groups; property owners and nonproperty owners; renters and homeowners; families with children and those without; old timers and newcomers, young and old, suburbanites and city dwellers; and traditional political party divisions.[3]

Increasingly in America's large cities, racial and ethnic conflicts are becoming more intense as the population makeup of urban areas is becoming more diverse. These conflicts are not always between minority groups and white residents. In some multiracial communities, the fiercest conflicts may be between several minority groups fighting with each other for resources and representation.

Coping with Dissatisfaction

How do individuals cope with community problems? If you are dissatisfied with the way things are going in your community, you have three choices: (1) resign yourself to the situation, do nothing, and just tolerate it; (2) move away and find a community that provides more satisfactions; (3) stay and make an attempt to change things. Political scientists tend to focus their attention on the people who try to change things, implying that this is the only way to respond rationally to community problems. However, economists have developed theories of residential mobility that focus on the individual's choice of community based on a rational calculation of personal costs and benefits.[4] (The theory is most applicable to metropolitan areas where many different kinds of communities are available.)

There are recognized negative **"push"** factors—crime, congestion, noise, overcrowding, racial conflict—and positive **"pull"**

When city residents see their own children drawing pictures focusing on crime, it often pushes them to move to the suburbs.

factors—more space, larger houses, better schools, "nice" playmates for the children—both of which affect decisions to move. One might move to the suburbs "for the kids," or move to the city to be close to good restaurants, fine entertainment, cultural events, and specialty shops, or to reduce the trip to work. In short, economists emphasize rational calculations and freedom of choice, which they assume most citizens possess.

How do people actually respond to community dissatisfactions? There is some evidence to suggest that, in the face of community problems[5]:

- Higher-status whites tend either to become politically active or to move out, with political activity somewhat more common.
- Lower-status whites tend to move out rather than become politically active.
- In the past, blacks have been more likely to become politically active in city politics rather than to move out, probably because of the increased difficulties most blacks face in residential relocation. Now many middle- and upper-class black professionals move to the suburbs rather than stay in the city and fight.[6]
- City residents are more likely to move out, whereas suburbanites are more likely to become politically active.
- Newly arrived immigrants are likely to stay put in the city but stay out of politics; it is the second or third generation of immigrants who become politically engaged.
- People who have been generally satisfied with the past performance of their local government, as well as people who have invested in home ownership or local businesses, are more likely to become politically active to solve a current problem, rather than to move out or do nothing.
- Dissatisfied affluent residents may choose to "privatize" the community services that distress them. The most common example is the choice of private schools over the public school system, but occasionally residents and businesses also turn to private police protection, security services, garbage collection, and so on.

Overall, the tendency to "move away" from urban problems has greatly accentuated the difficulties of the nation's largest central cities. Some of these cities are actually declining in population—losing middle-class residents to their surrounding suburbs and causing citizen satisfaction with services to deteriorate.[7] We will return to this problem in Chapter 12, but it is important to know how individual citizens as well as governments cope with community problems.

EIGHTY-EIGHT THOUSAND GOVERNMENTS

Local government is not mentioned in the U.S. Constitution. Although we regard the American federal system as a mixture of federal, state, and *local* governments, from a constitutional point of view, local governments are really parts of state governments. Communities have no right to self-government in the U.S. Constitution. All of their governmental powers legally flow from state laws and constitutions. Local governments—cities, townships, counties, special districts, and school districts—are creatures of the state, subject to the obligations, privileges, powers, and restrictions that state governments impose upon them. The state may create or destroy any or all units of local government. To the extent that local governments can collect taxes, regulate their citizens, and provide services, they are actually exercising *state* powers delegated to them by the state in either its constitution or its laws.

Communities have no right to self-government in the U.S. Constitution. All of their governmental powers legally flow from state laws and constitutions.

Do you know who to call if your house or apartment caught fire? Many citizens do not know which local government to contact when a crisis hits their own home. This poor understanding of which local government has what functional responsibility also makes it difficult to hold public officials accountable at election time.

Why Should You Care about the Structure of Local Government?

Most citizens see little need to understand the structure of the local governments that serve them—until there's a crisis or pressing need in our own neighborhood or a concern that touches members of our own household. Is there a pothole in the middle of the street that has been there for weeks? Who is to blame for the change in zoning that allowed a super Wal-Mart to be built two blocks from our home? Why have public swimming pools been built in every neighborhood except ours? How many more people have to be killed or injured before a traffic light is installed at the corner where we turn to go to work? Why has our community been judged to be "less than ready" for responding to a possible bioterrorism attack?

The Key to Holding Officials Accountable

The answers to these typical questions differ considerably depending on the structure of the local governments in our community. The bottom line is that we do not know whom to hold accountable for action—or inaction—unless we understand which official has the formal authority to deal with an issue or problem.

Regretfully, most Americans are unable to correctly identify which local government bears the major responsibility for delivering a specific service. (For example, is it the city or the county or the road district government that makes the decision about when and where to install a traffic light? Or is it the state?) This confusion is understandable. Each state determines which type of local government shall bear the major responsibility for providing major services and functions. The assignment of responsibility often differs across the states and even within the same state.

What does this complex local government landscape mean for the average citizen who moves several times in his or her lifetime? It means that we must make an effort to educate ourselves about which local governments and which officials do what within our community. If we don't make this effort, then we may place blame on the wrong local officials—and become quite frustrated and cynical when nothing happens.

What Should Citizens Focus on at the Local Level?

As a citizen, it is important to know who "hires and fires" various types of local officials. In the case of elected officials, we the citizens "hire and fire" them at the ballot box. In communities with a city, county, or town manager, the elected commissioners usually hire and fire the manager. Depending on the type of local government in place, department heads and their deputies may be hired and fired by the mayor, the manager, the commission or council, or several acting together.

It is equally important to know who has the major responsibility for preparing or drafting the budget and then approving it. After all, the budget is the single best statement about a government's priorities. No pothole will be filled, no swimming pool will be built, and no traffic light can be purchased and installed without funds being budgeted.

Another key to understanding a local government's modus operandi is determining the degree to which a local government's structure provides for separation of powers (checks and balances). Are the executive and legislative branches separate or do the same officials act as both branches? How much power does the chief executive have over the budget? In the hiring and firing of department heads? To veto the actions of the legislative body?

We also need to know who elects each of the commissioners. Do only voters living in his or her district elect a commissioner or is the commissioner elected by a citywide or countywide vote? Within your community, are some commissioners elected from districts while others run at-large? Why should this matter? An individual council member's or commissioner's priorities may differ considerably depending on his or her constituency base. For example, at budget time, a district-based commissioner may be more likely to say a budget is fair if it allocates as much to his or her district as to other districts. In contrast, a commissioner elected at-large may judge a budget that benefits the majority of the community as fair. The bottom line is that how local officials are elected affects their approach to policymaking and problem solving.

Local Government Functions Differ by State

Counties, cities, and townships are referred to as **general-purpose governments**. They provide a wide range of services, from law enforcement to parks and recreation, human services, roads, and public works.

Special districts and school districts are known as **special-purpose governments**. They are much more limited in the number of functions they perform for the public.

Different units of government are assigned different responsibilities by each of the states, so it is difficult to generalize about what each of these types of local governments is supposed to do. Indeed, even in the same state, there may be overlapping functions and responsibilities assigned to cities, counties, school districts, and special districts. Nevertheless, let us try to make some generalizations about what each of these types of government does, realizing of course that in any specific location the pattern of governmental activity may be slightly different:

COUNTIES
—*Rural*: Keep records of deeds, mortgages, births, marriages; assess and levy property taxes; maintain local roads; administer elections and certify election results to state; provide law enforcement through sheriff; maintain criminal court; maintain a local jail; administer state welfare programs.
—*Urban*: Most of same functions as rural counties (except police and court systems, which often become city functions), together with planning and control of new subdivisions; mental health; public health maintenance and public hospitals; care of the aged; recreation, including parks, stadiums, and convention centers; and perhaps some city-like functions.

CITIES
—Provide the "common functions" of police, fire, streets, sewage, sanitation, and parks; over half of the nation's large cities also provide welfare services and public education. (In other cities welfare is handled by county governments or directly by state agencies, and education is handled by separate school districts.)

GENERAL-PURPOSE GOVERNMENT

A government that provides a wide range of services, such as a county or city.

SPECIAL-PURPOSE GOVERNMENT

A government that performs a very specific function, such as a school district.

TOWNS AND TOWNSHIPS

—Midwestern townships: Generally subdivisions of counties with the same responsibilities as their county; provide roads and bridges, fire and rescue, and other basic services to rural areas.
—New England towns: Deliver extensive services similar to those provided by municipalities.[8]

SCHOOL DISTRICTS

—Organized specifically to provide public elementary and secondary education; community colleges may be operated by county governments or by special districts with or without state support.
—Most school districts are **independent**; but some are "**dependent**" because other governments (state, county, municipality, town or township) are responsible for the administration and operation of the public school system.

SPECIAL DISTRICTS

—Provide specific services that are not being supplied by existing general-purpose governments; most (92 percent) perform a **single function**, such as fire protection, mass transit, soil conservation, libraries, water and irrigation, mosquito control, sewage disposal, airports, sports, convention centers, and so on; some **multiple-function** special districts provide several related types of services such as water supply and sewerage services.

The fifty states vary a great deal in the numbers of local governments they authorize. (See "*Rankings of the States:* Local Governments.") Hawaii is the nation's most centralized state: There are only nineteen local governments in the Aloha State; fifteen of these are special districts without taxing power; three are counties; and one is the city of Honolulu. In contrast, there are 6,903 local governments in Illinois, including 1,291 cities, 102 counties, 1,431 townships, 934 school districts, and 3,145 special districts.

COUNTY GOVERNMENTS: RURAL AND URBAN

All states, with the exception of Connecticut and Rhode Island, have organized *county* governments. In Louisiana, counties are called "parishes," and in Alaska they are called "boroughs." Historically, states created counties as their administrative arms, which is why counties are often described as legal subdivisions of the state. It is difficult to generalize about the powers of the nation's 3,034 counties. The legal powers, organization, and officers of counties vary a great deal. Perhaps it would be best to begin a description of county government by distinguishing between *rural* and *urban* counties. Obviously there is a great deal of difference between Los Angeles County, with nearly 10 million people; Cook County, Chicago, with 5.3 million; and Harris County, Houston, with 3.9 million; and the more than 700 rural counties in the nation with populations of 10,000 or less. Loving County, Texas, has but fifty-two residents.

Counties range in area from 67 square kilometers (Arlington, Virginia) to 227,559 square kilometers (North Slope Borough, Alaska).

The number of county governments per state also differs widely, from the Texas total of 254 down to fewer than 20 in several states.

Rural Counties

Traditionally, the rural county was the most important unit of local government: It handled such essential matters as law enforcement, courts, roads, elections, poor relief, and the legal recording of property deeds, mortgages, wills, and marriages. Rural communities competed with each other for the location of the county seat, because the community named as county seat won social and political prestige, county jobs, a county fair, and

RANKINGS
of the STATES

Local Governments

All Local Governmental Units

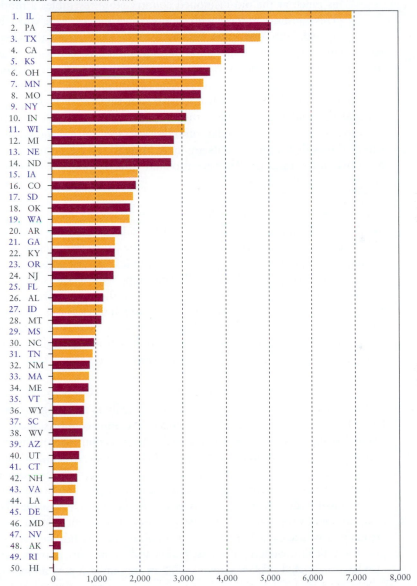

Rank	State
1.	IL
2.	PA
3.	TX
4.	CA
5.	KS
6.	OH
7.	MN
8.	MO
9.	NY
10.	IN
11.	WI
12.	MI
13.	NE
14.	ND
15.	IA
16.	CO
17.	SD
18.	OK
19.	WA
20.	AR
21.	GA
22.	KY
23.	OR
24.	NJ
25.	FL
26.	AL
27.	ID
28.	MT
29.	MS
30.	NC
31.	TN
32.	NM
33.	MA
34.	ME
35.	VT
36.	WY
37.	SC
38.	WV
39.	AZ
40.	UT
41.	CT
42.	NH
43.	VA
44.	LA
45.	DE
46.	MD
47.	NV
48.	AK
49.	RI
50.	HI

Note: Data are for 2002.
Source: U.S. Census Bureau, *Statistical Abstract of the United States* 2007, Table No. 416. Available at http://www.census.gov/prod/2006pubs/07statab/stlocgov.pdf

preferential treatment in county roads and public buildings. Moreover, many rural dwellers identify themselves as "coming from" a particular county. The county seat attracted retail business: Farm markets were generally located in county seats, where a farmer could transact both public and private business. Rural county government provided an arena for a folksy, provincial, individualistic, "friends and neighbors" type of politics. Rural county government was the province of amateurs rather than experts or professionals. Decision making was personalized and informal. Often rural counties resemble urban counties about as much as the old-fashioned country store resembles a modern supermarket. This is just fine to those who choose to live in rural areas, which have become more appealing to Americans. Beginning in the 1990s, rural areas began gaining population again—reversing a long period of population loss. The biggest gains have occurred in rural communities adjacent to metropolitan areas, in popular recreational and retirement counties more than in farming and mining communities.[9]

According to the Voices of Rural America national survey, over three-fourths of rural residents rate the quality of life in their community as either excellent or good. And contrary to conventional wisdom that rural residents feel isolated and physically detached, the survey shows that rural residents are more likely to feel connected to their small communities than urban residents. They are also quite content with "small-town" county politics.[10]

Urban Counties

Urban counties provide the traditional county functions like welfare, health care, roads, elections, and court systems for all county residents. But in urban areas, they also provide more traditional "city services" such as fire protection, water, sewers, and libraries to the unincorporated areas of the county, that is, to the areas not within the boundaries of cities. They may also provide "city-type" services to some incorporated areas, usually small municipalities, more cheaply than they could provide them to their own residents. Urban counties are the most likely to sell services to smaller cities in large metropolitan areas. In these areas, urban counties are increasingly providing more facilities and services that benefit an entire region, such as mass transit, convention centers, airports, sports stadiums, and pollution control (see Table 10–2).[11]

The Structure of County Government

Although county governments may differ markedly in their organization, they generally have (1) a governing body variously called the "**county commissioners**," "county board," "board of supervisors," or even "judges," which is composed of anywhere from three to fifty elected members, either elected by district or countywide; (2) a number of separately elected officials with countywide jurisdictions, such as sheriff, county attorney, auditor, recorder, coroner, assessor, judge, treasurer, and so on; (3) a large number of special boards or commissions that have authority over various functions, whose members may be elected or appointed by the county commissioners or may even include the county commissioners in an ex officio capacity; and (4) an appointed county bureaucracy in planning, transportation, health, welfare, libraries, parks, and so on. Larger, more urban counties may also have an elected chief executive and/or an appointed county administrator or manager.

Traditional County Commission Structure

Traditionally, county governments have been organized around the commission structure (see top of Figure 10–1). Nearly three-fourths of the nation's counties still operate

TABLE 10–2	County Functions	
Traditional, Rural	**Contemporary, Urban**	
Property tax assessment and collection	Mass transit	
Election administration	Airports	
Judicial administration, including civil and criminal courts, probate, etc.	Libraries	
	Water supply and sewage disposal	
Recording of deeds, mortgages, and other legal instruments	Water and air pollution control	
	Building and housing code enforcement	
Recording of vital statistics, including births, deaths, and marriages	Natural resource preservation	
	Planning and land use control	
Local roads and bridges, construction and maintenance	Community development and housing	
Law enforcement (sheriff and coroner)	Parks and recreation	
County jail maintenance	Stadiums, convention and cultural centers	
Administer state welfare and social service programs	Public health, including clinics	
Other: county fairs, agricultural extension service	Public hospitals	
	Disaster preparedness together with traditional functions	

under this structure. Typically there are three or five county commissioners, elected for overlapping four-year terms, and a large number of separately elected county officials. There is no single person responsible for administration of county functions. The commissioners may supervise some functions themselves and share supervision of other functions with other elected officials. Thus, for example, both the elected sheriff and the county commissioners share responsibility for the county jail, with the sheriff supervising day-to-day operations, but the commissioners deciding on its construction, repair, and financing. The commissioners usually decide on the **property tax** *rate* (or "**millage**," with one mill equal to one-tenth of a percent or $1 per $1,000 of assessed property value) to be imposed on property owners (subject to maximums usually set by the state legislature). But the tax *assessor* determines the value of each parcel of property in the county against which the rate is to be applied. And in some counties a separate tax *collector* actually sends out the tax bills and undertakes to collect the revenue. A separate *treasurer* may maintain the county's financial accounts and write the checks. Thus, responsibility for county government is fragmented and dispersed.

Reformers view this traditional structure of county government as lacking in efficiency and accountability. Governmental functions are usually in the hands of untrained nonprofessional county officeholders. County jobs are awarded to "friends and neighbors and relatives." Few voters, even in small rural counties, know enough about what goes on in various offices in the "county courthouse" to hold individual officers responsible for their administration. Typically, independently elected county officials are returned to office term after term with little or no opposition. Only the sheriff's race in rural counties stirs up much interest. But when small counties suddenly experience a growth spurt, county races can become more competitive, especially when new residents have different ideas about county services than longtime residents. Old-timer versus newcomer schisms often create intensely fierce local elections.

PROPERTY TAX MILLAGE (RATE)

1 mill = $1 per $1,000 per assessed valuation of property; rate is expressed in number of mills set by a government.

FIGURE 10–1 **Structures of County Government**

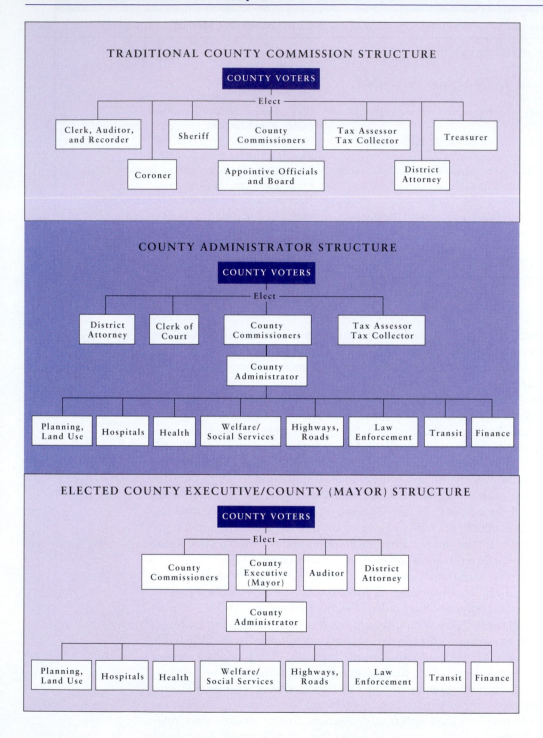

TRADITIONAL COUNTY COMMISSION STRUCTURE

COUNTY VOTERS

— Elect —

Clerk, Auditor, and Recorder | Sheriff | County Commissioners | Tax Assessor Tax Collector | Treasurer

Coroner | Appointive Officials and Board | District Attorney

COUNTY ADMINISTRATOR STRUCTURE

COUNTY VOTERS

— Elect —

District Attorney | Clerk of Court | County Commissioners | Tax Assessor Tax Collector

County Administrator

Planning, Land Use | Hospitals | Health | Welfare/ Social Services | Highways, Roads | Law Enforcement | Transit | Finance

ELECTED COUNTY EXECUTIVE/COUNTY (MAYOR) STRUCTURE

COUNTY VOTERS

— Elect —

County Commissioners | County Executive (Mayor) | Auditor | District Attorney

County Administrator

Planning, Land Use | Hospitals | Health | Welfare/ Social Services | Highways, Roads | Law Enforcement | Transit | Finance

County Administrator Structure

Urbanization and the proliferation of county functions usually result in demands for more professional administration of county government. When county commissioners find that they cannot cope with the volume and complexity of county business, they often seek professional assistance. The county-administrator or county-manager structure of government offers a solution. (See middle of Figure 10–1.) It is based on the council manager form of city government (see "Forms of City Government" later in this chapter). An appointed county administrator, responsible to the county commission, is placed in charge of the various county departments and agencies. The commission makes policy and appoints the administrator to *implement* policy. The administrator prepares the budget for the commission's approval and then implements it; the administrator hires and fires department heads and reports back regularly to the commission on county business. It seldom works out as neatly as it appears on the organization chart, but the use of the county administrator plan has grown rapidly throughout the United States in recent years. More than half of all U.S. counties are governed by such a structure. (See Figure 10–2.)

Voters lose some direct control over county functions with the adoption of the county-administrator structure. And county commissioners themselves are usually obliged to go through the county administrator to influence activities in a county department. But the advantage is the professional leadership, administrative efficiency, and functional accountability that the structure brings to county government. The role of the county administrator is similar to that of a city manager (see "City Managers in Municipal Politics" in Chapter 11).

Elected County Executive/County Mayor Structure

In recent years, more counties in the United States have adopted a governmental structure that features an elected "county executive." Voters elect both a county commission and a separate county executive officer, who exercises formal responsibility over county

COUNTY ADMINISTRATOR STRUCTURE
The organization of county government in which the elected commission appoints an administrator/manager who supervises county functions.

ELECTED COUNTY EXECUTIVE–COUNTY MAYOR
The organization of county government in which a chief executive officer is elected separately from the county commission.

FIGURE 10–2 Forms of County Government

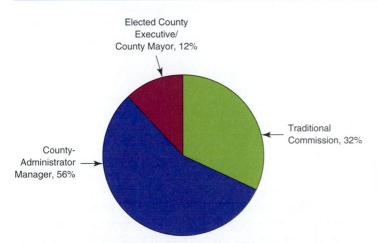

Elected County Executive/County Mayor, 12%

Traditional Commission, 32%

County-Administrator Manager, 56%

Note: Data are for 2002.
Sources: International City/County Management Association, *The 2004 Municipal Year Book*, p. 37; U.S. Census Bureau American Fact Finder.

HOME RULE CHARTER

A charter that authorizes a city or a county to exercise all powers not specifically prohibited by law or by charter.

DILLON'S RULE

The legal doctrine that cities possess only those powers expressly granted in their charter.

departments. (See bottom of Figure 10–1.) The elected county executive usually appoints the county administrator subject to approval of the commission. This structure envisions the separation of legislative and executive powers, much like American state and national governments. The elected county executive, like the county administrator, has won approval in many urban counties over recent years. Urban counties often experience more crises and emergencies and need a strong executive with the authority to act in such situations. Today, 12 percent of U.S. counties elect a county executive.

County Officials

Typically, county officials have the following duties:

Commissioners: Elected governing body with general responsibility for all county functions; most commissions have three to seven members with election by the county's voters at large.

Sheriff: Maintains jail; furnishes law enforcement in unincorporated areas; carries out orders of the county court.

Auditor: Maintains financial records; authorizes payment of county obligations.

County or district attorney: Serves as chief prosecuting attorney; conducts criminal investigations and prosecutes law violators.

Coroner: Conducts medical investigations to determine cause of death; maintains county morgue.

Tax collector: Collects taxes.

Treasurer: Maintains and disperses county funds; makes county fiscal reports.

Clerk: Registers and records legal documents including deeds, mortgages, subdivision plots, marriages, divorces, births; certifies election returns.

Tax assessor: Determines value of all taxable property in the county.

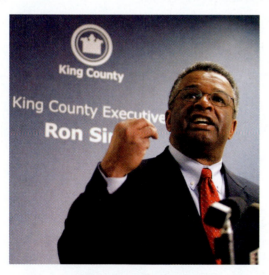

Ron Sims, the elected County Executive for King County, Washington won a prestigious *Governing* magazine Public Official of the Year award for being an "across-the-board innovator." Before becoming County Executive, he served on the county council.

The many separately elected county officials are generally considered an obstacle to the emergence of strong executive leadership at the county level. The ability of county governments to assume more important functions and responsibilities, particularly in urban areas, probably hinges on a reorganization of county government to provide for stronger executive leadership.

Home Rule Charter Counties

Most counties in America are still heavily dependent upon the state legislature to define their functions and cannot do anything that is not explicitly spelled out in state law (**Dillon's rule**). In its history of county government, the National Association of County Officials describes the legal status of most county governments: "Counties [have] to have specific enabling legislation to authorize whatever functions they might fulfill at the local level, and to respond to the changing needs of their citizens, they [have] to petition the [state] legislature for additional authority, which might or might not be granted."[12] The trend in county governance is for states to pass legislation allowing them to operate under a home rule charter. (A **county charter** is like a state constitution; it lays out the structure and powers of the local government for which it is written. It must be adopted by a majority of the county's voters.) A home rule charter grants a county more local control, greater policymaking authority, and more self-government than it is given by the state constitution or state statutes. California was the first state to allow home rule for its counties; Los Angeles County became the first county in the United States with a home rule charter. Today, thirty-seven states permit some form of home rule for at least some of their counties, usually the most populous counties. However, just 5 percent of all counties are home rule charter counties. When voters defeat proposals for a home rule charter, it is often because they fear higher taxes.[13]

Townships

Another interesting unit of local government is the "township," which is found in twenty states—the northern states from New England to the Midwest. Southern and western states have made little use of this unit of government. Most townships are subdivisions of counties and perform many of the functions of county governments at a grassroots level—elections, road repair, tax administration, fire protection, and even law enforcement through local justices of the peace. Most townships are unincorporated, which means they do not have charters from state governments guaranteeing their political independence or authorizing them to provide many municipal services. However, some states, like Michigan, grant townships a charter under certain conditions. The jurisdiction of townships may extend over many square miles of sparsely populated rural territory. More than 55 million people, or one-fifth of the U.S. population, live under township governments today. They are usually governed by an elected board of supervisors, trustees, or commissioners who oversee township operations; the structure is much like the traditional commission form of county government, although some have professional township managers. Some townships also elect other officials, such as a Clerk or a Constable.

Township governments vary considerably in their powers and organization. Perhaps it would be best to classify them as "rural townships" and "urban townships." Many rural townships outside of New England have lost much of their vitality in recent years. The school district consolidation movement (see Chapter 16) has centralized the control of public schools at the county level or in school districts that span villages and townships.

Some urban townships appear to have a brighter future as units of government than do rural townships. This is particularly true in certain suburban areas of larger cities where metropolitan growth has enveloped township governments. Some states, Pennsylvania for example, have authorized urban townships to exercise many of the powers and provide many of the services previously reserved to city governments.

The New England Town

In the New England states (Connecticut, Maine, Massachusetts, New Hampshire, Rhode Island, and Vermont), the "town" is a significant unit of local government, with long traditions and deep roots in the political philosophy of the people of the region. In fact, the New England "town meeting" is often cited by political philosophers as the ideal form of *direct* democracy as distinguished from *representative* democracy. For the **town meeting** was, and to some extent still is, the central institution of "town" government. The New England town included a village and all of its surrounding farms. The town meeting was open to all eligible voters; it was generally an important social as well as political event.

REPRESENTATIVE TOWN MEETING GOVERNMENT

Town meeting members are elected prior to a town meeting.

MUNICIPAL CORPORATION

A city government chartered by the state government.

CITY CHARTER

The document that grants powers to, and determines the structure of, a city government.

The town meeting would levy taxes, make appropriations, determine policy, and elect officers for the year. Between town meetings, a board of selected officials would supervise the activities of the town—schools, health, roads, care of the poor, and so on. Other officers include town clerk, tax assessors and collectors, justices of the peace, constables, road commissioners, and school board members. Although the ideal of direct democracy is still alive in many smaller New England towns, in the large towns, the pure democracy of the town meeting has given way to a representative system (**representative town meeting government**), in which town meeting members are elected prior to the town meeting. Moreover, much of the determination of the towns' financial affairs, previously decided at town meetings, has now been given over to elected officials, and many towns have appointed town managers to supervise the day-to-day administration of town services.

CITIES AS "MUNICIPAL CORPORATIONS"

Legally speaking, cities are "municipal corporations" that have received charters from state governments setting forth their boundaries, governmental powers and functions, structure and organization, methods of finance, and powers to elect and appoint officers and employees. In some ways, a charter may be thought of as a license to operate as a city granted to a community by the state. The **city charter** is intended to grant the powers of local self-government to a community. In this sense, a city charter is similar to a state constitution in that it establishes the city's structure and governing processes.

A city charter is similar to a state constitution in that it establishes the city's structure and governing processes.

Of course, the powers of self-government granted by a municipal charter are not unlimited. A state can change its charter or take it away, as it sees fit. Cities, like other local governments, have only the powers that state laws and constitutions grant them. They are still subdivisions of the state. And, of course, state laws operate within the boundaries of cities. In fact, municipal corporations are generally responsible for the enforcement of state law within their boundaries. However, they also have the additional power to make local laws, "ordinances," which operate only within their boundaries.

Dillon's Rule

Perhaps the most serious limitation on the powers of cities is the fact that American courts have insisted upon interpreting the powers granted in charters very narrowly. The classic statement of this principle of restrictive interpretation of municipal powers was made by John F. Dillon many years ago and is now well known as "Dillon's rule":

> It is a general and undisputed proposition of law that a municipal corporation possesses and can exercise the following powers, and no others: first, those granted in express words; second, those necessarily or fairly implied in or incident to the powers expressly granted; third, those essential to the accomplishment of the declared objects and purposes of the corporation—not simply convenient, but indispensable. Any fair, reasonable, substantial doubt concerning the existence of power is resolved by the courts against a corporation, and the power is denied.[14]

State Legislators Retain Local Powers

The restrictive interpretation of the powers of cities leads to rather lengthy city charters, since nearly everything a city does must have specific legal authorization in the charter. The city charter of New York, for example, is several hundred pages long. City charters must cover in detail such matters as boundaries, structure of government, ordinance-making powers, finances, contracts, purchasing, bonds, courts, municipal elections, property assessments, zoning laws and building codes, licenses, franchises, law enforcement, education, health, streets, parks, public utilities, and on and on. Since any proposed change in the powers, organization, or responsibilities of cities requires an act of a state legislature amending the city's charter, state legislatures are intimately involved in local legislation. This practice of narrowly interpreting city charters may appear awkward, but its effect is to increase the power of state legislators in city affairs. State legislators from cities acquire power because legislatures usually grant a local legislator the courtesy of accepting his or her views on local legislation that affects only that legislator's constituency.

Types of Municipal Charters

1. *Special act charters* State legislative control over cities is most firmly entrenched in special act charters. These charters are specially drawn for the cities named in them. Cities under special act charters remain directly under legislative control, and specific legislative approval for that city and that city alone must be obtained for any change in its government or service activities. Such charters give rise to local acts dealing with small details of city government in a specially named city, for example, "that West Fall River be authorized to appropriate money for the purchase of uniforms for the park police." Under special act charters, laws that apply to one city do not necessarily apply to others.

2. *General act charters* In contrast, general act charters usually classify cities according to their size and then apply municipal laws to all cities in each size classification. Thus, a state's municipal law may apply to all cities of less than 10,000 people, another law to all cities with populations of 10,000–24,999, another to cities with 25,000–49,999 people, and so on. These general act charters make it difficult to interfere in the activities of a particular city without affecting the activities of all cities of a similar size category. Yet in practice there are often exceptions and modifications to general act legislation. For example, since legislators know the populations of their cities, they can select size categories for municipal law that apply to only one city.

3. *Optional charters* Optional charter laws provide cities with some choice in the structure and organization of their governments. Such laws generally offer a choice of governmental forms: strong mayor and weak council, weak mayor and strong council, commission, city manager, or some modification of these.

4. *Home rule* Municipal home rule charters, like county home rule charters, are designed to give cities the power to adopt governmental forms and provide municipal services, as they see fit, without state legislative interference. Home rule charters may be given to cities by state constitutions or by legislative enactments; legislative home rule is considered less secure, since a legislature could retract the grant if it wished to do so. Beginning with Missouri in 1875, more than half the states have included in their constitutions provisions for the issuance of home rule charters. About two-thirds of the nation's cities with populations over 200,000 have some form of home rule. Any change in the charter must be approved by a majority of the voters.

The intended effect of home rule is to reverse Dillon's rule and enable cities to "exercise all legislative powers not prohibited by law or by charter." In other words, instead of preventing a city from doing anything not specifically authorized, home rule permits the city to do anything not specifically prohibited. The theory of home rule grants sweeping powers to cities; however, in practice, home rule has not brought self-government to cities.

Instead of preventing a city from doing anything not specifically authorized, home rule permits the city to do anything not specifically prohibited.

Home rule provisions in state constitutions range from those that grant considerable power and discretion over local affairs, to provisions that are so useless that no city has ever made use of them. First, these constitutional provisions may be too cumbersome or vague for effective implementation. In some states, cities feel that it is easier to use the general law charters, particularly if they provide for optional forms of government, than to use the cumbersome procedures for obtaining home rule.

Another important limitation on home rule is the distinction between "self-enforcing" and "non-self-enforcing," or "permissive," home rule provisions in state constitutions. Non-self-enforcing home rule provisions merely permit the state legislature to grant home rule to its cities; cities cannot acquire home rule without legislative action. Only about a dozen states have "self-enforcing" home rule provisions, which enable cities to bypass the state legislature and adopt home rule for themselves.

Finally, home rule may be limited by court interpretations of the language of the constitutional provisions granting power to home rule in cities. Constitutional provisions may grant to home rule cities the power to make "all laws and ordinances relating to municipal concerns," or the "powers of local self-government," or all powers "in respect to municipal affairs." Of course, ordinances passed under home rule authority cannot be in conflict with state law. Courts must distinguish between municipal and statewide concerns. In cases where doubt exists, legal traditions of municipal law require that courts resolve the doubt in favor of the state and against local powers of home rule. State legislatures can intervene in local affairs in home rule cities by simply deciding that a particular matter is of statewide concern.

Politics of Home Rule

The politics of home rule often pits reform groups, city mayors, and administrators against state legislators and large municipal taxpayers. State legislators are generally wary of giving up their authority over cities. Rural legislators have little reason to support city home rule, and even city legislators seldom welcome proposals to give up their authority over local bills. Sometimes city employees with good access to the legislature will oppose giving a mayor or a city manager too much control over their employment. Taxpayer groups may fear that home rule will give the city the ability to increase taxes. Local bills may be pictured as a distraction to legislators by reformers, but many legislators enjoy the power that it brings them in local affairs and welcome the opportunity to perform legislative services for their constituents. And so, even with reapportionment adding to the number of urban legislators, the League of Women Voters, good-government groups, and mayors may still be frustrated in their attempts to achieve genuine home rule for American cities.

Courts Restrict Local Powers

Courts figure prominently in municipal politics. This is because of the subordinate position of the municipal corporation in the hierarchy of governments, and legal traditions, such as Dillon's rule, which narrowly interpret the power of local governments. The power of courts over municipal affairs grants leverage to defenders of the status quo in any political battle at the local level. Proponents of a new municipal law or municipal service not only must win the battle over whether a city *ought* to pass the new law or provide the new service but also must win the legal battle over whether the city *can* pass the law or provide the service. Limitations and uncertainties abound about the validity of local enactments. Legal challenges to the authority of the city to pass new regulations or provide new services are frequent. The city attorney becomes a key official because he or she must advise the city about what it can or cannot do. Not only must the city obey the federal constitution (and adhere to federal mandates and strings attached to federal aid), but it is also subject to the restraints of the state constitution, state laws, its municipal charter, and of course, Dillon's rule. The result is to greatly strengthen courts, attorneys, and defenders of the status quo.

FORMS OF CITY GOVERNMENT

American city government comes in various structural packages (see Figure 10–3). There are some adaptations and variations from city to city, but generally one can classify the form of city government as mayor-council (strong mayor or weak mayor), commission, council-manager, town meeting, or representative town meeting. Over half of American cities now operate under council-manager governments (see Figure 10–4).

Commission

The traditional commission form of city government gives both legislative and executive powers to a small body, usually consisting of five members. The commission form originated at the beginning of the century as a reform movement designed to end a system of divided responsibility between mayor and council. One of the commission members is nominally the mayor, but he or she has no more formal powers than the other commissioners. The board of commissioners is directly responsible for the operation of city departments and agencies. In practice, one commission member may take on responsibility for the management of a specific department, such as finance, public works, or public safety. As long as the council members are in agreement over policy, there are few problems; but when commissioners differ among themselves and develop separate spheres of influence in city government, city government becomes a multiheaded monster, lacking in coordination. The results of a commission form of government were generally so disastrous that the reform movement abandoned its early support of this form of government in favor of the council-manager plan. Today, just 1 percent of U.S. cities, mostly those in the 10,000 to 25,000 population range, are still governed by this form.

Council-Manager

The council-manager form of government revived the distinction between legislative "policymaking" and executive "administration" in city government. Policymaking responsibility is vested in an elected council, and administration is assigned to an appointed professional administrator known as a manager. The council chooses the manager who is responsible to it. All departments of the city government operate under the direction of the manager, who has the power to hire and fire personnel within the limits set by the merit system. The council's role in administration is limited to selecting and dismissing the city manager. The plan is based on the idea that policymaking and administration are separate functions, and that the principal task of city government is to provide the highest level of services at the lowest possible costs—utilities, streets, fire and police protection, health, welfare, recreation, and so on. Hence, a professionally trained, career-oriented administrator is given direct control over city departments. The manager even prepares the budget. In recent years, an average of sixty communities a year have adopted the council-manager form of government. Today, it is used by 53 percent of all U.S. cities.

FIGURE 10–3 **Forms of City Government**

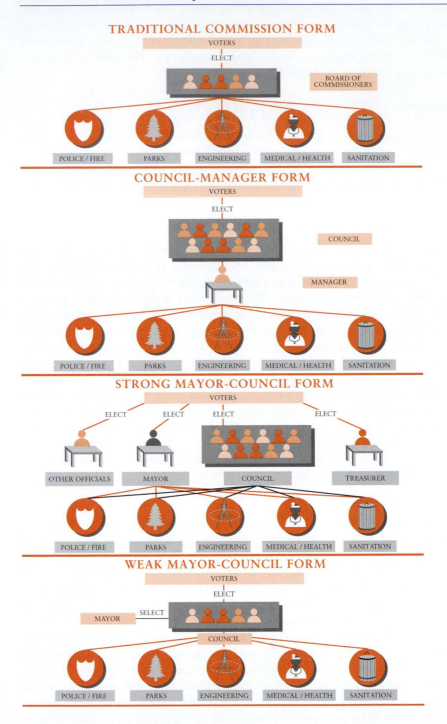

FIGURE 10–4 **American Cities: Forms of Government**

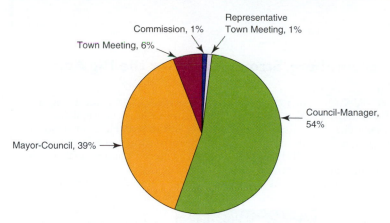

Commission, 1%

Representative
Town Meeting, 1%

Town Meeting, 6%

Council-Manager,
54%

Mayor-Council, 39%

Note: Population data are for 2001.
Source: The 2003 Municipal Year Book, p. 6; *The 2004 Municipal Year Book* (specific city form of government).

Elected Mayor (Hybrid Mayor-Manager Form of Government)   A **hybrid form of council-manager government** has emerged over the years.[15] The manager who is hired and fired by the council still functions as the chief executive but the voters also separately elect a mayor. Mayors in council-manager cities play two major roles. They are consensus builders and they guide the development and implementation of policies that improve community service delivery. By the early 2000s, 65 percent of all council-manager communities separately elected their mayor.[16]

Mayor-Council

There are two types of mayor-council government: strong mayor-council and weak mayor-council. The nation's largest cities tend to function under the "**strong mayor-council**" plan. This form of government is designed in the American tradition of separation of powers between legislature and executive. A strong mayor is one who is the undisputed master of the executive agencies of city government and who has substantial legislative powers in the form of budget making, vetoes, and opportunity to propose legislation. (See "*People in Politics:* Michael Bloomberg, Strong Mayor for the Big Apple.") Only a few cities make the mayor the sole elected official among city executive officers; it is common for the mayor to share powers with other elected officials—city attorney, treasurer, tax assessor, auditor, clerk, and so on. Yet many mayors, by virtue of their prestige, persuasive abilities, or role as party leader, have been able to overcome most of the weaknesses of their formal office.

In recent years, large cities have been adding to the formal powers of their chief executives. Cities have augmented the mayors' role by providing them with direction over budgeting, purchasing, and personnel controls; and independent boards and commissions and individual councilmen have relinquished administrative control over city departments in many cities. Moreover, many cities have strengthened their mayors' position by providing them with a **chief administrative officer**, "CAO," to handle important staff and administrative duties of supervising city departments and providing central management services.

HYBRID COUNCIL-MANAGER GOVERNMENT

A city manager who is hired and fired by a city council and functions as the chief executive but voters also separately elect a mayor.

STRONG MAYOR-COUNCIL GOVERNMENT

The form of city government in which legislative power is exercised by an elected council, and city departments are supervised by a separately elected mayor.

CHIEF ADMINISTRATIVE OFFICER

(CAO) In a strong mayor-council form of government, an official who functions as a city manager; is appointed by the mayor not the council.

PEOPLE in POLITICS

Michael Bloomberg, Strong Mayor for the Big Apple

New York City has a history of strong mayors—Ed Koch, Rudy Giuliani, and Michael Bloomberg. These mayors have all been national figures which is no doubt due to the fact that the City is the nation's financial and media center. It is also one of the nation's most diverse cities—America's melting pot—and one of the most challenging to govern. It is no surprise that the city's mayors believe they have the credentials to be president!

It is Bloomberg who holds the all-time record for campaign spending in a local election. The billionaire financier spent $73 million of his own personal fortune—nearly $100 per vote—to win the mayor's office in 2001. Bloomberg was a general partner in the Wall Street investment firm of Salomon Brothers, but he made most of his $6 billion fortune in his own investment company, Bloomberg L.P. He received his undergraduate education at Johns Hopkins University and his MBA from the Harvard Business School. In addition to funding his own political career, Bloomberg has engaged in substantial philanthropy, including support of the Johns Hopkins Bloomberg School of Public Health.

In 2001, Rudy Giuliani was ineligible for reelection as New York's mayor, having served two successive terms. Bloomberg, a lifelong Democrat, won Giuliani's endorsement to run for mayor as a Republican. Bloomberg won

Source: http://upload.wikimedia.org/wikipedia/commons/thumb/5/55/Michael_Bloomberg_speech.jpg/306pxMichael_Bloomberg_speech.jpg

in a close election—50 percent to 48 percent—against New York City Public Advocate Mark Green. Bloomberg outspent Green by over five to one. He campaigned in the aftermath of the terrorist attack of September 11, 2001, claiming that the city needed a businessman to help it recover.

As mayor, Bloomberg pursued what he termed a "results-based" management style: he placed his aides in an open bullpen office, similar to a Wall Street trading floor, in order to "promote accountability." More importantly, he reorganized the city's school system. (Unlike most cities with separate school districts with their own governing boards, New York City's mayor oversees the city's schools.) He extended the city smoking ban to all indoor public areas. And he backed a measure to require "potty parity"—requiring new buildings to install more women's toilets. As a social liberal, Bloomberg supports same-sex marriage; he is pro-choice and pro–gun control.

Bloomberg easily won re-election in 2005, equaling his earlier record-shattering campaign spending. He announced he was leaving the Republican Party and becoming an Independent. This switch prompted speculation that he might run as an independent candidate in the 2008 presidential election.

The **"weak mayor-council"** form of government is most common in cities under 10,000 in population, where both the mayor and the council serve on a part-time basis. In some cities the mayor is separately elected, but in most, the mayor is a member of the council who has been chosen mayor by his or her council peers. In both situations, the mayor is primarily an executive figurehead responsible for signing papers, cutting ribbons, etc. The council, not the mayor, has relatively strong appointment, budget, policy initiation, and management powers, although the powers of mayors even in this weak system are being expanded. Even so, such councils typically meet only once or twice a month because the issues they must deal with are not as complex or pressing as those facing big city councils.[17]

Town Meeting and Representative Town Meeting

Town-meeting and representative town-meeting governments are currently found in Connecticut, Maine, Massachusetts, New Hampshire, and Vermont. Most town meetings are held in response to the issuance of a warrant (agenda) by an elected town clerk and/or by the elected town council. The town meeting is open to all residents and it possesses full legislative authority. A town meeting may be called once or twice a year. In most town meetings, the passage of the annual budget is the most important item of business.

Town meetings usually choose a board to oversee business between meetings. Voters separately elect a town clerk, treasurer, assessor, constable, school board, and other officers. The town meeting may also elect a finance committee to prepare the budget.

While the town meeting has been celebrated by many political philosophers as "pure democracy," the reality is much less than full participatory democracy. Attendance at town meetings is usually less than 10 percent of the town's voters. In larger towns, the participation rate may be only 1 or 2 percent of the voters. The idealized town meeting democracy is really governance by a very small group of political activists. Special interest groups can easily pack a town meeting. Senior citizens attend these meetings in disproportionate numbers. And employees, members of the volunteer fire company, school teachers, and business and civic association members are also over-represented. Of course, attendance increases when controversial items are on the agenda. And in many town-meeting governments, a decision can be overturned by citizen initiative and referendum.[18]

Representative town-meeting (RTM) government is a hybrid political institution that seeks to combine features of the open town meeting with representative government. In RTM the voters elect a relatively large number of persons to vote at meetings, yet voters retain the right to attend and speak at town meetings themselves. However, in practice the number of candidates for town-meeting members is frequently equal to or even smaller than the number of town-meeting members to be elected. Town clerks often must recruit people to become town-meeting members. In theory, representative town-meeting members should be more attentive than townspeople because they accepted the responsibility of public office. But attendance is also a problem in RTM government.

Changing City Charters: The Trend toward Hybrid Forms

It is not uncommon for citizens to want to change some aspect of their city charter. Over the years, a number of mayor-council cities have adopted some elements of council-manager governments (e.g., professional administrator, civil service) and some council-manager governments have adopted several elements of the strong-mayor council form (e.g., separately elected mayor with veto power). "Fewer cities are now either distinctly mayor-council or council-manager in form, and most cities are structurally less distinct, constituting a newly merged or hybrid model of local government."[19] What prompts a city's voters to support changing the city charter? Often it is rapid growth, but any sharp shift in local conditions such as economic decline, government corruption, and/or rising crime rates may prompt change. Politically savvy community activists are often the catalysts for successful charter change movements.

WEAK MAYOR-COUNCIL GOVERNMENT The form of city government in which legislative and executive powers lie with an elected council and the mayor is primarily a figurehead.

NONPARTISAN ELECTIONS

Most of America's cities use the nonpartisan ballot to elect local officials. Reformers believed that nonpartisanship would take the "politics" out of local government and raise the caliber of candidates for elected offices (see Chapter 11). They believed that nonpartisanship would restrict local campaigning to local issues and thereby rule out extraneous state or national issues from local elections. They also believed that by eliminating party labels, local campaigns would emphasize the qualifications of the individual candidates rather than their party affiliations.

Nonpartisanship is found in both large and small cities. Nonpartisanship is even more widespread than council-manager government. However, there is a tendency for these two forms to be related: 85 percent of all council-manager cities have nonpartisan ballots, while only 65 percent of all mayor-council cities are nonpartisan (see Table 10–3). Party politics is still the prevailing style of local elections in eastern cities, except for New England. Elsewhere in the nation nonpartisanship prevails. The nonpartisan ballot is more likely to be adopted in homogeneous middle-class cities, where there is less social cleavage and smaller proportions of working-class and ethnic group members.

Do nonpartisan elections remove politics? To what extent has nonpartisanship succeeded in removing "politics" from local government? Of course, if *politics* is defined as conflict over public policy, then "politics" has certainly not disappeared with the elimination of party labels. There is no evidence that eliminating party ballots can reduce the level of community conflict. If we define *politics* to mean "partisanship," that is, *party* politics, then nonpartisanship can remove party influences from local government.

Apparently several types of political systems can be found in nonpartisan cities. First of all, in some nonpartisan cities, parties continue to operate effectively behind the scenes in local affairs. *Disguised party politics* is most likely to be found in big cities of

---

TABLE 10–3   Forms of Government and Type of Elections

	Percent	
	Partisan	**Nonpartisan**
Classification		
All Cities	22.7	77.3
Metropolitan Status		
Central city	19.4	80.6
Suburb	25.7	74.3
Independent city	18.2	81.8
Forms of Government		
Mayor-council	35.2	65.8
Council-manager	15.5	84.5
Commission	21.7	78.3
Town meeting	23.5	76.5
Rep. town meeting	15.2	84.8

Note: Data are for 2001.

Source: International City/County Management Association (ICMA), "Form of Government Survey 2001." Statistics calculated from data set provided to Susan A. MacManus by ICMA.

the Northeast and Midwest, in states where political parties are strong and competitive. In these cities, persons who are known Democratic and Republican candidates run in officially "nonpartisan" elections.

Another type of nonpartisan political system is one in which the major parties are inactive, but clear *coalitions* of socioeconomic groups emerge that resemble the national Democratic and Republican parties. These opposing coalitions may involve liberal, labor, Catholic, and black groups on one side; and conservative, business, Protestant, middle-class groups on the other.

Nonpartisan systems may feature the activities of independent community *groups* and organizations. Frequently, these groups are civic associations led by newspapers, chambers of commerce, or neighborhood associations. These organizations may "slate" candidates, manage their campaigns, and even exercise some influence over them while they are in office. These organizations are not usually as permanent as parties, but they may operate as clearly identifiable political entities over the years.

In still another type of nonpartisan political system, neither parties, nor coalitions, nor groups play any significant role, and there are no local slate-making associations. Individual candidates select themselves, collect their own money, and create their own temporary campaign organizations. Voting does not correlate with issues, or party identification, or socioeconomic groups, but instead tends to follow a *friends and neighbors* pattern. Indeed, voting in local nonpartisan elections often depends on factors such as incumbency, name recognition, position on the ballot (the first name on the list gets more votes), and very brief personal contacts (a handshake at the office or factory, a door-to-door canvass, or even a telephone call).

Possible Republican Advantage

Does nonpartisanship increase Republican influence in city government? It is sometimes argued that the removal of party designations from local elections hurt Democrats by disengaging their traditional support from urban voters—the low-income, labor, ethnic, and black groups that traditionally vote the Democratic ticket. Moreover, the well-educated, high-income groups and interests that are normally Republican have a natural edge in organization, communication, and prestige in the absence of parties. Republicans also have better turnout records in nonpartisan elections. Surveys of local officials elected under partisan and nonpartisan systems tend to confirm that nonpartisanship results in the election of more Republicans. However, this Republican advantage in nonpartisan elections is very modest; it appears to be limited to smaller cities and cities that are dominated by Democrats.[20]

Nonpartisan Candidates

Does nonpartisanship result in "better-qualified" candidates winning public office? Of course, the answer to this question depends on one's definition of better qualified. Nonpartisanship does result in more high-income, "respectable," older, white, Anglo-Saxon Protestants with prestigious jobs running for public office.[21] Working-class candidates are disadvantaged by nonpartisanship for several reasons. First, nonpartisanship reduces the turnout of labor, low-income, ethnic, Democratic voters and, consequently, increases the influence of well-educated, high income, white, Anglo-Saxon, Protestant Republican voters who continue to come to the polls in nonpartisan elections. In addition, nonpartisanship means that recruitment of candidates will be left to civic associations, or ad hoc groups of one kind or another, rather than to Democratic or Republican party organizations. This difference in recruitment and endorsement practices tends to give an advantage to middle-class candidates. Working-class candidates seldom have the organizational ties or memberships that would bring them to the attention of civic associations that recruit in nonpartisan elections.

Incumbent Advantage

Nonpartisanship appears to contribute to the reelection of incumbent council members, particularly when nonpartisanship is combined with at-large elections. Incumbent council members are reelected on the average about 80 percent of the time. When incumbents *are* defeated, they tend to suffer defeat in a group as a result of intensive community conflict.[22] Incumbents are more likely to have a name that is known to the voters. Incumbent council members in partisan cities are not reelected as often as incumbents in nonpartisan cities. This suggests that it is difficult to hold public officials accountable in nonpartisan elections. The voter does not have the opportunity to hear organized criticisms of incumbent officeholders from an opposition party. When the only challenge to an incumbent officeholder is an unknown name on the ballot, he or she is more likely to be reelected than if he or she is challenged by a candidate backed by an opposition party. The higher rates of reelection in nonpartisan systems suggest that accountability is harder to achieve where party labels are absent.

LOCAL ELECTION SYSTEMS: AT-LARGE, DISTRICT, AND COMBINATION

Local elected legislative officials—county commissioners, city council members, town and township board members, school board members, and special district board members—are usually elected one of two ways. The first is *at-large*—by the entire electorate (e.g., citywide, countywide, school districtwide). The second is *from a district*.

Some local governments elect all legislative officials at-large; others elect all from single-member districts; but a growing number elect some officials at-large, but others from single-member districts (a combination, or mixed, system). Today, roughly 64 percent of American cities elect their council members at-large, about 14 percent by districts, and 21 percent by a combination of at-large and district constituencies.[23]

Indeed, there are many hybrid local election systems used across the United States, which is very confusing to those who move from one community to another.

Types of At-Large Systems[24]

The city council has been selected as the local legislative body used to illustrate how different types of at-large electoral systems work. (They work the same for county commission, town board, township board of trustees, school board, or special district board elections.)

Under an at-large system, all council members run citywide and are voted on by all the voters in the city. Under a **pure at-large system**, if there are six seats up for election, each voter can vote for up to six candidates. The six candidates receiving the highest number of votes are elected. But there are other forms of at-large systems. In some cities, a person runs for a numerically or alphabetically labeled seat but is elected citywide (an **at-large by position system**). A person must decide whether he or she wants to run for Council Seat #1, or A, or Council Seat #2, or B, and so forth. The council

PURE AT-LARGE ELECTORAL SYSTEM

Elections in which candidates are chosen by all of the voters in a community; highest vote-getters win.

AT-LARGE BY POSITION ELECTORAL SYSTEM

A person runs for a numerically or alphabetically labeled seat but is elected citywide.

seat, regardless of how it is labeled, has no geographical basis. On Election Day, all voters in the city can select the candidates they prefer to hold each nongeographically defined seat up for election. If there are six seats up for election, each voter may cast six votes—one for each seat.

There is yet a third type of at-large election called the **at-large from residency district system**. The city is divided into equally populated, geographically defined districts. A candidate runs to represent the district he or she lives in (e.g., District 1), but all voters in the city get to vote on who shall represent that district. If there are six districts, each voter casts a ballot for a preferred candidate from each district. The intent of this type of system is to guarantee broader representation of geographical areas, while requiring candidates to take a citywide perspective.

Traditionally, reformers believed that district elections encourage parochial views, neighborhood interest, "logrolling," and other characteristics of "ward politics." These "undesirable" characteristics occur because council members are responsible to local majorities in the particular sections or wards from which they are elected. In contrast, council members elected at-large are responsible to citywide majorities; this should encourage impartial, communitywide attitudes. Moreover, in council-manager cities, it is argued that the manager can be more effective in serving the "general good" of the whole community if the manager is responsible to council members elected at-large rather than by districts. (Of manager cities, 70 percent elect council members at-large, compared to only 50 percent of mayor-council cities. Council-manager cities also tend to have more racially/ethnically homogeneous populations. Racial and ethnic groups have pressed for single-member district election systems.)

AT-LARGE RESIDENCY DISTRICT ELECTORAL SYSTEM

A candidate runs to represent the district he or she lives in, but all voters in the city get to vote on who shall represent that district.

SINGLE-MEMBER DISTRICT ELECTORAL SYSTEM

Elections in which candidates are chosen by voters in separate geographically defined districts.

Single-Member District Systems

A **single-member district election system** limits each voter's choice to a single contest. A voter must choose among the candidates who have filed to represent the district (sometimes called a "ward") in which the candidate and the voter both reside. (See Choctaw, Oklahoma in Figure 10–5.)

Minority spokespersons frequently argue that minority candidates have a better chance of winning when they run from districts, especially when they make up less than a majority of the city's voting age population but live in a residentially concentrated area. In such settings, switching to a district-based election system permits the drawing of a district in which minorities make up a majority of the electorate. District-based elections are also alleged to increase voter turnout rates and reduce campaign spending costs, although the data are clearly mixed on those counts. For example, there is some evidence that minority voter turnout declines once a minority candidate is elected and becomes an entrenched incumbent.

For racial/ethnic minorities, district-based elections have been shown to promote slightly higher levels of representation depending on the size of the group, their geographic concentration, their political cohesiveness, and their ability to coalesce with other groups.

However, there is considerable evidence that the size of the minority electorate within a community is a far more powerful predictor of a group's proportional representation on city council than the electoral system itself.[25] For example, one summary of this literature notes, "As black populations have grown, especially in large central cities, as black political participation rates (registration and turnout) have equaled or

FIGURE 10–5 Comparing Single-Member District and Mixed (Combination) Election Systems

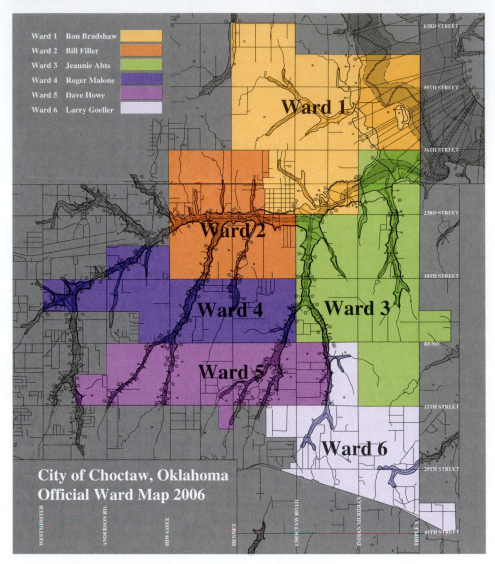

Ward 1   Ron Bradshaw
Ward 2   Bill Filler
Ward 3   Jeannie Abts
Ward 4   Roger Malone
Ward 5   Dave Howe
Ward 6   Larry Goeller

Ward 1
Ward 2
Ward 4
Ward 3
Ward 5
Ward 6

City of Choctaw, Oklahoma
Official Ward Map 2006

The City of Choctaw, Oklahoma elects its city council members using a single-member district election system, also referred to as a ward system. A citizen may only vote in one council race—the one featuring candidates running from the district in which the voter lives.
Source: http://www.choctawcity.org/pdf/2006ma/
City%20of%20Choctaw%20ward%20Map%202006%2011%5B1%5D.12.jpg

exceeded those of whites, and as successful black candidates have paved the way for others, the independent effect of electoral structure on black council representation levels has waned in certain parts of the country."[26] There is less evidence that the type of election system independently affects Hispanic or Asian representational levels.

FIGURE 10–5 (Continued)

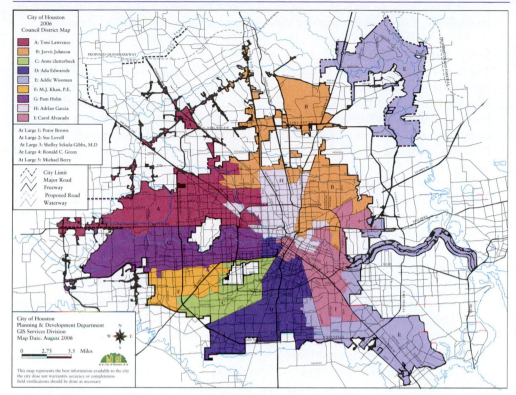

The City of Houston, Texas elects its city council members using a mixed, or combination, election system. Five members are elected citywide; nine are elected from single member districts. A citizen may vote in six council races—all five of the at-large races, and one district race (the one in which the voter resides). *Source:* http://www.houstontx.gov/council/maps/councildistricts.jpg

Even the importance of minority group size is beginning to weaken as more minorities capture at-large posts in big cities such as Houston and Kansas City or win seats in districts with less than majority-minority populations. This trend is expected to accelerate as more Americans begin to label themselves biracial or multiracial and cities become more multiethnic in composition.

Combination Election Systems

Voters in cities using a combination, or mixed, election system to choose council members can vote for all the at-large positions but for only one of the district-based council seats. For example, if a city has two at-large seats and four single-member district seats, each voter can cast three ballots (for the two at-large seats and for one district-based seat—the one in which he or she resides). (See Houston, Texas in Figure 10–5.)

Proponents of mixed systems promote them precisely because they retain some council members who bring a citywide perspective to matters before the council but allow other councilors to represent more narrow neighborhood or group perspectives. Minority groups (racial or partisan) who comprise a sizable portion of the population but are not concentrated in a specific neighborhood often prefer at least some at-large seats. This makes it possible for them to elect a candidate of their choice, or serve as the swing vote,

COMBINATION (MIXED) ELECTORAL SYSTEM
Some officials are elected at large; others are elected from single-member districts.

VOTING RIGHTS ACT OF 1982

Established a "totality of circumstances" test to be used in deciding whether at-large elections result in racial discrimination.

CUMULATIVE VOTING

Variation of at-large voting. Candidates run in multimember districts. Voters have as many votes as there are seats. Voters cast their votes for individual candidates and the winners are the ones with the most votes. Voters may also 'cumulate' or combine their votes on one or more candidates.

PROPORTIONAL REPRESENTATION

Racial and gender representation in government that is equal to that of their percentage makeup of the general population.

if they vote as a bloc. Term-limited district-based minority council members also favor having some at-large seats they can run for once the district seat term limits kick in. Increasingly, minorities are winning these at-large seats in combination systems.

Civil Rights Tests

The use of at-large elections to discriminate against racial minorities in their ability to participate in the political process and elect candidates of their own choice clearly violates the Equal Protection Clause of the Fourteenth Amendment and the federal Voting Rights Act. The U.S. Supreme Court in *Mobile* v. *Bolden* (1980) held that at-large elections are *not* unconstitutional in the absence of any evidence of discriminatory intent.[27] However, Congress amended the **Voting Rights Act in 1982** to substitute a *results test* for the more difficult to prove *intent test* in assessing discrimination. But Congress stopped short of declaring all at-large elections discriminatory and illegal. Instead Congress established a "totality of circumstances" test to be used in deciding whether at-large elections result in racial discrimination. The elements to be considered by the federal courts are as follows[28]:

- A history of official discrimination. (This test applies primarily to southern states.)
- A record of racial polarization in voting.
- Unusually large election districts.
- The existence of candidate slating by parties or groups, and whether minority members have been slated.
- The extent to which minorities have been adversely affected by local government decisions.
- Whether political campaigns have been characterized by racial appeals.
- The extent to which minority group members have been elected to office.

The federal courts are prepared to evaluate the use of at-large elections in each community by these tests.[29]

Federal Court Intervention

Federal court cases in recent years involving at-large elections suggest that it is becoming increasingly difficult for cities, counties, and even school districts to defend exclusive reliance on at-large elections. Civil rights groups have effectively utilized the "totality of circumstances" test to invalidate at-large elections across the country and especially in southern states. In some cases federal courts have ordered district elections for all officials, and in other cases federal courts have accepted combination plans—some council members elected by district and some at-large.

Some federal courts have ordered other elections systems put in place. **Cumulative voting** has been adopted in over forty localities to resolve federal voting rights cases, including Alamogordo, New Mexico; Amarillo, Texas; Peoria, Illinois; and Chilton County, Alabama.[30] Cumulative voting is actually a variation of at-large voting. "Candidates run in multimember districts. Voters have as many votes as there are seats. Voters cast their votes for individual candidates and the winners are the ones with the most votes. Voters may also 'cumulate' or combine their votes on one or more candidates instead of having to cast one vote for each candidate."[31] Supporters believe it enhances the chances of minority election and increases voter turnout slightly.[32]

The U.S. Supreme Court does *not* require **proportional representation** for minorities, that is, a council that is 20 percent black if the city's population is 20 percent black. However, lower federal courts have tended to compare the black proportion of the council with the black proportion of residents in determining whether the "totality of circumstances" suggests discrimination.

Minority Representation

Until recently, blacks were significantly *underrepresented* on city councils that elected their members at-large. In the 1970s several studies reported that blacks won fewer than 50 percent of the seats they deserved (based on their percentage of a city's population) in *at-large* cities, compared to 85 to 100 percent of the seats they deserved in cities that elected council members *by districts*.[33] However, by the late 1980s, black representation on city councils throughout the nation had increased dramatically, and it no longer made much difference in black representation whether councils were elected at-large or by district.[34] For cities with more than 10 percent and less than 50 percent black population, black representation on city councils is only slightly below black population percentages, and the difference between at-large and district elections is minuscule. For cities with black populations over 50 percent, "then it is whites who need district representation to obtain their proportional share of council seats."[35]

SPECIAL-PURPOSE LOCAL GOVERNMENTS

Counties and cities are referred to as general purpose local governments. They provide a wide range of services and programs. Special purpose local governments have narrower service responsibilities. School districts provide education. Special districts are formed for functions like transportation, mosquito control, hospitals, or parks, to name a few. The geographical area covered by special districts often is not the same as that covered by a county or city. In fact, special districts can cut across county lines.

School Districts

There are over 13,522 public school districts in the United States today. Local school districts are governed by an elected **school board** (legislative body) and an elected or appointed **superintendent** (chief executive). In some school districts, board members are appointed rather than elected, usually by city councils, county commissions, mayors, or even judges. (For a more detailed description of school system responsibilities and powers, see Chapter 16.)

There are fewer minorities and females on school boards than on other local governing bodies. A recent survey by the National School Boards Association found 86 percent of all school board members are white, 8 percent are African American, and 4 percent are Hispanic.[36] Minority and female representation levels are higher in larger school districts, which are typically more diverse. (See Table 10–4.)

Several factors deter minorities from running for school board posts: income, time commitment required, and lack of experience in holding leadership posts. In some districts, at-large elections may make it more difficult as well. Today, 57 percent of all school board members are elected at large, while 41 percent are elected by single member district. The rest are appointed.

SCHOOL BOARD
Legislative body that is either appointed or elected to govern schools.

SCHOOL SUPERINTENDENT
Chief Executive that is appointed or elected to oversee schools.

In most states, local school board members are elected. Minority and female representation levels are higher in larger school districts, which are typically more diverse. Issues brought before school boards are often highly contentious, ranging from sex education, school uniforms, and religious holidays, to teacher-student relationships.

TABLE 10–4　Minorities and Women on School Boards

Size of School District	Gender	Race-Ethnicity			
	Women (%)	White (%)	African American (%)	Hispanic (%)	Other (%)
25,000 or more	44.4	78.9	13	7.5	0.9
5,000–24,999	39.9	83.1	9.4	3.7	3.7
Fewer than 5,000	36.7	89.2	5.3	3.1	2.3
All Districts	38.9	85.5	7.8	3.8	2.3

Note: Data are for 2001.

Source: National School Board Association. Available at: www.nsba.org/site/docs/1200/1143.pdf

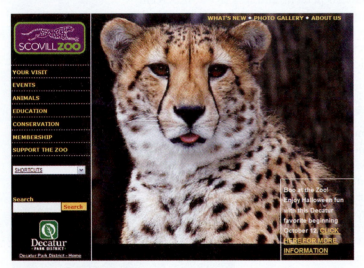

Special districts governments are the most common, but least understood, type of local government. Many have multimillion dollar budgets and perform a wide array of services. For example, the Decatur, Illinois Park District, established in 1924, manages and maintains an AZA-accredited zoo, forty-six parks, fifteen nature areas, sixty-three baseball diamonds, five golf courses, two swimming pools, an equestrian center, a tennis complex, bike trails, and the Decatur Airport. It also offers cultural arts programming, an indoor sports center, and a premier outdoor soccer complex that is home to MidState Soccer Club. Overall, the district controls 2,000 acres of parks and playgrounds, used by an estimated 1.2 million visitors each year.

Most school superintendents are appointed. Only two states permit the election of school superintendents—Florida and Mississippi.[37] The profile of school superintendents is even more white and male. A survey by the American Association of School Administrators finds that 87 percent of the school superintendents are male. Only 2 percent are black and 1 percent are Hispanic. Some say the "traditional path to the superintendency—becoming a high school principal or central office business administrator—favors male candidates. Women are more likely to be elementary school principals or curriculum coordinators—jobs that are not considered stepping-stones to the superintendency."[38]

Special Districts

There are over 35,000 special district governments across the United States. Many are governed by a quasi-independent board or commission. Most of these board members or commissioners are appointed by governors, legislators, and/or local elected officials such as mayors or county commissioners. Some board members serve by virtue of the fact that they hold another elective position. There is no national association of special districts so it is difficult to generalize about their structure or their diversity. *Special districts are the least understood of all the types of local government, yet they frequently control multimillion-dollar budgets. In a nutshell, there is little accountability to the general public.* The news media rarely covers special district activities unless there is a major crisis. (For a more detailed description of special district functions and responsibilities, see Chapter 12.)

Most citizens find discussions of local government structures and governance documents (charters) to be quite boring . . . and confusing. But when they want something done or they want to vote someone out of office whom they feel has been inept, irresponsible, or unresponsive, they soon recognize the importance of understanding which local government and public official has the authority to deal with their concern.

The Nation's Urban Areas Are Growing More Diverse

America's population is becoming more racially and ethnically diverse. Many minorities and new immigrants are drawn to large metropolitan areas areas, where jobs are more plentiful, minority neighborhoods already exist, and where ethnic shops and media abound. The multiplicity of local governments in such areas is quite confusing to newcomers and longtime residents alike. The job of governing is also considerably more difficult in these large, densely-populated areas, with more groups competing with each other for attention and services.

Metropolitan Areas That Had the Largest Gains in Minority Populations between 1990 and 2000

Hispanic	1990–2000 Hispanic Gains	2000 Hispanic Population	Percent of Total Population
1. Los Angeles–Riverside–Orange County, CA	1,819,370	6,598,488	40.3
2. New York–Northern New Jersey–Long Island, NY–NJ–CT–PA	992,185	3,849,990	18.2
3. Chicago–Gary-Kenosha, IL–IN–WI	600,810	1,498,507	16.4
4. Dallas–Ft. Worth, TX	594,836	1,120,350	21.5
5. Houston–Galveston–Brazoria, TX	575,098	1,348,588	28.9
6. Miami–Ft. Lauderdale, FL	501,543	1,563,389	40.3
7. Phoenix–Mesa, AZ	437,452	817,012	25.1
8. San Francisco–Oakland–San Jose, CA	413,258	1,383,661	19.7
9. San Diego, CA	240,184	750,965	26.7
10. Las Vegas, NV–AZ	232,978	322,038	20.6

Asians	1990–2000 Asian Gains	2000 Asian Population	Percent of Total Population
1. New York–Northern New Jersey–Long Island, NY–NJ–CT–PA	710,809	1,576,646	7.4
2. Los Angeles–Riverside–Orange County, CA	611,201	1,886,168	11.5
3. San Francisco–Oakland–San Jose, CA	554,326	1,446,563	20.6
4. Washington–Baltimore, DC–MD–VA–WV	212,350	454,702	6.0
5. Seattle–Tacoma–Bremerton, WA	183,134	358,255	10.1
6. Chicago–Gary–Kenosha, IL–IN–WI	179,537	428,819	4.7
7. Boston–Worcester–Lawrence, MA–NH–ME–CT	126,384	263,092	4.5
8. Dallas–Ft. Worth, TX	125,385	219,891	4.2
9. Houston–Galveston–Brazoria, TX	122,882	249,819	5.4
10. San Diego, CA	114,786	299,930	10.7

(continued)

Metropolitan Areas That Had the Largest Gains in Minority Populations between 1990 and 2000

African Americans	1990–2000 African American Gains	2000 African American Population	Percent of Total Population
1. Atlanta, GA	460,000	1,200,000	28.9
2. New York–Northern NJ–Long Island, NY–NJ–CT–PA	451,000	3,600,000	16.2
3. Washington–Baltimore, DC–MD–VA–WV	359,000	2,000,000	26.2
4. Miami–Ft.– Lauderdale, FL	241,000	798,000	20.4
5. Chicago–Gary-Kenosha, IL–IN–WI	181,000	1,700,000	18.7
6. Dallas–Ft. Worth, TX	176,000	732,000	13.8
7. Philadelphia–Wilmington–Atlantic City, PA–NJ–DC–MD	163,000	1,200,000	19.6
8. Houston–Galveston–Brazoria, TX	142,000	795,000	16.9
9. Los Angeles–Riverside–Orange County, CA	124,000	1,300,000	7.6
10. Detroit–Ann Arbor–Flint, MI	120,000	1,200,000	21.1

Source: U.S. Census Bureau. See also William H. Frey, "Micro Melting Pots," *American Demographics*, June 2001; "Trails South," *American Demographics*, July 2001.

The National Association of Counties (NACO): www.naco.org

This association provides extensive information on the nation's 3,000-plus counties, from the smallest (Loving County, Texas, with fifty-two people) to the largest (Los Angeles County, with its population of 9.9 million). NACO is the principal lobbying organization for counties in Washington. Its online database includes county policies, ordinances, codes, and model programs.

The National League of Cities: www.nlc.org

The league lobbies in Washington on behalf of city governments, "influencing national policy and building understanding and support for cities and towns." Its Web site includes policy positions on unfunded federal mandates, federal housing and community development programs, federal transportation programs, and other matters directly affecting cities.

Other very informative Web sites are as follows:

U.S. Conference of Mayors: **www.usmayors.org**

National Civic League: **www.ncl.org**

International City/County Management Association: **www.icma.org**

International Institute of Municipal Clerks: **www.iimc.com**

National Association of Towns and Townships: **www.natat.org**

National Center for Small Communities: **www.smallcommunities.org**

CHAPTER ELEVEN

PARTICIPATION IN COMMUNITY POLITICS

QUESTIONS TO CONSIDER

How competitive are local elections in your community?
- ■ Very
- ■ Moderately
- ■ Not very

How much corruption do you think takes place in your city government?
- ■ A great deal
- ■ Some
- ■ Hardly any

Should mayors have veto powers over the actions of city councils?
- ■ Yes   ■ No

What are the most influential interest groups in your community?
- ■ Business groups
- ■ Neighborhood associations
- ■ Environmentalists
- ■ Real estate developers
- ■ Other

COMMUNITARIAN
VIEW

Praises the many values
of direct citizen participation in community
affairs, not just by
voting, but, perhaps
more importantly, by
participating in groups
and forums, working
with neighbors to solve
the problems of the
community.

CITIZEN PARTICIPATION

A local business owner applies for a permit to build an adult business featuring "lap danc-ing." A police officer is arrested for selling drugs to high school students. The mayor pro-poses raising residential property tax rates by 10 percent during an economic downturn. A huge pothole causes a driver, swerving to miss it, to kill a dog beloved by an entire neighborhood. A weed-infested vacant lot has turned into a ready-made dump. A young girl is molested by a neighbor who is a registered sexual predator. City council passes an ordinance outlawing Satan (this really happened).[1] What do each of these happenings have in common? Where they occur, they are likely to prompt citizens to get involved in local community affairs who otherwise would not. At the community level, it's the little things that matter most—the things that directly affect someone's daily quality of life. Local politics is often said to be centered on police, potholes, porno, property, pets, pollution, "problem" neighbors, citizens' pocketbooks, and, of course, "politicians."

Ideally, democracy inspires widespread citizen participation in government—as voters, community activists, neighborhood association and interest group members, party workers, and candidates for public office. But in fact, rarely do many citizens participate actively in community politics.

A **"communitarian" view** praises the many values of direct citizen participation in community affairs, not just by voting, but, perhaps more importantly, by partic-ipating in groups and forums, and working with neighbors to solve the problems of the community. This view asserts that where neighbors talk about community affairs in face-to-face meetings, they learn from one another, become more tolerant of dif-ferent people with different views, create bonds of friendship, and look to common solutions to their problems.

In reality relatively few people are interested in com-munity political affairs. They are busy at their jobs and professions, concerned with raising their children, and more interested in watching sitcoms or sports on televi-sion than broadcasts of city council meetings. And it may be naive to believe that community political activism always engenders tolerance, respect, and common efforts to resolve problems. Often, increased participation inspires rancorous conflict, intolerant popular policy ini-tiatives, and even violence. Indeed, a surge of participa-tion, with resulting conflicting claims upon a government that cannot satisfy everyone, may simply engender cyni-cism and disrespect toward government. Citizen activists are not always well informed even on the issue on which they are most vociferous. Activism—particularly neigh-borhood NIMBY activity ("not in my backyard" oppo-sition to community projects)—may paralyze local government, preventing it from effectively addressing community-wide problems.[2]

Volunteering by citizens of all ages is a form of activism that helps build a sense of community. Here San Francisco students paint a wall in a housing project as part of their youth com-munity service activities.

Volunteering as Civic Participation

Many believe that "Americans are sitting in their homes and offices isolated from their communities and neighbors, shunning civic activities, and unwilling to get involved."[3] But surveys by groups like the Pew Partnership for Civic Change have reported that Americans are volunteering more than ever before and are helping neighbors to solve problems. Many citizens, especially younger ones, do not think of volunteering as a form of community participation. But volunteering for soup kitchens, domestic violence shelters, mentoring programs, and the like is a critical component of building a sense of community. Civic engagement is not limited to voting or joining organizations, although both are measures of a community's civic health.

Voters in Local Elections

Voter turnout in local elections is substantially lower than in state or national elections. While 55 percent of the nation's eligible voters may cast ballots in a presidential election, voter turnouts of 25 to 35 percent are typical in local elections. Local elections differ from national and state elections in several important ways. In *local* (county, city, town, township, and school board) elections:[4]

- Turnout is usually lower.
- Political parties and party allegiance play a less influential role, especially in smaller jurisdictions; 80 percent of all local governments have nonpartisan elections.
- Group identities and group interests (racial, ethnic, religious, union) are more important voting cues than political party identification.
- Campaigns focus more on "who gets what and at the expense of whom?"—the outputs of government (police and fire protection, garbage collection, parks and recreational facilities, the quality of roads and public schools, health care programs). The "zero-sum" nature of resource allocation is "front-and-center" in campaign debates.
- Issues are smaller in number, less complicated, but more personally relevant to individual voters.
- Certain types of issues, especially moral and fiscal, can be more important at promoting turnout than a candidate's personality or party, but usually personality and party dominate.
- The politics of "place" is more prevalent (e.g., eastside versus westside, north versus south, downtown business district versus residential areas).
- A wider variety of candidates run for office (candidate heterogeneity). It is easier to find someone of your own race, ethnicity, religion, social class, gender, or political ideology to vote for.
- Candidate and group get-out-the-vote (GOTV) strategies are typically narrowly targeted and group specific.
- Electoral coalitions are often the key to winning, but are constantly shifting as a community's demographic makeup changes. This is most common in fast-growing, increasingly diverse communities.
- The timing (when the election is held) can drastically affect turnout. Local election turnout is lowest in non–presidential election years (off-cycle).
- Media coverage, especially by television, of local campaigns is far less extensive. (See "*Up Close:* Broadcast Television Coverage of Local Campaigns Is Limited.") Mayoral races get far more coverage than county commission, city council, or school board races, even in local newspapers.

Nonpartisanship in local elections depresses voter turnout substantially. Voter turnout for municipal elections in nonpartisan cities averages closer to 25 percent,

More local governments are shifting to "on-cycle" elections to boost voter turnout rates and to save money.

compared to over 35 percent for cities with partisan elections. Partisan campaigns heighten voter turnout, in part because of the greater interest they generate and in part because of the role of party workers in getting out the vote. However, most local governments, especially municipalities, have nonpartisan elections.

Voter participation in local government can be further reduced by holding municipal elections at odd times of the year when no other state or national elections are being held. Approximately 60 percent of the nation's cities hold municipal elections that are completely independent of state or national elections. Yet studies show that the voting rate in local election contests is 36 percent higher when they are held at the same time as the presidential election.[5] A common rationale for holding municipal elections at times other than state or national elections is to separate local issues from state or national questions, but the real effect of scheduling local elections independently is to reduce voter turnout and to increase the influence of groups who vote more regularly, especially senior voters. Consequently, more local governments are shifting to "on-cycle" elections to boost voter turnout rates and to save money. (Elections are expensive to conduct.)

Voter turnout in large cities with a strong mayor-council form of government and with partisan elections is higher than in smaller cities with a council-manager plan and nonpartisan elections. In summary, nonpartisanship, council-manager government, and separate municipal elections—all part of the municipal "reform" movement—operate to reduce voter turnout and probably strengthen the influence of middle-class and older voters at the polls.

Voter turnout in municipal elections is also affected by the social character of cities. Social cleavages, especially race, increase voter turnout. Mayoral elections in which the racial or ethnic backgrounds of the candidates are well publicized inspire heavy voter turnout.[6] Latino and African American turnout rates often exceed white turnout rates in such elections. Minority group turnout rates increase sharply when a candidate from that group stands a good chance of being elected and would be the first member of that group to hold local office. Social homogeneity, on the other hand, is associated with lower voter interest.

Having a "hot issue" on the ballot increases turnout.

Turnout is also affected by the presence of a local issue on the ballot (permissible in states allowing local governments to utilize the tools of direct democracy—iniative, referendum, and recall). Having a "hot issue" on the ballot increases turnout by 4 percent or so.[7]

In summary, voter turnout in municipal elections can be described as follows:

Lower voter turnout is expected with	Higher voter turnout is expected with
■ Nonpartisan electoral systems	■ Partisan elections with competitive parties
■ Council-manager form of government	■ Strong mayor form of government
■ City elections held separately from state and national elections	■ City elections held concurrently with state and national elections
■ Small or middle-sized cities	■ Large cities
■ Middle-class, homogeneous cities	■ Ethnic, heterogeneous cities
■ No issue on the ballot	■ Issue on the ballot

up CLOSE

Broadcast Television Coverage of Local Elections Is Limited

Candidates for local offices are often frustrated with the lack of *local election coverage* aired on broadcast television stations in their hometowns. Coverage of local races is especially limited during a presidential or gubernatorial election year. A national study of local election coverage by the Lear Center Local News Archive found that

■ Only 8 percent of evening news broadcasts (5:00 P.M. to 11:30 P.M.) carried a story about a local candidate's race.

■ There was eight times more coverage of stories about accidental injuries and 12 times more coverage of sports and weather than coverage of *all local races combined*.

■ Less than 5 percent of the election stories featured local or state ballot initiatives (issues to be voted on).

■ The average campaign story was eighty-six seconds long.

■ Candidate sound bites featuring a candidate in his or her own words appeared in just 28 percent of the stories; the average sound bite was twelve seconds long.

FIGURE 11–1 Elements in a Typical Half-Hour of Local News

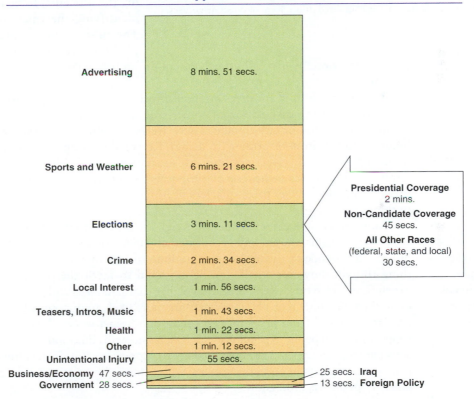

Advertising	8 mins. 51 secs.
Sports and Weather	6 mins. 21 secs.
Elections	3 mins. 11 secs.
Crime	2 mins. 34 secs.
Local Interest	1 min. 56 secs.
Teasers, Intros, Music	1 min. 43 secs.
Health	1 min. 22 secs.
Other	1 min. 12 secs.
Unintentional Injury	55 secs.
Business/Economy	47 secs.
Government	28 secs.

Presidential Coverage 2 mins.
Non-Candidate Coverage 45 secs.
All Other Races (federal, state, and local) 30 secs.

25 secs. **Iraq**
13 secs. **Foreign Policy**

Source: Martin Kaplan, Ken Goldstein, and Matthew Hale, "Local News Coverage of the 2004 Campaigns: An Analysis of Nightly Broadcasts in 11 Markets," The Lear Center Local News Archive, USC Annenberg School for Communication, Los Angeles, California, February 15, 2005.

Many states permit citizens to sign petitions to recall (revote) on an already-elected local official before his or her term is completed. It is a form of direct democracy.

Local Referenda Voters

In all but three states, citizens are given at least some tools to "take local government into their own hands" through the initiative, referendum, and recall processes.[8] Of these direct democracy devices, the *recall* is the most widely available, especially in larger, more diverse cities and in West and Pacific Coast communities.[9] Recall is the process whereby citizens can remove an elected official before his or her term is completed. The process typically begins with the circulation of a petition among registered voters asking for a recall election to be held, naming the official(s) to be recalled, and identifying the cause for removal. The most common causes are misuse of the office or failure to perform duties. Occasionally a recall effort centers on an official's "unusual" behavior or demeanor.[10]

The referendum is another common direct democracy tool. It gives voters the final say about the disposition of some issue or proposal put on the ballot by a county commission or city council. There are several different forms, binding, non-binding, and petition or protest (to delay). **Referenda voting** is an important aspect of local politics—an aspect not found at the national level. City charters frequently require that referenda be held on all proposals to increase indebtedness or to increase property taxation. Over three-quarters of American cities have referenda provisions in their charters.

Many voters in local referenda will weigh the benefits that will come to them from a bond issue against the amount of the tax that will fall on them as a result of the expenditure. Non–property owners, having nothing to lose by the expenditure and something to gain, however small, can be expected to favor the passage of bond and expenditure referenda. (Renters seldom realize that landlords will pass the tax increase on to them in higher rent.) Homeowners are more likely to oppose public expenditures that are financed from property taxes than non-homeowners. Among homeowners, support for local public expenditures often *increases* with education, wealth, and income. This tendency of upper-class, liberal voters to support recreational, cultural, and environmental projects (e.g., parks, museums, stadiums, libraries, art centers) was once labeled "**public-regardingness.**"[11]

The initiative is another popular tool of direct democracy. Citizens use the petition process to propose changes to the structure of local government (charter, ordinance, home rule) or policy changes.

The types of issues that end up on local ballots for voter approval, whether through a referendum or initiative procedure, are as diverse as local governments themselves.

A sample of the wide range of issues placed before voters in the early 2000s and their resolution included the following:

- In San Francisco, California: Voters approved a $100 million bond issue to pay for solar power in public buildings; they also authorized city supervisors to underwrite renewable energy projects in homes and businesses without voter approval.
- In Carson, California, a Los Angeles suburb: Voters decided against seceding from the Los Angeles Unified School District.
- In Montrose, Colorado: Voters upheld a seven-month ban on smoking in public places.
- In Miami Beach, Florida: Voters said the city should provide employee benefits to gay and heterosexual domestic partners.
- In Portland, Maine: Voters approved a nonbinding resolution supporting the creation of a single-payer system of health care, based on a Canadian system.
- In Plymouth, California, population 1,090: Voters recalled the mayor and two city council members for supporting efforts by the Mikok Indian tribe to purchase 200 acres to build a casino inside the city limits.

Issues put on local ballots for voter approval, if controversial and high profile, may increase voter turnout. Campaign ads are likely to be run on both sides of the issue.

Campaign Contributors

Money is playing an increasingly influential role in politics at all levels of government.[12] The costs of campaigning, especially the costs of television advertising, are rising rapidly. Earlier we observed that it is not uncommon for candidates for governor in large states to raise and spend millions in an election, and campaigns for highly competitive state legislative seats in large states often require $50,000 to $500,000 (see "Money in State Politics" in Chapter 5). Tracking the amount of money raised by a candidate and those who are contributing to the campaign is a common way the media gauges the momentum of a local race.[13]

The costs of campaigning, especially the costs of television advertising, are rising rapidly.

In local politics it is still possible to run a low-budget, door-to-door "shoe leather" campaign, especially in suburbs and small towns. It is still possible for many candidates for city council and county commission to rely on small contributions from friends, neighbors, and relatives, or on their own pocketbooks, to pay for signs, brochures, and newspaper ads.[14]

But in big cities, candidates for mayor, as well as city council and county commission, must raise substantial campaign money. Mayoral campaigns in America's big cities may cost millions of dollars, and even city council campaigns may cost $50,000 or more. Wealthy individuals may choose to finance their own campaigns. (See "*People in Politics:* Michael Bloomberg: Strong Mayor for the Big Apple" in Chapter 10.)

Who contributes to candidates for local office? A careful inspection of candidate campaign contributors offers great insights into the range of individuals and interest groups involved in any community's political process. Traditionally the largest sources of campaign contributions for city and county offices have come from business interests with direct contacts with these governments—real estate developers, builders, contractors, professional service providers (law, accounting, public relations/advertising), and nonprofit human service agencies.[15] They seek to "invest" in winners in order to establish access and goodwill among the officials who will be deciding on contracts for a variety of goods and services, zoning and

GROWTH MANAGEMENT

In local government, efforts to limit or restrict population growth and commercial and industrial development.

INCUMBENT

The person currently serving in a public office.

The "political" rule of thumb is that even if a link between a contributor and an elected official is legal, if it doesn't pass the "smell test" it may be perceived by the public as unethical.

land-use questions, building and construction codes, environmental regulations, and various **"growth management"** policies (see Chapter 13, "Community Power, Land Use, and the Environment"). Their campaign contributions usually go to **incumbents** running for re-election on the (correct) assumption that they are likely to remain in office. A local officeholder must be particularly anti-growth in order to lose the contributions of developers and builders. Neighborhood associations that oppose development, environmental groups, and affluent residents occasionally combine their contributions to challenge the monetary advantage of prodevelopment candidates. Municipal employee unions, including police, firefighters, and sanitation workers, are another common source of campaign contributions in big cities. Law and accounting firms, printing and construction companies, and other businesses that have contracts with the city and county are also likely to be contributors, again usually to incumbents.

It is difficult to say whether money "buys" local elections. Incumbents raise and spend much more money than challengers, and incumbents almost always win re-election. But name recognition, friendships, contacts, and gratitude for services and favors, accumulated by incumbents during their terms of office, may be more important than the money they spend on their re-election campaigns. In open-seat elections the best financed candidate usually wins, but this may be because contributors correctly judged that he or she would be the winner.

A more serious question is whether campaign contributions to a winning candidate "buy" influence and a favorable vote on an issue of high priority to the contributor. State laws and local ordinances spell out rules governing the link between campaign contributors, gifts, lobbyists, and elected officials, although in many cases the rules are not very explicit. Election commissions and/or ethics commissions investigate complaints and impose penalties unless the allegation is a criminal offense in which case it would be investigated by state or federal prosecutors. Defeated opponents and citizen watchdog groups are most often the source of official complaints. But local newspapers often play a key role in publicizing perceived wrongdoings. The "political" rule of thumb is that even if a link between a contributor and an elected official is legal, if it doesn't pass the "smell test" it may be perceived by the public as unethical.

PARTIES IN BIG-CITY POLITICS

While political parties play less of a role in local politics than national or state politics, their presence in big-city politics is still observable. This is true whether a city elects its mayor and council members via partisan (e.g., New York, Chicago, Philadelphia, Boston) or nonpartisan (e.g., Los Angeles, Detroit, Miami) elections. Traditionally, Democrats have dominated politics in the nation's large central cities, even while their surrounding suburbs have usually been governed by Republicans. Social groups that normally vote Democratic—white ethnic groups, Catholics and Jews, African Americans, Latinos (excluding Cubans in Miami), union members, low-income families—tend to be concentrated in big cities. Since the formation of the modern "New Deal" Democratic party coalition under President Franklin D. Roosevelt in the 1930s, most big cities in the United States have been governed by Democrats. This has been true whether the city's electoral system has been officially partisan or nonpartisan.

Party identification patterns of the various ethnic groups in cities are quite diverse. African Americans, Jewish Americans, and Hispanics are the most solidly Democratic (78 percent, 66 percent, and 57 percent, respectively). Arabs, Italians, and Asians are much more divided. While 38 percent of Arab Americans are Democrats, 36 percent are Republicans, and 21 percent are Independents. Italian Americans are similarly split, while Asian Americans are 36 percent Democrat, 26 percent Republican, and 31 percent Independents. However, party identification is not always the best predictor of policy positions. Even within each group, there are differences of opinion, often depending on how long an individual has been in the United States. Immigrants tend to be more conservative than native-born residents, with the exception of Asians. It is also important to recognize that because many minorities are recent immigrants and not yet citizens, they are not registered voters. This is particularly true of Hispanic and Asian immigrants. This means that 34 percent of Hispanic Americans and 32 percent of Asian Americans are not yet registered to vote.[16]

Since the formation of the modern "New Deal" Democratic party coalition under President Franklin D. Roosevelt in the 1930s, most big cities in the United States have been governed by Democrats.

Splits among Urban Democrats

Political cleavages within the Democratic party have been a driving force in big-city politics over the years. Political conflict in many of America's largest cities has centered on differences between working-class, Catholic, white ethnic (especially Irish, Italian, Polish) Democrats versus upper-class, white, liberal Protestants and Jews, allied with black and Latino Democratic voters. These factions within the Democratic party have frequently battled over such issues as affirmative action hiring in city government, busing in schools to achieve racial balance, and the behavior of police and prosecutors in crime control. And they have often differed over the burdens of public spending for welfare, health, and public housing—with working-class white ethnics, who are often homeowners and property tax payers, opposed to higher taxes and spending for these services; and upper-class liberals and blacks, many of whom are renters whose property taxes are hidden in rent payments, supporting these expenditures (see "Minorities and Women in Local Politics" later in this chapter).

Political cleavages within the Democratic party have been a driving force in big-city politics over the years.

Occasionally Democratic party organizations have been strong enough to hold these diverse Democratic groups together. Traditional **party "machines"** would slate candidates for city office with an eye to racial and ethnic group balance. But as these party machines lost influence over time, intraparty factional conflict—especially between working-class white ethnics and minorities—intensified in many cities.[17]

The growing Hispanic vote in many of America's largest cities adds another potentially unstable element to the Democratic party coalition. Both African Americans and Hispanics have suffered discrimination in a predominantly white, "Anglo" society, and both have higher-than-average rates of poverty and unemployment and lower median family incomes. But a number of studies have shown this coalition to be unstable, occasionally engaging in competition over city jobs, language issues, and representation (e.g., as in Chicago, Denver, Miami, Houston, and Los Angeles).

MACHINE

In politics, a tightly disciplined political organization, historically centered in big cities, which traded patronage jobs, public contracts, services, and favors for votes.

Republican Big-City Resurgence?

Splits among urban Democrats, combined with continuing big-city ills—huge deficits, violent crime, racial and ethnic conflicts—have opened up new opportunities for Republican candidates. Despite overwhelming Democratic registration, big-city voters have elected a number of Republican mayors to cope with urban problems. Republican prosecuting attorney Rudolph Giuliani was first elected mayor of New York in 1994, the first Republican to govern that city in over twenty years. Richard Riordan, a multi-millionaire lawyer-businessman, was elected mayor of Los Angeles in 1993, the first Republican to hold that office in twenty years. Since that time, other Republicans (Michael Bloomberg in New York City) and some conservative Democrats have won unexpected victories in heavily Democratic cities in recent elections. When Republicans have won in Democratic-dominated areas, certain common themes have driven their campaigns: a crackdown on crime, cutting the size of the city bureaucracy, reducing city deficits, easing tax burdens, and stimulating the city's economy. Republicans have also heavily targeted the Hispanic vote, especially in cities with sizable black and Hispanic populations. But it is not clear yet whether these Republican inroads in big-city politics are temporary responses to voter frustration or a more permanent resurgence of Republican strength.

Some political analysts argue that partisan politics is less important to voters these days as more citizens see themselves as independents and split-ticket voters. Others stick to the theory that local politics is much more about issues than parties. Still other urban experts believe the reason why party doesn't seem to matter as much anymore is because both national political parties pretty much ignore cities.

OLD-STYLE MACHINE POLITICS

Machine politics has gone out of style. Machines—tightly disciplined party organizations, held together and motivated by a desire for tangible benefits rather than by principle or ideology and run by professional politicians—emerged in the nation's large cities early in the nineteenth century. This style of city politics has historical importance. Between the Civil War and the New Deal, every big city had a machine at one time or another, and it is sometimes easier to understand the character of city politics today by knowing what went on in years past. A more important reason for examining the machine style of politics is to understand the style of political organization that employs personal and material rewards to achieve power. These kinds of rewards will always be important in politics, and the big-city machine serves as a prototype of a style of politics in which ideologies and issues are secondary and personal friendships, favors, and jobs are primary.

The political machine was essentially a large brokerage organization. Its business was to get votes and control elections by trading off social services, patronage, and petty favors to the urban masses, particularly the poor and the recent immigrants. To get the money to pay for these social services and favors, it traded off city contracts, protection, and privileges to business interests, which paid off in cash. Like other brokerage organizations, a great many middlemen came between the cash paid for a franchise for a trolley line or a construction contract and a Christmas turkey sent by the ward chairman to the Widow O'Leary. However, the machine worked. It performed many important social functions for the city.

Personal Attention

First, the political machine personalized government. With keen social intuition, the machine recognized the voter as a person, generally living in a neighborhood, who had specific problems and wants. The machine provided individual attention and recognition. As Tammany Hall **boss** George Washington Plunkitt, the philosopher king of old-style machine politics, explained, "I don't trouble them with political arguments. I just study human nature and act accordin'."[18] The machine also performed the functions of a welfare agency. According to Plunkitt, "What tells in holdin' your grip on your district is to go right down among the poor families and help them in the different ways they need help."[19] In the absence of government unemployment insurance or a federal employment service, **patronage** was an effective political tool, particularly in hard times. Not only were city jobs at the disposal of the machine, but the machine also had its many business contacts. Yet it was not so much the petty favors and patronage that won votes among urban dwellers as it was the sense of friendship and humanity that characterized the "machine" and its "boss."[20]

Assimilation

The machine also played an important role in educating recent immigrants and assimilating them into American life.[21] Machine politics provided a means of upward social mobility for ethnic group members, which was not open to them in businesses or professions. City machines sometimes met immigrants at dockside and led them in groups through naturalization and voter registration procedures. Machines did not keep out people with "funny"-sounding names but instead went out of the way to put these names on ballots. Politics became a way "up" for the bright sons of Irish and Italian immigrants. Few woman ran for local offices in those days.

"Getting Things Done"

Finally, for businesses, and particularly for public utilities and construction companies with government contracts, the machine provided the necessary franchises, rights of way, contracts, and privileges. As Lincoln Steffens wrote, "You cannot build or operate a railroad, or a street railway, gas, water, or power company, develop and operate a mine, or cut forests or timber on a large scale, or run any privileged business, without corrupting or joining in the **corruption** of government."[22] The machine also provided the essential protection from police interference, which is required by illicit businesses, particularly gambling. In short, the machine helped to centralize power in large cities. It could "get things done at city hall" (see "*People in Politics:* The Daleys of Chicago").

REFORMERS AND DO-GOODERS

A reform style of politics appeared in the United States shortly after the Civil War to battle the "bosses." Beginning in 1869, scathing editorials in the *New York Times* and cartoons by Thomas Nast in *Harper's Weekly* attacked the "Tammany Society" in New York City, a political organization that controlled the local Democratic party. William M. Tweed was president of the board of supervisors of New York County and undisputed boss of "Tammany Hall," as the New York County Democratic committee was called, after its old meeting place on Fourteenth Street. This early reform movement achieved

---

BOSS

The acknowledged leader of a political machine, who may or may not occupy a public office.

PATRONAGE

Rewards granted by government office-holders to political supporters in the form of government jobs.

CORRUPTION

In politics, the use of public office for private gain, including bribery, conflict of interest, and the misuse and abuse of power.

REFORM

In local government, a general reference to efforts to eliminate political machines, patronage, and party influence, and to install professional city management, nonpartisan elections, at-large districts, and the merit system.

temporary success under the brilliant leadership of Samuel J. Tilden, who succeeded in driving the "Tweed Ring" out of office and went on in 1876 to be the only presidential candidate ever to win a majority of popular votes and then be denied the presidency through the operation of the Electoral College.

Early municipal reform is closely linked to the Progressive movement in American politics. Leaders such as Robert M. La Follette of Wisconsin, Hiram Johnson of California, Gifford Pinchot of Pennsylvania, and Charles Evans Hughes of New York backed municipal reform at the local level as well as the direct primary and direct election of senators and woman's suffrage at the national level.[23] In 1912 social worker Jane Addams, who labored in slums and settlement houses, sang "Onward Christian Soldiers" at the Progressive party convention that nominated Teddy Roosevelt for president. Lincoln Steffens wrote in *The Shame of the Cities*, "St. Louis exemplified boodle [bribery]; Minneapolis, police graft; Pittsburgh, a political industrial machine; and Philadelphia (the worst city in the country), general civic corruption."[24]

Social Bases of Reform

From its beginning, reform politics was strongly supported by the upper-class, Anglo-Saxon, Protestant, longtime residents of cities whose political ethos was very different from that which the new immigrants brought with them. The immigrant, the machine that relied upon his or her vote, and the businessperson who relied upon the machine for street railway and other utility franchises, had formed an alliance in the nineteenth century that had displaced the native, old family, Yankee elite that had traditionally dominated northern cities. This upper-class elite fought to recapture control of local government through the municipal reform movement.

Machine politicians catered to ethnic groups, organized labor, blue-collar workers, and other white working-class elements of the city. The reform politician appealed to the upper- and middle-class affluent Americans who were well educated and public-service minded. Reform was popular among liberals, newspaper reporters, college professors, and others who considered themselves "intellectuals."

Reform Goals

Reform politics included a belief that there was a "public interest" that should prevail over competing, partial interests in a city. The idea of balancing competing interests or compromising public policy was not part of the reformers' view of political life. Rather, the reform ethos included a belief that "politics" was distasteful. Enlightened people should agree on the public interest; municipal government is a technical and administrative problem rather than a political one. City government should be placed in the hands of those who are best qualified, by training, ability, and devotion to public service, to manage public business. These best-qualified people can decide on policy and then leave administration to professional experts. Any interference by special interests in the politics or administration of the best-qualified people should be viewed as corruption.

The objectives of early reform movements were as follows:

- *Eliminate corruption.* The elimination of corruption in public office, and the recruitment of "good people" (educated, upper-income individuals who were successful in private business or professions) to replace "politicians" (who were no more successful than their constituents in private life and who were dependent upon public office for their principal source of income).

PEOPLE in POLITICS

The Daleys of Chicago

For over two decades Mayor Richard J. Daley governed Chicago in the style of traditional machine politics. (When Mayor Daley himself was asked about his "machine," he replied, "Organization, not machine. Get that Organization, not machine.") In Chicago, few others understood so well the labyrinths of formal and informal power. Daley won election to six four-year terms as mayor of Chicago, beginning in 1955. He remained the captain of his old Eleventh Ward Democratic committee, and he was chairman of the Cook County Democratic committee. He picked candidates' slates, ran the patronage machinery, and worked his will on nearly all of Chicago's city council. Illinois Democratic governors were usually responsive to his wishes, and Chicago's nine-member delegation to the U.S. House of Representatives also acted promptly on Daley's recommendations. The Cook County Democratic delegation to the Illinois legislature was firmly in his hands. No presidential candidate could ignore Daley's political "clout," either in the Democratic National Convention or in the general election. Daley may have been the most successful mayor in America, not only for his political acumen, but also for his ability to manage a great metropolis.[a]

Conflict Management

As a political broker, Daley was seldom the initiator of public policy. His approach to policy questions was more like that of an arbitrator between competing interests. When political controversies developed, Daley waited on the sidelines without committing himself, in the hope that public opinion would soon "crystallize" behind a particular course of action. Once the community was behind a project—and this determination Daley made himself after

lengthy consultations with his political advisors—he then awarded his stamp of approval. This suggests that in policy matters many political "bossess" were not so much bosses as referees among interested individuals and groups. The boss was really "apolitical"

when it came to policy matters. He was really more concerned with resolving conflict and maintaining his position and organization than he was with the outcome of public policy decisions. Boss Daley's politics: "Don't make no waves; don't back no losers."

The Machine Loses Clout

When Mayor Daley died in office in 1976, a lackluster machine replacement, Michael Bilandic, tried unsuccessfully to fill the shoes of the nation's most successful "boss." However, the once powerful Cook County Democratic committee gradually lost its direction, leadership, and "clout." Mayor Bilandic failed to hold together the coalition of white ethnic groups, blacks, Catholics, labor unions, and city employees, which were the backbone of the machine. In 1979 Jane Byrne defeated Bilandic and became Chicago's first female mayor. As the machine stumbled, the city's black voters became increasingly restless. In the 1983 Democratic mayoral primary the black community, under the leadership of Congressman Harold Washington, split from the Democratic machine. The machine went into the 1983 election hopelessly fractured. Mayor Byrne sought re-election and claimed control over city job holders; state attorney Richard M. Daley, son of the late mayor, challenged Byrne's control of the machine and called upon old loyalties to the family name; and Harold Washington worked hard to register and mobilize the city's black residents, 40 percent of Chicago's total population. The resulting split in the Democratic primary was: Washington, 37 percent; Byrne, 33 percent; Daley, 30 percent.

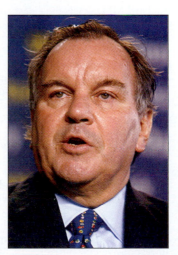

In the general election, several prominent white Democratic machine politicians deserted the Democratic candidate. Race

(*continued*)

dominated the campaign. Voter turnout in Chicago's 1983 mayoral election was a record 82 percent of registration. Washington won with 51.4 percent. He had the near-unanimous support of black voters combined with just enough "Lakefront liberal" white voters to provide a thin margin of victory. But most white voters, including the white ethnic voters who provided the machine with its traditional base of support, cast their ballots against the black Democratic nominee.[b]

Racial Politics

The demise of the old Daley political machine allowed racial divisions to surface as the major force in the city's political life. Harold Washington faced formidable opposition among many white city workers, police officers and firefighters, and a majority of white council members elected from wards. As council meetings deteriorated from parliamentary pandemonium to near fistfights, the courts were called upon to resolve many city issues.

Harold Washington's personal popularity among blacks and Hispanics and a significant portion of affluent, liberal whites was a major factor in his success as mayor. The city itself was almost evenly divided between white and black residents, with Hispanics comprising a smaller but important constituency. Washington's popularity, together with the gradual decline of the white percentage of the city's population, led many observers to believe that Chicago had seen its last white mayor. But Washington's untimely death in 1988 brought a new administration to the city.

Old Name, New Style

Richard M. Daley is the eldest son of the former mayor and long-time boss of Chicago's politics, Richard J. Daley. His father found him a job in the city attorney's office and later persuaded an incumbent state senator to give up his seat so that young "Richie" could start a political career. At the state capital, young Daley was unswervingly loyal to his father's machine. But after the mayor's death, and the personal tragedy of the death of a severely handicapped child, Richard M. Daley began to emerge as his own man.

In 1989 Daley won the Democratic primary against a black candidate with 56 percent of the vote. He held on to white ethnic voters who had so long supported his father, won the Hispanic vote, and won back many white liberals who were convinced the younger Daley stood for reform.

As mayor, Daley presented himself not as a "politician" but rather as a "manager" trying to reform a costly, unresponsive city bureaucracy. While critics claim that Daley's image as a reformer is only a cover for his political ambition, Daley's growing popularity in the job indicates that governmental reform is good politics. Chicago's voters seem to agree. Daley won the Democratic primary in 1991 with 63 percent of the vote (surpassing the best primary showing ever posted by his father), and then won an overwhelming 71 percent of the vote in the general election.

Daley's efforts to reform the city bureaucracy present an ironic twist to the long history of machine and reform politics in Chicago. Daley's father had overstaffed city hall with patronage appointees who worked his precincts at election time. But over time, the courts had given most city workers civil service protection as a "reform" of patronage practices. The result was a bloated bureaucracy unresponsive to either the mayor or the council. "You get elected mayor to make decisions, and then you find out the bureaucracy is against you," complained Daley. "Their attitude is 'we're going to be here when you leave!'"[c] Daley pushed to contract out to private firms—to "privatize"—many city functions, from janitorial services and parking fine collections to towing of abandoned cars.

Privatization efforts have always been bitterly opposed by Chicago's public employee unions, especially the American Federation of State, County and Municipal Employees (AFSCME). By pursuing privatization, Daley cut the political ties between the city's employee unions and the mayor's office, a strategy his father would never have considered. But the "Son of Boss" put together a new political coalition, consisting of the city's white ethnic groups and its rapidly growing Hispanic population. Black leaders charge that Daley's privatization schemes have disproportionately impacted black employees, who were concentrated in service and maintenance jobs, those easiest to privatize. But Daley's style is to appeal to *taxpayers:* "Minorities are taxpayers. You go out to a homeowner—who is black, Hispanic, female, or Asian—and they pay taxes!"[d]

Perhaps Mayor Daley's boldest move was his 1995 decision to intervene in Chicago's failing school system. Decades of poor classroom performance and administrative chaos made the move look hopeless. But Daley installed his own school board members, who promptly dismissed dozens of poorly performing teachers and administrators. Both discipline and test scores began to improve.[e] Later, he took over the dysfunctional Chicago Housing Authority. In 2005, *Time* magazine rated him as "the nation's top urban executive."

As he faced re-election to his sixth term in 2007, some of his staff was being investigated by the FBI for corruption—bribery and illegal hiring practices. In spite

(continued)

of the corruption scandal, Daley (who himself was not indicted) won with a landslide, getting 71 percent of the vote and carrying all fifty wards. At the end of his term, he will have served twenty-two years as mayor, making him Chicago's longest serving mayor. Daley remains one of the nation's most powerful mayors. Even his dad did not have as much power as "Richard the Second." "He has used it to steer the Windy City into a period of impressive stability, with declining unemployment and splashy growth."[f]

[a]For an excellent description of the functions of Mayor Daley's political organization in Chicago, see Edward C. Banfield, *Political Influence* (Glencoe, IL: The Free Press, 1961). For a hostile account of Mayor Daley, see Mike Royko, *Boss: Richard J. Daley of Chicago* (New York: E. P. Dutton, 1971).
[b]Michael B. Preston, "The Election of Harold Washington," *P.S. Political Science* (Summer 1983): 486.
[c]Quoted in *U.S. News & World Report*, March 23, 1992, p. 41.
[d]Quoted in Charles Mahtesian, "Taking Chicago Private," *Governing* (April 1994): 26–31.
[e]See *Governing* (December 1997), p. 22.
[f]David E. Thigpen, "The 5 Best Big-City Mayors: Richard the Second," *Time*, April 25, 2005, p. 17.

- *Nonpartisanship.* The elimination of parties from local politics by nonpartisan elections.
- *Manager government.* The establishment of the council-manager form of government, and the separation of "politics" from the "business" of municipal government.
- *At-large districts.* The establishment of at-large citywide constituencies in municipal elections in lieu of "district" constituencies in order to ensure that an elected official would consider the welfare of the entire city in public decision making and not merely his or her own neighborhood or "ward."
- *Short ballot.* The reorganization of local government to eliminate many separately elected offices (the "short-ballot" movement) in order to simplify the voters' task and focus responsibility for the conduct of public affairs on a small number of top elected officials.
- *Strong executive.* The strengthening of executive leadership in city government—longer terms for mayors, subordination of departments and commissions to a chief executive, and an executive budget combined with modern financial practices.
- *Merit system.* The replacement of patronage appointments with the merit system of civil service.
- *Home rule.* The separation of local politics from state and national politics by home-rule charters and the holding of local elections at times when there were no state and national elections.

MODEL CITY CHARTER

A guide for cities to use when writing or revising their charters, first written by the National Civic League, a good government reformminded organization.

All these objectives were interrelated. Ideally, a "reformed city" would be one with the manager form of government, nonpartisan election for mayor and council, a home-rule charter, a short ballot, at-large constituencies, a strong executive, a merit service personnel system, and honest people at the helm. Later, the reform movement added comprehensive city planning to its list of objectives—official planning agencies with professional planners authorized to prepare a master plan of future development for the city. The National Municipal League (now the National League of Cities) incorporated its program of reform into a **Model City Charter**, which continues today to be the standard manual of municipal reform.[25]

Reasons for the Machine's Decline

Parties in general are losing their appeal to many Americans. Increasing proportions of voters are identifying themselves as "independents," rather than as Democrats or Republicans. (See Chapter 5.) Party offices (precinct committee, ward chairperson, county committee, and so on) are vacant in many cities and counties. The general decline in parties has contributed to the decline of machine politics. Several additional factors might be cited as contributing to the decline of machine politics:

- *The decline in European immigration* and the gradual assimilation of white ethnic groups—Irish, Italians, Germans, Poles, Slavs.
- *Federal social welfare programs*, which undercut the machine's role in welfare work—unemployment insurance, workers' compensation, Social Security, and public assistance.
- *Rising levels of prosperity* and higher educational levels, which make the traditional rewards of the machine less attractive.
- *The spread of middle-class values* about honesty, efficiency, and good government, which inhibit party organizations in purchases, contracts, and vote buying, and other cruder forms of municipal corruption.
- *New avenues of upward social mobility* that have opened up to the sons and daughters of working-class families, and higher education, which has allowed many to join the ranks of professionals, corporate, executives, educators, and so on so that the party machine is no longer the only way "up" for persons at the bottom of the social ladder.
- *Structural reforms* such as nonpartisanship, better voting procedures, **city-manager** government, and—most important of all—civil service, which have weakened the party's role in municipal elections and administration.
- *The rise of self-financed candidates* who no longer need a political party's blessing or endorsement to enter an electoral contest or to mount a formidable campaign.
- *The emergence of television as the best way to get a candidate's message out to the voters*, rather than through party volunteers. Fewer Americans have time to volunteer for party get-out-the-vote efforts.

Today's local politics might be characterized as less party and more politician.

The New Personalized Machines

Some big-city mayors have been successful in building personal political organizations centered on the mayor's office. They have expanded their supply of patronage jobs by enlarging the mayoral office staff and creating public authorities and agencies that are directly responsible to the mayor's office. Appointees to these fairly high-paying staff and administrative positions form the nucleus of the mayor's personal campaign organization. A resourceful mayor can augment his or her immediate staff people ("the palace guard") with appointments to city economic development authorities, community rehabilitation agencies, housing authorities, and other quasi-governmental bureaucracies. Many of these bureaucracies are federally funded and their top posts can be filled by an astute mayor using "creative" personnel practices. In many large cities, elements of the old ward politics survive in particular neighborhoods. The neighborhood politician, perhaps a state senator or city council member, still strolls the sidewalks, glad-handing constituents, and promising to find a job for someone, fix a street light, and see about uncollected trash. Indeed, the modern neighborhood politician may enter each constituent's name in the office computer system and keep track of individual requests and favors rendered.[26] It still matters to many voters that their representative grew up in the neighborhood, still lives there, can be contacted day or night, knows their names, and gives personal attention to their problems.

CITY MANAGER

The chief executive of a city government, who is appointed by the city council and responsible to it.

It still matters to many voters that their representative grew up in the neighborhood, still lives there, can be contacted day or night, knows their names, and gives personal attention to their problems.

If we define patronage to include a wide range of tangible benefits—construction contracts, insurance policies, printing and office supplies, architectual services, and other government contracts for goods or services—then patronage is still important in many communities. Competitive bidding by potential government contractors is required in most states and cities, but it is not difficult to "rig" the process. The fact that the firms that do much of their business with government are also the largest contributors to political campaigns cannot be coincidence.[27] Another source of patronage is the power of courts to appoint referees, appraisers, receivers in bankruptcies, and trustees and executors of estates; these plums require little work and produce high fees for attorneys who are "well connected." Few cities have ever been able to remove zoning from politics: Rezoning property from lower-value classifications (single-family residential) to higher-value classifications (apartments, commercial, industrial) is one of the most important "goodies" available to municipal governments. In addition, municipal construction permits, inspection, and licensing can be slow and cumbersome, or fast and painless, depending on the political resources of the builder-developer. (See "*Up Close: Political Corruption.*")

NEW CONNECTIONS WITH CITIZENS

In today's high-tech society, governments are scrambling to improve their contact with the citizenry through the Internet and other interactive mechanisms. *Cities Online*, a report of the Pew Internet and American Life Project, has concluded that "the Internet is injecting new energy into many U.S. cities as public, private, and nonprofit institutions realize that a powerful new communications tool can transform the traditional roles of government and business. In social terms, this promises a closer, more interactive relationship between a community and its citizens. . . . The Internet is serving as a catalyst to change the 'rules of the game' that shape social capital—the informal norms and customs that grease the wheels of urban life."[28]

Professional associations like the International City/County Management Association routinely publish "how to" guides on local government Web site construction, maintenance, and ethics.[29] Winning a Web site design award is often as prestigious to a community as being designated an "All American City." The three standards commonly used to judge Web sites are information availability, service delivery, and public access. Not surprisingly, larger jurisdictions have better, more transparent, and more user friendly Web sites.[30]

Increasingly popular forms of local government interaction with their citizens are as follows[31]:

- *Interactive Web sites:* Allow citizens to "talk" to elected officials in online chat sessions, respond to surveys, register complaints, purchase licenses and permits online, pay parking and other fines online, bid on government contracts, and watch local government hearings via streamed video.
- *Citywide "wireless" zones or wi-fi "hot spots":* Communities see being on the leading edge of the broadband revolution as critical to maintaining and expanding strong residential and commercial sectors.
- *Government access cable television stations:* Citizens can watch public meetings, political debates, and forums, as well as learn about upcoming community events.

Exposing Political Corruption

Corruption is an ever-present theme in American political life. We all know that "politics is corrupt," but with the exception of some well-publicized cases we really do not know *how* much corruption takes place. Corruption may be more widespread in state and local politics than in national politics, because state and local officials avoid the spotlight of the national news media. One major problem in studying corruption is defining the term. What is "corrupt" to one observer may be "just politics" to another or merely "an embarrassment" to someone else.

For example, here is a list of hypothetical acts that state senators in twenty-four states were asked to rate as more or less corrupt, together with the percentage of senators who viewed each act as corrupt:[a]

- The driveway of the mayor's home being paved by the city crew—95.9 percent
- A public official using public funds for personal travel—95.2 percent
- A state assembly member, while chairman of the public roads committee, authorizing the purchase of land he or she had recently acquired—95.1 percent
- A legislator accepting a large campaign contribution in return for voting "the right way" on a legislative bill—91.9 percent
- A judge with $50,000 worth of stock in a corporation hearing a case concerning that firm—78.8 percent
- A presidential candidate promising an ambassadorship in exchange for campaign contributions—71.1 percent
- A secretary of defense owning $50,000 in stock in a company with which the Defense Department has a million-dollar contract—58.3 percent
- A member of Congress who holds a large amount of stock (about $50,000 worth) in Exxon working to maintain the oil depletion allowance—54.9 percent
- A member of Congress using seniority to obtain a weapons contract for a firm in his or her district—31.6 percent
- A public official using influence to get a friend or relative admitted to law school—23.7 percent

The line between unethical behavior and criminal activity is a fuzzy one. Unethical behavior includes lying and misrepresentation; favoritism toward relatives, friends, and constituents; and conflicts of interest, in which public officials decide issues in which they have a personal financial interest. Not all unethical behavior is criminal conduct. But **bribery** is a criminal offense—soliciting or receiving anything of value in exchange for the performance of a governmental duty.

How Much Corruption?

It is difficult to estimate the extent of corruption in American politics, in part because public officials do not usually volunteer information on their own corrupt behavior! The U.S. Justice Department reports on *federal* prosecutions of public officials for violations of criminal statutes. These figures do not include state prosecutions, so they do not cover all of the criminal indictments brought against public officials each year. (And, of course, they do not tell us how much corruption went undetected.) Nonetheless, these figures indicate that now over 1,200 public officials are indicted and convicted of criminal activity each year.

Explaining Corruption

Why do some government officials engage in corruption? We can think of at least three reasons: (1) for personal gain, that is, simply to enrich themselves; (2) to benefit friends, constituents, or ethnic groups with contracts, jobs, and aid; and (3) to bring coordination to fragmented government by exchanging favors simply "to get things done." Often we think of activities under these last two categories as less corrupt than efforts to achieve personal gain. Corruption for personal gain is less acceptable. Yet such corruption is almost an American tradition. Politicians over the years could echo Tammany Hall's George Washington Plunkitt, "I seen my opportunities and I took 'em."[b]

Prosecuting Corruption

Investigating and prosecuting state and local government officials for corrupt activity was once the exclusive responsibility of the state attorney general's office using state laws. But today U.S. attorneys have largely taken over this responsibility. Acting under broad federal statutes—federal laws dealing with mail fraud, tax fraud, and the RICO Act (Racketeer Influenced and Corrupt Organizations)—federal prosecutors have largely displaced state prosecutors in dealing with official corruption.[c] Federal prosecutors have the vast resources of the FBI, the Internal Revenue Service, the Postal Inspection Service, and a myriad of other federal agencies to assist them in investigations. Moreover, U.S. attorneys have great discretion in their investigatory and prosecutory decisions.

The Role of the Press: Protecting the Public

Journalists staunchly believe that they should play a major role in protecting the public by exposing the misdeeds of

(*continued*)

elected officials. The biggest prizes in the field of both print and electronic journalism (Pulitzers—newspapers; and Edward R. Murrows—television and radio) are usually given for stories that result in public officials being booted from office for corruption.

Voter Reaction

Do voters punish officials for corrupt activities? Sometimes . . . but not always. Voters sometimes re-elect officials who have been convicted of criminal offenses. There are various reasons for the continued voter support of corrupt politicians. First, *charges* of corruption are so frequent in election campaigns that voters disregard information about improprieties in office. Or voters may perceive both candidates as more or less corrupt and simply make their voting choices on other

factors. Second, if voters believe that officials' corrupt acts were designed to benefit their district or their race or their ethnic group, they may support them despite (or even because of) their corrupt acts. Third, corrupt politicians may be popular with their constituents, whether personally or because of their stand on issues; constituents may knowingly ignore corruption because they value the representation more. There are many other issues besides "honesty in government."[d]

A strategy of some disgraced officeholders today is to publicly acknowledge one's past errors, claim personal redemption, go on television talk shows, and ask voters to accept a restored and chastised candidate. Others just take the punishment, serve the time, and fade away from public life.

[a] John G. Peters and Susan Welch, "Political Corruption in America: A Search for Definitions and a Theory," *American Political Science Review* 72 (September 1978): 974–984.
[b] Riordan, *Plunkitt of Tammany Hall*, p. 3.
[c] See Arthur Maass, "Public Policy by Prosecution," *The Public Interest* (Fall 1987): 107–127.
[d] For some tests about voter reaction to corruption, see Barry S. Rundquist, Gerald S. Strom, and John G. Peters, "Corrupt Politicians and Their Electoral Support," *American Political Science Review* 71 (September 1977): 954–963.

Many local governments have their own public television stations that run on the cable networks licensed to operate in their area.
Source: http://www.nngov.com/video-production/images/48_home_page.jpg

- *Appearances by local officials on television and radio* call-in talk and news magazine (public affairs) shows.
- *Kiosks at malls:* Interactive computers let citizens send a message directly to city hall, on issues ranging from potholes to budget priorities; new voting technologies, such as touch-screen voting machines, are often put in malls to allow citizens to test them out before Election Day.
- *Better use of diverse communication skills:* Greater use of "signers" to reach hearing impaired citizens, braille to reach the sight-impaired, and multilingual communicators to interact with non-English-speaking residents.
- *Citizen satisfaction surveys:* These allow the concerns and policy preferences of average citizens to reach elected officials rather than just the views of the noisy few who can attend city council, county commission, or school board meetings.[32] Some local governments routinely use these surveys to find out how to better communicate with their citizens.
- *Annual performance reports mailed to each household:* Borrowing an idea from the corporate world, citizens (community shareholders) are sent an annual report highlighting services provided, facilities constructed, and the bottom line (the budget). A comment card is included soliciting citizen reaction to the government's "report card."
- *Citizen academies:* Small groups of citizens of all ages and backgrounds meet once a week or so to learn about government operations firsthand; they attend council or commission hearings, meet department heads, observe how the government delivers its services, and thereby gain a better understanding of how citizens can make a difference at city hall.
- *Active volunteer recruitment programs:* Virtually every department, from parks and recreation to health and hospitals, has stepped up its recruitment of volunteers from the community, knowing that such volunteerism increases civic engagement and political participation.[33]

Another trend in recent years has been for city councils to let voters make the final decision on highly explosive and divisive issues. Fiscal issues (taxing, spending, and borrowing) and moral issues (e.g., abortion, gay rights, gambling) top the list of issues typically laid in the laps of city voters by nervous council members.

RECRUITING CITY COUNCIL MEMBERS

Political ambition is the most distinguishing characteristic of elected officeholders at all levels of government. The people who run for and win public office are not necessarily the most intelligent, best-informed, wealthiest, or most successful business or professional people. At all levels of the political system, from presidential candidates, members of Congress, governors, and state legislators to city council and school board members, it is the most politically ambitious people who are willing to sacrifice time, family and private life, and energy and effort for the power and celebrity that comes with public office.

Most politicians publicly deny that personal ambition is their real motivation for seeking public office. Rather, they describe their motives in highly idealistic terms—"civic duty," "service to community," "reform the government," "protect the environment." These responses reflect the norms of our political culture: People are not supposed to enter politics to satisfy *personal* ambitions, but rather to achieve *public* purposes. Many politicians do not really recognize their own drive for power—the drive to shape their community according to their own beliefs and values. But if there were no personal rewards in politics, no one would run for office.

There are some gender-based differences in characteristics of those who ultimately run for local office. Men are more likely to become interested through being active in college government, while women began their activism in high school government. Men who run have more political acquaintances and, are married with pre-schoolers at home. Women who run are more likely to have experienced gender bias and see themselves as leaders.[34]

Professionalization

Politics is becoming increasingly professionalized. "**Citizen-politicians**"—people with business or professional careers who get into politics part time or for short periods of time—are being driven out of political life by **career politicians**—people who enter politics early in life as a full-time occupation and expect to make it their career. Politics is increasingly demanding of time and energy. At all levels of governments, from city council to state legislatures to the U.S. Congress, political work is becoming full time and year-round. It is not only more demanding to *hold* office than it was a generation ago, but also far more demanding to *run* for office. Campaigning has become more time-consuming, more technically sophisticated, and much more costly over time.

Traditionally, city council members and county commissioners were local businesspeople who were respected in the community and active in civic organizations. They were likely to own small businesses and to have many contacts among constituents—retail merchants, real estate brokers, insurance agents, and so on. (Seldom do executives of large corporations concern themselves with local affairs, although they may encourage lower-management personnel to do so.) The part-time nature of traditional community governance, combined with only nominal pay and few perks of office, made local office-holding a "community service." It attracted people whose business brought them into close contact with the life of the community and allowed them spare time to attend to community affairs.

These civic-minded small businesspeople are still politically dominant in many small towns and rural counties throughout the nation. But they are gradually being replaced by lawyers, government employees, teachers, and professional officeholders in medium to large cities. In these cities, council pay is higher, the work is more time-consuming, council members are afforded greater celebrity status (television interviews, newspaper stories, deference, and respect), and greater opportunities exist for political advancement.

Why Run for City Council?

Few Americans ever take the bold step of running for city council. To them, council salaries are too low, citizen expectations are unrealistic, politicians are held in low regard, and the media scrutiny of candidates is too intense.

The formal qualifications for city council members are actually quite minimal. Most cities require that a candidate for council be a registered voter, a U.S. citizen, and a resident of the community for a certain period of time (usually a year or less). Persons

PROFESSION-ALIZATION

In politics, a reference to running for and holding public office as a full-time career.

CITIZEN-POLITICIANS

People with business or professional careers who get into politics part time or for short periods of time.

CAREER-POLITICIANS

People who enter politics early in life as a full-time occupation and expect to make it their career.

At all levels of governments, from city council to state legislatures to the U.S. Congress, political work is becoming full time and year-round.

POLITICOS

Those who say they ran because they enjoy politics and hope to move on to another office.

COMMUNITY REGARDERS

Those who run more to serve the whole community than for personal gain.

PARTICULARISTS

Those who run because of an over-riding concern for a specific issue or issues; they tend to be outsiders—minorities or members of groups long underrepresented in government—and one-termers.

convicted of a felony offense and those formally certified as mental incompetents generally are prohibited from running unless they petition to have their voting rights restored (most states have provisions for this).[35]

So why *do* people choose to run for city council? One widely cited study classifies council members according to the reason they say they ran.[36] **Politicos** are those who say they ran because they enjoy politics and hope to move on to another office. **Self-regarders** are those who enter city politics intent on personal enrichment. **Community-regarders** run to serve the whole community and seek no personal gain. **Locals** run primarily to help friends and neighbors, not parties (*partisans*) or single-issue interest groups. **Particularists** run because of an overriding concern for a specific issue or issues; they tend to be outsiders—minorities or members of groups long underrepresented in government—and one-termers.

Motivations for running differ across age groups. Older voters, many of whom are retirees, report they initially decided to run because they finally had the time and resources to do so. Younger candidates are more likely to say they ran because no one else would or because it would give them experience in office before running for a higher office.[37] However, fewer young people are entering politics at the local level, choosing instead to make their first run for office for a state legislative seat.

Some council members choose not to run again after serving just a few terms, and the number is growing, especially those serving in big cities. The greatest source of frustration is conflict among council members, cited by 55 percent.[38] Conflict seems to be worse when councilors are elected from single-member districts with sharply divergent constituency profiles, creating "a sense of parochialism and feudalism" among them. "There are councils where bickering and infighting are so intense that the entire body acquires an image of irresponsible flakiness."[39] Other sources of anxiety come from special-interest group pressures (45 percent), amount of required reading (40 percent), and meeting frequency (35 percent). To these add low council salaries (43 percent), losses in private income (34 percent), media-related problems (36 percent), and rising campaign costs (49 percent), and it's a miracle anyone stays beyond a single term—except the overly ambitious. Today, the median length of service on city council is just five years.

City Councils: Terms and Elections

In most American cities, especially those with nonpartisan elections, getting elected to city council is a do-it-yourself project. Most party organizations and civic associations are unreliable as sources of money and workers. Candidates must mobilize their own resources and create their own organizations. It is generally unwise to challenge an incumbent; over 80 percent of all incumbent council members seeking reelection are returned to office.[40] When vacancies occur, there are likely to be many candidates in the race. Since local races lack the visibility of national or statewide races, most focus on the personality, style, or image of the candidate. Even when local issues divide the candidates, most voters in local elections will be unaware of the candidates' stands on these issues.

In this fluid setting, electoral success depends on (1) the social acceptability of candidates relative to the community (especially their race and ethnic background); (2) their personal recognition in the community (name recognition, contacts from business, church, civic activity, etc.); and (3) their political resources (endorsements by newspapers and civic associations, access to political contributors, people willing to serve as volunteer workers, etc.). These factors are especially important for first-time candidates.[41] In subsequent campaigns, candidates develop more stable political followings.

Most city councils have five or seven members, but large city councils with up to fifty-one members (New York City) are found in the larger, older cities of the Northeast and Midwest. Four-year terms for council members are most frequent, but some council members are elected for two- or three-year terms. (See Table 11–1.) In most cities, council member terms overlap, so that some council seats are filled at every municipal election. Presumably overlapping terms ensure continuity in the deliberations of the council. Although term limits for council members are growing in popularity, as yet fewer than 10 percent of cities have adopted them.

The mayor's role relative to the city council varies according to the form of government. In strong mayor-council cities, the mayor does not usually sit on the council. However, in over half of these cities the mayor can veto council-passed ordinances; the mayor's veto can usually be overridden by a vote of two-thirds of the council. In council-manager, commission, and some weak mayor-council cities, the mayor is usually a council member, often selected by the council itself or on the basis of seniority on the council. These mayors may perform symbolic functions (e.g., presenting the "keys to the city" to visiting celebrities), but they seldom can veto council ordinances.

In most American cities, especially those with non-partisan elections, getting elected to city council is a do-it-yourself project.

TABLE 11–1 City Councils	
Terms	**Cities with (%)**
One year	3
Two years	55
Three years	30
Four years	9
Other	4
Term limits	9
Mayor Sits on Council	
Mayor-council cities	41
Council-manager cities	85
Commission cities	92
Town meeting	90
Representative town meeting	78
Mayor Can Veto Council Ordinances	
Mayor-council cities	58
Council-manager cities	13
Commission cities	14
Town meeting	3
Representative town meeting	16

Source: The Municipal Year Book 2003, p. 10

Friends at City Hall

A surprising number of council members are initially *appointed* to their office to fill the unexpired terms of resigning members. Those appointees are likely to be personal friends of council members or to have held some other city job. Finally, 80 percent of incumbents running for reelection are successful. Voluntary retirement is the most common exit from community politics. Political scientists have observed that

> the election system provides advantages to those citizens who already have social and political resources; to those favorably located in the network of friendships which play such an important part in city politics; to those whose apprentice roles identify them as likely candidates for political office; to those who have natural organizational ties and support; and, finally, to those already in office if they choose to stand for reelection.[42]

COUNCIL MEMBERS: RESPONSIBLE POLICYMAKERS?

The typical city council member represents, legislates, oversees city management (checks the chief executive, city departments, and employees), and judges the fairness of government operations.

> Members of the city council . . . speak for and make decisions on behalf of the citizens of the community [their representation role], engage in "*lawmaking*"—policy leadership, enactment of ordinances and resolutions, debate, criticism, and investigation [their legislative role], . . . respond to problems their constituents have with administrative agencies by seeking to bring about corrective action . . . and oversee the *execution of policy* in order to insure that the purpose of their lawmaking is accomplished [their executive oversight role], . . . and fill a *judicial function* either in the informal sense that they serve as the "court of last resort" for certain kinds of appeals from citizens who feel they have been harmed by city government, or in the more formal sense, in a few cases, of following strict procedures to adjudicate regulations or settle legal disputes.[43]

The policymaking role of council members varies a great deal from city to city. Council members have more formal power in commission or weak-mayor forms of government, where the council itself sometimes appoints officials, prepares the budget, supervises departments, and performs other administrative tasks. However, in other cities—particularly strong mayor or manager cities—the council merely oversees city affairs. In these cities, the function of the council may be principally the representation of the interests of local constituents—forwarding complaints, making inquiries, pushing for new sidewalks or streetlights, and so forth.

Council members do *not* usually serve as either general policy innovators or general policy leaders. The role of the council is largely passive, granting or withholding approval in the name of the community when presented with proposals from a leadership outside of itself. The outside leadership is usually the manager, city departments, planning commission, citizen groups, or private enterprise.[44] In fact, research shows that city councils tend to adopt more innovative policies (e.g., privatization of services, public-private partnerships, quality in government programs, customer-oriented governance, and formal strategic planning) in cities with an effective manager or chief administrative officer (CAO).[45]

Accountability

Most constituents cannot even name their council member(s). The question is, How can citizens hold a council member accountable if they do not even know who represents them?[46] The problem of political accountability in local politics is aggravated by several factors:

1. *The frequency of appointment to elected office.* It is probable that as many as one-quarter of the nation's council members initially come into office by appointment rather than election. They are appointed, usually by the mayor, to fill unexpired terms.

2. *The effective constituency is very small.* Given the low turnout in municipal elections, and the small constituencies served by a council member, only a very few votes may elect a person to office. A council member's personal friends, immediate neighbors, business associates, fellow church members, and acquaintances at the Rotary Club may be enough for election.

3. *Limited contact with citizens.* Few citizens know how to contact city officials, and even fewer citizens actually do so. Moreover, citizen-initiated contacts are closely related to socioeconomic status, with higher-status individuals far more likely to contact city officials about a problem than middle- or lower-status persons.

4. *The infrequency of electoral defeat.* Incumbents running for reelection are hardly ever defeated. When they are defeated, it is frequently in groups, when several incumbents are turned out of office at once owing to a specific community controversy.

5. *The frequency of voluntary retirement from elected office.* The vast majority of council members voluntarily retire from office, over half of them after two terms. Officeholders simply conclude that the obligations of office exceed the rewards.

All these factors, together with the attitude of volunteerism, tend to distance municipal government from direct citizen control.

Representation

Despite this evidence of a lack of electoral accountability in local politics, some factors may compel council members to reflect the will of their constituents in policymaking. Moreover, council members tend to reflect, in their own socioeconomic background, the characteristics of their constituents. This does not *ensure* that council members share the same attitudes as their constituents on all matters; indeed, the experience of being a public official itself can help to shape a council member's views and give a different perspective on public affairs than the constituents'. However, if council members have deep roots in their communities (many social contacts and group memberships; shared socioeconomic, ethnic, racial, and religious characteristics with their constituents), they may reflect these in their policymaking, whether or not they are consciously aware of these "constituency influences." The effects of shared community life may be very influential in shaping decision making in small, homogeneous communities where uniformity of outlook may amount to compulsion. In short, although "electoral accountability" may have little direct influence over council members, "belief sharing" may still ensure some congruence between the views of community residents and the views of their representatives.[47]

CITY MANAGERS IN MUNICIPAL POLITICS

When council-manager government was first introduced as part of the municipal reform movement, managers were expressly admonished not to participate in community "politics." Early supporters of manager government believed in the separation of "politics"

ACCOUNTABILITY
In politics, the extent to which an elected official must answer to his or her constituents.

A majority of professionally trained city managers see themselves as "policy managers."

from "administration."[48] Politics, not only *party* politics but *policy* making as well, should be the exclusive domain of the elected city council. The manager was hired by the council to carry out its policy directives, and the manager could be removed by the council by majority vote at any time. This belief in the separation of policymaking from administration was intended to produce "nonpolitical," efficient, and economical government, which middle-class supporters of the reform movement valued so highly. Popular control of government was to be guaranteed by making the manager's tenure completely dependent upon the will of the elected council.

However, after a few years of experience with manager government in America, it became increasingly apparent to the managers themselves that they could not escape responsibility for policy recommendations. It turned out to be very difficult in practice to separate policymaking from administration. The first code of ethics of the International City Managers' Association (ICMA) stated flatly that "no manager should take an active part in politics." Managers agreed that they should stay out of partisan politics and election campaigns, but there was a great deal of debate about the role of managers in community policymaking. In 1938, the ICMA revised its code of ethics to recognize the positive role of managers in policy leadership.[49]

Managers as Policy Leaders

Today, we are likely to find varying role orientations among city managers. Some see themselves as "**policy managers**," providing community leadership through their recommendations to their councils on a wide variety of matters. They believe they should innovate and lead on policy matters. Others see themselves as "**administrative managers**," restricting themselves to the supervision of the municipal bureaucracy and avoiding innovative policy recommendations, particularly in controversial areas. Ambivalent about innovation and leadership on policy matters, these managers avoid involvement in community issues.

A majority of professionally trained city managers see themselves as "policy managers." Better-educated managers who have had experience in different cities and who aspire to move to larger cities and assume greater responsibilities are unlikely to settle for a restricted, administrative role. However, managers without professional training in city administration or those with engineering degrees, who have lived most of their lives in their own communities and who expect to remain there, are more likely to accept a fairly narrow administrative role.[50] Managers who have held their position for twenty years or longer (less than 5 percent of all managers) serve communities that are ethnically and racially homogeneous, with less fractious politics than those in larger cities.[51]

Managers as Administrators

While most managers see themselves as policy leaders, some council members see managers in their traditional role of administrators. This means that prudent managers will not wish to *appear* to be policymakers even when they are. They seek to have others present their policy proposals to the community and avoid the brasher methods of policy promotion. Like any successful politician, city managers try to avoid taking public stands on the more controversial issues facing the community. Their dependence upon the council for their jobs prevents them from being too extreme in policy promotion. Managers can push their councils, but they can seldom fight them with any success. Open disputes between the manager and the council are usually resolved by the dismissal of the manager. Managers who assume strong policy leadership roles have shorter tenures than those who do not.

Nevertheless, the manager is the most important policy initiator in most council-manager cities. Most managers determine the agenda for city council meetings. This permits them to determine the kinds of issues to be raised and the policy options to be considered. The council may not accept everything recommended by the manager, but the manager's recommendations will be given serious consideration. The city manager is the major source of information for most council members. The manager prepares the city budget; writes formal reports on city problems, defining the problems and proposing solutions; and advises and educates the council privately as well as publicly.

Managers in a Dual Role

Thus, managers really have two important roles in community politics: administration and policymaking. The administrative role involves the supervision of the municipal bureaucracy; this role requires administrative skills and technical expertise. Managers direct their personal staff, develop and control the city budget, and appoint and remove department heads. In most council-manager cities, managers try to guard these powers from direct council interference: These powers are the managers' most important formal resources. The policymaking role requires managers to make recommendations for action.

How Council Members View Managers

What kind of managers do mayors and council members want? Doubtlessly, some mayors and council members want to retain a larger policy role for themselves and resent a manager who wants to run the show. These elected officials might try to recruit "administrative managers" by avoiding applicants with forceful personalities, high professional qualifications, and experience in other cities. However, we have already suggested that many council members are "volunteers" who prefer a passive role in policymaking—approving or disapproving proposals brought before them by the manager and others. A weak manager can lengthen council meetings and significantly increase the council's workload. So we should not be surprised to find many council members welcoming policy leadership from the manager (as long as the manager avoids the appearance of dominating the council). Indeed, one study indicates that a majority of council members "expect the manager to take the lead" in budget decisions, hiring and firing personnel, reorganization of city departments, wage and salary negotiations, community improvements, and cooperative proposals with other communities.[52] Only in planning and zoning do council members say they want to retain leadership. Presumably these council members would try to recruit well-educated, professionally trained, experienced, and mobile managers to their community. However, past manager–council relations in a community may affect recruitment. Some communities may undergo cycles in council-manager relations: A council resentful of a strong manager replaces him or her with a weak one, only to find that their workload increases, decisions are postponed, complaints of inaction accumulate; and the council decides to find a new, stronger manager.

Professionalism

A high percentage of today's city managers are white males under fifty years of age, although the number of women and minorities in city manager positions is on the upswing. Most city managers are professionals who have been trained in university

Mayors are in the
"hot seat" of
American politics.

graduate programs in public administration. They are familiar with budgeting and fiscal administration, public personnel management, municipal law, and planning. They tend to move from city to city as they advance in their professional careers. They may begin their careers as a staff assistant to a city official and then move to assistant city manager, then manager of a small town, and later perhaps of a larger city. About three-quarters of all city manager appointments are made from outside the city, and only about one-quarter are local residents, which indicates the professionalism of city management. The average tenure of managers who resigned or were removed from office has been about five years.[53] One in ten managers reports having been fired at least once. Most of these found another job within six months but reported using up their savings or severance pay to survive between jobs. The three principal reasons given for having been fired were "poor working relationship with council," "politics," and "change in the council." All of these reasons might be termed political.[54] However, other managers move on because they have been offered more attractive professional opportunities. Most managers love their career choice, regardless of how long they serve in one place. They say they get the most satisfaction from having made specific significant contributions to the communities in which they have served.[55]

MAYORS IN CITY POLITICS

Today, more than ever before, the nation's cities need forceful, imaginative political leadership. The nation's major domestic problems—race relations, poverty, violence, congestion, poor schools, and fiscal crisis—are concentrated in cities. Mayors are in the "hot seat" of American politics; they must deal directly with these pressing issues. No other elected official in the American federal system must deal face-to-face, eyeball-to-eyeball with these problems.

Atlanta Mayor Shirley Franklin, the city's first female mayor, has won many awards for restoring trust in government by rooting out corruption and making tough fiscal choices. (Her predecessor's administration was the subject of a federal investigation for corruption related to the 1996 Olympic Games.) She was elected to a second term in a landslide and is one of *Time Magazine*'s top five mayors.

Limited Powers

The challenges facing big-city mayors are enormous; however, their powers to deal with these challenges are restricted on every side. Executive power in major cities is often fragmented among a variety of elected officials—city treasurer, city clerk, city comptroller, district attorney, and so on. The mayor may also be required to share power over municipal affairs with county officials. Many city agencies and functions are outside the mayor's formal authority: Independent boards and commissions often govern important city departments—for example, the board of education, board of health, zoning appeals board, planning commission, civil service board, library board, park commission, sewage and water board, and so on. Even if the mayor is permitted to appoint the members of the boards and commissions, they are often appointed for a fixed term, and the mayor cannot remove them. The mayor's power over the affairs of the city may also be affected by the many special district governments and public authorities operating within the city, including public housing, urban renewal, sewage and water, mass transit, and port authority. Traditionally, school districts have been outside the authority of the mayor or city government except in the nation's oldest cities in the Northeast and Midwest. Mayors' powers over city finances may even be restricted—they may share budget-making powers with a board of estimate, and powers over expenditures with an elected comptroller or treasurer. Civil service regulations and independent civil service boards can greatly hamper mayors' control over their own bureaucrats. The activities of federal and state agencies in a city are largely beyond the mayor's control.

Selecting Mayors

The method of selecting mayors also influences their powers over city affairs. Mayors in cities with weak mayor-council, council-manager, or commission forms of government are often selected by their city councils or commissions and generally have little more power than other council members or commissioners. Their job is generally ceremonial: They crown beauty queens, dedicate parks, lay cornerstones, lead parades, and sign official papers. Larger cities, usually strong mayor-council cities, generally elect their mayors, although now over half of all council-manager cities do, too. Mayors may be elected for anything from one to five years, but two-year and four-year terms are most common in American cities. Some mayors run at a very young age and win.

Legislative Powers

Mayors' legislative powers also vary widely. Of course, in all cities they have the right to submit messages to the council and to recommend policy. These recommendations will carry whatever prestige the mayor possesses in the community. Moreover, in council-manager and commission cities, mayors usually are themselves members of the council. In these cities where mayors are chosen by the council, they generally have voting power equal to that of other council members. In about one-third of mayor-council cities, the mayor also serves on the council; in about half of the mayor-council cities the mayor presides over meetings of the council and can cast a tie-breaking vote. In most cities where the mayor is *not* a member of the council, the mayor enjoys veto power over council-passed ordinances. The veto power helps distinguish between "strong-mayor" and "weak-mayor" cities.

Administrative Powers

Another distinction between "strong" and "weak" mayors is made on the basis of their powers of administration. Weak mayors have very limited appointing powers and even more limited removal powers. They have little control over separately elected boards and commissions or separately elected offices, such as clerk, treasurer, tax assessor, comptroller, and attorney. The council, rather than the mayor, often appoints the key administrative officers. No single individual has the complete responsibility for law enforcement or coordinating city administration.

Political Powers

In summary, a mayor's ability to provide strong leadership in many cities is limited by fragmented authority, multiple elected officials, limited jurisdiction over important urban services, civil service, state or federal interference, and constraints placed upon

POLITICAL
BROKER

Role calling for a mayor
to be a mediator—to
help resolve commu-
nity conflicts.

that power by "reform" and "good-government" arrangements. Nevertheless, even though it is recognized that mayors have few formal powers to deal with the enormous tasks facing them, it is frequently argued that mayors can and should exercise strong leadership as **"political brokers"**—mediating disputes, serving as a channel of communications, bringing conflicting groups together for reasonable discussions of their differences, and suggesting solutions that diverse groups can accept in coping with the city's problems. In other words, the "ideal" mayor overcomes limited formal powers by skill in persuasion, negotiation, and public relations. Each "success" in resolving a particular problem "pyramids" the mayor's prestige and influence, and he or she eventually accumulates considerable informal power. The mayor can then direct energy and power toward accomplishing one or more of the numerous goals set for mayors: reducing racial tensions, providing effective law enforcement, speeding redevelopment and renewal of downtown areas and the relocation of persons living there, improving public schools, constructing low-cost housing, cleaning up the urban environment, finding ways to move people and things about the city speedily and efficiently, and, most important of all, finding ways to finance these goals.

But this "ideal" city leadership requires that the mayor possess certain minimum resources[56]:

- Sufficient financial and staff resources in the mayor's office and in city government generally
- City jurisdiction over social-program areas—education, housing, urban renewal, etc.
- Mayor's jurisdiction within city government over these areas
- A salary that enables the mayor to spend full time on the job
- Friendly newspapers or television stations supportive of the mayor and his or her goals
- Political groups, including a political party, that the mayor can mobilize to attend meetings, parades, distribute literature, and so on, on his or her behalf

Successful mayors must rely chiefly upon their own personal qualities of leadership: their powers to persuade, to sell, to compromise, to bargain, and to "get things done."[57] Mayors are not usually expected to initiate proposals for new programs or to create public issues. Nor is their primary concern the administration of existing programs, although they must always seek to avoid scandal and gross mismanagement, which would give their administrations a bad public "image." They must rely upon other public agencies, planners, citizens' groups, and private enterprise to propose new programs, and they can usually rely upon their department heads and other key subordinates to supervise the day-to-day administration of city government. Mayors are primarily promoters of public policy: Their role is to promote, publicize, organize, and finance the projects that others suggest. The money side of the job is usually the toughest and getting more so by the day. The former mayor of Indianapolis put it like this: All "mayors are being so squeezed they don't have time for anything except to make ends meet. Their noses are so close to the grindstone that nobody can see their faces."[58]

MINORITIES AND WOMEN IN LOCAL POLITICS

Local politics is the entry level in the American political system for minorities as well as women. Currently about half of the one hundred largest cities in the United States have minority or women mayors. All but a few of these cities have had minority or women mayors in the recent past.

Minority Mayors

African Americans have served as mayors in many cities with majority white populations, including New York, Chicago, Los Angeles, and Philadelphia, as well as cities with majority black populations, including Detroit, Washington, DC, New Orleans, and Atlanta. In fact, by 1999, almost one-third of all cities over 200,000 had elected black or Hispanic mayors.[59] States with the most black mayors are Mississippi, Alabama, Texas, Louisiana, Arkansas, Georgia, and North Carolina.[60] Black mayors are most likely to be elected in cities where there is a large black population, black representation on city council, a more educated black population, and reformed governments.[61] States with the largest number of local Hispanic elected officials are Texas, California, New Mexico, Arizona, Colorado, Florida, New York, Illinois, and New Jersey. These nine states contain 82 percent of the Latino population and 97 percent of all Latinos elected in the United States.[62]

The success of blacks and Hispanics in city politics, especially in majority white and Anglo cities, suggests that race is becoming less important as a criterion in voter choice for municipal leadership. However, voting patterns in city elections in which minority and white candidates face each other indicate a continuing residue of racial politics. Black and Hispanic voters continue to cast their votes solidly for black and Hispanic candidates in these elections; white voters continue to give majority support to white candidates. The swing vote in these minority–white election confrontations usually rests with 30 to 40 percent of white voters who are prepared to support qualified minority candidates. Support patterns are more complex in multiracial/ethnic communities.

Successful black mayoral candidates in majority white cities have generally emphasized racial harmony and conciliation. They have stressed broad themes of concern to all voters—regardless of race. They have built coalitions that cut across racial, ethnic, and economic lines; many have worked their way up through the ranks of local organizations. They have avoided identification as "protest" candidates. However, in cities where blacks are a majority, black candidates favor a more highly racial campaign strategy.[63] In multiracial cities, race may play a major role in the candidate's first election, but job approval becomes more important when the minority candidate runs for re-election.[64] In general, blacks are less cohesive in local than national politics, often due to sizable socioeconomic differences within the black community.[65]

The strategies used by Hispanic mayoral candidates in areas where Latinos are in the minority are twofold. In more suburban areas where there are lots of middle- and upper-middle-class white homeowners, they campaign on platforms calling for preservation of property values, better schools, and tougher law enforcement. In urban areas, Hispanic candidates focus on building winning "biracial, multiracial, multiple issue, and labor–Latino alliances."[66] (See "*People in Politics*: Against All Odds: Los Angeles Mayor Antonio Villaraigosa.")

Across the United States, the trend is toward more racially pluralist cities, where no one racial or ethnic group makes up a majority of the population. Different, and shifting, electoral coalitions are more the rule in such cities. They vary as each racial and ethnic group changes in its relative group size, cohesion, resources, partisan makeup, residential concentration patterns, issue priorities, and candidates.

Across the United States, the trend is toward more racially pluralist cities, where no one racial or ethnic group makes up a majority of the population.

Minorities on Councils

In general, minority candidates for city council are the most successful in larger cities, with sizable, concentrated, cohesive minority populations and better-educated, liberal

Against All Odds:
Los Angeles Mayor Antonio Villaraigosa

No Hispanic had been elected mayor of Los Angeles, the nation's second largest city, since 1872. No challenger had beaten an incumbent mayor since 1973. He was running against the very person who had defeated him in the previous mayoral election. The incumbent who had beaten him in 2001 won by building a coalition of black and white voters in a city where Latinos make up less than one-fourth of the *registered* voters. (Overall, Los Angeles' 3.9 million population is 47 percent Hispanic, 29 percent white [non-Hispanics], 11 percent black, and 10 percent Asian.)

In spite of the seemingly insurmountable odds against him, Antonio Villaraigosa was elected Mayor of Los Angeles in 2005 by a landslide vote (59%–41%). He raised more money than his opponent, was endorsed by the *Los Angeles Times,* and put together a winning coalition of Latinos, blacks, and liberal whites, seen as nothing short of masterful.

> For in a metropolis fragmented by ethnicity, geography and social class—where candidates have struggled to patch together a winning coalition—Villaraigosa won big. He won the Latino vote—and the black vote, and the white vote. He won the working-class neighborhoods, and the prosperous San Fernando Valley. The longtime liberal even captured much of the Republican vote. Villaraigosa's landslide victory over one-term incumbent James K. Hahn, a fellow Democrat . . . in the nonpartisan election, left many of his supporters giddy about his potential to unify a city where so many groups have long been at odds."[a] Asians were the only racial group Villaraigosa did not win.

Villaraigosa's winning coalition is seen as the type of coalition likely to dominate big-city politics in the twenty-first century as the Latino population continues to grow. Said one UCLA political scientist: "Clearly this is an opportunity . . . for a new kind of multiracial coalition. This is different—Latinos in the lead with African-Americans playing a key role with white liberals and Jews. It's a different kind of pecking order."[b] Following his election, Alcalde (Mayor) Villaraigosa downplayed his own ethnicity and played up the need to represent all "Angelinos": "I'm an American of Mexican descent, and I'm proud of that. But I intend to be the mayor of all of Los Angeles. As the mayor of the most diverse city in the world, that's the only way it can work."[c]

Future Governor or White House Appointee?

Midway into his first term, Villaraigosa admitted having an affair with a popular anchor at Telemundo, the highly watched Spanish-language TV station. He also lost a court battle to take control over Los Angeles public schools and failed at getting bus fare increases to help fund much-needed Metropolitan Transit Authority projects. However, none of these setbacks kept U.S. Sen. Hillary Rodham Clinton (D-N.Y.) from naming him one of four national chairpersons of her 2008 presidential campaign, calling him "an honest optimist and a practical visionary." Nor did it stop *The Sacramento Bee* newspaper from running a headline touting him as a viable contender for governor should he run in 2010 or the *Los Angeles Times* from speculating about a possible Cabinet post should a Democrat be elected president in 2008.[d] Analysts are betting he will beat the odds again whatever he decides to do.

Villaraigosa Background

Age when elected: 52

B.A., history major, University of California at Los Angeles (UCLA); after being a high school dropout

Law degree: J.D., People's College of Law, Los Angeles

Former president: ACLU for Southern California

Previous elective offices: California Assembly, 1994–2000 (Assembly Speaker, 1998–2000); Los Angeles City Council, 2003–2005

Term of office: Four years

Voter turnout rate: 30 percent

[a] Amy Argetsinger and Kimberly Edds, "Villaraigosa Wins Easily in L.A. Mayoral Runoff," *The Washington Post*, May 19, 2005, p. A01.
[b] UCLA political scientist Franklin Gilliam Jr., quoted by Daniel Wood, *The Christian Science Monitor*, "L.A. Victory Boosts Hispanic Political Clout," *USA Today*, May 19, 2005, p. 4A.

(*continued*)

c John M. Broder, "Latino Victor in Los Angeles Overcomes Division," *The New York Times*, May 19, 2005, accessed at www.nytimes.com/2005/05/19/national/19angeles.html?pagewanted=print, May 19, 2005.

d Kevin Yamamura, "Despite Affair, Villaraigosa Still Seen as 2010 Contender," *The Sacramento Bee*, July 4, 2007; available at www .sacbee.com/111/v-print/story/2555858.html; Duke Helfand, "Mayor's Smooth Ride Has Gotten Bumpier," *Los Angeles Times*, June 1, 2007; available at www.latimes.com/news/local/la-me-meyor1june01,0,4216336,print.story?coll=la-home-center.

white populations willing to vote for minority candidates. Until recently, blacks were generally underrepresented on city councils across the country. That is to say, blacks held a smaller proportion of seats on city councils than the black percentages of city populations. But the steady rise in the number of black city council members and county commissioners over the last thirty years has brought black representation to rough proportionality in most American cities. In cities in which blacks constitute 10 to 50 percent of the population, black representation on city councils generally reflects the black population percentage (In cities in which the black population constitutes a majority (over 50 percent), black representation on city councils usually exceeds the black population percentage.[67]

In contrast, Hispanic representation on city councils is significantly below the Hispanic population percentages.[68] Earlier we observed that Hispanic voter turnout was significantly lower than that for other social groups (see Chapter 4). Lower voter turnout among Hispanics is frequently attributed to cultural and language barriers and the resident alien status of many Hispanics. These factors, along with lower candidacy rates, less residential concentration, and some structural features of reform government, including at-large elections in some settings, continue to create barriers to the political mobilization of Hispanics.[69] (See Table 11–2.) Asian candidates are confronted with similar hurdles.[70]

Historically, Asian American elected officials, mostly Chinese and Japanese Americans, were concentrated in two states: Hawaii and California. But by 2000, over 300 Asian Americans had been elected to office, mostly at the local level, in thirty-one states. While Chinese and Japanese Americans still make up 67 percent, other Asian ethnic groups (e.g., Filipino, Korean, and Vietnamese) are being elected as well. Asian Americans are more likely to be elected from non-Asian majority districts that are either heavily white or multiracial. They "must rely on political strategies that have a mainstream platform or a multiracial platform focusing on both inter- and intraracial coalition building in order to be successful."[71]

Policy Consequences

What are the policy consequences of increasing minority representation on city councils? Perhaps the most obvious consequence is increased minority *employment* in city jobs. For example, black employment at all levels of city administration—professional and managerial, police and fire, office and clerical, service and maintenance—tends to increase with increases in the black population of the city, as we might expect.[72] But the single most important determinant of minority employment in administrative and professional positions is the proportion of blacks, Hispanics, and Asians elected to city councils.[73] The employment of minorities in service and maintenance jobs does not require political representation. However, to get important city jobs, minorities must first win political power.[74]

Urban police departments have long been a focus of concern for minorities. Police policies have come under scrutiny for contributing to racial tensions, triggering riots,

TABLE 11–2 Black and Hispanic Local Elected Officials	
Blacks	**5452**
County Governments	**975**
County executive/mayors	4
County commission members	820
Other county bodies	73
Other county officials	78
City Governments	**4477**
Mayors	454
City council members	3538
Municipal board members	103
Neighborhood Advisory Commission members	269
Other municipal officials	113
Hispanics	**3962**
County officials	474
Municipal officials	1585
Education/school board members	1723
Special district officials	180

Note: Data for black elected officials is from 2001. Data for Hispanic elected officials is for 2004.

Sources: Black elected officials, 2001; David A. Bositis, *Black Elected Officials* (Washington, DC: Joint Center for Political and Economic Studies, 2003). Hispanic elected officials, 2004; NALEO Education Fund National Directory of Latino Elected Officials (Los Angeles, 2004).

blocking minority aspirations, and shaping minority perceptions of justice. Many black mayors have campaigned on explicit pledges to reform police departments and adopt policies designed to make police responsive and sensitive to the concerns of minorities. The adoption of minority-oriented police policies, including increases in the number of minority police officers, has occurred with increases in black population percentages in cities, regardless of whether cities elect black mayors and council members. However, there is some evidence that the election of black mayors results in (1) accelerated recruitment of black police officers and (2) the adoption of citizen review boards to oversee police actions.[75]

Yet to date there is *no* evidence that cities with greater minority representation on city councils, or even cities with minority mayors, pursue significantly different taxing, spending, or service policies than do cities with little or no minority representation. This is really not surprising; African American, Latino, and other minority city leaders face the same problems as white city leaders in raising revenue, fighting crime, improving housing, reducing congestion, removing garbage, and so on. It is possible, of course, that black neighborhoods receive better *delivery* of urban services under black leadership. However, the overall problems of cities may remain unaffected by substituting black leadership for white leadership. Research shows that while in office, black and white mayors are judged much more by their performance on the job than by their race.

Performance in office accounts for 16 to 25 percent of the typical mayor's performance evaluation, race just 1 to 6 percent.[76]

The presence of minorities on city councils is important for city politics even if there is little impact on taxing and spending policies. Blacks, Hispanics, Asians, and gays and lesbians in city government improve the image of that government among each group's residents; it helps to link minorities to city hall, to provide role models, and to sensitize white officials to minority concerns. "When minorities talk to the city council now, council members nod their heads rather than yawn."[77]

Women in Local Politics

Women's participation in local politics has risen dramatically in recent years. Women occupy about 14 percent of mayors' offices across the country. Women mayors are more prevalent in larger cities with racially and ethnically diverse, and more affluent and better-educated, populations. As of the mid-2000s, 16 percent of the 243 mayors of U.S. cities with populations over 100,000 were women, including two African Americans and five Latinas.[78] Today, of the approximately 21,000 municipal council members serving in cities with populations over 10,000, over 21 percent are women.[79] As late as 1975 this figure was estimated to be only about 4 percent.

Women have made major gains in capturing county commission and school board seats. The percent of female county commissioners across the United States jumped from 3 percent in 1975 to 24 percent in 1998.[80] Women comprised 26 percent of all school board members in 1978 but 39 percent by 2001. The movement of women into politics generally is attributed to the movement of women into the workforce and the changing cultural values redefining women's role in American society. At the local level, women may find fewer obstacles to political officeholding than at the state or national level. Local offices do not require women to move away from their home communities to the state capital or to Washington. (Women candidates, unlike men, are seldom relieved of all of their home responsibilities when running for or occupying political office.[81]) Plus, local offices often have higher salaries than state- or national-level positions.

Women (and men) who have been more active in civic and professional associations are more likely to get elected than those who have not. Winners of both sexes attribute at least part of their victory to this connection. Female city council candidates traditionally have received more support than have male candidates from neighborhood organizations, single-issue groups, and women's organizations. Male candidates still tend to get a marginally higher level of support from business groups, although this is changing, too.[82]

Some of the long-standing myths about the role of gender in city council elections have been refuted. We now know that, when compared with male candidates, females win at the same rate; raise as much or more campaign money; are not disadvantaged by at-large elections, nonpartisan elections, runoff elections (second primaries), or newspaper or political party endorsements of male candidates; and are not deterred from running by steep filing fees. Media coverage of women candidates, relative to their male counterparts, has improved in frequency and content, although some women still complain that media coverage focuses too much on their clothing and appearance.

Age also is no longer much of a barrier. Formerly, younger and middle-aged professional women were the most likely to enter local politics, but that trend has changed considerably. Older women are running in record numbers, as the notion that politics is "a male thing" has rapidly eroded.

It is increasingly common for female candidates to end up running against other females for the same position—a marked change from the past.

For years, black and Hispanic females did not run or win as often as did white females, even when they run against minority males. For these minority women, gender was seen as a bigger barrier to their election to city councils than their race.[83] It still is for Latinas. But now African American women are getting elected to office at a faster rate than black men, paralleling college graduation rates, which are higher among black women than black men.[84]

Today, there are few city councils with no female members. And it is increasingly common for female candidates to end up running against other females for the same position—a marked change from the past. Women opposing women is simply one more piece of evidence that women are not a politically monolithic group. Gender actually is a fairly weak voting cue compared to age, race, education, income, or religion.

Women are elected at the school board level at a higher rate than for other local offices. Few women (or men) run for school board thinking they will use the office as a stepping-stone to higher office, although some do. Virtually all school board members say they ran to make the community a better place. However, one study has found that "men are more likely than women to say that a desire to apply their religious beliefs to policy and return schools to traditional values was important to their initial decision to seek a school board seat."[85]

What are the policy consequences of increased women's representation on city councils? Several studies have shown that women are more likely than men to favor greater representation of underrepresented groups and to put higher priorities on social issues. Female council members regard themselves as better prepared than their male counterparts, who believe women ask too many questions.[86]

INTEREST GROUPS IN COMMUNITY POLITICS

Interest group activity may be more influential in community politics than in state or national political affairs. Since the arena of local politics is smaller, the activities of organized interest groups may be more obvious at the local level. The types of groups that are active at the local level reflect the activities and services over which local governments have the most control.[87] (See Tables 11–3 and 11–4.)

TABLE 11–3   Local Policy Arenas: Level of Activity and Influence
Policy Areas in Which Local Interest Groups Are Very Active and Very Influential

Policy Area	High Level of Activity (% Citing)	Very Influential (% Rating)
Economic development	68	58
Police/law enforcement	62	54
Land-use planning	59	51
Public safety	58	49
Zoning	57	46
Housing	49	29

TABLE 11-3 (Continued)

Policy Areas in Which Local Interest Groups Are Very Active and Very Influential

Policy Area	High Level of Activity (% Citing)	Very Influential (% Rating)
Recreation/parks	47	40
Fire	45	33
Art/culture	43	31
Traffic	41	25
Education	40	31
Taxes	36	29
Roads	31	23
Refuse collection	22	17
Personal social services	22	17
Health	18	15
Electricity	17	16
Public transportation	26	17
Vocational education	6	4

Source: Christopher A. Cooper, Anthony J. Nownes, and Steven Roberts, "Perceptions of Power: Interest Groups in Local Politics," *State and Local Government Review* 37(3) 2005: 211.

TABLE 11-4 Local Interest Groups: Types and Influence

Types of Local Interest Groups That Are Very Active and Very Influential

Type of Interest Group	Level of Activity	Level of Influence
Neighborhood associations	64	49
Business associations	59	46
Public employee unions	42	31
Cultural/recreational groups	35	27
Ethnic/minority groups	28	27
Homeowner groups	27	26
Environmental groups	35	23
Antigrowth groups	30	12
Private-sector groups	27	22
Single-Issue groups	26	13
Utilities	18	19
Taxpayer groups	18	11
Religious/church groups	17	18
Business firms	16	16
Women's groups	6	4
Farm groups	1	3
Professional associations	1	2

Source: Christopher A. Cooper, Anthony J. Nownes, and Steven Roberts, "Perceptions of Power: Interest Groups in Local Politics," *State and Local Government Review* 37(3) 2005: 212.

CIVIC ASSOCIA-
TIONS

In local politics, an
organization of citizens
that works to further
its own view of the
best interest of the
community.

TAXPAYER
GROUPS

Interest groups that
generally stand for
lower taxes and fewer
governmental activities
and services.

ENVIRONMENTAL
GROWTH-
MANAGEMENT
GROUPS

Interest groups that
are generally opposed
to community growth,
highway construction,
street widening, tree
cutting, increased traf-
fic, noise and pollution,
commercial or indus-
trial development, or
anything else that
offends their aesthetic
preferences.

NEIGHBORHOOD
ASSOCIATIONS

In local politics, an
organization of the
residents of a specific
neighborhood that
works to protect
property values.

The Civic Associations

At the local level, interest groups frequently assume the form of civic associations. Few communities are too small to have at least one or two associations devoted to civic well-being, and larger cities may have hundreds of these organizations. Council members usually name civic associations (service clubs, citizens' commissions, improvement associations) as the most influential groups or organizations that are active and appear before the council. This does not necessarily mean that economic interests or taxpayer associations are less active than civic associations, but probably that civic associations are the predominant style of organized interest group activity at the local level. Businesspeople, reform groups, taxpayer associations, merchants, service clubs, developers, and so on organize themselves into civic associations for action at the local level. Civic associations generally make their appeals in terms of the "welfare of the community," the "public interest," "civic responsibility," "making Janesville a better place to live." In other words, civic associations claim to be community-serving rather than self-serving. Members belong to these groups as a hobby, because of the sense of prestige and civic participation they derive from membership. Occasionally, of course, participation in civic associations can be a stepping-stone to local office.

Taxpayer Groups

Organized taxpayer groups generally stand for lower taxes and fewer governmental activities and services. Their most enthusiastic support comes from the community's larger taxpayers, generally businesspeople with large investments in commercial or industrial property in the community. However, when the economy is in a downturn, middle-class citizens become quite active "anti-taxers."

Environmental and "Growth-Management" Groups

Environmental groups and opponents of residential and commercial development have become major forces in community politics throughout the nation. These groups are generally opposed to community growth, although they employ the term *growth management* to imply that they do not necessarily oppose all growth. But they are generally opposed to highway construction, street widening, tree cutting, increased traffic, noise and pollution, commercial or industrial development, or anything else that offends their aesthetic preferences. These groups generally reflect liberal reformist views of upper-middle-class residents who are secure in their own jobs and own their own homes. Indeed, restrictions on new housing construction directly benefit them by increasing the value of existing property. Municipal government offers many tools to restrict growth—planning regulations, zoning laws, building permits, environmental regulations, developmental charges and restrictions, street and utility access, and so on. (For further discussion, see Chapter 13.) Often, environmental "growth-management" groups combine with neighborhood associations to oppose specific developmental projects.

Neighborhood Groups

Neighborhood associations frequently spring up when residents perceive a threat to their property values. They may be formed to oppose a rezoning that would allow new business and unwanted traffic in their neighborhood, or to oppose a new mobile home park, or to petition for stoplights or sidewalks or pothole repairs. Sometimes neighborhood associations will fight to keep out "undesirables," whose presence they feel will reduce property values. Neighborhood groups may protest the location of low-income housing, halfway houses for parolees, or mental health facilities. Neighborhood associations may also lead the fight *against* development, where residents will be displaced or their lifestyle threatened. They may oppose road building, urban renewal, or industrial and commercial development in or near their neighborhood. The NIMBY (not in my backyard) forces may be closely identified with "growth-management" efforts to slow or halt development. This posture places them in opposition to the local growth-oriented "power structure"—"the growth promoters" (businesses, banks, contractors, real estate developers).

Business Groups

Traditionally, *business interests* were the most influential of all groups in community politics. Many businesspeople or "economic notables" occupied an important role in the structure of community decision making or the "power structure." (See Chapter 13.) Business interests are also represented in local politics by organized groups: The chamber of commerce and the junior chamber of commerce, or "Jaycees," are found in nearly every community, representing the general views of business. The program of the chamber of commerce is likely to be more general than the interests of particular sectors of the business community—banks, utilities, contractors, real estate developers, downtown merchants, or bar and club owners. The chamber or the Jaycees can be expected to support lower taxes and more economy and efficiency in government operations. They are also active "promoters" of community growth and business activity. They can be expected to back civic improvements so long as it does not raise the tax rate too much. "Service to the community" creates a "favorable image," which the chamber and businesspeople are anxious to cultivate.

Generally, the active members of the chamber of commerce or the Jaycees are younger business owners in the community who are still on their way "up" in business. Owners of larger businesses, banks, utilities—the "big powers" in the community—are more likely to function informally in the community's power structure than to take an overt role in organized interest group activity.

The so-called service clubs—the Lions, Kiwanis, Rotarians, and others—are basically for businesspeople. Their interests are likely to be more social than political, but their service projects often involve them in political activity and their meetings provide an excellent opportunity for speechmaking by political candidates.

The businesses most active in community affairs are those most directly affected by policies of local government, such as department stores, banks, utilities, contractors, real estate developers, bar and club owners, and television and newspaper interests.

Banks

Banks often own, or hold the mortgages on, downtown business property. They have an interest in maintaining business, commercial, and industrial property values. Banks are also interested in the growth and prosperity of the city as a whole, particularly large business enterprises who are their primary customers. Banks are influential because they decide who is able to borrow money in a community and under what conditions. Banks are directly involved in local governments in financing municipal bond issues for public works, school buildings, and so on, and in pledging financial backing for urban renewal projects. Banks are also influential in land development, for they must provide the financial backing for real estate developers, contractors, businesses, and home buyers; hence they are interested in business regulation, taxation, zoning, and housing.

Contractors

Contractors are vitally interested in city government because the city has the power of inspection over all kinds of construction. Local governments enforce building, plumbing, electric, and other codes, which are of great interest to contractors. Some contractors, particularly road-grading and surfacing companies, depend on public contracts, and they are concerned with both city policy and the personnel who administer this policy. While municipal contracts are generally required by law to be given to the "low bidder" among "responsible" contractors, definitions about what is or is not a "low bid," and who is or who is not a "responsible" contractor, make it important for contractors to maintain close and friendly relationships with municipal officials. It is no accident that builders, contractors, and developers are a major source of campaign contributions for local office seekers.

Real Estate Developers

Real estate developers are particularly interested in planning, zoning, and subdivision control regulations and urban renewal programs. (These are discussed at length in Chapter 13.) Developers of residential, commercial, and industrial property must work closely with city government officials to coordinate the provision of public services—especially streets, sewage, water, and electricity. They must also satisfy city officials regarding planning and zoning regulations, building codes, fire and safety laws, and environmental regulations. Today, real estate developers must be highly skilled in governmental relations.

Newspapers, Television, and Radio

The media are an important force in community politics, especially newspapers, which can engage in more investigative reporting than television and radio. The influence of the press would be relatively minor if its opinions were limited to its editorial pages. The influence of the press arises from its power to decide what is "news," thereby focusing public attention on the events and issues that are of interest to the press. Newspaper writers must first decide what proportion of space in the paper will be devoted to local news in contrast to state, national, and international news. A big-city paper may give local news about the same amount of space that it gives to national or foreign news. Suburban or small-town papers, which operate within the circulation area of a large metropolitan daily, may give a greater proportion of the news space to local events than to national and international affairs. Crime and corruption in government are favorite targets for the press. Editors believe that civic crusades and the exposure of crime and corruption help sell newspapers. Moreover, many editors and writers believe they have a civic responsibility to use the power of the press to protect the public. (See "*Up Close*: Exposing Political Corruption.") In the absence of crime or corruption, newspapers may turn to crusades on behalf of civic improvements—like a city auditorium or cultural center.

The politics of newspapers can be understood in part by some insight into the economics of the newspaper business. Newspapers get two-thirds of their revenue from advertising. Over the years the newspapers' percentage of all advertising dollars has declined in the face of stiff competition from television and the Internet. Many big-city newspapers have either merged or gone out of business because of a lack of sufficient advertising revenue to offset increasing costs; it was not a lack of readers that brought about their collapse. Moreover, it is important to know that downtown department stores provide the largest source of advertising revenue. Big-city newspapers have been hurt by the flight of the middle class to the suburbs and the declining role of downtown department stores in retail sales in the metropolitan areas. In metropolitan affairs, one can expect big-city newspapers to support the position of downtown interests. This means support for urban renewal, mass transit, downtown parking, and other procentral-city policies in metropolitan affairs. On the other hand, suburban daily and weekly newspapers are supported by the advertising from suburban shopping centers, and they can be expected to take a pro-suburban position on metropolitan issues.

Newspapers are more influential in the absence of strong party organizations, which would compete with newspapers as channels of communication to the voters. Nonpartisanship, lengthy ballots, and numerous referenda all contribute to the influence of newspapers. Any situation that tends to obscure candidates or issues to the voter contributes to the power of newspapers, since the voter is obliged to rely upon them for information. Newspapers doubtlessly have more influence in local than in state or national politics because of (1) the relative importance in local politics of middle-class groups who read newspapers, (2) the relative obscurity of local politics to voters in their reliance upon newspapers for information about local affairs, and (3) the relative weakening of party affiliations in local politics.

But the role of local television news and talk radio should not be underestimated. (See Chapter 4.) Particularly in large metropolitan area markets, television and radio stations compete with each other for viewers and listeners. The most popular stations earn more advertising money. And nothing makes a better story to boost ratings than exposing some corrupt, inept, inefficient, or ridiculous action by a local public official.

The faith communities may become quite involved in local politics, particularly when a moral issue surfaces. In such situations, members of the clergy often testify before city councils, county commissions, or school boards. When they do, they get the attention of elected officials, who are well aware that persons who attend a religious service are more likely to turn out to vote. However, most local churches are careful *not* to tell their members which candidates to vote for, fearing loss of their tax-exempt status with the Internal Revenue Service.

Churches

Any listing of influential interest groups in local politics should include the community's churches and church-related organizations. Ministers, priests, rabbis, and leaders of religious lay groups are frequently participants in community decision making. Active church members feel less isolated from their community through involvement in social service-related activities.[88] The Catholic Church and its many lay organizations are vitally concerned with the operation of parochial schools. Protestant ministerial associations in large cities may be concerned with public health, welfare, housing, and other social problems. Ministers and church congregations in small towns may be concerned with the enforcement of blue laws, limitations on liquor sales, prohibitions on gambling, and other public policies relative to "vice" and public morality, ranging from free needle exchanges to gay rights ordinances. Morality politics is more prevalent at the local level than at the national or state levels.[89]

Municipal Employees

No one has a greater personal stake in municipal government than municipal employees—police, firefighters, street crews, transit employees, welfare workers, sanitation workers, clerks, secretaries. There are some 19 million state and local government employees in the nation (5 million state employees, and 14 million employees of cities, counties, school districts, and special districts). Their rate of voter turnout in municipal elections is very high, and they are politically influential in small towns and suburbs whether they are organized into unions or not.

Who Solves Community Problems Best?

Americans believe that solutions to community problems come from a *variety* of sources—government, organizations, and individual citizens. When asked to identify the best problem solvers in their own community, they point to local police departments, religious institutions, nonprofit organizations, and friends and neighbors, as well as local governments and school boards[90]:

- Fifty-eight percent rate local police departments as crucial or important to problem solving. While whites are more likely than nonwhites to view the police as playing a strong role in the solution of local problems, even among nonwhites the police ranked extremely high compared with other institutions.

- Fifty-six percent say that local churches, synagogues, and mosques are important or crucial to finding solutions. African Americans (38 percent) are more likely than whites (29 percent) to rank religious institutions as crucial to local problem solving.

- Fifty-three percent say that nonprofit organizations such as the Salvation Army, Habitat for Humanity, and Goodwill Industries are crucial or very important to the solution of community problems.

- More than 50 percent say that friends and neighbors are problem solvers in their community. This holds true across race and income levels and it is even more evident among those age 65 and older. Nearly two-thirds of the seniors believe friends and neighbors are important problem solvers.

- Other problem solvers that received high marks as being crucial or very important are parent–teacher organizations (47 percent), local government officials (43 percent), local foundations and United Ways (39 percent), neighborhood organizations (39 percent), school boards (38 percent), and local businesses (36 percent).

At the local level, people usually get involved in politics when something promises to directly affect them, often at the urging of friends and neighbors and groups to which they belong.

did **YOU** know?

Americans Serve Their Communities by Volunteering

More than 61 million volunteers dedicate over 8 billion hours of service in communities across the U.S. It is a measure of what is called a community's "*social capital*"—social connectedness or social networks. In the fifty largest metropolitan areas, volunteer rates ranged from 14.4 percent to 40.5 percent. Within metro areas, voluntarism rates are higher in the suburbs and rural areas than in the more populous urban core. Women volunteer more than men and middle-age persons more than younger or older generations. Volunteering is more prevalent in areas with high homeownership rates, higher educational levels, and more organized nonprofit organizations. It is lower in areas with long commuting times. Volunteering often gets one involved in local politics as well and can be a launching pad for running for county, city, or school board offices.

National Volunteer Trends

Category	National Average	
	Hours per Volunteer	Percent Who Volunteer
Area of Residence		
Total Area	50	28.1
Urban	51	23.7
Suburban	50	29.3
Gender		
Male	52	24.3
Female	50	31.6
Age		
16–24	39	23.4
25–34	37	24.7
35–44	48	33.3
45–54	52	32.2
55–64	60	29.3
65–74	96	27.5
75+	100	20.9

Volunteer Efforts: Type of Organization

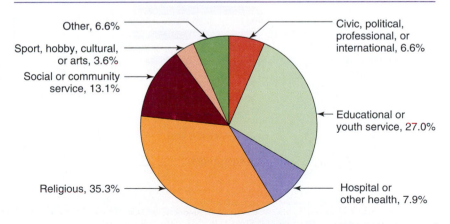

Other, 6.6%

Sport, hobby, cultural, or arts, 3.6%

Social or community service, 13.1%

Religious, 35.3%

Civic, political, professional, or international, 6.6%

Educational or youth service, 27.0%

Hospital or other health, 7.9%

(*continued*)

Volunteering: Metropolitan Areas

Rankings of Metro Area

1.	Minneapolis-St. Paul, MN
2.	Salt Lake City, UT
3.	Austin, TX
4.	Omaha, NE
5.	Seattle, WA
6.	Portland, OR
7.	Kansas City, MO
8.	Milwaukee, WI
9.	Charlotte, NC
10.	Tulsa, OK
11.	Cincinnati, OH
12.	Columbus, OH
13.	Pittsburgh, PA
14.	Bridgeport, CT
15.	Washington, DC
16.	Louisville, KY
17.	Denver, CO
18.	St. Louis, MO
19.	Nashville, TN
20.	Dallas, TX
20.	Oklahoma City, OK
22.	New Haven, CT
23.	Hartford, CT
23.	San Francisco, CA
25.	San Diego, CA
26.	Baltimore, MD
27.	Albuquerque, NM
28.	Indianapolis, IN
29.	Richmond, VA
30.	Boston, MA
30.	Cleveland, OH
32.	Chicago, IL
33.	San Jose, CA
34.	Detroit, MI
35.	San Antonio, TX
36.	Philadelphia, PA
37.	Sacramento, CA
38.	Atlanta, GA
39.	Houston, TX
39.	Tampa, FL
41.	Phoenix, AZ
42.	Honolulu, HI
42.	Providence, RI
44.	Los Angeles, CA
45.	Orlando, FL
46.	Riverside, CA
47.	Virginia Beach, VA
48.	New York, NY
49.	Miami, FL
50.	Las Vegas, NV

Note: Data are based on a three-year average from 2004, 2005, and 2006.
Source: Corporation for National Community Service. Volunteering in America: 2007 City Trends and Rankings. Washington, DC: CNCS, p. 13, 16. Available at http://www.nationalservice.gov/pdf/VIA_CITIES/VIA_cities_fullreport.pdf

Most of the nation's city managers are members of the International City/County Management Association (ICMA). Each year ICMA publishes the *Municipal Year Book*, the most comprehensive collection of information on American cities. Unfortunately, the *Municipal Year Book* is *not* on the ICMA Web site, but the site does provide directions to sources of information important to city managers. These include a series of books on how to manage various aspects of city government, from planning, personnel, and budgeting to waste disposal, environmental protection, and mass transit. The ICMA Web site at

www.icma.org

does offer information on local government management issues.

The U.S. Conference of Mayors exercises considerable influence in Washington. Its annual meeting regularly attracts hundreds of mayors as well as presidential candidates and other national figures seeking to use this popular platform to express their views. The U.S. Conference of Mayors represents mayors of cities of 30,000 or more people. Its announced purpose is to "aid in the development of effective national urban policy." It lobbies heavily in Washington on behalf of federal grant-in-aid programs to cities. Its Web site at

www.usmayors.org

includes the official policy positions of the organization on a wide variety of urban issues.

The National Civic League was formed more than a century ago to advance the municipal reform movement. Theodore Roosevelt was one of its founders. Today it continues to encourage city government reform. It is probably best known for its All American City Awards, which it presents annually to cities that it considers innovative and progressive, as well as "honest, efficient, and effective." Its Web site at

www.ncl.org

includes stories of how particular cities dealt effectively with problems ranging from race relations to economic development and quality of life.

CHAPTER TWELVE

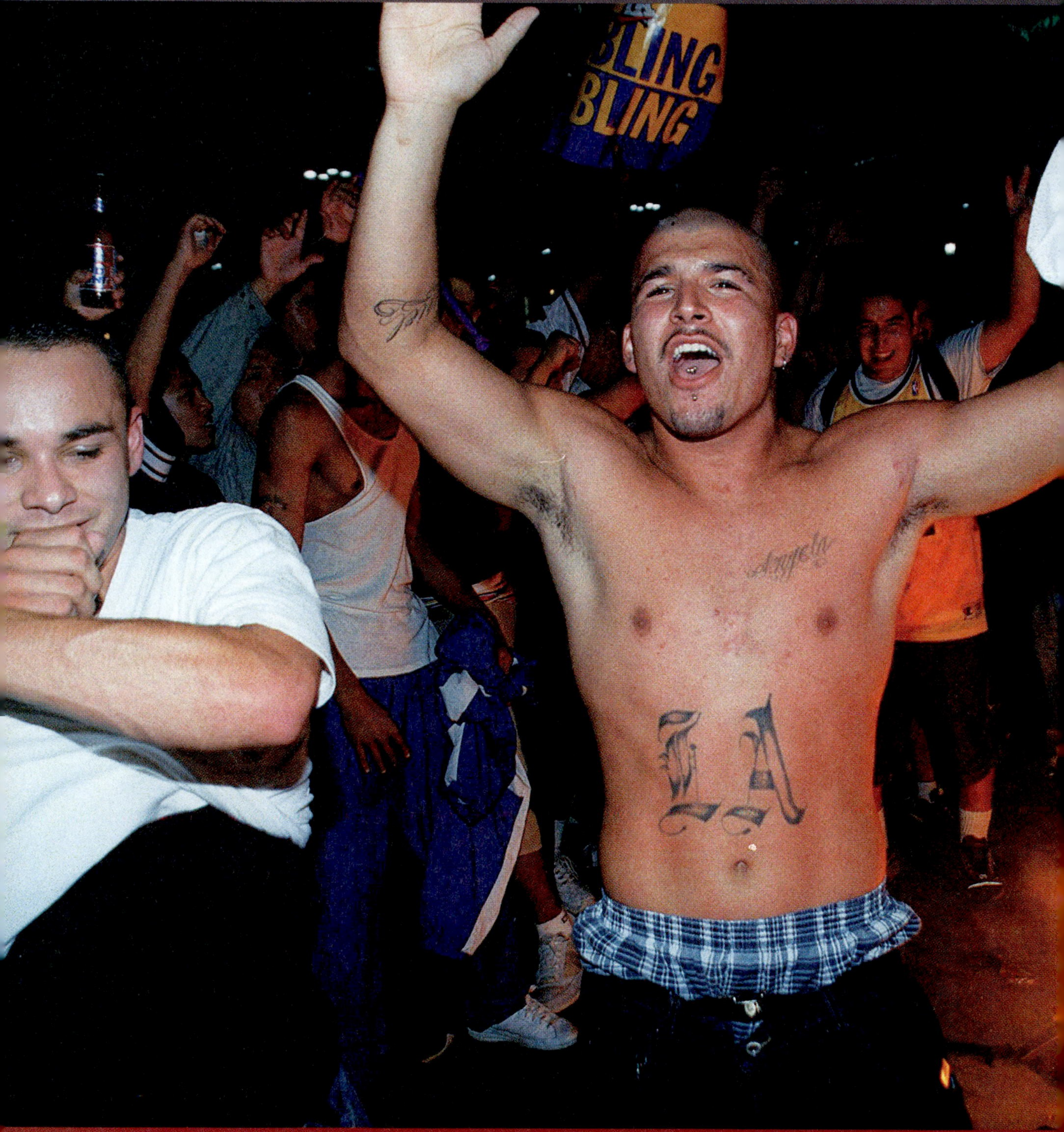

12

METROPOLITICS: CONFLICT IN THE METROPOLIS

QUESTIONS TO CONSIDER

Do you believe that suburban growth should be managed by government to prevent "sprawl"?
■ Yes   ■ No

Would a single metropolitan-wide government provide better and cheaper public services than the multiple governments currently functioning in most metropolitan areas?
■ Yes   ■ No

Do multiple governmental units in large metropolitan areas provide people with better residential choices in terms of taxes and services?
■ Yes   ■ No

Are special district governments the best way to provide such services as water supply and sewerage, fire protection, and mass transit, on a metropolitan-wide basis?
■ Yes   ■ No

THE METROPOLIS: SETTING FOR CONFLICT

Where will you live after you graduate? A big city? A suburb on the outskirts of a big city? A small town or some remote rural area? Will your choice of where to live be dictated by housing costs? Proximity to your job? The quality of local schools? Crime rates? Taxes? If faced with the choice of buying an affordable home on the outskirts of a large metropolitan area or living in an apartment or condo closer to where you work to reduce the long commute, which would you prefer? Are you moving to the Washington, DC, metropolitan area? If so, will you live in "the District"? In one of the northern Virginia suburbs like Arlington, Alexandria, Manassas, Leesburg, or Woodbridge? Or in a southern Maryland suburban community like Bethesda, Rockville, Beltsville, Columbia, or Frederick? (Democrats are more likely to choose Maryland; Republicans, Virginia!)

The Census Bureau divides the nation's metropolitan area geographies into two categories: metropolitan (urban) and micropolitan (suburban). (See Figure 12–1). One category represents the heavily-urbanized core city area; the other category, the smaller, more newly urbanized, more suburban-like areas beyond the core. Together, they encompass many cities and counties and contain 93 percent of the U.S. population. The other 7 percent live in rural areas. We are indeed a metropolitan nation.

A **"metropolitan statistical area"** (MSA) is a city of 50,000 or more people together with adjacent counties that have predominantly urban populations with close ties to the central city as measured by commuting patterns. A **micropolitan statistical area** (M-PSA) has a population cluster of at least 10,000 but less than 50,000, plus adjacent territory

FIGURE 12–1 Metropolitan Statistical Areas

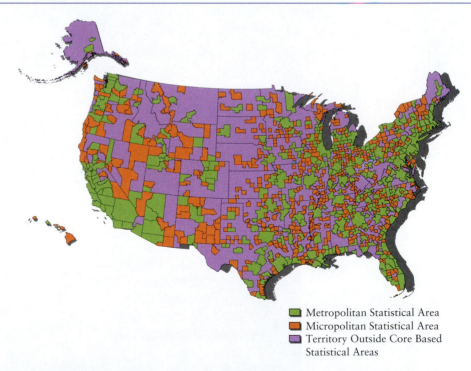

- Metropolitan Statistical Area
- Micropolitan Statistical Area
- Territory Outside Core Based Statistical Areas

Source: U.S. Census Bureau, http://www.census.gov/prod/2006pubs/07statab/app2.pdf, No. 439

that has a high degree of social and economic interconnectedness with the urban core or central city.

Some metropolitan areas adjoin each other, creating a continuous urban environment over an extended area. One such **"megalopolis"** is the New York–Northern New Jersey–Long Island area, encompassing parts of four states, fifteen MSAs, and over 21 million people. While hundreds of local governments partition these metropolitan areas, people travel over these municipal boundaries often several times a day. Media markets—television, radio, newspapers—extend throughout these metropolitan areas. Most businesses depend on metropolitan-wide markets for workers, suppliers, and customers. Cultural, restaurant, and entertainment centers serve people from throughout the metropolis.

The states have become "metropolitanized." Today all fifty states have more than half of their populations concentrated in MSAs and M-PSAs; in twenty-eight states, it is more than 90 percent. (See "*Rankings of the States:* Metropolitanization in the States.")

The very definition of metropolitan life involves *large numbers* of *different* types of people living *close together* who are socially and economically *dependent* upon one another.[1] *Numbers, density, heterogeneity,* and *interdependence* are said to be distinguishing characteristics of metropolitan life. It is not difficult to envision a metropolitan area as a large number of people living together; we can see these characteristics in metropolitan life from a map or an airplane window. However, it is more difficult to understand the heterogeneity and interdependence of people living in metropolitan areas.

Growth Engines of the U.S. Economy

America's metropolitan areas make up a huge part of the nation's economy. If treated as nations, U.S. metropolitan areas would make up forty-seven of the world's largest economies. In fact, if the nation's five largest metropolitan areas were treated as a single country, it would rank as the fourth largest economy in the world. In 2000 alone, U.S. metropolitan areas generated nearly 85 percent of the nation's employment, income, and production of goods and services (gross domestic product). The combined gross economic output of the ten largest metropolitan areas was $2.43 trillion—an amount greater than the combined economic output of thirty-one states.[2] Even the smaller metro areas contribute billions of dollars to the economy.

Heterogeneity

The modern economic system of the metropolis is based on a highly specialized and complex division of labor. Highly specialized jobs account for much of the heterogeneity in urban populations. Different jobs produce different levels of income, dress, and styles of living. People's jobs shape the way they look at the world and their evaluations of social and political events. In acquiring their jobs, people attain a certain level and type of education that also distinguish them from those in other jobs with different educational requirements. Metropolitan living concentrates people with all these different economic, educational, and occupational characteristics in a very few square miles. But America's metropolitan areas are as diverse as the nation itself. Some are magnets for the young, others for the old. Some are more "wired" than others. Do you like to go to live theater? Eat out? Travel? Buy electronics? Shop for clothes? Different metro areas rate better than others for these activities.

MEGALOPOLIS
Metropolitan areas that adjoin each other, creating a continuous urban environment over an extended area.

HETEROGENEITY
In metropolitan areas, differences among people in occupation, education, income, race, and ethnicity.

In fact, if the nation's five largest metropolitan areas were treated as a single country, it would rank as the fourth largest economy in the world.

America's metropolitan areas are as diverse as the nation itself.

Metropolitanization in the States

Metropolitan Population Percentage

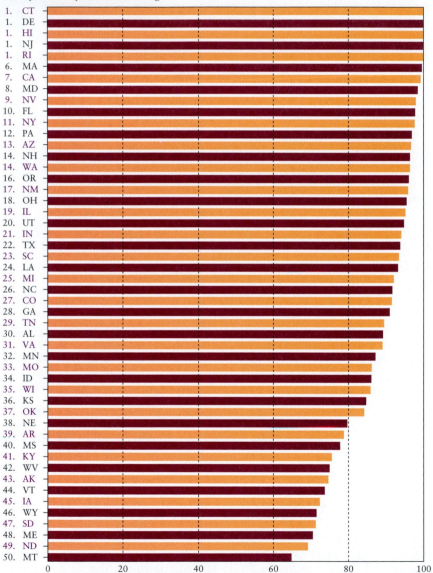

Rank	State
1.	CT
1.	DE
1.	HI
1.	NJ
1.	RI
6.	MA
7.	CA
8.	MD
9.	NV
10.	FL
11.	NY
12.	PA
13.	AZ
14.	NH
14.	WA
16.	OR
17.	NM
18.	OH
19.	IL
20.	UT
21.	IN
22.	TX
23.	SC
24.	LA
25.	MI
26.	NC
27.	CO
28.	GA
29.	TN
30.	AL
31.	VA
32.	MN
33.	MO
34.	ID
35.	WI
36.	KS
37.	OK
38.	NE
39.	AR
40.	MS
41.	KY
42.	WV
43.	AK
44.	VT
45.	IA
46.	WY
47.	SD
48.	ME
49.	ND
50.	MT

Note: Each metropolitan statistical area must have at least one urbanized area of 50,000 or more inhabitants. Each micropolitan statistical area must have at least one urban cluster of at least 10,000 but less than 50,000 population.

Source: U.S. Census Bureau, *Statistical Abstract of the United States 2007*, Table 28. Available at http://www.census.gov/prod/2006pubs/07statab/pop.pdf.

Note: Abstract includes both metropolitan and micropolitan areas.

Ethnic and Racial Diversity

Ethnic and racial diversity are also present. In the nineteenth and early twentieth centuries, opportunities for human betterment in the cities attracted immigrants from Ireland, Germany, Italy, Poland, and Russia, which is why some demographers have labeled these areas as "metro melting pots."[3] African Americans in search of opportunities migrated to cities from the rural South. Today America's cities attract waves of immigrants from Mexico and other Latin American countries, Asia and the Philippines, and Haiti and other less developed nations of the world. Newcomers to the metropolis bring with them different needs, attitudes, and ways of life. The "melting pot" tends to reduce some of this diversity over time, but the pot does not "melt" people immediately, and there always seem to be new arrivals.

Interdependence

Despite social and economic differences, urban dwellers are highly dependent upon one another in their daily activities. Suburbanites, for example, rely upon the central city for newspapers, entertainment, hospitalization, and a host of other modern needs. Many also rely upon the central city for employment opportunities. Conversely, the central city relies upon the suburbs to supply both employees and customers. This interdependence involves an intricate web of economic and social relationships, a high degree of communication, and a great deal of daily physical interchange among residents, groups, and firms in a metropolitan area.

Fragmented Government

However, another characteristic of metropolitan areas is "fragmented" government. Suburban development, spreading out from central cities, generally ignored governmental boundaries and engulfed counties, townships, towns, and smaller cities. Some metropolitan areas even spread across state lines, and four metropolitan areas of the United States—Detroit, San Diego, El Paso, and Laredo—adjoin urban territory in Canada and Mexico. This suburbanization has meant that hundreds of governments may be operating in a single metropolitan area. Thus, while metropolitan areas are characterized by social and economic interdependence, and consequently require coordinating mechanisms, metropolitan government is generally "fragmented" into many smaller jurisdictions, none of which is capable of governing the entire metropolitan area in a unified fashion.

Potential for Conflict

The metropolis presents a serious problem in *conflict* management. Because a metropolitan area consists of a large number of different kinds of people living closely together, the problem of regulating conflict and maintaining order assumes tremendous proportions. Persons with different occupations, incomes, and ethnic ties are known to have different views on public issues. People

It is not hard to imagine why residents of poor neighborhoods surrounding downtowns with shiny skyscrapers may view life as a conflict between the "haves" and the "have nots."

FRAGMENTED GOVERNMENT

Multiple governmental jurisdictions, including cities, townships, school districts, and special districts, all operating in a single metropolitan area.

well equipped to compete for jobs and income in a free market view government housing and welfare programs differently than others not so well equipped. People at the bottom of the social ladder look at police—indeed, governmental authority in general—differently from the way those on higher rungs do. Homeowners and renters usually look at property taxation in a different light. Families with children and those without children have different ideas about school systems. And so it goes. Differences in the way people make their living, in their income levels, in the color of their skin, in the way they worship, in their style of living—all are at the roots of political life in a metropolis.

CITIES VERSUS SUBURBS

Suburbs account for most of the growth of America's metropolitan areas. New suburbs, most built since the 1970s on the outer fringes of metropolitan areas, are capturing increasing shares of both population and employment growth. Many central cities, especially in the Northeast and Midwest, actually lost people and jobs over the last two decades. These were mostly older industrial cities. These cities have had trouble transitioning from a manufacturing-based to a more knowledge-based economy.[4]

Some central cities are showing signs of a second life. New waves of immigrants seeking welcoming populations; an aging Boomer population that prefers to be near top-notch hospitals and health care; young people delaying marriage, having fewer children, and choosing to live closer to colleges and universities, and environmentalists concerned about auto emission pollutants—all are trends that offer some promise of slowly revitalizing central cities.

Suburban growth patterns vary across the nation. While most suburbs (73 percent) have grown in size over the past few decades, some have not.[5] Declining suburbs are predominantly located in slow-growing metropolitan areas in the Northeast and Midwest; fast-growing suburbs are located in the South and West.

Suburbanization

America's suburbanization was a product of technological advances in transportation—the automobile and the expressway.[6] In the nineteenth century an industrial worker had to live within walking distance of his or her place of employment. This meant that the nineteenth-century American city crowded large masses of people into relatively small central areas, often in tenement houses and other high-density neighborhoods. However, modern modes of transportation—first the streetcar, then the private automobile, and then the expressway—eliminated the necessity of workers living close to their jobs. The same technology that led to the suburbanization of residences also influenced commercial and industrial location. Originally industry was tied to waterways or railroads for access to suppliers and markets. This dependence was reduced by the development of motor truck transportation, the highway system, and the greater mobility of the labor force. Many industries located in the suburbs, particularly light industries, which did not require extremely heavy bulk shipments that could only be handled by rail or water. When industry and people moved to the suburbs, commerce followed. Giant suburban shopping centers sprang up to compete with downtown stores. Thus, metropolitan areas become decentralized over time as people, business, and industry spread themselves over the suburban landscape. Today, 35 percent of all jobs in metropolitan areas are in places more than 10 miles away from the central business district (CBD), 43 percent are between 3 and 10 miles away. Just 22 percent are located within 3 miles from the CBD.[7] (Some refer to this as **"job sprawl."**)

First Suburbs

One-fifth of Americans live in first suburbs that are neither fully urban nor completely suburban. They are usually in the first ring of suburbs that sprung up around central cities right after World War II. They were the nation's first "bedroom communities." But today, they face a unique set of challenges: "concentrations of elderly and immigrant populations as well as outmoded housing and commercial buildings."[8] At the same time, they are home to some of the nation's wealthiest and most highly educated residents. First suburbs can be places were income, education, and racial divides are the widest in a metropolitan area.

The New "Boomburbs"

The newest form of suburb has been labeled a "boomburb."[9] A boomburb is a city with more than 100,000 residents located within a metropolitan area but which is *not* the central city and which has maintained a double-digit growth rate in recent years. Most are located in the Southwest. The Phoenix metropolitan area, for example, has seven boomburbs. Boomburbs typically contain a more economically and racially diverse population than smaller suburbs. While most are affluent, virtually all have low-income neighborhoods. But boomburbs are not just residential communities. They have vibrant commercial sectors as well. "These drive-by cities of highways, office parks, and shopping malls are much more horizontally built and less-pedestrian friendly than older suburbs."[10] At the same time, many are facing buildout by 2020 and competition from their "exurbs"—new suburbs that have sprung up beyond the boomburbs.

City–Suburban Differences

Social, economic, and racial conflict can be observed at all levels of government, but at the metropolitan level, it is most obvious in the conflict that occurs between central cities and their suburbs. At the heart of city–suburban conflict are the differences in the kinds of people who live in cities and suburbs. City–suburban conflict is at the heart of the "metropolitan problem"; that is, the failure to achieve metropolitan-wide consensus on public policy questions affecting the entire metropolitan area and the failure to develop metropolitan government institutions. Social, economic, and racial differences between cities and suburbs are major obstacles to the development of metropolitan-wide policies and government institutions.[11]

Of course, generalizing about cities and suburbs is a dangerous thing. Although we will talk about some common characteristics of cities and suburbs, students are cautioned that individual suburbs may be quite different from one another. There are, for example, industrial suburbs, residential suburbs, black suburbs, wealthy suburbs, and working-class suburbs.[12] There are declining "at-risk" first suburbs close in proximity to old central cities and fast-growing suburbs ("boomburbs" and "exurbs" or "edge cities") located at the outer extremities of metropolitan areas. Some suburbs (usually the older or "first suburbs") look more like cities in their social and economic composition than others. Nevertheless, a clear perception of the social distance between cities and suburbs is important in understanding metropolitan politics, particularly why it is so hard to build city–suburban and regional coalitions.[13]

Social, economic, and racial differences between cities and suburbs are major obstacles to the development of metropolitan-wide policies and government institutions.

Life for a child growing up in an inner city is drastically different from that for children raised in the suburbs. The "social distance" between central-city and suburban residents is generally greater in larger metropolitan areas.

Social Class

Cities and suburbs can be differentiated, first of all, on the basis of social class—the occupation, income, and educational levels of their population. The cultured class of an earlier era established "country" living as a symbol of affluence; widespread prosperity has made possible mass imitation of the aristocracy by an upwardly mobile middle-class population. The suburbs house greater proportions of white-collar employees, college graduates, and affluent families than any other sector in American life.

Status differentials in favor of suburbs are more pronounced in larger metropolitan areas, although in some of the largest areas in California, Texas, and New York, class differences are beginning to shrink.[14] (See Table 12–1.) Status differentials in smaller metropolitan areas are not as great as in larger areas, and sometimes even favor the city rather than the suburbs. However, on the whole, suburban living still reflects middle-class values.

Familism

Cities and suburbs can also be differentiated on the basis of "familism," or lifestyle. Perhaps the most frequently mentioned reason for a move to the suburbs is "the kids." Family after family list consideration of their young as the primary cause for their move to suburbia. A familistic, or child-centered, lifestyle can be identified in certain social statistics. A larger percentage of suburban families have children under age eighteen than city families. In addition, the single-family, owner-occupied, freestanding

Central-city residents are more likely to rent apartments rather than to own their own home like suburbanites. When rents are raised rather sharply, affordable housing and tenants' rights protests increase.

Rank	Metro Area	Lower Income	Middle Income	Higher Income
	TABLE 12–1 Middle Income Neighborhoods Are Shrinking in Some Large Metropolitan Areas			
1	Scranton–Wilkes-Barre–Hazelton, PA	13.2	74.2	12.6
2	Nassau–Suffolk, NY	15.1	64.7	20.2
3	Grand Rapids–Muskegon–Holland, MI	23.7	59.4	17.0
4	Tacoma, WA	21.9	58.1	20.0
5	Harrisburg–Lebanon–Carlisle, PA	24.6	57.2	18.1
6	Allentown–Bethlehem–Easton, PA	23.9	55.1	21.0
7	Sarasota–Bradenton, FL	22.4	54.5	23.1
8	Greenville–Spartanburg–Anderson, SC	26.7	54.4	18.9
9	Wilmington–Newark, DE-MD	24.5	54.0	21.6
10	Seattle–Bellevue–Everett, WA	22.6	53.9	23.5
91	Tucson, AZ	34.9	32.8	32.3
92	Orange County, CA	30.9	32.7	36.4
93	El Paso, TX	38.9	32.5	28.6
94	Bakersfield, CA	33.6	32.1	34.3
95	Dallas, TX	39.2	31.3	29.5
96	Newark, NJ	39.5	30.4	30.2
97	Houston, TX	39.7	30.0	30.3
98	Memphis, TN-AR-MS	41.8	29.7	28.5
99	New York, NY	34.5	29.6	35.9
100	Los Angeles–Long Beach, CA	37.3	28.3	34.4

Note: Low-income neighborhoods have median family incomes under 80 percent of metropolitan area median family income. The range for middle-income neighborhoods is 80 to 120 percent, and 120 percent and above for high-income neighborhoods. Data are for 2000.
Source: Jason C. Booza, Jackie Cutsinger, and George Galster, "Where Did They Go? The Decline of Middle-Income Neighborhoods in Metropolitan America" (Washington, DC: The Brookings Institution, June 2006).

home has become symbolic of familistic living in an affluent society. In central cities there are proportionately fewer children and more rental apartment living.

Race

Perhaps the most important difference between cities and suburbs is their contrasting *racial composition*. Overall, America's surburban population is only about 10 percent nonwhite, while the nation's overall central city population is over 20 percent nonwhite. However suburbia has become more racially and ethnically diverse over the past decade. African Americans, Hispanics, and Asians are moving to the suburbs at a somewhat faster pace than whites.[15] Today more than one in four suburban households are minority[16] and some of the nation's richest neighborhoods now have substantial proportions of foreign-born and Asian residents.[17] The suburbs of virtually all metropolitan areas are more integrated today than a decade ago. "Melting pot metros"[18] (e.g., Los Angeles, Chicago, Washington, DC, Houston, and New York) have the largest minority suburban populations. In these areas, there is less dissimilarity between the racial composition of the city and the suburbs.

Poverty

Low-income, low-education, unskilled populations are concentrated in the central cities. Social problems are also concentrated in central cities—racial imbalance, crime, violence, inadequate education, poverty, slum housing, and so on. The poverty rate among central city residents is nearly twice that of suburbanites. By moving to the suburbs, middle-class families not only separate themselves from minorities and poor people but also place physical distance between themselves and the major social problems that confront metropolitan areas. This permits them, for the time being, to avoid the problems associated with poverty, although in "first suburbs" there are growing numbers of poor neighborhoods.

Parties

In general, large cities are much more Democratic than their suburban rings, which generally produce more Republican votes. While temporary shifts may occur from one election to another, this general pattern of Democratic cities and Republican suburbs is likely to prevail for the near future. As long as the national Democratic party represents central-city, low-income, ethnic, labor, and racial constituencies, and the Republican party represents middle-class, educated, managerial, white, Anglo-Saxon Protestant constituencies, the political coloration of cities and suburbs is likely to be different. Of course, the pattern of Democratic central cities and Republican suburbs is less evident in the "melting pot metros" where the suburbs house substantial minority populations.

Costs of Government

Large central cities show substantially higher operating expenditures per capita than their suburbs. The maintenance of a large physical plant for the entire metropolitan area requires city residents to make higher per capita operating expenditures than those required for suburbanites. In addition, many living costs in suburban communities are shifted from public to private spending (private septic tanks instead of public sewers, private instead of public recreation, and so on). Differences in the public services provided by city and suburban governments are greatest in the area of police protection, recreation, and health. This reflects a concentration in the city of people who are likely to require these public services, in contrast to the suburbs.

Taxes

The tax bill in suburbs is only slightly lower than in central cities. Taxes had much to do with the migration of the "pioneer" suburbanites, those who moved to the suburbs in the 1930s and 1940s. At that time, suburban living offered a significant savings in property taxation over what were thought to be heavy city taxes. However, the tax advantage of the suburbs turned out partly to be a "self-denying prophecy": The more people who fled to the suburbs to avoid heavy taxes, the greater the demand for public services in these new suburban communities, and the higher suburban taxes became to meet these new demands. Yet the tax bill in most suburbs remains lower than in central cities. The difference in tax burden between city and suburb would be even greater if suburbanites did not choose to spend more per pupil in education than city residents, which produces higher school taxes in the suburbs. The suburbs also manage to limit their indebtedness more than cities, and most of the indebtedness incurred by the suburbs is for school rather than municipal purposes.

Exceptions

Finally, it should be noted that differences between cities and suburbs in smaller metropolitan areas do not appear to be as great as differences between cities and suburbs in larger metropolitan areas. In fact, all these generalizations about cities and suburbs are, indeed, generalizations. Individual cities and suburbs can be found that do not conform to these national patterns.

Is Bad News Coverage the Problem?

Some urban scholars have come to the conclusion that the major media are at least partially to blame for reinforcing overly harsh and negative stereotypes of life in metropolitan America:

> The images from the nightly news, newsweeklies, and daily newspapers are an unrelenting story of social pathology—mounting crime, gangs, drug wars, racial tension, homelessness, teenage pregnancy, AIDS, inadequate schools, and slum housing. . . . Government programs are typically covered as well-intentioned but misguided, plagued by mismanagement, inefficiency, and, in some cases, corruption. . . . More important, the drumbeat of negativism has its political consequences. Many Americans have concluded that problems such as poverty and crime may be intractable.[19]

Others see the media as essential to the rebirth of urban areas—as necessary vehicles to promote economic development, civic pride, and cooperation.

SUBURBAN "SPRAWL"

Suburban sprawl is often cited as the root cause of social, economic, and governmental problems in the nation's metropolitan areas. **New urbanists**, who favor more compact, livable communities, are disdainful of suburbs, which they describe as places "where the internal-combustion engine is king and the garage its castle, is seen by many land planners as a gas-wasting, fume-choked mess where the desolation is broken only by patches of high-maintenance grass and ornamental plants."[20] Sprawl—the outward extension of new low-density residential and commercial development from the core city—is seen by "smart growth" proponents as underlying many of the problems of inner-city life:

> Central cities and older inter-ring suburbs have been left behind. They have lost millions of residents, particularly middle-class families who were the economic and social backbone of sustainable communities. Consequently these once-proud places now harbor higher and higher concentrations of the poor, particularly the minority poor, without the fiscal capacity to grapple with the consequences: joblessness, family fragmentation, failing schools, and deteriorating commercial districts.[21]

But sprawl is also seen as increasingly problematic for suburban residents themselves:

> Suburban sprawl is eating our open spaces, creating mind-boggling traffic jams, bestowing on us endless strip malls and housing developments, and consuming an ever-increasing share of our resources.[22]

Identifying Suburban Sprawl

It is argued that *not* all suburbanization can be castigated as sprawl. Rather, unwanted sprawl can be identified by the following characteristics:

- Unlimited outward extension of new development
- Low-density residential and commercial settlements
- Leapfrog development jumping out beyond established settlements
- Fragmentation of powers over land use among many small localities

- Dominance of transportation by private automobiles
- Widespread development of commercial strips
- Great fiscal disparities among localities
- Reliance mainly on trickle-down to provide housing to low-income households.[23]

Regardless of whether sprawl is wanted or unwanted, what we're seeing now is the urbanization of suburbia as the burbs continue to grow.

The Causes of Sprawl

Suburban sprawl actually occurs because it is the preferred lifestyle of most Americans. Critics of sprawl—reformers, city planners, environmentalists—are reluctant to recognize the popular appeal of single-family homes on large lots with lawns, shrubs, and trees; open spaces for recreation; and quiet residential streets. Commercial businesses—supermarkets, shopping centers, malls—must follow their customers to the suburbs. And increasingly, industries, particularly financial, insurance, and other service companies, together with high-tech firms, want to be located nearer to the homes of their middle-class employees and to enjoy pleasant working surroundings. More commuting now takes place from suburb to suburb than from suburb to central city.

It is true, of course, that government policies have facilitated suburban sprawl. Suburbanization was accelerated after the federal Interstate and Defense Highway Act of 1955 provided the financial support for the interstate "I Highway" system (see "Transportation Policy" in Chapter 13). Federal housing insurance—FHA (Federal Housing Administration) and VA (Veterans Administration) mortgages—enabled millions of American families to fulfill their dream of owning their own suburban home. Even the deductibility of home mortgage interest payments from federal income taxation is cited as a contributor to suburbanization.

Open land is easier and cheaper to build upon than downtown areas that must first be cleared of older buildings. Federal aid has long been available to city governments to assist in the redevelopment of blighted areas (see "Community Development and Revitalization Policy" in Chapter 13). But city bureaucracies have been slow and cumbersome in the implementation of urban redevelopment. City regulatory agencies frequently make the costs of complying with building codes, zoning regulations, and planning and environmental controls so high that builders and developers cannot produce affordable homes for middle-class residents, let alone the poor, in downtown areas. Redevelopment plans for these areas often favor commercial or high-income residential projects that promise to both beautify the city and add to its taxable property value. Indeed, "**gentrification**" of downtown residential areas—attracting upper-class residents and trendy high-priced restaurants and boutiques—is often the deliberate design. In such areas, proponents of new urbanism strongly favor "**walkable urbanism**"—an approach to development that features pedestrian-oriented, mixed-use, and mixed-income areas within the same neighborhood. Finally, municipal governments in the suburbs contribute to sprawl when they themselves restrict growth, causing development to "leapfrog" to areas still farther from the central city . . . "the exurbs." Suburban residents use the tools of municipal government to exclude low-income housing and other "undesirable" development (see Chapter 13).

Regardless of whether sprawl is wanted or unwanted, what we're seeing now is the urbanization of suburbia as the burbs continue to grow.

GENTRIFI-CATION

The movement of upper-class residents and trendy high-priced restaurants and boutiques back to downtown locations.

WALKABLE URBANISM

An approach to development that features pedestrian-oriented, mixed-use, and mixed-income areas within the same neighborhood.

Conflict over Sprawl

Urban planners, environmentalists, "growth management," and "smart growth" advocates argue that sprawl increases the costs of highway building, water and sewer services, school busing, and other public infrastructure that must be extended over a wider area to accommodate low-density development. "Compactness" is said to equal "efficiency." But the evidence to support this argument is scanty; city governments actually tax and spend more per resident than suburban governments. Only public school costs are higher in suburbs, a fact that probably reflects residents' desire for better schools rather than inefficiency.

Environmentalists argue that sprawl devours green spaces, that increased automobile commuting fouls the air, that paving over land adds to global warming, and that precious farmland is being lost. Yet the automobile remains the near universal choice of Americans for transportation because of the freedom and flexibility it provides. Despite billions of dollars in federal, state, and local government taxpayer subsidies to mass transit (see "Transportation Policy" in Chapter 13), transit use remains at historical lows. And land is no longer the key factor in food production; each year American farmers grow more crops using less land.

But serious questions have been raised about government efforts to contain sprawl. First, land is cheaper and housing more affordable further away from the central city. Forcing more compact development in metropolitan areas may have negative impacts for low-income and minority populations. Second, higher population and housing densities (less sprawl) reduce the amount of park and recreational land, increase traffic congestion, and worsen air pollution in core cities. Finally, antisprawl efforts come "perilously close to a campaign against the American Dream"—living in a single-family home with a yard and play area in a quiet community.[24]

CONSOLIDATION OR FRAGMENTATION?

The brawl over sprawl has renewed the debate on how a metropolitan area can be governed most efficiently and effectively. Is it best to govern the area as a *regional* entity by centralizing or consolidating the common activities of existing local governments (**regionalism**)? Or is it better to continue governing via the existing decentralized and fragmented system of competing local governments (**localism**)? There are good arguments for each approach.[25] (See Table 12–2 for a list of the various types of approaches.)

THE CASE FOR METROPOLITAN CONSOLIDATION

"**Fragmented**" **government**—that is, the proliferation of governments in metropolitan areas and the lack of coordination of public programs—adds to the metropolitan problem. The objective of the metropolitan reform movement of the last forty years has been to reorganize, consolidate, and enlarge government jurisdictions. The goal is to rid metropolitan areas of "ineffective multiple local jurisdictions" and "governments that

REGIONALISM

Centralizing or combining activities of local governments in a metropolitan area; consolidation.

LOCALISM

Allowing individual local governments to provide services within their own communities; fragmentation.

FRAGMENTED GOVERNMENT

The large number of local governments existing within a metropolitan area.

FUNCTIONAL CONSOLIDATION

Several local governments jointly provide a service, such as emergency management.

do not coincide with the boundaries of the metropolis."[26] Some regionalists favor consolidating county and municipal *governments* but others propose combining certain *services* currently delivered independently by each local government. The latter approach is known as "**functional consolidation.**"

Public Services

Many advantages are claimed for metropolitan governmental reorganization. First, the reorganization and consolidation of metropolitan governments is expected to bring about improved public services as a result of centralization. Consolidation of governments is expected to achieve many economies of large-scale operations and enable government to provide specialized public services, which "fragmented" units of government cannot provide. For example, larger water treatment plant facilities can deliver water at lower per gallon costs, and larger sewage disposal plants can handle sewage at a lower per gallon cost of disposal.[27]

The problem with this argument is that most studies show that larger municipal governments are *un*economic and fail to produce improved services. Only in very small cities (with populations under 25,000) can economies of scale be achieved by enlarging the scope of government. In cities of over 250,000, further increases in size appear to produce *dis*economies of scale and lower levels of public service per person.

TABLE 12–2 Approaches to Solving Problems in Metropolitan Areas		
	Government Structure	**Governance**
Regionalism and Cooperative Responses (Consolidated Approach)	• Annexation and mergers • City–county consolidation • Two-tier metropolitan government • Regional tax sharing • Multipurpose metropolitan districts • Regional coordinating agencies • Federal and state grants and policies encouraging regionalism	• Urban county • Consolidation of functions • Regional governance processes
Autonomy and Independent Responses (Fragmented Approach)	• Suburban development • Easy incorporation laws • Addition of different forms of general-purpose government	• Single-purpose districts • Interlocal agreements • Privatization • Federal and state grants and policies supporting fragmentation • Regional councils with no authority • Neighborhood government in central cities

Coordination

Second, it is argued that metropolitan consolidation will provide the necessary *coordination of public services* for the metropolis. Study after study report that crime, fire, traffic congestion, air pollution, water pollution, homeland security, and so on do not respect municipal boundary lines. The transportation problem is the most common example of a coordination problem. Traffic experts have pleaded for the development of a balanced transportation system in which mass transit carries many of the passengers currently traveling in private automobiles. Yet mass transit requires decisive public action by the entire metropolitan area. Certainly, the city government is in a poor position to provide mass transit by itself without the support of the suburbanites. In the post-9/11 and post-Katrina eras, studies have shown the importance of coordination among first responders of all local governments. Federal funding formulas have promoted metropolitan-wide (regional) approaches to improve coordination.

Equality

The third major argument for metropolitan consolidation stresses the need to eliminate *inequalities in financial burdens* throughout the metropolitan area. Suburbanites who escaped many city taxes continue to add to the cities' traffic and parking problems, use city streets and parks, find employment in the cities, use city hospitals and cultural facilities, and so on. By concentrating the poor, uneducated, unskilled minorities in central cities, we also saddle central cities with costly problems of public health and welfare, crime control, fire protection, slum clearance, and the like—all the social problems that are associated with poverty and discrimination. We concentrate these costly problems in cities at the same time that middle-class tax-paying individuals, tax-paying commercial enterprises, and tax-paying industries are moving into the suburbs. Thus, metropolitan-government fragmentation often succeeds in segregating financial needs from resources. The result is serious financial difficulty for many central cities.

Responsibility

It is also argued that metropolitan government will *clearly establish responsibility for metropolitan-wide policy.* One of the consequences of "fragmented" government is the scattering of public authority and the decentralization of policymaking in the metropolis. This proliferation in the number of autonomous governmental units reduces the probability of developing a consensus on metropolitan policy. Each autonomous unit exercises a veto power over metropolitan policy within its jurisdiction; it is often impossible to secure the unanimity required to achieve metropolitan consensus on any metropolitan-wide problem. An opponent of any particular solution need only find, among the countless independent governmental bodies whose consent is required, one that can be induced to withhold its consent in order to obstruct action. The dispersion of power among a large number of governmental units makes it possible for each of them to reach decisions without concern for the possible spillover effects, which may be harmful to other governments or residents of the metropolis. Finally, citizens rarely know who to hold accountable for inaction or obstruction when so many local governments are involved.

DE FACTO SEGREGATION Concentration of radical minorities in an area as a result of demographics or economics, not by law.

The dispersion of power among a large number of governmental units makes it possible for each of them to reach decisions without concern for the possible spillover effects, which may be harmful to other governments or residents of the metropolis.

THE CASE FOR "FRAGMENTED" GOVERNMENT

Suburb "bashing" is a common theme among central-city politicians, city newspaper columnists, and many reform minded scholars who would prefer centralized metropolitan government.[28] But the suburbs house well over half of the nation's population, and it is important to try to understand why so many suburbanites prefer "fragmented" government. Many citizens do not look upon the "optimum development of the metropolitan region" as a particularly compelling goal. Rather, there are a variety of social, political, and psychological values at stake in maintaining the existing "fragmented" system of local government.

Identity

The existence of separate and independent local governments for suburbs plays a vital role in developing and maintaining a sense of community *identity*. Suburbanites identify their residential community by reference to the local political unit. They do not think of themselves as residents of the "New York metropolitan region," but rather as residents of Scarsdale or Mineola. Even the existence of community problems, the existence of a governmental forum for their resolution, and the necessity to elect local officials heighten community involvement and identity. The suburban community, with a government small in scale and close to home, represents a partial escape from the anonymity of mass urban culture. The institutional apparatus of government helps the suburban community to differentiate itself from the "urban mass" by legislating differences in the size and design of buildings, neighborhood and subdivision plans, school policies, types and quality of public services, and tax expenditure levels.

Access

The political advantages of a fragmented suburbia cannot easily be dismissed. The existence of many local governments provides *additional forums* for the airing of public grievances. People feel better when they can publicly voice their complaints against governments, regardless of the eventual outcome of their grievance. The additional points of access, pressure, and control provided by a decentralized system of local government give added assurance that political demands will be heard and perhaps even acted upon. Opportunities for individual participation in the making of public policy are expanded in a decentralized governmental system.

Effectiveness

Maintaining the suburb as an independent political community provides the individual with a sense of *personal effectiveness* in public affairs. The individual can feel a greater sense of manageability over the affairs of a small community. A smaller community helps relieve feelings of frustration and apathy, which people often feel in their relations with larger bureaucracies. Suburbanites feel that their votes, their opinions, and their political activities count for more in a small community where they are more likely to know their local officials.[29] They cling to the idea of grassroots democracy in an organizational society.

Influence

Fragmented government clearly offers a larger number of groups the opportunity to *exercise influence* over government policy. Groups that would be minorities in the metropolitan area as a whole can avail themselves of government position and enact diverse public policies. This applies to blacks in the central city as well as to whites in the suburbs. Fragmented government creates within the metropolitan area a wide range of government policies. Communities that prefer, for example, higher standards in their school system at higher costs have the opportunity to implement this preference. Communities that prefer higher levels of public service or one set of services over another or stricter enforcement of particular standards can achieve their goals under a decentralized governmental system. Communities that wish to get along with reduced public services in order to maximize funds available for private spending may do so.

Schools

Racial imbalance and the plight of central-city schools are important forces in maintaining the political autonomy of suburban school systems in the nation's large metropolitan areas. Many suburbanites, whites and minorities alike, left the central city to find "a better place to raise the kids," and this means, among other things, better schools. As we have already observed, suburbs generally spend more on the education of each child than central cities. Moreover, the increasing concentration of minorities and newly arrived immigrants in central cities has resulted in racial imbalance in center-city schools. Efforts to end **de facto segregation** within the cities frequently involve busing school children into and out of ghetto schools in order to achieve racial balance. In Chapter 15 we will discuss de facto segregation in greater detail. However, it is important to note here that independent suburban school districts are viewed by many suburbanites as protection against the possibility that their children might be bused to inner-city schools. Autonomous suburban school districts lie outside the jurisdiction of city officials. While it is possible that federal courts may some day order suburban school districts to cooperate with cities in achieving racial balance in schools, the political independence of suburban schools helps to ensure that their children will not be used to achieve racial balance in city schools.

METROPOLITAN GOVERNMENT AS MARKETPLACE

Fragmented metropolitan government means many different mixes of municipal services, public schools, and tax levels in the same metropolitan area. So why can't people "shop around" among local communities and move into the community where the mix of services, schools, and taxes best suits their individual preferences?

The Tiebout Model

Economist Charles Tiebout argues that the existence of many local governments in the same area, all offering "public goods" (public schools, police and fire protection, water and sewer, refuse collection, streets and sidewalks) and various "prices" (taxes), provides a competitive and efficient government marketplace.[30] Families can choose for themselves what public goods they want at what price by simply moving to the community that best approximates their own preferences. Both families and businesses can

An economic theory that asserts that families and businesses in metropolitan areas can maximize their preferences for services and taxes by choosing locations among multiple local governments.

DE FACTO SEGREGATION
Concentration of racial minorities in an area as a result of demographics or economics, not by law.

The existence of many local governments in the same area, all offering "public goods" and various "prices" (taxes), provides a competitive and efficient government marketplace.

"vote with their feet" for their preferred "bundle" of municipal services and taxes. Local governments must compete for residents and businesses by offering high-quality public services at the lowest possible tax rates. This encourages efficiency in local government.

Mobility?

The Tiebout model of efficient local government assumes that metropolitan residents have a high degree of *mobility*; that is, they can move anywhere in the metropolitan area anytime they wish. The major criticism of this model is that many metropolitan residents do not enjoy unlimited mobility. The poor are limited by meager financial resources from "shopping" for the best governmental services. And minorities often confront barriers to residential mobility regardless of their economic resources.

Equity?

Moreover, the Tiebout model in its original formulation ignores the interdependence of the metropolis. Many public services are metropolitan-wide in scope—urban expressways, mass transit, clean air and water, public health and hospitals, homeland security, for example. These services cannot be provided by small local governments. Suburbanites use public facilities and services of cities when they work in the city or go to the city for entertainment. If they do not share in the costs of these services and facilities, they become **"free riders,"** unfairly benefiting from services paid for by others. The major social problems of the city—poverty, racial tension, poor housing, crime and delinquency—are really problems of the entire metropolis.[31]

Satisfaction?

The Tiebout model is correct in asserting that there is a great variety of lifestyles, housing types, governmental services, and costs *within* large metropolitan areas, and that most families take this into account when choosing a place of residence. And judging by the subjective evaluations of residents, many different types of neighborhoods are judged satisfactory by the people living in them. Quality-of-life studies usually ask respondents how "satisfied" they are with their neighborhoods. These studies reveal that people living in *all* types of neighborhoods express satisfaction with them. Indeed, even lower-income people living in substandard housing or areas considered slums by outsiders report being satisfied. (However, attachment to friends and relatives is a major source of their satisfaction, rather than governmental services.[32]) The fact that residents of many different kinds of communities express satisfaction with them lends implicit support to the Tiebout model. There is also evidence that business locational decisions within the metropolis are influenced by the "bundle" of governmental services and taxes offered by local governments.[33]

MANAGING METROPOLITAN AREAS

In most of America's metropolitan areas, there are tremendous cross-pressures to coordinate governmental activity across a region, while at the same time protecting the values of suburban independence. A wide variety of approaches to accomplishing this difficult balancing act are used.

Annexation

The most obvious method of achieving some degree of governmental consolidation in the metropolitan areas would be for the central city to annex unincorporated suburban areas. Annexation continues to be the most popular integrating device in the nation's metropolitan areas. Not all cities, however, have been equally successful in annexation efforts. In some states, there are rather strong constraints on the annexation powers of local governments.[34] Opposition to central-city annexation is generally more intense in the larger metropolitan areas. The bigger the metropolis, the more one can expect that suburbanites will defend themselves against being "swallowed up" or "submerged" by the central city. While central cities expect fiscal gains from annexation, suburbanites often fear tax hikes. In reality, the pattern is mixed.[35]

Central cities in smaller urbanized areas experience more success in annexing people than cities in large urbanized areas. Yet size does not appear to be the most influential factor affecting annexation success. Actually, the "age" of a city seems more influential than its size in determining the success of annexation efforts. Over three-fourths of the area and population annexed to central cities in the nation in recent decades have been in newer cities of the West and South. City boundary lines in "older" metropolitan areas are relatively more fixed than in "newer" areas. Perhaps the immobility of boundaries is a product of sheer age. Over time, persons and organizations adjust themselves to circumstances as they find them. The longer these adjustments have been in existence, the greater the discomfort, expense, and fear of unanticipated consequences associated with change.[36] Annexation battles increasingly pit counties versus municipalities. Counties fear cities will "cherry-pick" wealthier residential and commercial unincorporated areas to annex, leaving the counties to deliver services to unincorporated areas with heavier concentrations of low-income residents and less lucrative tax bases.

City–County Consolidation

Three-quarters of the nation's metropolitan areas lie within single counties. From the standpoint of administration, there is much to be said for city–county consolidation. It would make sense administratively to endow county governments with the powers of cities and to organize them to exercise these powers effectively. Yet important political problems—problems in the allocation of influence over public decision making—remain formidable barriers to strong county government. Many central-city minorities oppose consolidation. They fear loss of political control and cultural identity.[37] Suburbanites are likely to fear that consolidation will give city residents a dominant voice in county affairs. Suburbanites may also fear that city–county consolidation may force them to pay higher taxes to help support the higher municipal costs of running the city. (Actually, county governments usually do provide more benefits to city than suburban residents, while receiving more tax revenues from suburbanites than city residents.[38]) Suburbanites may not welcome uniform, countywide policies in taxation or zoning or any number of other policy areas. Suburbanites who had paid for their own wells and septic tanks will hardly welcome the opportunity to help pay for city water or sewer services. Suburbanites with well-established, high quality public school systems may be unenthusiastic about integrating their schools with city schools in a countywide system, and so on. A variety of policy differences may exist between city and suburb, which will reflect themselves in any attempt to achieve city–county consolidation.

> *Annexation continues to be the most popular integrating device in the nation's metropolitan areas.*

ANNEXATION
The extension of city boundaries over adjacent territory.

CITY–COUNTY CONSOLIDATION
The merger of a county and a city government into a single jurisdiction.

The track record for
getting voters to
approve city–county
consolidation propo-
sals is not very good.

The track record for getting voters to approve city–county consolidation proposals is not very good. Since 1921, over 140 city and county governments have attempted consolidation but just 32 have been successful.[39] Most of those passed in the 1960s and 1970s. (See Table 12–3.) One of the few consolidations to pass in recent years—the merger of the City of Louisville and Jefferson County, Kentucky—promised a different benefit to the voters: economic advantage.

Merger will make us money. We'll vault from 65th largest U.S. city to 23rd. We'll be on the radar screen of major metropolises. We'll attract more jobs. Our young people won't have to go elsewhere for economic opportunity.[40]

Has this approach been successful at managing the sprawl of cities into unincorporated areas of the county or at improving the efficiency of service delivery by eliminating duplication of services? Not entirely, primarily because these consolidations involve the central city and the county, but allow smaller cities in the county to opt out of the new structure. Thus, the city–county consolidation approach utilized so far has elements of both regionalism and localism.[41]

Sometimes, just changing the name of a county to include the major city helps create an image of a more coordinated areawide entity. For example, the county in which the City of Miami is located was formerly known as Dade County. But in 1997, voters approved renaming the county Miami-Dade County.

TABLE 12–3	City–County Consolidation Attempts: 1990–2000	
1990	Gainesville/Alachua County, Florida	Fail
1990	Sacramento/Sacramento County, California	Fail
1990	Roanoke/Roanoke County, Virginia	Fail
1990	Owensboro/Davis County, Kentucky	Fail
1990	Bowling Green/Warren County, Kentucky	Fail
1990	**Athens/Clarke County, Georgia**	**Pass**
1991	Griffin/Spalding County, Georgia	Fail
1992	Ashland and Catlettsburg/Boyd County, Kentucky	Fail
1992	**Lafayette/Lafayette Parish, Louisiana**	**Pass**
1994	Des Moines/Polk County, Iowa	Fail
1994	Douglasville/Douglas County, Georgia	Fail
1994	Metter/Candler County, Georgia	Fail
1995	Wilmington/New Hanover County, North Carolina	Fail
1995	Spokane/Spokane County, Washington	Fail
1995	**Augusta/Richmond County, Georgia**	**Pass**
1997	Griffin/Spalding County, Georgia	Fail
1997	**Kansas City/Wyandotte County, Kansas**	**Pass**
2000	Hawkinsville/Pulaski County, Georgia	Fail
2000	**Louisville/Jefferson County, Kentucky**	**Pass**
2000	**Hartsville/Troosdale County, Tennessee**	**Pass**

Source: National Association of Counties.

Special Districts

One of the more popular approaches to metropolitan integration is the creation of **special districts** or **authorities**. (See *"Rankings of the States:* Special District Governments in the States.") These special-purpose governments are charged with administering a particular function or service on a metropolitan-wide or at least an intermunicipal level, such as a park, sewerage, water, parking, airport, planning, other district, or authority. Because the special district or authority leaves the social and governmental status quo relatively undisturbed, important integrative demands are met with a minimum of resistance with this device. The autonomy of suburban communities is not really threatened, loyalties are not disturbed, political jobs are not lost, and the existing tax structure is left relatively intact. Special districts or authorities may be preferred by suburban political leaders when they believe it will lessen the pressure for annexation by the central city. Special districts or authorities may also be able to incur additional debt after existing units of government have already reached their tax and debt limits.[42] Thus, special districts or authorities may be able to operate in an area wider than that of existing units of governments and at the same time enable governments to evade tax or debt limits in financing a desired public service. The nation's largest special districts—New York's Metropolitan Transportation Authority, Boston's Massachusetts Bay Transportation Authority, Washington's Metro Area Transit Authority, Los Angeles County Transportation Commission, Port Authority of New York and New Jersey—collect and spend billions of dollars each year.

Yet experience in the cities that have relied heavily upon special districts or authorities has suggested that these devices may create as many problems as they solve. Many special districts and authorities are governed by a quasi-independent board or commission, which once established, becomes largely immune from popular pressures for change. These agencies may be quite independent of other governmental jurisdictions in the metropolis; their concerns might be water, air or water pollution control, city planning, and so on. Remoteness from popular control or close political responsibility often results in the professional administrators of these authorities exercising great power over their particular function. While authorities and special districts are supposed to be nonprofit governmental agencies, they often act very much like private enterprises, concentrating their resources on those activities that produce revenue and ignoring equally important non-revenue-producing responsibilities. Independent authorities often borrow money, collect tolls and service charges, and otherwise control their own finances in a manner very much like a private business.

The structure of these districts and authorities usually confuses the voters and makes it difficult for the average citizen to hold officials of these agencies responsible for their decisions. Moreover, since these special districts and authorities are usually created for a single purpose, they often come to define the public interest in terms of the promotion of their own particular function—recreation, mass transit, water, parks, and so on—without regard for other metropolitan concerns. This "single-mindedness" can lead to competition and conflict between authorities and other governmental agencies in the region. Sooner or later, the problem of coordinating the activities of these independent authorities or special districts arises. Thus, even from the point of view of administrative efficiency, it is not clear whether the special district or authority, with its maze of divided responsibility, reduces or compounds the problem of governmental coordination in the metropolis in the long run.[43] What it may do, if the governing board is elected, is to rely less on property taxes than user fees.[44]

SPECIAL DISTRICTS
Local governmental units charged with performing a single function, often overlapping municipal and county boundaries.

AUTHORITY
Special-purpose governments with taxing, spending, and borrowing powers; can cut across county and state lines.

Sooner or later, the problem of coordinating the activities of these independent authorities or special districts arises.

RANKINGS
of the STATES

Special District Governments in the States

Special District Governments

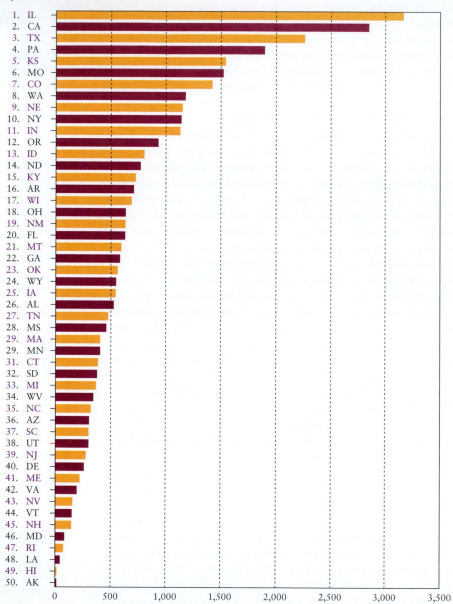

1. IL
2. CA
3. TX
4. PA
5. KS
6. MO
7. CO
8. WA
9. NE
10. NY
11. IN
12. OR
13. ID
14. ND
15. KY
16. AR
17. WI
18. OH
19. NM
20. FL
21. MT
22. GA
23. OK
24. WY
25. IA
26. AL
27. TN
28. MS
29. MA
29. MN
31. CT
32. SD
33. MI
34. WV
35. NC
36. AZ
37. SC
38. UT
39. NJ
40. DE
41. ME
42. VA
43. NV
44. VT
45. NH
46. MD
47. RI
48. LA
49. HI
50. AK

0   500   1,000   1,500   2,000   2,500   3,000   3,500

Note: Single-function districts only. Data are for 2002.

Source: U.S. Census Bureau, *Statistical Abstract of the United States, 2007*, Table No. 416. Available at http://www.census.gov/prod/2006pubs/07statab/stlocgov.pdf

Interjurisdictional Agreements

Another approach to metropolitan integration is the interjurisdictional agreement. Voluntary cooperative agreements between governments in a metropolitan area are common. Agreements may take the form of informal verbal understandings that might involve, for example, the exchange between welfare departments of information on cases, or cooperation among police departments in the apprehension of a lawbreaker, or agreements among local fire departments to come to the assistance of each other in the event of a major fire. Agreements may also be *formal* interjurisdictional agreements among governments, perhaps to build and operate a major facility such as a garbage incinerator or a sewage treatment plant. Interjurisdictional agreements may provide for (1) one government performing a service or providing a facility for one or more other governments on a contractual basis, (2) two or more governments performing a function jointly or operating a facility on a joint basis, or (3) two or more local governments agreeing to assist and supply mutual aid to each other in emergency situations.

One of the attractions of interjurisdictional agreements is that they provide a means for dealing with metropolitan problems on a voluntary basis while retaining local determination and control. Interjurisdictional agreements do not threaten the existence of communities or governments. They do not threaten the jobs of incumbent public officials. Yet at the same time they enable governments to achieve the economies of scale and provide the specialized services that only a larger jurisdiction can make possible.[45]

Councils of Government

Metropolitan councils of governments (COGs) are another form of integration in metropolitan areas. Metropolitan councils are associations of governments or government officials that provide an opportunity for study, discussion, and recommendations regarding common metropolitan problems. Not governments themselves, these COGs have no power to implement decisions but must rely instead upon compliance by member governments. Metropolitan councils provide an arena where officials of metropolitan governments can come together regularly, discuss problems, make recommendations, and, hopefully, coordinate their activities. Regional associations are the most successful when top-level local elected officials actively participate in them as opposed to their staffers.

"Metro" Government

The American experience with federalism at the national level has prompted consideration of federated

Toledo Metropolitan Area Council of Governments

Our Vision: Toledo Metropolitan Area Council of Governments will be the governmental partner of choice to coordinate regional assets, opportunities, and challenges.

Administration
Calendar
Contact Us
Employment
FAQ's
History of TMACOG
Location
Members
Newsroom
Regional &
Membership maps

Mission Statement
To improve quality of life in the Region, TMACOG will:

- Promote a positive identity for the Region.
- Enhance awareness of the Region's assets and opportunities.
- Be an impartial broker of Regional disputes and challenges
- Provide stakeholders a voice in Regional decision-making.
- Support opportunities for Regional stakeholder networking.

The Toledo Metropolitan Area Council of Governments is made up of local governments from two states—Michigan and Ohio. The major benefit of Councils of Governments is to allow local officials in a metropolitan area to meet regularly to discuss common problems and possible solutions to them. Councils of Governments have no power to implement decisions. They rely upon the "good will" of their member governments.

COGs have no power to implement decisions but must rely instead upon compliance by member governments.

**"METRO"
GOVERNMENT**

A federated system of
government for
metropolitan areas in
which powers are
divided between a
comprehensive
government
encompassing the
entire area and
multiple local
governments operating
within the area.

governmental structures for metropolitan areas. A **"metro" government** with authority to make metropolitan-wide policy in selected fields might be combined with local control over functions that are "local" in character. Metropolitan federation, in one form or another and at one time or another, has been proposed for many major metropolitan regions in the nation. Yet with the exception of Toronto, Miami, and Nashville, proposals for metropolitan federation have been consistently rejected by both voters and political leaders. While metropolitan federation promises many of the advantages of governmental consolidation listed earlier—administrative efficiency, economy of large-scale operation, elimination of financial inequalities, and public accountability for metropolitan-wide policy—it seriously threatens many of the social, political, and psychological values in the existing "fragmented" system of local government in the metropolis. Metropolitan federation also poses a problem discussed earlier, that of deciding what is a "metropolitan" problem. In order to allocate functions to a "metro" government in a federation arrangement, one must first determine what is a metropolitan problem in which all the citizens of the area have a responsibility.

Governance versus Government Structure

Can simply altering the structure of governments in metropolitan areas solve regional problems in fragmented areas? "No," say the urban scholars who have studied the impact of consolidating various cities and counties. Their research has shown that "there is no hard evidence that consolidated government will be a better, more honest, more efficient, more effective, or more democratic and responsive governmental structure."[46] Besides, "structure is really only a framework for how governance occurs and that structure is filtered through and colored by local political practices, historical patterns of behavior, and local civic cultures or ways of governance."[47] These scholars believe that voluntary cooperative efforts (governance) linking governmental and nongovernmental organizations are likely to be more effective than drastically altering existing governmental structures, which is often quite difficult. Examples of governance activities include "community visioning initiatives, collaborative planning processes, service integration efforts, community collaboratives, study circles, civic journalism projects, community disputes resolved through mediation, and multisectoral partnership."[48] The Internet, videoconferencing, government access cable television, and other telecommunication technologies have made it easier to build an infrastructure for community collaboration.

Even with the greater emphasis on regional cooperation in certain areas, metropolitics is a tough game to win.

Other scholars believe cooperative governance approaches can only go so far—but not far enough. To them, cooperation merely "serves to protect and preserve the status quo—governmental fragmentation, local government autonomy, and the absence of authoritative areawide decision making."[49] Why? Because it only works for highly local matters, not tough-to-solve metropolitan-wide issues such as suburban sprawl or city–suburban fiscal and social disparities. As we have seen in this chapter, even with the greater emphasis on regional cooperation in certain areas,[50] metropolitics is a tough game to win.

America's Ten Most Livable Metropolitan Areas

Communities love to be ranked by national publications as great places to live. A wide array of groups and publications routinely rank Metropolitan Statistical Areas on everything from housing costs, education, and job opportunities to cultural amenities, hurricane vulnerability, and life for singles. One of the most widely cited rankings gives the most weight to nine factors: ambience, housing, the local economy, transportation, education, health care, crime, recreation, and climate.

Top 10 Metropolitan Areas

1. Pittsburgh, PA
2. San Francisco, CA
3. Seattle, WA
4. Portland, OR
5. Philadelphia, PA
6. Rochester, NY
7. Washington, DC
8. San Jose–Sunnyvale, CA
9. Boston, MA
10. Madison, WI

Pittsburgh, Pennsylvania

Note: Rankings are for 2007. Rankings are changed annually. Updates are available at www.placesrated.com.
Source: David Savageau, *Places Rated Almanac*, 7th ed., (Washington, DC: Places Rated Books, LLC, 2007.)

ON THE WEB

www.governing.com

The official Web site for *Governing* magazine, the nation's leading monthly publication directed at state and local government officials. *Governing* also publishes an annual *State and Local Sourcebook*, which contains comparative governmental information on states, counties, and cities.

www.miamidade.gov

Metropolitan Miami-Dade County is one of the nation's very few "metro" governments. It is a strong federation of thirty municipalities (the largest is the city of Miami), together with the unincorporated areas of Dade County. It has an elected mayor as well as an elected board of county commissioners. The Web site describes this unique two-tiered system of local government. It contains the official charter of the metropolitan government as well as descriptions of all metro government services.

www.knowledgeplex.org

One of the best Web sites for various studies about demographic trends, growth, affordable housing, and community development is maintained by the U.S. Department of Housing and Urban Development. It is an easy-to-use Web site designed for practitioners, scholars, and policymakers.

www.brook.edu/es/urban/urban.htm

The Brookings Institution Center for Urban and Metropolitan Policy Web site has excellent analyses of Census data.

Other useful sites:

www.sprawlwatch.org The Funders' Network for Smart Growth and Livable Communities

www.narc.org The National Association of Regional Councils (NARC)

www.neighborhoodcoalition.org The National Neighborhood Coalition

www.smartgrowth.org The Smart Growth Network

www.sustainable.org Sustainable Communities Network (SCN)

CHAPTER THIRTEEN

ZONING REQUEST

NO.: G 823

FROM: R60 RESIDENTIAL

TO: C1 COMMERCIAL

AREA: 13371 SQ. FT.

FOR INFO. 240-777-6666

DRINK Coca-Cola IN

COMMUNITY POWER, LAND USE, AND THE ENVIRONMENT

13

QUESTIONS TO CONSIDER

Do your local elected public officials or a behind-the-scenes power structure make important decisions in your community?

■ Elected public officials make important decisions.

■ Power structure runs things behind the scenes.

Should economic growth in your community be limited in order to preserve the community's character and lifestyle?

■ Yes   ■ No

Do you believe that property owners should be compensated by taxpayers when government regulations reduce the value of their land?

■ Yes   ■ No

Will building more commuter rail systems greatly reduce the number of individuals who currently drive to work?

■ Yes   ■ No

Do you believe environmental protection should be given priority, even at the risk of curbing economic growth, or should economic growth be given priority even if the environment may suffer to some extent?

■ Environment should get priority

■ Economic growth should get priority

ELITE MODEL OF COMMUNITY POWER

In community politics, the theory that power is concentrated in the hands of relatively few people, usually top business and financial leaders.

PLURALIST MODEL OF COMMUNITY POWER

In community politics, the theory that power is widely dispersed with different leaders in different issue areas responding to the wishes of various interest groups as well as voters.

LAND USE, ECONOMICS, AND COMMUNITY POLITICS INTERTWINED

All local governments operate within specific geographical boundaries. How land is used within those boundaries greatly affects the economic and personal well-being of the citizens who live there and the finances and politics of the local governments that serve them. Land use rules and regulations affect the quantity and type of housing units (single-family homes, condos, townhomes, mobile homes, apartments) permitted in an area, the number and type of jobs available, the types of business establishments in existence and the conditions under which they operate, and the proportion of the land area that is used for public purposes (e.g., roads, mass transit systems, parks, water and sewer lines, convention centers, sports stadiums, and public housing). Land use decisions also affect the type of transportation system that will take residents to and from their jobs (cars, buses, subways, rail, air, water). And land use decisions can greatly affect the environment.

In rundown, deteriorating areas, government tax and redevelopment incentives to private-sector entities are often the key to revitalization while in fast-growing areas, government fees on developers may ensure growth-related public-sector needs are paid for by newcomers rather than by long-standing property owners. In rundown areas, pro-growth ("pro-jobs") policies are favored, while in fast-growing areas anti-growth, pro-environment coalitions often emerge. Because the land available is finite, the politics over any proposed changes in land use often evoke tremendous political and neighborhood involvement—and conflicts. The politics of land use can be brutally fierce, causing clashes between those who have different priorities.

A careful analysis of which individuals and groups are involved in local debates over land use–related issues—housing, planning, zoning, permitting, economic development and redevelopment, transportation, the environment—is one way to get a good glimpse of the political and economic power structures within a community.

MODELS OF COMMUNITY POWER

Who runs this town? Do the elected public officials actually make the important decisions? Or is there a "power structure" in this community that really runs things? If so, who is in the power structure? Are public officials "gofers" who carry out the orders of powerful individuals who operate "behind the scenes"? Or are community affairs decided by democratically elected officials acting openly in response to the wishes of many different individuals and groups? Is city government of the people, by the people, and for the people? Or is it a government run by a small "elite," with the "masses" of people largely apathetic and uninfluential in public affairs?

Social scientists have differed over the answers to these questions. Some social scientists posit an **elite model of community power**—that power in American communities is concentrated in the hands of relatively few people, usually top business and financial leaders. They believe that this "elite" is subject to relatively little influence from the "masses" of people. Other social scientists posit a **pluralist model of community power**—that power is widely shared in American communities among many leadership groups who represent segments of the community and who are held responsible by the people through elections and group participation. Interestingly, both elitist and pluralist models seem to agree that decisions are made by small minorities in the community. Direct, widespread, individual citizen participation in community decision making is more of an ideal than a reality. The *elite model describes a monolithic structure of power*, with a single leadership group making decisions on a variety of issues. The pluralist model *describes a polycentric structure of power*, with different leaders active in different issues and a great deal of competition, bargaining, and sharing of power among them.

Most "real" communities will probably fall somewhere in between—that is, along a continuum from the monolithic elite model of power to a diffused and polycentric pluralist model. Many social scientists are neither confirmed "elitists" nor "pluralists," but they are aware that different structures and power may exist in different communities. Yet these ideal models of community power may be helpful in understanding the different ways in which community power can be structured.

The Elite Model

European social theory has long been at odds with democratic political writers about the existence and necessity of elites. Italian political theorist Gaetano Mosca, in his book *The Ruling Class*, wrote, "In all societies . . . two classes of people appear—a class that rules and a class that is ruled."[1] For Mosca, elitism is explained by the nature of social organization. Organization inevitably results in the concentration of political power in the hands of a few. Organized power cannot be resisted by an unorganized majority in which each individual ". . . stands alone before the totality of the organized minority. A hundred men acting uniformly in concert, with a common understanding, will triumph over a thousand men who are not in accord and can therefore be dealt with one by one."[2] Since organized power will prevail over individual effort in politics, sooner or later, organizations will come to be the more important actors in political life. And organizations cannot function without leaders. In the words of European sociologist Robert Michels, "He who says organization, says oligarchy."[3]

Power in "Middletown"

One of the earliest studies of American communities, the classic study of Middletown, conducted by sociologists Robert and Helen Lynd in the mid-1920s and again in the mid-1930s, confirmed a great deal of elitist thinking about community power.[4] The Lynds found in Muncie, Indiana, a monolithic power structure dominated by the owners of the town's largest industry. Community power was firmly entrenched in the hands of the business class, centering on, but not limited to, the "X family."[5] The power of this group was based on its control over the economic life in the city, particularly its ability to control the extension of credit. The city was run by a "small top group" of "wealthy local manufacturers, bankers, the local head managers of . . . national corporations with units in Middletown, and . . . one or two outstanding lawyers." Democratic procedures and governmental institutions were so much window dressing for business control. The Lynds described the typical city official as a "man of meager calibre" and as "a man whom the inner business control group ignores economically and socially and uses politically."

Perhaps the most influential elitist study of community politics was sociologist Floyd Hunter's *Community Power Structure*, a study of Atlanta, Georgia. According to Hunter, no one person or family or business dominated "Regional City" (a synonym for Atlanta), as might be true in a smaller town.[6] Instead, Hunter described several tiers of community influentials, with business leaders dominating the top tier. The top

A community in which organized interest groups get heavily involved in a variety of issues would be an example of the pluralist model of community power. The "pluralist model" sees power as fragmented—shared by different small groups of active citizens pressuring elected officials on different issues.

decision makers were not formally organized but frequently met informally and passed down decisions to government leaders, city organizations, and other "figure heads."

The Pluralist Model

Modern pluralism does not mean a commitment to "pure democracy," where all citizens participate directly in decision making. The underlying value of individual dignity continues to motivate contemporary pluralist thought, but it is generally recognized that the town-meeting type of pure democracy is not really possible in an urban industrial society. To modern pluralists, individual participation has come to mean membership in *organized groups*. Interest groups become the means by which individuals gain access to the political system. Government is held responsible, not directly by individuals, but by organized interest groups and political parties. Pluralists believe that competition between parties and organized groups, representing the interests of their citizen members, can protect the dignity of the individual and offer a viable alternative to individual participation in decision making.

The pluralist model of community power stresses the fragmentation of authority, the influence of elected public officials, the importance of organized group activity, and the role of public opinion and elections in determining public policy. Who rules in the pluralist community? "Different small groups of interested and active citizens in different issue areas with some overlap, if any, by public officials, and occasional intervention by a large number of people at the polls."[7]

Power in New Haven

Perhaps the most influential of the pluralist community studies was Robert A. Dahl's *Who Governs?*, a detailed analysis of decision making in New Haven, Connecticut. Dahl chose to examine sixteen major decisions on redevelopment and public education in New Haven and on nominations for mayor in both political parties for seven elections. Dahl found a polycentric and dispersed system of community power in New Haven, in contrast to Hunter's highly monolithic and centralized power structure in Atlanta. Influence was exercised from time to time by many individuals, each exercising power over some issue but not over others. When the issue was one of urban renewal, one set of individuals was influential; in public education, a different group of leaders was involved. Business elites, who were said by Hunter to control Atlanta, were only one of many different influential groups in New Haven. The mayor of New Haven was the only decision maker who was influential in most of the issue areas studied, and his degree of influence varied from issue to issue.

ECONOMIC ELITES IN COMMUNITIES

Great power derives from control of economic resources. Most of the nation's economic resources are controlled by national institutions—industrial corporations, banks, utilities, insurance companies, investment firms, and the national government. Most of the forces shaping life in American communities arise outside of these communities; community leaders cannot make war or peace, or cause inflation or recession, or determine interest rates or the money supply. But there is one economic resource—land—that is controlled by communities. Land is a valuable resource: Capital investment, labor and management, and production must be placed somewhere.

There is one economic resource—land—that is controlled by communities.

Local Control of Land Use

Traditionally, community power structures were composed primarily of economic elites whose goals were to maximize land values, real estate commissions, builders' profits, rent payments, and mortgage interest, as well as to increase revenues to commercial enterprises serving the community. Communities were traditionally dominated by mortgage-lending banks, real estate developers, builders, and landowners. They were joined by owners or managers of local utilities, department stores, attorneys and title companies, and others whose wealth was affected by land use. Local bankers who financed the real estate developers and builders were often at the center of the elite structure in communities. Unquestionably these community elites competed among themselves for wealth, profit, power, and preeminence. But they shared a consensus about intensifying the use of land. Corporate plants and offices, federal and state office buildings, and universities and colleges all contributed to the increased land values, not only on the parcels used by these facilities but also on neighboring parcels.

Growth as Shared Elite Value

Growth was the shared elite value. The community elite was indeed a "growth machine."[8] Economic growth expands the workforce and disposable income within the community. It stimulates housing development, retail stores, and other commercial activity. The economic elite understand that they all benefit, albeit to varying degrees, when economic growth occurs within the community. Not only must a community compete for new investments, but it must also endeavor to prevent relocation of investments it already has.

Attracting investors requires the provision of good transportation facilities—highways, streets, rail access, and water and airport facilities. It requires the provision of utilities—water, gas and electrical power, solid waste disposal, and sewage treatment. It requires the provision of good municipal services, especially

When major land use changes are proposed, fights between pro-development and anti-development forces often become intense and the police have to be called in to maintain order.

fire and police protection; the elimination of harassing business regulations and the reduction of taxes on new investments to the lowest feasible levels; the provision of a capable and cooperative labor force, educated for the needs of productive capital and motivated to work; and finally, the provision of sufficient amenities—cultural, recreational, aesthetic—to provide the corporate managers with a desirable lifestyle.

Elites Striving for Consensus

Community economic elites usually strive for consensus. They believe that community economic growth—increased capital investment, more jobs, and improved business conditions—benefits the entire community. According to Paul E. Peterson, community residents share a common interest in the economic well-being of the city:

> Policies and programs can be said to be in the interest of cities whenever the policies maintain or enhance the economic position, social prestige, or political power of the city as a whole.[9]

Community economic elites themselves would doubtlessly agree with Peterson. He adds that the interests of the city as a whole are closely bound to its export industries. These industries add net wealth to the community at large, while support and service industries merely transfer wealth within the community.

> Whatever helps them prosper rebounds to the benefit of the community as a whole— perhaps four or five times over. It is just such an economic analysis (of the multiplier effect of export industries) that has influenced many local government policies. Especially the smaller towns and cities may provide free land, tax concessions, and favorable utility rates to incoming industries.[10]

The less economically developed a community, the more persuasive the argument on behalf of export industries.

Growth as Good Politics

Economic elites expect local government officials to share in the growth consensus.

In many American communities, older economic elites have been replaced by newer political elites.

Economic elites expect local government officials to share in the growth consensus. Economic prosperity is necessary for protecting the fiscal base of local government. Growth in local budgets and public employment, as well as governmental services, depends on growth in the local economy. Governmental growth expands the power, prestige, and status of government officials. Moreover, economic growth is usually good politics. Growth-oriented candidates for public office generally have larger campaign treasuries than antigrowth candidates, unless they are running in an area that has become "antigrowth." Growth-oriented candidates routinely solicit contributions from the local community power structure. Finally, according to Peterson, most local politicians have a "sense of community responsibility." They know that if the economy of the community declines, "local business will suffer, workers will lose employment opportunities, cultural life will decline, and city land values will fall."[11] If that happens, they are sure to be defeated at the ballot box.

POLITICAL ELITES IN COMMUNITIES

Today, in many American communities, older economic elites have been replaced by newer political elites. Many of the old economic elites sold their businesses to national corporations and vacated their positions of community leadership. Locally owned stores and factories became manager-directed plants and chain stores. The result was a weakening of community loyalties in the business sector. The new corporate managers could easily decide, in response to national economic conditions, to close the local plant or store with minimal concern for the impact on the community. Local banks were merged into national banking corporations and local bankers were replaced by banking executives with few community ties. City newspapers that were once independently owned by families who lived in the communities were bought up by giant newspaper and publication chains. Instead of editors and reporters who expected to live the lives of their communities, city newspapers came to be staffed with people who hope to move up in the corporate hierarchy— people who strive primarily to advance their own careers, not the interests of the local community.

Professional politicians have moved into this vacuum in city after city, largely replacing the local bankers, real estate developers, chambers of commerce, and old-style newspaper editors who had dominated community politics for generations. The earlier economic elites were only part-time politicians who used local government to promote their economic interests. The new professional political elites work full time at local politics. They are drawn primarily by personal ambition, not so much for the wealth as for the power and celebrity that accompany running for and winning public office. They are not "screened" by economic elites or political parties, but rather they nominate themselves, raise their own funds, organize their own campaigns, and create their own publicity.

Some Political Elites Opposed to Growth

Consensus on behalf of economic growth is sometimes challenged by political elites in communities. However much the economic elite may strive for consensus, some people do not like growth, and they are willing to use political power to stop it. Indeed, it has become fashionable in upper middle-class circles today to complain loudly about the problems created by growth— congestion, pollution, noise, unsightly development, or the replacement of green spaces with concrete slabs. People who already own their houses and do not intend to sell them, people whose jobs are secure in government bureaucracies or tenured professorships, people who may be displaced from their homes and neighborhoods by new facilities, people who see no direct benefit to themselves from growth, and businesses or industries who fear the new competition that growth may bring to the community, all combine to form potentially powerful political alliances.[12]

It has become fashionable in upper middle-class circles today to complain loudly about the problems created by growth.

Not all of the opposition to growth is upper middle class in character. Students of community power have described the struggle of blacks and low-income neighborhood groups in opposing urban renewal and downtown city development. (Minorities and the poor fear being displaced by redevelopment.) In the past, community elites were likely to be successful against this kind of opposition because minorities and low-income residents had very little political clout. But this has changed. Cities have become more diverse. More minorities are being elected to governing bodies. Federal aid programs require recipient governments to solicit citizen input from minorities in order to receive redevelopment funding. Thus, today's elites can no longer ignore the voices of minorities and the poor when they oppose growth because it threatens their homes and neighborhoods.

No-growth movements are *not* mass movements. They do *not* express the aspirations of workers for jobs or renters for their own homes. Instead, they reflect upper-middle-class

NIMBY

An acronym for "not in my backyard," referring to residents who oppose nearby public or private projects or developments.

SMART GROWTH

Promotion of higher density growth so more livable communities can be created.

lifestyle preferences of educated, affluent, articulate homeowners. They see growth as bringing ugly factories, cheap commercial outlets, hamburger stands, fried chicken franchises, and "undesirable" residents. Even if new business or industry would help hold down local taxes, these affluent citizens would still oppose it. They would rather pay the higher taxes associated with no growth than change the appearance or lifestyle of their community. They have secure jobs themselves and own their homes; they are relatively unconcerned about creating jobs or building homes for less affluent citizens.

No-growth political movements have challenged traditional economic elites in many large and growing cities in the West and South. The no-growth leaders may themselves have been beneficiaries of community growth only five or ten years ago, but they quickly perceive their own interest in slowing or halting additional growth. Now that they have climbed the ladder to their own success, they are prepared to knock the ladder down to preserve their own style of living. They often ignore the fact that America's population is growing and that people must have somewhere to live. As an international observer of urban growth explains: "Urban populations and commercial activities can only grow in four directions: *in* (by crowding), *up* (as in Manhattan's skyscrapers), *down* (as in Tokyo's 700 subterranean mah-jongg parlors), and *out* (as on the peripheries of cities nearly everywhere except Gibraltar)."[13]

The NIMBY Syndrome

Opponents of growth can usually count on help from community residents who will be directly inconvenienced by specific projects. Even people who would otherwise support new commercial or housing developments or new public facilities may voice the protest, "Not in my backyard!" earning them the **NIMBY** label. Many Americans want growth; they just do not want it near them.[14]

NIMBYs may be the noisiest of protest groups. They are the homeowners and voters who are most directly affected by a proposed private or public project. (And virtually every project inspires NIMBY opposition.) NIMBYs are particularly active regarding waste disposal sites, incinerators, highways, prisons, halfway houses, mental health facilities, low-income public housing projects, power plants, pipelines, airports, and factories. NIMBYs are formidable opponents. While they may constitute only a small portion of the community, they have a very large stake in defeating a project. They have a strong motivation to become active participants—meeting, organizing, petitioning, parading, demonstrating against a project, while seeking and attracting media attention. The majority of the community may benefit from the project, but because each person has only a small stake in its completion, no one has the same strong motivation to participate as the NIMBYs. Government agencies and private corporations seeking to locate projects in communities are well advised to conduct professional public relations campaigns well in advance of groundbreaking. When the power of the NIMBYs is added to that of "no-growth" forces, economic development can be stalemated, just as it can by "restricted growthers."

Restricted Growthers (The "Smart Growth" Movement)

Persons who favor the "right kind of growth" like to describe themselves as proponents of "growth management" or "**smart growth**." Their major premise is that by dictating the right kind of growth, more livable communities can be created. (More will be said about livable communities later in the chapter.) Smart growth proponents argue restricted, directed growth "preserves community character, protects open space and the environment, strengthens the local economy, and uses taxpayer dollars efficiently."[15] Growth management supporters favor restricting growth through zoning laws, subdivision-control restrictions, utility regulations, building permits, environmental regulations, and even municipal land purchases. Zoning laws can rule out multifamily dwellings or specify only large, expensive lot sizes for homes. Zoning laws can exclude heavy or "dirty" industrial development, or restrict "strip" commercial development along highways. Opposition to street widening, road building, or tree cutting can slow or halt development. Public utilities needed for development—water lines, sewage disposal, firehouses, and so on—can be postponed indefinitely. High development fees, utility hookup charges, or building permit costs can all be used to discourage growth. Unrealistic antipollution laws can also discourage growth. If all else fails, a community can buy up vacant land itself or make it a "wildlife refuge."

"Smart-growthers" have become influential in many large and growing cities—for example, Austin, Denver, Phoenix, San Francisco, San Jose, and Tucson. But they are also politically powerful in *many upper-middle-class suburban communities* (even those in metropolitan areas with declining core cities) that view growth restrictions as in their own interest. Smart growthers, like no-growthers and NIMBYs, are concentrated among well-educated, upper-middle-class, white residents who own their own homes. Within these households, it is women who first adopt no growth attitudes.[16]

Restricting land use changes in such communities often inflates the prices of existing homes (and thereby limits the amount of affordable housing in the community). Hence it is in the economic interest of homeowners, once they have acquired their own homes, to oppose further development. Note that the burden of these policies falls not only on builders and developers (who are the most influential opponents of "no-growth" policies), but also on the poor, the working class, minorities, and non–property owners. These groups need the jobs that business and industry can bring to a community, and they need reasonably priced homes in which to live.

Land use policies that restrict the supply of housing in a community increase its costs. Higher housing costs restrict access for minorities and the poor. Indeed, many "growth-management" policies do not limit population growth but rather discourage the movement of minorities and the poor into a community.[17]

When suburban communities restrict growth, they are often distributing population to other parts of the metropolitan area.[18] The people kept out do not cease to exist; they find housing elsewhere in the metropolitan area. They usually end up imposing greater costs on other municipalities—central cities or larger, close-in suburbs—which are less able to absorb these costs than the wealthier upper-middle-class communities that succeeded in excluding them. What appears to be a local "growth" issue may be in reality a metropolitan "distribution" issue.

The bottom line is that more communities with highly restrictive housing policies are now facing "affordable housing" problems, which threaten to keep out teachers, nurses, firefighters, police officers, and other working families who are vital to the well-being of the community. Political activists fighting for government-imposed affordable housing policies argue that "If we don't keep fighting this fight, then those people we rely on—to teach our children, for example—won't be able to live in the communities in which they work and want to call home."[19] There is a widening gap between those who can afford to buy a home and those who cannot.

PLANNING AND ZONING

MASTER PLAN

A city map showing the location of present and future streets and public facilities.

City planning began in antiquity with the emergence of the first cities. Governing authorities have long determined the location of streets, squares, temples, walls, and fortresses. Most early American cities were planned as a gridiron of streets and squares in the fashion of William Penn's plan for Philadelphia in 1682. A notable exception to the gridiron pattern was Pierre L'Enfant's 1791 plan for Washington, DC, with radial streets slashing through the gridiron.[20] Until the early twentieth century, city planning was focused almost exclusively on the layout of streets and the location of public buildings and parks. A city's "**master plan**" was a map showing the location of present and future streets and public facilities. There was relatively little regulation of the use of private property.

> *"Comprehensive planning" involves not only the determination of the location of public facilities but also the control of private land uses.*

Comprehensive Planning

But the reform movement of the early twentieth century (see "Reformers and Do-Gooders" in Chapter 11) brought with it a much broader definition of planning. "Comprehensive planning" involves not only the determination of the location of public facilities but also the control of private land uses.

Comprehensive planning involves the identification of community goals, the development of plans to implement these goals, and the use of governmental tools to influence and shape private and public decision making to serve these goals. Community goals are identified not only in land use and physical development policies, but also in those for population growth, health and safety, housing and welfare, education, transportation, economic development, culture, lifestyle and beautification, historic preservation, and environmental protection. According to the American Institute of Planners (AIP), planning is a "comprehensive, coordinated and continuing process, the purpose of which is to help public and private decision makers arrive at decisions which promote the common good of society."[21] Obviously this extended definition of planning plunges the planner deep into the political life of the community.

State laws authorize and often mandate that cities develop comprehensive plans. Traditionally the comprehensive plan was prepared by semi-independent *planning commissions* composed of private citizens appointed by the mayor and approved by the city council. These commissions rely heavily on **professional planners** to prepare the comprehensive plan. Professional planners are mostly university graduates in city planning. They are organized into the American Institute of Planners, which publishes its own journal and grants professional credentials to planners. Over time, however, independent citizen planning commissions were gradually replaced with planning departments within city government that are directly responsible to the mayor and council. Federal (and many state) laws now mandate community and regional planning as conditions of fiscal assistance, especially for transportation.

PROFESSIONAL PLANNERS

University graduates in city planning. They are organized into the American Institute of Planners (AIP), which publishes its own journal and grants professional credentials to planners.

Developing Political Support for Planning

Citizen planning commissions are still retained in many communities to facilitate citizen input into the planning process and to develop political support for the comprehensive plan. Planning commissions often hold public hearings on the comprehensive plans and proposed changes to it.

The decisions of professional planners and planning commissions are officially considered advisory. That is, the comprehensive plan must be enacted by the city council to become law. The recommendations of the planning commission can be overturned by the city council. But the advice of a prudent planning staff, with the support of influential private citizens on the planning commission, cannot be easily ignored.

Planners, like reformers generally, claim to represent the welfare of the community as a whole. They are usually hostile to what they perceive to be narrow, self-serving interests in the community, especially businesspeople, real estate developers, and property owners.

The Influence of Planners

While the formal role of planners is advisory, they can have a substantial influence on community policy. In smaller cities, planners may be preoccupied with the day-to-day administration of the zoning and subdivision control ordinances. They may have insufficient time or staff to engage in genuine long-range comprehensive planning. In large cities, the planning staff may be the only agency that has a comprehensive view of community development. Although they may not have the power to "decide" about public policy, they can "initiate" policy discussions through their plans, proposals, and recommendations. The planners can project the image of the city of the future and thereby establish the agenda of community decision making. Their plans can initiate public discussion over the goals and values to be implemented in the community. The current thrust of planning is to create **"livable" communities** by emphasizing the design and protection of neighborhoods and the environment. ("Conservation subdivisions" utilize the natural landscape in their design and have a common open space rather than individual backyards.[22]) Planning and the smart growth movement go hand in hand.

Planners can project the image of the city of the future and thereby establish the agenda of community decision making.

Opposition to Planning

There are, of course, some limitations on the influence of planners. First of all, many important decisions in community development are made by private enterprise rather than by government. Real estate interests, developers, builders, and property owners make many of the key decisions that shape the development of the community. Their actions are often determined by the economics of the marketplace. Property owners will try to find a way to make the most profitable use of their land, the ideas of the planners notwithstanding. Second, the planners can only advise policymakers; they are just one voice among many attempting to influence public decisions about land use and physical development.

The free market usually does a better job of allocating resources in a society than does government. Opponents of government planning and land use control argue that the decisions of thousands of individual property owners result in a better allocation of land than the decisions of government bureaucrats. Decentralized marketplace decisions allow more rapid adjustment to change and satisfy the preferences of more people than centralized bureaucratic decision making. Marketplace prices signal the most appropriate uses of land, just as they do the most appropriate uses of other resources.

Opponents also argue that requiring government permits for land uses—for new commercial, industrial, or residential developments and for new homes, buildings, or

ZONING ORDINANCES

Local government regulations that divide communities into various residential, commercial, and industrial zones, and that require landowners to use their land in conformity with the regulations for the zone in which it is located.

ZONING VARIANCE

An exception to the zoning ordinance applied to a particular piece of property.

other structures—adds to the time and costs of development and the size of government bureaucracy. By adding to the costs of housing, planning places owning homes beyond the reach of many middle-class families. By adding to the costs of industry, or banning new industrial development altogether, planning limits the number of jobs created in a community. By empowering local officials to describe how land will be used, individual citizens are deprived of an important individual freedom.

Zoning

Planning agencies usually prepare the zoning ordinance for the approval of the city council. The **zoning ordinance** divides the community into districts for the purpose of regulating the use and development of land and buildings. Zoning originated as an attempt to separate residential areas from commercial and industrial activity, thereby protecting residential property values. The zoning ordinance divides the community into residential, commercial, and industrial zones, and perhaps subdivisions within each zone, such as "light industrial" and "heavy industrial," or "single-family residential" and "multifamily residential." Owners of land in each zone must use their land in conformity with the zoning ordinance; however, exceptions are made for people who have used the land in a certain way before the adoption of the zoning ordinance. An ordinance cannot prevent a person from using the land as one has done in the past; thus, zoning laws can only influence land use if they are passed prior to the development of a community. Many new and rapidly expanding communities pass zoning ordinances too late—after commercial and industrial establishments are strung out along highways, ideal industrial land is covered with houses, good park and recreational land has been sold for other purposes, and so on.

Since the planning agency prepares the zoning ordinances as well as the comprehensive plan, the ordinance is expected to conform to the plan. In many communities, the role of the planning agency is strengthened by the requirement that a city council *must* submit all proposed changes in the zoning ordinance to the planning agency for its recommendation before any council action.

Changes in the zoning ordinance usually originate at the request of property owners. They may wish to change the zoning classification of their property to enhance its value—for example, to change it from single-family to multifamily residential, or from residential to commercial. Usually the planning agency will hold a public hearing on a proposed change before sending its findings and recommendation to the city council. The city council may also hold a public hearing before deciding on the change.

City councils can and sometimes do ignore the recommendations of their planning agencies when strong pressures are exerted by neighborhood groups or environmentalists opposed to rezoning, or by developers and property owners supporting it. However, the recommendations of planning agencies prevail in the vast majority of rezoning cases, indicating the power of the planners in community affairs.[23]

A **zoning "variance"** is a request for a limited and specific variation from the strict standards in a zoning ordinance as applied to a particular piece of property. Some cities create special boards to hear requests for zoning variances, and other cities allow their planning agency to grant zoning variances. The zoning variance may be the most abused of all zoning procedures. It is not intended to encourage "spot" zoning, grant special privileges, or circumvent the interest of the zoning ordinance, but this is frequently what happens. Local zoning decisions may also conflict with regional planning efforts.[24]

Subdivision Control

Another means of implementing the master plan is **subdivision regulations**, which govern the way in which land is divided into smaller lots and made ready for improvements. Subdivision regulations, together with the zoning ordinance, may specify the minimum size of lots, the standards to be followed by real estate developers in laying out new streets, and the improvements developers must provide, such as sewers, water mains, parks, playgrounds, and sidewalks. Often planning agencies are given direct responsibility for the enforcement of subdivision regulations. Builders and developers must submit their proposed **"plats"** for subdividing land and for improvements to the planning commission for approval before deeds can be recorded.

Official Map

The planning agency also prepares the **official map** of the city for enactment by the council. The official map shows proposed, as well as existing, streets, water mains, public utilities, and the like. Presumably, no one is permitted to build any structures on land that appears as a street or other public facility on the official map. Many cities require the council to submit to the planning agency for their recommendation any proposed action that affects the plan of streets or the subdivision plan and any proposed acquisition or sale of city real estate.

Building and Construction Codes

Most cities have building codes designed to ensure public health and safety. These codes are lengthy documents specifying everything from the thickness of building beams and the strength of trusses, to the type of furnaces, electric wiring, ventilation, fireproofing, and even earthquake resistance that must be incorporated into buildings. No construction may be undertaken without first obtaining a building permit, which must be prominently displayed at the building site. Building inspectors are then dispatched periodically to the site to see if work is progressing in conformance with the building codes. The planning agency does not usually administer the code (that is normally the function of a building or housing department), but the planners are usually consulted about proposed changes in the building code.

Housing codes are designed to bring existing structures up to minimum standards. They set forth minimum requirements for fire safety, ventilation, plumbing, sanitation, and building condition. As with building codes, enforcement is the responsibility of city government, but the planning commission is normally consulted about changes in the code.

Capital Improvements

Comprehensive planning can also be implemented through a **capital improvement program**. This program is simply the planned schedule of public projects by the city—new public buildings, parks, streets, and so on. Many larger cities instruct their planning agencies to prepare a long-range capital improvement program for a five- or ten-year period. Of course, the council may choose to ignore the planning commission's long-range capital improvement program in its decisions about capital expenditures, but at least the planning commission will have expressed its opinions about major capital investments.

SUBDIVISION REGULATIONS
Regulations governing the dividing of land areas into lots.

PLATS
Plans for subdividing land and for improvements that must be submitted to a planning commission for approval before deeds can be recorded.

OFFICIAL MAP
Shows proposed and existing streets, water mains, public utilities, and other public facilities; must be approved by city council.

BUILDING CODES
Local government regulations requiring building permits and inspections of new construction to ensure compliance with detailed specifications that protect the public's health and safety.

CAPITAL IMPROVEMENT PROGRAM (CIP)
The planned schedule of new public projects by a local government; usually for a five- or ten-year period.

Environmental Regulations

Governments have increasingly turned to environmental laws and regulations to assert control over community development. State laws or local ordinances may designate "**areas of critical concern**" in an effort to halt development. Designation of such areas is usually very subjective; they may be swamps, forests, waterfront, or wildlife habitats, or even historic, scenic, or archeological sites. "Critical" may also refer to flood plains or steep hillsides or any other land on which governments wish to halt construction.

States and cities are increasingly requiring developers to prepare "**environmental impact statements**"—assessments of the environmental consequences of proposed construction or land use change. These statements are usually prepared by professional consultants at added cost to builders and developers.

In most cities and counties, enforcement of environmental regulations is the responsibility of separate environmental departments. This means that landowners and developers usually must deal with two separate bureaucracies. Planning departments are generally consulted in the preparation of environmental regulations.

INNOVATIVE PLANNING PRACTICES: MORE DISCRETIONARY

The formal instruments of land use control are often considered too inflexible for optimum planning. Local governments and private property owners frequently seek ways to avoid the rigidities of zoning and subdivision ordinances and construction codes.[25] These regulations, when applied strictly and uniformly, often limit the freedom of architects and developers, produce a sterile environment through separation of land uses, and lead to excessive court litigation. So planners have increasingly turned to a variety of practices intended to minimize some of the worst consequences of land use regulation.

PUDs

One technique that has grown in popularity in recent years is **planned urban development** (PUD). PUD ordinances vary but typically they allow developers with a minimum number of acres (e.g., ten, twenty, or more) to have the option of abiding by conventional zoning, subdivision, and building codes, or alternatively submitting an overall site plan for the approval of the planning agency and council. PUD designs usually incorporate mixed residential and commercial uses, perhaps with single-family homes and apartments or condominiums, retail shops, hotels and restaurants, parks and open spaces, all included. Planners and councils often exercise considerable discretion in approving or rejecting or forcing modifications in PUDs, depending on their own preferences.

Exactions and Impact Fees

Many communities require developers to pay substantial fees or give over land to local government in exchange for approval of their land use plans.[26] This practice, known as "**exaction**," is often defended as a charge to pay the local government's costs in connection with the new development, for example, additional roads or sewers needed or additional schools or parks required for new residents. A closely related practice is that of charging developers "**impact fees**" that are supposed to compensate the community for increased costs imposed by the development *beyond* the added tax revenues that the development will generate when completed. But it is virtually impossible to accurately calculate impact costs, if indeed a development actually does impose more costs on a community than the revenues it produces. So impact fees become just another cost to developers that are passed on to homebuyers and (through commercial tenants) to consumers.

Developer Agreements

Often conflict between local governments and developers are settled through *developer agreements*. Some states (e.g., California) specifically authorize municipalities to enter into such agreements, bypassing zoning, subdivision, and construction ordinances. In other states, often lawsuits, or the threat of lawsuits, by developers force municipalities into such agreements. The municipality benefits by being able to specify the details of a project. The developer benefits by obtaining a legally binding contract that cannot be changed later by the municipality as the project proceeds to completion.

Designing "Livable" Communities

The "New Urbanism" or "Livable Communities" movement began in the 1990s. It is a *design-oriented* approach to planning, initially developed by architects but now subscribed to by some demographers, sociologists, criminologists, political scientists, and community activists. "The basic unit of planning is the *neighborhood*, which is limited in physical size, has a well-defined edge, and has a focused center."[27]

CONSTITUTIONAL CONCERNS—THE TAKINGS CLAUSE

How far can government go in regulating the use of property without depriving individuals of their property rights? The U.S. Constitution (Fifth Amendment) states clearly, "nor shall private property be taken for public use without just compensation." Taking land for highways, streets, and public buildings, even when the owners do not wish to sell, is known as **eminent domain**. A city or state must go to court and show that the land is needed for a legitimate public purpose; the court will then establish a fair price *(just compensation)* based on testimony from the owner, the city or state, and impartial appraisers. Eminent domain is a constitutional protection to American citizens against arbitrary government seizure of their land.

But what if a government does not "take" ownership of the property, but instead restricts the owner's use of it through regulation? Zoning ordinances, subdivision regulations, environmental regulations, or building and housing codes may reduce the value of the property to the owner. Should the owner be compensated for loss of use?

Courts have always recognized that governments can make laws to protect the health, safety, and general welfare of its citizens. Owners of property have never been entitled to any compensation for obeying laws or ordinances with a clear public purpose. But it was not clear that zoning restrictions were legitimate public purposes until 1926 when the U.S. Supreme Court upheld city zoning ordinances as "a proper exercise of police powers."[28] Cities are *not* required to compensate

IMPACT FEES

Fees required from developers by local governments in exchange for approval of plans, presumably compensating for the increased governmental costs created by the new development.

TAKINGS CLAUSE

The clause in the U.S. Constitution's Fifth Amendment that prohibits government from taking private property without just (fair) compensation.

EMINENT DOMAIN

The judicial process by which government can take private property for public use by providing fair (just) compensation.

Eminent domain is a constitutional protection to American citizens against arbitrary government seizure of their land.

Local governments have the right to "take" privately owned property for public use (e.g., road, school) under their eminent domain power if they adequately compensate the property owner. But when local governments use their eminent domain power to take privately owned land for economic revitalization and turn it over to a private developer, citizens get up in arms. A number of state legislatures have passed laws prohibiting this practice.

owners for lost value as a result of zoning regulations. Yet it was still argued that some planning and zoning provisions, especially those designed for beauty and aesthetics, had no relation to public health, safety, and welfare. They simply enacted somebody's taste over that of their neighbor. But in 1954 the U.S. Supreme Court upheld a very broad interpretation of the police power: "It is within the power of the legislature to determine that the community should be beautiful as well as healthy, spacious as well as clean, well-balanced as well as carefully patrolled."[29] So it is difficult to challenge the constitutionality of planning and zoning as a "taking" of private property without compensation.

"Takings"—When Cities Go Too Far

The U.S. Supreme Court has held that a regulation that denies a property owner *all* economically beneficial use of land (e.g., a state coastal zone management regulation preventing any construction on a beach lot) was a "taking" that required just compensation to the owner in order to be constitutional.[30] The Takings Clause of the Constitution's Fifth Amendment was designed to protect private property from unjust taking by government. Its purpose is "to bar Government from forcing some people alone to bear public burdens which, in all fairness and justice, should be borne by the public as a whole."[31] If a community wants open spaces, wildlife preserves, environmental havens, historic buildings, or other amenities, these should be paid for by all of the citizens of the community. Property should not be taken from private owners, even for public purposes, without compensation. All citizens should share in the costs of providing community amenities, not just the owners of particular properties.

The question remains, however, how far can government go in regulating land use without compensating property owners? Depriving landowners of *all* beneficial uses of their land without compensation is clearly unconstitutional. But what if their use of their land is devalued by 50 percent or 25 percent? Are governments constitutionally required to compensate them in proportion to their losses? In the past, federal courts have ruled that "mere diminution" in the value of property is not a "taking" within the meaning of the Fifth Amendment and hence does not require government to compensate landowners. However, in recent years both Congress and the federal courts, as well as some states, have undertaken to reconsider "how far" government can go in depriving property owners of valued uses of their land. Increasingly, regulatory devaluations of 50 percent or more are becoming highly suspect, and property owners have a reasonable chance of recovering compensation from governments.

"Takings" For Public Use (Economic Development)

Can governments use eminent domain to take privately owned land in order to turn it over to private developers to improve it and sell it for their own profit? Is this a "public use" under the Constitution, or a private use? The City of New London, Connecticut, exercised eminent domain in its "economic development" program to take private homes for a more expensive private development that would produce higher tax revenues for the city. Owners objected that this was not a "public use" such as highways, sewers, or schools but rather simply a means of forcibly transferring property from some private owners to other private owners who would build more expensive homes and sell them for a profit. The city would then collect higher taxes from the new owners. The U.S. Supreme Court, in a 5–4 decision, approved of this type of "taking" as a "public use," that is, economic development.[32] The ruling created quite an outcry from many citizens, prompting state legislators in a number of states to pass their own laws restricting their local governments' use of the eminent domain power.

MORTGAGE INSURANCE
Federal guarantees of home mortgages that allow lenders to offer homebuyers lower down payments and lower interest charges.

HOUSING POLICY

For over a half century, the federal government has pursued a national goal of "a decent home and suitable living environment for every American family." And the nation has made impressive strides toward achieving that goal. Homeownership continues to be an important part of the American Dream. Today two-thirds of all Americans own their own homes. (See Table 13–1.) Yet problems remain.

Low-cost, affordable housing is in short supply. Homeownership is declining, especially among younger families. Indeed, liberals and conservatives alike agree that "affordability" is the principal problem facing American housing today, particularly for the young, poor, and minority populations, many of whom live in metropolitan areas.[33]

The national effort in housing is centered in the U.S. Department of Housing and Urban Development (HUD). HUD is the federal department concerned primarily with **mortgage insurance,** public housing, community development, and related programs. Increasingly, states and localities are playing an even bigger role in these policy areas than the national government.[34] It has become apparent that top-down, one-size-fits-all federal policies do not work as well as initially expected.[35]

Low-cost, affordable housing is in short supply.

Traditional Federal Housing Assistance

The federal government began as early as 1934 to guarantee private mortgages against default by the individual home buyer. The Federal Housing

Americans place a high value on homeownership. Liberals and conservatives alike agree that affordable housing is the principal problem facing many young, poor, and minority populations, especially in metropolitan areas.

Homeowners Associations: "Buddies" or "Bullies"?

It is not only government that some property owners have to deal with regarding control of their land. It is their neighbors, bonded together in **homeowners associations**. Homebuyers are often obligated by deeds to their property to belong to these associations, obey their rules, and pay dues to them. These associations are "private corporations with government-like powers."[a] Some 8,000 new households a year become members of these groups. The number of associations has skyrocketed from just 10,000 in 1970 to 230,000. They collect dues each year "to manage billions of dollars in communal assets—everything from the walls and roofs of condominiums and townhouses to streets, sidewalks, swimming pools, playgrounds, parks, clubhouses, roads, and more."[b] Homeowners elect association board members to make these decisions.

Local government officials often see these associations as "partners . . . in participatory planning processes, community policing efforts, and conservation" and sometimes even in service delivery.[c] Developers believe these associations "give neighborhoods aesthetic purity, high property values, recreational facilities and grassroots democracy, too." And some homeowners "see them as protection from obnoxious neighbors who let their property deteriorate, paint their homes offensive colors or keep rusty old cars on blocks in the front yard."[d]

To others, these associations are bullies—"trampling individual liberties with invasive regulations and iron-fisted enforcement." Critics cite pettiness, favoritism, and unneighborly behavior as the modus operandi of these associations, with the result being more, rather than less, community conflict. The State of Nevada has appointed an ombudsman to handle complaints by homeowners against their associations. Typical of the types of complaints received: "An elderly gentleman is fined for leaving his lawn half-mowed while seeking a brief respite from the desert sun. An association board decrees that children can't play on the grass in front of their homes." In Harris County (Houston), Texas, over 4,000 homeowners since 1995 had their property foreclosed by homeowner associations for minor violations.[e] Complaints against homeowners associations are escalating in many high-growth areas, which are prompting more state and local governments to reexamine the legal position of these groups. Large-scale organized complaints about *privately* owned homes are a relatively recent phenomenon whereas complaints about government housing policies and *public* housing have been around for quite some time.

Where you live, are homeowners associations perceived as "buddies" or "bullies"?

HOMEOWNERS ASSOCIATIONS

Private associations of neighborhood homeowners who are required by property deeds to obey their rules and pay their dues.

[a]Christopher Conte, "Boss Thy Neighbor," *Governing*, 14 (April 2001): 38–40.
[b]Ibid.
[c]Kathryn Stratos, "Neighborhood Associations," *IQ Report*, 33 (November 2001), Washington, DC: International City/County Management Association.
[d]Christopher Conte, "Boss Thy Neighbor," *Governing*, 14 (April 2001): 38–40.
[e]Ibid.

Administration (FHA), now a part of HUD, insures home mortgages and thereby helps banks, savings and loan associations, and other lending agencies to provide long-term, low-down-payment mortgages for Americans wishing to buy their own homes. After checking the credit rating of the prospective buyer, FHA assures the private mortgage lender—bank, savings and loan company, or insurance company—of repayment of the loan in case the homebuyer defaults. This reduces the risk and encourages mortgage lenders to offer more loans, lower down payments, and longer repayment periods. While these advantages in borrowing assist middle-class homebuyers, note that the direct beneficiaries of mortgage insurance are the banks and mortgage-lending companies who are insured against losses. The Department of Veterans Affairs also provides VA insurance for veterans seeking mortgages.

TABLE 13–1	Homeownership Rates by Race/Ethnicity	
	All Locations	
	Percent Own	**Percent Rent**
All Households	67	33
White	70	30
Black	46	54
Asian and other races	53	47
Hispanic*	45	55

*Hispanic householders may be of any race.

Note: The tabulation by race is based on the race of householder. Percentages may not add up to 100.0 due to rounding. The tabulation by Hispanic origin is based on the Hispanic origin of householder. Data are for 1999.

Source: U.S. Census Bureau, *Current Population Survey*, March 1999.

PUBLIC HOUSING
Federally aided housing programs carried out by local government agencies for low-income residents.

FHA and VA mortgage insurance has been extremely successful in promoting home-ownership among millions of middle-class Americans who have financed their homes through federally insured mortgages. A great many of these mortgages financed *suburban* homes. In fact, the success of mortgage insurance programs may have contributed to the deterioration of the nation's central cities by enabling so many middle-class white, and more recently middle-class minority, families to acquire homes in the suburbs and leave the city behind. The FHA's mortgage insurance program is an entirely federal program, but its impact on city and suburban governments should not be underestimated.

HUD also subsidizes and insures apartment projects for low- and moderate-income families and housing projects for the elderly and handicapped. However, "subsidized housing tends to be disproportionately located in distressed inner city and older suburban neighborhoods because wealthier suburbs practice exclusionary zoning and limit affordable housing within their borders."[36] HUD also provides flood insurance and risk insurance in areas where private insurance is difficult to obtain. While these programs have helped, they have increasingly come under attack for not doing enough to provide affordable housing. Overall, studies have concluded that most federal housing programs aimed at helping low- and moderate-income households "by their design, discourage ownership of housing" due to "strong disincentives . . . which often cut off public benefits for those who own."[37]

Public Housing

The Housing Act of 1937 initiated federal public housing programs to provide low-rent public housing for the poor who could not afford decent housing on the private market. The public housing program was designed for people without jobs or incomes sufficient to enable them to afford homeownership, even with the help of FHA mortgage insurance. HUD makes loans and grants to local public housing authorities established by local governments to build, own, and operate low-cost public housing. These housing authorities keep rents low in relation to their tenants' ability to pay. This means that local housing authorities operate at a loss and the federal government reimburses them. No community is required to have a public housing authority; it must apply to Washington and meet federal standards in order to receive federal financial support.

**URBAN
RENEWAL**

The original term for
federally aided pro-
grams carried out by
local government agen-
cies to rebuild blighted
areas of central cities.

**COMMUNITY
DEVELOPMENT
BLOCK GRANT
(CDBG)**

A federal grant
program administered
by HUD that helps
local governments
improve low- and
moderate-income
neighborhoods via
planning, redevelop-
ment, and housing.

Public Housing Today

Today there are about 3,300 local public housing authorities nationwide. They house about 1.3 million households.[38] Most of their income is in the form of government welfare payments; only about one-quarter of public housing residents depend primarily on earned income. Over one million eligible families are on the waiting lists of public housing authorities for units to become available. Many "troubled" local housing authorities and projects have been taken over by HUD.[39] Some of the worst buildings have been demolished, and HUD now encourages local authorities to evict drug dealers.

COMMUNITY DEVELOPMENT AND REVITALIZATION POLICY

In the original Housing Act of 1937, the ideal of "**urban renewal**" was closely tied to public housing. Slums were to be torn down as public housing sites were constructed. Later in the Housing Act of 1949, the urban renewal program was separated from public housing, and the federal government undertook to support a broad program of urban redevelopment to help cities fight a loss in population and to reclaim the economic importance of the core cities. After World War II, the suburban exodus had progressed to the point where central cities faced slow decay and death if large public efforts were not undertaken. Urban renewal could not be undertaken by private enterprise because it was not profitable; suburban property was usually cheaper than downtown property, and it did not require large-scale clearance of obsolete buildings. Moreover, private enterprise did not possess the power of eminent domain, which enables the city to purchase the many separately owned small tracts of land needed to ensure an economically feasible new investment.

For many years, the federal government provided financial support for specific renewal projects in cities. By the early 1960s, it was obvious that federal urban renewal programs created by the Housing Act of 1949 were not working as intended. By the 1970s, the images of urban renewal were "of destruction and delay rather than renaissance and reconstruction." The National Commission on Urban Problems reported that the average urban renewal project took between ten and thirteen years to complete. In looking back at the lessons from the failure: "It was a valuable experiment that taught certain lessons necessary to later urban revitalization initiatives. It exposed the social and political costs of big bulldozer schemes and revealed the limitations inherent in federal policy."[40] It led to the adoption of federal block grant programs that gave localities funding with fewer strings attached than the old programs.

Community Development Block Grants

In the Housing and Community Development Act of 1974, federal development grants to cities were consolidated into community development block grant (CDBG) programs. Cities and counties were authorized to receive these grants to assist them in eliminating slums; increasing the supply of low-income housing; conserving existing housing; improving health, safety, welfare, and public service; improving planning; and preserving property with special value. Today, local governments with 50,000 or more residents, central cities of metropolitan areas, and urban counties with populations of at least 200,000 are eligible for CDBG funds directly. (A state CDBG program provides funds to states, which they, in turn, allocate among localities that are not large enough to qualify for direct aid.) Each year, the grant funds available for entitlement communities are allocated according to relative need on the basis of the higher of two formulas—both of which have a housing component. The first considers the presence of overcrowded housing in the locality, its population, and the poverty rate. The second formula uses housing age, population growth lag, and poverty rate.[41] No local "matching" funds are required. Communities are required to submit an annual application that describes their housing and redevelopment needs, and a comprehensive strategy for meeting those needs.

To ensure that the CDBG program remains targeted on the poor, the legislation requires localities and states to certify that not less than 70 percent of their CDBG funds are spent on activities that benefit low- and moderate-income persons. Low- and moderate-income persons are defined as those persons whose income does not exceed 80 percent of the median income for the area.

Community development block grants can be used by local authorities to acquire blighted land, clear off or modernize obsolete or dilapidated structures, and make downtown sites available for new uses. When the sites are physically cleared of the old structures, they can be resold to private developers for residential, commercial, or industrial use, and the difference between the costs of acquisition and clearance and the income from the private sale to the developers is paid for by the federal government. In other words, local authorities sustain a loss in their redevelopment activities, and this loss is made up by federal grants.

No city is required to engage in redevelopment, but if cities wish federal financial backing, they must show in their applications that they have developed a comprehensive program for redevelopment and the prevention of future blight. They must demonstrate that they have adequate building and health codes, good zoning and subdivision control regulations, sufficient local financing and public support, and a comprehensive plan of development with provisions for relocating displaced persons.

HUD's CDBG program is one of the largest federal grant programs, serving nearly 1,000 of the largest localities in the nation, plus scores of smaller jurisdictions. While the rehabilitation of affordable housing has traditionally been the largest single use of CDBG funds, the program has increasingly become "an important catalyst for economic development activities that expand job and business opportunities for lower income persons and neighborhoods."[42]

Economics of Development

Urban redevelopment is best understood from an economic standpoint. The key to success is to encourage private developers to purchase the land and make a heavy investment in middle- or high-income housing or in commercial or industrial use. In fact, before undertaking a project, local authorities frequently "find a developer first, and then see what interests that developer." The city cannot afford to purchase land, thereby taking it off the tax rolls, invest in its clearance, and then be stuck without a buyer. A private developer must be encouraged to invest in the property and thus enhance the value of the central city. Over time a city can more than pay off its investment by increased tax returns from redeveloped property and hence make a "profit." Thus, many people can come out of a project feeling successful—the city increases its tax base and annual revenues, the private developer makes a profit, and mayors can point to the physical improvements in the city that occurred during their administrations.

COMMUNITY DEVELOPMENT CORPORATIONS (CDCS)

Organizations incorporated to provide programs, offer services, and engage in other activities that promote and support a community.

Urban redevelopment in many cities has become the responsibility of semiautonomous **community development corporations (CDCs)** or authorities (CDAs). An estimated 2,000 to 2,200 of these now exist. Many were initially formed in the 1980s when federal aid to local governments declined, making it necessary to involve public, private, and nonprofit entities in the financing of urban redevelopment. Over time, CDC activity "has expanded beyond the traditional focus on housing and business development into human services, community empowerment, and building social capital."[43]

Enterprise Empowerment Zones

Yet another federally aided effort at community renewal is the "enterprise" or "empowerment" zone. Beginning in the 1980s, the federal government offered assistance to communities for **enterprise zones**—federal grants, tax incentives, loans, and technical assistance to communities within areas of high unemployment and poverty to help them develop partnerships with businesses to revitalize distressed neighborhoods. Most states have also created their own enterprise zone programs. They differ considerably in the specific tax incentives offered, how they define an area eligible for zone status, and what eligibility criteria they use for businesses seeking tax breaks or subsidies. Do they work? The results are mixed, especially with regard to the effectiveness of tax incentives and job creation.[44] One of the reasons is that after the zones are adopted, political pressures take hold. Soon more zones are being created which negates the initial targeting of areas of need.[45]

ENTERPRISE ZONE

A specific geographical area that is economically distressed and eligible for federal grants, tax incentives, and loans to help revitalize it.

Relocation

Relocation is the most sensitive problem in redevelopment.

Relocation is the most sensitive problem in redevelopment. Most people relocated by redevelopment are poor minorities. They have no interest in moving simply to make room for middle- or higher-income housing, or business or industry, or universities, hospitals, and other public facilities. Even though relocated families are frequently given priority for public housing, there is not nearly enough space in public housing to contain them all. They are simply moved from one slum to another. The slum landowner is paid a just price for the land, but the renter receives only a small moving allowance. Redevelopment officials assist relocated families in finding new housing and generally claim success in moving families to better housing. However, frequently the result is higher rents, and redevelopment may actually help to create new slums in other sections of the city. Small business owners are especially vulnerable to relocation. They often depend on a small, well-known neighborhood clientele, and they cannot compete successfully when forced to move to other sections of the city.

"Brownfields"

BROWNFIELDS

Abandoned, idle, or underused industrial or commercial property that may be environmentally contaminated.

In the late 1990s and early 2000s, many advocates of urban redevelopment began focusing their attention—and hopes—on cleaning up "brownfields." "A brownfield is an abandoned, idle, or underused industrial or commercial property where more effective use is hindered by real or perceived contamination."[46] Brownfields, particularly those that are heavily polluted or contaminated, are the most problematic because they have a spillover effect.

Advocates of brownfield cleanup and development believe it will "generate jobs and tax revenues, revitalize neighborhoods, and control urban sprawl."[47] Others are less optimistic, in light of industry relocations to the suburbs (where the workers live) and

Many federal, state, and local agencies are involved in cleaning up brownfields. A brownfield is an abandoned, idle, or underused property that is contaminated. Brownfield cleanup, like other forms of urban redevelopment, is often controversial. Some believe it will create jobs and generate tax revenues, while others believe it is a form of environmental injustice since such efforts may displace minorities or poor residents.

minority concerns about relocation. At a minimum, both sides agree that brownfields and vacant land in declining inner cities tend to go hand-in-hand with crime, unemployment, health, and other social problems for areas surrounding them. This explains why so many federal agencies are currently involved in combating brownfields. The Environmental Protection Agency, HUD, the Department of Transportation, and the Economic Development Administration, along with many state and local agencies, have programs aimed at brownfield redevelopment. However, for some minority residents, brownfields have become a symbol of environmental injustice.[48]

Politics and Development

Political support for redevelopment has come from mayors who wish to make their reputation by engaging in large-scale renewal activities that produce impressive "before" and "after" pictures of the city. Business owners wishing to preserve downtown investments and developers working to acquire land in urban centers have provided a solid base of support for downtown renewal. Mayors, planners, the press, and the good-government forces have made urban redevelopment politically much more popular than public housing.

TRANSPORTATION POLICY

Roads take land. (And so do subways and light rail.) As we have seen, taking land creates conflicts. Yet transportation systems are critical to the economy and are to many citizens a measure of the quality of life in the area in which they live.

Cars, Cars, and More Cars

Few inventions have had such a far-reaching effect on the life of the American people as the automobile. Henry Ford built one of the first gasoline-driven carriages in America in 1893, and by 1900 there were 8,000 automobiles registered in the United States. The Model T was introduced in the autumn of 1908. By concentrating on a single unlovely but enduring model, and by introducing the assembly line processes, the Ford Motor Company began producing automobiles for the masses. Today, there are over 241 million registered motor vehicles in the nation and nearly 4 million miles of roads.

Highway Politics

Highway politics are of interest not only to the automotive industry and the driving public, but also to the oil industry, the American Road Builders Association, railroads, the trucking industry, farmers, the outdoor advertising industry, and county commissioners, taxpayer associations, ecologists and conservationists, and neighborhood improvement associations. These political interests are concerned with the allocation of money for highway purposes, the sources of funds for highway revenue, the extent of gasoline and motor vehicle taxation, the regulation of traffic on the highways, the location of highways, the determination of construction policies, the division of responsibility among federal, state, and local governments for highway financing and administration, the division of highway funds between rural and urban areas, and many other important outcomes in highway politics.

Early Federal Aid

It was in the Federal Aid Road Act of 1916 that the federal government first provided regular funds for highway construction under terms that gave the federal government considerable influence over state policy. For example, if states wanted to get federal money, they were required to have a highway department, and to have their plans for highway construction approved by federal authorities. In 1921, federal aid was limited to a connected system of principal state highways, now called the "federal aid primary highway system." Uniform standards were prescribed and even a uniform numbering system was added, such as "US 1," or "US 30." The emphasis of the program was clearly rural. Later, the federal government also designated a federal aid "secondary" system of farm-to-market roads and provided for "urban extensions" of primary roads, in addition to the federal aid for the primary highway system.

The Interstate System

Congress authorized a national system of interstate and defense highways in 1956 ("I" highways). The interstate system is the most important feature of the federal highway policy. Costs are allocated on the basis of 90 percent federal and 10 percent state. The Federal Highway Act of 1956, as amended, authorized 46,000 miles of highway, designed to connect principal metropolitan areas and industrial centers and thereby shifted the emphasis of federal highway activity from rural to urban needs. Although the system constitutes less than 2 percent of the total surfaced roads in the nation, it carries over 20 percent of all highway traffic. The U.S. Department of Transportation has been given strong supervisory powers, including the selection of routes, but administration and execution are still left to state highway departments. Federal monies are paid to the states, not to the contractors, as the work progresses.

RANKINGS of the STATES

Road Mileage and Gasoline Taxes

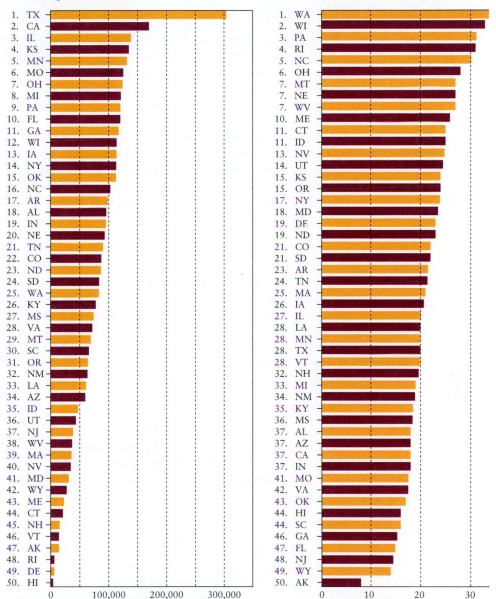

Road mileage

Rank	State
1.	TX
2.	CA
3.	IL
4.	KS
5.	MN
6.	MO
7.	OH
8.	MI
9.	PA
10.	FL
11.	GA
12.	WI
13.	IA
14.	NY
15.	OK
16.	NC
17.	AR
18.	AL
19.	IN
20.	NE
21.	TN
22.	CO
23.	ND
24.	SD
25.	WA
26.	KY
27.	MS
28.	VA
29.	MT
30.	SC
31.	OR
32.	NM
33.	LA
34.	AZ
35.	ID
36.	UT
37.	NJ
38.	WV
39.	MA
40.	NV
41.	MD
42.	WY
43.	ME
44.	CT
45.	NH
46.	VT
47.	AK
48.	RI
49.	DE
50.	HI

State Gasoline Tax Rates (*cents per gallon*)

Rank	State
1.	WA
2.	WI
3.	PA
4.	RI
5.	NC
6.	OH
7.	MT
7.	NE
7.	WV
10.	ME
11.	CT
11.	ID
13.	NV
14.	UT
15.	KS
15.	OR
17.	NY
18.	MD
19.	DE
19.	ND
21.	CO
21.	SD
23.	AR
24.	TN
25.	MA
26.	IA
27.	IL
28.	LA
28.	MN
28.	TX
28.	VT
32.	NH
33.	MI
34.	NM
35.	KY
36.	MS
37.	AL
37.	AZ
37.	CA
37.	IN
41.	MO
42.	VA
43.	OK
44.	HI
44.	SC
46.	GA
47.	FL
48.	NJ
49.	WY
50.	AK

Source: U.S. Department of Transportation, Federal Highway Administration "Highway Statistics 2005" (Table HM-10) Available at http://www.fhwa.dot.gov/policy/ohpi/hss/index.htm

Source: U.S. Federal Highway Administration, Highway Statistics, annual. Data are for 2003.

Federal Highway Money

Revenue from the federal gasoline tax has long been "earmarked" for the Federal Highway Trust Fund. Since 1983, the Federal Highway Trust Fund has contained a highway account and a mass transit account. The current federal gasoline tax is 18.4 cents per gallon, the revenue from this tax alone is insufficient to repair and maintain the nation's highway system. Congress generally recognizes the need to rebuild the nation's highways and bridges. The real political fireworks center on requirements that Congress attaches to the receipt of federal highway funds.

Speed Limits

An example of the controversies generated by federal highway policy was the long battle over speed limits. Prior to 1974 most states had speed limits of 70 miles per hour on interstate highways. A national speed limit of 55 was enacted by Congress that year as a means of saving gasoline. Congress mandated that a state be denied 10 percent of its federal highway aid if it failed to enact and enforce a 55-mph speed limit. But truckers and others who drive a great deal, particularly over long open stretches of interstate highway in the western United States, lobbied hard to eliminate the 55-mph national speed limit. They argued that the costs in billions of additional hours spent on the road were unreasonable, that the 55-mph speed limit was widely ignored anyway, and that it eroded respect for the law.

The national speed limit was also seen as symbolic of federal intrusion in state affairs and a threat to American federalism. However, insurance companies and consumer safety groups lobbied hard to keep the 55-mph speed limit. In 1987 Congress relented; the speed limit on rural portions of interstate highways was raised to 65 mph. Finally in 1995, twenty-one years after first imposing a national speed limit, Congress returned control of speed limits to the states. Arguments over speed and safety are now heard again in state capitals across the country. Proponents of lower limits argue that "speed kills" and that drivers will always exceed posted limits by 10 mph. Opponents contend that most drivers exceed speed limits only when they are set too low, and that safety is more closely related to enforcement of drunk driving and seat belt laws, as well as with improved auto safety, than with speed limits. Most eastern states have retained the 65-mph limit, but several western states have upped their limit to 70 or 75 mph.

The Twenty-One-Year-Old Drinking Age

Currently, federal law also mandates that the Department of Transportation withhold 10 percent of a state's highway funds if it fails to enact a twenty-one-year-old minimum age for the purchase of alcoholic beverages. (See "*Up Close:* Federalism and the Drinking Age" in Chapter 3.)

Auto Insurance

All states currently require drivers to have automobile liability insurance. Minimum amounts of coverage vary across the states. Most states require proof of insurance for annual automobile registration and authorize police to demand proof of insurance as well as drivers' licenses when stopping motorists. Auto insurance rates are regulated in most states. Insurance rates and regulations inspire a near-constant political conflict in state capitols.

Traffic Safety

States have the responsibility for licensing drivers and vehicles and enforcing traffic laws. Prominent state efforts to improve traffic safety include mandatory seat belt laws and stronger enforcement of laws prohibiting driving under the influence of alcohol (DUI). Mandatory seat belt laws have been shown to more than double seat belt usage; usage is higher in states where a violation is considered primary (where a driver can be ticketed for nonusage alone) rather than secondary (where a driver can be ticketed for seat belt violation only if stopped for another reason).[49] Studies have generally found that increased seat belt usage (as well as air bags) have resulted in lower traffic fatality rates. Stepped-up enforcement of DUI laws has also been shown to reduce fatalities.[50]

The growing popularity of bicycles and motorcycles has generated helmet laws in many states and communities. Beginning in the 1960s, the U.S. Department of Transportation required states to enact motorcycle helmet laws in order to receive federal highway funds. DOT eliminated the requirement in 1976 but many states initially kept them in place. Proponents of motorcycle helmet laws cite statistics showing that motorcyclists experience sixteen to eighteen fatalities per mile traveled—more than automobile drivers. Opponents see the issue as one of personal choice and political freedom, rather than public safety. Some states have recently bowed to pressures from Baby Boomer motorcyclists and repealed their helmet laws.

Driver Distraction

Driver distraction is the newest safety issue. The National Highway Traffic Safety Administration estimates that driver distraction is involved in over one-third of all accidents.[51] Eating, drinking, smoking, putting in a CD or tape, moving objects in the car, adjusting climate control, and using hand-held cell phones cause motorist distraction. New York was the first state to ban handheld phones while driving. Most of the others have considered cell phone restrictions in response to high-profile crashes involving cell phones, both hand-held and hands-free.[52] New technological distractions are likely to emerge in the future.

Driver distraction is the newest safety issue.

Auto Safety

Under pressure from consumer lobbies and the U.S. Department of Transportation, auto manufacturers gradually improved the safety of their products. The traffic fatality rate in the United States (the number of deaths from motor vehicle accidents per 100 million miles traveled) was 4.7 in 1970. This rate has dropped dramatically over the years to 1.5 in 2005. This reduction in auto fatalities is primarily a result of manufacturers' safety improvements including airbags.

State Gasoline Taxes

State motor fuel taxes pay over two thirds of total highway costs; the remainder comes from federal highway funds. Every state adds to the federal gasoline tax of 18.5 cents per gallon. State gasoline taxes range from 7.5 to 30 cents per gallon (see "*Rankings of the States*: Gasoline Taxes").

Automoblie and highway interests make vigorous efforts in state capitals to separate gasoline taxes from general revenues and to ensure that these taxes are used exclusively for highways. They strongly oppose "raiding" state highway tax funds for other purposes. In contrast, environmentalists and metropolitan interests frequently seek to use gasoline tax revenues for mass transit—buses, trains, subways.

Fuel Efficiency

The federal government requires automobile manufacturers to maintain corporate average fuel efficiency (**CAFE**) **standards** in the production of automobiles and light trucks. These averages are calculated from highway miles-per-gallon figures for all models of cars and light trucks produced by each manufacturer. In recent years, the CAFE standards for cars has been 27.5 miles per gallon. For light trucks, vans, and sports utility vehicles, the CAFE standard is much lower—20.7 miles per gallon. Determining CAFE standards engenders near constant political conflict in Washington, pitting auto manufacturers against environmental and consumer groups. The increased popularity of pick-up trucks, mini-vans, and sports utility vehicles in recent years has meant that overall fuel efficiency on the roads has improved very little. Alternative fuel vehicles—cars powered entirely or in part by electricity, natural gas, hydrogen, ethanol, etc.—constitute less than five percent of new vehicle sales. Some states, like California and Florida, have moved toward more stringent fuel efficiency standards than even the national government.

The Highway Lobby

Traditionally, highway interests in the states sought to separate highway departments from general state government and to separate gasoline tax revenues from general state revenues. Highway interests believed that their road-building programs would fare better when organization and funding were not in competition with other state programs. They succeeded in most states in obtaining (1) the creation of separate highway boards and commissions, and (2) the establishment of separate highway trust funds to receive gasoline tax revenues "earmarked" for highway construction and maintenance. Indeed, some states passed constitutional amendments preventing the "diversion" of gasoline taxes for non-highway purposes. These policies guaranteed a continual flow of road-building funds and gave highways preferential treatment over other public programs. Today some southern and western states retain these special organizational and funding arrangements for highways.

Infrastructure Investment and Economic Growth

Highway construction, and infrastructure development generally, is widely recognized as a key component of economic development. Nonetheless, while overall government spending has skyrocketed in recent decades, spending for public infrastructure (highways, bridges, ports, airports, sewers, etc.) has not kept pace with growth. Despite evidence that spending for highways is linked to economic development,[53] state and local government spending for highway construction and maintenance has declined from about 20 percent of total spending in 1962 to about 5 percent in 2005.[54] This suggests not only that the nation is failing to invest in *new* public infrastructure, but also that older existing highways, bridges, sewers, and water mains are deteriorating over time.

The Mass Transportation Movement

An alliance of environmentalists, social equity activists, bicycling advocates, transit supporters, architects, planners, community groups, the elderly, and others, has recently emerged to oppose highway building in favor of mass transportation. The coalition has pushed for changes in U.S. transportation policy: "more equitable transportation outcomes, better environmental quality, improved public health and safety, stronger communities, and a thriving economy."[55]

"Anti-sprawlists" believe that transportation reform is necessary to stop sprawl. To get people out of their cars, they favor creating convenient, walkable neighborhoods that are served by public transit. Pedestrian and bicycle-friendly places will, in their judgment, improve residents' health and safety, while saving the environment. Most metropolitan areas are not bicycle or pedestrian friendly. In a *Mean Streets 2000* report,[56] a reform organization labeled many large metro areas as "dangerous" places to walk. "The riskiest places are characterized by spread-out growth and wide, high-speed streets that often lack sidewalks and crosswalks."

Metropolitan Transportation

City planners, urban reformers, and transportation specialists argue that the only way to relieve traffic congestion and preserve central cities is to get people out of private automobiles and onto public transit, that is, "to move people, not cars." Automobiles on expressways can move about 2,000 people per lane per hour; buses can move between 6,000 and 9,000; rail systems can carry up to 60,000 people per hour. In other words, one rail line is estimated to be equal to twenty or thirty expressway lanes of automobiles in terms of its ability to move people.

Nationwide, approximately two-thirds of all commutes last less than 30 minutes and just 17 percent are 45 minutes or longer.[57] More time is spent commuting in the largest metropolitan areas like Los Angeles, San Francisco, Houston, and Seattle. (See Table 13–2.)

The average citizen has a large investment in the automobile. Few Americans want to see their financial investment sit in a garage all day. Americans clearly prefer private automobile transportation and costly expressways to mass transit, regardless of the arguments of transportation experts. Only about 5 percent of Americans use buses or trains to commute to work (see Table 13–3). The result is that mass transit facilities almost always lose money.

Nearly all cities now experience heavy expressway congestion at rush hour and a resulting increase in time and cost to the average automobile commuter. But predictions about future expressway "gridlock" may prove inaccurate. The proportion of daily commuters who drive from the suburbs to work in central cities is gradually decreasing as more businesses move to the suburbs. Intersuburban commuting is increasing over time; circumferential expressways circling cities now carry more traffic than expressways leading into central cities. Rail-based mass transit facilities are usually designed for city–suburban commuting.

Americans clearly prefer private automobile transportation and costly expressways to mass transit, regardless of the arguments of transportation experts.

TABLE 13–2 The Most Congested Urban Areas	
Urban Area	**Per Person Annual Hours of Delay**
Los Angeles, CA	50
San Francisco, CA	37
Houston, TX	36
Dallas, TX	35
Atlanta, GA	34
Washington, DC	34
Denver, CO	31
Detroit, MI	30
U.S. Average	26

Source: U.S. Census Bureau, *Statistical Abstract of the United States,* 2006, p. 713.

TABLE 13–3 How Americans Get to Work	
How?	**Percent**
Drive Alone	77.8
Carpool	10.4
Mass Transit	4.8
Works at Home	3.5
Walk	2.3
Other	1.2

Source: U.S. Census Bureau *Statistical Abstract of the United States, 2006,* p. 714.

As the central city fades as a center for employment and shopping, and more people travel from suburb to suburb, the ridership for mass transit decreases.

The Case for Subsidies

It is necessary to provide public subsidies to commuter rail companies or to have governments operate these facilities at a loss if commuter service is to be maintained. Only a small portion of the costs of public transit come from the fares charged riders. However, it is argued that the cost of mass transit subsidies is very small in comparison with the cost of building and maintaining expressways. Thus, mass transit is considered cost-effective for many cities, even if fares do not meet operating expenses. Moreover, new, speedier, more comfortable, air-conditioned, high-capacity trains with fewer stops and more frequent trips may lure many riders back to public transportation.

Commuter rail systems have to be subsidized by government. Fares alone pay only a small portion of the costs of public transit. But to the governments with mass transit systems, subsidizing them is still cheaper than building and maintaining new expressways.

Federal Mass Transit Aid

For many years the federal government has subsidized the building of highways, particularly the interstate highways, where the federal government assumed 90 percent of the costs. It was not until the 1970s that the federal government showed any comparable interest in mass transit. (Indeed, the *interstate* highway system, despite its name, has carried a major share of *intra*metropolitan city–suburban traffic.) The energy crisis accelerated federal efforts in mass transit. In the Urban Mass Transit Act of 1974, the U.S. Department of Transportation was authorized to make grants to cities for both construction and operation of mass transit systems. In many cities, this simply meant the creation of a local mass transit authority and the purchase of buses. However, in some cities, massive new mass transit programs were developed with federal funds.

Among the most striking efforts in mass transit were San Francisco's BART (Bay Area Rapid Transit), Washington, DC's METRO, and Atlanta's MARTA (Metropolitan Atlanta Rapid Transit Authority). These are large projects into which the cities and the federal government pumped hundreds of million of dollars. They incorporated all of the latest features of modern, pleasant, rapid, convenient, and efficient mass transit. Nonetheless, ridership cannot pay for continuing operating costs, let alone the enormous costs of construction. Perhaps the worst example of federally subsidized mass transit is Miami's Metrorail. The costs were so great and the ridership so small that critics estimated it would have been cheaper for the federal government to buy every regular rider a Rolls-Royce.

The battle for mass transit is filled with trade-off decisions. Certainly one goal of mass transit is to reduce the number of cars on the road in metropolitan areas and to thereby reduce air pollution. But as with roads, it is often necessary to "take" land to construct rail systems and that is never an easy fight, particularly when it may involve relocating residents living in the inner city.

ENVIRONMENTAL PROTECTION

Historically, the principal responsibility for the protection of the environment rested with local governments—removing and disposing of trash, maintaining sewers and treating sewage, providing drinkable water, cleaning streets, and maintaining parks and recreation facilities. But over time, the national government has assumed ever greater responsibilities in environmental protection. Federal environmental policymaking began in earnest in 1970 with the creation of the Environmental Protection Agency (EPA) and the subsequent passage of clean air and water acts. Potentially the EPA is the most powerful and far-reaching bureaucracy in Washington, with legal authority over any activity in the nation that affects the air, water, or ground.

The air and water in the United States are far cleaner today than in previous decades. This is true despite growth in population and an even greater growth in waste products. Nonetheless, genuine concern for the environment centers on the disposal of solid waste (especially hazardous waste), water pollution, and air pollution.

Solid Waste Disposal

Every American produces over 4 pounds of solid waste *each* day. (See Table 13–4.) There are essentially three methods of disposing of solid waste—landfills, incineration, and recycling. Modern landfills have nearly everywhere replaced town dumps. Landfills are

TABLE 13–4 Growth in Solid Wastes						
Waste Measure	**1960**	**1970**	**1980**	**1990**	**2000**	**2004**
Gross waste (millions of tons)	87.5	120.5	151.2	205.2	231.9	236.2
Waste per person per day (lb)	2.6	3.2	3.7	4.5	4.5	4.4
Percent recycled	NA	NA	9.6	16.4	30.1	30.0

Source: U.S. Census Bureau, *Statistical Abstract of the United States*, 2006, p. 229.

usually lined with clay so that wastes do not seep into the water system. In addition, hazardous wastes are separated from those that are not hazardous and handled separately. Contrary to popular rhetoric, there is no "landfill crisis"; the nation is not "running out of land." However, both government agencies and private waste disposal firms are being stymied by powerful organized NIMBYs. Landfill sites are plentiful in most areas but local opposition is strong in every area.

Another alternative is to burn the garbage. Modern incinerators are special plants, usually equipped with machinery to separate the garbage into different types, with scrubbers to reduce air pollution from the burning. They may be sited alongside electric generation plants that can be powered by the heat from the garbage fire. One problem with this method is that the substances emitted from the chimney of the incinerator pollute the air. Another problem: The garbage separated during the screening phase still has to be disposed of; the need for landfill sites is only reduced, not eliminated.

A third method of reducing the amount of solid waste is recycling. Recycling is the conversion of waste into useful products. Newspapers are recycled into cardboard, insulation, and cat litter, and some of it is recycled into newsprint. Overall, about 30 percent of all solid waste in the United States is recycled for reuse. This is a notable achievement over the mere 10 percent that was recycled years ago.[58]

Toxic Waste

Toxic or hazardous wastes are those that pose a significant threat to public health or the environment because of their "quantity, concentration, or physical, chemical, or infectious characteristics."[59] The EPA has the authority to determine which substances are toxic, and to establish separate rules for toxic waste disposal. Hazardous wastes from old sites also constitute an environmental problem. The EPA is committed to clean up such sites under the **Superfund laws**. The EPA has developed a National Priority List of sites based on a hazard ranking system. The EPA has listed about 1,500 hazardous waste sites, but relatively few have undergone complete cleanup to date, often causing state and local officials to get quite angry at Washington.

Water Pollution

Water pollution comes from domestic sewage, industrial waste, agricultural runoff of fertilizers and pesticides, and silt deposits and sedimentation which may be caused by nearby construction. **Primary sewage treatment**—which uses screens and settling chambers, where filth falls out of the water and sludge—is fairly common. **Secondary sewage treatment** removes organic wastes, usually by trickling water through a bed of rocks three to 10 feet deep, where bacteria consume the organic matter. Remaining bacteria are killed by chlorination. **Tertiary sewage treatment** uses chemical filtration processes to remove almost all contaminants from water. Federal water pollution abatement goals call for the establishment of secondary treatment in all American communities. Tertiary treatment is expensive, costing two or three times as much to build and operate as a secondary treatment plant.

The federal government has provided financial assistance to states and cities to build sewage treatment plants ever since the 1930s. The Water Pollution Control Act of 1972 sets a "national goal" for the elimination of all pollutants from navigable waters; it requires industries and municipalities to install "the best available technology." The Act gave the EPA authority to initiate legal actions against pollution caused by private firms or governments. The EPA was authorized by the Safe Drinking Water Act of 1974 to set minimum standards for water quality throughout the nation. Water quality has improved significantly over the last thirty years.

TERTIARY SEWAGE TREATMENT
Expensive chemical filtration processes to remove almost all contaminants from water.

Air Pollution

The air we breathe is about one-fifth oxygen and a little less than four-fifths nitrogen, with traces of other gases, water vapor, and waste products. Most air pollution is caused by the gasoline-powered internal combustion engines of cars, trucks, and buses. Motor vehicles account for more than 60 percent of the total polluting materials sent into the atmosphere every year. The largest industrial polluters are petroleum refineries, smelters, and foundries. Electrical power plants also contribute to total air pollution by burning coal or oil for electric power. Home heating is also a source of pollution, as is the incineration of garbage, trash, and other refuse by governments and industries.

The EPA sets limits on fine particulate matter (silt, dust) in the air. But many large cities, Los Angeles, for example, regularly exceed these limits. Nonetheless, the air we breathe is significantly cleaner today than thirty years ago. The Environmental Protection Agency claims that the Clean Air Act of 1970 and subsequent amendments to it have resulted in an overall reduction in principal pollutants of 48 percent over thirty years.[60] This improvement in air quality has come about despite increases in the gross domestic product (economic growth), vehicle miles traveled, energy consumption, and population. However, the political reality is that environmentalists have become much more powerful in state and local politics and are increasingly effective at pressuring state and local governments to become more "green."

The air we breathe is significantly cleaner today than thirty years ago.

Environmental Politics

Everyone is opposed to pollution. Environmental groups (see Table 13–5) begin with a psychological and political advantage: they are "clean" and their opponents are "dirty." Environmental groups, the news media, Congress and executive agencies can be moved to support environmental protection measures with relatively little consideration of their costs—job loss, price increases, increased dependence on foreign sources of energy. The electric power companies, oil and gas companies, chemical companies and coal companies must fight a rearguard action, continually seeking delays, amendments, and

Noise is a form of air pollution in some neighborhoods, punishable by a fine.

WHITE PHENOMENON

The perception that the environmental movement is a higher priority for whites than for racial minorities.

TABLE 13–5 Leading Environmental Organizations	
National Wildlife Federation	Natural Resources Defense Council
Greenpeace	Environmental Defense Fund
National Audubon Society	Defenders of Wildlife
Sierra Club	Friends of the Earth
Wilderness Society	Union of Concerned Scientists

adjustments and federal standards. But these industries are suspect; environmentalists can charge that industry opposition to environmental protection is motivated by greed for higher profits. And the charge is partially true, although most of the cost of anti-pollution efforts is passed on to the consumer in the form of higher prices.

The environmental movement is generally supported by upper-middle-class or upper-class individuals whose income and wealth are secure. Their aesthetic preferences for a no-growth, clean, unpolluted environment take precedence over jobs and income. Workers and small business people whose jobs and income depend on energy production, oil reining, forestry, mining, smelting, or manufacturing, are unlikely to be ardent environmentalists. Minority opinion is split; some minority interests argue that minorities live closer to the sources of pollution and environmental degradation and therefore should support regulation; yet minorities are generally more concerned with jobs than with a clean environment.[61] Indeed, environmentalism is sometimes seen as a **"white phenomenon."** Overall, public opinion supports environmental measures when they are posed in the abstract, but public opinion is divided when environmental concerns are matched against economic growth (see Figure 13–1).

Environmental groups have powerful allies in the nation's NIMBYs. Even people who otherwise recognize the general need for new commercial or industrial developments, highways, power plants (electric and nuclear), pipelines, waste disposal sites, nonetheless voice loud opposition when any of these are planned for placement in their neighborhood.

Environmental activists are more likely to be upper-middle-class or upper-class individuals whose income and wealth are secure. Poorer individuals whose jobs may be eliminated do not have the time to attend protest rallies and are often outnumbered at protest events.

Greening of the States and Cities

Since the creation of the Environmental Protection Agency in 1970, environmental protection has been a national responsibility. However, states and communities have undertaken important initiatives in the field, in addition to their traditional responsibilities for solid waste disposal, sewerage treatment, and the provision of safe drinking water. State initiatives are encouraged by the use of federal partial standard preemptions which permits states to regulate activities in a field already regulated by the federal government as long as state regulatory standards

FIGURE 13–1 Public Opinion: Environment and Economic Growth

Do you think the environmental movement has done more good than harm, or more harm than good?

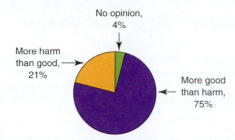

With which one of these statements about the environment and the economy do you most agree: protection of the environment should be given priority, even at the risk of curbing economic growth, or economic growth should be given priority, even if the environment suffers to some extent?

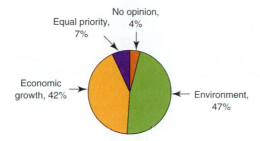

Source: Various polls reported in www.publicagenda.org

are at least as strict as those of the federal government. To receive such a preemption or waiver for an environmental protection initiative, states must usually submit their regulations to the EPA for approval.

Environmental groups often feel that the federal government has not gone far enough in mandating restrictions on air pollution. (An international Rio Treaty in 1992 and its follow-up Kyoto Protocol in 1987 set national goals for reducing greenhouse gases below 1990 levels. The United States failed to ratify the Treaty, citing the economic dislocations required to fully comply with it.) Environmentalists have increasingly turned to the states and cities to enact a wide variety of measures to reduce air and water pollution.

California Governor Arnold Schwarzenegger committed his state to automobile fuel emission standards well beyond those of the federal government. He has even threatened to sue EPA if it fails to grant California a partial standard preemption to implement these tougher standards. Schwarzenegger also established a "Green Buildings" program, ordering all state buildings to be designed and reengineered to make them more energy efficient. New York City ordered its fleet of 13,000 taxis to go green over five years by substituting smaller hybrid-fueled cabs for larger gas-guzzling taxis. Dozens of other states and cities have initiated pollution control programs.

Land use battles continue to be fierce in many communities—reflective of major power struggles for control of a scarce resource.

did **YOU** know?

The Nation's Biggest Landowner

Few people realize that the nation's largest landowner is the U.S. government. It owns over one-fourth of the total land area of the United States. Its land use policies are largely determined by the U.S. Department of the Interior. Federal land use policies are particularly important in those states where the U.S. government owns half or more of the total land area.

Federal Land Ownership			
By Percent of State			
Nevada	84.5	Washington	30.3	Mississippi	7.3
Alaska	69.1	Montana	29.9	Arkansas	7.2
Utah	57.5	Hawaii	19.4	South Dakota	6.2
Oregon	53.1	New Hampshire	13.5	Minnesota	5.6
Idaho	50.2	North Carolina	11.8	Wisconsin	5.6
Arizona	48.1	Michigan	10.0	Kentucky	5.4
California	45.3	Virginia	9.9	Louisiana	5.1
Wyoming	42.3	Florida	8.2	Missouri	5.0
New Mexico	41.8	Vermont	7.5		
Colorado	36.6	West Virginia	7.4		
Less Than 5%			
Georgia	3.8	Delaware	2.0	Kansas	1.2
Oklahoma	3.6	Indiana	2.0	Maine	1.1
Tennessee	3.2	Massachusetts	1.9	Iowa	0.8
New Jersey	3.1	Texas	1.9	New York	0.8
South Carolina	2.9	Illinois	1.8	Connecticut	0.4
Maryland	2.8	Ohio	1.7	Rhode Island	0.4
North Dakota	2.7	Alabama	1.6		
Pennsylvania	2.5	Nebraska	1.4		

Note: Data are for 2004.

Source: Government Services Administration, Office of Governmentwide Real Property Policy, 2004. Available at http://www.gsa.gov/realpropertyprofile

ON THE WEB

The American Planning Association and its professional arm, the American Institute of Certified Planners, represents more than 30,000 planners, officials, and citizens involved in urban planning. It lobbies in Washington to strengthen planning requirements as conditions for federal grants to states and cities. Its Web site at

www.planning.org

provides extensive information about planning and related subjects. It includes some articles from the organization's monthly publication, *Planning*. For students, it includes a catalog of books on planning, as well as information on how to become a certified planner. The U.S. Department of Housing and Urban Development (HUD) maintains a Web site at

www.hud.gov

It contains information on all HUD programs including federal home loans, rental assistance, community development grants, and planning grants. A particularly interesting feature at this site is "HUD in Your Community," which allows users to click to their own state and their own city to learn what HUD programs are currently in operation there.

Other Web Sites

Housing

National Association of Home Builders Housing Facts and Figures: **www.nahb.org**

Joint Center for Housing Studies of Harvard University: **www.jchs.harvard.edu**

Fannie Mae Foundation Knowledgeplex: **www.knowledgeplex.org**

National Association of Housing and Redevelopment Officials: **www.nahro.org**

National Association of Realtors: **www.realtor.org**

National Council of State Housing Agencies: **www.ncsha.org**

National Low Income Housing Coalition: **www.nlihc.org**

Economic Development

Economic Development Administration: **www.eda.gov**

Minority Business Development Agency: **www.mbda.gov**

EPA Brownfields Initiative: **www.epa.gov/swerosps/bf**

U.S. Department of Commerce: **www.doc.gov**

U.S. Department of Agriculture Rural Development: **www.rurdev.usda.gov**

National Rural Development Partnership: **www.rurdev.usda.gov/nrdp**

THE POLITICS OF TAXATION AND FINANCE

14

QUESTIONS TO CONSIDER

What do you think is the fairest tax?
- ■ Income tax
- ■ Sales tax
- ■ Property tax
- ■ Cigarette tax

Do you believe that state governments should operate lotteries?
- ■ Yes   ■ No

Should state legislatures have constitutional limits placed on their taxing authority?
- ■ Yes   ■ No

If your city government is forced to reduce spending, do you think it should do so?
- ■ Across the board on all services?
- ■ Selectively on only certain services?

AN OVERVIEW OF GOVERNMENT FINANCES

Hate taxes but love government programs? Many Americans feel just that way, yet the many services, activities, and facilities we enjoy somehow have to be paid for. As in many households, money-related decisions are often the most difficult—and contentious—and misunderstood. An individual's preferences for their state or locality's taxing, spending, and borrowing decisions are often driven by his or her own personal economic situation and level of understanding of economics, which, for many, is limited. The sheer dollar amounts of revenues raised and monies spent are quite intimidating to the average taxpayer who is simply trying to make ends meet in his or her own household. Occasionally, governments, like individuals, struggle economically and have to tighten their belts.

Government Finances and the GDP

Dollar figures in government budgets are often mind-boggling. The federal government spends almost $2.5 *trillion* each year, and all state and local governments combined spend an additional $1.4 *trillion*. To better understand what these dollar figures mean, it is helpful to view them in relation to the nation's **gross domestic product** (**GDP**), the sum of all the goods and services produced in the United States in a year.

In 1929 total governmental spending—federal, state, and local combined—amounted to only about 10 percent of the GDP. Today total governmental spending amounts to about 31 percent of the GDP (see Figure 14–1). *Federal* spending accounts for about 20 percent of the GDP, and spending by all *state and local* governments adds another 11 percent.

State and Local Government Spending

State and local governments direct most of their spending toward education, social services (welfare and health), public safety (police and fire), and transportation. Spending patterns are different between states and local governments, primarily because they differ in the functions for which they have primary financial and service delivery responsibilities (see Figure 14–2).

FIGURE 14–1 Government Expenditures as a Percentage of GDP

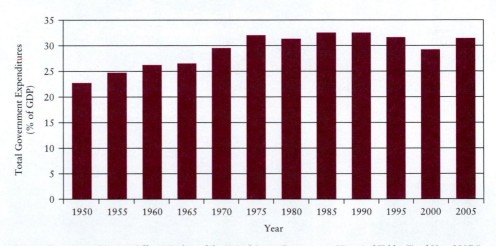

Source: Government Printing Office, "Budget of the United States Government: Historical Tables Fiscal Year 2007," Table 15.3. Available at http://www.gpoaccess.gov/usbudget/fy07/sheets/hist10Z1.xls

FIGURE 14–2 Revenues and Expenditures: States versus Localities

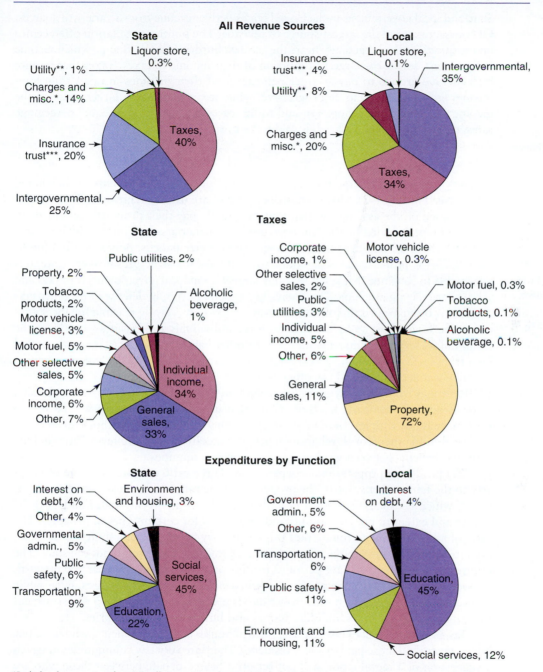

All Revenue Sources

State
- Liquor store, 0.3%
- Utility**, 1%
- Charges and misc.*, 14%
- Insurance trust***, 20%
- Intergovernmental, 25%
- Taxes, 40%

Local
- Insurance trust***, 4%
- Liquor store, 0.1%
- Intergovernmental, 35%
- Utility**, 8%
- Charges and misc.*, 20%
- Taxes, 34%

Taxes

State
- Public utilities, 2%
- Property, 2%
- Tobacco products, 2%
- Motor vehicle license, 3%
- Motor fuel, 5%
- Other selective sales, 5%
- Corporate income, 6%
- Other, 7%
- Alcoholic beverage, 1%
- Individual income, 34%
- General sales, 33%

Local
- Corporate income, 1%
- Motor vehicle license, 0.3%
- Other selective sales, 2%
- Public utilities, 3%
- Individual income, 5%
- Other, 6%
- General sales, 11%
- Motor fuel, 0.3%
- Tobacco products, 0.1%
- Alcoholic beverage, 0.1%
- Property, 72%

Expenditures by Function

State
- Interest on debt, 4%
- Other, 4%
- Governmental admin., 5%
- Public safety, 6%
- Transportation, 9%
- Environment and housing, 3%
- Social services, 45%
- Education, 22%

Local
- Government admin., 5%
- Other, 6%
- Transportation, 6%
- Public safety, 11%
- Environment and housing, 11%
- Interest on debt, 4%
- Education, 45%
- Social services, 12%

*Includes charges = user fees: Miscellaneous general revenue includes interest earnings, special assessments, sale of property, and other general revenue.

**Includes water, electric power, gas supply, and transit.

***Includes unemployment compensation, employee retirement, workers' compensation, and other insurance trust revenue.

Note: Data are for 2005.

Source: U.S. Census Bureau. "State and Local Government Finances by Level of Government and by State: 2004–2005, Table 1." Available at http://www.census.gov/govs/estimate/0500uss1_1.html

TYPES OF TAXES AND TAX POLITICS

State and local governments in the United States derive revenue from a variety of sources. Of course, taxes are the largest source of revenue. The politics of taxation often center on the question of who actually bears the greatest **burden of a tax,** that is, which income groups must devote the largest proportion of their income to taxes. Taxes that require high-income groups to pay a larger percentage of their incomes in taxes than low-income groups are said to be **progressive**, while taxes that take a larger share of the income of low-income groups are said to be **regressive**. Taxation at equal percentage rates, regardless of income level, is said to be **proportional**.

Local Property Taxes

Property taxes are the largest source of revenue for *local* governments in the United States. (see Figure 14–2). However, property taxes are usually regressive. This conclusion is based on the assumption that renters actually pay their property taxes through increased rentals levied by the landlord, and the further assumption that high-income groups have more wealth in untaxed forms of property (stocks, bonds, mutual funds, etc.). Since the property tax is the foundation of local tax structures in every state, it is reasonable to conclude that states that rely largely upon local governments for taxes and services are relying more upon regressive tax structures. Yet, in defense of property taxation, it is often argued that no other form of taxation is really feasible for local governments. Local sales and income taxes force individuals and businesses to leave the communities levying them; real estate, on the other hand, is less easy to move about and hide from local tax assessors. Real estate taxes are the only type of taxes that can be effectively collected by local tax officials.

Revenues from property taxation depend on the property wealth of a community. Dependence upon property taxation means that wealthier communities will be able to raise more funds with less burden on taxpayers than communities without much property wealth. In other words, reliance on property taxation results in inequalities in burdens and benefits between wealthier and poorer communities.

The burden of property taxes depends on (1) the ratio of **assessed value** of property to the fair **market value** of the property; (2) the rate at which assessed property is taxed, which is usually expressed in **mills** or tenths of a percent; and, finally, (3) the nature and extent of tax exemptions and reductions for certain types of property. The ratio of assessed value to full market value may vary from one community to the next, even in states with laws requiring uniform assessment ratios throughout the state. The failure of communities to have periodic, professional and computer-generated tax evaluation means that taxes continue to be levied on old assessment figures, even while market values go up. The result, over time, is a considerable lowering of assessment ratios, and therefore taxes, on older homes and businesses and industries.

Tax assessors usually know the sale price of houses of newer residents, who must pay higher taxes than those paid by older residents. There are very few communities in which a suggestion of a reevaluation will not set off a heated debate between those who are enjoying a low assessment and those who are not. If new tax revenues are needed, it is much easier to simply increase the rate or millage to be applied against the assessed value of property. Many communities face state restrictions on maximum tax rates, or they are required to submit any proposed increase in tax rates to the voters in a referendum. These restrictions are usually favored by low-tax forces, which have succeeded in obtaining legislation at the state level that impairs the taxing abilities of local governments.

Some categories of property are exempt from taxation; these usually include properties that are used for nonprofit, charitable, religious, educational, and other public purposes. Occasionally, such exemptions are attacked by those who feel that they are, in effect, subsidies to the exempted organizations; this is particularly true regarding exemptions for religious property. Exemptions for educational or public properties sometimes work a hardship on communities in which large public facilities or educational institutions are located. However, the exemptions that arouse the greatest controversy are usually those given by state and local governments to new business and industry, in an effort to induce them to locate in the state or community granting the exemption.

State Sales Taxes

While the property tax is the most important source of revenue for local communities, the general sales tax is the most important source of tax revenue for state governments. Consumers are a notoriously weak pressure group. It is difficult for them to count pennies dribbled away four or five at a time; the tax does not involve obvious payroll deductions, as in income taxation, or year-end bills, as in property taxation. Only five states do *not* impose a general sales tax (Alaska, Delaware, Montana, New Hampshire, and Oregon). Some states get over half of their revenue from sales taxes.

State and local sales taxes are often considered regressive, that is, the poor are believed to devote a larger percentage of their income to paying these taxes than the wealthy. The regressivity of sales taxation is based on the assumption that low-income groups must use most, if not all, of their income for purchases, while high-income groups devote larger shares of their income to savings. However, many states exclude some of the necessities of life from sales taxation, such as packaged food, rent, and medical expenses, in order to reduce the burden of sales taxation on the poor. Because of these exclusions, sales taxes in many states are not highly regressive.

States generally rely more heavily on sales taxation than on income taxation. However, reliance upon one or the other type of tax varies from state to state. The decision to place primary reliance upon sales or income taxation is one of the most important policy choices facing state government. The yield from both types of taxation can be quite large.

There are several arguments on behalf of sales taxation in the states. The first is that sales taxation is the only major source of revenue left to the states—local governments must rely on property taxes, and the federal government has placed such a heavy tax burden on incomes that taxpayers will not countenance an additional state bite out of their paychecks. Moreover, sales taxes are not as visible as income or property taxes, since sales taxes are paid pennies at a time. Generally, the customer considers the sales tax as part of the price of an item. Taxpayers never add up the total they have paid in sales taxes, so sales taxation appears to be a relatively "painless" form of taxation. In

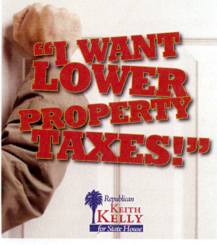

Candidates from both parties often run on a platform promising to lower homeowners' property taxes. This clever ad was a very effective one for the candidate to hand to potential supporters as he campaigned door-to-door through neighborhoods.

The general sales tax is the most important source of tax revenue for state governments.

PROGRESSIVE STATE INCOME TAX

Income tax rates rise with increases in income.

"ABILITY TO PAY" PRINCIPLE

Wealthier individuals pay a higher tax rate than poorer individuals.

SIXTEENTH AMENDMENT

Created the federal income tax, a progressive tax based on ability to pay.

FLAT RATE TAX

Income tax rate stays the same, regardless of taxable income.

addition, sales taxes ensure that low-income groups who benefit from public services will share in the costs of government. Actual hardships for the poor from sales taxes can be reduced by excluding food and other necessities from taxation, but the poor will pay taxes when purchasing luxury items. Finally, sales taxes are useful in reaching mobile populations, that is, tourists, commuters, and transients—people who derive benefits from a host state but who would not otherwise help pay for these benefits.

Selective Sales (Excise) Taxes: Cigarette, Alcohol, Gas

States vary considerably in the sales taxes they place on certain selected items. Two of these selective sales taxes are sometimes referred to as "sin taxes" (cigarettes and alcohol). Few people object to raising either tax, unless they use or produce the product. Often these sorts of taxes are earmarked to specific programs—for example, cigarette taxes to help pay for indigent health care; alcohol taxes to fund domestic violence shelters, etc. In 2007 alone, ten states raised their rates on cigarettes. A majority of states have tax rates over 80 cents per pack. Eight states charge more than $2.00 per pack, and New Jersey's $2.58 rate is the highest in the nation. Alcohol tax rates differ by type of booze—wine, beer, hard liquor. Gas taxes, too, are often earmarked; they must be used on roads. But gas taxes are a lot more political than cigarette or alcohol taxes because gas is a necessity for most people.

State Income Taxes

Today all but seven states tax individual income. (See Table 14–1.) Connecticut was the most recent state to enact an income tax in 1991. Fiscal pressures on state government continue to stir debate in the non–income tax states over the adoption of the tax.

Progressive state income taxes—income taxes with rates that rise with increases in income—are usually defended on the principle of "**ability to pay**"; that is, the theory that high-income groups can afford to pay a larger percentage of their income into taxation at no more of a sacrifice than that required of low-income groups who devote a smaller proportion of their income to taxation. The principle of a graduated (progressive) income tax based on ability to pay, a principle accepted at the federal level in 1913 with the passage of the **Sixteenth Amendment**, together with the convenience, economy, and efficiency of income taxes, is generally cited by proponents of income taxation.

State income taxes in several states are "**flat rate**" taxes on personal income: 3 percent (Illinois), 5.95 percent (Pennsylvania), 4.8 percent (Colorado), and 5.9 percent (Massachusetts). In other income tax states, the rates are "progressive"—rising from 1 or 2 percent, to 7 or 8 percent, with increases in income levels. Rhode Island and Vermont tie their *state* personal income tax to the *federal* income tax, by specifying that state taxes will be a specific percentage of federal taxes. Most states also have their own systems of exemptions.[1]

A proposal to levy a 10-cent-per-cup tax on expresso was roundly defeated by voters in Seattle, Washington—birthplace of the Starbucks Corporation. Opponents argued the tax would negatively impact small businesses (coffeehouses) and their employees. Proponents who signed petitions to get the issue on the ballot saw the consumption tax as a way to raise money for underfunded early childhood education programs. www.usefulwork.com/shark/LatteTaxProtestZoka.jpg

TABLE 14–1 Income Taxation in the States

States Without an Individual Income Tax

Alaska	South Dakota	Wyoming
Florida	Texas	
Nevada	Washington	

State Individual Income Tax Rates (rate ranges in parentheses)

Alabama (2.0–5.0)	Louisiana (2.0–6.0)	North Dakota (2.1–5.54)
Arizona (2.59–4.57)	Maine (2.0–8.5)	Ohio (0.712–7.185)
Arkansas (1.0–7.0)	Maryland (2.0–4.75)	Oklahoma (0.5–5.65)
California (1.0–9.3)	Massachusetts (5.3)	Oregon (5.0–9.0)
Colorado (4.63)	Michigan (3.9)	Pennsylvania (3.07)
Connecticut (3.0–5.0)	Minnesota (5.35–7.85)	Rhode Island[b]
Delaware (2.2–5.95)	Mississippi (3.0–5.0)	South Carolina (2.5–7.0)
Georgia (1.0–6.0)	Missouri (1.5–6.0)	Tennessee[a]
Hawaii (1.4–8.25)	Montana (1.0–6.9)	Utah (2.3–6.98)
Idaho (1.6–7.8)	Nebraska (2.56–6.84)	Vermont (3.6–9.5)
Illinois (3.0)	New Hampshire[a]	Virginia (2.0–5.75)
Indiana (3.4)	New Jersey (1.4–8.97)	West Virginia (3.0–6.5)
Iowa (0.36–8.98)	New Mexico (1.7–5.3)	Wisconsin (4.6–6.75)
Kansas (3.5–6.45)	New York (4.0–6.85)	
Kentucky (2.0–6.0)	North Carolina (6.0–8.0)	

[a]State income tax is limited to dividends and interest only.
[b]Federal tax liability.
Source: The Book of the States, 2007, vol. 39, p. 383.

Corporate Taxes

In addition to property taxes paid to local governments, corporations in forty-five states pay a **corporate income tax**. (Nevada, South Dakota, Texas, Washington, and Wyoming do not tax corporate income.) These taxes range from a 5 percent flat rate to sliding scales of 1 to 10 percent of net profits. Raising corporate taxes is popular with voters; however, while individuals do not pay corporate taxes directly, these taxes may be passed along to consumers in higher prices. The greatest barrier to higher state corporate taxes is the possibility that such taxes will cause corporations to locate in another state. It is difficult for a state to maintain a "good business climate" if its corporate taxes are high. Most studies find that industrial-location decisions are influenced by many factors other than taxes—for example, access to markets, raw materials, skilled labor, and energy. However, businesses expect their taxes to be kept in line with those of their competitors. In addition to corporate profits taxes, business looks at **unemployment compensation** and **workers' compensation "premiums"** (taxes) and the costs of environmental regulations.

Lottery and Gambling Revenue

Most states now have public lotteries as a means of raising money. However, lotteries bring in just 2 percent of all state–local government revenue. The administrative costs, including prize money, run over 50 percent of the gross revenue. This compares very unfavorably with the estimated 5 percent cost of collecting income taxes, and with the

CORPORATE INCOME TAX

Tax on the net profits of corporations.

UNEMPLOYMENT COMPENSATION

Payment received by unemployed workers, who become unemployed through no fault of their own.

WORKERS' COMPENSATION

A form of insurance held by employers that provides medical care and compensation for employees who are injured in the course of employment.

Lotteries have big jackpots but actually raise less than 2 percent of all state and local government revenue. Administrative costs, including payouts, take over half of the gross revenue.

only slightly higher cost of collecting sales taxes. Some states also receive income from horse racing, dog racing, casino gambling, and video gaming devices. Nevada leads the way with nearly a quarter of its revenue coming directly from gambling taxes. Most states restrict gambling to parimutuel betting on the racetrack. The total revenues raised from such sources, however, make up less than 0.5 percent of all state–local revenues. Opponents of gambling-based revenue sources complain that they are very regressive forms of taxation, while supporters say they are a "voluntary" tax—no one has to play. States downplay lottery and gambling as revenue sources, choosing instead to promote them as entertainment. From a player's perspective, the odds are pretty bad. (See "Fat Chance.")

USER CHARGES

The fastest growing source of revenue; charges levied on specific users by a government agency for the services they use; only those who use a service pay the charge.

User Charges

User charges are currently the fastest-growing source of state and local government revenue. Today, charges and miscellaneous revenues constitute nearly 25 percent of state–local revenue. (This figure is really a combination of user charges, utility and liquor store revenues, and miscellaneous revenues.) User charges directly link the benefits and costs of public goods in the fashion of the marketplace. Only those persons who actually use the government service pay for it. User charges include charges for water and sewerage,

Gambling proposals generate NIMBY (not-in-my-back-yard) protests, especially when it is a celebrity like Donald Trump who proposes to build a casino in the neighborhood.

Fat Chance: Odds of a Variety of Unlikely Occurrences*

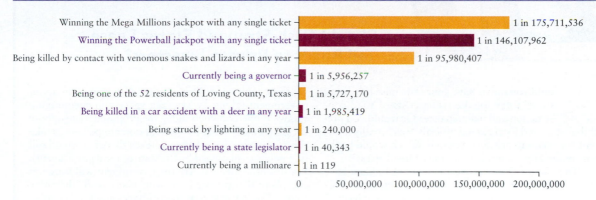

Winning the Mega Millions jackpot with any single ticket	1 in 175,711,536
Winning the Powerball jackpot with any single ticket	1 in 146,107,962
Being killed by contact with venomous snakes and lizards in any year	1 in 95,980,407
Currently being a governor	1 in 5,956,257
Being one of the 52 residents of Loving County, Texas	1 in 5,727,170
Being killed in a car accident with a deer in any year	1 in 1,985,419
Being struck by lighting in any year	1 in 240,000
Currently being a state legislator	1 in 40,343
Currently being a millionare	1 in 119

*Odds make use of most recent data and refer to all U.S. residents

Source: "Fat Chance" from "Observer" by Alan Greenblatt in *Governing*, January 2006. Copyright © 2006 by Congressional Quarterly, Inc. Reprinted by permission of Governing Magazine. (Sources: Megamillions. com, Multi-State Lottery Association, National Safety Council, U.S. Census Bureau, State Farm, National Weather Service, National Conference of State Legislatures, Capgemini and Merrill Lynch & Co.)

garbage collection, electricity supplied by municipalities, transit fares, toll roads, airport landing fees, space rentals, parking meters, stadium fees, admissions to parks, zoos, swimming pools, and so on. States and localities have gotten very creative in getting much needed revenue from user fees. (See "*What Do You Think?* Should Cash-Strapped States Lease Toll Roads to Private Investors?")

EXPLAINING STATE TAX SYSTEMS

What accounts for differences in tax policy among the states? Total state–local *tax revenues* vary from a high of over $5,258 per person in New York, to a low of $2,332 in Alabama (see "*Rankings of the States:* Per Capita State and Local Government Tax Revenue"). This means that per capita tax levels of some states are twice as high as those of other states.

Tax burdens, that is, taxes in relation to personal income, also vary considerably among the states. The concept of tax *burden* generally refers to taxes paid in relation to personal income. Because of differences among the states in income levels, states with the highest per capita *levels of taxation* are not necessarily the same states with the highest *tax burdens*. The total tax burden in a state is measured by "state and local tax revenues as a percent of personal income." (See "*Rankings of the States:* Tax Burdens," right column.) The state–local tax burden averages about 10.5 percent of personal income in the United States.

Progressivity and Regressivity

It is difficult to evaluate the overall progressivity or regressivity of state tax systems. It is generally believed that *overall* state and local government taxes are regressive.[2] This regressivity is largely attributed to state and local government reliance on sales and property taxation, rather than progressive income taxation. However, this belief fails to consider the many types of exemptions to sales taxes found in various states (food, rent, medical care, etc.); these exemptions make sales taxes less regressive. It also fails to consider many property tax exemptions ("**homestead**" exemptions) found in many states that offer relief to owners of less expensive homes. Nevertheless,

HOMESTEAD EXEMPTION

Excludes a certain portion of the value of owner-occupied homes from property taxes.

Should Cash-Strapped States Lease Toll Roads to Private Investors?

Would you rather have your state raise its gas tax to help pay for the rising costs of road construction and maintenance? Or would you prefer that state and local elected officials "sell" (really lease) some toll roads to private investors? Which would be the most politically palatable in a time of fiscal stress?

The City of Chicago and the State of Indiana have already opted for the leasing approach, "in return for a big upfront payment of guaranteed year-by-year paybacks." Chicago entered into a 99-year lease of the Chicago Skyway toll road (8 miles long) with Australian and Spanish investors. The deal raised $1.8 billion for the city. Indiana Gov. Mitch Daniels (R) leased the 157-mile-long Indiana Toll Road to private investors for 75 years, generating $3.85 billion. Some states, like Texas and Virginia, have entered into similar agreements on a smaller scale, while still others are still seriously toying with the idea.

Turning over toll roads to private investors is risky business *politically*, especially when it involves a proposed, yet-to-be built road. Environmentalists complain about government taking away green space and encouraging sprawl. Property owners along the proposed route oppose the government using its eminent domain powers to take private property for private use (even though it would still be a public road owned by the state or local government). Fiscal conservatives worry the government will lease too cheaply or that private firms will "cherry pick" lucrative routes, leaving government to finance the less lucrative ones.

Proponents of toll road leasing, often elected officials and the private investors, say it is easier to do politically at a time when money for roads is difficult to generate. In the words of one investor, "Private financiers can produce bank loans and major equity capital far more easily than governments can raise taxes. And they can also outdo governments in introducing road-building innovations and on-time construction performance."

Source of photo: http://www.tfhrc.gov/pubrds/06mar/images/pooll.jpg

Source: Neal Peirce, "Selling Our Toll Roads: Good or Retrograde Idea?" *Government Finance Review* 23 (June 2007): 81–82.

it is generally argued that states that rely more on income taxes (especially those states with progressive rate structures rather than flat rates) have more progressive tax systems.[3] Progressivity *increases* with higher levels of state income. It appears to be easier to make tax systems more progressive when the size of the economic pie is expanding.[4]

RANKINGS of the STATES

Tax Burdens

Per Capita State and Local Government Tax Revenue

1. NY
2. CT
3. NJ
4. WY
5. MA
6. MD
7. RI
8. HI
9. MN
10. ME
11. CA
12. WI
13. VT
14. AK
15. DE
16. NE
17. IL
18. WA
19. PA
20. NV
21. OH
22. KS
23. VA
24. MI
25. CO
26. NH
27. FL
28. IA
29. IN
30. ND
31. NC
32. OR
33. LA
34. TX
35. GA
36. AZ
37. NM
38. MO
39. KY
40. WV
41. UT
42. ID
43. OK
44. SC
45. MT
46. SD
47. TN
48. AR
49. MS
50. AL

(x-axis: 0, 1,000, 2,000, 3,000, 4,000, 5,000, 6,000)

Note: Data are for 2004.
Source: Bureau of the Census, Governments Division "State and Local Government Finances: 2003–2004." Available online at http://www.census.gov/govs/www/estimate04.html

Combined State and Local Tax Burdens

1. VT
2. ME
3. NY
4. RI
5. HI
5. OH
7. WI
8. CT
9. NE
10. NJ
11. CA
11. MN
13. AR
14. KS
14. MI
16. WA
17. IA
17. LA
17. NC
20. KY
20. WV
22. IL
22. MD
22. PA
25. IN
25. SC
27. UT
28. MA
29. MS
30. CO
31. AZ
31. GA
33. VA
34. ID
34. MO
34. NV
37. FL
37. OR
39. ND
40. NM
41. MT
42. WY
43. TX
44. OK
44. SD
46. AL
46. DE
48. TN
49. NH
50. AK

(x-axis: 0, 3, 6, 9, 12, 15)

Note: Tax burden data are for 2007.
Source: Bureau of Economic Analysis, Department of Commerce, and Tax Foundation calculations, available online at http://www.taxfoundation.org/taxdata/show/336.html

PROPERTY TAX
LIMITS

Limits on property tax
millage rates or annual
assessment (appraised
value) rate increases.

REVOLTING AGAINST TAXES

The United States is the land of tax revolts. The national tradition of revolting against taxes includes the Boston Tea Party in 1773, a leading event in the movement toward independence; Shays' Rebellion in 1786, an important stimulus to creating the Constitution of the United States; and the Whisky Rebellion of 1794, forcefully extinguished by President George Washington. The political culture of the nation has always reflected a distrust of government power. The total tax burden in the United States is less than most other advanced industrialized nations of the world. Yet opinion polls regularly show that many Americans believe their taxes are "too high." Polls also show that some taxes are regarded as less fair than others. (See Figure 14–3.)

Popular Opposition to Rising Taxes

Voters appear to be very sensitive to levels of state and local taxation. That is to say, popular dislike of taxes rises with increases in real levels of taxation. (This is not as obvious a conclusion as it might seem; state and local taxes are not as visible to most people as federal taxes, and few people are informed or attentive to state and local matters.) Indeed, as state income taxes rise above 4 percent, levels of dislike begin to rise exponentially.[5] Likewise, when sales tax levels rise above 5 percent, opposition increases rapidly. Homeowners are much more likely to object to property taxation than renters, while renters are more likely to object to sales taxes than homeowners.

Tax Limitations

Constitutional limits on taxes fall into several general categories. Of course, any specific plan may vary in details from the outlines described here.

■ *Property tax limits* Some limitations are specifically directed at property taxes. These proposals may limit allowable tax rates to 10 or 15 mills of full value of property, limit annual assessment increases, and/or allow reassessments only when the property is sold. This form of limitation applies mainly to local governments and school districts and may actually increase state taxes if state governments simply take over local services.

FIGURE 14–3 **Citizen Opinions about the Fairness of Federal and State Taxes**

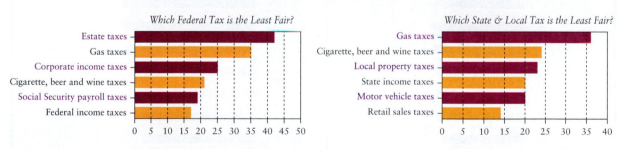

Source: From pp. 9 and 10 in *Special Report: What Does America Think About Taxes: The 2007 Annual Survey of U.S. Attitudes on Taxes and Wealth* by Andrew Chamberlain, March 2007, No. 154. Copyright © 2007 by Tax Foundation. Reprinted by permission of Tax Foundation.

**STATE
EXPENDITURE
LIMITS**

Limits rate of increase
in expenditures to the
cost of living or con-
sumer price index.

**PERSONAL
PROPERTY**

Automobiles, boats,
furniture, stocks and
bonds, and the like,
whose true value is
difficult to identify.

**CIRCUIT
BREAKER
PROGRAM**

Limits the proportion
of an individual's
income that is used to
pay property taxes;
designed to protect
poor property owners
from losing their home
as property values
escalate.

■ *Personal income limits* A somewhat more complex scheme promises to limit state taxes to a certain percentage of the state's personal income revenue. For example, if state taxes currently amount to 7 percent of a state's total personal income, a constitutional amendment could be offered to voters that limits all future state and local taxes to a total of no more than 7 percent of personal income. This prevents state government from growing at a faster rate than personal income, but it does allow tax revenues to rise.

■ *State expenditure limits* Similar restrictions can be placed on total state *expenditures*— limiting spending to a certain percentage of a state's total personal income. Presumably expenditure limits would hold down taxes over the long run, and therefore expenditure limits can be considered as an indirect form of tax limitation.

■ *Prohibitions on specific taxes* State constitutions can be written or amended to prohibit certain types of taxes or require specific types of exemptions. For example, if the state constitution bars an income tax, this is a very effective tax limitation. States may also exempt specific items from sales taxes; some common exemptions include groceries, medicines, rents, and purchases by religious, educational, or charitable organizations.

■ *Exemptions and special treatments* The *homestead exemption* is an increasingly popular method of excluding some part of the value of owner-occupied homes from property taxes. Homestead exemptions go only to homeowners, not to businesses; these exemptions may be expressed in dollar amounts of assessed value (where the first $10,000 or $25,000 of assessed value of a home is nontaxable). **Personal property** tax exemptions are common—exemptions of automobiles, boats, furniture, stocks and bonds, and the like—in part because of the difficulty in identifying and assessing the true value of these types of property. Some states have adopted **circuit-breaker programs** that exempt property from taxation for individuals who are poor, aged, disabled, and so forth.

Impact of Limits

What impacts have tax limits had on the state and local government operations? The consequences of tax limits have been greater for local than for state governments. Constitutional provisions limiting state government taxing or spending have generally failed to have any discernible effect on state taxing or spending levels.[6] However, local property tax limits have had the effect of increasing reliance of local governments on state aid as well as fees and charges.[7]

EXPLAINING TAX REVOLTS

Why do people support tax limitation measures? A variety of explanations have been offered and tested in opinion polls, but no single explanation seems to explain why people vote for or against tax limitations.[8]

*No single expla-
nation seems to
explain why people
vote for or against
tax limitations.*

The Self-Interest Explanation

People who benefit most from government spending should oppose tax limitation measures, while people whose tax burdens are heaviest should support these measures. Despite the popularity of "rational" theory, this explanation finds only limited support in opinion surveys; high-income homeowners are only slightly more supportive of tax limits than beneficiaries of government services.

The High-Tax Explanation

People who pay high taxes should support tax limitations, while people who pay modest taxes should show little interest in the tax revolt. Again, there is very little solid evidence to support this theory. Although people who say taxes are "high" tend to vote in favor of tax limitations, the states that have passed limitations are not necessarily the high tax-burden states.

The "Waste-in-Government" Explanation

People who think government wastes a lot of money should support tax limitation proposals. Opinion polls do show a relationship between perceived waste and support for tax limits. This implies that tax limitation referenda can be defeated if people can be convinced that tax dollars are not wasted.

The Ideological Explanation

According to this explanation, conservatives should support tax limits, while liberals should oppose them. Indeed, according to this rationale, the tax revolt itself is a product of increasing conservatism of the electorate in the late 1970s and early 1980s. There is some support for this explanation in opinion polls: Conservatives and Republicans tend to support tax limitation measures more than liberals or Democrats.

The Fairness Explanation

People who perceive the tax system as "unfair" should be more likely to vote for tax limitations than people who do not. Again, there is some limited evidence in opinion polls to support this explanation.

The Alienation Explanation

This explanation views the tax revolt as a reflection of declining confidence in government. Negative feelings about government go beyond perceptions of waste, or fairness, or burdensome taxation, and tap deeply felt resentment and alienation from the political system. Again, there is some limited support for this explanation in opinion polls.

It is not surprising that no single explanation of the tax revolt can be offered. Indeed, even a combination of all of the explanations mentioned here does not fully explain voting on tax proposals. Other explanations may be derived from *the specific characteristics of politics in the states* in which tax limitation referenda have been voted on. Still other explanations may focus on *the specific provisions of the tax limitation amendments* being voted upon.

WHEN SPENDING CUTS ARE NECESSARY: CUTBACK MANAGEMENT

Fiscal stress does *not* refer to the annual struggle to balance the budget without raising taxes or cutting services. This struggle occurs in every city. **Fiscal stress** refers to a financial condition so unfavorable as to impair borrowing ability, require reduction of municipal services, pose a threat to public health and safety, and thus diminish the quality and satisfaction of urban life.[9] Fiscal stress occurs when cities have large municipal payrolls, large socially dependent populations, and heavy tax burdens, yet an eroding tax base, a weak or declining economy, and population loss.

FISCAL STRESS
Unfavorable financial conditions that impair borrowing ability, require the reduction of services, and may threaten public health and safety.

Fiscal stress occurs when cities have large municipal payrolls, large socially dependent populations, and heavy tax burdens, yet an eroding tax base, a weak or declining economy, and population loss.

CUTBACK MANAGEMENT

Deciding how to reduce spending and services in order to relieve fiscal stress.

DECREMENTS

Cutbacks made a little at a time, over time.

"ACROSS-THE-BOARD" CUTS

Every agency or program is cut back by the same percentage during economic downturns.

TARGETED CUTS

Reductions in spending higher in some agencies or programs than in others; established by prioritization.

EFFICIENCY

Getting the biggest bang for the buck.

EQUITY

Fairness in spending; can be defined in terms of people or geography.

Fiscal stress has widespread impact.[10] As a city tries to solve its budget problems, it raises taxes; imposes fees; reduces its workforce; cuts back on maintenance of streets, bridges, buildings, and parks; and postpones capital construction projects. These measures further hurt the local economy. Businesses move away and cancel plans to expand. Unemployment increases as well as demands for help from government. As a city's deficits grow, its bonds become hard to sell to banks and investors. This forces up interest costs that further hurt the city's budget.

Fiscal stress imposes new administrative tasks for mayors and managers. These tasks have been labeled as "**cutback management.**" Managing organizational decline—cutting back on spending and organizational activity, deciding who will be let go, what programs will be scaled down or terminated, and what citizens will be asked to make sacrifices—is not as much fun as managing an expanding organization.

Difficult Decisions

Cutback management presents a host of problems for government officials. These include the following considerations:

- *Resist cutting or smooth the decline.* Should officials resist cutting by claiming it cannot be done without great injury to the city? Should they cut vital and popular programs first in order to stir opposition to the cut? By taking police and firefighters off the streets or closing the schools? By refusing to cut back until paydays are missed and loans are defaulted? Or should officials try to smooth the cutback by cutting low-prestige programs, administrative personnel, social programs, and less vital services?

- *Take one deep gouge or a series of **decrements**.* Should officials try to improve city finances with a single very difficult year by making one set of deep cuts in the budget? Or should they plan a series of smaller cuts over several years to minimize the impact of the cuts and hope that the financial condition of the city may turn around and the cutting can stop?

- *Share the pain or target the cuts.* Should city officials cut all programs "**across the board**" in order to minimize pain, avoid conflict, maintain morale, and build team spirit in the organization? Or should they make hard decisions about what programs are not really necessary? **Targeting cuts** requires officials to identify and rank priorities; it generates intense political conflict and tends to be avoided until things get very bad and across-the-board cuts are no longer feasible.

- *Promote efficiency or equity.* Should city officials favor the most efficient programs, usually police and fire protection, streets and sanitation, over the more costly social-service programs? Or should city officials act to protect the most dependent elements of the population?

Cutback Strategies

What strategies can be employed by cities facing retrenchment? We have attempted to summarize some general strategies available to governments in confronting cutbacks.[11]

- *The no-change strategy: across-the-board cuts, seniority retention, and hiring freezes.* Across-the-board cuts appear to be popular. They distribute the pain of budget reductions equally across agencies and among services. However, eventually across-the-board strategies must be abandoned "as officials become aware that the reductions are permanent . . . that equal cuts are not fair, as some programs are more important than others."[12] A hiring freeze is also a convenient and popular short-run strategy to minimize the pain of cutbacks. Hiring freezes rely on "**natural attrition**" through resignations and retirements to cut down the size of the workforce. It does not require politically difficult decisions about which employees are most essential. If natural attrition does not occur fast enough to meet budget deficits, the next strategy is seniority retention. A "**last-in–first-out**" **rule** in layoffs may be viewed by most employees as fair, although it may result in disproportionate harm to women and minorities if they were recruited to government more recently.

■ *A hierarchy-of-community-needs strategy.* An alternative strategy is for cities to set priorities for essential services. Decisions about what services are essential may differ from city to city, but in general we can expect a ranking (from most essential to least essential): public safety (police and fire), public works (streets, sewers, sanitation), administrative services, human services, leisure services.

■ *A "privatizing" strategy.* Some city services are "priceable"—users can be charged for them. Cities can charge users for garbage collection, water supply, ambulance service, special police services, transit, licensing, libraries, recreation, and so forth. So one retrenchment strategy is to increase the number and types of user charges for city services. A related strategy is to transfer these services to private enterprise (**privatization**), which can usually perform them cheaper than can the city government. User charges are politically popular because citizens can "see" what they are buying and they are not forced to buy anything they do not want.

■ *A reduction in capital spending strategy.* When tough times hit, one of the first responses is to cut back on capital spending—canceling or postponing new equipment purchases, new construction, major repairs. There are short-term advantages to this strategy; city employees can keep their jobs and service levels can be maintained. But over the longer term, this strategy can produce costly results, as streets, bridges, buildings, and equipment fail. Some capital investments can save money over the long run if they improve productivity and reduce labor costs.

■ *A reduction in labor strategy.* Cities may finally confront the necessity to reduce personnel costs—hiring freezes, layoffs, renegotiated labor contracts. The most labor-intensive city functions are police and fire protection, together with hospitals and schools in those cities that have these responsibilities. Cutbacks in police and fire personnel are politically unpopular. Indeed, city officials may threaten such cutbacks to force a reconsideration of the rollbacks, but that can backfire if taxpayers feel the government has been wasteful.

NATURAL ATTRITION

The elimination of jobs due to death, retirement, resignation, transfers, or moving.

"LAST-IN–FIRST-OUT" RULE

When cutbacks have to be made, the last person hired is the first person that has to go.

PRIVATIZATION

Transfer of services to private enterprise, on the premise that a service will be delivered more cheaply than if delivered by government.

CAPITAL SPENDING

Spending on building, facilities, machinery—expensive items with a multiple year lifespan.

WHEN ENDS DON'T MEET: STATE AND LOCAL DEBT

What happens when revenues fail to match expenditures in state and local government budgets? Most state constitutions require the operating budget of the state government, and those of local governments as well, to be balanced. In other words, most state constitutions prohibit deficits in operating budgets. Revenue estimates must match authorized expenditures in the appropriation act. If actual revenues fail to meet the estimates during the fiscal year, expenditures must be cut so that no deficit occurs at the end of the year.

Most state constitutions require the operating budget of the state government, and those of local governments as well, to be balanced.

Capital Financing

State constitutions generally permit state and local governments to borrow funds for capital improvements, with provisions for repayment of the debt during the useful life of the project. State and local governments may sell bonds to finance traditional

RANKINGS
of the STATES

Spending and Borrowing

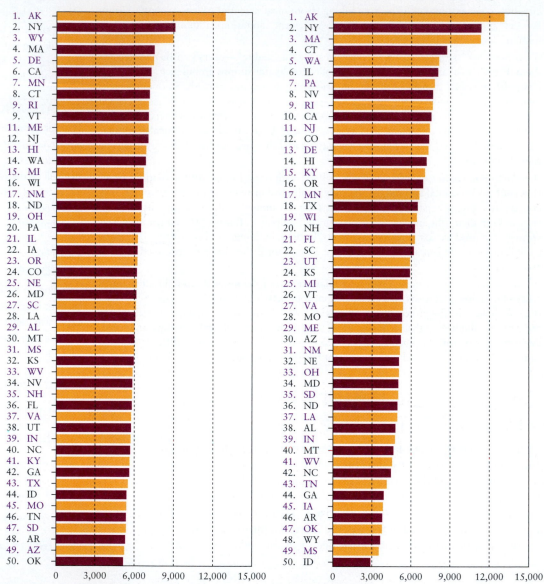

Per Capita State and Local Direct Expenditures

1. AK
2. NY
3. WY
4. MA
5. DE
6. CA
7. MN
8. CT
9. RI
9. VT
11. ME
12. NJ
13. HI
14. WA
15. MI
16. WI
17. NM
18. ND
19. OH
20. PA
21. IL
22. IA
23. OR
24. CO
25. NE
26. MD
27. SC
28. LA
29. AL
30. MT
31. MS
32. KS
33. WV
34. NV
35. NH
36. FL
37. VA
38. UT
39. IN
40. NC
41. KY
42. GA
43. TX
44. ID
45. MO
46. TN
47. SD
48. AR
49. AZ
50. OK

Per Capita State and Local Debt Outstanding

1. AK
2. NY
3. MA
4. CT
5. WA
6. IL
7. PA
8. NV
9. RI
10. CA
11. NJ
12. CO
13. DE
14. HI
15. KY
16. OR
17. MN
18. TX
19. WI
20. NH
21. FL
22. SC
23. UT
24. KS
25. MI
26. VT
27. VA
28. MO
29. ME
30. AZ
31. NM
32. NE
33. OH
34. MD
35. SD
36. ND
37. LA
38. AL
39. IN
40. MT
41. WV
42. NC
43. TN
44. GA
45. IA
46. AR
47. OK
48. WY
49. MS
50. ID

0   3,000   6,000   9,000   12,000   15,000

0   3,000   6,000   9,000   12,000   15,000

Note: Data are for 2004.
Source: U.S. Bureau of the Census, Governments Division "State and Local Government Finances: 2003–2004." Available online at http://www.census.gov/govs/www/estimate04.html

508   CHAPTER 14

"essential functions"—roads, schools, parks, libraries, prisons, and government office buildings. These governments may also sell bonds to finance water and sewage systems, airports, ports, mass transportation facilities, solid waste disposal plants, hazardous waste disposal, single- and multifamily housing projects, and hospitals. In the world of municipal finance, these are referred to as "nonessential functions," even though we might argue that they are essential to a community. Finally, government may sell bonds to finance "private activities"—industrial development projects, trade and convention centers, sports arenas.

When governments borrow using bonds, they must pay back the investors who loan them the money, plus interest. (Most individual investors invest in government bonds through mutual funds.) Governments can borrow money more cheaply if they have higher credit ratings; the bet-

Many local governments sell bonds to pay for sports stadiums, roads, libraries, prisons, parks, and other expensive capital improvement projects. The Washington-King County Stadium Authority sold bonds to finance part of the construction of Safeco Field, home of the Seattle Mariners. The rest of the financing came from the owner.

ter the credit rating, the lower the interest rate. To get a credit rating on the proposed project for which the government is borrowing, state and local governments can hire three major rating firms—Standard & Poor's, Fitch, or Moodys Investors Service. These firms analyze five factors: the local economy, debt already incurred, financial condition of the government, the demographic make-up of the community, and management practices. (For a look at some of the most damaging financial management practices, see "*Did You Know?*: Three Sure Roads to Financial Disaster.")

Constitutional Restrictions

State constitutions may place restrictions on these debts in the form of **debt ceilings**, limiting the total amount of money that a government can borrow (usually expressed as a percentage of the total assessed value of taxable property in the community); and bond referenda provisions, requiring that any bonded indebtedness (and the taxes imposed to pay off this indebtedness) be approved by the voters in a referendum. These restrictions usually apply only to general obligation bonds.

General Obligation versus Revenue Bonds

Bonds issued by state and local governments may be either general obligation bonds or revenue bonds. **General obligation bonds** are backed by the "full faith and credit" of the government that issues them. This pledges the full taxing powers of the government to pay both the principal and interest due on the bonds. Because these bonds are more secure, lenders are willing to accept lower interest rates on them. This saves the government (and the taxpayer) money in interest payments. **Revenue bonds** are not guaranteed by the issuing government but instead are backed by whatever revenues the project itself generates. Both the interest and principal of revenue bonds are paid from fees, and charges or rents ("revenues") generated by the project, rather than tax revenues of the government. Because these bonds are not backed by the full taxing powers of the government, lenders face greater risks and therefore require higher interest payments. Revenue bonds are not usually subject to constitutional debt ceilings or referendum

DEBT CEILING

Limits the amount of money a government can borrow to a proportion of the tax base.

GENERAL OBLIGATION (GOBs) BONDS

Bonds issued by governments that pledge their "full faith and credit," including tax revenues, to repayment.

REVENUE BONDS

Bonds issued by governments for specific projects and backed only by whatever revenues the projects generate.

**INDUSTRIAL
DEVELOPMENT
BONDS (IDBs)**

Revenue bonds issued
by a municipality to
obtain funds to pur-
chase land and build
facilities for private
businesses.

**POLLUTION
CONTROL
REVENUE BONDS**

Bonds issued by
municipalities to obtain
funds to provide indus-
tries with air and water
pollution control
facilities.

**SINGLE-FAMILY
MORTGAGE
REVENUE BONDS**

Government bonds
sold to assist home
buyers, builders, and
developers.

**HOSPITAL
REVENUE BONDS**

Government bonds
sold to assist private
as well as public
hospitals in the
community.

requirements, although when the proposed project is extremely costly, elected officials may choose to let the voters decide (e.g., sports stadiums).

Industrial Development Bonds (IDBs)

Competition between municipalities for economic development has led to a vast expansion in industrial development bonds. These are revenue bonds issued by a municipality to obtain funds to purchase land and build facilities for private businesses. **Pollution control revenue bonds** are issued by municipalities to obtain funds to provide industries with air and water pollution control facilities. Municipalities sometimes issue **single-family mortgage revenue bonds** to assist home buyers, builders, and developers. Municipalities may issue **hospital revenue bonds** to assist private as well as public hospitals in the community. These types of revenue bonds blur the distinction between public and private business. At one time most state and local indebtedness was in the form of general obligation bonds. But industrial development, pollution control, mortgage revenue, and hospital bonds have become so popular that these nonguaranteed revenue bonds now constitute well over half of the outstanding municipal debt in the nation.

Municipal Bond Interest Deductibility

Traditionally, the federal government did not levy individual or corporate income taxes on the interest that lenders received from state and local government bonds. All municipal bond interest income was deductible from gross income for federal tax purposes. The original rationale for this deductibility was based on the federal ideal: The national government should not interfere with the operations of state governments and their subdivisions. "The power to tax is the power to destroy,"[13] and therefore neither level of government should tax the instrumentalities of the other. Later this rationale was replaced by more practical considerations: By not taxing municipal bond interest, the federal government was providing an incentive for investment in public infrastructure—schools, streets, hospitals, sewers, airports. Because the federal government forgoes taxing municipal bond income, we might consider these lost federal revenues as a subsidy to state and local governments and the people who lend money to them.

The deductibility of municipal bond interest from federal income taxation makes these bonds very attractive to high-income investors. This attraction allows state and local governments to pay out less interest on their tax-free bonds than corporations must pay out on comparable taxable corporate bonds. Thus, for example, if average *corporate* AAA-rated thirty-year bonds are paying 7 percent interest (taxable), average *municipal* AAA-rated thirty-year bonds might only pay 5 percent interest (tax free). Many investors would prefer the lower rate because it is tax free. In short, federal deductibility allows state and local governments to borrow money relatively cheaply.

Public Bonds for Private Uses

Controversy arises when private businesses ask municipal governments to issue revenue bonds on their behalf—bonds that businesses use to finance everything from the purchase of single-family homes and the development of luxury apartments, to the building of industrial plants and commercial offices. Business prefers municipal revenue bond financing over its own direct financing because municipal bond interest rates are cheaper owing to federal deductibility. In other words, the issuance of municipal "private-purpose" revenue bonds is really a device to obtain cheaper interest rates for business at the expense of lost revenues to the federal government.

Federal Tax Reform and Municipal Finance

The Federal Tax Reform Act of 1986 distinguishes among **"essential function" bonds** (bonds issued for roads, schools, parks, libraries, prisons, and government buildings), **"nonessential function" bonds** (bonds issued for water and sewer, transportation, multifamily housing, hazardous waste disposal, and health and education facilities), and **"private activities" bonds** (bonds for industrial development, pollution control, parking facilities, and sports and convention centers). Only essential function bond income is completely free of all federal income taxation. Nonessential bond income is subject to the federal alternate minimum tax (AMT), which means it may be taxable if the taxpayer has a large amount of tax-free income. And income from "private-purpose" municipal bonds no longer enjoys tax-free status. These separate treatments complicate the municipal bond market for both governments and investors.

Debt Patterns

In examining total indebtedness, we should consider both general obligation and revenue indebtedness. The total debt per person of all governments within a state ranges from $2,884 in Idaho to over $13,000 in Alaska. (See "*Rankings of the States*: Spending and Borrowing.") Of course, some local governments avoid debt altogether, preferring "pay-as-you-go" (PAYGO) financing of capital projects. Indebtedness appears to be greater in cities in the Northeast, cities that undertake a wide variety of functions and services, and cities under fiscal strain.[14]

WHEN A LOCAL GOVERNMENT GOES BUST

What happens when a city continually spends more than it receives in revenues, when its annual deficits pile up into a huge city debt, when banks and other lenders finally decide not to lend a city any more money? A number of large American cities have gone bust or come close to it, including New York City in 1975, Cleveland in 1979, Philadelphia in 1991, and Washington, DC, in 1995. But rather than officially declare bankruptcy and have federal bankruptcy courts take over fiscal control, these cities have been "rescued" by state and federal governments. Rescue, however, generally requires the city to turn over control of its financial affairs to a control board. Control board members are appointed by the state or federal government. In exchange for an infusion of state or federal money, the control board imposes fiscal discipline on the city.

ESSENTIAL FUNCTION BONDS

Government bonds sold to assist traditional services, such as road maintenance, schools, law enforcement, prisons, parks, and the running of government offices.

NONESSENTIAL FUNCTION BONDS

Government bonds sold to assist services not necessarily undertaken by all local governments, such as mass transit, airports, housing, and hospitals.

PRIVATE ACTIVITIES BONDS

Government bonds sold to assist industrial development projects performed by the private sector (e.g., trade and convention centers and sports arenas).

Three Sure Roads to Financial Disaster

ad financial decisions can lead to catastrophic results—not just in one's personal life, but in the public sector as well. Government finance experts have identified three of the most dangerous financial practices as follows:

- *Balancing the budget by repeatedly using one-time sources of revenue:* Relying on last year's reserves or **rainy day (savings) fund** or the proceeds from sale of an asset, like a parcel of property or a building. This is particularly a bad practice if the one-time monies are used to fund on-going top priority items in the operating budget (e.g., police officers and firefighters).

- *Deferring current costs to the future:* Postponing expenditures for maintenance and replacement of capital assets, or deferring pension liabilities. Delaying maintenance of repair of buildings, structures, etc. can result in considerably higher costs in the future either in the form of higher replacement costs or totally new construction.

- *Ignoring long-range or lifecycle costs of a liability:* Deciding to build or purchase a capital asset without calculating the full lifecycle costs of owning, operating, and maintaining that asset. This would be the equivalent of budgeting only for the cost of a car and not budgeting for insurance, gas, maintenance, licensing, etc.

Delaying repairs and maintenance can cause major financial meltdowns as well as deaths. Using one-time revenues for ongoing services can lead to cutbacks and layoffs in tough times.

Source: Craig Clifford, chief financial officer of the City of Scottsdale, Arizona, in "The Road to Fiscal Sustainability." *Government Finance Review*, August 2005, p. 37.

Budget information for most states and large cities and counties can be accessed through their home pages. This information usually includes both sources of *revenue* and categories of *expenditures*.

The federal government's executive budget is prepared by the Office of Management and Budget (OMB). Each year's federal budget can be accessed at:

http://www.gpo.gov/usbudget/index.html

OMB provides summary pages of revenue sources and expenditure categories.

The National Taxpayers Union lobbies in Congress and state legislatures "to fight for the American taxpayer." The organization offers arguments in support of constitutional amendments to curtail spending, in support of lower taxes and taxpayer rights, and in opposition to wasteful government spending. The Web site is at:

www.ntu.org

The Tax Foundation is a nonpartisan research-based organization located in Washington, D.C. whose purpose is to educate taxpayers about tax policy and the tax burden at all levels of government. The Web site is at:

www.taxfoundation.org

Other useful sites are as follows:

Government Finance Officers Association, a professional association of state, provincial and local finance officers in the United States and Canada:

www.gfoa.org

National Association of State Budget Officers, a professional membership organization for state financial officers:

www.nasbo.org

CHAPTER FIFTEEN

POLITICS AND CIVIL RIGHTS

15

QUESTIONS TO CONSIDER

Do city government policies change significantly with the election of minority group members to the offices of mayor or city council?

■ Yes   ■ No

Should state and local governments be color-blind with respect to the races in all of their laws and actions?

■ Yes   ■ No

Do you generally favor affirmative action programs for women and minorities?

■ Yes   ■ No

Should governments pay for abortions for poor women?

■ Yes   ■ No

FROM PROTEST TO POWER

African Americans and Hispanics have made significant progress in urban politics in recent years. The progress of these minorities in city government has important implications for the future of the American political system, because these are the two largest minority groups in the country. Minorities were almost totally excluded from significant influence in city politics prior to the 1960s. We have already discussed increases in minority representation in city councils (Chapter 11) and state legislatures (Chapter 6), and minority political power in the nation's largest cities is a recognized fact of American politics. As former Atlanta Mayor Andrew Young said, "It's like the old preacher says: we ain't what we oughta be; we ain't what we gonna be; but thank God we ain't what we was."[1] While the earliest civil rights fights in the states primarily focused on racial discrimination, in recent years the battles have extended to gender, disability, and sexual preference.

Policy Consequences of Minority Representation

Do city government policies change as a result of minority incorporation into the political system? Black elected officials in cities perceive poverty and unemployment as more severe problems than do white officials in the same cities; and black officeholders are more likely to add race relations and racial balance in the distribution of city jobs and services to the policy agenda.[2] Another consequence of the election of blacks to public office, especially the mayor's office, is an increase in political participation among black citizens.[3] And it appears that the election of black mayors reduces fears among whites about the consequences of electing blacks and reduces racial polarization in voting.[4]

But many city government policies, especially taxing and spending policies, are severely constrained by economic conditions and by limits and mandates set by the state and federal governments.[5] So it is unrealistic to expect major shifts in these policies to accompany the election of African Americans or Hispanics to city office. The policies that respond to minority representation in city government are those that deal directly with minority presence in government. Broad taxing and spending policies are largely unaffected by minority influence in government. Examples of the kind of policy changes directly attributable to minority representation in government include the creation of police review boards, the appointment of more minorities to city boards and commissions, increasing use of minority contractors, and a general increase in the number of programs oriented toward minorities. Perhaps the most significant policy impact of minority representation on city councils is an increase in the number of minorities in city employment and their employment in higher-grade positions.[6]

The most significant policy impact of minority representation on city councils is an increase in the number of minorities in city employment and their employment in higher-grade positions.

THE STRUGGLE AGAINST SEGREGATION

The Fourteenth Amendment of the U.S. Constitution declares that

> all persons born or naturalized in the United States, and subject to the jurisdiction thereof, are citizens of the United States and of the State wherein they reside. No State shall make or enforce any law which shall abridge the privileges or immunities of citizens of the United States; nor shall any State deprive any person of life, liberty, or property, without due process of law; nor deny to any person within its jurisdiction the equal protection of the laws.

The language of the Fourteenth Amendment and its post–Civil War historical context leave little doubt that its original purpose was to achieve the full measure of citizenship and equality for African Americans. Some "radical" Republicans were prepared in 1867 to carry out the revolution in southern society that this amendment implied. Under military occupation, southern states adopted new constitutions that awarded the vote and full civil liberties to African Americans, and southern states were compelled to ratify the Thirteenth, Fourteenth, and Fifteenth Amendments to the U.S. Constitution. African Americans were elected to southern state legislatures and to the Congress; the first African American to serve in Congress, Hiram R. Revels, took over the U.S. Senate seat from Mississippi previously held by Confederate President Jefferson Davis.

However, by 1877 Reconstruction was abandoned. The national government was not willing to carry out the long and difficult task of really reconstructing society in the eleven states of the former Confederacy.[7] In what has been described as the "Compromise of 1877," the national government agreed to end military occupation of the South, give up its efforts to rearrange southern society, and lend tacit approval to white supremacy in that region. In return, the southern states pledged their support of the Union, accepted national supremacy, and agreed to permit the Republican candidate, Rutherford B. Hayes, to assume the presidency after the disputed election of 1876.

"Separate but Equal"

The Supreme Court adhered to the terms of the compromise. The result was an inversion of the meaning of the Fourteenth Amendment so that by 1896 it had become a bulwark of **segregation**. State laws segregating the races were upheld so long as persons in each of the separated races were treated equally. The constitutional argument on behalf of segregation under the Fourteenth Amendment was that the phrase "equal protection of the laws" did not prevent state-enforced separation of the races. Schools and other public facilities that were "separate but equal" won constitutional approval.[8] This separate but equal doctrine remained the Supreme Court's interpretation of the Equal Protection Clause of the Fourteenth Amendment until 1954.

As a matter of fact, of course, segregated facilities, including public schools, were seldom if ever equal, even with respect to physical conditions. In practice, the doctrine of segregation was "separate and unequal." The Supreme Court began to take notice of this after World War II. While it declined to overrule the segregationist interpretation of the Fourteenth Amendment, it began to order the admission of individual blacks to white public universities, where evidence indicated that separate black institutions were inferior or nonexistent.[9]

NAACP

Leaders of the newly emerging civil rights movement in the 1940s and 1950s were not satisfied with court decisions that examined the circumstances in each case to determine if separate school facilities were really equal. The National Association for the Advancement of Colored People (NAACP), led by Roy Wilkins, its executive director, and Thurgood Marshall, its chief counsel, pressed for a court decision that segregation itself meant inequality within the meaning of the Fourteenth Amendment, whether or not facilities were equal in all tangible respects. In short, they wanted a complete reversal of the "separate but equal" interpretation of the Fourteenth Amendment, and a holding that laws *separating* the races were unconstitutional.

SEGREGATION

Separation of people by race; mandated by law in schools and public facilities in southern states prior to the U.S. Supreme Court decision in *Brown v. Board of Education of Topeka, Kansas* in 1954, and prior to the Civil Rights Act of 1964.

"SEPARATE BUT EQUAL"

The ruling by the U.S. Supreme Court in 1896 that segregated facilities were lawful as long as the facilities were equal; a ruling reversed by the Court in *Brown v. Board of Education of Topeka, Kansas* in 1954.

NAACP

The largest African American civil rights organization; sponsored historic desegregation case in 1954.

The civil rights groups chose to bring suit for desegregation in Topeka, Kansas, where segregated black and white schools were equal with respect to buildings, curricula, qualifications and salaries of teachers, and other tangible factors. The legal strategy was to prevent the Court from ordering the admission of a black because *tangible* facilities were not equal and to force the Court to review the doctrine of segregation itself.

Brown v. Board of Education of Topeka, Kansas

On May 17, 1954, the Court rendered its decision in *Brown v. Board of Education of Topeka, Kansas:*

> Segregation of white and colored children in public schools has a detrimental effect upon the colored children. The impact is greater when it has the sanction of law, for the policy of separating the races is usually interpreted as denoting the inferiority of the Negro group. A sense of inferiority affects the motivation of a child to learn. Segregation with the sanction of law, therefore, has a tendency to retard the educational and mental development of Negro children and to deprive them of some of the benefits they would receive in a racially integrated school system.[10]

The 1954 *Brown* v. *Board of Education of Topeka, Kansas* ruling by the U.S. Supreme Court declared that segregation in public schools is unconstitutional. Here the jubilant attorneys who successfully argued the case against segregation, George E. C. Hayes, Thurgood Marshall, and James Nabrit, Jr., stand arm-in-arm on the steps of the Court. Thurgood Marshall would later become a U.S. Supreme Court Justice.

The symbolic importance of the original *Brown v. Board of Education of Topeka, Kansas* decision cannot be overestimated. While it would be many years before any significant number of black children would attend formerly segregated white schools, the decision by the nation's highest court undoubtedly stimulated black hopes and expectations. African-American sociologist Kenneth Clark writes,

> This [civil rights] movement would probably not have existed at all were it not for the 1954 Supreme Court school desegregation decision which provided a tremendous boost to the morale of Negroes by its *clear* affirmation that color is irrelevant to the rights of American citizens. Until this time the Southern Negro generally had accommodated to the separatism of the black from the white society.[11]

STATE RESISTANCE TO DESEGREGATION

The Supreme Court had spoken forcefully in the *Brown* case in 1954 in declaring segregation unconstitutional. From a constitutional viewpoint, any state-supported segregation of the races after 1954 was prohibited. Article VI of the Constitution declares that the words of that document are "the supreme law of the land . . . anything in the constitution or laws of any state to the contrary notwithstanding." From a political viewpoint, however, the battle over segregation was just beginning.

Segregation in the States

In 1954, the practice of segregation was widespread and deeply ingrained in American life. Seventeen states required the segregation of the races in public schools:

Alabama	North Carolina	Kentucky
Arkansas	South Carolina	Maryland
Florida	Tennessee	Missouri
Georgia	Texas	Oklahoma
Louisiana	Virginia	West Virginia
Mississippi	Delaware	

The Congress of the United States required the segregation of the races in the public schools of the District of Columbia.[12] Four additional states—Arizona, Kansas, New Mexico, and Wyoming—authorized segregation upon the option of local school boards. (See Figure 15–1.)

Thus, in deciding *Brown* v. *Board of Education of Topeka, Kansas* the Supreme Court struck down the laws of twenty-one states and the District of Columbia in a single opinion. Such a far-reaching decision was bound to meet with difficulties in implementation. The Supreme Court did not order immediate nationwide desegregation, but instead it turned over the responsibility for desegregation to state and local authorities under the supervision of federal district courts.

The six border states with segregated school systems—Delaware, Kentucky, Maryland, Missouri, Oklahoma, and West Virginia—together with the school districts in Kansas, Arizona, and New Mexico that had operated segregated schools, chose not to resist desegregation. The District of Columbia also desegregated its public schools the year following the Supreme Court's decision.

FIGURE 15–1 Segregation Laws in the United States in 1954

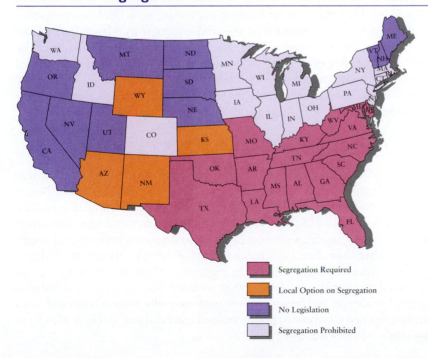

Segregation Required
Local Option on Segregation
No Legislation
Segregation Prohibited

DE FACTO SEGREGATION

Racial imbalances not directly caused by official action but rather by neighborhood residential patterns.

Resistance

Resistance to school integration was the policy of the eleven states of the Old Confederacy. Refusal of a school district to desegregate until it was faced with a federal court injunction was the most common form of delay. Other schemes included state payment of private school tuition in lieu of providing public schools, amendment of compulsory attendance laws to provide that no child shall be required to attend an integrated school, the requirement that schools faced with desegregation orders cease operation, and the use of pupil-placement laws to avoid or minimize the extent of integration. State officials also attempted to delay desegregation on the grounds that it would endanger public safety.[13] On the whole, those states that chose to resist desegregation were quite successful in doing so during the ten-year period from 1954 to 1964. Ten years after *Brown* v. *Board of Education of Topeka, Kansas* only about 2 percent of the black schoolchildren in the eleven southern states were attending integrated schools.

Federal Funds

In the Civil Rights Act of 1964, Congress finally entered the civil rights field in support of court efforts to achieve desegregation. Among other things, the Civil Rights Act of 1964 provided that every federal department and agency must take action to end segregation in all programs and activities receiving federal financial assistance. It was specified that this action was to include termination of financial assistance if states and communities receiving federal funds refused to comply with federal desegregation orders. Acting under the authority of Title VI, the U.S. Office of Education (now the Department of Education) required all school districts in the seventeen formerly segregated states to submit desegregation plans as a condition of federal assistance. Progress toward desegregation was speeded up.

Unitary Schools

The last vestige of legal justification for delay in implementing school desegregation collapsed in 1969 when the Supreme Court rejected a request by Mississippi school officials for a delay in implementing school desegregation plans in that state. The Supreme Court declared that every school district was obligated to end dual school systems "at once" and "now and hereafter" to operate only unitary schools.[14] The effect of the decision—fifteen years after the original *Brown* case—was to eliminate any further legal justification for the continuation of segregation in public schools.

RACIAL BALANCING IN SCHOOLS

In *Brown* v. *Board of Education of Topeka, Kansas*, the Supreme Court found that segregation had "a tendency to retard the educational and mental development of Negro children and to deprive them of some of the benefits they would receive in a racially integrated school system." The U.S. Civil Rights Commission reported that even when segregation was "**de facto**," that is, a product of segregated housing patterns and neighborhood schools rather than direct discrimination, the adverse effects on African-American students were still significant.[15] In northern urban school districts, the commission reported, predominantly black schools were less likely to have good libraries or advanced courses in sciences and languages than predominantly white schools and more likely to have overcrowded classrooms, poorly trained teachers, and teachers who were dissatisfied with their school assignments.

Racial Balance

Ending racial isolation in the public schools frequently involved **busing** schoolchildren into and out of segregated neighborhoods. The objective was to achieve a racial "balance" in public schools, so that each had roughly the same percentages of minorities and whites as are found in the total population of the entire school district.

Federal Court Supervision

Federal district judges enjoy wide freedom in fashioning remedies for past or present discriminatory practices by governments. If a federal district court anywhere in the United States finds that any actions by governments or school officials have contributed to racial imbalance (e.g., in drawing school district attendance lines), the judge may order the adoption of a desegregation plan to overcome racial imbalances produced by official action. A large number of cities have come under federal district court orders to improve racial balances in their schools through busing.

In the case of *Swan v. Charlotte-Mecklenburg Board of Education*, the Supreme Court upheld (1) the use of racial balance requirements in schools and the assignment of pupils to schools based on race, (2) "close scrutiny" by judges of schools that are predominantly of one race, (3) gerrymandering of school attendance zones as well as "clustering" or "grouping" of schools to achieve equal balance, and (4) court-ordered busing of pupils to achieve racial balance.[16] The Court was careful to note, however, that racial imbalance in schools is not itself grounds for ordering these remedies, unless it is also shown that some present or past governmental action contributed to the imbalance.

Cross-District Busing

In the absence of any governmental actions contributing to racial imbalance, states and school districts are *not* required by the Fourteenth Amendment to integrate their schools. Thus, for example, where central-city schools are predominantly black, and suburban schools are predominantly white, owing to residential patterns, cross-district busing is not constitutionally required, unless it is shown that some official action brought about these racial imbalances. The Supreme Court threw out a lower federal court order for massive busing of students between Detroit and fifty-two suburban school districts. Although Detroit city schools were 70 percent black, none of the Detroit-area suburban school districts segregated students within their own boundaries.[17] This important decision means the largely black central cities, surrounded by largely white suburbs, will remain de facto segregated because there are not enough white students living within the city to achieve integration.

When is Desegregation Complete?

Many school districts in the South and elsewhere have operated under federal court supervision for many years. How long should court supervision continue, and what standards are to be used in determining when desegregation has been achieved once and for all? In recent years the Supreme Court has undertaken to free some school districts from direct federal court supervision. Where the last vestiges of state-sanctioned discrimination have been removed "as far as practicable," the Supreme Court has allowed lower federal courts to dissolve racial balancing plans even though imbalances due to residential patterns continue to exist.[18]

When is Racial Balancing Constitutional?

"STRICT SCRUTINY"

Supreme Court standard requiring race-based actions by governments to be necessary to remedy past discrimination, or to advance clearly identified and compelling government needs, and to be narrowly tailored to minimize the effects on nonminority individuals.

All racial classifications by governments are subject to **strict scrutiny** by the courts. This means that racial classifications must be "narrowly tailored" to achieve a "compelling government interest."[19] School districts that engage in racial balancing must show that the interest they seek to achieve is a compelling one and that the means they have chosen are the least disruptive of all the means available.

When a Seattle school district voluntarily adopted student assignment plans that relied on race to determine which schools certain children would attend, the U.S. Supreme Court held that the district had violated the Fourteenth Amendment's guarantee of equal protection of the laws.[20] (Inasmuch as the Seattle district had no history of segregation, its racial balancing was subject to the strict scrutiny test.) The Court reasoned that although achieving "diversity" in the student body may be a compelling interest in a university context,[21] it was not proven to be a compelling interest in public elementary and secondary schools. Moreover, the Seattle district's racial balancing plan was not narrowly tailored; the district failed to consider race-neutral assignment plans that might achieve the same interest in racial diversity. The Court noted that the Seattle plan considered race exclusively and not in a broader definition of diversity. The effect of the decision is to force school districts across the country to reconsider voluntary racial balancing plans.

Continuing Racial Separation and "White Flight"

"WHITE FLIGHT"

The movement of white residents away from central cities to suburbs in response to increasing numbers and percentages of minorities in neighborhoods and schools in the central cities.

Minority students now comprise the overwhelming majority of public school pupils in many large cities (including Detroit, Philadelphia, Boston, Atlanta, Chicago, Baltimore, Cleveland, Memphis, New Orleans, Newark, Richmond, St. Louis, and Washington, DC). In some cities, where extensive busing has been employed, **"white flight"** from the public schools is so widespread that the schools have ended up more racially separated than before racial balancing was imposed.[22] Currently over two-thirds of all black public school pupils in the United States attend schools that have a majority of black students.[23] The most racially separated schools are found in Illinois, Michigan, New York, New Jersey, and Pennsylvania (in that order) with over half of their black pupils attending schools that are 90 to 100 percent black. And racial separation in public schools is *increasing* over time.[24]

Over two-thirds of all black public school pupils in the United States attend schools that have a majority of black students.

THE CIVIL RIGHTS ACT OF 1964

The initial objective of the civil rights movement in America was to prevent discrimination and segregation as practiced by or supported by *governments*, particularly states, municipalities, and school districts. However, even while important victories for the civil rights movement were being recorded in the prevention of discrimination by governments, particularly in the *Brown* case, the movement began to broaden its objectives to include the elimination of discrimination in all segments of American life, private as well as public.

The Constitution does not govern the activities of private individuals. It is the laws of Congress and the states that govern the conduct of private individuals. When the civil rights movement turned to combating private discrimination, it had to carry its fight into the legislative branch of government. The federal courts could help restrict discrimination by state and local governments and school authorities, but only Congress,

White supremacy groups still exist in the twenty-first century. The rights of such groups to exist and march are protected by the U.S. Constitution. When local governments issue them parade permits, it generally evokes a large turnout by African Americans.

state legislatures, and city councils could restrict discrimination practiced by private owners of restaurants, hotels and motels, private employers, and other individuals who were not government officials.

The Civil Rights Act of 1964 passed both houses of Congress by better than a two-thirds favorable vote; it won the overwhelming support of both Republican and Democratic members of Congress. It was signed into law on July 4, 1964. It ranks with the Emancipation Proclamation, the Fourteenth Amendment, and *Brown* v. *Board of Education of Topeka, Kansas* as one of the most important steps toward full equality for African Americans in America. (See "*People in Politics:* Martin Luther King, Jr.")

Among other things, the Civil Rights Act of 1964 dictated the following:

■ That it is unlawful to discriminate or segregate persons on the grounds of race, color, religion, or national origin in any place of public accommodation, including hotels, motels, restaurants, movies, theaters, sports arenas, entertainment houses, and other places which offer to serve the public. This prohibition extends to all establishments whose operations affect interstate commerce or whose discriminatory practices are supported by state action. (Title II)

■ That each federal department and agency shall take action to end discrimination in all programs or activities receiving federal financial assistance in any form. This action shall include termination of financial assistance. (Title VI)

■ That it shall be unlawful for any employer or labor union with twenty-five or more persons after 1965 to discriminate against any individual in any fashion in employment, because of his or her race, color, religion, sex, or national origin, and that an Equal Employment Opportunity Commission shall be established to enforce this provision by investigation, conference, conciliation, persuasion, and, if need be, civil action in federal court. (Title VII)[25]

PEOPLE in POLITICS

Martin Luther King, Jr.

The leadership in the struggle to eliminate discrimination and segregation from private life was provided by a young African-American minister, Martin Luther King, Jr. King's father was the pastor of one of the South's largest and most influential congregations, the Ebenezer Baptist Church in Atlanta, Georgia. Martin Luther King, Jr., received his doctorate from Boston University and began his ministry in Montgomery, Alabama. In 1955 the black community of Montgomery began a year-long boycott with frequent demonstrations against the Montgomery city buses over segregated seating practices. The dramatic appeal and the eventual success of the boycott in Montgomery brought nationwide attention to its leader and led to the creation in 1957 of the Southern Christian Leadership Conference.

Nonviolent Direct Action

Under King's leadership the civil rights movement developed and refined political techniques for minorities in American politics, including *nonviolent direct action*. Nonviolent direct action is a form of protest that involves breaking "unjust" laws in an open, "loving," nonviolent fashion. The general notion of civil disobedience is not new; it played an important role in American history, from the Boston Tea Party to the abolitionists who illegally hid runaway slaves, to the suffragettes who demonstrated for women's voting rights, to the labor organizers who formed the nation's major industrial unions, to the civil rights workers of the early 1960s who deliberately violated segregation laws. The purpose of nonviolent direct action is to call attention, or to "bear witness," to the existence of injustice. In the words of Martin Luther King, Jr., civil disobedience "seeks to dramatize the issue so that it can no longer be ignored." There should be no violence in true civil disobedience, and only "unjust" laws are broken. Moreover, the law is broken "openly, lovingly," with a willingness to accept the penalty.[a]

Marches in Birmingham and Washington

Perhaps the most dramatic confrontation between the civil rights movement and the southern segregationists occurred in Birmingham, Alabama, in the spring of 1963. In support of a request for desegregation of downtown eating places and the formation of a biracial committee to work out the integration of public schools, Martin Luther King, Jr., led several thousand Birmingham blacks in a series of orderly street marches. The demonstrators were met with strong police action, including fire hoses, police dogs, and electric cattle prods. Newspaper pictures of blacks being attacked by police and bitten by dogs were flashed all over the world. More than 25,000 demonstrators, including Dr. King, were jailed.

The Birmingham protest set off demonstrations in many parts of the country; the theme remained one of nonviolence, and it was usually whites rather than blacks who resorted to violence in these demonstrations. The culmination of the nonviolent philosophy was a giant, yet orderly, march on Washington, held on August 28, 1963. More than 200,000 blacks and whites participated in the march, which was endorsed by various labor leaders, religious groups, and political figures. The march ended at the Lincoln Memorial, where Martin Luther King, Jr., delivered his most eloquent appeal, "I Have a Dream."[b] It was in response to this march that President John F. Kennedy sent a strong civil rights bill to Congress, which was passed after his death—the landmark Civil Rights Act of 1964. On the night of April 4, 1968, the world's leading voice of nonviolence was killed by an assassin's bullet.

[a]Martin Luther King, Jr., "Letter from Birmingham City Jail," April 16, 1963.
[b]Martin Luther King, Jr., August 28, 1963, at the Lincoln Memorial, Washington, DC.

Fair Housing

For many years "fair housing" had been considered the most sensitive area of civil rights legislation. Discrimination in the sale and rental of housing was the last major civil rights problem on which Congress took action. Discrimination in housing had not been mentioned in any previous legislation; even the comprehensive Civil Rights Act of 1964 made no reference to housing. Prohibiting discrimination in the sale or rental of housing affected the constituencies of northern members of Congress more than any of the earlier, southern-oriented legislation. The prospects for a fair housing law were not very good at the beginning of 1968. When Martin Luther King, Jr., was assassinated, however, the mood of the nation and of Congress changed dramatically, and many felt that Congress should pass a fair housing law as a tribute to the slain civil rights leader. The Civil Rights Act of 1968 prohibited the following forms of discrimination:

- Refusal to sell or rent a dwelling to any person because of race, color, religion, or national origin.
- Discrimination against a person in the terms, conditions, or privileges of the sale or rental of a dwelling, or advertising the sale or rental of a dwelling indicating a preference or discrimination based on race, color, religion, or national origin.

The Act applied to all apartments and houses, rented or sold by either real estate developers or by private individuals who used the services of real estate agents. It exempted private individuals who sold their own homes without the services of a real estate agent, provided they did not indicate any preference or discrimination in advertising in the sale or rental of a house.

FAIR HOUSING
Anti-discrimination in the sale and rental of housing to minorities.

AFFIRMATIVE ACTION BATTLES

Although the gains of the civil rights movement were immensely important, they were primarily gains in *opportunity*, rather than in *results*. The civil rights movement of the 1960s did not bring about major changes in the conditions under which most African Americans lived in America. Racial politics today center on the actual inequalities between minorities and whites in incomes, jobs, housing, health, education, and other conditions of life.

Continuing Inequalities

The issue of inequality is often posed today as differences in the "life chances" of whites, blacks, and Hispanics. Figures can reveal only the bare outline of the life chances in American society (see Table 15–1). The average income of a black family is about 64 percent

TABLE 15–1 Minority Life Chances				
Median Income of Families				
Race	**1980**	**1990**	**2000**	**2005**
White	38,621	41,668	45,860	48,554
Black	22,250	24,917	30,980	30,858
Asian and Pacific Islander	N/A	51,299	58,255	61,094
Hispanic	28,218	29,792	34,636	35,967
				(continued)

TABLE 15-1 (Continued)				
Persons below Poverty Level				
Race	**1980 (%)**	**1990 (%)**	**2000 (%)**	**2005 (%)**
White	10.2	10.7	9.5	10.6
Black	32.5	31.9	22.5	24.9
Asian and Pacific Islander	N/A	12.2	9.9	11.1
Hispanic	25.7	28.1	21.5	21.8

Persons over 25 Completing		
Race	**High School (%)**	**Bachelor's Degree (%)**
White	85.8	28.2
Black	80.6	17.6
Asian and Pacific Islander	88.4	49.3
Hispanic	58.4	12.1

Unemployment Rate			
Race	**1992**	**2000**	**2005**
White	5.5	2.6	3.9
Black	11.0	5.4	8.1
Asian and Pacific Islander		2.7	3.8
Hispanic	9.8	4.4	5.7

Note: Education data are for 2004.

Source: Statistical Abstract of the United States 2006, pp. 460, 412, 148; U.S. Bureau of the Census, "Income, Poverty and Health Insurance Coverage 2005." www.census.gov/prod/2006pubs/p60–231.pdf

AFFIRMATIVE ACTION

Programs pursued by governments or private businesses to overcome the results of past discriminatory treatment of minorities and/or women by giving these groups special or preferential treatment in employment, promotion, admissions, and so forth.

of the average white family's income. Nearly 25 percent of all black families are below the recognized poverty line, while only 11 percent of white families live in poverty. The unemployment rate for blacks is over twice as high as that for whites. Blacks are less likely to hold prestigious white collar jobs in professional, managerial, clerical, or sales work. They do not hold many skilled craft jobs in industry but are concentrated in operative, service, and laboring positions. The civil rights movement opened up new opportunities for black Americans. But equality of *opportunity* is not the same as *absolute* equality.

Policy Choices

What public policies should be pursued to achieve equality in America? Is it sufficient that government eliminate discrimination, guarantee "equality of opportunity," and apply "color-blind" standards to both minorities and whites? Or should government take "**affirmative action**" to overcome the results of past unequal treatment of minorities— that is, preferential or compensatory treatment to assist minority applicants for university admissions and scholarships, job hiring and promotion, and other opportunities for advancement in life?

The early emphasis of government policy, of course, was nondiscrimination. This approach began with President Harry Truman's decision to desegregate the armed forces in 1948 and was carried through to Title VI and Title VII of the Civil Rights Act of 1964 to eliminate discrimination in federally aided projects and private employment. Gradually, however, policy shifted from the traditional aim of *equality of opportunity* through nondiscrimination alone to affirmative action to establish "goals and timetables" to achieve greater *equality of results* between minorities and whites. While avoiding the term *quota*, the notion of affirmative action tests the success of equal opportunity by observing whether minorities achieve admissions, jobs, and promotions in proportion to their numbers in the population.

Constitutional Issues—The Bakke Case

The constitutional question posed by "affirmative action" programs is whether or not they discriminate against whites in violation of the Equal Protection Clause of the Fourteenth Amendment. The U.S. Supreme Court first dealt directly with this question in *Regents of the University of California v. Bakke* (1978).[26] The Court struck down a special admissions program for minorities at a state medical school on the grounds that it excluded a white applicant because of his race and violated his rights under the Equal Protection Clause. Allan Bakke applied to the University of California Davis Medical School two consecutive years and was rejected; in both years black applicants with significantly lower grade point averages and medical aptitude test scores were accepted through a special admissions program that reserved sixteen minority places in a class of one hundred.[27] The University of California did not deny that its admission decisions were based on race. Instead, it argued that its racial classification was "benign," that is, designed to assist minorities, not to hinder them. The Supreme Court held that race and ethnic origin *may* be considered in reviewing applications to a state school without violating the Equal Protection Clause. However, the Court held that a *separate* admissions program for minorities with a specific quota of openings that were unavailable to white applicants violated the Equal Protection Clause. The Court ordered Bakke admitted to medical school and the elimination of the special admissions program. It recommended that California consider an admissions program developed at Harvard that considered disadvantaged racial or ethnic background as a "plus" in an overall evaluation of an application but did not set numerical quotas or exclude any persons from competing for all positions.

Affirmative Action as a Remedy for Past Discrimination

The Supreme Court has generally approved of affirmative action programs when there was evidence of past discriminatory practices. In *United Steelworkers of America v. Weber* (1979), the Supreme Court approved a plan developed by a private employer and a union to reserve 50 percent of higher-paying, skilled jobs for minorities.[28] In *United States v. Paradise* (1987), the Court upheld a rigid 50 percent black quota system for promotions in the Alabama Department of Safety, which had excluded blacks from the ranks of state troopers prior to 1972 and had not promoted any blacks higher than corporal prior to 1984. In a 5–4 decision, the majority stressed the long history of discrimination in the agency as a reason for upholding the quota system. Whatever burdens were imposed on innocent parties were outweighed by the need to correct the effects of past discrimination.[29]

Cases Questioning Affirmative Action

The Supreme Court has continued to express concern about whites who are directly and adversely affected by government action solely because of their race. In *Firefighters*

REGENTS OF THE UNIVERSITY OF CALIFORNIA v. BAKKE
Early case challenging affirmative action; ruling that race may be *considered* a "plus" factor in evaluating admissions applications but banning specific quotas.

The Supreme Court has generally approved of affirmative action programs when there was evidence of past discriminatory practices.

SET-ASIDE
PROGRAM

Governments requiring
a certain percentage of
contracts to go to
minority contractors.

CALIFORNIA
CIVIL RIGHTS
INITIATIVE

A initiative that changed
California's constitution
to include a ban on race
or gender preferences,
which made some
forms of affirmative
action illegal.

Local Union v. *Stotts* (1984), the Court ruled that a city could not lay off white firefighters in favor of black firefighters with less seniority.[30] In *Richmond* v. *Crosen* (1989), the Supreme Court held that a minority set-aside program in Richmond, Virginia, which mandated that 30 percent of all city construction contracts must go to "blacks, Spanish-speaking, Orientals, Indians, Eskimos, or Aleuts," violated the Equal Protection Clause of the Fourteenth Amendment.[31]

Affirmative Action and "Strict Scrutiny"

It is important to note that the Supreme Court has never adopted the color-blind doctrine first espoused by Justice John Harlan in his *dissent* from *Plessy* v. *Ferguson*—that "our constitution is color-blind and neither knows nor tolerates classes among citizens." If the Equal Protection Clause requires that the laws of the United States and the states be truly color-blind, then *no* racial preferences, goals, or quotas would be tolerated. This view has occasionally been expressed in minority dissents and concurring opinions.[32]

However, the Court has held that racial classifications in law must be subject to "strict scrutiny." This means that race-based actions by government—any disparate treatment of the races by federal, state, or local public agencies—must be found necessary to remedy past proven discrimination, or to further clearly identify, compelling, and legitimate government objectives. Moreover, it must be "narrowly tailored" so as not to adversely affect the rights of individuals. In striking down a federal construction contract **"set-aside" program** for small businesses owned by racial minorities, the Court expressed skepticism about governmental racial classifications: "There is simply no way of determining what classifications are 'benign' and 'remedial' and what classifications are in fact motivated by illegitimate notions of racial inferiority or simple racial politics."[33] The membership of the Supreme Court appears to be closely split over the meaning and use of "strict scrutiny" in affirmative action cases (see *"Up Close:* 'Diversity' in Universities").

Ending Racial Preferences by Initiative and Referenda

While leaders in business and government generally support affirmative action, many voters oppose granting preferential treatment to minorities. The initiative and referenda devices in American state politics allow voters to bypass political leadership (see Chapter 2).

California voters led the way in 1996 with a citizens' initiative (Proposition 209) that added the following to that state's constitution:

> Neither the State of California nor any of its political subdivisions or agents shall use race, sex, color, ethnicity or national origin as criterion for either discriminating against, or granting preferential treatment to, any individual or group in the operation of the State's system of public employment, public education or public contracting.

The key words are "or granting preferential treatment to." Supporters of this **"California Civil Rights Initiative"** argued that it leaves all existing federal and state civil rights protections intact, while extending the rights of specifically protected groups to all of the state's citizens. They contended that governmental racial classifications violate the fundamental principle of equality under the law—that America cannot "make up" for past discrimination by "discrimination in the opposite direction." Even some early supporters of affirmative action argued that race-conscious programs are no longer

up CLOSE — "Diversity" in Universities

Most colleges and universities in the United States—public as well as private—specify "diversity" as an institutional goal. The term refers to racial and ethnic representation in student body and faculty.

University administrators argue that students benefit when they interact with others from different cultural heritages. There are claims that racial and ethnic diversity on the campus improve students' "self-evaluation," "social-historical thinking," and "intellectual engagement." There is some evidence that students admitted under policies designed to increase diversity do well in postcollege careers. But despite numerous efforts to develop scientific evidence that racial or ethnic diversity on the campus improves learning, no definitive conclusions have emerged. Educational research on this topic is clouded by political and ideological conflict. There is no conclusive evidence that racial diversity does in fact promote the expression of ideas on campus or change perspectives or viewpoints of students.

Diversity requires racial classifications and the U.S. Supreme Court has held that such classifications be subject to "strict scrutiny." The Supreme Court held in 2003 that diversity may be a "compelling government interest" because it "promotes cross-racial understanding, helps break down racial stereotypes, and enables [students] to better understand persons of different races." This opinion was written by Justice Sandra Day O'Connor in a case involving the University of Michigan Law School's affirmative action program. In a 5–4 decision, O'Connor said that the Constitution "does not prohibit the law school's narrowly tailored use of race in admissions decisions to further a compelling interest in obtaining the educational benefits that flow from a diverse student body."[a]

However, in a case involving University of Michigan's affirmative action program for *undergraduate* admissions, the Supreme Court held that the admissions policy was "not narrowly tailored to achieve the asserted interest in diversity" and therefore violated the Equal Protection Clause of the Fourteenth Amendment.[b] The Court rejected the University's affirmative action plan that made race the *decisive* factor for even minimally qualified minority applicants. Yet the Court restated its support for limited affirmative action programs that use race as a "plus" factor, the position the Court has held since the *Bakke* case in 1978.

Can colleges and universities achieve diversity without using racial preferences? The U.S. Department of Education recommends (1) preferences based on socioeconomic status, (2) recruitment outreach efforts targeted at students of traditionally low-performing schools, and (3) admissions plans for students who finished in the top of their high school classes without regard to SAT scores.[c] California, along with Texas and Florida, abandoned racial preferences yet managed to retain roughly the same percentages of minority students as they had under racial preference admissions policies. These states currently give preference to students who stand at or near the top of their class (perhaps the top 10 or 20 percent) in each of their states' high schools. This allows students from high schools with heavy minority enrollments to gain admission without reliance on standardized test scores. However, admissions to law and medical schools and graduate programs do not lend themselves to this approach.

[a] *Grutter* v. *Bollinger*, 539 U.S. 306 (2003).
[b] *Gratz* v. *Bollinger*, 523 U.S. 244 (2003).
[c] U.S. Department of Education, Office of Civil Rights, "Race-Neutral Alternatives in Postsecondary Education," March 2003.

necessary, that disadvantages in society today are more class-based than race-based, and that if preferences are to be granted at all they should be based on *economic* disadvantage, not race. In addition, it was argued that affirmative action may unfairly stigmatize the supposed beneficiaries, resulting in stereotyping that "stamps minorities with a badge of inferiority that may cause them to develop dependencies or to adopt an attitude that they are 'entitled' to preferences."[34]

Opponents argued that it sets back the civil rights movement, that it will end the progress of minorities in education and employment, and that it denies minorities the opportunity to seek assistance and protection from government. Supporters of racial preferences argue that discrimination still exists in American society. Race-conscious policies are a continuing necessity to remedy current discrimination as well as the effects of past discrimination. They contend that America is not now nor has ever been a "color-blind" society, and that racial preferences remain a necessary tool in achieving equality of opportunity.

Following its adoption, opponents of the California Civil Rights Initiative filed suit in federal court arguing that it violated the Equal Protection Clause of the U.S. Constitution because it denied minorities and women an opportunity to seek preferential treatment by government. But a federal Circuit Court of Appeals held, and the U.S. Supreme Court affirmed, that a "ban on race or gender preferences, as a matter of law or logic, does not violate the Equal Protection Clause [of the Constitution]." The Court reasoned that the Constitution allows some race-based preferences to correct past discrimination, but does not prevent states from banning racial preferences altogether.[35]

California voters approved of this initiative by a margin of 54 to 46 percent. But the overall margin of victory obscured serious divisions within the California electorate over racial preferences. Men voted in favor of the ban (61 to 39 percent) while women opposed it (48 to 52 percent). Whites voted for it (63 to 37 percent), while blacks voted against it (26 to 74 percent). Hispanics also opposed it (24 to 76 percent).

The success of the California Civil Rights Initiative inspired similar mass movements in other states: Washington adopted a similarly worded state constitutional amendment in 1998, and Michigan approved a statewide ban on racial preferences in public education, employment, and state contracts in 2006. In Michigan this initiative was opposed by elites in the political, business, and academic worlds, including both Democratic and Republican gubernatorial candidates. Nonetheless, 58 percent of Michigan voters favored banning racial preferences. "Proposition 2" in that state gathered the most support from men (60 to 40 percent) and whites (59 to 39 percent). It gathered less support from women (47 to 53 percent) and very little support from blacks (14 to 86 percent). Following voter approval of the referendum, the president of the University of Michigan announced her intention "not to allow our University" to end its affirmative action efforts.

HISPANICS IN AMERICA

Hispanics—persons of Spanish-speaking ancestry and culture—are now the nation's largest minority (see Table 15–2). When adult Hispanics were asked in a 1999 national poll, "Which term do you prefer most for people who are of Spanish or Latin American dissent, Hispanic or Latino?", the results were Hispanic—55 percent, Latino—22 percent, No Difference—21 percent.[36] Most are of Mexican descent (64 percent) and reside in California, Texas, Arizona, and New Mexico. Puerto Ricans (11 percent) are concentrated in New York and Cuban Americans (5 percent) are concentrated in South Florida. Increasing immigration from other Latin American countries (20 percent) also contributes to the nation's Hispanic population.

There is some evidence that each of these Hispanic groups identify themselves separately, rather than as Hispanics.[37] But if all Hispanics are grouped together for statistical comparisons, their median family income level is below that of whites (see "Minority Life Chances," Table 15–1). Hispanic poverty and unemployment rates are also higher than those of whites. The percentage of Hispanics completing high school

TABLE 15–2   Minorities in America

	Number	Percent of U.S. Population
Hispanic Americans	41,322,000	14.1
African Americans	37,502,000	12.8
Asian	12,326,000	4.2
Native Americans, Eskimos, Aleuts	2,825,000	1.0
Native Hawaiian and Other Pacific Islanders	506,000	0.1
Total Population	293,655,000	100.0*

*In the 2000 Census, for the first time, some people were recognized as "two or more races" (1.5%).
Note: Data are for 2005.
Source: Statistical Abstract of the United States, 2006, p. 15. Available at http://www.census.gov/prod/2004pubs/04statab/pop.pdf

and college education is below that of both whites and blacks, suggesting that language or other cultural obstacles adversely affect education.

Mexican Americans

For many years, agricultural businesses encouraged immigration of Mexican farm laborers willing to endure harsh conditions for low pay. Many others came to the United States as *indocumentados*—undocumented, or illegal, aliens. In the Immigration Reform Act of 1986 Congress offered amnesty to all undocumented workers who had entered the United States prior to 1982. But the Act also required employers, under threat of penalties, to hire only people who can provide documentation of their legal status in the country. The result has been a booming business in counterfeit green (employment) and Social Security cards.

Although Mexican Americans have served as governors of Arizona and New Mexico and have won election to the U.S. Congress, their political power does not yet match their population percentages. Mexican American voter turnout is lower than for other ethnic groups, perhaps because many are resident aliens or illegal immigrants not eligible to vote, or perhaps because of cultural factors that discourage political participation.

Puerto Ricans

Puerto Rico is a **commonwealth** of the United States. Its commonwealth government resembles that of a state, with a constitution and elected governor and legislature, but the island has no voting members of the U.S. Congress and no electoral votes for president (see "The Commonwealth of Puerto Rico" in Chapter 1). As citizens, Puerto Ricans can move anywhere in the United States; many have immigrated to New York City.

Puerto Ricans have long debated whether to remain a commonwealth of the United States, apply for statehood, or seek complete independence from the United States. All of the participants in the debate agree that Puerto Ricans themselves should vote on the matter by referendum. In various nonbinding referenda votes, Puerto Ricans have voted to remain a commonwealth.

Cuban Americans

Many Cuban Americans, especially those in the early waves of refugees from Castro's revolution in 1959, were skilled professionals and businesspeople, and they rapidly set about

*INDOCUMENTADOS/
UNDOCUMENTEDS*
Illegal immigrants living within the United States.

**COMMON-
WEALTH**
A government that resembles that of a state, with a constitution and elected governor and legislature, but with no voting members in the U.S. Congress and no electoral votes in presidential elections.

building Miami into a thriving economy. Although Cuban Americans are the smallest of the Hispanic subgroups, today they are better educated and enjoy higher incomes than the others. They are well organized politically, and they have succeeded in electing Cuban Americans to local office in Florida and to the U.S. Senate and House of Representatives.

Political Mobilization

For many decades American agriculture encouraged Mexican American immigration, both legal and illegal, to labor in fields as *braceros*. Most of these migrant farm workers lived and worked under very difficult conditions; they were paid less than minimum wages for backbreaking labor. Farm workers were not covered by the federal National Labor Relations Act and therefore not protected in the right to organize labor unions. But civil rights activity among Hispanics, especially among farm workers, grew during the 1960s under the leadership of Ceasar Chavez and his United Farm Workers union. Chavez organized a national boycott of grapes from California vineyards that refused to recognize the union or improve conditions. *La Raza*, as the movement was called, finally ended in a union contract with the growers and later a California law protecting the right of farm workers to organize unions and bargain collectively with their employers. More importantly, the movement galvanized Mexican Americans throughout the Southwest to engage in political activity.[38]

However, inasmuch as many Mexican American immigrants were noncitizens, and many were *indocumentados*, the voting strength of Mexican Americans never matched their numbers in the population. The Immigration Reform and Control Act of 1986 granted amnesty to illegal aliens living in the United States in 1982. But the same Act also imposed penalties on employers who hired illegal aliens. The effect of these threatened penalties on many employers was to make them wary of hiring Hispanics, especially as permanent employees. At the same time, industries in need of cheap labor—agriculture, health and hospitals, restaurants, clothing manufacturers, and so on—continued to encourage legal and illegal immigration to fill minimum- and even subminimum-wage-level jobs with few, if any, benefits.

In 1994 California voters approved a referendum, Proposition 187, which would have barred welfare and other benefits to persons living in the state illegally. Most Hispanics opposed the measure believing that it was motivated by prejudice. A federal court later declared major portions of Proposition 187 unconstitutional; and earlier the U.S. Supreme Court held that a state may not bar the children of illegal immigrants from attending public schools.[39] Although Proposition 187 was approved, the battle over it in California helped to mobilize Hispanic voters everywhere.[40]

> *While Hispanic voter turnout has been low, population projections forecast an ever-growing role for Hispanics in state, national, and local politics.*

HISPANIC POLITICS

Hispanic voters are a growing force in American politics. While Hispanic voter turnout has been low, population projections forecast an ever-growing role for Hispanics in state, national, and local politics. Already it is estimated that Hispanics make up about 36 percent of the electorate in New Mexico, 13 percent in California, and 16 percent in Texas.

Political Diversity

Overall, most Hispanics identify with the Democratic Party (see Table 15–3). Among Hispanic groups only Cuban Americans tend to identify with the Republican

TABLE 15–3 Hispanic Politics

	Total (%)	Mexican (%)	Puerto Rican (%)	Cuban (%)	Other (%)
"In politics today do you consider yourself a Republican, a Democrat, an Independent, or something else?"					
Democrat	37	33	52	29	39
Republican	16	15	17	34	12
Independent	33	37	17	27	35
"Do you think abortion should be legal in all cases, illegal in most cases, or illegal in all cases?"					
Legal	40	36	60	49	32
Illegal	58	61	39	49	66
"Do you think the government should provide health insurance for Americans without insurance, or is this something the government should not do?"					
Should	83	83	84	87	86
Should not	14	14	15	11	11
"Should colleges sometimes take a student's racial and ethnic background into consideration when they decide which student to admit, or should they select students without considering their racial or ethnic backgrounds?"					
Consider	22	21	17	17	21
Don't consider	75	76	78	82	76
"Do you favor or oppose offering government financial aid or 'vouchers' to pay parents some of the cost of sending their children to private and parochial schools?"					
Favor	40	40	46	49	37
Oppose	18	16	12	22	23

Source: As reported in *Public Perspective*, May/June 2000, from a *Washington Post* survey of adult Hispanics nationwide; "Don't know" and "other" responses not shown. From "National Survey on Latinos in America" (#3023), The Henry J. Kaiser Family Foundation, May 2000. This information was reprinted with permission from the Henry J. Kaiser Family Foundation. The Kaiser Family Foundation, based in Menlo Park, California is a non-profit, private operating foundation focusing on the major health care issues facing the nation and is not associated with Kaiser Permanente or Kaiser Industries.

Party. Polls suggest that Hispanics are generally conservative on social issues (opposing abortion, opposing racial preferences, favoring government vouchers to pay parochial school tuitions), but liberal on economic issues (favoring government provision of health insurance for all, favoring a larger federal government with many services).

The Republican Party under President George W. Bush began aggressively seeking "outreach" to Hispanic voters. (President Bush and former Governor Jeb Bush of Florida both speak Spanish, Jeb more fluently than the President.) In Texas gubernatorial elections, George W. Bush won nearly half of the Mexican American vote in that state. In the 2000 and 2004 presidential elections, Bush won over 35 percent of the Hispanic vote nationwide. President Bush proposed reversing the traditional Republican opposition to immigration and pushed for a more open border with Mexico. But many other prominent Republicans have not, which has reversed some of the gains Republicans made with Hispanics in the 2004 presidential election.

Voter Turnout

Various explanations have been advanced for the lower voter participation of Mexican Americans. Language barriers may still discourage some voters, even though ballots in many states are now available in the Spanish language. Illegal immigrants, of course, cannot vote. Lower education and income levels are also associated with lower voter turnout. Nonetheless, Hispanic voting is on the increase throughout the nation and both Democratic and Republican candidates are increasingly aware of the importance of the Hispanic vote.

NATIVE AMERICANS AND TRIBAL GOVERNMENT

Christopher Columbus erred in his estimate of the circumference of the globe. He believed he had arrived in the Indian Ocean when he first came to the Caribbean. He mistook the Arawaks for people of the East Indies, calling them "Indios," and this Spanish word passed into English as Indians—a word that came to refer to all Native American peoples. But at the time of the first European contacts, these peoples had no common identity; there were hundreds of separate cultures and languages thriving in the Americas.

Although estimates vary, most historians believe that in the fifteenth century, 7 to 12 million people lived in the land that is now the United States and Canada; 25 million more lived in Mexico; and 60 to 70 million lived in the Western Hemisphere, a number comparable to Europe's population at the time. But in the centuries that followed, the native population of the Americas was devastated by warfare, famine, and, most of all, by epidemic diseases brought from Europe. Overall, the native population fell by 90 percent, the greatest human disaster in world history.

The Trail of Broken Treaties

In the Northwest Ordinance of 1787, Congress, in organizing the western territories of the new nation, declared that "the utmost good faith shall always be observed toward the Indians. Their lands and property shall never be taken from them without their consent."

And later, in the Intercourse Act of 1790, Congress declared that public treaties between the United States government and the independent Indian "nations" would be the only legal means of obtaining Indian land. As president, George Washington forged a treaty with the Creeks: In exchange for land concessions, the United States pledged to protect the boundaries of the "Creek Nation" and allow the Creeks themselves to punish all violators of their laws within these boundaries. This semblance of legality was reflected in hundreds of treaties to follow. (And indeed, in recent years some Indian tribes have successfully sued in federal court for reparations and return of lands obtained in violation of the Intercourse Act of 1790 and subsequent treaties.) Yet Indian lands were constantly invaded by whites. The resulting Indian resistance would typically lead to wars that would ultimately result in great loss of life among warriors and their families and the further loss of tribal land. The cycle of invasion, resistance, military defeat, and further land concessions continued for a hundred years.

Indian Wars

The "Indian wars" were fought between the Plains Indian tribes and the U.S. Army between 1864 and 1890. Following the Civil War, the federal government began to assign boundaries to each tribe and created a Bureau of Indian Affairs (BIA) to "assist and protect" Indian peoples on their "reservations." But the reservations were repeatedly reduced in size until subsistence by hunting became impossible. Malnutrition and demoralization of the native peoples were aided by the mass slaughter of the buffalo; vast herds, numbering perhaps as many as seventy million, were exterminated over the years. The most storied engagement of the long war occurred at the Little Big Horn River in Montana on June 25, 1876, where Civil War hero General George Armstrong Custer led elements of the U.S. Seventh Cavalry to destruction at the hands of Sioux and Cheyenne warriors led by Chief Crazy Horse, Sitting Bull, and Gall. But Custer's Last Stand inspired renewed army campaigns against the Plains tribes; the following year Crazy Horse was forced to surrender. In 1881, destitute Sioux under Chief Sitting Bull returned from exile in Canada to surrender themselves to reservation life. Among the last tribes to hold out were the Apaches, whose famous warrior, Geronimo, finally surrendered in 1886. Sporadic fighting continued until 1890, when a small, malnourished band of Lakota Sioux were wiped out at Wounded Knee Creek.

Federal Policy Reversals

The Dawes Act of 1887 governed federal Indian policy for decades. The thrust of the policy was to break up tribal lands, allotting acreage for individual homesteads in order to assimilate Indians into the white agricultural society. Farming was to replace hunting, and tribal life and traditional customs were to be shed for English language and schooling. But this effort to destroy Indian culture never really succeeded. While Indian peoples lost over half of their 1877 reservation land, few lost their communal ties or accumulated much private property. The Dawes Act remained federal policy until 1934, when Congress finally reversed itself in the Indian Reorganization Act of 1934 and reaffirmed tribal ownership of land. Life on the reservations was often disparate. Indians suffered the worst poverty of any group in the nation, with high rates of infant mortality, alcoholism, and other diseases. The BIA, notoriously corrupt and mismanaged, encouraged dependency, and regularly interfered with Indian religious affairs and tribal customs.

Native Americans Today

Today about 2.4 million people—less than 1 percent of the nation's population—identify themselves as American Indians. About 800,000 of these people live on tribal reservations and trust land, the largest of which is the Navaho and Hopi enclave in the southwestern United States (see Figure 15–2). Yet these peoples remain the poorest and least healthy in America, with high incidences of infant mortality, suicide, and alcoholism. Approximately half of all Indians live below the poverty line.

Tribal Government

The U.S. Constitution (Article I, Section 8) grants Congress the full power "to regulate Commerce . . . with the Indian Tribes." States are prevented from regulating or taxing Indian tribes or extending their courts' jurisdiction over them, unless authorized by Congress. The Supreme Court recognizes Native Americans "as members of quasi-sovereign tribal entities"[41] with powers to regulate their own internal affairs, establish their own courts, and enforce their own laws, all subject to congressional supervision. Thus, for example, many Indian tribes chose to legalize gambling, including casino gambling, on reservations in states that otherwise prohibited the activity. As American citizens, Indians have

The Supreme Court recognizes Native Americans "as members of quasi-sovereign tribal entities" with powers to regulate their own internal affairs, establish their own courts, and enforce their own laws, all subject to congressional supervision.

FIGURE 15–2 Native American Reservations and Trust Land

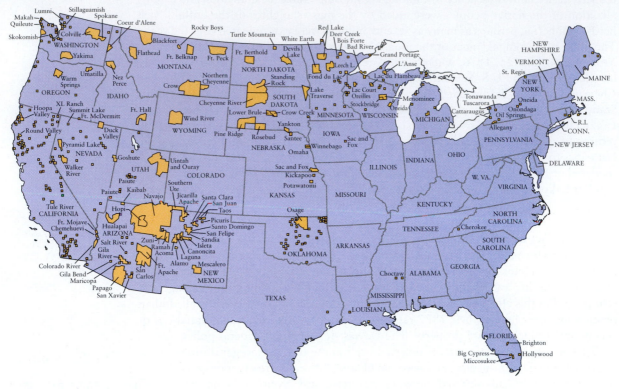

Source: U.S. Bureau of the Census.

the right to vote in state as well as national elections. Indians living off of reservations have the same rights and responsibilities as anyone else. Indians enrolled as members of tribes and living on reservations are entitled to certain benefits established by law and treaty. The BIA in the Department of Commerce continues to supervise reservation life.

Tribes versus States

In recent years, many tribal governments have reasserted their sovereignty and rights to self-government. The result has often led to strained relations with state and local governments. Disputes have arisen over casino gambling on reservations; state collection of taxes on gasoline, liquor, and cigarettes sold on reservations; and the enforcement of state environmental, natural resource, and wildlife protection laws within reservations. Some states have succeeded in negotiating compacts and agreements with tribal governments.

Under federal law, the Indian Gaming Regulatory Act of 1988, tribes must enter into compacts with states before they can open gambling casinos on tribal land. States must bargain "in good faith" in negotiating these compacts. States cannot tax the income from Indian casinos, but they may negotiate reimbursement for regulation and administration. About half of the states have negotiated such compacts. But in several states, including California, Texas, and Florida, tribes have opened casinos without state approval. State governments have been reluctant to enforce prohibitions on tribes: "I don't want another war with the Seminoles."[42]

AMERICANS WITH DISABILITIES

Throughout most of our nation's history, little thought was given to making public or private buildings or facilities accessible to blind, deaf, or mobility-impaired people.[43] But in 1990, Congress passed the sweeping Americans with Disabilities Act (ADA), which prohibits discrimination against the disabled in private employment, government programs, public accommodations, and telecommunications.

ADA

The Act is vaguely worded in many of its provisions, requiring "reasonable accommodations" for the disabled that do not involve "undue hardship." But the ADA mandates that:

Sight-impaired members of the Capital City Council of the Blind of Washington demonstrate to ask the legislature for more funding for the Washington Talking Book & Braille Library. One member said, "It's important because its information that people need to have . . . to see what the world is doing."

1. The disabled cannot be denied employment or promotion if, with "reasonable accommodation," they can perform the duties of the job.

2. The disabled cannot be denied access to government programs or benefits. New buses, taxis, and trains must be accessible to disabled persons, including those in wheelchairs.

3. The disabled must enjoy "full and equal" access to hotels, restaurants, stores, schools, parks, museums, auditoriums, and the like. To achieve equal access, owners of existing facilities must alter them "to the maximum extent feasible"; builders of new facilities must ensure that they are readily accessible to disabled persons unless doing so is structurally impossible.

These federal mandates for accommodations of the disabled were not accompanied by any federal funds to employers or state and local governments to implement them (see "Coercive Federalism: Preemptions and Mandates" in Chapter 3).

Mental and Learning Disabilities

The ADA protects the rights of people with learning and psychiatric disabilities, as well as physical disabilities. The U.S. Equal Employment Opportunity Commission has received almost as many complaints about workplace discrimination against the mentally disabled as it has received from people claiming back injuries. But it is far more difficult for employers to determine how to handle a depressed or anxiety-ridden employee than an employee with a visible physical disability. How can employers distinguish uncooperative employees from those with psychiatric disorders?

The American Council on Education reports that the percentage of students in colleges and universities claiming a "learning disability" jumped from 3 to 10 percent after the enactment of ADA.[44]

The federal Help America Vote Act of 2002 mandates that precincts have voting machines that can be used by disabled voters. The machine shown here features speakers, a computer screen, and a printer into which the actual ballot is fed.

A decision by the U.S. Department of Education that "attention deficit disorder" is covered by the ADA has resulted in another significant rise in students claiming disabilities. Colleges and universities are required to provide special accommodations for students with disabilities, including tutors, extra time on examinations, oral rather than written exams, and so on.

Lawsuits

In recent years the ADA has produced a flood of lawsuits against private businesses claiming that their facilities were not reasonably accessible to employees or customers. The law requires buildings open to the public to have designated parking for the disabled and no steps or curbs blocking the entrance. Bathrooms and aisles must be able to accommodate patrons in wheelchairs. Counters cannot be too high. The law allows attorneys for the disabled to file lawsuits and collect damages and fees from offending businesses. Many business owners complain that frivolous lawsuits are being driven by lawyers' fees.

GENDER EQUALITY

Traditionally, gender issues were decided largely by *states*, particularly state laws governing marriage, divorce, employment, and abortion. State laws frequently differentiated between the rights and responsibilities of men and women. Women had many special protections in state laws, but often these protections limited opportunities for advancement and encouraged dependence upon men. State laws governing employment considered women as frail creatures in need of special protections against long hours, heavy work, night work, and so on.

State laws and employer practices that differentiate between men and women in hours, pay, retirement age, and so on have been struck down.

Employment

Today, Title VII of the federal Civil Rights Act of 1964 prohibits sexual (as well as racial) discrimination in hiring, pay, and promotions. The Equal Employment Opportunity Commission, which is the federal agency charged with eliminating discrimination in employment, has established guidelines barring stereotyped classifications of "men's jobs" and "women's jobs." State laws and employer practices that differentiate between men and women in hours, pay, retirement age, and so on have been struck down.

Gender Classifications

Over the years, the Supreme Court ruled that states could no longer set different ages for men and women to become legal adults[45] or purchase alcoholic beverages[46]; women could not be barred from police or firefighting jobs by arbitrary height and weight requirements[47]; insurance and retirement plans for women must pay the same monthly benefits even though women on the average live longer[48]; and schools must pay coaches in girls' sports the same as coaches in boys' sports.[49] However, all-male and all-female schools are still permitted[50]; and Congress may draft men for military service without drafting women.[51] Gender protection under the Equal Protection Clause was also extended to men: The Supreme Court struck down a state law that allowed wives to obtain alimony from husbands but did not permit husbands to obtain alimony from wives.[52]

Education

Title IX of the Federal Education Act Amendment of 1972 dealt with sex discrimination in education. This federal law barred discrimination in admissions, housing, rules, financial aid, faculty and staff recruitment, pay, and—most troublesome of all—athletics. The latter problem has proven very difficult because men's football and basketball programs have traditionally brought in the money to finance all other sports and have received the largest share of school athletic budgets. (See also "*Up Close: Sexual Harrassment.*")

The Earnings Gap

The federal Equal Pay Act of 1963 prevents employers from discriminating against women by paying them less than men for work performed under similar conditions in requiring "equal skill, effort and responsibility." When it was signed, women were earning about 59 cents for every dollar earned by a man.

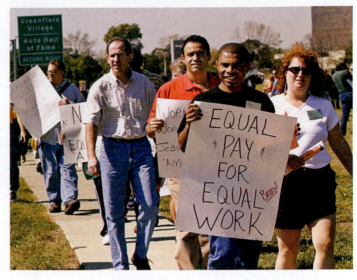

The wage gap between men and women is narrowing. But women today still earn annually about 78 percent of what men earn. The existence of a "dual" labor market is a large part of the problem. Female-dominated jobs pay less than male-dominated occupations.

Today women earn annually about 78 percent of what men earn. Despite federal laws barring direct gender discrimination in employment, the existence of a "dual" labor market, with male-dominated "blue-collar" jobs distinguishable from female-dominated "pink-collar" jobs, continues to be a major obstacle to economic equality between men and women. These occupational differences can be attributed to cultural stereotyping, social conditioning, and training and education that narrow the choices available to women. While significant progress has been made in recent years in reducing occupational sex segregation, nonetheless, many observers doubt that sexually differentiated occupations will be eliminated soon.

Comparable Worth

As a result of a growing recognition that the wage gap is more a result of occupational differentiation than direct discrimination, some feminist organizations have turned to another approach—the demand that pay levels in various occupations be determined by "comparable worth" rather than by the labor market. Comparable worth means more than paying men and women equally for the same work; it means paying the same wages for jobs of comparable value to the employer. It means that traditionally male and female jobs would be evaluated by governmental agencies or courts to determine their "worth" to the employer, perhaps by considering responsibilities, effort, knowledge, and skill requirements. Jobs adjudged to be comparable would have equal wages. Government agencies or the courts would replace the labor market in the determination of wage rates.

To date, the U.S. Equal Employment Opportunity Commission has rejected the notion of comparable worth and declined to recommend wages for traditionally male and female jobs. And so far the federal courts have refused to declare that different wages in traditionally male and female occupations are evidence of sexual discrimination in

COMPARABLE WORTH

The argument that pay levels for traditionally male and traditionally female jobs should be equalized either by employers themselves or by government laws and regulations.

upCLOSE Sexual Harassment

The Civil Rights Act of 1964 (Title VII) makes it "an unlawful employment practice to discriminate against any individual with respect to . . . conditions or privileges of employment because of an individual's race, color, religion, sex, or national origin." The U.S. Supreme Court has declared that "sexual harassment" is a condition of employment that is outlawed by the Civil Rights Act. But what constitutes "sexual harassment"?

The Supreme Court has wrestled with the question of sexual harassment over the years. In 1986, the Court provided the following definition:

> Unwelcome sexual advances, requests for sexual favors, and other verbal or physical conduct of a sexual nature constitute sexual harassment when (1) submission to such conduct is made either explicitly or implicitly a term or condition of an individual's employment; (2) submission to or rejection of such conduct by an individual is used as the basis for employment decisions affecting such individual; or (3) such conduct has the purpose or effect of unreasonably interfering with an individual's work performance or creating an intimidating, hostile, or offensive working environment.[a]

There is no real difficulty in defining sexual harassment when jobs or promotions are conditioned on the granting of sexual favors. But problems arise in defining what is an "intimidating, hostile, or offensive working environment." This phrase may include dirty jokes, sexual innuendoes, the display of X-rated photos, or perhaps even unwanted proposals for dates. All of these definitions raise First Amendment questions regarding how far speech may be curtailed by law in the workplace. Moreover, some of these definitions about what is "offensive" or "unwanted" depend more on the subjective feelings of the individual employee than any objective standard of law.

Justice Sandra Day O'Connor tried to clarify some of these questions in 1993. Writing for the Court majority, she held that the particular words or actions objected to must be serious enough to make a "reasonable person," not just the plaintiff, perceive the work environment to be hostile. She indicated that a single incident is unlikely to constitute harassment; rather, courts should consider "the frequency of the discriminatory conduct, . . . its severity," and whether it "unreasonably interferes with an employee's work performance."[b]

What does a "reasonable person" believe to be sexual harassment? Some polls show that neither women nor men are likely to believe that sexual harassment includes repeated requests for a date, or the telling of dirty jokes, or comments on attractiveness—even though these behaviors often inspire formal complaints. Many college and university policies go well beyond the Supreme Court definition of sexual harassment, including the following:

- remarks about the person's clothing.
- suggestive or insulting sounds.
- leering or ogling a person's body.
- remarks that degrade a person's gender.

Overly broad and vague definitions of sexual harassment can undermine academic freedom and inhibit classroom discussions of important yet sensitive topics. Both faculty and students must feel free to express their views without fear of being labeled "insensitive" or charged with making others feel "uncomfortable." Students especially must feel free to express themselves on matters of gender, whether or not their ideas are immature or crudely expressed.

[a]*Meritor Savings Bank* v. *Vinson*, 477 U.S. 57 (1986).
[b]*Harris* v. *Forklift*, 126 L. Ed. 2d 295 (1993).

PRO-CHOICE

Those who feel that a woman should be permitted to choose whether she has an abortion.

violation of federal law. However, some state governments and private employers have undertaken to review their own pay scales to determine if traditionally female occupations are underpaid.

BATTLES OVER ABORTION

Arguments over abortion touch on fundamental moral and religious principles. Proponents of legalized abortion, who often refer to themselves as "**pro-choice**," argue that a woman should be permitted to control her own body and should not be forced by law to have unwanted children. They cite the heavy toll in lives lost in criminal abortions and the psychological and emotional pain of an unwanted pregnancy. Opponents of abortion, who often refer to themselves as **"pro-life,"** generally base their belief on the sanctity of life, including the life of the unborn child, which they believe deserves the protection of law—"the right to life." Many believe that the killing of an unborn child for any reason other than the preservation of the life of the mother is murder.

Early State Laws

Historically, abortions for any purpose other than saving the life of the mother were criminal offenses under state law. About a dozen states acted in the late 1960s to permit abortions in cases of rape or incest, or to protect the physical health of the mother, and in some cases her mental health as well. Relatively few legal abortions were performed under these laws, however, because of the red tape involved—review of each case by several concurring physicians, approval of a hospital board, and so forth. Then, in 1970, New York, Alaska, Hawaii, and Washington enacted laws that in effect permitted abortion at the request of the woman involved with the concurrence of her physician.[53]

Roe v. Wade

The U.S. Supreme Court's decision in *Roe* v. *Wade* was one of the most important and far-reaching in the Court's

Issues that touch on a person's moral and religious beliefs often generate the most intense courtroom battles. Abortion has been just such an issue for several decades, creating intense and emotionally-charged debates between Americans described as "pro-life" and those labeled "pro-choice." Meanwhile, public opinion surveys show that many in the public-at-large have mixed views on the subject.

history.[54] The Supreme Court ruled that the constitutional guarantee of "liberty" in the Fifth and Fourteenth Amendments included a woman's decision to bear or not to bear a child. The Supreme Court ruled that the word *person* in the Constitution did not include the unborn child. Therefore, the Fifth and Fourteenth Amendments to the Constitution, guaranteeing "life, liberty and property," did not protect the "life" of the fetus. The Court also ruled that a state's power to protect the health and safety of the mother could not justify *any* restriction of abortion in the first three months of pregnancy. Between the third and sixth month of pregnancy, a state could set standards for abortion procedures in order to protect the health of women, but a state could not prohibit abortions. Only in the final three months could a state prohibit or regulate abortion to protect the unborn.

Reactions in the States

The Supreme Court's decision did not end the controversy over abortion. Congress declined to pass a constitutional amendment restricting abortion or declaring that the guarantee of life begins at conception. However, Congress banned the use of federal funds under Medicaid (medical care for the poor) for abortions (except to protect the life of a woman, and, later, in cases of rape and incest). The Supreme Court upheld the constitutionality of federal and state laws *denying tax funds for abortions.*[55]

PRO-LIFE

Those who support a ban on most abortions, generally based on their belief in the sanctity of life, including the life of the unborn child, which they believe deserves the protection of law.

While women retained the right to an abortion, the Court held that there was no constitutional obligation for governments to pay for abortions; the decision about whether to pay for abortions from tax revenues was left to Congress and the states.[56] However, efforts by the states to directly restrict abortion ran into Supreme Court opposition.[57]

Abortions in the States

About 1.3 million abortions are performed each year in the United States. This is about 32 percent of the number of live births. About 85 percent of all abortions are performed at abortion clinics; others are performed in physicians' offices or in hospitals, where the cost is significantly higher. Most of these abortions are performed in the first three months; about 10 percent are performed after the third month. Abortion rates are higher in some states (New York, Delaware, Rhode Island, and Florida) than in other states (Mississippi, Utah, Colorado, Kentucky, Indiana).

Why are abortions more frequent in some states than in others? A careful study of this question by political scientist Susan B. Hansen revealed that abortion rates were *not* related to unwanted pregnancies, that is, the "demand" for abortions.[58] Rather, abortion rates were related to state policies affecting the availability of abortion services, that is, to government policies affecting the "supply" of abortions. Among the reported findings were that abortion rates are higher in states that permitted abortion before *Roe* v. *Wade*; some states with low abortion rates (Utah and Idaho) have large Mormon populations; and greater state legislative support for abortion facilities and health services leads to higher abortion rates.

State Restrictions

Opponents of abortion won a victory in the *Webster* case in 1989 when the Supreme Court upheld a Missouri law sharply restricting abortions.[59] The right to abortion under *Roe* v. *Wade* was not overturned, but narrowed in application. The effect of the decision was to return the question of abortion restrictions to the states for decision.

The Court held that Missouri could deny public funds for abortions that were not necessary for the life of the woman and could deny the use of public facilities or public employees in performing or assisting in abortions. More important, the Court upheld the requirement for a test of "viability" after twenty weeks and a prohibition of an abortion of a viable fetus except to save a woman's life. The Court recognized the state's "interest in the protection of human life when viability is possible."

Reaffirming *Roe v. Wade*

Abortion has become such a polarizing issue that pro-choice and pro-life groups are generally unwilling to search out a middle ground. Yet the current Supreme Court appears to have chosen a policy of affirming a woman's right to abortion while upholding modest restrictions.

Pennsylvania is a state where pro-life forces won the support of the governor and legislature for a series of restrictions on abortion—physicians must inform women of risks and alternatives; a twenty-four-hour waiting period is required; minors must have consent of parents or a judge; spouses must be notified. These restrictions reached the Supreme Court in the case of *Planned Parenthood of Pennsylvania* v. *Casey* in 1992.[60]

Justice Sandra Day O'Connor took the lead in forming a moderate, swing bloc on the Court; her majority opinion strongly reaffirmed the fundamental right to abortion:

> Our law affords constitutional protection to personal decisions relating to marriage, procreation, contraception, family relationships, child rearing, and education. . . . These matters, involving the most intimate and personal choices a person may make in a lifetime, choices central to personal dignity and autonomy, are central to the liberty protected by the Fourteenth Amendment. . . . A woman's liberty is not so unlimited, however, that from the outset the State cannot show its concern for the life of the unborn, and at a later point in fetal development the State's interest in life has sufficient force so that the right of the woman to terminate the pregnancy can be restricted. We conclude the line should be drawn at viability, so that before that time the woman has a right to choose to terminate her pregnancy. . . .[61]

Justice O'Connor went on to establish a standard for constitutionally evaluating state restrictions: They must not impose an "undue burden" on women seeking abortion or place "substantial obstacles" in her path. All of Pennsylvania's restrictions were upheld except spousal notification.

The likelihood of states adopting restriction on abortion appears to be related to the size of their Catholic populations. It is in the states with large Catholic populations that pro-choice and pro-life forces are well organized and active in lobbying legislatures.[62]

Standard for constitutionally evaluating state restrictions: They must not impose an "undue burden" on women seeking abortion or place "substantial obstacles" in her path.

Abortion Battles in the States

Contentious debates over abortion continue in virtually all state capitals. Various legal restrictions on abortions have been passed in the states, including (1) *denial of public financing:* prohibitions on public financing of abortions; (2) *conscience laws:* laws granting permission to doctors and hospitals to refuse to perform abortions; (3) *fetal disposal:* laws requiring humane and sanitary disposal of fetal remains; (4) *informed consent:* laws requiring physicians to inform patients about the development of the fetus and the availability of assistance in pregnancy; (5) *parental notification:* laws requiring that parents of minors seeking abortion be informed (upheld by the U.S. Supreme Court)[63]; (6) *spousal verification:* laws requiring spouses to be informed (struck down by the U.S. Supreme Court)[64]; (7) *hospitalization requirement:* laws requiring that late abortions be performed in hospitals; and (8) *clinic licensing:* laws setting standards of cleanliness and care in abortion clinics.

"Partial-Birth" Abortions

But perhaps the most inflamed arguments have been inspired by efforts in the states to ban "partial-birth" abortions of viable fetuses. The procedure is relatively rare. A physician induces a breech delivery with forceps, pulls out the fetus's legs and body, and then pierces the as-yet-undelivered skull and vacuums out the brain; the delivery is then completed. In 1996 and 1997, Congress passed national bans on the procedure, only to have them vetoed by President Clinton. The "partial-birth" abortion issue energized anti-abortion pro-life supporters in the states to seek bans on the procedure. By 2000, over half of the states had enacted such bans. The U.S. Supreme Court decided in 2000 (by 5–4) that a Nebraska law prohibiting "partial-birth abortion" was an unconstitutional "undue burden" on a woman's right to choose whether to have an abortion.[65]

The Nebraska law failed to make an exception for the procedure when it was considered necessary to save a woman's life.

Congress passed and President George W. Bush signed into law a Partial Birth Abortion Ban Act in 2003 that carefully defined the procedure as one that "deliberately and intentionally vaginally delivers a living fetus until, in the case of a head-first presentation, the entire fetal head is outside the body . . . for the purpose of performing an overt act that the person [doctor] knows will kill the partially delivered living fetus." Moreover, the Act makes an exception for the procedure where it is determined by appropriate medical authorities to be "necessary to save the life of a mother."

Lower courts initially declined to enforce the ban believing that it was an unconstitutional undue burden on a woman's right to choose an abortion. But in 2007, the Supreme Court upheld the Act, citing its specificity in describing the prohibited procedure and granting an exception for the preservation of a woman's life.[66] The case was decided by 5–4 margin with President Bush's new appointees, justices Roberts and Alito, joining the majority. The decision upholding the ban reignited efforts in the states not only to prohibit partial-birth abortions, but also to enact other limitations on abortion.

In summary, throughout history, civil rights battles have evoked some of the fiercest battles at the state and local level, with Congress and the federal courts often having to resolve the issues at hand. The newest issue involves rights related to sexual preference (See "*Did You Know?*: Same-Sex Marriage in the States.")

did YOU know?

Same-Sex Marriage in the States

In 2003, the U.S. Supreme Court held that homosexuals' "right to liberty under the Due Process Clause gives them the full right to engage in private conduct without government interference."[a] This decision was an important victory for the gay rights movement in America and generated additional cases involving the legal status of homosexual relations.

Among the issues confronting homosexuals is that of same-sex marriage. Anticipating that some states might pass laws allowing same-sex marriage, or that some state courts might rule that such marriages were constitutionally protected in their states, Congress passed a Defense of Marriage Act in 1996. The Act declared that marriage is between a man and a woman and that "no state . . . shall be required to give effect to any public act, record, or judicial proceeding of any other state respecting a relationship between persons of the same sex that is treated as a marriage." This provision was designed to circumvent the Full Faith and Credit Clause of Article IV of the U.S. Constitution requiring every state to recognize the public acts and judiciary proceedings of every other state.

Vermont decided in 2000 to sanction "**civil unions**" between same-sex couples. While avoiding the term *marriage*, the Vermont law allows ceremonies to be performed by a judge or clergy member and the couple to be entitled to all the benefits, protections, and responsibilities that are granted to married couples. And in 2003, the Massachusetts Supreme Court ruled that same-sex couples had a right to marriage under the Massachusetts state constitution. However, most states have laws or constitutional provisions prohibiting same-sex marriage.

CIVIL UNIONS

A legal status some states give to same-sex couples that provide rights, responsibilities, and benefits similar to those of opposite-sex civil marriages.

[a]*Lawrence v. Texas.* (02–102) 539 U.S. (2003).
Source: Stateline.org, March 1, 2007.

Same-Sex Marriage in the States

Recognizes Same-Sex Marriage

Massachusetts

Recognizes Civil Unions and/or Domestic Partnerships

California, Connecticut, Hawaii, Maine, New Jersey, Vermont

Prohibits Same-Sex Marriage by Law

Arizona, Delaware, Florida, Illinois, Indiana, Iowa, Maryland, Minnesota, New Hampshire, Pennsylvania, Washington, West Virginia, Wyoming

Prohibits Same-Sex Marriage in State Constitution

Alabama, Alaska, Arkansas, Colorado, Georgia, Idaho, Kansas, Kentucky, Louisiana, Michigan, Mississippi, Missouri, Montana, Nebraska, Nevada, North Dakota, Ohio, Oklahoma, Oregon, South Carolina, South Dakota, Tennessee, Texas, Utah, Virginia, Wisconsin

No State Law or Constitutional Provision Regarding Same-Sex Marriage

New Mexico, New York, Rhode Island

A vast array of information on civil rights topics exists on the Internet. Many civil rights organizations have elaborate Web sites with sections on current topics, press releases, legislative affairs, programs, and publications. Among the more important sites is that of the National Association for the Advancement of Colored People (NAACP) at

www.naacp.org

The NAACP is the oldest and largest civil rights organization in the United States. It was founded in 1909 by black and white citizens committed to overcoming social injustices. It has a network of more than 2,200 local branches throughout the United States; its total membership exceeds 500,000. Its principal publication, *Crisis Magazine*, can be found at most libraries.

The National Organization for Women (NOW) is the most prominent feminist organization in the nation with 250,000 members in more than 500 chapters throughout the country. It was founded in 1966 "to take actions to bring about equality for all women." Its Web site at

www.now.org

contains a wealth of information on topics such as abortion and reproductive rights, affirmative action, sexual harassment, global feminism, lesbian rights, and violence against women.

The American Civil Liberties Union (ACLU) labels itself "the nation's foremost advocate of individual rights—litigating, legislating, and educating the public on a broad array of issues affecting individual freedom in the United States." It was founded in 1920 initially to assist people who were prosecuted for holding antiwar views during World War I. Today the ACLU focuses its attention on a wide variety of civil rights issues—arts censorship, capital punishment, lesbian and gay rights, immigrants' rights, privacy and technology, prisoners' rights, voting rights, and women's rights. Its Web site at

www.aclu.org

includes information and advocacy on these and related topics.

The American Civil Rights Institute (ACRI) is a relatively new organization created to oppose racial and gender preferences in affirmative action programs. The organization grew out of California's Proposition 209, the successful citizens' initiative that prohibits racial and gender preferences in that state's education, employment, and contracting. The institute's Web site at

www.acri.org

provides information on efforts in other states to pass legislation and/or generate citizens' initiatives to ban racial preferences.

CHAPTER SIXTEEN

THE POLITICS OF EDUCATION

16

QUESTIONS TO CONSIDER

Are SAT scores a good measure of the qualitative output of public schools?
☐ Yes   ☐ No

Should private groups in a community be allowed to operate "charter" schools with public funds?
☐ Yes   ☐ No

Do you favor the state providing tax-supported vouchers to parents to use at any public or private school of their choice?
☐ Yes   ☐ No

Should school district superintendents be directly elected by the voters or appointed by school board members?
☐ Directly elected
☐ Appointed by school board

Should public schools be allowed to begin the day with voluntary prayer?
☐ Yes   ☐ No

GOALS IN EDUCATIONAL POLICY

The primary responsibility for American public education rests with the fifty state governments and their local school districts. It is the largest and most costly of state and local functions. Today about 55 million pupils are in grade schools and high schools in America. About 49 million are in public schools and 6 million in private schools. About 17 million students are enrolled in institutions of higher education: community colleges, colleges, and universities.

Educating Citizens

In 1647 the Massachusetts colonial legislature first required towns to provide for the education of children out of public funds. The rugged individualists of earlier eras thought it outrageous that one person should be taxed to pay for the education of another person's child. They were joined in their opposition to public education by those aristocrats who were opposed to arming the common people with the power that knowledge gives. However, the logic of democracy led inevitably to public education. The earliest democrats believed that the safest repository of the ultimate powers of society was the people themselves. If the people make mistakes, the remedy was not to remove power from their hands, but to help them in forming their judgment through education. Congress passed the **Northwest Ordinance** in 1787 offering land grants for public schools in the new territories and giving succeeding generations words to be forever etched on grammar school cornerstones: "Religion, morality, and knowledge being necessary to good government and the happiness of mankind, schools and the means for education shall ever be encouraged." When American democracy adopted universal suffrage, it affected every aspect of American life, and particularly education. If the people were to be granted the right of suffrage, they must be educated to the task. This meant that public education had to be universal, free, and compulsory.

> *If the people were to be granted the right of suffrage, they must be educated to the task. This meant that public education had to be universal, free, and compulsory.*

Advancing Social Goals

If there ever was a time when schools were only expected to combat ignorance and illiteracy, that time is far behind us. Today, schools are expected to do many things: resolve racial conflict and build an integrated society; improve the self-image of minority children; inspire patriotism and good citizenship; offer various forms of recreation and mass entertainment (football games, bands, choruses, cheerleaders, and the like); teach children to get along well with others and appreciate multiple cultures; reduce the highway accident toll by teaching students to be good drivers; eliminate unemployment and poverty by teaching job skills; end malnutrition and hunger through school lunch and milk programs; produce scientists and other technicians to continue America's progress in science and technology; fight drug abuse and educate children about sex and sexually transmitted diseases; and act as custodians for teenagers who have no interest in education, but are not permitted to work or roam the streets unsupervised. In other words, nearly all the nation's problems are reflected in demands placed on schools. And, of course, these demands are frequently conflicting.

Strengthening the Economy

Governors, legislators, and candidates for almost every office regularly extol education as the key to economic development in their states. As governor of Arkansas, Bill Clinton was once quoted as saying that "low education levels of the workforce are perhaps the biggest stumbling block to economic growth."[1] It is theorized that a well-educated workforce creates the "human capital" that becomes the stimulus to economic development, especially in the "information age." University-based "research parks" are promoted in the states as a magnet for high-tech industry.[2]

But regrettably there is little systematic evidence that state spending for education—for either public elementary and secondary schools or for higher education—has any *direct* impact on economic growth rates in the states.[3] (Even average state SAT scores are *un*related to economic growth rates.) Direct state investment in physical infrastructure, especially transportation, is the only public expenditure that consistently correlates with economic growth in the states.[4] However, over the long run education and economic development are related. "If you think education is expensive, you should try ignorance."

EDUCATIONAL PERFORMANCE MEASUREMENT

Too often educational reports focus on **inputs**—measures of resources expended on education—rather than **outputs**—measures of what, if anything, pupils are learning. Professional educators frequently resist performance measurement, especially comparisons between states or school districts. It is true that many performance measures, especially test scores, are controversial; many commentators argue that they do not measure the qualitative goals of education or that they are biased in one fashion or another. Certainly all interested citizens will welcome future refinements in educational performance measurement. But we cannot ignore performance simply because our measures are unrefined. We need to make reasoned use of the best available comparative measures of educational performance.

Educational Attainment

Educational attainment is measured by the years of school completed, rather than by student knowledge. In educational attainment, the nation has an enviable record, with 85 percent of the overall population now graduating from high school and 28 percent

Intense debates among teachers, students, and parents over how to measure student achievement are ongoing. Any sort of testing tied to graduation is seen by some as "unfair" but to others is regarded as an essential element of holding schools accountable for educating students.

graduating from college. Discrepancies between white and black educational attainment have diminished (see Figure 16–1). High school graduation rates of blacks and whites are nearing parity. Only Hispanic education levels still appear to lag.

A college education is now fairly common. The white college graduation rate has reached 28 percent and the black college graduation rate about 18 percent. Again, the Hispanic rate seems to lag. As late as 2000, women's educational attainment rates were below those of men. But that condition has changed; today, women have higher educational attainment rates than men.

The Dropout Rate

Certainly one measure of an educational system's performance is its ability to retain and graduate its students. National studies have consistently shown that high school dropouts tend to experience more unemployment and earn less over a lifetime than high school graduates. Yet often schools fail to convince young people that staying in school is a worthwhile endeavor.

The conflict over dropouts begins with arguments over how to measure the dropout rate. Two separate measures are regularly employed:

1. *Event dropouts:* Persons who are recorded by the schools as having stopped attending during the tenth, eleventh, and twelfth grades, as a percentage of total attendance. This figure is preferred by professional educators because it is very low, about 4 percent.

2. *Status dropouts:* Persons age 18–24 who are not attending school and have not graduated from high school, as a percentage of all 18–24-year-olds. The national status dropout rate is about 13 percent.

FIGURE 16–1 Educational Attainment by Race

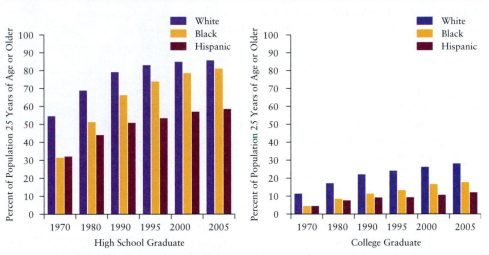

Source: U.S. Census Bureau, *Statistical Abstract of the United States, 2007*, Table No. 214. Available at http://www.census.gov/prod/2006pubs/07statab/educ.pdf

The good news is that high school dropout rates are declining over time, however they are measured. Even so, dropout rates differ by race and ethnicity; the percentage of white 18–24-year-olds not attending or not graduated from school is about 12 percent; for blacks it is about 14 percent, and for Hispanics about 32 percent.[5] Dropout rates are higher than the national average in southern states and states with large Hispanic populations.

SAT Scores

For many years critics of modern public education cited declining scores on standardized tests, particularly the Scholastic Assessment Test (SAT), as evidence of the failure of the schools to teach basic reading and mathematics skills.[6] SAT scores declined dramatically

No school principal likes to have an "F" grade posted on the marquis in front of his or her school for all to see. In many states, individual schools are given grades from A to F, depending on how well their students score on standardized tests given statewide.

during the 1960s and 1970s, ironically during a period in which per pupil educational spending was rising and the federal government initiated federal aid to education. (See Figure 16–2.) When the decline ended in 1982, it was attributed to increasing emphasis on basic skills and standardized testing. But changes in these test scores are also a function of how many students take the test. During the declining years, increasing numbers of students were taking the test—students who never aspired to college in the past and whose test scores did not match those of the earlier, smaller group of college-bound test takers.

Professional educators generally oppose efforts to assess state educational performance by comparing average SAT scores. Indeed, the College Board "strongly cautions against comparing states based on SAT scores alone." (But see "*Rankings of the States*: Educational Performance.") In some states, more than 75 percent of graduating students take the test, while in other states fewer than 20 percent do so. Average scores are higher when only a small select group takes the test.

SAT score increases in recent years have been attributed to the increased emphasis in schools on testing for basic skills. An influential 1983 report by the Commission on Excellence in Education entitled "A Nation at Risk" recommended, among other things, standardized tests for promotion and graduation.[7] Many states responded to the demand for greater achievement in basic skills by requiring minimum competency testing in the schools. The U.S. Department of Education began giving tests each year to a sample of fourth-, eighth-, and twelfth-grade students and

SAT SCORES

Verbal and math scores obtained on the national College Board Scholastic Assessment Test, required for admission to many colleges and universities.

RANKINGS
of the STATES

Educational Performance

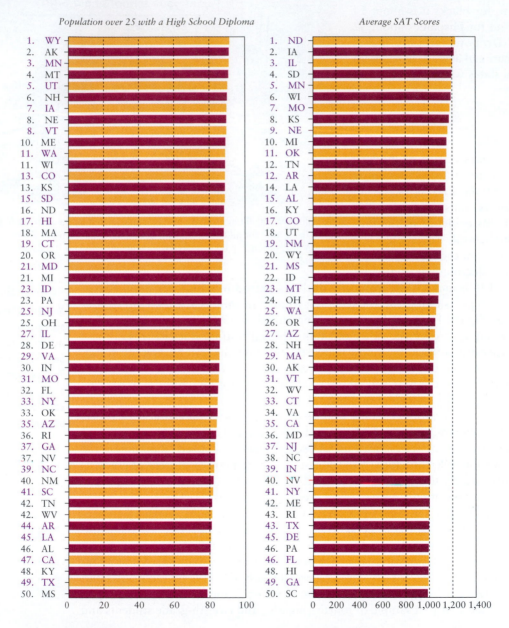

Population over 25 with a High School Diploma	Average SAT Scores
1. WY	1. ND
2. AK	2. IA
3. MN	3. IL
4. MT	4. SD
5. UT	5. MN
6. NH	6. WI
7. IA	7. MO
8. NE	8. KS
8. VT	9. NE
10. ME	10. MI
11. WA	11. OK
11. WI	12. TN
13. CO	12. AR
13. KS	14. LA
15. SD	15. AL
16. ND	16. KY
17. HI	17. CO
18. MA	18. UT
19. CT	19. NM
20. OR	20. WY
21. MD	21. MS
21. MI	22. ID
23. ID	23. MT
23. PA	24. OH
25. NJ	25. WA
25. OH	26. OR
27. IL	27. AZ
28. DE	28. NH
29. VA	29. MA
30. IN	30. AK
31. MO	31. VT
32. FL	32. WV
33. NY	33. CT
33. OK	34. VA
35. AZ	35. CA
36. RI	36. MD
37. GA	37. NJ
37. NV	38. NC
39. NC	39. IN
40. NM	40. NV
41. SC	41. NY
42. TN	42. ME
42. WV	43. RI
44. AR	43. TX
45. LA	45. DE
46. AL	46. PA
47. CA	46. FL
48. KY	48. HI
49. TX	49. GA
50. MS	50. SC

Note: Data are for 2005.
Source: U.S. Census Bureau, *Statistical Abstract of the United States, 2007*. Available at http://www.census.gov/prod/2006pubs/07statab/educ.pdf, No. 218

Note: Data are for 2006.
Source: College Board 2006.

FIGURE 16–2 SAT Score Trends

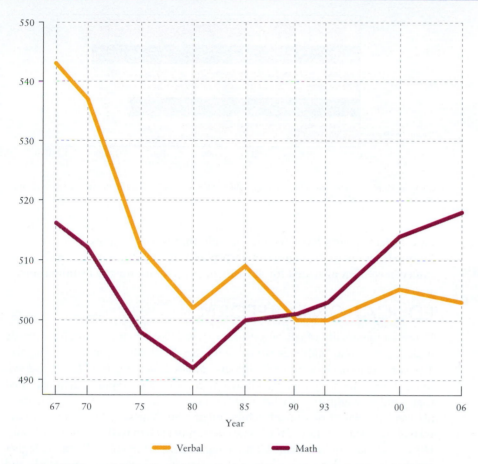

publishing the results. This National Assessment of Educational Progress gave added emphasis to the testing movement. But testing finally became nationwide with the passage of the No Child Left Behind Act in 2001 (see "No Child Left Behind" later in this chapter).

Minority group leaders often charge that tests are racially biased. Average scores of African-American students are frequently lower than those of white students on standardized tests (see Figure 16–3). Larger percentages of black students are held back from promotion and graduation by testing than are white students. However, to

FIGURE 16–3 Average SAT Scores by Race, Ethnicity

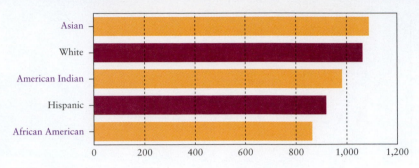

Note: Data are for 2006.
Source: College Bound Seniors: Total Group Report. Copyright © 2006, CollegeBoard.com. Reproduced with permission. All rights reserved. www.collegeboard.com

> *Federal courts have declined to rule that testing requirements for promotion or graduation are discriminatory, as long as sufficient time and opportunity have been provided for all students to prepare for the examinations.*

date, federal courts have declined to rule that testing requirements for promotion or graduation are discriminatory, as long as sufficient time and opportunity have been provided for all students to prepare for the examinations.

EDUCATIONAL REFORM

How can the quality of education be improved? Systematic research has made it clear that money alone does not guarantee good educational performance. The early landmark work of sociologist James Coleman, *Equality of Educational Opportunity* (popularly known as the **Coleman report**), demonstrated that pupil expenditures, teacher salaries, classroom size, facilities, and materials were *un*related to student achievement.[8] Student success is more closely related to characteristics of the home environment than to those of the schools. However, Coleman later demonstrated that student achievement levels are higher in schools in which there is a high expectation for achievement, an orderly and disciplined learning environment, an emphasis on basic skills, frequent monitoring of student progress, and teacher–parent interaction and agreement on values and norms.[9]

Educational Spending

There is no evidence that increased spending for public education improves student achievement. Public elementary and secondary school spending per pupil has risen dramatically over the years (see Figure 16–4). Indeed, since 1980 spending per pupil has quadrupled, yet SAT scores have improved only modestly (see Figure 16–2). The apparent failure of money alone, including federal aid, to significantly affect student achievement directed the focus of educational improvements to new and sometimes controversial reforms.

School-Based Management

One approach in public education reform is **school-based management**—decentralized decision making in individual schools by principals, teachers, parents, and community members, rather than central offices of school districts. It is designed to give flexibility to

FIGURE 16–4 Public Elementary and Secondary School Expenditures Per Pupil

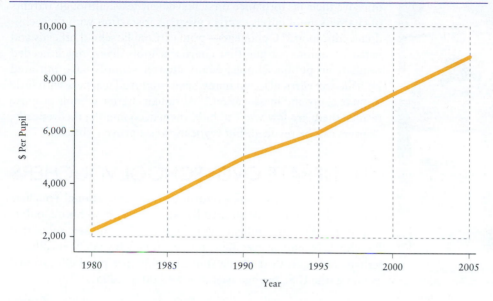

Source: U.S. Department of Education, National Center for Educational Statistics.

people closest to the students and to foster within the community a sense of ownership and responsibility for the quality of education. Presumably principals, teachers, and parents at each school would decide about goals, curriculum, discipline, and perhaps even personnel. But it seldom works out that way. School-based councils often end up in conflict with central school district administrators, elected school boards, state and federal regulations, budgetary restrictions, and so on. Principals and teachers often feel that it takes time away from teaching, or requires additional efforts to reach community consensus.

Magnet Schools

Another common reform proposal is the magnet school. High schools choose to specialize, some emphasizing math and science, others the fine arts, others business, and still others vocational training. Some schools might be "adopted" by businesses, professional organizations, or universities. Magnet schools, with reputations for quality, specialized instruction, are frequently recommended for inner-city areas in order to attract white pupils and reduce racial isolation.

Charter Schools

Yet another reform that has been advanced in a limited number of states is the charter school. Community educational groups, including public school teachers and parents, sign a "charter" with their school district or state education department to establish their own school. They receive waivers from most state and school district regulations to enable them to be more innovative; in exchange for this flexibility they promise to show specific student achievement. They receive tax money from the state and school district based on their enrollment.

SCHOOL-BASED MANAGEMENT
Reforms designed to decentralize educational decision making to individual schools rather than central school district administrations.

MAGNET SCHOOLS
Schools emphasizing instruction in particular areas in an effort to improve quality and attract students.

CHARTER SCHOOLS
Schools operated with public funds by private community groups under a charter from a public school district.

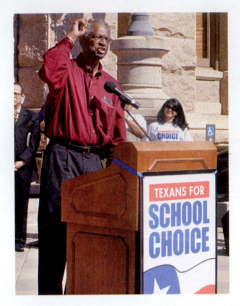

The experience with charter schools to date is very uneven. There is no clear evidence that pupils transferring to charter schools improve their performance on achievement tests, although parents of charter school pupils express greater satisfaction with their children's education.[10] Opponents—primarily public school officials and teachers' unions—argue that charter schools divert much-needed funds from public schools. Many charter schools have initiated unorthodox curricula, and many have employed teachers with little or no background in education.[11] Although charter schools promise results, there are few ways to hold them accountable; theoretically, charters can be revoked, but revocation has proven difficult.

THE DEBATE OVER SCHOOL VOUCHERS

An even more controversial reform involves **educational vouchers** that are given to parents to spend at any school they choose, public or private. State governments would redeem the vouchers submitted by schools by paying specified amounts for each student enrolled— perhaps the equivalent of the state's average per pupil educational spending (the U.S. average was over $8,800 in 2005).

"My child, my choice" reflects the sentiment of school voucher supporters. Among the strongest proponents are parents from poor or disadvantaged homes whose children do not have the same option as children from more affluent homes of fleeing poorly performing public schools and enrolling in private schools.

The Pro-Voucher Argument

Proponents of vouchers argue that parental choice among schools would promote competition and enhance achievement. Vouchers would inspire both public and private schools to compete equally for students. State education funds would flow to those schools that succeeded in enrolling more students. Competition would encourage all schools to satisfy parental demands for excellence. Racial or religious or ethnic discrimination would be strictly prohibited in any private or public school receiving vouchers. It is argued that providing vouchers for children from poor or disadvantaged homes, or children who are currently attending poor public schools, is the most effective way of serving their needs. These children currently do not have the same option as children from more affluent homes of fleeing the public schools and enrolling in private academies.[12]

Opponents of vouchers argue that public education will be harmed by diverting public money from public to private schools.

Opposition to Vouchers

Yet there is strong opposition to the voucher idea.[13] The most vocal opposition comes from professional school administrators and state educational agencies. They argue that giving parents the right to move their children from school to school disrupts educational planning and threatens the viability of schools that are perceived as inferior. It may lead to a stratification of schools into popular schools that attract the best students, and less popular schools that are left with the task of educating students whose parents were unaware of or uninterested in their children's education. Other opponents of choice plans fear that public education may be undermined by diverting public money from public to private schools.

Voters Reject Vouchers

The voucher movement was dealt a major setback in 1993 when California voters soundly defeated a citizens' initiative known as Proposition 174, Parental Choice in Education. Professional educators, teachers' unions, and liberal groups joined together to mount an expensive, highly publicized campaign to defeat the measure. Proposition 174 promised to "empower parents" by granting each schoolchild a "scholarship" (voucher) equal to about one-half of the average amount of state and local government aid per pupil in California. The money was to be paid directly to the schools in which parents chose to enroll their children. Either public or private schools could qualify as "scholarship-redeeming schools"; schools that discriminated on the basis of race, ethnicity, color, or national origin would not be eligible.

Opposition groups, including the powerful California Teachers Association, argued that the proposal would create a "two-tier system of schools, one for the haves, one for the have-nots." They portrayed vouchers as "an entitlement program offering wealthy families a private-school subsidy for their children, paid for by the taxpayers,"[14] noting that there was no means test for the vouchers. About 10 percent of California's schoolchildren were in private schools already; their parents would enjoy an immediate windfall benefit from the program. Opponents warned that public education would suffer grievously if both money and gifted students were removed from public schools. Although only half of the costs of educating a public school student would go into a voucher, it was argued that public schools would face financial difficulties from the implementation of the program. The initial costs of vouchers for pupils already attending private schools posed a major financial problem. No one could accurately estimate how many pupils would eventually transfer from public to private schools. Finally, opponents made inroads in the electorate by warning that taxpayers' money would go to religious schools and noting that the content of instruction and credentials of teachers were unregulated in the proposal.

Subsequent school voucher initiatives have suffered a similar fate in several states, including Utah in 2007.

Vouchers as a Constitutional Issue

School vouchers paid to religious schools by states raised the issue of whether or not these payments violated the First Amendment's prohibition against the "establishment of religion." Earlier Supreme Court decisions had invalidated programs that provided *direct* government subsidies to religious schools. But the Court had approved of state and federal scholarships granted directly to students who then used them to enroll in religious colleges and universities.

When Ohio initiated a "Scholarship Program" that provided tuition aid to certain students in the Cleveland City School District who could choose to use this aid to attend either public or private or religious schools of their parents' choosing, opponents challenged the program in federal court arguing that it "advanced a religious mission" in violation of the No Establishment Clause of the First Amendment. Although parents could use

Vouchers given to parents to pay for their children's education at schools of their own choosing, redeemable by the schools in public funds from the state and school district.

the vouchers to send their children to other public schools or nonreligious private schools, over 90 percent of the students participating in the scholarship program were enrolled in religiously affiliated schools. Sixty percent of the students were from families at or below the poverty line. In 2002 the U.S. Supreme Court held (in a narrow 5–4 decision) that the program did *not* violate the Constitution. The Court reasoned that the program was neutral with respect to religion and provided assistance directly to citizens who, in turn, directed this aid to religious schools wholly as a result of their own independent private choices. The incidental advancement of a religious mission is reasonably attributed to the individual recipients, not the government, "whose role ends with the distribution of benefits."[15]

THE FEDERAL ROLE IN EDUCATION

Today state governments have taken major responsibility for public education.

The federal share of educational spending is less than 10 percent.

LAND-GRANT COLLEGES

Grants of federal land to each state for the establishment of colleges specializing in agricultural and mechanical arts.

Traditionally, education in America was a community responsibility. But today state governments have taken major responsibility for public education. The federal government has taken the lead in guaranteeing racial equality in education, and separating religion from public schools, but it has never assumed any significant share of the costs of education. The federal share of educational spending is less than 10 percent. (See Table 16–1.)

Early Federal Aid

The federal government's role in education, however, is a longstanding one. In the famous Northwest Ordinance of 1787, Congress offered land grants for public schools in the new territories. Then in 1862 the Morrill Land Grant Act provided grants of federal land to each state for the establishment of colleges specializing in agricultural and mechanical arts. These became known as "**land-grant colleges.**" In 1867, Congress established a U.S. Office of Education, which became the Department of Education in 1979. The Smith–Hughes Act of 1917 set up the first program of federal grants-in-aid to promote vocational education and enabled schools to provide training in agriculture, home economics, trades, and industries. In the National School Lunch and Milk programs, begun in 1946, federal grants and commodity donations are made for nonprofit lunches and milk served in public and private schools. In the Federal Impacted Areas Aid Program, begun in 1950, federal aid is authorized in "federally impacted" areas of the nation. These are areas where federal activities create a substantial increase in school enrollments or a reduction in taxable resources because of federally owned property. In response to the Soviet Union's success in launching *Sputnik*, the first satellite in space, in 1957, Congress became concerned that the American educational system might not be keeping abreast of advances made in other

TABLE 16–1	Sources of Funds for Public Education in the United States					
	Percentage of Public Educational Revenues by Source					
	1980	1985	1990	1995	2000	2005
Federal	9.2	6.7	6.3	6.9	7.1	8.6
State	49.1	49.0	48.3	47.6	49.8	48.0
Local	41.7	44.3	45.4	45.4	43.1	43.4

Source: U.S. Census Bureau, *Statistical Abstract of the United States, 2006,* p. 164.

nations, particularly in science and technology. In the National Defense Education Act (NDEA) of 1958, Congress provided financial aid to states and public school districts to improve instruction in science, mathematics, and foreign languages.

Elementary and Secondary Education Act (Title I)

The Elementary and Secondary Education Act of 1965 (ESEA) marked the first large breakthrough in federal aid to education. Yet even ESEA was not a *general* aid-to-education program—one that would assist all public and private schools in school construction and teachers' salaries. The main thrust of ESEA is in "poverty-impacted" schools, instructional materials, and educational research and training. The Education Consolidation and Improvement Act of 1981 consolidated ESEA and related education programs into a single "Title I" block grant allowing the states greater discretion in how federal funds can be spent for compensatory education. This remains the largest federal aid-to-education program, accounting for over half of all federal elementary and secondary education spending.

However, it is difficult to demonstrate that federal aid programs improve the quality of education in America.[16] Indeed, during the years in which federal aid was increasing, student achievement scores were *declining*. Raising the educational achievement levels of America's youth depends less on the amount spent than on *how* it is spent.

Head Start

The most popular federal educational aid program is Head Start, which began in President Lyndon B. Johnson's "War on Poverty" in the 1960s. Its purpose is to provide special preschool preparation to disadvantaged children before they enter kindergarten

Early childhood education first got a lot of attention under the federal Head Start program. Today state and local officials are also focusing more attention on pre-K and kindergarten as research has shown positive results from early childhood learning programs.

or first grade. Over the years it has enjoyed great popularity among parents, members of Congress, and both Republican and Democratic presidents. However, despite an avalanche of research by professional educators seeking to prove the value of the program, the results can best be described as mixed. Much of the value of Head Start preparation disappears after a few years of schooling; disadvantaged pupils who attend Head Start do not perform much better in later years than disadvantaged pupils who did not attend. Nevertheless, Head Start remains politically very popular.

NO CHILD LEFT BEHIND

Upon taking office, President George W. Bush made education his first domestic priority. His approach to comprehensive educational reform is embodied in the No Child Left Behind Act of 2001. While this act is officially only an amendment to Title I of the Elementary and Secondary Education Act of 1965, it really defines the federal role in public education. It has been controversial almost from its inception.

Testing

The preferred phraseology is "accountability"—requiring states to establish standards in reading and mathematics and undertaking to test annually all students in grades 3–8.

The No Child Left Behind Act (NCLB) relies primarily on testing as a means to improve performance of America's elementary and secondary schools. The preferred phraseology is "accountability"—requiring states to establish standards in reading and mathematics and undertaking to test annually all students in grades 3–8. (Testing under this act is in addition to the U.S. Department of Education's National Assessment of Educational Progress tests given each year to a sample of public and private school students in the fourth, eighth, and twelfth grades; results of these NAEP tests are frequently cited as indicators of educational achievement for the nation.) Among the goals of testing is to ensure that every child can read by the end of third grade.

Test results and school progress toward proficiency goals are published, including results broken out by poverty, race, ethnicity, disability, and limited-English proficiency, in order to ensure that no group is "left behind." School districts and individual schools that fail to make adequate yearly progress (AYP) toward statewide proficiency goals face "corrective action" and "restructuring measures" designed to improve their performance. Student achievement and progress are measured according to tests that are given to every child every year. Annual report cards on school performance give parents information about their child's school and all other schools in their district.

Parental Choice

Parents whose children attend schools that fail to make AYP are to be given the opportunity to send their children to another public school or a public charter school within the school district. The school district is required to use its own money for transportation to the new school and to use Title I federal funds to implement school choice and supplemental educational services to the students. The objective is to ensure that no pupil is "trapped" in a failing school, and to provide an incentive for low-performing schools to improve. Schools that wish to avoid losing students, along with a portion of their annual budgets typically associated with these students, are required to make AYP. Schools that fail to make AYP for five years run the risk of "restructuring."

Flexibility

The Act promises the states "flexibility in accountability." It allows the states themselves to design and administer the tests and decide what constitutes low performance and adequate yearly progress. States are encouraged to use Title I federal funds to improve low-performing schools.

Controversy

The No Child Left Behind Act has inspired considerable controversy in Washington, state capitols, and educational circles. The National Education Association—the powerful teachers' union—contends that NCLB is "fundamentally flawed." Professional educators object, first, to the emphasis on testing for basic skills, reading and mathematics. They argue that this emphasis leads to narrow "test-taking" education rather than comprehensive preparation for life. Teachers are obliged to neglect other instructional topics in order to concentrate on reading and mathematics. Even some supporters of NCLB urge that history and civics as well as science be added to the tests.

The federal No Child Left Behind Act of 2001 is actually an amendment to Title I of the Elementary and Secondary Education Act of 1965. It has become highly controversial, primarily because of its heavy reliance on testing as a measure of how well teachers and the school system overall are performing and its use of test scores over time for funding decisions. Proponents argue that it is working—student test scores are rising and the gap between minority and white students' scores is narrowing. The bottom line is that the Act has become a key issue in local school board elections.

Professional educators also argue that states, school districts, and schools should all participate in developing "accountability systems" based on multiple measures of student success. States should have greater "flexibility" in implementing NCLB. Moreover, measures of progress, or lack of it, "should not be used to penalize schools or teachers."[17] Measures of AYP should be used to provide increased support and assistance to schools needing help, not to penalize them. The National Education Association strongly opposes providing transfers or vouchers to students in low-performing schools.

Opposition to testing has also arisen from minority group leaders, who charge that the tests are racially biased. Average black student scores are frequently lower than average white student scores. Denying a disproportionate number of black students advancement because of the school's failure to teach basics is viewed as a form of discrimination. Proponents of NCLB argue that testing for basic skills has improved student performance in recent years. AYP measures inspire school administrators and teachers to bring about improvement in student achievement. And proponents also contend that disparities between whites and minorities in test scores have been narrowing as teachers concentrate more on instruction in basic skills.

ORGANIZING PUBLIC EDUCATION IN THE STATES

The fifty state governments, by means of enabling legislation, establish local school districts and endow them with the authority to operate public schools. There are about 13,500 local school districts, governed by 80,000 school board members, who are chosen usually, but not always, by popular election. State laws authorize these boards to levy and collect taxes, borrow money, engage in school construction, hire instructional personnel, and make certain determinations about local school policy.

Only Hawaii governs its schools centrally from the state capital. Other states vary considerably in the number of local school districts functioning within their boundaries.

State Supervision

In every state, the authority of local school districts is severely limited by state legislation.

Yet in every state, the authority of local school districts is severely limited by state legislation. State law determines the types and rates of taxes to be levied, the maximum debt that can be incurred, the number of days schools shall remain open, the number of years of compulsory school attendance, the minimum salaries to be paid to teachers, the types of schools to be operated by the local boards, the number of grades to be taught, the qualifications of teachers, and the general content of curricula. In addition, many states choose the textbooks, establish course outlines, recommend teaching methods, establish statewide examinations, fix minimum teacher–pupil ratios, and stipulate course content in great detail. In short, the responsibility for public education is firmly in the hands of state governments.

State responsibility for public education is no mere paper arrangement. States ensure local compliance with state educational policy through: (1) bureaucratic oversight, involving state boards of education, state commissioners or superintendents of education, and state departments of education; and (2) financial control through state allocation of funds to local school districts.

State Boards of Education

Traditionally, state control over education was vested in state boards of education. In most states these boards are appointed by the governor; in some states they are composed of state officials; and in four states (Alabama, Hawaii, Nevada, and Utah) they are directly elected by the voters. These boards generally have the formal power to decide everything from teacher certification to textbook selection. However, in practice these boards rely heavily on the recommendations of the state commissioner of education and the state department of education.

State Commissioners of Education

All states have chief education officers, variously entitled commissioner of education, state school superintendent, or superintendent of public instruction. In fourteen states this official is elected (Arizona, California, Georgia, Idaho, Indiana, Montana, North Carolina, North Dakota, Oklahoma, Oregon, South Carolina, Washington, Wisconsin, and Wyoming). In other states this official is appointed by the governor or the state education board. The chief education officer may exercise the most important influence over education in the state, as public spokesperson for education, in testimony before the legislature, and as the head of the state department of education.

State Departments of Education

State educational bureaucracies have greatly expanded in size and power over the years. They disburse state funds to local schools, prepare statewide curricula, select textbooks and materials, determine teacher qualifications, establish and enforce school building codes, and supervise statewide testing. Their principal tool in enforcing their control over local schools is the allocation of state educational money.

RANKINGS
of the STATES

Financing Public Schools

Per Pupil Spending

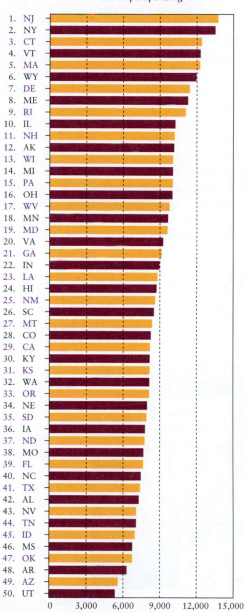

1.	NJ	
2.	NY	
3.	CT	
4.	VT	
5.	MA	
6.	WY	
7.	DE	
8.	ME	
9.	RI	
10.	IL	
11.	NH	
12.	AK	
13.	WI	
14.	MI	
15.	PA	
16.	OH	
17.	WV	
18.	MN	
19.	MD	
20.	VA	
21.	GA	
22.	IN	
23.	LA	
24.	HI	
25.	NM	
26.	SC	
27.	MT	
28.	CO	
29.	CA	
30.	KY	
31.	KS	
32.	WA	
33.	OR	
34.	NE	
35.	SD	
36.	IA	
37.	ND	
38.	MO	
39.	FL	
40.	NC	
41.	TX	
42.	AL	
43.	NV	
44.	TN	
45.	ID	
46.	MS	
47.	OK	
48.	AR	
49.	AZ	
50.	UT	

0   3,000   6,000   9,000   12,000   15,000

Note: Per pupil spending data are for 2005–2006.
Sources: U.S. Department of Education, National Center for Education Statistics, www.nces.ed.gov/ccd; National Education Association, *Rankings and Estimates: Rankings of the States 2005* and *Estimates of School Statistics 2006*; www.nea.org

School District Consolidation

One of the most dramatic reorganization and centralization movements in American government in this century was the successful drive to reduce, through consolidation, the number of local school districts in the United States. In a thirty-year period (1950–1980), three out of every four school districts were eliminated through consolidation. Support for school district consolidation came from *state* school officials in every state. Opposition to consolidation was *local* in character. Beginning in the 2000s, however, some reformers began proposing smaller school districts again and arguing that huge school districts are ineffective and unresponsive.

State Financial Control

States ensure the implementation of state educational policies through state grants of money to local school districts. Every state provides grants in one form or another to local school districts to supplement locally derived school revenue. This places the superior taxing powers of the state in the service of public schools operated at the local level. In every state, an equalization formula in the distribution of state grants to local districts operates to help equalize educational opportunities in all parts of the state. This enables the state to guarantee a minimum "foundation" program in education throughout the state. In addition, since state grants to local school districts are administered through state departments of education, state school officials are given an effective tool for implementing state policies, namely, withholding or threatening to withhold state funds from school districts that do not conform to state standards. The growth of state responsibility for school policy was accomplished largely by the use of money—state grants to local schools.

BATTLES OVER SCHOOL FINANCES

Public elementary and secondary schools enroll about 49 million students. Nationwide over $8,800 per year is spent on the public education of each child.[18] Yet national averages can obscure as much as they reveal about the record of the states in public education. Fifty state school systems establish policy for the nation, and this decentralization results in variations from state to state in educational policy. Only by examining public policy in all fifty states can the full dimension of American education be understood.

While research has shown that money alone is not the answer to improving schools, any proposal to cut back funding is likely to generate protests against it by persons of all ages and headlines in local newspapers.

Variation among States

In 2005, for example, public school expenditures for each pupil ranged from $5,216 in Utah to $14,117 in New Jersey. (See "*Rankings of the States: Financing Public Schools*.") Why is it that some states spend more than twice as much on the education of each child as other states? Economic resources are the principal determinant of a state's willingness and ability to provide educational services.

Polls show that Americans prefer smaller classes and expect smaller class size to improve student learning. Smaller class size mandates approved by voters require building more classrooms and hiring more teachers. This is not always easy, especially when the economy is in a slump and there is a teacher shortage because of low salaries.

Inequalities among School Districts

A central issue in the struggle over public education is that of distributing the benefits and costs of education equitably. In every state except Hawaii, local school boards must raise money from property taxes to help finance their schools. This means that communities that do *not* have much taxable property cannot finance their schools as well as communities that are blessed with great wealth. Frequently, wealthy communities can provide better education for their children at lower tax rates than poor communities can provide at higher tax rates, simply because of disparities in the value of taxable property from one community to the next. Disparities in educational funding among school districts *within* states can also be quite large.

Wealthy communities can provide better education for their children at lower tax rates than poor communities can provide at higher tax rates, simply because of disparities in the value of taxable property from one community to the next.

School Inequalities as a Constitutional Issue

Do disparities among school districts within a state deny "equal protection of laws" guaranteed by the Fourteenth Amendment of the U.S. Constitution and similar guarantees found in most state constitutions? The U.S. Supreme Court ruled that disparities in financial resources among school districts in a state, and resulting inequalities in educational spending per pupil across a state, do *not* violate the Equal Protection Clause of the Fourteenth Amendment. There is no duty under the U.S. Constitution for a state to equalize educational resources within the state.[19]

However, in recent years *state courts* have increasingly intervened in school financing to ensure equality among school districts based on their own interpretation of *state* constitutional provisions. Beginning with an early California state supreme court decision requiring that state funds be used to help equalize resources among the state's school districts,[20] many state courts have pressured their legislatures to come up with equalization plans in state school grants to overcome disparities in property tax revenues among school districts. State court equalization orders are generally based on *state* constitutional provisions guaranteeing equality.

Attracting and keeping good teachers is a major challenge for local school systems.

State Funds versus Local Property Taxes

Local school district reliance on property taxation, combined with inequalities in property values among communities, creates an equity problem: Should less money be spent on children in poorer districts because of where their parents live? Heavy reliance on local

SCHOOL BOARD

The elected governing body of a school district.

SCHOOL SUPER- INTENDENT

The chief executive officer of a school district; may be directly elected or appointed by the school board.

property taxes to fund schools generally ensures that fiscal disparities among school districts will exist. But many school districts across the country have sued their respective state governments, claiming that heavy reliance on local property taxes to fund schools discriminates unfairly against poorer communities. A number of state supreme courts in recent years have agreed, and cases are currently pending in many other states. To achieve equity in school funding among communities, state courts are increasingly ordering their legislatures to substitute state general revenues for local property taxes.

GOVERNING LOCAL SCHOOLS

Responsibility for many basic decisions in public education lies with the 13,500 separate school districts in America. In theory, these school districts are under local control. The people of the local school district are supposed to exercise that control through an elected **school board** and an elected or appointed **superintendent** who acts as the chief executive of the community schools. There is some variation to that pattern—in approximately a quarter of the nation's school districts, the boards are appointed rather than elected, usually by city councils, county commissions, mayors, or even judges. In theory, school boards exercise control over curriculum (that is, what should be taught in the schools), buildings and facilities, personnel (including both administrators and teachers), and, perhaps most important of all, financing. In practice, however, as we have already seen, the concept of local control over education is heavily circumscribed by both state and federal laws.

THE SCHOOL DISTRICT SUPERINTENDENTS

The school district superintendents are usually professionally trained educators, either appointed by the local school board or separately elected on a nonpartisan ballot. The superintendent is responsible for the management of the public schools—hiring and supervising teachers and principals, planning and organizing the schools, preparing budgets and overseeing expenditures, and recommending policy to the board.

Responsibilities

School superintendents have three major responsibilities. First, the superintendent sets the agenda for school board decisions. Second, the superintendent makes policy recommendations. Most agenda items will carry a recommendation. Third, the superintendent implements board decisions. In performing these responsibilities, superintendents, even more than city managers, provide strong leadership—advocating policy changes and selling programs to the community. Moreover, many superintendents, in contrast to city managers, involve themselves in school board elections, providing encouragement to candidates whom they respect.

Leadership

Professional superintendents do not expect to be overruled by their boards. Many of them have a "trust me or fire me" attitude that often makes compromise difficult. Nonetheless, the average tenure of appointed school superintendents is fairly long, about eight years. This is slightly longer than the average tenure of city managers (seven years).

SCHOOL BOARDS: RESPONSIBLE POLICYMAKERS?

Even if we accept the notion that schools should be governed by a democratically elected board, how can we know whether board members are accurately reflecting their constituents' desires and aspirations?

Recruitment and Selection

Like most decision makers, the nation's 80,000 school board members are unrepresentative of their constituents in their socioeconomic background. Specifically, board members come disproportionately from "educational families"; many members have relatives in education, usually their spouse. Many school board members report that they were first prompted to run for the school board by friends already on the board; this suggests a perpetuation of similar kinds of people on school boards. Most school board elections are nonpartisan. Many members originally came to the board as appointees to replace individuals who left the board with unexpired terms. Seldom are incumbents defeated for reelection; two-thirds of the board members who leave office do so voluntarily. The average tenure of board members is about five years, compared to over eight years for superintendents. School board members do not ordinarily aspire to, or gain, higher political office. All of this suggests "volunteerism" among board members and difficulty in holding members accountable through the threat of electoral defeat.

> Most school board elections are nonpartisan.

Minority Representation

Black membership on the nation's large central-city school district boards reflects fairly accurately the black population in central cities.[21] Black representation on school boards has been linked to a variety of school policies: increased employment of black teachers; fewer black students disciplined, suspended, or dropping out; fewer black students assigned to special education classes; and more black students in gifted programs. Hispanics, Asians, and other racial/ethnic minorities are underrepresented on school boards, relative to their proportional makeup in the population, primarily due to the higher incidence of noncitizens within their ranks.

Teachers' Unions

The struggle for power over the schools between interested citizens, school board members, and professional educators has now been joined by still another powerful force—the nation's teachers' unions. Most of the nation's 2 million teachers are organized into either the older, larger National Education Association (NEA) or the smaller American Federation of Teachers (AFT), an affiliate of the American Federation of Labor-Congress of Industrial Organizations (AFL-CIO). Since its origin, the AFT has espoused the right to organize, bargain collectively, and strike, in the fashion of other labor unions. The AFT is small in numbers, but its membership is concentrated in the nation's largest cities, where it exercises considerable power. Traditionally, the NEA was considered a "professional" organization of both teachers and administrators. However, today state and district chapters of the NEA are organized as labor unions, demanding collective bargaining rights for their members and threatening to strike to achieve them. Both AFT and NEA chapters have shut down schools to force concessions by superintendents, board members, and taxpayers—not only in salaries and benefits, but also in pupil–teacher ratios, classroom conditions, school discipline, and other educational matters. As the teachers' unions grow stronger, the traditional question

Teachers' unions are very active in politics, most often in support of Democratic Party candidates. However, not all teachers support the union's goals and tactics, particularly when it comes to partisan campaigns. The U.S. Supreme Court has ruled that states may require a nonunion member's *affirmative consent* before a public sector union (the teachers union) may use fees paid by nonmembers for collective bargaining for political purposes. (Unions collect fees from all teachers, regardless of whether they are members, for representing them in collective bargaining.) (*Washington v. Washington Education Association* and *Davenport v. Washington Education Association*, 2007.)

of whether citizens or professional administrators should run the schools will be made more complex: What role should teachers' unions have in determining educational policy?

THE POLITICS OF HIGHER EDUCATION

States have been involved in public higher education since the colonial era. State governments in the Northeast frequently made contributions to support private colleges in their states. The first university to be chartered by a state legislature was the University of Georgia in 1794. Before the Civil War, northeastern states relied exclusively on private colleges, and the southern states assumed the leadership in public higher education. The early curricula at southern state universities, however, resembled the rigid classical studies of the early private colleges—with heavy emphasis on Greek and Latin, history, philosophy, and literature.

Early Federal Support

It was not until the Morrill Land Grant Act of 1862 that public higher education began to make major strides in the American states. Interestingly, the eastern states were slow to respond to the opportunity afforded by the Morrill to develop public universities; eastern states continued to rely primarily on their private colleges and universities. The southern states were economically depressed in the post–Civil War period, and leadership in public higher education passed to the midwestern states. The philosophy of the Morrill Act emphasized agricultural and mechanical (A and M) studies, rather than the classical curricula of eastern colleges, and the movement for A and M education spread rapidly in the agricultural states. The early groups of midwestern state universities were closely tied to agricultural education, including agricultural extension services. State universities also took over the responsibility for the training of public school teachers in colleges of education. The state universities introduced a broad range of modern subjects in the university curricula—business administration, agriculture, home economics, education, engineering. It was not until the 1960s that the eastern states began to develop public higher education (notably the State University of New York multicampus system).

Public Higher Education

Today, public higher education enrolls three-quarters of the nation's college and university students. Perhaps more importantly, the nation's leading state universities can challenge the best private institutions in academic excellence. The University of California at Berkeley, the University of Michigan, the University of Virginia, the University of Texas, and the University of North Carolina–Chapel Hill are deservedly ranked with Harvard, Yale, Princeton, Penn, Stanford, and Chicago.

Higher education in America is mass education. No other nation sends so large a proportion of its young people to college. About 17 million Americans are enrolled in colleges and universities. Almost two-thirds of all high school graduates enroll in college.

Community Colleges

In most states, community colleges are separate from state colleges and universities; the community colleges are really part of local government. They receive revenue from local property taxes as well as grants from the state and federal government. They are usually governed by a local board, whose members are elected or appointed from the communities served by the college.

Community colleges have been the fastest growing sector of American higher education. (See Table 16–2.) These colleges are designed to reflect the local area's requirements for higher education, and they usually offer both a general undergraduate curriculum that fulfills the first two years of a baccalaureate degree, and vocational and technical programs that fulfill community needs for skilled workers. Moreover, community colleges usually offer special programs and courses in adult higher education, often in association with community groups.[22]

No other nation sends so large a proportion of its young people to college.

TABLE 16–2 Higher Education in America					
Institutions (Thousands)	**1970**	**1980**	**1990**	**2000**	**2005**
Total	2,556	3,231	3,559	4,182	4,169
Four-year colleges and universities	1,665	1,957	2,141	2,450	2,324
Two-year colleges	891	1,274	1,418	1,732	1,844
Faculty (thousands)	474	686	817	990	1,175
Percent full-time	75	66	61	(N/A)	54
Enrollment (Thousands)	**1970**	**1980**	**1990**	**2000**	**2005**
Total	8,581	12,097	13,819	15,312	16,612
Four-year colleges and universities	6,290	7,571	8,579	9,364	10,082
Two-year colleges	1,630	4,526	5,240	5,948	6,529
Public	5,800	9,457	10,845	11,753	12,752
Private	2,120	2,640	2,974	3,560	3,860
Graduate	1,031	1,343	1,586	1,850	2,035
Undergraduate	7,376	10,495	11,959	13,155	14,257

Source: U.S. Census Bureau *Statistical Abstract of the United States, 2007,* No. 175–176.

University Governance

The organization and governance of public higher education varies a great deal from state to state. Most states have established **boards of trustees** (or **"regents"**) with authority to govern the state universities. One of the purposes of the boards is to insulate higher education from the vicissitudes of politics. Prominent citizens who are appointed to these boards are expected to champion higher education with the public and the legislature, as well as set overall policy guidelines for colleges and universities. In the past, there were separate boards for each institution and separate consideration by the governor's office and the legislature of each institution's budgetary request. However, the resulting competition caused state after state to create unified "university system" boards to coordinate higher education. These university system boards consolidate the budget requests of each institution, determine systemwide priorities, and present a single budget for higher education to the governor and the legislature. The stronger and more independent the university system board, the less likely that university and college funding will be distributed in a pork-barrel fashion by legislators seeking to enhance their local constituencies.

The Presidents

The key figures in university politics are the presidents. They are the chief spokespersons for higher education, and they must convince the public, the regents, the governor, and the legislature of the value of state universities. The presidents' crucial role is one of maintaining support for higher education in the state; they frequently delegate administrative responsibilities for the internal operation of the university to the vice-presidents and deans. Support for higher education among the public and its representatives can be affected by a broad spectrum of university activities, some of which are not directly related to the pursuit of knowledge. A winning football team can stimulate legislative enthusiasm and win appropriations for a new classroom building. University service-oriented research—developing new farm crops or feeds, assessing the state's mineral resources, advising state and local government agencies on administrative problems, analyzing the state economy, advising local school authorities, and so forth—may help to convince the public of the practical benefits of knowledge. University faculty may be interested in advanced research and the education of future Ph.Ds, but legislators and their constituents are more interested in the quality and effectiveness of undergraduate teaching.

The Faculty

The faculty traditionally identified themselves as professionals with strong attachments to their institutions. The historic pattern of college and university government included faculty participation in policymaking—not only in determining academic requirements but also in budgeting, the hiring and firing of personnel, building programs, and so forth. However, government by faculty committee has proven cumbersome, unwieldy, and time-consuming in an era of large-scale enrollments, multimillion-dollar budgets, and increases in the size and complexity of academic administration. Increasingly, concepts of public accountability, academic management, cost control, centralized budgeting, and purchasing have transferred power in colleges and universities from faculty to professional academic administrators.

Yet another infringement on the powers of faculty is the increasing employment by colleges and universities of part-time or **"adjunct" faculty**. Today almost half of all courses are taught by part-time faculty. Employing adjuncts rather than full-time faculty saves money for the institution. Adjuncts are paid on a per-course-taught basis, almost always much less than full-time faculty teaching the same number of courses. And adjuncts rarely receive medical, retirement, or other benefits. Whether or not these savings result in diminished quality of teaching is a hotly debated topic on many campuses.

The Unions

The traditional organization for faculty was the American Association of University Professors (AAUP); historically, this group confined itself to publishing data on faculty salaries and officially "censoring" colleges or universities that violated longstanding notions of academic freedom or tenure. (**Tenure** ensures that faculty members who have demonstrated their competence by service in a college or university position for three to seven years cannot thereafter be dismissed except for "cause"—a serious infraction of established rules or dereliction of duty, provable in an open hearing.) In recent years, some faculty have become convinced that traditional patterns of *individual* bargaining over salaries, teaching load, and working conditions in colleges and universities should be replaced by *collective* bargaining in the style of unionized labor. The American Federation of Teachers of the AFL-CIO, as well as the National Education Association and the AAUP, has sought to represent faculty in collective bargaining. Many states now authorize collective bargaining with the faculty of public colleges and universities if the faculty votes for such bargaining.

State Legislatures

The costs of public higher education are borne largely by taxpayers. Rarely does tuition at state colleges and universities pay for more than one-quarter of the costs of providing an education. Each year's higher education appropriations bill provides state legislatures with the opportunity to exercise their oversight of the state university system.

In recent years, public higher education has faced increased austerity as the demands for state spending on Medicaid, social services, and prison construction have risen dramatically. In most states, higher education is today receiving a *smaller* share of the state budget than in previous years. Moreover, state legislatures are increasingly interjecting themselves into college and university policy-making, often intruding on the traditional powers of independent trustees and regents, as well as presidents and faculty.

The thrust of legislative interventions is to increase teaching loads and responsibilities of faculty. State legislators are rarely impressed with the research activities of faculty, even when these activities are funded by grants and contracts from federal agencies or private foundations. And legislators are more concerned with teaching *under*graduates than graduate students. Legislators often receive complaints from parents about closed or overcrowded classes encountered by

TENURE

Ensures that faculty members who have demonstrated their competence by service in a college or university position for three to seven years cannot thereafter be dismissed except for "cause"—a serious infraction of established rules or dereliction of duty, provable in an open hearing.

Rarely does tuition at state colleges and universities pay for more than one-quarter of the costs of providing an education.

Public colleges and universities enroll three-quarters of the nation's college students. With growing pressures to fund kindergarten, elementary, and secondary schools, state legislatures may propose cutting higher education funding. Such a move is likely to prompt college students to storm the state capitol in protest.

the sons and daughters of their constituents, or the inability of a state university to admit qualified students. Many state legislators are demanding greater faculty "productivity," usually defined as teaching more classroom hours each week to more undergraduate students.[23]

Federal Role

Federal aid to colleges and universities comes in a variety of forms. Historically, the Morrill Act of 1862 provided the groundwork for federal assistance in higher education. In 1890 Congress initiated several federal grants to support the operations of the land-grant colleges, and this aid, although very modest, continues to the present. Federal support for scientific research has also had an important impact on higher education. In 1950 Congress established the National Science Foundation (NSF) to promote scientific research and education through direct grants to university faculty and departments. (In 1965 Congress established a National Endowment for the Arts and Humanities, but these fields receive only a fraction of the amounts given to NSF.) In addition to NSF, many other federal agencies—the Department of Defense, the Department of Education, the U.S. Public Health Service, the Department of Health and Human Services, the Department of Housing and Urban Development, and so forth—grant research contracts to universities for specific projects. Thus, research has become a very big item in university life.

Federal Student Aid

The federal government directly assists students with a variety of federal grant and loan programs. Federal "Pell Grants" (named for the program's original sponsor Senator Claiborne Pell, D-RI) offer students in good standing a money grant each year, based on the amount their families could reasonably be expected to contribute to their educational expenses. Today over five million students receive Pell grants, worth an average of about $3,400. In addition, a Federal Direct Student Loan (FDSL) program allows students to borrow money with no interest charged while the student is in college; repayment is delayed until after the student leaves school. About three million students borrow federal money; the default rate on repayment is high (over 18 percent) but declining over time. And a national work-study program uses federal funds to allow colleges and universities to employ students part time while they continue to go to school.

READING, WRITING, AND RELIGION

The First Amendment to the Constitution of the United States contains two important guarantees of religious freedom: (1) "Congress shall make no law respecting an establishment of religion," and (2) "or prohibiting the free exercise thereof." The Due Process Clause of the Fourteenth Amendment made these guarantees of religious liberty applicable to the states and their subdivisions as well as to Congress.

"Free Exercise" and Private Religious Schools

Most of the debate over religion in the public schools centers on the **No Establishment Clause** of the First Amendment rather than the Free Exercise Clause. However, it was respect for the **Free Exercise Clause** that caused the Supreme Court in 1925 to declare unconstitutional an attempt on the part of a state to prohibit private religious schools and to force all children to attend public schools. In the words of the Supreme Court, "The fundamental theory of liberty upon which all governments in this Union repose excludes any general power of the state to standardize its children by forcing them to accept instruction from public teachers only. The child is not the mere creature of the state."[24] This decision protects the entire structure of private religious schools in this nation.

The Meaning of "No Establishment"

A great deal of religious conflict in America has centered on the meaning of the No Establishment Clause, and the public schools have been the principal scene of this conflict. One interpretation of the clause holds that it does not prevent government from aiding religious schools or encouraging religious beliefs in the public schools, so long as it does not discriminate against any particular religion. Another interpretation of the No Establishment Clause is that it creates a "wall of separation" between church and state in America, which prevents government from directly aiding religious schools or encouraging religious beliefs in any way.

Support for Public Aid to Religious Schools

The Catholic Church in America enrolls about half of all private school students in the nation, and the Catholic Church has led the fight for an interpretation of the No Establishment Clause that would permit government to aid religious schools. As Catholic spokespeople see it, Catholic parents have a right to send their children to Catholic schools; and since they are taxpayers, they also expect that some tax monies should go to the aid of church schools. To do otherwise, they argue, would discriminate against parents who choose a religious education for their children.

Those who favor government aid to religious schools frequently refer to the language found in several cases decided by the Supreme Court, which appears to support the idea that government can *in a limited fashion* support the activities of church-related schools. In *Cochran* v. *Board of Education* (1930), the Court upheld a state law providing free textbooks for children attending both public and parochial schools on the grounds that this aid benefited the *children* rather than the Catholic Church and hence did not constitute an "establishment" of religion within the meaning of the First Amendment.[25] In *Everson* v. *Board of Education* (1947), the Supreme Court upheld the provision of school bus service to parochial school children at public expense on the grounds that the "wall of separation between church and state" does not prohibit the state from adopting a general program that helps *all* children, regardless of religion, to proceed safely to and from schools.[26] In *Mueller* v. *Allen* (1983), the court upheld a state income tax deduction for educational expenses even though the vast majority of deductions were used for religious school expenses.[27] These cases suggest that the Supreme Court is willing to permit some forms of aid to parochial school *children* that indirectly aids religion, so long as this is not directly used for the teaching of religion.

Proponents of public aid for church schools argue that these schools render a valuable public service by instructing millions of children who would have to be instructed by the state, at additional expense, if church schools were not available. Moreover, there are many precedents for public support of religious institutions: Church property has always been exempt from taxation; church contributions are deductible from federal

> A great deal of religious conflict in America has centered on the meaning of the No Establishment Clause, and the public schools have been the principal scene of this conflict.

income taxes; chaplains are provided in the armed forces as well as in the Congress of the United States; student federal grant and loan monies can be used to finance college educations in Catholic and other religious universities.

Opposition to Public Aid to Religious Schools

Opponents of aid to church schools argue that free public schools are available to the parents of all children regardless of religious denomination. If religious parents are not content with the type of school that the state provides, they should expect to pay for the establishment and operation of special schools. The state is under no obligation to finance the religious preferences in education of religious groups. In fact, opponents contend that it is unfair to compel taxpayers to support religion directly or indirectly; furthermore, the diversion of any substantial amount of public education funds to church schools would weaken the public school system.

The Supreme Court has also voiced the opinion that the No Establishment Clause of the First Amendment should constitute a "wall of separation" between church and state. In the words of the Court:

> Neither a state nor the federal government can set up a church. Neither can pass laws which aid one religion, aid all religions, or prefer one religion over another. Neither can force nor influence a person to go to or to remain away from church against his will, or force him to profess a belief or disbelief in any religion. No person can be punished for entertaining or professing religious beliefs or disbeliefs, for church attendance or nonattendance. No tax in any amount, large or small, can be levied to support any religious activities or institutions, whatever they may be called, or whatever form they may adopt to teach or practice religion. Neither a state nor the federal government can openly or secretly, participate in the affairs of any religious organizations or groups, and vice versa.[28]

"Excessive Entanglement" and the "Lemon Test"

One of the more important Supreme Court decisions in the history of church–state relations in America came in 1971 in the case of *Lemon* v. *Kurtzman*.[29] The Supreme Court set forth a three-part *Lemon test* for determining whether a particular state law constitutes "establishment" of religion and thus violates the First Amendment. To be constitutional, a law affecting religious activity:

- Must have a secular purpose.
- As its primary effect, must neither advance nor inhibit religion.
- Must not foster "an excessive government entanglement with religion."

Using this three-part test, the Supreme Court held that it was unconstitutional for a state to pay the costs of teachers' salaries or instructional materials in parochial schools. The justices argued that this practice would require excessive government controls and surveillance to ensure that funds were used only for secular instruction and thus would create an "excessive entanglement between government and religion."

However, the Supreme Court has upheld the use of tax funds to provide students attending church-related schools with nonreligious textbooks, lunches, transportation, sign-language interpreting, and special education teachers. And the Court has upheld a state's granting of tax credits to parents whose children attend private schools, including religious schools.[30] The Court has also upheld government grants of money to church-related colleges and universities for secular purpose.[31] The Court has ruled that if school buildings are open to use for secular organizations, they must also be open to use by religious organizations.[32] And the Court has held that a state institution (the University of Virginia) not only can but must grant student activity fees to religious organizations on the same basis as it grants these fees to secular organizations.[33] But the Court held that a Louisiana law requiring the teaching of creationism along with evolution in the public schools was an unconstitutional establishment of a religious belief.[34]

Prayer in the Schools

Religious conflict in public schools also centers on the question of prayer and Bible-reading ceremonies conducted by public schools. The practice of opening the school day with prayer and Bible-reading ceremonies was once widespread in American public schools. Usually the prayer was a Protestant rendition of the Lord's Prayer, and Bible reading was from the King James version. To avoid the denominational aspects of these ceremonies, the New York State Board of Regents substituted a nondenominational prayer, which it required to be said aloud in each class in the presence of a teacher at the beginning of each school day:

> Almighty God, we acknowledge our dependence upon Thee, and we beg Thy blessings upon us, our parents, our teachers, and our country.

New York argued that this prayer ceremony did not violate the No Establishment Clause, because the prayer was denominationally neutral and because student participation in the prayer was voluntary. However, in *Engle* v. *Vitale* (1962), the Supreme Court stated that "the constitutional prohibition against laws respecting an establishment of a religion must at least mean in this country it is no part of the business of government to compose official prayers for any group of the American people to recite as part of a religious program carried on by government."[35] The Court pointed out that making prayer voluntary did not free it from the prohibitions of the No Establishment Clause; that clause prevented the *establishment* of a religious ceremony by a government agency, regardless of whether the ceremony was voluntary or not:

> Neither the fact that the prayer may be denominationally neutral, nor the fact that its observance on the part of the students is voluntary can serve to free it from the limitations of the establishment clause, as it might from the free exercise clause, of the First Amendment, both of which are operative against the states by virtue of the 14th Amendment. . . . The establishment clause, unlike the free exercise clause, does not depend on any showing of direct governmental compulsion and is violated by the enactment of laws which establish an official religion whether those laws operate directly to coerce nonobserving individuals or not.[36]

One year later, in the case of *Abbington Township* v. *Schempp*, the Court considered the constitutionality of Bible-reading ceremonies in the public schools.[37] Here again, even though the children were not required to participate, the Court found that Bible reading as an opening exercise in the schools was a religious ceremony. The Court went to some trouble in its opinion to point out that they were not "throwing the Bible out of the school," for they specifically stated that the study of the Bible or of religion, when presented objectively as part of a secular program of education, did not violate the First Amendment, but religious *ceremonies* involving Bible reading or prayer, established by a state or school, did so.

State efforts to encourage "voluntary prayer" in public schools have also been struck down by the Supreme Court as unconstitutional. When the state of Alabama authorized a period of silence for "meditation or voluntary prayer" in public schools, the Court ruled that this was an "establishment of religion." The Court said the law had

The "Best-Educated" State Populations: College versus High School Grads

Approximately 28 percent of the U.S. population over age twenty-five has completed a bachelor's degree or more. But the *college-educated* population spreads itself unevenly across the states. College graduates make up the highest proportion of the adult population in Connecticut (36.8 percent) and the lowest in West Virginia (15.1 percent). Actually, the District of Columbia, with its hordes of federal bureaucrats, can boast of the largest proportion of college-educated adults—46.9 percent.

However, if "best-educated" is defined as the highest percentage of adult *high school graduates*, then Wyoming (91.3 percent) is ranked number one, and Mississippi (78.5 percent) is ranked number fifty. (See "*Rankings of the States:* Educational Performance.")

States Ranked by Percent College-Educated Population

Top Ten (%)		Average (%)		Bottom Ten (%)	
Connecticut	36.8	Hawaii	30.4	Nevada	23.4
Massachusetts	36.6	Kansas	30.4	Ohio	23.0
Maryland	36.3	New York	30.4	Indiana	22.6
New Jersey	36.3	Utah	29.8	Wyoming	21.9
Colorado	35.5	Illinois	29.6	Mississippi	21.8
Vermont	34.4	Rhode Island	29.2	Tennessee	21.5
Minnesota	34.2	Oregon	29.0	Alabama	19.8
New Hampshire	32.8	Alaska	28.6	Louisiana	19.6
Washington	30.9	Arizona	28.0	Kentucky	18.9
California	30.6	New Mexico	27.4	Arkansas	17.5
Virginia	30.6	North Dakota	27.2	West Virginia	15.1
		Georgia	27.1		
		Pennsylvania	26.0		
		Idaho	25.9		
		Delaware	25.6		
		Texas	25.5		
		Florida	25.4		
		Montana	25.4		
		Nebraska	25.4		
		North Carolina	25.3		
		Missouri	25.0		
		South Dakota	25.0		
		Wisconsin	25.0		
		Michigan	24.6		
		Iowa	24.5		
		Maine	24.3		
		South Carolina	24.2		
		Oklahoma	24.0		

Note: Data are for 2005.

Source: U.S. Census Bureau. Available at http://www.census.gov/population/www/socdemo/education/cps2005.html

no secular purpose, that it conveyed "a message of state endorsement and promotion of prayer," and that its real intent was to encourage prayer in public schools.[38] (In a stinging dissenting opinion, then Chief Justice Warren Burger noted that the Supreme Court itself opened its session with a prayer, that both houses of Congress opened every session with prayers led by official chaplains paid by the government: "To suggest that a moment of silence statute that includes the word *prayer* unconstitutionally endorses religion, manifests not neutrality but hostility toward religion.") In 2000, the Supreme Court ruled that the delivery of an invocation at public high school football games over the school's public address system was an unconstitutional state-sponsored endorsement of religion.[39]

In summary, the public places a high priority on the need for a high quality education system, from K–12, to community colleges and institutions of higher learning. The biggest conflicts are over how to structure the system in an effective and equitable manner and how to pay for it. Everyone thinks they are an expert on education.

ON THE WEB

Most state education departments have their own Web sites that can be accessed through the state government homepages. These sites usually provide extensive information on the organization and functioning of educational agencies of the state. Many larger school districts throughout the nation also maintain their own Web sites.

Other very useful education-related Web sites and the groups sponsoring them are as follows:

www.nea.org The National Education Association, whose membership is primarily teachers.

www.aasa The American Association of School Administrators

www.aaup.org The American Association of University Professors (AAUP)

www.nas.org The National Association of Scholars (NAS), a conservative faculty group.

www.ed.gov The official site of the U.S. Department of Education; describes all federal aid to education programs, including loans and financial aid programs for college students.

CHAPTER SEVENTEEN

THE POLITICS OF POVERTY, WELFARE, AND HEALTH

17

QUESTIONS TO CONSIDER

**Should public welfare programs be run
by the federal government or by the
states?**
■ Federal government
■ States

**Should welfare payments be limited to
two years?**
■ Yes   ■ No

**Should the federal government provide
health insurance for all Americans, not
just the aged and poor?**
■ Yes   ■ No

**Who should be responsible for dealing
with the problem of obesity, the
individual or the government?**
■ Individual
■ Government

POVERTY IN AMERICA

Political conflict over poverty in America begins with disagreement over its nature and extent, and then it proceeds to disputes over its causes and remedies.

How Many Poor?

How much poverty really exists in America? According to the U.S. Census Bureau, there are about 37 million poor people in the United States. The **official poverty rate** (the number of people living in poverty as a percentage of the total population) has ranged between 11 and 15 percent in recent years (see Figure 17–1). This official definition of poverty includes all those Americans whose annual cash income falls below that which is required to maintain a decent standard of living. The dollar amounts of the poverty level change each year to take into account the effect of inflation.

Liberal Criticism

This official definition of poverty has many critics. Some liberals believe poverty is underestimated because: (1) the official definition does not take into account regional differences in the cost of living, climate, or accepted styles of living; (2) the official definition includes cash income from welfare and Social Security (without this government assistance, the number of poor would be much higher, perhaps 25 percent of the total population); and (3) the official definition does not count the many "near poor." There are nearly 50 million Americans or about 18 percent of the population living below 125 percent of the poverty level.

Conservative Criticism

Some conservatives also challenge the official definition of poverty: (1) it does not consider the value of family assets. People (usually older people) who own their own mortgage-free homes, furniture, and automobiles may have current incomes below the poverty line yet not suffer hardship; (2) there are many families and individuals who are officially counted as poor but who do not think of themselves as "poor people"—students, for example, who deliberately postpone income to secure an education; (3) more importantly, the official definition of poverty excludes **"in kind"** (**noncash**) **benefits**

FIGURE 17–1 Poverty in America

Source: U.S. Census Bureau.

given to the poor by governments. These benefits include, for example, food stamps, free medical care, public housing, and school lunches. If these benefits were "costed out" (calculated as cash income), there may be only half as many poor people as shown in official statistics.

Variations among the States

The official poverty rate varies considerably among the states (see "*Rankings of the States*: Poverty and Lack of Health Insurance"). Poverty in some states (notably Mississippi, Louisiana, and New Mexico) ranges up to 19 percent. Inasmuch as minority populations tend to experience poverty in greater proportions than others, it is not surprising that southern states with larger African-American populations and southwestern states with larger Hispanic populations have higher poverty rates (see Figure 17–2).

WHO ARE THE POOR?

Poverty occurs in many kinds of families and in all races and ethnic groups. However, some groups experience poverty in greater proportions than the national average.

FIGURE 17–2 **Three-Year Average Poverty Rate by State (Poverty Most Severe in Deep South)**

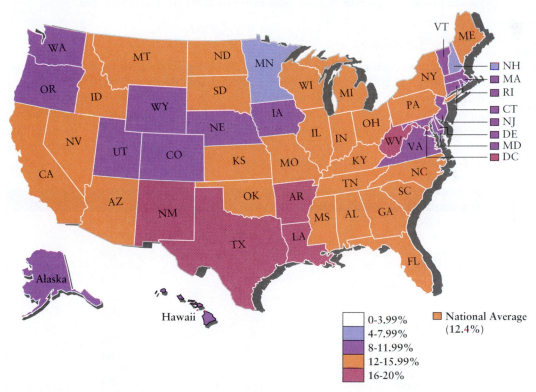

Legend:
- 0-3.99%
- 4-7.99%
- 8-11.99%
- 12-15.99%
- 16-20%
- National Average (12.4%)

Note: Data are average for 2002–2004.
Source: Current Population Survey, 2003 to 2005 Annual Social and Economic Supplements, *Wall Street Journal*, http://interactive.wsj.com/documents/info-poverty0604-25.html?printVersion=true

Families headed by single moms are more likely to be poor than a two-parent household.

Family Structure

Poverty is most common among female-headed families. The incidence of poverty among these families in 2005 was over 36 percent, compared to about 5 percent for married couples (see Table 17–1). These women and their children comprise over two-thirds of all of the persons living in poverty in the United States. These figures describe the **"feminization of poverty"** in America. Clearly, poverty is closely related to the family structure. Today the disintegration of the traditional husband–wife family is the single most influential factor contributing to poverty.

TABLE 17–1 Poverty in America	
Poverty Definition 2005	$19,971
Number of poor	37.0 million
Poverty percentage of total population	12.6
Race (% poor)	
White	9.9
Black	23.7
Hispanic	21.8
Age (% Poor)	
Under 18	17.6
Over 65	10.1
Family (% Poor)	
Married couple	5.1
Single parent, mother only	36.2

Source: U.S. Census Bureau, available at www.census.gov

Poverty and Lack of Health Insurance

Percentage of Population in Poverty

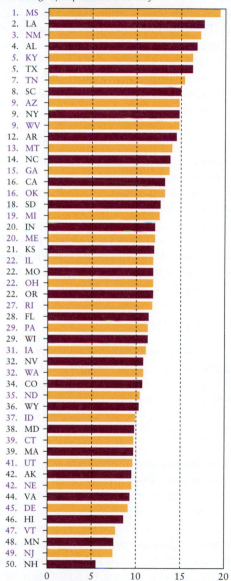

1. MS
2. LA
3. NM
4. AL
5. KY
5. TX
7. TN
8. SC
9. AZ
9. NY
9. WV
12. AR
13. MT
14. NC
15. GA
16. CA
16. OK
18. SD
19. MI
20. IN
20. ME
21. KS
22. IL
22. MO
22. OH
22. OR
27. RI
28. FL
29. PA
29. WI
31. IA
32. NV
32. WA
34. CO
35. ND
36. WY
37. ID
38. MD
39. CT
39. MA
41. UT
42. AK
42. NE
44. VA
45. DE
46. HI
47. VT
48. MN
49. NJ
50. NH

0   5   10   15   20

Note: Data are for 2005.
Source: U.S. Census Bureau *Statistical Abstract of the United States,* 2004–2005. Available at http://www.census.gov/hhes/www/poverty/poverty05/table8.html

Lacking Health Insurance

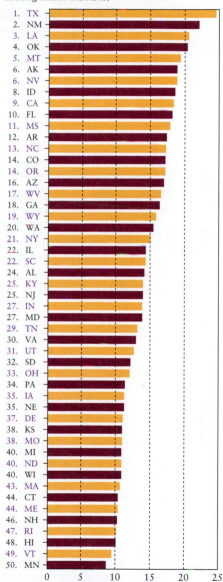

1. TX
2. NM
3. LA
4. OK
5. MT
6. AK
6. NV
8. ID
9. CA
10. FL
11. MS
12. AR
13. NC
14. CO
14. OR
16. AZ
17. WV
18. GA
19. WY
20. WA
21. NY
22. IL
22. SC
24. AL
25. KY
25. NJ
27. IN
27. MD
29. TN
30. VA
31. UT
32. SD
33. OH
34. PA
35. IA
35. NE
37. DE
38. KS
38. MO
40. MI
40. ND
40. WI
43. MA
44. CT
44. ME
46. NH
47. RI
48. HI
49. VT
50. MN

0   5   10   15   20   25

Note: Data are for 2003.
Source: U.S. Census Bureau *Statistical Abstract of the United States,* 2006, "Health and Nutrition," Table 143. Available at http://www.census.gov/prod/2006pubs/07statab/health.pdf

Race/Ethnicity

African Americans and Hispanics experience poverty in much greater proportions than whites. Over the years the poverty rate among blacks in the United States has been over twice the poverty rate among whites.

Age

The aged in America experience *less* poverty than the nonaged. The aged are not poor, despite the popularity of the phrase "the poor and the aged." The poverty rate for persons over sixty-five years of age is *below* the national average. Moreover, the aged are much wealthier than the nonaged. They are more likely than younger people to own homes with paid mortgages. A large portion of their medical expenses is paid by Medicare. With fewer expenses, the aged, even with relatively smaller cash incomes, experience poverty in a different fashion than young mothers with children. Continuing increases in Social Security benefits over the years are largely responsible for this singular "victory" in the war against poverty.

Wealth

WEALTH

The net worth of all one's possessions.

Wealth is the net worth of all one's possessions—home value minus mortgage, auto value minus loan, business value minus debts, money in bank accounts, savings, stocks and bonds, and real estate. All calculations of poverty consider income, not wealth. It is theoretically possible for persons to have considerable wealth (e.g., to own a mortgage-free home and a loan-free automobile and have money in savings and investments) yet fall within the official definition of poverty because current cash income is low. Indeed, many of the *aged* who are counted as poor because their incomes are low have substantial accumulations of wealth. The U.S. Census Bureau estimates that the *net worth* of the median family over age 65 is ten times higher than the median family under age 35.[1]

INEQUALITY IN AMERICA

Inequality in America has been increasing over the last thirty years.

Inequality in America has been increasing over the last thirty years. Income differences among American families decreased for most of the last century but have widened ominously in recent years. This reversal of historical trends has generated both political rhetoric and serious scholarly inquiry about its causes and consequences.

Measuring Inequality

INCOME DISTRIBUTION

A measure of inequality; generally the percent of total family income received by each quintile (20 percent) of families from highest to lowest in terms of income.

Inequality is generally measured by **income distribution** among American families. Table 17–2 divides all families into five groups—from the lowest one-fifth of personal income to the highest one-fifth—and shows the percentage of total family personal income received by each of these groups over the years. (If perfect income equality existed, each fifth of American families would receive 20 percent of all family personal income, and it would not be possible to rank fifths from highest to lowest.) The poorest one-fifth received 3.5 percent of all family personal income in 1929; by 1947, however, this group had increased its percentage of all family personal income to 5.0. (Most of this increase occurred during World War II.) The highest one-fifth received 54.4 percent of all family personal income in 1929; by 1947, however, this percentage had declined to 43.0. Another measure of income inequality is the percentage of income received by the top 5 percent in

TABLE 17–2 Distribution of Family Income by Quintiles and Top 5 Percent, Selected Years

Quintiles	1929	1947	1954	1968	1979	1990	2000	2005
Lowest	3.5	5.0	4.5	5.6	5.4	4.6	3.6	3.4
Second	9.0	11.9	12.1	12.4	11.6	10.8	8.9	8.6
Third	13.8	17.0	17.7	17.7	17.5	16.6	14.9	14.6
Fourth	19.3	23.1	23.9	23.7	24.1	23.8	23.0	23.0
Highest	54.4	43.0	41.8	40.5	41.4	44.3	49.7	50.4
Top 5 Percent	30.0	17.5	16.3	15.6	15.3	17.4	21.9	22.5

Source: U.S. Census Bureau

America. The top 5 percent received 30.0 percent of all family personal income in 1929, but only 17.5 percent in 1947.

Rising Inequality

But note that since 1968, the long-term trend toward greater equality in America has been reversed. The percentage of total family income received by the poorest one-fifth of families declined from 5.6 percent in 1968 to 3.4 percent in 2005. In contrast, the richest one-fifth of all families increased their share of total income from 40.5 to 50.4 percent.

Explaining Increases in Inequality

A variety of explanations have been put forth to explain this trend toward greater inequality: the decline of the manufacturing sector of the economy with its relatively high-paying blue-collar jobs; the rise in the number of two-wage families, making single-wage families relatively less affluent; and demographic trends, which include larger portions of female heads of households. But the globalization of trade is emerging as the principal cause of increasing inequality in America. America's unskilled and semiskilled workers are now competing with people around the world, including very low-wage workers in developing nations. In contrast, our high-tech workers, entrepreneurs, and investors benefit significantly from world trade. The result is that inequality has worsened among Americans even though the aggregate income of the nation has risen.

AN OVERVIEW OF WELFARE POLICY

Public welfare has been a recognized responsibility of government in the United States since colonial days. As far back as the Poor Relief Act of 1601, the English Parliament

Income inequality in the U.S. has been increasing over the past thirty years, prompting poor persons and their advocates to call for imposing more taxes on the rich.

provided workhouses for both the "able-bodied poor" (the unemployed) and poorhouses for widows and orphans, the aged, and the handicapped. Today, about half of all families in America receive some type of government payments (see Table 17–3).

Social Security

The key feature of the Social Security Act is the Old-Age, Survivors, and Disability Insurance (OASDI) program; this is a compulsory social insurance program which gives individuals a legal right to benefits in the event of certain occurrences

TABLE 17-3   Social Welfare for Everyone

U.S. Population Receiving Government Payments

Social Insurance Programs (No Means Test for Entitlement to Benefits)	Beneficiaries (Millions)
Social Security	47.7
Medicare	41.1
Government Retirement	3.3
Veteran's Benefits	3.4
Unemployment Compensation	8.4

Public Assistance Programs (Means-Tested Entitlement)	Beneficiaries (Millions)
Cash Aid	
Temporary Assistance for Needy Families (formerly AFDC)	4.8
SSI	6.9
Earned income tax credit	21.7
Medical Care	
Medicaid	50.9
Veterans	1.6
Food Benefits	
Food stamps	23.9
School lunches	18.0
School breakfasts	6.7
Women, infants, children	7.5
Housing Benefits	
Total	3.3
Education Aid	
Stafford Loans	5.6
Pell Grants	4.8
Head Start	0.9
Job Training	
Total	0.8
Energy Assistance	
Total	4.6

Source: Data from *Statistical Abstract of the United States*, 2005–2006, pp. 363, 364, 366, 369, 372, 373, 375, 376.

that cause a reduction in their income—old age, death of the head of the household, or permanent disability.[2] Both employees and employers must pay equal amounts toward employees' OASDI insurance. Upon retirement, an insured worker is entitled to monthly benefit payments based upon age at retirement and the amount earned during his or her working years. OASDI also ensures benefit payments to survivors of an insured worker, including the spouse if there are dependent children. However, if the spouse has no dependent children, benefits will not begin until he or she reaches retirement age. Finally, OASDI ensures benefit payments to people who suffer permanent and total disabilities that prevent them from working more than one year.

OASDI is a completely federal program, administered by the Social Security Administration in the Department of Health and Human Services. However, OASDI has an important indirect effect on state and local welfare programs, by removing people in whole or in part from welfare roles. Social Security has doubtlessly reduced the welfare problems that state and local governments would otherwise face.

Unemployment Compensation

Another feature of the Social Security Act was that it induced states to enact unemployment compensation programs through the imposition of the **payroll tax** on all employers. A federal unemployment tax was levied on the payroll of employers of four or more workers, but employers paying into state insurance programs that meet federal standards could use these state payments to offset their federal unemployment tax. In other words, the federal government threatened to undertake an unemployment compensation program and tax if the states did not do so themselves. This federal program succeeded in inducing all fifty states to establish unemployment compensation programs. Federal standards are flexible, and the states have some freedom in shaping their own unemployment programs. In all cases, unemployed workers must report in person and show that they are willing and able to work in order to receive unemployment compensation benefits, and states cannot deny workers benefits for refusing to work as strikebreakers or refusing to work for rates lower than prevailing rates.

Supplemental Security Income (SSI)

The federal government also directly aids certain categories of welfare recipients—the aged, the blind, and the disabled—under a program called Supplemental Security Income (SSI). A loose definition of "disabled"—including alcoholism and drug abuse among adults and attention deficiency among children—has led to rapid growth in the number of SSI recipients.

Family Assistance

Family Assistance, officially **Temporary Assistance to Needy Families,** (formerly AFDC, or Aid to Families with Dependent Children), is a grant program to enable the *states* to assist needy families. States now operate the program and define "need"; they set their own benefit levels and establish (within federal guidelines) income and resource limits. Prior to welfare reform in 1996, AFDC was a *federal* entitlement program.

Food Stamps

The federal food stamp program now distributes billions in federal monies to improve food and nutrition among the poor. Eligible persons may receive food stamps, generally

SOCIAL SECURITY

The federal government's Old-Age, Survivors, and Disability Insurance program; for all employed Americans it is a compulsory program.

Social Security has doubtlessly reduced the welfare problems that state and local governments would otherwise face.

PAYROLL TAX

Tax that is levied on and withheld from an employee's wages to pay for unemployment compensation systems.

SUPPLEMENTAL SECURITY INCOME (SSI)

Direct federal cash assistance to the needy, aged, blind, and disabled.

TEMPORARY ASSISTANCE TO NEEDY FAMILIES (TANF)

Federal aid for state programs of cash assistance to poor families; replaced the AFDC federal entitlement program.

from county welfare departments, which may be used to purchase food at supermarkets. This program has mushroomed very rapidly since its origins; eligibility for food stamps now extends to many people who are not poor enough to qualify for public assistance.

Earned Income Tax Credit

The Earned Income Tax Credit (EITC) is designed to assist the working poor. It not only refunds their payroll taxes, but also provides larger refunds than they actually paid in taxes during the previous year. Thus, the EITC is in effect a "negative" income tax. The program applies only to those poor who actually work and who apply for the credit when filing their income tax.

Other Social Programs

Public assistance recipients are generally eligible for participation in a variety of other social programs. These include school lunch and milk; housing assistance; job training; various educational and child-care programs and services; special food programs for women, infants, and children (WIC); home heating and weatherization assistance; free legal services; and more.

Political conflict over welfare policy arises in part from a clash of values over individual responsibility and social compassion.

WELFARE REFORM

Political conflict over welfare policy arises in part from a clash of values over individual responsibility and social compassion. As Harvard sociologist David Ellwood explains,

Welfare brings some of our most precious values—involving autonomy, responsibility, work, family, community and compassion—into conflict. We want to help those who are not making it but in so doing, we seem to cheapen the efforts of those who are struggling hard just to get by. We want to offer financial support to those with low incomes, but if we do we reduce the pressure on them and their incentive to work. We want to help people who are not able to help themselves but then we worry that people will not bother to help themselves. We recognize the insecurity of single-parent families but, in helping them, we appear to be promoting or supporting their formation.[3]

A political consensus developed over the years that welfare policy in America was in need of reform. A variety of problems were commonly cited: the work disincentives created by the pyramiding of multiple forms of public assistance, the long-term social dependency that welfare programs seemed to encourage, and the adverse effects welfare assistance appeared to have on families.

Work Disincentives

In most states, if a recipient of assistance took a full-time job, assistance checks were stopped. If the former recipient was then laid off, it took some time to get back on welfare. In other words, employment was uncertain, while assistance was not. Moreover, a family on the welfare rolls was generally entitled to participate in the food stamp program, to receive health care through Medicaid, to gain access to free or low-rent public housing, to receive free lunches in public schools, and to receive a variety of other social and educational benefits at little or no cost to themselves.

Social Dependency

About half of the people receiving welfare benefits at any one time were doing so temporarily; that is, they would leave the welfare rolls within two years. For these recipients, welfare payments were a relatively short-term aid that helped them over life's difficult times. But for others, welfare became a more permanent part of their lives. An "**underclass**" of persistently poor became dependent on welfare payments for much of their lives. About half of welfare recipients received aid for five years or more.

Family Effects

Traditional welfare policies also provided many disincentives to family life. Unwed parenthood has risen rapidly since 1970. Today about one-third of all births are to unmarried women (see Table 17–4). Many poor, young, unmarried women became dependent on welfare payments as teenagers when they first gave birth. It was argued that the availability of welfare cash payments, food stamps, Medicaid, and housing encouraged teenagers to have children, or at least removed the traditional hardships once associated with teenage pregnancy. Welfare benefits accompanying motherhood allowed these young women to live independently of the families in which they were raised, and to live independently of the child's father, thus encouraging these men to abandon their child support responsibilities. These concerns gave rise to efforts at welfare reform in the 1990s.

Welfare Reform

After a great deal of controversy and two presidential vetoes, welfare reform finally became law in 1996. It was passed by a Republican Congress and signed by a Democratic president, but it was bitterly opposed by groups representing social workers, minorities, and the poor.

Welfare reform—officially Temporary Assistance to Needy Families (TANF)—ended the sixty-year-old federal cash entitlement program for low-income families with children—Aid to Families with Dependent Children (AFDC). TANF reflects the philosophy of "devolution" of responsibility to the states. TANF is essentially a federal block grant program that allocates lump sums to the states for cash welfare payments. Benefits and eligibility requirements for cash assistance are now largely decided by the states. However, conservatives in Congress imposed some tough-minded "strings" to this federal aid, including a two-year limit on continuing cash benefits and a five-year lifetime limit; a "family cap" that denies additional cash benefits to women already on welfare

UNDERCLASS
Persistently poor persons; economically-disadvantaged portion of a society.

WELFARE REFORM
Officially, the Temporary Assistance to Needy Families (TANF) program enacted in 1996, which included the "devolution" of responsibility for cash assistance programs to the states.

TABLE 17–4	Rising Births to Unmarried Women		
	All Races	**Whites**	**Blacks**
1950	5.0	4.0	17.0
1970	10.7	5.6	37.0
1975	14.3	7.3	46.8
1980	17.8	10.2	55.5
1985	22.0	14.5	60.1
1990	26.6	16.9	66.7
1995	32.2	25.3	69.9
2000	33.2	27.1	68.5
2005	34.0	28.5	68.2

Source: Statistical Abstract of the United States, 2006, p. 68.

Is Welfare Reform a Success?

Supporters of welfare reform have declared it a success. Their claim is based primarily on the rapid exodus of over 8 million people from the nation's welfare rolls (see the figure in this box).

The number of welfare recipients in the nation has now dropped below 5 million—the lowest number in more than forty years. Only about 2 percent of Americans are now receiving cash welfare—the smallest proportion since 1970. No doubt some of this decline is attributable to growth of the economy: Declines in welfare rolls began *before* Congress passed its welfare reform law, and some decline may have occurred without reform. Many states initiated their own reforms under "waivers" from the federal government even before Congress acted.

Virtually all states have now developed work programs for welfare recipients. Applicants for welfare benefits are now generally required to enter job-search programs, to undertake job training, and to accept jobs or community service positions.

Yet although nearly everyone agrees that getting people off welfare rolls and onto payrolls is the main goal

This mother of six and one grandchild from Washington, DC, spent ten years on public assistance while she raised her children. She then enrolled in a welfare-to-work program with the Plumbers Union Local and began a job earning nearly $13 per hour.

of reform, there are major obstacles to the achievement of this goal. First, many long-term welfare recipients have handicaps—physical disabilities, chronic illnesses, learning disabilities, alcohol or drug abuse problems—that prevent them from holding a full-time job. Many long-term recipients have no work experience at all, and two-thirds of them did not graduate from high school. Almost half have three or more children, making day-care arrangements a major obstacle. It is unlikely that any counseling, education, job training, or job placement programs could ever succeed in getting these people into productive employment.

Early studies of people who left the welfare rolls following welfare reform suggest that over half and perhaps as many as three-quarters have found work, although most at minimum or near-minimum wages.[a] However the early dramatic reductions in welfare case loads (see figure) began to level off after 2000. There are probably 4 to 6 million people who have so many physical, psychological, and social problems that it is simply impossible for them to work.

[a]*Governing*, April 1999, pp. 21–26.

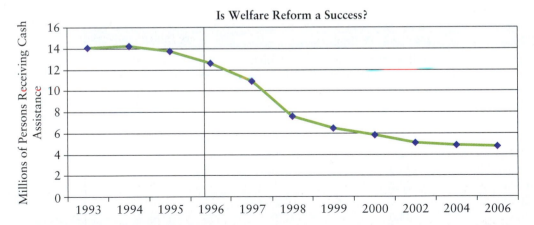

Is Welfare Reform a Success?

Y-axis: Millions of Persons Receiving Cash Assistance (0 to 16)
X-axis: 1993, 1994, 1995, 1996, 1997, 1998, 1999, 2000, 2002, 2004, 2006

Note: Line reflects year federal Welfare Reform Act was passed.
Source: Statistical Abstract of the United States, 2007.

who bear more children; and the denial of cash welfare to unwed parents under eighteen years of age unless they live with an adult and attend school. Liberals in Congress obtained some modifications to the welfare reform act: exemptions from time limits and work requirements for some portion of welfare recipients, and community service alternatives to work requirements. (See "*What Do You Think?*: Is Welfare Reform a Success?")

HEALTH CARE POLICY

Good health correlates best with factors over which doctors and hospitals have no direct control: heredity, lifestyle (smoking, eating, drinking, exercise, stress), and the physical environment. Historically, most of the reductions in death rates have resulted from public health and sanitation improvements, including immunization against smallpox, clean public water supplies, sanitary sewage disposal, and increased standards of living. Many of the leading causes of death today, including heart disease, stroke, cirrhosis of the liver, AIDS, accidents, and suicides, are closely linked to personal habits and lifestyles. Nearly 60 percent of the nation's population is overweight.[4] Thus, for many, the greatest contribution to better health is likely to be found in altered personal habits and lifestyles, rather than in more medical care.

> *The greatest contribution to better health is likely to be found in altered personal habits and lifestyles, rather than in more medical care.*

Community Public Health and Hospitals

Public health and sanitation are among the oldest functions of local government. Keeping clean is still one of the major tasks of cities today, a task that includes street cleaning, sewage disposal, garbage collection, and the provision of a clean water supply. Very often these services are taken for granted in the United States, but in many underdeveloped countries of the world, health and sanitation are still major concerns.

Local public health departments are directly concerned with the *prevention* of disease. They engage in vaccination and immunization, as well as regulatory activity and the safeguarding of water supplies.

In addition to the preventive activities of the public health departments, state and local governments also provide extensive, tax-supported hospital care. State and local governments provide both general and specialized hospitals, health centers, and nursing homes and very often subsidize private hospitals and medical facilities as well. New York City operates the nation's largest city hospital system, but almost every community subsidizes hospital facilities in some way. City and county hospitals and heavily subsidized private hospitals are expected to provide free emergency care to indigent patients. Thus, when revenue shortfalls hit local governments, the impact can be quite negative for governments, hospitals, doctors who may not get reimbursed, and the poor.

Medicare

The federal government added Medicare to the Social Security program in 1965. **Medicare** provides for prepaid hospital insurance for the *aged*, and low-cost voluntary medical insurance for the aged under federal administration. Medicare includes: (1) a compulsory basic health insurance plan covering hospital costs for the aged, which is

MEDICARE
Federal health insurance for the aged.

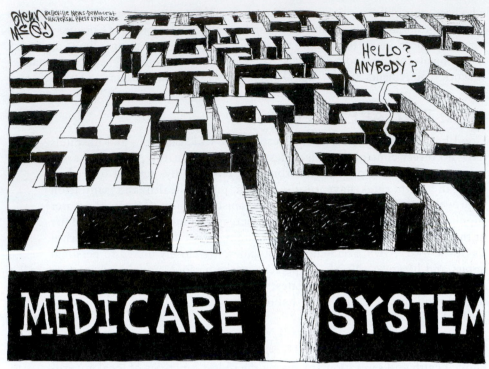

Medicare is a federal program serving only the elderly. It is a very confusing program, but one that senior citizens depend on heavily. Prescription drug coverage was added to the program in 2004. Some worry that as the baby boomers age, the Social Security system and the Medicare programs will go broke. *Source:* Glenn McCoy, Copyright © 2006 Belleville News-Democrat. Distributed by Universal Press Syndicate. Reprinted with permission. All rights reserved.

financed through payroll taxes collected under the Social Security system; and (2) a voluntary but supplemental medical program that will pay doctors' bills and additional medical expenses, financed in part by contributions from the aged and in part by the general tax revenues. Only aged persons are covered by Medicare.

Prescription drug coverage was added to Medicare in 2004. Medicare pays 75 percent of annual health costs up to $2,250; individuals must pay the next $3,600 out-of-pocket; the government pays 95 percent of costs after $5,100. The $3,600 "hole" or "gap" in coverage is one of the principal objections to the current program. The federal government is barred from mandating or negotiating prices with drug companies, although there is growing pressure on Congress to change this.

Medicaid is a federally funded program that requires states to provide medical services to the poor—regardless of their age.

Medicaid

The federal government also provides federal funds under Medicaid to enable states to guarantee medical services to the *poor*. Each state operates its own Medicaid program. Unlike Medicare, Medicaid is a welfare program designed for needy persons; no prior contributions are required, and recipients of Medicaid services are generally welfare recipients. States can extend coverage to other medically needy persons if they choose to do so. Medicaid pays virtually all health care costs, including nursing home care.

Medically Uninsured

Most Americans are covered by either private group health insurance plans (mostly employer provided) or by Medicare or Medicaid (see Figure 17–3). But about 15 percent of Americans have no health insurance at all. (Among age categories, young people age 18 to 24 are the least likely to have insurance.) Most of the medically uninsured are working people and their families who are not poor enough to qualify for Medicaid or old enough for Medicare.

SCHIP

Under the **State Children's Health Insurance Program (SCHIP)** the federal government provides grants to states to extend health insurance to children who would not otherwise qualify for Medicaid. The program is generally targeted toward families with incomes below 200 percent of the poverty level. But each state may set its own eligibility limits and each state has flexibility in the administration of the program. States may expand their Medicaid programs to include children or develop separate child health programs. The future of SCHIP funding and eligibility requirements lies with Congress. It has been very controversial beginning in 2007 when President Bush vetoed a bill based on proposed changes to the program.

Coping with Costs

Various efforts have been made to counter rising costs of health care. (See Figure 17–4.) Private insurers have negotiated discounts with groups of physicians and with hospitals (so-called **preferred provider organizations—PPOs**) and have implemented rules to guide

FIGURE 17–3 Health Insurance Coverage in the United States

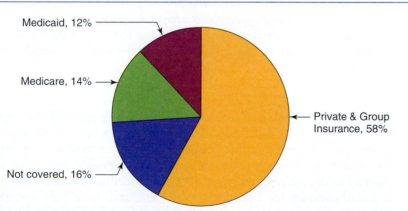

Medicaid, 12%
Medicare, 14%
Not covered, 16%
Private & Group Insurance, 58%

Source: Statistical Abstract of the United States, 2006, p. 109.

MEDICAID

Federal aid to the states to provide health insurance for the poor.

STATE CHILDREN'S HEALTH INSURANCE PROGRAM (SCHIP)

Federal grants to states to extend health insurance to low income children who would not otherwise qualify for Medicaid and whose families cannot afford private coverage.

PREFERRED PROVIDER ORGANIZATION (PPO)

A health care organization composed of physicians and hospitals which provides health care services at a reduced rate or discount.

HEALTH MAINTENANCE ORGANIZATIONS (HMOs)

Private health care organizations that provide medical services for fixed fees.

FIGURE 17–4 **National Health Care Expenditures: 1970 to 2015**

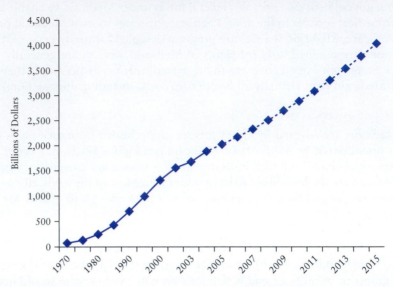

Source: U.S. Census Bureau, http://www.census.gov/compendia/statab/tables/07s0120.xls

MANAGED CARE

An insurance company's or health care organization's rules governing patient-doctor relations; limits ability of physicians to decide patient care.

physicians about when patients should and should not receive costly diagnostic and therapeutic procedures (so-called **managed care**). The government has replaced payments to hospitals under Medicare based on costs incurred, with payment of fixed fees based on primary and secondary diagnoses at the time of admission. Government and private insurers have encouraged the expansion of **health maintenance organizations** (HMOs) that promise to provide a stipulated list of services to patients for a fixed fee and that are able to provide care at lower total costs than can other providers.

However, many of the efforts by both private insurance companies and governments to control health care costs have created new problems. Cost-control regulations and restrictions add to administrative costs and create a mountain of paperwork for physicians and hospitals. Many insurance companies require preapproval of treatments. Patients and doctors complain that preapproval removes medical decision making from the physician and patient and places it in the hands of non-medically trained insurance company employees. These problems are now reflected in many state legislative debates about HMO and medical insurance company practices.

Many of the efforts by both private insurance companies and governments to control health care costs have created new problems.

Patients' Bill of Rights

These kinds of complaints have fueled a drive for a **patients' bill of rights**. The most common provisions in proposed patients' rights bills are allowing patients to see specialists without first obtaining permission from a representative of their health care plan; providing emergency care without securing prior approval from a health plan representative; allowing immediate appeals when a patient is denied coverage for a particular treatment; and, most controversial of all, giving patients the right to sue their health plans for medical mistakes. The health insurance industry, including HMOs, argues that the latter proposal would significantly increase the cost of health insurance. They argue that any law opening themselves to patients' lawsuits would be "just a lawyer's bill of rights."

Medicaid in the States

Medicaid is the costliest of all public assistance programs. States must pay about 45 percent of Medicaid's costs, with the federal government paying the remainder. Medicaid is the most rapidly growing item in the budget of most states.

Medicaid is increasingly becoming the last resort for people who have no medical insurance and for those whose insurance does not cover long-term illness or nursing home care. People confronted with serious or "catastrophic" illnesses that exhaust their private insurance or Medicare coverage are often forced to impoverish themselves in order to qualify for Medicaid. (Medicare pays for only 60 days of hospital care and 100 days of nursing home care.) Moreover, as the number and proportion of the very old in society rise (those 80 years and over comprise the nation's fastest-growing age group), the need for long-term nursing home care grows. Medicaid is the only program that covers nursing home care, but middle-class people must first "spend down" their savings or transfer their wealth to others in order to qualify for Medicaid. Nursing home care is now the single largest item in Medicaid spending.

Mentally incapacitated people living out of shopping carts are often taken off the streets and put in jail because there is no housing for them.http://newstandardnews.net/content/photos/cart.jpg

Medicaid is the most rapidly growing item in the budget of most states.

POLITICS AND HEALTH CARE REFORM

Health care reform centers on two central problems: controlling costs and expanding access. These problems are related: expanding access to Americans who are currently uninsured and closing gaps in coverage require increases in costs, even while the central thrust of reform is to bring down overall health care costs.

Approximately 85 percent of the population of the United States is covered by either private health insurance, mostly through their employers, or government health insurance, including Medicare and Medicaid. However, about 16 percent of the population has *no* medical insurance (see *"Rankings of the States: Lacking Health Insurance"*). Most of the uninsured are working Americans and their families—people who are neither poor enough to qualify for Medicaid nor old enough to qualify for Medicare. These people may postpone or go without needed medical care or be denied medical care except in emergencies. Confronted with serious illnesses, they may be obliged to impoverish themselves in order to become eligible for Medicaid. Their unpaid medical bills must be absorbed by hospitals and state and local government support of them or shifted to paying patients and their insurance companies.

PATIENT'S BILL OF RIGHTS

Policy dictating that patients be informed about their medical treatments, appeals processes, and their right to sue.

State Reforms

The states, rather than the federal government, have so far taken the lead in heath care reform. Medicaid has been the fastest-growing item in the state budgets over the last decade. Inasmuch as states cannot run deficits in the fashion of the federal government, considerable effort has been made in the states to contain Medicaid costs. Prior to 1997 states were required to obtain waivers from the U.S. Department of Health and Human Services in order to experiment with Medicaid cost containment. But in that year Congress eliminated the waiver requirement and states began to place their Medicaid recipients in managed care plans. Today, nationwide about 60 percent of all Medicaid patients are in managed care plans. (See "*Up Close*: The Rise and Fall of 'TennCare'.")

Massachusetts Mandated Health Insurance

Should states mandate that everyone have health insurance? The aged would be covered by Medicare, the poor by Medicaid, employers with more than ten workers would be required to provide health insurance, and those who cannot afford private insurance would qualify for a state health insurance program. Massachusetts is the first state in the nation to experiment with this approach to health care reform. In 2006, Republican Governor Mitt Romney and the Democratic-controlled state legislature, together with an unlikely alliance of business leaders and consumer advocates, agreed on this "bold, positive, and necessary" program. Beginning in 2008, Massachusetts residents are required to provide health insurance information on their state income tax forms or face a financial penalty. Polls report that a majority of Massachusetts residents support mandated health insurance. Initially at least, the program is receiving political support from across the nation and capturing the attention of other states.

Managed Care

Managed care programs, including HMOs, dominate the private health insurance market. State managed care programs vary widely, but most resemble private health insurance organizations. The states pay health insurance organizations a fixed amount for each person enrolled. These organizations have financial incentives to limit costs, by monitoring patient care, often requiring primary care physicians to obtain permission before referring patients to specialists or before performing specific procedures. The object is to minimize unnecessary care and costs, but, of course, physicians, hospitals, and patients themselves are often frustrated with delays and adverse decisions by outside personnel who have no direct contact with patients. Moreover, overall Medicaid spending continues to rise dramatically.

Interest Group Battles

While there is widespread public support for the general goals of health care reform—expanding coverage and reducing costs—there is no agreement among the principal interest groups on health care politics about the details of reform. *Insurance companies* are unhappy with the notion of health insurance purchasing organizations that would bargain down insurance premiums or even bypass insurance companies and deal directly with hospitals and physicians' groups. *Physicians* strongly oppose price controls and treatment guidelines; they also oppose any program that takes away patient choice of physicians. *Hospitals*, both public and private profit making, oppose

up CLOSE   The Rise and Fall of "TennCare"

In 1994 Tennessee enacted the most comprehensive health care program in the Unites States, even more generous in benefits and broader in coverage than the federal Medicare and Medicaid programs. It expanded health care coverage well beyond Medicaid recipients to include all uninsured children in the state, all medically needy adults with incomes too high for Medicaid, uninsured adults whose preexisting health conditions left them uninsurable, and other adults who did not have access to employer-based insurance. TennCare recipients were not obliged to join HMOs but could choose their own doctors. Virtually all services were covered, from prescription drugs to laboratory and x-ray expenses and even preventative care checkups.

TennCare was a very popular program. Over 22 percent of the state's population—1.3 million people—were enrolled, the highest proportion of any state's population in government-sponsored health care programs.

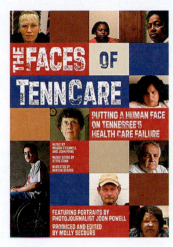

But eventually TennCare's generous benefits and virtually open eligibility led to fiscal crisis. By 2004 the state was spending one-third of its budget on TennCare, depriving education, welfare, highways, and many other state programs of vitally needed dollars. Lawsuits over virtually every aspect of the program added to the crisis. What had begun as a widely praised state health program threatened to bankrupt the state.

In 2005 Governor Phil Bredesen (D) was obliged to announce dramatic reductions in the persons covered by TennCare, as well as significant reduction in the services provided. Over one-third of the beneficiaries were to be dropped from the roles. Moreover, all beneficiaries would be placed in HMOs in an effort to contain costs. The Governor expressed the hope that children in the program would be spared any enrollment or benefit reductions. "We're putting limits into what has been the most generous healthcare program in the nation."[a]

[a]WATE, "TennCare to Be Saved, with Cuts," WATE.com, January 10, 2005; accessed at www.wate.com/global/story.asp?s=2788723&ClientType=Printable, July 15, 2005.

government payment schedules. *Drug companies* want to see prescription drugs paid for by government-sponsored insurance, but they vigorously oppose price controls on drugs. Powerful *senior citizens'* lobbies want added benefits for the aged, including broader coverage for drugs, dental care, and nursing homes, but they oppose folding Medicare into other health care systems. *Opponents and supporters of abortion rights* battle over whether abortion services should be included in taxpayer-paid programs. All of these groups have strong lobbying organizations in state capitals and in Washington, DC, and all have PACs that contribute heavily to state and national political campaigns.

Public assistance (welfare) and health care costs are becoming ever larger slices of state and local government budgets. Generational, gender, and racial divides over how to best address the problem of poverty are on the upswing; so, too, is the divide among the rich, the poor, and the middle class.

State government homepages generally provide direct links to state welfare agencies; these agencies frequently bear names such as "Children and Families," "Human Services," "Health Care," and so on.

The U.S. Department of Health and Human Services (HHS) maintains a Web site at

www.dhhs.gov

It describes in detail all major federal health and welfare programs. Each of these programs has its own Web site linked to that of HHS. Among the more important program sites is that of the Administration for Children and Families (AFC); this is the agency that administers Temporary Assistance for Needy Families (TANF), the federal program that assists states in providing cash welfare aid. Another important site is the Health Care Finance Administration (HCFA), the agency that administers federal-state Medicaid programs.

The Social Security Administration maintains its own Web site at

www.ssa.gov

that not only describes the various benefits available under Social Security, but also provides information on how to apply for old age and disability insurance benefits as well as Medicare. Individuals can also submit a request for their own "Personal Earnings and Benefit Estimate Statement" over the Internet; this uses their personal Social Security account information.

The Children's Defense Fund is perhaps the most influential lobby group in Washington representing the poor. Its Web site at

www.childrensdefense.org

presents arguments in support of increased funding for TANF, in opposition to welfare reform measures that limit benefits, and in support of the expansion of Medicaid to all children. The site also includes statistical information on "Children in the States," with each state separately listed.

NOTES

CHAPTER 1

1. Kim Geron, *Latino Political Power* (Boulder, CO: Lynne Rienner, 2005).

2. Wendy K. Tam Cho and Suneet P. Lad, "Subcontinential Divide: Asian Indians and Asian American Politics," *American Politics Quarterly*, 32 (May 2004): 239–263.

3. "Native American Nations," www.tribal-institute.org/lists/nations.htm, accessed May 10, 2005; U.S. Census Bureau, "The American Indian and Alaska Native Population: 2000," Census 2000 Brief, February 2002.

4. *Plyer v. Doe*, 457 US 202 (1982).4. American Security Council, *The Illegal Immigration Crisis* (Washington, DC: ASC, 1994).

5. For a debate over how to measure a state's ideology and whether it changes, see a series of articles in *State Politics & Policy Quarterly* 7 (2) (Summer 2007): 111–166.

6. Virginia Gray, "The Socioeconomic and Political Context of States," in Virginia Gray and Russell L. Hanson, eds., *Politics in the American States: A Comparative Analysis*, 8th ed. (Washington, DC: CQ Press, 2004), 1–30.

7. Robert S. Erikson, John P. McIver, and Gerald C. Wright, "State Political Culture and Public Opinion," *American Political Science Review* 81 (September 1987): 797–813. The most conservative state in terms of voter self-identification was Utah, followed by Indiana. The most liberal states were Massachusetts, New York, and New Jersey.

8. 2004 presidential exit poll—National Election Pool (or NEP) Exit Poll, conducted by Edison/Mitofsky, November 2004 (available at http://www.cnn.com/ELECTION/2004/pages/results/states/US/P/00/epolls.0.html).

9. Gerald C. Wright, Robert S. Erikson, and John P. McIver, "Public Opinion and Policy Liberalism in the American States," *American Journal of Political Science*, 31 (November 1987): 980–1001. See also William D. Berry et al., "Measuring Citizen and Government Ideology in the American States," *American Journal of Political Science* 42 (January 1998): 327–348.

10. Daniel Elazar, *American Federalism: A View from the States* (New York: Thomas Y. Crowell, 1966). For a well-developed theory of America's political subcultures, ethnic migrations, and generational changes, see Daniel Elazar, *The American Mosaic* (Boulder, CO: Westview Press, 1994).

11. See Kenneth D. Wald, *Religion and Politics in the United States*, 4th ed. (New York: Rowman and Littlefield, 2003).

12. John C. Green, *The American Religious Landscape and Political Attitudes: A Baseline for 2004*, The Pew Research Forum on Religion and Public Life, accessed at http://pewforum.org/publications/surveys/green-full.pdf. The Pew Forum on Religion and Public Life, "A Faith-Based Partisan Divide" (Washington, DC: Pew Research Center, 2005).

13. Linda Lyons, "U.S. Government: Champion of Traditional Values?" The Gallup Organization, November 9, 2004; Pew Research Center, "Politics and Values in a 51%–48% Nation," *Trends 2005*, press release, January 24, 2005.

14. Alexander Hamilton, *The Federalist*, Number 43.

15. For further reading on U.S. territories, see Pedro A. Malavet, *America's Colony: The Political and Cultural Conflict Between the United States and Puerto Rico* (New York: New York University Press, 2004); Arnold H. Leibowitz, *Defining Status: A Comprehensive Analysis of United States Territorial Possessions* (New York: Springer Publishing Company, 1989).

CHAPTER 2

1. Bil's Blog, November 1, 2004.

2. See Bruce E. Cain and Roger G. Noll (eds.), *Constitutional Reform in California* (Berkeley, CA: Institute of Governmental Studies, 1995).

3. For a history of the initiative, see Joseph F. Zimmerman, *The Initiative: Citizen Law-Making* (Westport, CT: Praeger, 1999).

4. See Richard Hofstadter, *The Age of Reform* (New York: Knopf, 1955).

5. For a balanced summary and evaluation of direct democracy, see Thomas E. Cronin, *Direct Democracy: The Politics of Initiative, Referendum and Recall* (Cambridge, MA: Harvard University Press, 1989).

6. Ibid., p. 227.

7. Rasmussen Research poll, March 3, 1998; see also John R. Hibbing and Elizabeth Thiess-Morse, "Policy Preferences and American Politics," *American Political Science Review* 95 (March 2001): 145–153.

8. Alan Rosenthal, *The Decline of Representative Democracy* (Washington, DC: Congressional Quarterly Press, 1998), 337.

9. Daniel A. Smith, "Initiatives and Referendums: The Effects of Direct Democracy on Candidate Elections," paper presented at the Graduate Program in Political Campaigning, University of Florida, Gainesville, February 24–25, 2005.

10. Susan B. Hansen, *The Politics of Taxation* (New York: Praeger, 1983).

11. Jerry Seper, "Arizona Initiative Inspires Others," *The Washington Times*, November 10, 2004.

12. The U.S. Supreme Court has held that a state may not prohibit financial payments for the circulation of petitions. *Meger v. Grant*, 486 U.S. 414 (1988).

13. Frederick J. Boehmke, "Sources of Variation in the Frequency of Statewide Initiatives: The Role of Interest Group Populations," *Political Research Quarterly* 58 (4) (December 2005): 565–576; Shaun Bowler and Robert Hanneman, "Just How Pluralist is Direct Democracy? The Structure of Interest Group Participation in Ballot Proposition Elections," *Political Research Quarterly* 59 (4) (December 2006): 557–568.

14. Council of State Governments, *The Book of the States, 1994–95*, p. 286.

15. Kellyanne Conway, president and CEO of the Polling Company, quoted in Elizabeth Fulk, "State Ballot Initiatives May Play Large Role in '04 Elections; Candidates Ignore Them 'at their own peril,' Pollster Says," *The Hill* (September 23, 2004), accessed at www.thehill.com/news/092304/ballot.aspx.

16. Stephen Nicholson, *Voting the Agenda: Candidates, Elections, and Ballot Propositions* (Princeton, NJ: Princeton University Press, 2005).

17. Political consultant David Hill quoted in Elizabeth Fulk, "State Ballot Initiatives May Play Large Role in '04 Elections; Candidates Ignore Them 'at their own peril,' Pollster Says," *The Hill* (September 23, 2004), accessed at www.thehill.com/news/092304/ballot.aspx.

18. Caroline Tolbert, Ramona McNeal, and Daniel A. Smith, "Enhancing Civic Engagement: The Effect of Direct Democracy on Political Participation and Knowledge," *State Politics & Policy Quarterly* 3 (2003): 23–41; Todd Donovan and Daniel A. Smith, "Turning On and Turning Out: Assessing the Indirect Effects of Ballot Measures on Voter Participation," paper presented at the Conference on State Politics and Policy, Kent State University, Kent, OH, April 30–May 2, 2004; Robert J. Lacey, "The Electoral Allure of Direct Democracy: The Effect of Initiative Salience on Voting, 1990–96," *State Politics & Policy Quarterly* 5(2) (Summer 2005):168–181.

19. Elizabeth A. Gerber, "Legislative Response to the Threat of Popular Initiatives," *American Journal of Political Science*, 40 (February 1996): 99–128. However, for evidence that public policy and public opinion are no closer in initiative states than noninitiative states (i.e., for evidence that initiative states are no more "responsive" than noninitiative states), see Edward L. Lascher, Jr. et al., "Gun Behind the Door? Ballot Initiatives, State Politics and Public Opinion," *Journal of Politics* 58 (August 1996): 760–775.

20. Rasmussen Research, March 3, 1998.

21. *Bates* v. *Jones*, U.S. Ninth Circuit Court of Appeals, December 1997.

22. *Bates* v. *Jones*, U.S. Supreme Court, March 23, 1998.

23. Quotation from *U.S. Term Limits* v. *Thornton* (1995).

24. National Conference of State Legislatures, "NCSL's Online Term Limits Poll," November 2000.

CHAPTER 3

1. Other definitions of federalism in American political science include, "Federalism refers to a political system in which there are local (territorial, regional, provincial, state, or municipal) units of government as well as a national government, that can make final decisions with respect to at least some governmental authorities and whose existence is especially protected." James Q. Wilson, *American Government*, 4th ed. (Lexington, MA: D.C. Heath, 1989), 47; "Federalism is the mode of political organization that unites smaller polities within an overarching political system by distributing power among general and constituent units in a manner designed to protect the existence and authority of both national and subnational systems enabling all to share in the overall system's decision-making and executing processes." Daniel J. Elazar, *American Federalism: A View from the States* (New York: Thomas Y. Crowell, 1966), 2.

2. James Madison, Alexander Hamilton, and John Jay, *The Federalist*, Number 51 (New York: Modern Library, 1958).

3. David Osborne, *Laboratories of Democracy* (Cambridge, MA: Harvard Business School, 1988).

4. The arguments for "competitive federalism" are developed at length in Thomas R. Dye, *American Federalism: Competition Among Governments* (Lexington, MA: Lexington Books, 1990). The book argues that competitive decentralized government has many advantages over centralized "monopoly" governments: greater overall responsiveness to citizen preferences; incentives for government to become efficient and provide quality services at the lowest costs; restraints on the overall burdens of taxation and nonproportional taxes; encouragement of economic growth; and innovation in policies designed to improve the well-being of citizens.

5. For conflicting arguments, see Paul E. Peterson and Mark C. Rom, *Welfare Magnets* (Washington, DC: Brookings Institution, 1990); Scott W. Allard and Sheldon Danzinger, "Welfare Magnets: Myth or Reality?" *Journal of Politics* 62 (May 2000): 350–368; Robert R. Preuhs, "State Policy Components of Interstate Migration in the States," *Political Research Quarterly* 52 (September 1999): 527–549; Robert C. Lieberman and Greg M. Shaw, "Looking Inward, Looking Outward: The Politics of State Welfare Innovation under Devolution," *Political Research Quarterly* 52 (June 2000): 215–240.

6. *Texas* v. *White*, 7 Wallace 700 (1869).

7. See Val Burris, "Who Opposed the ERA? An Analysis of the Social Basis for Antifeminism," *Social Science Quarterly* 64 (June 1983): 305–317.

8. See Ruth Ann Strikland, "The Twenty-Seventh Amendment and Constitutional Change by Stealth," *P.S. Political Science and Politics* 26 (December 1993): 716–722.

9. *Massachusetts* v. *Mellon* 262 U.S. 447 (1923).

10. See Daniel J. Elazar, *The American Partnership: Inter-Governmental Cooperation in Nineteenth-Century United States* (Chicago: University of Chicago Press, 1962).

11. Robert M. Stein, "The Allocation of Federal Aid Monies: The Synthesis of Demand-Side and Supply-Side Explanations," *American Political Science Review* 75 (June 1981): 334–343.

12. John Kincaid, "Trends in Federalism: Continuity, Change and Polarization," in *The Book of the States*, 2004 edition, Vol. 36 (Lexington, KY: The Council of State Governments, 2004), 21–27.

13. Edwin Benton, "George W. Bush's Federal Aid Legacy," *Publius: The Journal of Federalism* 37 (3) (Summer 2007): 371–389.

14. Morton Grodzins, *The American System* (Chicago: Rand McNally, 1966), 8–9.

15. Ibid., p. 265.

16. Charles Press, *State and Community Governments in the Federal System* (New York: John Wiley, 1979), 78.

17. *Garcia* v. *San Antonio Metropolitan Transit Authority* 469 U.S. 528 (1985).

18. *Gregory* v. *Ashcraft*, 11 S. Ct. 2395 (1991).

19. *Tarbels Case*, 13 Wall. 397 (1872). Also cited and discussed in Deil S. Wright, *Understanding Intergovernmental Relations* (Boston: Duxbury Press, 1978), p. 22.

20. Paul Posner, "The Politics of Coercive Federalism in the Bush Era," *Publius: The Journal of Federalism* 37 (3) (Summer 2007): 390–412. Tim Conlan and John Dinan, "Federalism, the Bush Administration, and the Transformation of American Conservatism." *Publius: The Journal of Federalism* 37 (3) (Summer 2007): 279–303.

21. *Pollock* v. *Farmers Loan and Trust Company*, 157 U.S. 429 (1895).

22. *South Carolina* v. *Barker* 485 U.S. 505 (1988).

23. Joseph F. Zimmerman, "The Nature and Political Significance of Preemption," *PS: Political Science and Politics*, 38 (July 2005): 358–362, and "Congressional Preemption: Removal of State Regulatory Powers," pp. 375–378; in the same volume, see also Paul L. Posner, "The Politics of Preemption: Propects for the States," pp. 371–374.

24. John Kincaid, "Trends in Federalism: Continuity, Change and Polarization," in *The Book of the States*, 2004 edition. Vol. 36 (Lexington, KY: The Council of State Governments, 2004), 21–27.

25. See Timothy Conlan, *From New Federalism to Devolution* (Washington, DC: Brookings Institution, 1998).

26. *United States* v. *Lopez* 63 L.W. 4343 (1995).

27. *Puintz* v. *U.S.* 521 U.S. 890 (1997).

28. *Seminole Tribe* v. *Florida* 517 U.S. 44 (1996).

29. *Aldin* v. *Maine*, June 23, 1999.

30. *Nevada Department of Human Resources* v. *Hibbs*, 123 S. Ct. 1972 (2003).

31. *U.S.* v. *Morrison*, May 15, 2000.

32. Ann O'M. Bowman, "Trends and Issues in Interstate Cooperation," in *The Book of the States*, 2004 edition. Vol. 36.

CHAPTER 4

1. Richard Niemi and Michael Hanmer, "College Students in the 2004 Election," Center for Information and Research on Civic Learning and Engagement, November 2004.

2. Lee Sigelman et al., "Voting and Nonvoting: A MultiElection Perspective," *American Journal of Political Science* 29 (November 1985): 749–765.

3. Susan A. MacManus, *Targeting Senior Voters: Campaign Outreach to Elders and Others with Special Needs* (Lanham, MD: Rowman and Littlefield, 2000).

4. Sara E. Helms, "Youth Volunteering in the States: 2002 and 2003," Fact Sheet, Center for Information and Research on Civic Learning and Engagement, August 2004.

5. William H. Riker and Peter C. Ordeshook, "A Theory of the Calculus of Voting," *American Political Science Review* 62 (March 1968): 25–42.

6. J. A. Ferejohn and Morris Fiorina, "The Paradox of Voting," *American Political Science Review* 18 (March 1974): 525–536.

7. Brad T. Gomez, Thomas G. Hansford, and George A. Krause, "The Republicans Should Pray for Rain: Weather, Turnout, and Voting in U.S. Presidential Elections," *The Journal of Politics* 69 (3) (August 2007): 649–663.

8. Joshua J. Dyck and James G. Gimpel, "Distance, Turnout, and the Convenience of Voting," *Social Science Quarterly* 86 (3) (September 2005): 531–549. Moshe Haspel and H. Gibbs Knotts, "Location, Location, Location: Precinct Placement and the Costs of Voting," *Journal of Politics* 67 (2) (May 2005): 560–573.

9. For an excellent review of this literature, see Jan E. Leighley and Arnold Vedlitz, "Race, Ethnicity, and Political Participation: Competing Models and Contrasting Explanations," *Journal of Politics* 61 (November 1999): 1092–1114.

10. James G. Gimpel and Jason E. Schuknecht, "Interstate Migration and Electoral Politics," *Journal of Politics* 63 (February 2001): 207–231.

11. Robert D. Brown, Robert A. Jackson, and Gerald C. Wright, "Registration, Turnout, and State Party Systems," *Political Research Quarterly* 52 (September 1999): 463–479.

12. Douglas L. Kruse, Kay Schriner, Lisa Schur, and Todd Shields, *Empowerment Through Civic Participation: A Study of the Political Behavior of People with Disabilities*, Final Report to the Disability Research Consortium, Bureau of Economic Research, Rutgers University and New Jersey Developmental Disabilities Council, April 1999; Susan A. MacManus, *Targeting Senior Voters*, op. cit.; United States General Accounting Office, *Voters with Disabilities: Access to Polling Places and Alternative Voting Methods* (Washington, DC: GAO), October 2001.

13. Martin P. Wattenberg, "Getting Out the Vote: Half the Nation Stands Still," *Public Perspective* 12 (January/February 2001): 16–17.

14. Wattenberg, "Getting Out the Vote," p. 16. Also see Mary Fitzgerald, "Greater Convenience But Not Greater Turnout: The Impact of Alternative Voting Methods on Electoral Participation in the United States," *American Politics Research* 33 (6) (November 2005): 842–867.

15. See Staci L. Rhine, "Registration Reform and Turnout Change in the American States," *American Politics Quarterly* 23 (October 1995): 409–426; Stephen Knack, "Does Motor-Voter Work? Evidence from State Level Data," *Journal of Politics* 57 (August 1995): 796–811.

16. Benjamin Highton and Raymond E. Wolfiner, "Estimating the Effects of the National Voter Registration Act of 1993," *Political Behavior* 20(2) 1998: 79–104.

17. Brown, Jackson, and Wright, "Registration, Turnout, and State Party Systems," op. cit., p. 477.

18. Raymond E. Wolfinger, Benjamin Highton, and Megan Mullin, "How Postregistration Laws Affect the Turnout of Citizens Registered to Vote," *State Politics & Policy Quarterly* 5 (1) (Spring 2005): 1–23.

19. Samuel C. Patterson and Gregory A. Caldeira, "Getting Out the Vote: Participation in Gubernatorial Elections," *American Political Science Review* 77 (September 1983): 675–689.

20. For excellent analyses of the states' implementation of HAVA, see Sarah F. Liebschutz and Daniel J. Palazzolo, "HAVA and the States," editors of a special issue of *Publius: The Journal of Federalism* 35 (4) (Fall 2005). Daniel J. Palazzolo and Vincent G. Moscardelli, "Policy Crisis and Political Leadership: Election Law Reform in the States after the 2000 Presidential Election," *State Politics & Policy Quarterly* 6 (3) (Fall 2006): 300–321.

21. Warren J. Mitofsky, "Fool Me Twice: An Election Nightmare," *Public Perspective* 12 (May/June 2001): 35–38.

22. Daniel J. Palazzolo and James W. Caesar, eds., *Election Reform: Politics and Policy* (Boulder, CO: Lexington Books, 2005).

23. Election Data Services, "Voting Equipment Summary By Type as of 11/02/2004, August 5, 2004. www .electiondataservices.com.

24. Jim Drinkard, "Push to Replace Voting Machines Spurs Confusion," *USA Today*, May 8, 2005; accessed at www.usatoday .com/news/nation/2005-05-08-votingmachines_x.htm.

25. Laurence Arnold, "Carter-Baker Commission Weighs U.S. Voting Changes (Update 1)," Bloomberg.com, April 18, 2005.

26. Jill E. Fuller, "Equality in Cyberdemocracy? Gauging Gender Gaps in On-Line Civic Participation," *Social Science Quarterly* 85 (December 2004): 938–957.

27. Yvette Alez-Assensoh and A. B. Assensoh, "Inner-City Contexts, Church Attendance, and African-American Political Participation," *Journal of Politics* 63 (August 2001): 886–901; Peter W. Wielhouwer, "Releasing the Fetters: Parties and the Mobilization of the African-American Electorate," *Journal of Politics* 62 (February 2000): 206–222; Avaluara L. Gaither and Eric C. Newburger, *The Emerging American Voter: An Examination of the Increase in the Black Vote in November 1998*, Population Division Working Paper No. 44 (Washington, DC: U.S. Census Bureau): June 2000; Priscilla Southwell and Kevin Pirch, "Defying the National Trend: Rising Voter Turnout Among Blacks," paper presented at the annual meeting of the American Political Science Association, 2001.

28. John R. Arvizu and F. Chris Garcia, "Latino Voting Participation: Explaining and Differentiating Latino Voting Turnout," *Hispanic Journal of Behavioral Sciences* 18 (May 1996): 104–128; Robert A. Jackson, "Latino Electoral Participation," paper presented at the annual meeting of the Southern Political Science Association, 2001; David L. Leal, Matt A. Barreto, Jongho Lee, and Rodolfo O. de la Garza, "The Latino Vote in the 2004 Election," *PS: Political Science and Politics* 38 (1) (January 2005): 41–50.

29. Atiya Kai Stokes-Brown, "Racial Identity and Latino Vote Choice," *American Politics Research* 34 (5) (September 2006): 627–652.

30. Wendy K. Tam Cho, "Naturalization, Socialization, Participation: Immigrants and (Non-) Voting," *Journal of Politics* 61 (November 1999): 1140–1155; Louis DeSipio, "Making Citizens or Good Citizens? Naturalization as a Predictor of Organizational and Electoral Behavior Among Latino Immigrants," *Hispanic Journal of Behavioral Sciences* 18 (May 1996): 194–213.

31. Matt Barreto, Ricardo Ramirez, and Nathan D. Woods, "Are Naturalized Voters Driving the California Latino Electorate? Measuring the Effect of IRCA Citizenship on Latino Voting," *Social Science Quarterly* 86 (4) (December 2005): 792–811; Matt Barreto, "Latino Immigrants at the Polls: Foreign Born Voter Turnout in the 2002 Election," *Political Research Quarterly* 58 (1) (March 2005):79–86.

32. *Voting and Registration in the Election of November 2004* (Washington, DC: U.S. Census Bureau); accessed at http://www .census.gov/population/wwwsocdemo/voting/cps2004.html, May 28, 2005.

33. Paul M. Ong and Don T. Nakanishi, "Becoming Citizens, Becoming Voters: The Naturalization and Political Participation of Asian Pacific Immigrants," in Bill Ong Hing and Ronald Lee, eds., *Reframing the Immigration Debate* (Los Angeles, CA: LEAP Public Policy Institute and UCLA Asian American Studies Center, 1996), 275–305.

34. *Smith* v. *Allright*, 321 U.S. 649 (1944).

35. *Harper* v. *Virginia State Board of Elections*, 383 U.S. 663 (1966).

36. *South Carolina* v. *Katzenbach*, U.S. 301 (1996).

37. United States Department of Justice, Civil Rights Division, Voting Section. "Introduction to Federal Voting Rights Laws." www.usdoj.gov/crt/voting/intro/intro_c.htm, January 18, 2002; Pei-te Lien, Dianne M. Pinderhuges, Carol Hardy-Fanta, and Christine M. Sierra, "The Voting Rights Act and the Election of Nonwhite Officials," *PS: Political Science and Politics* (July 2007): 489–494.

38. Congress had earlier passed the Voting Rights Act of 1970, which (1) extended the vote to eighteen-year-olds regardless of state law; (2) abolished residency requirements in excess of thirty days; and (3) prohibited literacy tests. However, there was some constitutional debate about the power of Congress to change state laws on voting age. While Congress can end *racial* discrimination, extending the vote to eighteen-year-olds was a different matter. All previous extensions of the vote had come by constitutional amendment. Hence, Congress quickly passed the Twenty-Sixth Amendment.

39. *Mobile* v. *Bolden*, 446 U.S. 50 (1980).

40. See Susan A. MacManus, "Racial Representation Issues," *Political Science and Politics* 18 (Fall 1985): 759–769.

41. *Thornburg* v. *Gingles*, 478 U.S. 30 (1986).

42. Kevin A. Hill, "Does the Creation of Majority Black Districts Aid Republicans?" *Journal of Politics* 57 (May 1995): 384–401.

43. *Shaw* v. *Reno* (1993).

44. *Miller* v. *Johnson* (1995).

45. Bernard Grofman and Lisa Handley, "The Impact of the Voting Rights Act on Black Representation in Southern State Legislatures," *Legislative Studies Quarterly* 16 (February 1991): 111–128; Benjamin Radcliff and Martin Saiz, "Race, Turnout, and Public Policy in the States," *Political Research Quarterly* 48 (December 1995): 775–794; Baodong Liu, "Whites as a Minority and the New Racial Coalition in New Orleans and Memphis," *PS: Political Science and Politics* 39

(January 2006) (1): Robert M. Stein, Stacey G. Ulbig, and Stephanie Shirley Post, "Voting for Minority Candidates in Multiracial/Multiethnic Communities," *Urban Affairs Review* 41 (2) (November 2005): 157–181.

46. Phil Tajitsu Nash, "Reaching Out to Asian Americans and Latinos," *Campaigns and Elections* (February 2003): 40–42; Atiya Kai Stokes, "Latino Group Consciousness and Political Participation," *American Politics Research* 31 (July 2003): 361–378.

47. Center for American Women and Politics, "History of Women Governors." January 2007. Available at http://www.cawp.rutgers.edu/Facts/Officeholders/govhistory.pdf.

48. Center for American Women and Politics, "Women In Elective Office 2007." July 2007. Available at http://www.cawp.rutgers.edu/Facts/Officeholders/elective.pdf.

49. Kira Sanbonmatsu, "Gender Pools and Puzzles: Charting a 'Women's Path' to the Legislature," *Politics & Gender* 2 (3) (September 2006): 387–399.

50. Kira Sanbonmatsu, "Do Parties Know That 'Women Win'? Party Leader Beliefs about Women's Electoral Chances," *Politics & Gender* 2 (4) (December 2006): 431–450.

51. Sue Thomas, "The Impact of Women on State Legislative Policies," *Journal of Politics* 53 (November 1991): 958–976. See also Michelle A. Saint-Germain, "Does Their Difference Make a Difference?" *Social Science Quarterly* 70 (December 1989): 956–968; Sue Tolleson-Rinehart and Jyl J. Josephson, eds., *Gender and American Politics*, 2nd ed. (Armonk, NY: M.E. Sharpe, 2005).

52. Lyn Kathlene, "Alternative Views of Crime: Legislative Policymaking in Gendered Terms," *Journal of Politics* 57 (August 1995): 696–723.

53. Susan A. MacManus, *Young vs. Old: Generational Conflict in the 21st Century* (Boulder, CO: Westview Press, 1996), 23.

54. Andrea Louise Campbell, "The Non-distinctiveness of Senior Voters in the 2004 Election," *Public Policy and Aging Report* 15 (Winter 2005): 1, 3–6; Lawrence R. Jacobs and Melanie Burns, "Don't Lump Seniors," *Public Policy and Aging Report* 15 (Winter 2005): 7–9; Susan A. MacManus, "Florida's Senior Voters in Election 2004: Results, Top Issues, Reforms, and New Concerns," *Public Policy and Aging Report* 15 (Winter 2005): 10–13.

55. CIRCLE staff, "Fact Sheet: Youth Voting in the 2004 Election," Center for Information and Research on Civic Learning and Engagement, January 25, 2005.

56. See Benjamin Radcliff and Martin Saiz, "Labor Organization and Public Policy in the American States," *Journal of Politics*, 60 (February 1998): 113–125.

57. Quotations reported in *Tallahassee Democrat*, January 12, 1992.

58. Christopher A. Cooper, Anthony J. Nownes, and Martin Johnson, "Interest Groups and Journalists in the States," *State Politics & Policy Quarterly* 7 (1) (Spring 2007): 39–53.

59. Anthony J. Nownes and Patricia Freeman, "Interest Group Activity in the States," *Journal of Politics* 60 (February 1998): 86–112.

60. See, for example, William Browne, "Variations in the Behavior and Style of State Lobbyists and Interest Groups," *Journal of Politics* 47 (May 1985): 450–468.

61. Quotations from legislators in Lester Milbrath, *The Washington Lobbyists* (Chicago: Rand McNally, 1963), 241–243.

62. Alan J. Cigler and Burdett A. Lomis, *Interest Group Politics*, 4th ed. (Washington, DC: Congressional Quarterly Press, 1995), 395.

63. Nownes and Freeman, "Interest Group Activity."

64. Stacy B. Gordon, "All Votes Are Not Created Equal: Campaign Contributions and Critical Votes," *Journal of Politics* 63 (February 2001): 249.

65. Benjamin Radcliff and Martin Saiz, "Labor Organizations and Public Policy in the American States," *Journal of Politics* 60 (February 1998): 113–125.

66. Robert E. Hogan, "State Campaign Finance Laws and Interest Group Electioneering Activities," *The Journal of Politics* 67 (3) (August 2005): 887–906.

67. Clive S. Thomas and Robert J. Hrebenar, "Interest Groups in the States," in Virginia Gray et al., *Politics in the American States*, 5th ed. (New York: HarperCollins, 1990), 141.

68. Sarah McCally Morehouse, *State Politics, Parties and Policy* (New York: Holt, Rinehart and Winston, 1981), 118.

69. See Charles W. Wiggins, Keith E. Harmun, and Charles G. Bell, "Interest-Group and Party Influence Agents in the Legislative Process: A Comparative State Analysis," *Journal of Politics* 54 (February 1992): 82–100.

70. See Special Issue on the Impact of State Legislative Term Limits, *State Politics & Policy Quarterly* 6 (4) (Winter 2006); Thad Kousser, "The Limited Impact of Term Limits: Contingent Effects on the Complexity and Breadth of Laws," *State Politics & Policy Quarterly* 6 (4) (Winter 2006): 410–429.

71. William Safire, "Netroots," *The New York Times*, November 19, 2006; available at nytimes.com/2006/11/19/magazine/19wwln_safire.html.

72. For an inspiring essay on "nonviolent direct action" and civil disobedience in a modern context, read Martin Luther King, Jr., "Letter from Birmingham City Jail," April 16, 1963.

73. For a more detailed examination of the purposes, functions, and rationale of civil disobedience, see Paul F. Power, "Civil Disobedience as Functional Opposition," *Journal of Politics* 34 (February 1972): 37–55; and "On Civil Disobedience in Recent American Thought," *American Political Science Review* 64 (March 1970): 35–47.

74. Michael Lipsky, *Protest in City Politics* (Chicago: Rand McNally, 1970); Peter K. Eisinger, "The Conditions of Protest Behavior in American Cities," *American Political Science Review* 67 (March 1973): 11–29; Paul D. Schumaker, "Policy Responsiveness to Protest Group Demands," *Journal of Politics* 37 (May 1975): 488–521.

75. Michael Lipsky, "Protest as a Political Resource," *American Political Science Review* 62 (December 1968): 1144–1158.

CHAPTER 5

1. The Pew Research Center for The People and The Press, "The 2005 Political Typology: Beyond Red v. Blue: Republicans Divided About Role of Government—Democrats By Social and Personal Values," May 10, 2005.

2. E. E. Schattschneider, *Party Government* (New York: Rinehart, 1942), 1.

3. John C. Green and Paul S. Herrnson, eds. *Responsible Partisanship? The Evolution of American Political Parties Since 1950* (Lawrence: University Press of Kansas, 2003); John C. Green and Rick Farmer, eds., *The State of the Parties: The Changing Role of Contemporary American Parties*, 4th ed. (Lanham, MD: Rowman & Littlefield, 2003); Gerald M. Pomper, "Parliamentary Government in the United States: A New Regime for a New Century?" in *The State of the Parties*, pp. 267–286.

4. See John F. Bibby, "State and Local Parties in a Candidate-Centered Age," in Robert E. Weber and Paul Brace, *American State and Local Politics* (New York: Chatham House, 1999), pp. 194–212.

5. John F. Bibby and Thomas M. Holbrook, "Parties and Elections," in Virginia Gray and Russell L. Hanson, eds., *Politics in the American States: A Comparative Analysis*, 8th ed. (Washington, DC: CQ Press, 2004), 62.

6. *California Democratic Party et al. v. Jones*, 120 S.Ct. 2402 (2000).

7. See Charles S. Bullock and Loch K. Johnson, "Sex and the Second Primary," *Social Science Quarterly* 66 (December 1985): 933–942.

8. Charles S. Bullock and A. Brock Smith, "Black Success in Local Run-off Elections," *Journal of Politics* 52 (November 1990): 1205–1220.

9. Charles S. Bullock III and Loch Johnson, *Runoff Elections in the United States* (Chapel Hill: University of North Carolina Press, 1992); Joseph Stewart, James F. Sheffield, and Margaret E. Ellis, "The Mechanisms of Runoff Primary Disadvantage," *Social Science Quarterly* 76 (December 1995): 807–822.

10. Robert J. Huckshorn, *Party Leadership in the States* (Amherst: University of Massachusetts Press, 1976), p. 1.

11. Joel Paddock, "Explaining State Variation in Interparty Ideological Differences," *Political Research Quarterly* 51 (September 1981): 765–780.

12. See Harold Clarke, Frank B. Feigert, and Marianne C. Stewart, "Different Contents, Similar Packages: The Domestic Political Beliefs of Southern Local Party Activists," *Political Research Quarterly* 48 (March 1995): 151–167.

13. John F. Bibby, "State and Local Parties in a Candidate Centered Age," in Ronald E. Weber and Paul Brace, *American State and Local Politics* (New York: Chatham House, 1999), p. 209.

14. Huckshorn, *Party Leadership*, p. 46.

15. James L. Gibson et al., "Whither the Local Parties?" *American Journal of Political Science* 29 (February 1985): 139–160.

16. See Steven E. Finkel and Howard A. Scarrow, "Party Identification and Party Enrollment," *Journal of Politics* 47 (May 1985): 624–642.

17. See Kerin M. Leyden and Stephen A. Borrelli, "The Effect of State Economic Conditions on Gubernatorial Elections: Does Unified Government Make a Difference?" *Political Research Quarterly* 48 (June 1995): 275–290.

18. Cynthia J. Bowling and Margaret R. Ferguson, "Divided Government, Interest Representation, and Policy Differences," *Journal of Politics* 63 (February 2001): 182–206.

19. See also Robert D. Brown, "Party Cleavages and Welfare Effort in the American States," *American Political Science Review*, 89 (March 1995): 23–33.

20. Costas Panagopoulos, "Political Consultants, Campaign Professionalizatin, and Media Attention," *PS: Political Science and Politics* 39 (4) (October 2006): 867–870.

21. Judith S. Trent and Robert V. Friedenberg, *Political Campaign Communication*, 5th ed. (Boulder, CO: Rowman & Littlefield, 2004).

22. Todd Meredith, "Open the Envelope: Getting People to Look at the Direct Mail They Receive," *Campaigns and Elections* (December 2004/January 2005): 76.

23. Hal Malchow, "Influencing the Late Deciding Voter," *Campaigns and Elections* (February 2005): 40.

24. Thomas B. Edsall and James V. Grimaldi, "On Nov. 2, GOP Got More Bang for Its Billion, Analysis Shows," *The Washington Post*, December 30, 2004, p. A01.

25. Michael D. Cohen, "Polls as the Key to Victory," *Campaigns and Elections* (July 2004): 35.

26. Matthew A. Baum and Angela S. Jamison, "The Oprah Effect: How Soft News Helps Inattentive Citizens Vote Consistently," *Journal of Politics* 68 (4) (November 2006): 946–959; Markus Prior, "News vs. Entertainment: How Increasing Media Choice Widens Gaps in Political Knowledge and Turnout," *American Journal of Political Science* 49 (3) (July 2005): 577–592.

27. David W. Nickerson, Ryan D. Driedrichs, and David C. King, "Partisan Mobilization Campaigns in the Field: Results from a Statewide Turnout Experiment in Michigan," *Political Research Quarterly* 59 (1) (March 2006): 85–98.

28. Bill Adair, "Steal the Playbook, Democrats," *St. Petersburg Times*, December 5, 2004.

29. Barbara Allen, Daniel P. Stevens, Gregory Marfleet, John Sullivan, and Dean Alger, "Local News and Perceptions of the Rhetoric of Political Advertising," *American Politics Research* 35 (4) (July 2007): 506–540.

30. Pew Research Center, *Trends 2005*, Chapter 5 ("More Voices, Less Credibility"), 2005.

31. Kim L. Fridkin and Patrick J. Kenney, "Do Negative Messages Work? The Impact of Negativity on Citizens' Evaluations of Candidates," *American Politics Research*, 32 (September 2004): 570–605. See also Ted Brader, "Striking a Responsive Chord: How Political Ads Motivate and Persuade Voters by Appealing to Emotions," *American Journal of Political Science* 49 (April 2005): 388–405.

32. Ron Faucheux, "Ask, and You Shall Receive: Seven Fundamentals of Candidate Fund Raising," *Campaigns and Elections* (April 2005): 25.

33. See Sarah M. Morehouse, "Money versus Party Effect: Nominating for Governor," *American Journal of Political Science* 34 (August 1990): 706–724.

34. W. P. Welch, "The Effectiveness of Expenditures in State Legislative Races," *American Politics Quarterly* 4 (July 1976): 333–356.

35. Frank J. Sorauf, *Money in American Elections* (Boston: Scott, Foresman, 1988).

36. Welch, "The Effectiveness of Expenditures."

37. Larry Sabato, *Goodbye to Good-Time Charlie*, 2nd ed. (Washington, DC: Congressional Quarterly Press, 1983), 152.

38. Michael J. Malbin, *Money and Politics in the United States* (Washington, DC: American Enterprise Institute, 1984).

39. Ruth S. Jones and Anne H. Hopkins, "State Campaign Fund Raising," *Journal of Politics* 47 (May 1985): 427–449.

40. Thad Beyle, "Governors, Elections, Campaign Costs, Profiles, Forced Exits and Powers," in *The Book of the States 2004*. (Lexington, KY: Council of State Governments, 2004), 145–156.

41. Thad Kousser, "The California Governor's Recall," in *The Book of the States 2004* (Lexington, KY: Council of State Governments, 2004), 308.

42. Sid Salter, "$40 Mil in Campaign Finance for this Junk?" *The Clarion-Ledger*, April 24, 2005.

43. "Campaign Finance: Why States Regulate Money in Elections," National Conference of State Legislatures, available at http://ncsl.org/programs/legman/about/campfin.htm.

44. *Buckley* v. *Valeo* 424 U.S. 1 (1976).

45. *McConnell* v. *Federal Elections Commission* 540 U.S. 93 (2003).

46. *Federal Elections Commission* v. *Wisconsin Right to Life*, June 25, 2007.

47. *Randall* v. Sorrell, June 26, 2006.

48. Jennifer Drage, "Do Campaign Finance Laws Make a Difference?" *State Legislatures* 26 (September, 2000): 25.

49. Joseph E. Sandler and Neil P. Reiff, "New Campaign Finance Rules and the 2004 Elections," *Campaigns and Elections* (February 2005): 35–36.

CHAPTER 6

1. *Tampa Tribune*, July 27, 1987.

2. National Conference of State Legislatures, "Legislator Demographics," accessed at http://ncsl.org/programs/legman/about/demographic_overview.htm, May 30, 2005.

3. See Paul J. Hain and James E. Pierson, "Lawyers and Politics Revisited: Structural Advantages of Lawyer-Politicians," *American Journal of Political Science* 19 (February 1975): 41–51.

4. Wayne L. Francis, "Costs and Benefits of Legislative Service in the American States," *American Journal of Political Science* 29 (August 1985): 626–642.

5. Karl T. Kurtz, Gary Moncrief, Richard G. Niemi, and Lynda W. Powell, "Full-Time, Part-Time, and Real Time: Explaining State Legislators' Perceptions of Time on the Job," *State Politics & Policy Quarterly* 6 (3) (Fall 2006): 322–338.

6. Minority statistics (as of January 2006) are from Pei-te Lien, Dianne M. Pinderhuges, Carol Hardy-Fanta, and Christine M. Sierra, "The Voting Rights Act and the Election of Nonwhite Officials," *PS: Political Science and Politics* (July 2007): 489–494; statistics on women (2007) are from the Center For American Women and Politics, "Women Officeholders Fact Sheets and Summaries," www.cawp.rutgers.edu/Facts.html.

7. Byron D'Andra Orey, L. Marvin Overby, and Christopher W. Larimer, "African-American Committee Chairs in U.S. State Legislatures," *Social Science Quarterly* 88 (3) (September 2007): 619–639; Robert R. Preuhs, "The Conditional Effects of Minority Descriptive Representation: Black Legislators and Policy Influence in the American States," *The Journal of Politics* 68 (3) (August 2006): 585–599.

8. Mary Herring, "Legislative Responsiveness to Black Constituents in Three Southern States," *Journal of Politics* 52 (August 1990): 740–758; for a report on the differing experiences of black legislators, see David Hedge, James Button, and Mary Spear, "Accounting for the Quality of Black Legislative Life," *American Journal of Political Science* 40 (February 1996): 82–98. See also Kerry L. Haynie, *African American Legislators in the American States* (New York: Columbia University Press, 2001).

9. Data are from the Gender and Multi-Cultural Leadership (GMCL) Project as reported in Pei-te Lien, Dianne M. Pinderhuges, Carol Hardy-Fanta, and Christine M. Sierra, "The Voting Rights Act and the Election of Nonwhite Officials," *PS: Political Science and Politics* (July 2007): 489–494.

10. See Emmy F. Werner, "Women in State Legislatures," *Western Political Quarterly* 21 (March 1968): 40–50; Paula J. Dubeck, "Women and Access to Political Office," *Sociological Quarterly* 17 (March 1976): 42–52; Susan Welch, "The Recruitment of Women to Public Office," *Western Political Quarterly* 19 (June 1978): 372–380.

11. Wilma Rule, "Why More Women Are State Legislators," *Western Political Quarterly* 43 (June 1990): 437–448.

12. Sue Vandenbosch, "A Negative Relationship Between Religion and the Percentage of Women State Legislators in the United States," *Journal of Legislative Studies* 2 (Winter 1996): 322–338.

13. Susan A. MacManus, Charles S. Bullock III, Karen Padgett, and Brittany Penberthy, "Women Winning At the Local Level: Are County and School Board Positions Becoming More Desirable and Plugging the Pipeline to Higher Office?" in Lois Duke Whitaker, ed. *Women in Politics*, 4th ed. (Upper Saddle River, NJ: Prentice Hall, 2005); see also H. W. Jerome Maddox, "Opportunity Costs and Outside Careers in U.S. State Legislatures," *Legislative Studies Quarterly* 29 (November 2004): 517–544.

14. Susan Welch et al., "The Effect of Gender on Electoral Outcomes in State Legislative Races," *Western Political Quarterly* 38 (September 1985): 464–475.

15. Susan Welch and Lee Sigelman, "Changes in Public Attitudes Toward Women in Politics," *Social Science Quarterly* 63 (June 1982): 321–322.

16. David Niven, "Throwing Your Hat Out of the Ring: Negative Recruitment and the Gender Imbalance in State Legislative Candidacy," *Politics & Gender* 2 (4) (December 2006): 473–491.

17. Virginia Sapiro, "Private Costs of Public Commitments: Family Roles versus Political Ambition," *American Journal of Political Science* 26 (May 1982): 265–279.

18. Carol Nechemias, "Geographic Mobility and Women's Access to State Legislatures," *Western Political Quarterly* 38 (March 1985): 119–131.

19. Kevin Arceneaux, "The Gender Gap in State Legislature Representation," *Political Research Quarterly* 54 (March 2000): 143–160.

20. Lesley Dahlkemper, "Growing Accustomed to Her Face," *State Legislatures* (July/August 1996): 37–45.

21. R. Darcy, "Women in the State Legislative Power Structure," *Social Science Quarterly* 77 (December 1996): 888–898.

22. Sue Thomas, *How Women Legislate* (New York: Oxford University Press, 1994).

23. Lyn Kathlene, "Power and Influence in State Legislative Policymaking: The Interaction of Gender and Position in Committee Hearing Debates," *American Political Science Review* 88 (September 1994): 560–576.

24. Michelle Swers, "Understanding the Policy Impact of Electing Women," *PS Political Science* 34 (June 2001): 217–220. See also Beth Reingold, *Representing Women: Sex, Gender, and Legislative Behavior in Arizona and California* (Chapel Hill: University of North Carolina Press, 2000). Kathleen A. Bratton and Kerry L. Haynie, "Agenda Setting and Legislative Success in State Legislatures," *Journal of Politics* 61 (August 1999): 658–679.

25. Beth Reingold, *Representing Women*, op. cit.

26. Zach Patton, "Chasing the Shadow," *Governing* 19 (9) (June 2006): 43–45.

27. Alan E. Wiseman, "Partisan Strategy and Support in State Legislative Elections: The Case of Illinois," *American Politics Research* 33 (3) (May 2005): 376–403.

28. Robert E. Hogan, "Sources of Competition in State Legislative Primary Elections," *Legislative Studies Quarterly* 28 (February 2003): 103–126.

29. Ronald E. Weber, "The Quality of State Legislative Representation," *Journal of Politics* 61 (August 1999): 609–627.

30. David Ray and John Havick, "A Longitudinal Analysis of Party Competition in State Legislative Elections," *American Journal of Political Science* 25 (February 1981): 119–128.

31. Ronald Weber, Harvey Tucker, and Paul Brace, "Vanishing Marginals in State Legislative Elections," *Legislative Studies Quarterly* 16 (February 1991): 29–47.

32. Alan Abramowitz, "Don't Blame Redistricting for Uncompetitive Elections," *Sabato's Crystal Ball*, 111 (10), accessed at http://www.centerforpolitics.org/crystalball, May 26, 2005.

33. Malcolm E. Jewell, "State Legislative Elections," *American Politics Quarterly* 22 (October 1994): 483–509.

34. Emily Van Dunk, "Challenger Quality in State Legislative Elections," *Political Research Quarterly* 50 (December 1997): 793–807.

35. Quotations of legislators from William J. Keefe and Morris S. Ogul, *The American Legislative Process: Congress and the States*, 8th ed. (Englewood Cliffs, NJ: Prentice Hall, 1993).

36. William B. Berry, Michael B. Berkman, and Stewart Schneiderman, "Legislative Professionalism and Incumbent Reelection," *American Political Science Review* 94 (December 2000): 859–874.

37. Jennifer A. Steen, "The Impact of State Legislative Term Limits on the Supply of Congressional Candidates," *State Politics & Policy Quarterly* 6 (4) (Winter 2006): 430–447.

38. Michael Berkman and James Eisenstein, "State Legislators as Congressional Candidates," *Political Research Quarterly* 52 (September 1999): 481–498.

39. H. W. Jerome Maddox, "Opportunity Costs and Outside Careers in U.S. State Legislatures," *Legislative Studies Quarterly* 29 (November 2004): 517–544. He concludes that the prevalence of outside careers declines as legislative salary increases, regardless of party, education, or sex.

40. Richard A. Clucas, "Legislative Professionalism and the Power of State House Leaders," *State Politics & Policy Quarterly* 7 (1) (Spring 2007): 1–19.

41. Alan Rosenthal, *Governors and Legislatures* (Washington, DC: CQ Press, 1990), 63.

42. For a comprehensive look at the ins-and-outs of redistricting, see the series of articles published in *PS: Political Science and Politics* 39 (1) (January 2006).

43. *Baker* v. *Carr*, 369 U.S. 186 (1962).

44. *Reynold* v. *Sims*, 84 S. Ct. 1362 (1964).

45. *Wesberry* v. *Sanders*, 84 S. Ct. 526 (1964).

46. *Gray* v. *Sanders*, 83 S. Ct. 801 (1963), p. 809.

47. *Karchev* v. *Daggett*, 462 U.S. 725 (1983).

48. *Brown* v. *Thompson*, 462 U.S. 835 (1983).

49. For an excellent discussion of the issues and rulings, see National Conference of State Legislatures, "Shifting Sands of Redistricting Law," 2005, accessed at http://www.ncsl.org/programs/legman/elect/law-article.htm, May 30, 2005.

50. Kevin B. Smith, Alan Greenblatt, and John Buntin, *Governing States and Localities* (Washington, DC: CQ Press, 2005), 193.

51. *Davis* v. *Bandemer*, 106 S. Ct. 2797 (1986).

52. Charles Backstrom, Samuel Krislov, and Leonard Robins, "Desperately Seeking Standards: The Court's Frustrating Attempts to Limit Political Gerrymandering." *PS: Political Sicence and Politics* 39 (3) (July 2006): 409–416.

53. *Vieth* v. *Jubelirer*, 241 F. Supp. 2d 478 (2004).

54. See Harry Basehart, "The Seats/Vote Relationship and the Identification of Partisan Gerrymandering in State Legislature," *American Politics Quarterly*, 15 (October 1987): 484–498. See

also Gerard S. Gryski, Bruce Reed, and Euel Elliot, "The Seats–Vote Relationship in State Legislative Elections," *American Politics Quarterly*, 18 (April 1990): 141–157, for an estimate of bias for each state prior to 1990 redistricting.

55. *Davis* v. *Bandemer*, 106 S. Ct. 2797 (1986).

56. *Fortson* v. *Dorsey*, 179 U.S. 433 (1965).

57. *Thornburg* v. *Gingles*, 478 U.S. 30 (1986).

58. *Hunt* v. *Cromartie*, 532 U.S. 234 (2001).

59. Taren Stinebrickner-Kauffman, "The Prison Effect on Political Landscape," *The Christian Science Monitor*, May 17, 2004; accessed at http://www.csmonitor.com/2004/0517/p09s02-coop .htm, May 28, 2005; see also Peter Wagner, "Importing Constituents: Prisoners and Political Clout in New York," *Prison Policy Initiative*, April 22, 2002.

60. *Connor* v. *Johnson*, 407 U.S. 640 (1971).

61. *White* v. *Regester*, 412 U.S. 755 (1973).

62. See Harry Basehart and John Comer, "Redistricting and Incumbent Reelection in State Legislatures," *American Politics Quarterly* 23 (April 1995): 241–253.

63. Alan Abramowitz, "Don't Blame Redistricting for Uncompetitive Elections," *Sabato's Crystal Ball*, 111(10), accessed at http://www.centerforpolitics.org/crystalball, May 26, 2005.

64. National Conference of State Legislatures, "Shifting Sands of Redistricting Law," 2005, accessed at http://www .ncsl.org/programs/legman/elect/law-article.htm, May 30, 2005.

65. Harvey J. Tucker, "Legislative Logjams: A Comparative State Analysis," *Western Political Quarterly* 38 (September 1985): 432–446.

66. The "institutionalization" theme was first developed to understand changes in the U.S. House of Representatives by Nelson Polsby, "The Institutionalization of the U.S. House of Representatives," *American Political Science Review* 62 (March 1968): 144–168.

67. Peverill Squire, "Measuring State Legislative Professionalism: The Squire Index Revisited," *State Politics & Policy Quarterly* 7 (2) (Summer 2007): 211–227.

68. Neal D. Woods and Michale Baranowski, "Legislative Professionalism and Influence on State Agencies," *Legislative Studies Quarterly* 31 (4) (November 2006): 585–610. Neil Malhotra, "Government Growth and Professionalism in U.S. State Legislatures," *Legislative Studies Quarterly* 31 (4) (November 2006): 563–584.

69. William D. Berry, Michael B. Berkman, and Stuart Schneiderman, "Legislative Professionalism and Incumbent Reflection," *American Political Science Review* 94 (December 2000): 859–865.

70. Alan Rosenthal, *Governors and Legislatures: Contending Powers* (Washington, DC: CQ Press, 1990), 63.

71. Kim U. Hoffman, "Legislative Fiscal Analysts: Influence in State Budget Development," *State and Local Government Review* 38 (1) (2006): 41–51.

72. For a good overview of a job description for a legislative staffer, see "Career Prospects in Virginia: Legislative Staffers," April 7, 2005, accessed at http://www.careerprospects.org/ briefs/Print/K-O/LegislativeStaff.shtml, May 28, 2005.

73. James Coleman Battista, "Committee Theories and Committee Votes: Internal Committee Behavior in the California Legislature," *State Politics & Policy Quarterly* 6 (2) (Summer 2006): 117–150.

74. L. Marvin Overby and Thomas A. Kazee, "Outlying Committees in the Statehouse," *Journal of Politics* 62 (August 2000): 701–728; L. Marvin Overby, Thomas A. Kazee, and David W. Prince, "Committee Outliers in State Legislatures," *Legislative Studies Quarterly* 29 (February 2004): 81–108.

75. Keith E. Hamm, Ronald D. Hedlund, and Nancy Martorano, "Measuring State Legislative Committee Power: Change and Chamber Differences in the 20th Century," *State Politics & Policy Quarterly* 6 (1) (Spring 2006): 88–111.

76. Thomas H. Little, "A Systematic Analysis of Members' Environments and Their Expectations of Elected Leaders," *Political Research Quarterly* 47 (September 1994): 733–747.

77. National Conference of State Legislatures, *State Legislative Priorities* (Denver: NCSL, 1995, 2005).

78. Christopher A. Cooper and Lilliard E. Richardson, Jr., "Institutions and Representational Roles in American State Legislatures," *State Politics & Policy Quarterly* 6 (2) (Summer 2006): 174–194.

79. Hanna Pitkin, *The Concept of Representation* (Berkeley: University of California Press, 1967), 154.

80. Ronald D. Hedlund and H. Paul Friesma, "Representatives' Perceptions of Constituency Opinion," *Journal of Politics* 34 (August 1971): 730–752.

81. Robert S. Erikson, Norman R. Luttbeg, and William V. Holloway, "Knowing One's District: How Legislators Predict Referendum Voting," *American Journal of Political Science* 19 (May 1975): 231–241.

82. John M. Carey, Richard G. Niemi, Lynda W. Powell, and Gary F. Moncrief, "The Effects of Term Limits on State Legislatures: A New Survey of the 50 States," *Legislative Studies Quarterly* 31 (1) (February 2006): 105–134.

83. D. E. Appollonio and Raymond J. La Raja, "Term Limits, Campaign Contributions, and the Distribution of Power in State Legislatures," *Legislative Studies Quarterly* 31 (2) (May 2006): 259–282.

84. Marjorie Sarbaugh-Thompson, Lyke Thompson, Charles D. Elder, Meg Comins, Ricahred C. Elling, and John Strate, "Democracy Among Strangers: Term Limits' Effects on Relationships Between State Legislators in Michigan," *State Politics & Policy Quarterly* 6 (4) (Winter 2006): 384–409.

85. Thad Kousser, "The Limited Impact of Term Limits: Contingent Effects on the Complexity and Breadth of Laws," *State Politics & Policy Quarterly* 6 (4) (Winter 2006): 410–429.

86. Rebekah Herrick and Sue Thomas, "Do Term Limits Make a Difference?" *American Politics Research* 33 (3) (September 2005): 726–747.

87. William M. Salka, "Term Limits and Electoral Competition: An Analysis of California Legislative Races," *State and Local Government Review* 37 (2) (2005): 116–127.

88. Jeffrey Lazarus, "Term Limits' Multiple Effects on State Legislators' Career Decisions," *State Politics & Policy Quarterly* 6 (4) (Winter 2006): 357–383

89. Lilliard E. Richardson, Jr., David Valentine, and Shannon Daily Stokes, "Assessing the Impact of Term Limits in Missouri," *State and Local Government Review* 17 (1) (2005): 177–192. Scot Schraufnagel and Karen Halperin, "Term Limits, Electoral Competition, and Representational Diversity: The Case of Florida," *State Politics & Policy Quarterly* 6 (4) (Winter 2006): 448–462.

90. National Conference of State Legislatures, "Ethics Issues Overview," 2005, accessed at http://ncsl.org/programs/ethics/overview_ethics.htm, May 27, 2005.

91. Beth A. Rosenson, "The Impact of Ethics Laws on Legislative Recruitment and the Occupational Composition of State Legislatures," *Political Research Quarterly* 59 (4) (December 2006): 619–628.

92. See Robert Harmel and Keith E. Hamm, "Development of a Party Role in a No-Party Legislature," *Western Political Quarterly*, 39 (March 1986): 79–92. See also Cole Blease Graham and Kenny J. Whitby, "Party-Based Voting in a Southern State Legislature," *American Politics Quarterly* 17 (April 1989): 181–193.

93. Christopher A. Cooper, "Media Tactics in the State Legislature," *State Politics & Policy Quarterly* 2 (Winter 2002): 353–371.

94. Nicole Casal Moore, "Adversaries Always," *State Legislatures* 31 (May 2005): 21.

95. Ibid.

96. The Irrigation Association, "State Lobbying: Vital For Our Industry and Your Livelihood," *The Irrigation Association Statesman* (September/October, 2002): 1–2.

97. Ibid.

98. Christopher A. Mooney, "Peddling Information in the State Legislature: Closeness Counts," *Western Political Quarterly* 44 (June 1991): 433–444.

99. Harmon Zeigler and Michael A. Baer, *Lobbying: Interaction and Influence in American State Legislatures* (Belmont, CA: Wadsworth, 1969), 107.

100. Ibid.

101. Mary Ellen Klas, "Special-Interest Ties Persist," *The Miami Herald*, May 22, 2005, accessed at http://www.miami.com/mld/miamiherald/news11705823.htm, May 28, 2005.

102. Robert Morlino and Leah Rush, "Hired Guns: Lobbyists Spend Loads of Money to Influence Legislators—And In Many States, With Too Little Scrutiny," May 15, 2003, accessed at http://www.publicintegrity.org/hiredguns/printer-friendly.aspx?aid=165, May 31, 2005.

103. Cynthia Opheim, "Explaining the Differences in State Lobbying Regulation," *Western Political Quarterly* 44 (June 1991): 405–421.

104. Kevin Bogardus, "Statehouse Revolvers," Public Integrity .com, October 12, 2006; available at http://publicintegrity.org/hiredguns/report.aspx?aid=747.

105. William Keefe, "Reform and the American Legislature." In Donald Herzberg and Alan Rosenthal, eds. *Strengthening the States: Essays on Legislative Reform*. New York: Doubleday & Co., 1971:190.

106. Alan Rosenthal, *The Decline of Representative Democracy: Process, Participation, and Power in State Legislatures*. Washington, DC: CQ Press, 1997.

107. Ronald E. Weber, "The Quality of State Legislative Representation," *Journal of Politics* 61 (August 1999): 609–627.

CHAPTER 7

1. Charles Howe, "Animal House," *The Wall Street Journal*, April 14, 2005; accessed at http://online.wsj.com/article_print/0,,SB111344065143306651,00.html, April 14, 2005.

2. Greg D. Adams and Peverill Squire, "A Note on the Dynamics and Idiosyncrasies of Gubernatorial Popularity," *State Politics and Policy Quarterly* (Winter 2001): 380; See also Robert E. Crew, Jr., David Branham, Gregory R. Weiher, and Ethan Bernick, "Political Events in a Model of Gubernatorial Approval," *State Politics & Policy Quarterly* 2 (Fall 2002): 283–297; Jay Barth and Margaret R. Ferguson, "American Governors and Their Constituents: The Relationship Between Gubernatorial Personality and Public Approval," *State Politics & Policy Quarterly* 2 (Fall 2002): 268–282.

3. Sarah McCally Morehouse, *The Governor and Party Leader* (Ann Arbor: University of Michigan Press, 1998).

4. Steve L. B. Lem and Conor M. Dowling, "Picking Their Spots: Minor Party Candidates in Gubernatorial Elections," *Political Research Quarterly* 59 (September 2000): 471–480.

5. John A. Hamman, "Career Experience and Performing Effectively as Governor," *American Review of Public Administration* 34 (June 2004): 151–163.

6. Thad Beyle, "The Governors," in Virginia Gray and Russell L. Hanson, eds., *Politics in the American States: A Comparative Analysis*, 8th ed. (Washington, DC: CQ Press, 2004), 194–231.

7. See Robert M. Stein, "Economic Voting for Governor and U.S. Senator," *Journal of Politics* 52 (February 1990): 29–53.

8. Susan B. Hansen, "Life Is Not Fair: Governors' Job Performance Ratings and State Economies." *Political Research Quarterly* 52 (March 1999): 167–188.

9. Daniel Coffey, "Measuring Gubernatorial Ideology: A Content Analysis of State of the State Speeches," *State Politics & Policy Quarterly* 5 (Spring 2005): 97.

10. John E. Chubb, "Institutions, the Economy and the Dynamics of State Elections," *American Political Science Review* 82 (March 1988): 151. However, for contrary evidence showing that retrospective evaluations of a state's economy affect voter choice, see Craig J. Svoboda, "Retrospective Voting in Gubernatorial Elections," *Political Research Quarterly* 48 (March 1995): 117–134; Richard G. Niemi, Harold W. Stanley, and Ronald J. Vogel, "State Economies and State Taxes: Do Voters Hold Governors Accountable?" *American Journal of Political Science* 39 (November 1995): 936–957.

11. Dennis M. Simon, "Presidents, Governors and Electoral Accountability," *Journal of Politics* 51 (May 1989): 286–304; Thomas M. Holbrook-Provow, "National Factors in Gubernatorial Elections," *American Politics Quarterly* 15 (October 1987): 471–483.

12. James D. King, "Incumbent Popularity and Vote Choice in Gubernatorial Elections," *Journal of Politics* 63 (May 2001): 585–597.

13. James D. King and Jeffrey E. Cohen, "What Determines a Governor's Popularity?" *State Politics & Policy Quarterly* 5 (Fall 2005): 225–247.

14. Thomas M. Casey, *Campaign Dynamics: The Race for Governor* (Ann Arbor: University of Michigan Press, 2000).

15. Andrew D. McNitt and Jim Seroka, "Intraparty Challenges of Incumbent Governors and Senators," *American Politics Quarterly* 9 (July 1981): 321–340.

16. Peverill Squire and Christina Fastnow, "Comparing Gubernatorial and Senatorial Elections," *Political Research Quarterly* 47 (September 1994): 703–720.

17. Susan L. Kane and Richard F. Winters, "Taxes and Voting: Electoral Retribution in the American States," *Journal of Politics*, 55 (February 1993): 22–40.

18. Robert A. Jackson, "Gubernatorial and Senatorial Campaign Mobilization of Voters," *Political Research Quarterly* 55 (December 2002): 825–844.

19. Kedron Bardwell, "Campaign Finance Laws and the Competition for Spending in Gubernatorial Elections," *Social Science Quarterly* 84 (December 2003): 810–825.

20. Thad Beyle, "The Governors," in Virginia Gray and Russell L. Hanson, eds., *Politics in the American States: A Comparative Analysis*, 8th ed. (Washington, DC: CQ Press, 2004), 194–231.

21. Kendra A. Hovey and Harold A. Hovey, *CQ's State Fact Finder, 2003* (Washington, DC: CQ Press, 2003).

22. Alan Rosenthal, *Governors and Legislatures: Contending Powers* (Washington, DC: Congressional Quarterly Press, 1990), 170.

23. F. Ted Hebert, Jeffrey L. Brudney, and Deil S. Wright, "Gubernatorial Influence and State Bureaucracy," *American Politics Quarterly* 11 (April 1983): 243–244.

24. See Keith J. Muller, "Explaining Variation and Change in Gubernatorial Power," *Western Political Quarterly* 85 (September 1985): 424–431.

25. Thad Beyle, "The Governors," op. cit., p. 214.

26. Charles Barrilleaux and Michael Berkman, "Do Governors Matter? Budgeting Rules and the Politics of State Policymaking," *Political Research Quarterly* 56 (December 2003): 409–417.

27. Daniel Coffey, "Measuring Gubernatorial Ideology: A Content Analysis of State of the State Speeches," *State Politics & Policy Quarterly* 5 (1) (Spring 2005): 88–103.

28. Charles Wiggins, "Executive Vetoes and Legislative Overrides in the American States," *Journal of Politics* 42 (November 1980): 1110–1117.

29. Thad Beyle and Robert Dalton, *Being Governor: The View from the Office* (Durham, NC: Duke University Press, 1983), 135.

30. Rosenthal, *Governors and Legislatures*, p. 69.

31. Ibid., pp. 47, 294, 296–298.

32. See Kevin M. Leyden and Stephen A. Borrelli, "The Effect of State Economic Conditions on Gubernatorial Elections: Does Unified Government Make a Difference?" *Political Research Quarterly* 48 (June 1995): 275–290.

33. See Sarah McCally Morehouse, *The Governor and Party Leader*, op cit.; Laura A. Van Assendelft, *Governors, Agenda Setting and Divided Government* (Lanham, MD: University Press of America, 1997).

34. The study *The American Journalist in the 21st Century* was conducted by David Weaver, Randal Beam, Bonnie Brownlee, G. Cleveland Wilhoit, and Paul Voakes in collaboration with the Indiana University School of Journalism. *Source:* "Landmark Research into the Backgrounds of American Journalists Continues," Indiana University Media Relations, April 10, 2003, accessed at http://nesinfo.iu.edu/news/page/normal/895.html, June 4, 2005. For an extensive compilation of media political leaning studies by the Media Research Center, see "Media Bias Basics," www.mediaresearch.org/biasbasics/welcome.asp, accessed June 3, 2005.

35. S. Robert Lichter, *The Media Elite: America's New Powerbrokers* (New York: Adler Publishing Company, 1986).

36. William T. Gormley, "Coverage of State Government in the Mass Media," *State Government* 52 (December 1979): 46–51.

37. Thad Beyle, "Governors: Elections, Campaign Costs, Profiles, Forced Exits and Powers," in the Council of Sate Governments, *The Book of the States 2004* (Lexington, KY: Council of State Governments, 2004), 155.

38. John A. Hamman, "Career Experience and Performing Effectively as Governor," *American Review of Public Administration* 34 (June 2004): 151–163.

39. Thad Beyle, "The Governors," op. cit., p. 218.

40. Richard L. Fox and Zoe Me. Oxley, "Does Running with a Woman Help? Evidence from U.S. Gubernatorial Elections," *Politics & Gender* 1 (4) (December 2005): 525–546.

CHAPTER 8

1. Jonathan Walters, "Did Someone Say Downsizing?" *Governing*, 11 (February 1998): 17–20.

2. Christine A. Kelleher and Susan Webb Yackee, "Who's Whispering in Your Ear? The Influence of Third Parties Over State Agency Decisions," *Political Research Quarterly* 59(4) (December 2006): 629–644.

3. David Osbourne and Ted Gaebler, *Reinventing Government* (Reading, MA: Addison-Wesley, 1992), 24.

4. *Elrod* v. *Burns*, 96 S. Ct. 2673 (1976); *Branti* v. *Finkel*, 445 U.S. 507 (1980).

5. James B. Carroll and David A. Moss, *State Employee Worker Shortage: The Impending Crisis* (Lexington, KY: Council of State Governments, October 2002).

6. "Appointed Policy Makers in State Government: Five-Year Trend Analysis: Gender, Race, and Ethnicity," A Report of the Center for Women in Government and Civil Society, University at Albany, SUNY, Winter 2004, accessed at www.cwig.albany.edu/APMSG-advancecopy.htm, June 7, 2005.

7. Ibid.

8. Sue A. Frank and Gregory B. Lewis, "Government Employees: Working Hard or Hardly Working?" *American Review of Public Administration* 34 (March 2004): 36–51.

9. Ibid.

10. For a summary of research on this topic, see Gregory B. Lewis and Lana Stein, "Unions and Municipal Decline," *American Politics Quarterly* 17 (April 1989): 202–222.

11. Zogby International, "Nationwide Attitudes Toward Unions," for the Public Service Research Foundation, February 26, 2004, accessed at http://www.psrf.org/info/Nationwide_Attitudes_Toward_Unions.pdf, June 7, 2005.

12. Brian J. Gerber and Paul Teske, "Regulatory Policymaking in the American States," *Political Research Quarterly* 53 (December 2000): 849–886.

13. Dan B. Wood, "Principal-Agent Models of Political Control of Bureaucracy," *American Political Science Review* 83 (December 1989): 851–859.

14. Richard Elling, "Administering State Programs: Performance and Politics," in Virginia Gray and Russell L. Hanson, eds., *Politics in the American States: A Comparative Analysis*, 8th ed. (Washington, DC: CQ Press, 2004), 283.

15. Philip K. Howard, *The Death of Common Sense* (New York: Random House, 1995), 10.

16. E. S. Savas, *Privatizing the Public Sector* (Chatham, NJ: Chatham House, 1982), 25.

17. *The Municipal Year Book, 1987* (Washington, DC: ICMA, 1988), 44–53.

18. Former Michigan Governor John Engler (R), quoted by Keon S. Chi, Kelley A. Arnold, and Heather M. Perkins, "Privatization in State Government: Trends and Issues," in The Council of State Governments, *The Book of the States, 2004* (Lexington, KY: Council of State Governments, 2004), 465–482.

19. Keon S. Chi, Kelley A. Arnold, and Heather M. Perkins, "Privatization in State Government: Trends and Issues," in The Council of State Governments, *The Book of the States, 2004* (Lexington, KY: Council of State Governments, 2004), 465.

20. U.S. General Accounting Office, *Privatization: Lessons Learned by State and Local Governments* (Washington, DC: U.S. General Accounting Office, 1997).

21. David Osbourne, "Privatization: One Answer, Not *the* Answer," *Governing* (April 1992): 83.

22. Osbourne and Gaebler, *Reinventing Government*.

23. See Thomas Osborne, *Laboratories of Democracy* (Boston: Harvard Business School, 1988), chap. 3, "Arkansas: The Education Model."

24. See National Performance Review, *Creating a Government That Works Better and Costs Less* (Washington, DC: Government Printing Office, 1994).

25. In addition to Osborne and Gaebler, *Reinventing Government*, see National Commission on State and Local Government Public Service, *Hard Truths/Tough Choices: An Agenda for State and Local Government Reform* (Washington, DC: Government Printing Office, 1993).

26. Kevin B. Smith, Alan Greenblatt, and John Buntin, *Governing States and Localities* (Washington, DC: CQ Press, 2005), 326.

27. "Ethics Report on State Legislature Counteracts Public Perceptions, *NCSL News*, 2002, accessed at www.ncsl.org/programs/press/2002/pr020724.htm, June 7, 2005.

28. "Grading the States 2005: A Report Card on Government Performance," special issue of *Governing* magazine, February 2005. Available at http://results.gpponline.org/states.aspx.

29. The federal government's fiscal year is October 1 to September 30.

30. David Osborne and Peter Hutchinson, "About the Book: The Price of Government: Getting the Results We Need in an Age of Permanent Fiscal Crisis," *Governing*, accessed at www.governing.com/books/price.htm, June 23, 2004.

31. James E. Alt and Robert C. Lowry, "Divided Government, Fiscal Institution, and Budget Deficits," *American Political Science Review* 88 (December 1994): 811–828.

CHAPTER 9

1. A Harris Interactive Survey, "Arbitration: Simpler, Cheaper, and Faster Than Litigation," conducted for the U.S. Chamber Institute for Legal Reform, April 2005.

2. Ibid.

3. *Gitlow v. New York*, 268 U.S. 652 (1925).

4. See Donald R. Souger and Ashlyn Kuersten, "The Success of Amici in State Supreme Courts," *Political Research Quarterly* 48 (March 1995): 31–42.

5. John C. Kilwein and Richard A. Brisbin, Jr., "Policy Convergence in a Federal Judicial System," *American Journal of Political Science* 41 (January 1997): 122–148.

6. Valerie Hoekstra, "Competing Constraints: State Court Responses to Supreme Court Decisions and Legislation on Wages and Hours," *Political Research Quarterly* 58 (2) (June 2005): 317–328.

7. National Center for State Courts, *Examining the Work of State Courts, 2003* Williamsburg, VA: National Center for State Courts, 2003, accessed at http://ncsconline.org/D_Research/CSP/2003_Files/2003_Main_Page.html, June 16, 2005.

8. Henry R. Glick, "Courts: Politics and the Judicial Process," in Virginia Gray and Russell L. Hanson, eds., *Politics in the American States: A Comparative Analysis*, 8th ed. (Washington, DC: CQ Press, 2004), 237–238.

9. David B. Rottman, "Trends and Issues in the State Courts: Challenges and Achievements," *The Book of the States, 2004* (Lexington, KY: Council of State Governments, 2004), 236–238.

10. National Center for State Courts, *Examining the Work of State Courts*, 2003 (Williamsburg, VA: National Center for State Courts, 2003), 12.

11. Ibid., p. 13.

12. National Center for State Courts, "Grand Juries: Frequently Asked Questions," n.d., accessed at ncsconline.org, June 16, 2005.

13. *Miller-El* v. *Dretke*, 545 U.S. _____ (June 13, 2005); *Johnson* v. *California*, 545 U.S. _____ (2005) (June 13, 2005).

14. *Batson* v. *Kentucky*, 476 U.S. 79 (1986).

15. Charles Lane, "Justices Overturn Verdict, Cite Race," *Washington Post*, June 14, 2005, p. A01, accessed at http://www.washingtonpost.com/wp-dyn/content/article/2005/06/13/AR2005061300531_pf.html

16. James P. Wenzel, Shaun Bowler, and David J. Lanoue, "The Sources of Public Confidence in State Courts," *American Politics Research* 31 (March 2003): 191–211; Stefanie A. Lindquist, George W. Dougherty, and Mark D. Bradbury, "Evaluating Performance in State Judicial Institutions: Trust and Confidence in the Georgia Judiciary," *State and Local Government Review* 38 (3) 2006: 176–190.

17. *Gideon* v. *Wainwright*, 372 U.S. 335 (1963).

18. *Argersinger* v. *Hamlin*, 407 U.S. 25 (1972).

19. "Public-Defense Alternatives," *The Seattle Times*, April 6, 2004, accessed at http://seattletimes.nwsource.com/news/local/unequaldefense/stories/three/alternatives.html, June 22, 2005.

20. Henry R. Glick, "Courts: Politics and the Judicial Process," in Virginia Gray and Russell L. Hanson, eds., *Politics in the American States: A Comparative Analysis*, 8th ed. (Washington, DC: CQ Press, 2004), 238.

21. See Gregory A. Caldereira, "On the Reputations of State Supreme Courts," *Political Behavior* 5 (1983): 89.

22. Philip L. Dubois, "Voter Turnout in State Judicial Elections," *Journal of Politics* 41 (1979): 865–887.

23. Philip L. Dubois, "The Significance of Voting Cues in State Supreme Court Elections," *Law and Society Review* 13 (Spring 1979): 759–779.

24. Charles A. Johnson, Roger C. Schaefer, and R. Neal McKnight, "The Salience of Judicial Candidates and Elections," *Social Science Quarterly* 59 (September 1978): 371–378.

25. *Republican Party of Minnesota* v. *White*, 536 U.S. 765 (2002).

26. William Jenkins, "Retention Elections: Who Wins When No One Loses," *Judicature*, 61 (August 1977): 79–86.

27. "Methods of Removing State Judges," American Judicature Society, accessed at www.ajs.org/ethics/eth_impeachement.asp, June 16, 2005.

28. Ibid.

29. Melinda Gann Hall, "State Supreme Courts in American Democracy," *American Political Science Review* 95 (June 2002): 315–333.

30. Chris W. Bonneau, "Electoral Verdicts: Incumbent Defeats in State Supreme Court Elections," *American Politics Research* 33 (6) (November 2005): 818–841; Melinda Gann Hall and Chris W. Bonneau, "Does Quality Matter? Challengers in State Supreme Court Elections," *American Journal of Political Science* 50 (1) (January 2006): 20–33; Chris W. Bonneau, "Campaign Fundraising in State Supreme Court Elections," *Social Science Quarterly* 88 (1) (March 2007: 68–85; Mathew Manweller, "The 'Angriest Crocodile': Information Costs, Direct Democracy Activists, and the Politicization of State Judicial Elections," *State and Local Government Review* 37 (2) (2005): 86–102; Chris W. Bonneau, "What Price Justice? Understanding Campaign Spending in State Supreme Court Elections," *State Politics & Policy Quarterly* 5 (2) (Summer 2005): 107–125.

31. Austin Sarat, "Judging Trial Courts," *Journal of Politics* 39 (May 1977): 368–398.

32. Stuart Nagel, "Political Party Affiliation and Judges' Decisions," *American Political Science Association* 55 (1961): 843–851; and Sidney Ulmer, "The Political Party Variable on the Michigan Supreme Court," *Journal of Public Law* 11 (1962): 352–362.

33. Paul Brace and Melinda Gann Hall, "Studying Courts Comparatively," *Political Research Quarterly* 48 (March 1995): 5–29.

34. Henry R. Glick, "Courts: Politics and the Judicial Process," in Virginia Gray and Russell L. Hanson, eds., *Politics in the American States: A Comparative Analysis*, 8th ed. (Washington, DC: CQ Press, 2004), 236.

35. Jerome Frank, *Law and the Modern Mind* (New York: Coward-McCann, 1930); Benjamin N. Cardozo, *The Nature of the Judicial Process* (New Haven, CT: Yale University Press, 1921); and Roscoe Pound, *Justice According to Law* (New Haven, CT: Yale University Press, 1951).

36. See John Patrick Hagan, "Patterns of Activism on State Supreme Courts," *Publius* 18 (Winter 1988): 97–115.

37. John M. Scheb, Terry Bowen, and Gary Anderson, "Ideology, Role Orientations and Behavior in State Courts of Last Resort," *American Politics Quarterly* 19 (July 1991): 324–335.

38. Paul Brace, Laura Langer, and Melinda Gann Hall, "Measuring the Preferences of State Supreme Court Judges," *Journal of Politics*, 62 (May 2000): 287–413.

39. Donald R. Songer and Susan J. Tabrizi, "The Religious Right in Court: The Decision Making of Christian Evangelicals in State Supreme Courts," *Journal of Politics* 61 (May 1999): 507–526.

40. National School Safety and Security Services, "School Related Deaths, School Shootings, and School Violence Incidents (2004–2005 School Year)," accessed at www.schoolsecurity.org/trends/school_violence04-05.html, June 20, 2005.

41. Associated Press, "7,500 U.S. Hate Crimes in 2003," November 22, 2004, accessed at http://election.cbsnews.com/stories/2004/11/22/national/main657048.shtml, June 20, 2005.

42. Brad Knickerbocker, "National Acrimony and a Rise in Hate Crimes," *The Christian Science Monitor*, July 5, 2005; accessed at http://www.csmonitor.com/2005/0603/p03s01-ussc.html, June 20, 2005.

43. Mark Potok, "The Year In Hate, 2005," Southern Poverty Law Center, 2007; available at www.splcenter.org/intel/itelreport/article.jsp?aid=627

44. Rebecca Stotzer, "Comparison of Hate Crime Rates Across Protected and Unprotected Groups," The Williams Institute, June 2007, p. 1.

45. U.S. Bureau of Justice Statistics, *Criminal Victimization in the United States*, annual.

46. Elaine B. Sharp, "Policing Urban America: A New Look at the Politics of Agency Size," *Social Science Quarterly* 87 (2) (June 2006): 291–307.

47. John MacDonald and Robert J. Stokes, "Race, Social Capital, and Trust in the Police," *Urban Affairs Review* 41 (1) (January 2006): 358–375.

48. Bureau of Labor Statistics, U.S. Department of Labor, *Occupational Outlook Handbook, 2004–05 Edition*, "Police and Detectives," accessed at http://www.bls.gov/oco/ocos160.htm, June 21, 2005.

49. For a summary, see John J. Dilulio, Jr., "Arresting Ideas: Tougher Law Enforcement Is Driving Down Crime," *Policy Review* (Fall 1995): 12–16.

50. Bureau of Justice Statistics, "Criminal Victimization, 2005," September 2006. Available at http://www.ojp.usdoj.gov/bjs/pub/pdf/cv05.pdf

51. John M. Dawson, "Prosecutors in State Courts," 1990, Bureau of Justice Statistics Bulletin, NCJ-134500, March 1992.

52. The following discussion relies on evidence presented by Robert A. Carp, "The Behavior of Grand Juries: Acquiescence or Justice," *Social Science Quarterly* 55 (March 1975): 853–870.

53. National Center for Policy Alternatives, "Privatizing Prisons," http://www.stateaction.org/issues/issue.cfm/issue/PrivatizingPrisons.xml, accessed June 22, 2005.

54. Jeff Yates and Richard Fording, "Politics and State Punitiveness in Black and White," *The Journal of Politics* 67 (4) (November 2005): 1099–1121; S. Fernando Rodriguez, Theodore R. Curry, and Gang Lee, "Gender Differences in Criminal Sentencing: Do Effects Vary Across Violent, Property, and Drug Offenses?" *Social Science Quarterly* 87 (2) (June 2006): 318–339.

55. Bureau of Justice Statistics, *Survey of State Prison Inmates* (1994).

56. John J. Dilulio, Jr., "Punishing Smarter," *Brookings Review* (Summer 1989): 8.

57. Richard B. Abell, "Beyond Willie Horton: The Battle of the Prison Bulge," *Policy Review* 47 (Winter 1989): 32–35.

58. Dilulio, "Punishing Smarter," 3–12.

59. "Aged Inmates' Care Stresses State Prison Budget," *The Arizona Republic*, May 9, 2005, accessed at http://www.tucsoncitizen.com/index.php?page=local&story_id=050805a6_prisonaging, June 22, 2005.

60. James J. Stephan, "State Prison Expenditures, 2001," Bureau of Justice Statistics Special Report, June 2004, accessed at http://www.ojp.usdoj.gov/bjs/pub/pdf/spe01.pdf, June 22, 2005.

61. See Abell, "Beyond Willie Horton," pp. 32–35.

62. Angela Munoz, "U.S. Prison Population Hits All-Time High," PBS *Online NewsHour EXTRA*, accessed at http://www.pbs.org/newshour/extra/teachers/lessonplans/math/incarceration_story_9-05.html, June 22, 2005.

63. Death Penalty Information Center, "DPIC Summary: Innocence Protection Act of 2004," accessed at http://www.deathpenaltyinfo.org/article.php?scid=40&did=1234, June 22, 2005.

64. *Furman* v. *Georgia*, 408 U.S. 238 (1972).

65. *Gregg* v. *Georgia*, 428 U.S. 153 (1976).

66. *Atkins* v. *Virginia*, 536 U.S. 304 (2002).

67. *Roper* v. *Simmons* 112 S. W. 3d 397, affirmed (2005).

68. Arline Kaplan, "When Is It 'Cruel and Unusual Punishment'? Supreme Court Bans Juvenile Death Penalty," *Psychiatric Times*, 22 (May 2005), accessed at http://www.psychiatrictimes.com/showArticle.jhtml?articleId=164303063, June 22, 2005.

69. Kavan Peterson, "Death Penalty: Lethal Injection on Trial," stateline.org, January 17, 2007; available at www.stateline.org/live/printable/story?contentId=171776.

70. *House* v. *Bell*, 597 U.S. (2006). June 12, 2006.

71. S. Kavan Peterson, "Death Penalty—34 States Permit Executions," Stateline.org, April 19, 2005, accessed at http://www.stateline.org/live/ViewPage.action?siteNodeId=136&languageId=1&contentId=25995, June 22, 2005.

CHAPTER 10

1. See David Jacobson, *Place and Belonging in America* (Baltimore, MD: Johns Hopkins University Press, 2001); Tom Christensen and Per Laegreid, "Trust in Government: The Relative Importance of Service Satisfaction, Political Factors, and Demography," *Public Performance and Management Review* 28 (June 2005): 487–511.

2. Arizona State University, *The Phoenix Area Social Survey: Community and Environment in a Desert Metropolis* (Tempe, AZ: Center for Business Research, Center for Environmental Studies, Department of Social and Behavioral Sciences, Department of Sociology, Survey Research Laboratory, School of Planning and Landscape Architecture, March 2003), 3.

3. For some empirical support for these speculations, see Gordon S. Black, "Conflict in the Community: A Theory of the Effect of Community Size," *American Political Science Review* 68 (September 1974): 1245–1261; see also Timothy A. Almy, "Residential Locations and Electoral Cohesion," *American Political Science Review* 67 (September 1973): 914–923, who argues that conflict is greater in communities where different social groups are residentially segregated.

4. The widely cited classic essay is Charles M. Tiebout, "The Pure Theory of Local Expenditure," *Journal of Political Economy* 64 (October 1956): 416–424.

5. David Swindell and Janet Kelly, "Performance Measurement Versus City Service Satisfaction: Intra-City Variations in Quality," *Social Science Quarterly* 86 (3) (September 2005): 704–723.

6. John M. Orbell and Toru Uno, "A Theory of Neighborhood Problem Solving: Political Action versus Residential Mobility," *American Political Science Review*, 66 (June 1972): 471–489; William E. Lyons and David Lowery, "Citizen Response to Dissatisfaction in Urban Communities," *Journal of Politics* 51 (November 1989): 841–868.

7. David Whelan, "Black Boom in the 'Burbs," *American Demographics* (July 2001).

8. National Association of Towns and Townships, "Grassroots Governments and the People They Serve," accessed at www .michigantownships.org/township_history.htm, January 2002.

9. Nancy Thorne, "Census 2000: Perspectives on Small Communities," *Small Community Quarterly* (Winter 2001).

10. Pew Partnership, "Voices of Rural America: National Survey Results," accessed at *www.pew.partnership.org/pubs/ voicesofRuralAmerica.html*, January 5, 2002.

11. J. Edwin Benton, *Counties as Service Delivery Agents: Changing Expectations and Roles* (New York: Praeger, 2002).

12. National Association of County Officials, "The History of County Government, Part I," accessed at *www.naco.org/*.

13. David R. Berman, "State–Local Relations: Authority, Finances, Takeovers," *The 2004 Municipal Year Book* (Washington, DC: International City/County Management Association, 2004), 48–50.

14. John F. Dillon, *Commentaries on the Laws of Municipal Corporations*, 5th ed. (Boston: Little, Brown, 1911), 448.

15. William DeSoto, Hassan Tajalli, and Cynthia Opheim, "Power, Professionalism, and Independence: Changes in the Office of the Mayor," *State and Local Government Review* 38 (3) (2006): 156–164.

16. Susan A. MacManus and Charles S. Bullock III, "The Form, Structure, and Composition of America's Municipalities in the New Millennium," *The 2003 Municipal Year Book* (Washington, DC: International City/County Management Association), 3–18.

17. Susan A. MacManus, "The Resurgent City Councils," in Ronald E. Weber and Paul Brace, eds., *American State and Local Politics: Directions for the 21st Century* (New York: Chatham House, 1999).

18. See Joseph F. Zimmerman, "The New England Town Meeting: Pure Democracy in Action?" *Municipal Yearbook, 1984* (Washington, DC: International City Managers' Association, 1984), 102–106.

19. H. George Frederickson, Gary Alan Johnson, and Curtis Wood, "The Changing Structure of American Cities: A Study of the Diffusion of Innovation," *Public Administration Review* 64 (May/June 2004): 320.

20. Susan Welch and Timothy Bledsoe, "The Partisan Consequences of Nonpartisan Elections," *American Journal of Political Science* 30 (February 1986): 128–139.

21. Carol A. Cassel, "Social Background Characteristics of Nonpartisan City Council Members," *Western Political Quarterly*, 38 (September 1985): 495–501.

22. John J. Kirlen, "Electoral Conflict and Democracy in Cities," *Journal of Politics* 37 (February 1975): 262–269.

23. Susan A. MacManus and Charles S. Bullock III, "The Form, Structure, and Composition of America's Municipalities in the New Millennium," *The 2003 Municipal Year Book* (Washington, DC: International City/County Management Association), 3–18.

24. This section is from MacManus, "The Resurgent City Councils."

25. Richard Engstrom and Michael McDonald, "The Election of Blacks to City Councils," *American Political Science Review*, 75 (June 1981): 344–355; Susan Welch, "The Impact of At-Large Elections on the Representation of Blacks and Hispanics," *Journal of Politics* 52 (November 1990): 1050–1057.

26. Susan A. MacManus and Charles S. Bullock III, "Women and Racial/Ethnic Minorities in Mayoral and Council Positions," in *Municipal Year Book*, 1993 (Washington, DC: International City/County Management Association, 1993), 57–69.

27. *Mobile v. Bolden*, 446 U.S. 55 (1980).

28. For a discussion of federal court applications of these tests, see Susan A. MacManus and Charles S. Bullock, "Racial Representation Issues," *PS* 18 (Fall 1985): 759–769.

29. *Thornburg v. Gingles*, 106 S. Ct. 2752 (1986).

30. Edward Still and Robert Ritchie, "Alternative Electoral Systems as Voting Rights Remedies," *Journal of Election Administration* 18 (1997).

31. Douglas J. Amy, *Behind the Ballot Box: A Citizen's Guide to Voting Systems* (Westport, CT: Praeger, 2000.) See Chapter 5, "Semiproportional Voting Systems."

32. Shaun Bowler, David Brockington, and Todd Donovan, "Election Systems and Voter Turnout: Experiments in the United States," *Journal of Politics* 63 (August 2001): 902–915.

33. Albert K. Karnig, "Black Representation on City Councils," *Urban Affairs Quarterly* 12 (December 1976): 223–243; Thomas R. Dye and Theodore P. Robinson, "Reformism and Black Representation on City Councils," *Social Science Quarterly* 59 (June 1978).

34. Susan Welch, "The Impact of At-Large Districts on the Representation of Blacks and Hispanics," *Journal of Politics* 52 (November 1990): 1050–1076. See also Charles S. Bullock and Susan M. MacManus, "Municipal Electoral Structure and the Election of Councilwomen," *Journal of Politics* 53 (February 1991): 75–89.

35. Ibid, p. 1072.

36. Kathleen Vail, "The Changing Face of Education," *Education Vital Signs*, a supplement to the *American School Board Journal* (December 2001).

37. Education Commission of the States, "Local Superintendents," accessed at *http://mb2ecs.org/reports/Report.aspx?id=171*, July 4, 2005.

38. Kathleen Vail, "The Changing Face of Education," *Education Vital Signs*, a supplement to the *American School Board Journal* (December 2001).

1. The town was Inglis, Florida. The proclamation read, "Be it known from this day forward that Satan, ruler of darkness, giver of evil, destroyer of what is good and just, is not now, nor ever again will be, a part of this town of Inglis . . ." Todd Lewan, Associated Press, "A Town Asks Itself: Did Banning Satan Make a Difference?" accessed at www.jacksonville.com/tu-online/apnews/stories/031304/D819HN580.shtml, March 13, 2004.

2. Arguments over value of direct citizen participation are as old as democracy itself. See "Direct versus Representative Democracy" in Chapter 2. And see Samuel P. Huntington, *American Politics: The Promise of Disharmony* (Cambridge, MA: Harvard University Press, 1981); and Jeffrey M. Berry, Kent E. Portney, and Ken Thompson, *The Rebirth of Urban Democracy* (Washington, DC: Brookings Institution, 1993).

3. Carole Hamner, "New Survey Dispels Myths on Citizen Engagement," in *Ready, Willing, and Able: Citizens Working For Change* (Charlottesville, VA: Pew Partnership for Civic Change, 2001).

4. These uniquenesses of local elections are discussed in detail in Karen M. Kauffmann, *The Urban Voter: Group Conflict and Mayoral Voting Behavior in American Cities* (Ann Arbor: University of Michigan Press, 2004).

5. Zoltan L. Hajnal and Paul G. Lewis, "Municipal Institutions and Voter Turnout in Local Elections," *Urban Affairs Review* 38 (May 2003): 645–668.

6. Kauffman, *The Urban Voter*, Elaine Sharp, "Political Participation in Cities," in John P. Pelissero, *Cities, Politics, and Policy: A Comparative Analysis* (Washington, DC: CQ Press, 2003), 68–96.

7. Hajnal and Lewis, "Municipal Institutions."

8. Tari Renner, "Local Initiative and Referendum in the United States," Initiative and Referendum Institute, www.iandrinstitute.org, January 8, 2002.

9. Richard C. Feoick and Seung-Bum Yang, "Factors affecting Constitutional Choice: The Case of the Recall in Municipal Charters," *State and Local Government Review* 37 (1) 2005: 40–48; Sharon Lawrence, "Initiative and Referendum—A Direct Voice for County Voters," Issue Brief, National Association of Counties, January 1996, accessed at www.naco.org/pubs/research/issues/initiative.cfm.

10. Jennifer Hamilton, "Stripper Mayor Faces Stripping: Exposure Charges Pose Challenge to Stripper-Turned-Mayor," abcNEWS.com, December 4, 2001.

11. Early arguments over public-regardingness are found in James Q. Wilson and Edward C. Banfield, "Public Regardingness as a Value Premise in Voting Behavior," *American Political Science Review* 58 (December 1964): 876–887; and Roger Durand, "Ethnicity, Public-Regardingness and Referenda Voting," *Midwest Journal of Political Science*, 16 (May 1972): 259–268. More recent evidence that wealth and income lead citizens to be more supportive of public services is found in Evel Elliot, James Regens, and Barry Sheldon, "Exploring Variation in Public Support for Environmental Protection," *Social Science Quarterly* 76 (March 1995): 41–52.

12. Herbert C. Alexander, *Reform and Reality: The Financing of State and Local Campaigns* (New York: Twentieth Century Fund Press, 1991).

13. Timothy B. Krebs and David B. Holian, "Media and Momentum: Strategic Contributing in a Big-City Mayoral Election," *Urban Affairs Review* 40 (May 2005): 614–633.

14. Arnold Fleischmann and Lana Stein, "Campaign Contributions in Local Elections," *Political Research Quarterly* 51 (September 1998): 673–690.

15. Timothy B. Krebs, "Urban Interests and Campaign Contributions: Evidence From Los Angeles," *Journal of Urban Affairs* 27 (2, 2005): 165–176.

16. See Raphael Sonenshein, "Bi-Racial Coalition Politics in Los Angeles," *PS: Political Science and Politics,* 19 (September 1986): 582–590; "The Dynamics of Bi-Racial Coalitions," *Western Political Quarterly* 42 (June 1989): 333–353; and Rufus Browning, Dale Rogers Marshall, and David Tabb, *Protest Is Not Enough* (Berkeley: University of California Press, 1984). The data reported in this paragraph are from a report entitled "What Ethnic Americans Really Think: The Zogby Culture Polls." The survey was conducted by Zogby International and sponsored by the National Italian American Foundation and the Center for Study of Culture and Values at Catholic University of America. The results were reported in "Race and Politics," *American Demographics* 23 (August 2001): 11–13. See also Rufus P. Browning, Dale Rogers Marshall, and David H. Tabb, eds., *Racial Politics in American Cities*, 2nd ed. (New York: Longman, 1997); Paula D. McClain and Joseph Stewart, Jr., "Can We All Get Along?" in *Racial and Ethnic Minorities in American Politics* (Boulder, CO; Westview Press, 1998); Rufus P. Browning, Dale Rogers Marshall, and David H. Tabb, "Taken In or Just Taken? Political Incorporation of African Americans in Cities," in Richard E. Keiser and Katherine Underwood, eds., *Minority Politics at the Millennium* (New York: Garland Publishing, 2000), 131–156.

17. See Paula D. McClain and Joseph Stewart, Jr., "Can We All Get Along?" in *Racial and Ethnic Minorities in American Politics*, 3rd ed. (Boulder, CO: Westview Press, 2002); Rodney E. Hero, "Crossroads of Equality: Race/Ethnicity and Cities in American Democracy," *Urban Affairs Review* 40 6 (July 2005): 695–705.

18. William L. Riordan, *Plunkitt of Tammany Hall* (New York: McClure, Phillips, 1905), 46.

19. Ibid., p. 52.

20. Edward C. Banfield and James Q. Wilson, *City Politics* (Cambridge, MA: Harvard-MIT Press, 1963), chap. 9.

21. See Elmer E. Cornwell, Jr., "Bosses, Machines, and Ethnic Groups," *Annals of the American Academy of Political and Social Science* (May 1964): 27–39.

22. Lincoln Steffens, *Autobiography* (New York: Harcourt, Brace & World, 1931), 168.

23. See Richard J. Hofstadter, *The Age of Reform* (New York: Knopf, 1955); and Lorin Peterson, *The Day of the Mugwump* (New York: Random House, 1961).

24. Lincoln Steffens, *The Shame of the Cities* (New York: Sagamore Press, 1957), 10.

25. Jim Svara, "Possible Approaches to the Model Charter Revision," The National Civic League, 2001, accessed at www.ncl.org/npp/chater/artciles/possible_U.S._approaches.html, January 3, 2002; and "Do We Still Need Model Charters? The Meaning and Relevance of Reform in the Twenty-First Century," *National Civic Review* 90 (Spring 2001): 19–33.

26. John F. Persimos, "Ward Politics 21st-Century Style," *Governing* (October 1989): 46–50.

27. Roland Zullo, "Public-Private Contracting and Political Reciprocity," *Political Research Quarterly* 59 (2) (June 2006): 273–281.

28. John B. Horrigan, *Cities Online: Urban Development and the Internet* (Washington, DC: Pew Internet and American Life Project, 2001).

29. League of Minnesota Cities and the International City/County Management Association, *Local Government Web Site Development Manual*, November, 2001, available at govoffice.com.

30. James K. Scott, "E-Services: Assessing the Quality of Municipal Government Web Sites," *State and Local Government Review* 37 (2) (2005): 151–165.

31. For an extensive list of ways to faciliate public participation, see James L. Creighton, *The Public Participation Handbook: Making Better Decisions Through Citizen Involvement* (San Francisco: Jossey-Bass, 2005). See also Suzanne W. Morse, *Smart Communities: How Citizens and Local Leaders Can Use Strategic Thinking to Build a Brighter Future* (San Francisco: Jossey-Bass, 2004).

32. International City/County Management Association, *Citizen Surveys: How to Do Them, How to Use Them, and What They Mean*, 2nd ed. (Washington, DC: ICMA, 2000); Christine H. Roch and Theodore H. Poister, "Citizens, Accountability, and Service Satisfaction: The Influence of Expectations," *Urban Affairs Review* 41 (3) January 2006: 292–308.

33. Louis Ayala, "Trained for Democracy: The Differing Effects of Voluntary and Involuntary Organizations on Political Participation," *Political Research Quarterly* 53 (March 2000): 99–115; Gary M Segura, Harry Pachon, and Nathan P. Woods, "Hispanics, Social Capital, and Civic Engagement," *National Civic Review* 90 (Spring 2001): 85–96; Tom Lando, "Public Participation in Local Government: Points of View," *National Civic Review* 88 (Summer 1999): 109–122; J. Eric Oliver, "City Size and Civic Involvement in Metropolitan America," *American Political Science Review* 94 (June 2000): 361–373.

34. Robert G. Moore, "Religion, Race, and Gender Differences in Political Ambition," *Politics & Gender* 1 (4) (December 2005): 577–596.

35. Much of the material in this section is from Susan A. MacManus, "The Resurgent City Councils," in Ronald E. Weber and Paul Brace, eds., *American State and Local Politics: Directions for the 21st Century* (New York: Chatham House, 1999), 185–193.

36. Timothy Bledsoe, *Careers in City Politics: The Case for Urban Democracy* (Pittsburgh, PA: University of Pittsburgh Press, 1993); Timothy B. Krebs also notes that people are more likely to run if there is an open seat or a vulnerable incumbent, in "The Political and Demographic Predictors of Candidate Emergence in City Council Elections," *Urban Affairs Review* 35 (November 1999): 279–300.

37. MacManus, op. cit.

38. James Svara, *Survey of America's City Councils* (Washington, DC: National League of Cities, 1991).

39. Rob Gurwitt, "Are City Councils a Relic of the Past?" *Governing* (April 2003): 20–24.

40. Timothy B. Krebs, "The Determinants of Candidate's Vote Share and the Advantage of Incumbency in City Council Elections," *American Journal of Political Science* 42 (July 1998): 921–935.

41. See Joel Lieske, "The Political Dynamics of Urban Voting Behavior," *American Journal of Political Science* 33 (February 1989): 150–174.

42. Kenneth Prewitt, *The Recruitment of Political Leaders: A Study of Citizen-Politicians* (Indianapolis: Bobbs-Merrill, 1970), 148.

43. James Svara, *Official Leadership in the City: Patterns of Conflict and Cooperation* (New York: Oxford University Press, 1990), 122.

44. Of course, council members themselves are not likely to agree that their role is a passive one. They like to think of themselves as policy innovators—people of vision and leadership—who follow their own convictions in public affairs regardless of what others want them to do.

45. Douglas Ihrke, Rick Proctor, and Jerry Gabris, "Understanding Innovation in Municipal Government: City Council Member Perspectives," *Journal of Urban Affairs* 25 (1, 2003): 79–90.

46. Studies show citizens tend to contact municipal bureaucrats instead of elected officials when they are less familiar with or interested in local government. John Clayton Thomas and Julia E. Melkers, "Citizen Contacting of Municipal Officials: Choosing Between Appointed Administrators and Elected Officials," *Journal of Public Administration Research and Theory* 11 (1, 2000): 51–71.

47. See David R. Morgan, "Political Linkage and Public Policy: Attitudinal Congruence Between Citizens and Officials," *Western Political Quarterly* (June 1973): 209–223.

48. Leonard D. White, *The City Manager* (Chicago: University of Chicago Press, 1927).

49. See Harold A. Stone, Don K. Price, and Kathryn H. Stone, *City Manager Government in the United States* (Chicago: Public Administration Service, 1940).

50. See Timothy A. Almy, "Local-Cosmopolitanism and U.S. City Managers," *Urban Affairs Quarterly* 10 (March 1975): 243–277.

51. Douglas J. Watson and Wendy L. Hassett, "The 20-Year Manager: Factors of Longevity," *Public Management* (October 2003): 22–25.

52. Alan L. Saltzstein, "City Managers and City Councils: Perceptions of the Division of Authority," *Western Political Quarterly* 27 (June 1974): 275–287.

53. David N. Ammons and Matthew J. Bosse, "Tenure of City Managers: Examining the Dual Meanings of 'Average' Tenure," *State and Local Government Review* 37 (1, 2005): 61–71.

54. William J. Pammer, Jr., Herbert A. Marlowe, Jr., Joseph G. Jarret, and Jack L. Dustin, "Managing Conflict and Building Conflict in Council-Manager Cities: Insights on Establishing a Resolution Framework," *State and Local Government Review* 31 (Fall 1999): 202–213; James B. Kaatz, P. Edward French, and Hazel Prentiss-Cooper, "City Council Conflict as a Cause of Psychological Burnout and Voluntary Turnover Among City Managers," *State and Local Government Review* 31 (Fall 1999): 162–172.

55. Doyle W. Buckwalter and Robert J. Parsons, "Local City Managers' Career Paths: Which Way to the Top?" in International City/County Management Association, *The 2000 Municipal Year Book* (Washington, DC: ICMA, 2000), 20–21.

56. Jeffrey L. Pressman, "Preconditions of Mayoral Leadership," *American Political Science Review* 66 (June 1972): 511–524.

57. See Melvin G. Holli, "American Mayors: The Best and the Worst Since 1960," *Social Science Quarterly* 78 (March 1997): 149–157. The five best: Richard J. Daley (Chicago, 1955–1976); Henry Cisneros (San Antonio, 1981–1989); Tom Bradley (Los Angeles, 1973–1993); Dianne Feinstein (San Francisco, 1978–1987); and Andrew Young (Atlanta, 1982–1990).

58. Haya El Nasser, "Few Big Names Run Big Cities Now," *USA Today,* March 24, 2004, p. 3A.

59. Neil Kraus and Todd Swanstrom, "The Continuing Significance of Race: Black and Hispanic Mayors, 1967–1999," paper presented at the annual meeting of the American Political Science Association, August 30–September 2, 2001; Nicholas O. Alozie, "The Promise of Urban Democracy: Big-City Black Mayoral Service in the Early 1990s," *Urban Affairs Review* 35 (January 2000): 422–434.

60. David A. Bositis, *Black Elected Officials: A Statistical Summary 2001* (Washington, DC: The Joint Center for Political and Economic Studies, 2003).

61. Melissa J. Marshall and Anirudh V.S. Ruhil, "The Pomp of Power: Black Mayoralties in Urban America," *Social Science Quarterly* 87 (December 2006): 828–850.

62. Rodney E. Hero, F. Chris Garcia, John Garcia, and Harry Pachon, "Latino Participation, Partisanship, and Office Holding," *PS: Political Science and Politics* 33 (September 2000).

63. David Haywood Metz and Katherine Tate, "The Color of Urban Campaigns," in Paul E. Peterson, ed., *Classifying by Race* (Washington, DC: The Brookings Institution, 1995), 262–277.

64. Robert M. Stein, Stacey G. Ulbig, and Stephanie Shirley Post, "Voting for Minority Candidates in Multiracial/Multiethnic Communities," *Urban Affairs Review* 41 (2) (November 2005): 157–181.

65. Baodong Liu, "Whites as a Minority and the New Racial Coalition in New Orleans and Memphis," *PS: Political Science and Politics* 39 (January 2006)(1): 69–76.

66. Susan Welch, "The Impact of At-Large Elections on the Representation of Blacks and Hispanics," *Journal of Politics,* 52 (November 1990): 1050–1076.

67. See Rufus P. Browning, Dale Rodgers Marshall, and David H. Tabb, *Protest Is Not Enough* (Berkeley: University of California Press, 1984): Rodney E. Hero, "Hispanics in Urban Government," *Western Political Quarterly* 43 (June 1990): 403–414; Jerry L. Polinard, Robert D. Wrinkle, and Thomas Longovia, "The Impact of District Elections on the Mexican American Community," *Social Science Quarterly* 72 (September 1991): 609–614.

68. Charles S. Bullock III, "The Opening Up of State and Local Election Processes," in Ronald E. Weber and Paul Brace, eds., *American State and Local Politics: Directions for the 21st Century* (New York: Chatham House, 1999), 220–221.

69. Kim Geron and James S. Lai, "Transforming Ethnic Politics: A Comparative Analysis of Electoral Support for and Policy Priorities of Asian American and Latino Elected Officials," paper presented at the annual meeting of the American Political Science Association, August 30–September 2, 2001.

70. Geron and Lai, op. cit., p. 7.

71. Geron and Lai, "Transforming Ethnic Politics."

72. Peter K. Eisinger, "Black Employment in Municipal Jobs," *American Political Science Review* 76 (June 1982): 380–392.

73. Thomas R. Dye and James Renick, "Political Power and City Jobs," *Social Science Quarterly* 62 (September 1981): 475–486. See also Matthew Hutchins and Lee Sigelman, "Black Employment in State and Local Government," *Social Science Quarterly* 62 (March 1981): 79–87.

74. For an argument that black and Hispanic mayors do not increase minority city employment, but that black and Hispanic council members do so, see Brinck Kerr and Kenneth Mladenka, "Does Politics Matter?" *American Journal of Political Science* 38 (November 1994): 918–943.

75. Grace Hall Saltzstein, "Black Mayors and Police Policies," *Journal of Politics* 51 (August 1989): 525–544.

76. Susan E. Howell and Huey L. Perry, "Black Mayors/White Mayors: Explaining Their Approval," *Public Opinion Quarterly* 68 (Spring 2004): 57–80.

77. Browning, Marshall, and Tabb, *Protest Is Not Enough*, p. 41.

78. Center for American Women and Politics, "Women Mayors in U.S. Cities 2006: CAWP Fact Sheet," CAWP, 2006.

79. Center for the American Woman in Politics, Eagleton Institute of Politics, Rutgers University, 1998.

80. Susan A. MacManus and Charles S. Bullock, III, "'Winning in My Own Back Yard': County Government, School Board Positions Steadily More Attractive to Women Candidates," in Lois Duke Whitaker, ed., *Women in Politics*, 3rd ed. (Upper Saddle River, NJ: Prentice Hall, 1999), 121–187.

81. Ruth B. Mandel, *In the Running: The New Woman Candidate* (New Haven, CT: Ticknor and Fields, 1981), 63–97.

82. Robert Darcy, Susan Welch, and Janet Clark, *Women, Elections, and Representation,* 2nd ed. (New York: Longman, 1994).

83. Linda L.M. Bennett and Stephen E. Bennett, "Changing Views About Gender Equality in Politics: Gradual Change and Lingering Doubts," in Lois Lovelace Duke, ed., *Women and Politics: Have the Outsiders Become Insiders?,* 2nd ed. (Englewood Cliffs, NJ: Prentice Hall, 1996) 38.

84. Bositis, *Black Elected Officials: A Statistical Summary 2001.*

85. Melissa Deckman, "Gender Differences in the Decision to Run For School Board," *American Politics Research* 35 (4) (July 2007): 541–563.

86. See James Svara, "Council Profile: More Diversity, Demands, and Frustration," *Nation's Cities Weekly* 14 (November 18, 1991): 4; Susan Adams Beck, "Rethinking Municipal Governance: Gender Distinctions on Local Councils," in Debra L. Dodson, ed., *Gender and Policymaking: Studies of Women in Office* (New Brunswick, NJ: Center for the American Women and Politics, 1991).

87. Christopher A. Cooper, Anthony J. Nownes, and Steven Roberts, "Perceptions of Power: Interest Groups in Local Politics," *State and Local Government Review* 37 (3) (2005): 206–216.

88. Paul A. Djupe and Christopher P. Gilbert, "The Resourceful Believer: Generating Civic Skills in Church," *The Journal of Politics* 68 (1) (February 2006): 116–127.

89. Elaine B. Sharp, "Culture, Institutions, and Urban Officials' Responses to Morality Issues," *Political Research Quarterly* 55 (December 2002): 861–884.

90. Pew Partnership for Civic Change, *Ready, Willing, and Able: Citizens Working for Change* (Charlottesville, VA: Pew Partnership for Civic Change, 2001).

CHAPTER 12

1. See John Bollens and Henry Schmandt, *The Metropolis* (New York: Harper & Row, 1985).

2. U.S. Conference of Mayors, *U.S. Metro Economies: A Decade of Prosperity* (Washington, DC), July 10, 2001.

3. William H. Frey, "Micro Melting Pots," *American Demographics* 23 (June 2001): 21–23.

4. Jennifer S. Vey, "Restoring Prosperity: The State Role in Revitalizing America's Older Industrial Cities," The Brookings Institution, May 2007. Available at www.brookings.edu/metro/pubs/20070520_oic.htm.

5. William H. Lucy and David L. Phillips, "Suburbs and the Census: Patterns of Growth and Decline" (Washington, DC: The Brookings Institution Center on Urban and Metropolitan Policy, December 2001), Survey Series, p. 1.

6. Lewis Mumford, *The City in History* (New York: Harcourt, Brace, & World, 1961), 34.

7. Bruce Katz, Metropolitan Policy Program, The Brookings Institution, "The State of American Cities and Suburbs," presentation to Habitat Urban Conference, March 18, 2005, citing Glaeser, Kahn, and Chu, "Job Sprawl: Employment Location in U.S. Metropolitan Areas," 2001.

8. Robert E. Land and Jennifer LeFurgy, *Boomburbs: The Rise of America's Accidental Cities* (Washington, DC: Brookings Institution Press, 2007).

9. Robert E. Lang and Patrick A. Simmons, "Boomburbs': The Emergence of Large, Fast Growing Suburban Cities in the United States," Fannie Mae Foundation Census Note 06 (June 2001).

10. Robert Puentes and David Warren, "One-Fifth of America: A Comprehensive Guide to America's First Suburbs" (Washington, DC: The Brookings Institution, February 2006), p. 1.

11. Richard Child Hill, "Separate and Unequal: Government Inequality in the Metropolis," *American Political Science Review* 68 (December 1974): 1557–1568.

12. Kenneth Jackson, *Crabgrass Frontier: The Suburbanization of the United States* (New York: Oxford University Press, 1985).

13. Margaret Weir, Harold Wolman, and Todd Swanstrom, "The Calculus of Coalitions: Cities, Suburbs, and the Metropolitan Agenda. *Urban Affairs Review* 40 (6) (July 2005): 730–760.

14. Jason C. Booza, Jackie Cutsinger, and George Galster, "Where Did They Go? The Decline of Middle-Income Neighborhoods in Metropolitan America" (Washington, DC: The Brookings Institution, June 2006).

15. Edward L. Glaeser and Jacob L. Vigdor, "Racial Segregation in the 2000 Census: Promising News" (Washington, DC: The Brookings Institution, April 2001).

16. Katz, "The State of American Cities and Suburbs," op. cit.

17. Barrett A. Lee and Matthew Marlay, "The Right Side of the Tracts: Affluent Neighborhoods in the Metropolitan United States," *Social Science Quarterly* 88 (3) (September 2007): 766–830.

18. William H. Frey, "Melting Pot Suburbs: A Census 2000 Study of Suburban Diversity" (Washington, DC: The Brookings Institution Center on Urban and Metropolitan Policy, Census 2000 Series, June 2001).

19. Peter Dreier, "How the Media Compound Urban Problems," *Journal of Urban Affairs* 27 (2, 2005): 193–194.

20. Robert Johnson, "Why 'New Urbanism' Isn't For Everyone," *The New York Times*, February 20, 2005; accessed at www.nytimes.com/2005/02realestate/20nati.html?pagewanted==printer&positions=, February 20, 2005.

21. Bruce Katz and Scott Bernstein, "The New Metropolitan Agenda," *Brookings Review* 16 (Fall 1998): 5.

22. Christine Todd Whitman, "The Metropolitan Challenge," *Brookings Review* 16 (Fall 1998): 3.

23. See Anthony Downs, "How America's Cities Are Growing," *Brookings Review* 16 (Fall 1998): 8.

24. For other criticisms, see John Carlisle, *The Campaign Against Urban Sprawl: Declaring War on the American Dream* (Washington, DC: National Center for Public Policy Research, report #239, April 1999).

25. Roger B. Parks and Ronald J. Oakerson, "Regionalism, Localism, and Metropolitan Governance: Suggestions From the Research Program on Local Public Economies," *State and Local Government Review* 32 (Fall 2000): 169–179; see also Donald F. Norris, "Whither Metropolitan Governance?" *Urban Affairs Review* 36 (March 2001): 532–550; David Lowery, "A Transaction Costs Model of Metropolitan Governance: Allocation Versus Redistribution in Urban America," *Journal of Public Administration Research and Theory* 10 (January 2000): 49–78.

26. John Harrigan, *Political Change in the Metropolis* (Boston: Little, Brown, 1985).

27. However, see Arthur C. Nelson and Kathryn A. Foster, "Metropolitan Governance Structure and Income Growth," *Journal of Urban Affairs* 21 (3, 1999): 309–324.

28. For an excellent analysis of the political values of scholars who study urban problems, see Brett W. Hawkins and Stephen L. Percy, "On Anti-Suburban Orthodoxy," *Social Science Quarterly* 72 (September 1991): 478–490.

29. For a good discussion of this view, see Stan Humphries, "Who's Afraid of the Big, Bad Firm: The Impact of Economic Scale on Political Participation," *American Journal of Political Science* 45 (July 2001): 678–699; for a somewhat different view, see Avery M. Guest, "The Mediate Community: The Nature of Local and Extralocal Ties Within the Metropolis," *Urban Affairs Review* 35 (May 2000): 603–627.

30. Charles Tiebout, "A Pure Theory of Local Expenditures," *Journal of Political Economy* 64 (October 1956): 416–424.

31. Bollens and Schmandt, *The Metropolis*.

32. See Barrett A. Lee, "The Urban Unease Revisited: Perceptions of Local Satisfaction Among Metropolitan Residents," *Social Science Quarterly* 62 (December 1987): 611–629; Craig St. John and Frieda Clark, "Race and Social Class Differences in the Characteristics Desired in Residential Neighborhoods," *Social Science Quarterly* 65 (September 1984): 803–813.

33. See Mark Schneider, "Suburban Fiscal Disparities and the Location Decisions of Firms," *American Journal of Political Science* 29 (August 1985): 587–605.

34. Jered B. Carr and Richard C. Feoick, "State Annexation 'Constraints' and the Frequency of Municipal Annexation," *Political Research Quarterly* 54 (June 2001): 459–470.

35. Mary Edwards, "Annexation: A 'Winner-Take-All' Process?" *State and Local Government Review* 31 (Fall 1999): 221–231.

36. See Arnold Fleischmann, "The Politics of Annexation," *Social Science Quarterly* 67 (March 1986): 128–141; Gary J. Miller, *Cities by Contract: The Politics of Municipal Incorporation* (Cambridge, MA: MIT Press, 1981).

37. John A. Powell, "Addressing Regional Dilemmas for Minority Communities," Chapter 8 in Bruce Katz, ed., *Reflections on Regionalism* (Washington, DC: The Brookings Institution, 2000).

38. See Brett W. Hawkins and Rebecca M. Hendrick, "Do County Governments Reinforce City–Suburban Inequalities?" *Social Science Quarterly* 25 (December 1994): 755–771.

39. Jacqueline J. Byers, "The Consolidation Question," *County News Online*, National Association of Counties, 29 (May 12, 1997).

40. Neal R. Pierce, "Louisville Votes Merger—First Since Indy in 1969," *County News Online*, National Association of Counties 32 (December 18, 2000).

41. See Mark S. Rosentraub, "City–County Consolidation and the Rebuilding of Image: The Fiscal Lessons from Indianapolis's UniGov Program," *State and Local Government Review* 32 (Fall 2000): 180–191; Timothy D. Mead, "Governing Charlotte-Mecklenburg," *State and Local Government Review* 32 (Fall 2000):

192–197; Arnold Fleischmann, "Regionalism and City–County Consolidation in Small Metro Areas," *State and Local Government Review* 32 (Fall 2000): 213–226; Jered B. Carr, Sang-Seok Bae, and Wenjue Lu, "City-County Government and Promises of Economic Development: A Tale of Two Cities," *State and Local Government Review* 38 (3) 2006: 131–141.

42. Jered B. Carr, "Local Government Autonomy and State Reliance on Special District Governments: A Reassessment," *Political Research Quarterly* 59 (September 2006): 481–492.

43. For an excellent overview of the role of state rules regarding special districts, see Barbara Coyle McCabe, "Special-District Formation Among the States," *State and Local Government Review* 32 (Spring 2000): 121–131.

44. Nicholas Bauroth, "The Influence of Elections on Special District Revenue Policies: Special Democracies or Automatons of the State?" *State and Local Government Review* 17 (1) (2005): 193–205.

45. David K. Hamilton, "Organizing Government Structure and Governance Functions in Metropolitan Areas in Response to Growth and Change: A Critical Overview," *Journal of Urban Affairs* 22 (1, 2000): 65–84.

46. James H. Seroka, "City–County Consolidation: Gaining Perspective on the Limits of Our Understanding," *State and Local Government Review* 37 (1, 2005): 75. The essay reviewed two edited volumes on city–county consolidation: Suzanne M. Leland and Kurt Thurmaier, eds., *Case Studies of City–County Consolidation: Reshaping the Local Government Landscape* (Armonk, NY: M.E. Sharpe, 2004); and Jered Carr and Richard Feiock, eds., *City–County Consolidation and Its Alternatives: Reshaping the Local Government Landscape* (Armonk, NY: M.E. Sharpe, 2004).

47. Laura A. Reese, "Same Governance, Different Day: Does Metropolitan Reorganization Make a Difference?" *Review of Policy Research* 21 (4, 2004): 608.

48. William R. Potapchuk, "Building an Infrastructure of Community Collaboration," *National Civic Review* 88 (Fall 1999): 165.

49. Donald F. Norris, "Whither Metropolitan Governance?" *Urban Affairs Review* 36 (March 2001): 532–550.

50. For an excellent overview of the rise of regionalism, see entire issue of *State and Local Government Review* 32 (Fall 2000), which is a symposium on new regionalism and its policy agenda edited by H. V. Savitch and Ronald K. Vogel.

CHAPTER 13

1. Gaetano Mosca, *The Ruling Class* (New York: McGraw-Hill, 1939), 50.

2. Ibid., p. 51.

3. Robert Michels, *Political Parties* (Glencoe, IL: The Free Press, 1949).

4. Robert S. Lynd and Helen M. Lynd, *Middletown* (New York: Harcourt Brace & World, 1929); and *Middletown in Transition* (New York: Harcourt Brace & World, 1937). Other classic community studies include W. Lloyd Warner et al., *Democracy in Jonesville* (New York: Harper & Row, 1949); and August B. Hollingshead, *Elmtown's Youth* (New York: John Wiley, 1949).

5. The "X family," never identified in the Lynds' books, was actually the Ball family, glass manufacturers. As late as 1975 the Ball family exercised a controlling influence over the Ball Corporation, Ball Brothers Foundation, Ball Memorial Hospital, Muncie Aviation Corp., and Muncie Airport, Inc.; and E. F. Ball served as a director of American National Bank and Trust of Muncie, Borg-Warner Corp., Indiana Bell Telephone Co., Merchants National Bank of Muncie, and Wabash College. Ball State University in Muncie is named for the family.

6. Floyd Hunter, *Community Power Structure* (Chapel Hill: University of North Carolina Press, 1953).

7. Aaron Wildavsky, *Leadership in a Small Town* (Totowa, NJ: Bedminster Press, 1964), 8.

8. See Harvey Molotch, "The City as Growth Machine," *American Journal of Sociology* 82 (September 1976): 309–330; and "Capital and Neighborhood in the United States," *Urban Affairs Quarterly* 14 (March 1979): 289–312.

9. Paul E. Peterson, *City Limits* (Chicago: University of Chicago Press, 1981), 20.

10. Ibid., p. 23.

11. Ibid., p. 29.

12. For a parallel argument, see Heywood T. Sanders and Clarence N. Stone, "Developmental Politics Reconsidered," *Urban Affairs Quarterly* 22 (June 1987): 521–539; and Mark Schneider, "Undermining the Growth Machine," *Journal of Politics* 54 (February 1992): 214–230.

13. Pietro S. Nivola, *Laws of the Landscape: How Policies Shape Cities in Europe and America* (Washington, DC: Brookings Institution Press, 1999).

14. See Kent E. Portney, "Allaying the NIMBY Syndrome," *Hazardous Waste* 1 (1984): 411–421; and "Coping in the Age of NIMBY," *New York Times*, June 19, 1988.

15. The EcoOutlet, "Smart Growth," accessed at http://shop.ecoiq .com.acb.showdetl.cfm?&DID=23&Product_ID=1548&CATID =155, July 13, 2005.

16. Robert W. Wassmer and Edward L. Lascher, Jr., "Who Supports Local Growth and Regional Planning to Deal With Its Consequences?" *Urban Affairs Review* 41 (5) (May 2006): 621–645.

17. See Todd Donovan and Max Neiman, "Local Growth Control Policy and Changes in Community Characteristics," *Social Science Quarterly* 76 (December 1995): 780–793.

18. For discussions of why suburban communities adopt growth controls, see Mark Baldasarre, *Trouble in Paradise* (New York: Columbia University Press, 1986); John R. Logan and Min Zhou, "The Adoption of Growth Controls in Suburban Communities," *Social Science Quarterly* 71 (March 1990): 118–129.

19. PRNewswire, "Survey Shows Housing Issues of Concern, Says Florida Association of Realtors," press release, June 21, 2005, accessed at http://biz.yahoo.com/prnews/050621/ fltu003.html?.v=14, July 16, 2005.

20. See Anthony J. Catanese and James C. Snyder, *Urban Planning*, 2nd ed. (New York: McGraw-Hill, 1988).

21. American Institute of Planners, *AIP Planning Policies* (Washington, DC: Author, 1977).

22. Rayman Mohamed, "The Economics of Conservation Subdivisions: Price Premiums, Improvement Costs, and Absorption Rates," *Urban Affairs Review* 41 (3) (January 2006): 376–399.

23. See Arnold Fleischmann and Carol A. Pierannunzi, "Citizens, Development Interests, and Local Land-Use Regulation," *Journal of Politics* 52 (August 1990): 838–853.

24. Anthony Downs, "The Future of U.S. Ground Transportation From 2000 to 2020," testimony to the Subcommittee on Highways and Transit of the Committee on Transportation and Infrastructure, U.S. House of Representatives, March 21, 2001.

25. See Alan Ehrenhalt, "The Trouble with Zoning," *Governing* (February 1998): 28–34.

26. For a good overview of the legal basis for these fees, see Bruce W. Bringardner, "Exactions, Impact Fees, and Dedications: National and Texas Law After *Dolan* and *Del Monte Dunes*," *The Urban Lawyer* 32 (Summer 2000): 561–585.

27. Susan Fainstein, "New Directions in Planning Theory," *Urban Affairs Review* 35 (March 2000): 451–478.

28. *Village of Euclid, Ohio* v. *Amber Realty Company*, 272 U.S. 365 (1926).

29. *Berman* v. *Parker*, 348 U.S. 26 (1954).

30. *Lucas* v. *South Carolina Coastal Council*, 112 Sup.Ct. 2886 (1992).

31. *Dolan* v. *City of Tigard* (1994).

32. *Kelo* v. *City of New London*, June 23, 2005.

33. Urban Land Institute, "A Nation Divided by Haves and Have Nots? *Urban Land* Sizes up America's Housing Affordability Problem," January 10, 2001; Anthony Downs, "Housing Policies in the New Millennium," HUD Conference on Housing Policies for the Millennium, October 3, 2000.

34. Antonio R. Villaraigosa, "America's Urban Agenda: A View From California," *Brookings Review* 18 (Summer 2000): 46–49.

35. Bruce Katz, "Enough of the Small Stuff: Toward a New Urban Agenda," *Brookings Review* 18 (Summer 2000): 4–9; see also Jon C. Teaford, "Urban Renewal and its Aftermath," *Housing Policy Debate*, 11 (2, 2000); Ronald D. Utt, "Cities and Suburbs: Promoting Innovative Solutions to Community Problems" (Washington, DC: The Heritage Foundation, 2000); Rolf Pendall, "Why Voucher and Certificate Users Live in Distressed Neighborhoods," *Housing Policy Debate* 11 (4, 2000).

36. Bruce Katz, "The Need to Connect Smart Growth and Affordable Housing," Vermont Affordable Housing Conference, November 29, 2000.

37. Adam Carasso, Elizabeth Bell, Edgar O. Olsen, and C. Eugene Steuerle, "Improving Homeownership Among Poor and Moderate-Income Households," Washington, DC: The Urban Institute, Opportunity and Ownership Project, No. 2, June 2005.

38. U.S. Department of Housing and Urban Development, "HUD's Public Housing Program," December 5, 2000.

39. See William Fulton, "Do Housing Authorities Have a Future?" *Governing* (February 1998): 40–43.

40. Jon C. Teaford, "Urban Renewal and Its Aftermath," *Housing Policy Debate* 11 (2, 2000): 443–465.

41. U.S. Department of Housing and Urban Development, "Community Development Block Grant (CDBG) Entitlement Communities Program," www.hud.gov, February 4, 2002.

42. Ibid.

43. Spencer M. Cowan, William Roh, and Esmail Baku, "Factors Influencing the Performance of Community Development Corporations," *Journal of Urban Affairs* 21 (3, 1999): 325.

44. Marion G. Boarnet, "Enterprise Zones and Job Creation: Linking Evaluation and Practice," *Economic Development Quarterly* 15 (August 2001): 242–254; Laura Langer, "The Consequences of State Economic Development Strategies on Income Distribution in the American States, 1976–1994," *American Politics Research* 29 (July 2001): 392–415.

45. Robert C. Turner and Mark K. Cassell, "When Do States Pursue Targeted Economic Development Policies? The Adoption and Expansion of State Enterprise Zone Programs," *Social Science Quarterly* 88 (1) (March 2007): 86–103.

46. Michael Greenberg, Karen Lowrie, Laura Solitare, and Latoya Duncan, "Brownfields, Toads, and the Struggle for Neighborhood Redevelopment: A Case Study of the State of New Jersey," *Urban Affairs Review* 35 (May 2000): 717–718. For other studies of the vacant land problem, see John Accordino and Gary T. Johnson, "Addressing the Vacant and Abandoned Property Problem," *Journal of Urban Affairs* 22 (3, 2000): 301–315; Ann O'M. Bowman and Michael A. Pagano, "Transforming America's Cities: Policies and Conditions of Vacant Land," *Urban Affairs Review* 35 (March 2000): 559–581.

47. Michael Greenberg, Karen Lowrie, Laura Solitare, and Latoya Duncan, "Brownfields, Toads, and the Struggle for Neighborhood Redevelopment: A Case Study of the State of New Jersey," *Urban Affairs Review* 35 (May 2000): 717–718.

48. Manuel Pastor, Jr., Jim Sadd, and John Hipp, "Which Came First? Toxic Facilities, Minority Move-In, and Environmental Justice," *Journal of Urban Affairs* 23 (1, 2001): 1–12.

49. Jerome S. Legge, "Policy Alternatives and Traffic Safety," *Western Political Quarterly* 43 (September 1990): 597–612.

50. For a summary of previous research on the effects of state traffic safety, as well as well-crafted original research, see David J. Houston, Lilliard E. Richardson, and Grant W. Neeley, "Legislating Traffic Safety," *Social Science Quarterly* 76 (June 1995): 328–345.

51. Sandy Graham, "Driving to Distraction," *Traffic Safety* 1 (November/December), 18–21.

52. Consumer Reports, "The Distraction Factor," www.consumerreports.org January 23, 2002.

53. See Thomas R. Dye, "Taxing, Spending, and Economic Growth in the States," *Journal of Politics* 42 (November 1980), 1085–1087.

54. *Statistical Abstract of the United States*, 2007.

55. Don Chen and Nancy Jakowitsch, "Transportation Reform and Smart Growth: A Nation at the Tipping Point," Funders' Network for Smart Growth and Livable Communities, Surface Transportation Policy Project, Paper No. 6 (August 2001), p. 4.

56. Barbara McCann and Bianca DeLille, *Mean Streets 2000: Pedestrian Safety, Health and Federal Transportation Spending*, (Washington DC: Surface Transportation Policy Report, 2000).

57. John Fetto, "The Grid: Congestion Ahead," *American Demographics* 22 (June 2000): 49–50.

58. Resource Conservation and Recovery Act of 1976.

59. *Statistical Abstract of the United States* 2006, p. 229

60. Environmental Protection Agency, "National Air Quality and Emission Trends 2006"; www.epa.gov

61. Matthew Whittaker, Gary M. Segura, and Shaun Bowler, "Racial Group Attitudes Toward Environmental Protection," *Political Research Quarterly* 58 (September 2005): 435–447.

CHAPTER 14

1. See Edward T. Howe and Donald J. Reed, "The Historical Evolution of State and Local Tax Systems," *Social Science Quarterly* 78 (March 1997): 109–121.

2. Robert McIntyre, *A Far Cry from Fair* (Washington, DC: Citizens for Tax Justice, 1991).

3. See David R. Morgan, "Tax Equity in the American States," *Social Science Quarterly* 75 (September 1994): 510–523.

4. Neil Berch, "Explaining Changes in Tax Incidence in the States," *Political Research Quarterly* 48 (September 1995): 629–642.

5. Shawn Bowler and Todd Donovan, "Popular Responsiveness to Taxation," *Political Research Quarterly* 48 (March 1995): 61–78.

6. James Cox and David Lowery, "The Impact of the Tax Revolt Era State Fiscal Caps," *Social Science Quarterly* 71 (September 1990): 492–509.

7. Phillip G. Joyce and Daniel R. Mullins, "The Changing Fiscal Structure of State and Local Public Sector: The Impact of Tax and Expenditure Limits," *Public Administration Review* 51 (May/June 1991): 240–253.

8. The following discussion relies on the theoretical concepts and reports of opinion surveys in David Lowery and Lee Sigelman, "Understanding the Tax Revolt: Eight Explanations," *American Political Science Review* 75 (December 1981): 963–974; James M. Buchanan, "The Potential for Taxpayers Revolt in American Democracy," *Social Science Quarterly* 59 (March 1979): 691–696; Paul Allen Beck and Thomas R. Dye, "Sources of Public Opinion on Taxes," *Journal of Politics* 44 (February 1982): 172–182; Carl Ladd, "The Polls: Taxing and Spending," *Public Opinion Quarterly* 43 (Spring 1979): 126–135; Susan Hansen, *The Politics of Taxation* (New York: Praeger, 1983).

9. David T. Stanley, "Cities in Trouble," in Charles H. Levine, ed., *Managing Fiscal Stress* (Chatham, NJ: Chatham, 1980).

10. Various measures of fiscal stress have been devised and applied to American cities. See Richard P. Nathan and Charles Adams, "Understanding Central City Hardship," *Political Science Quarterly* 91 (Spring 1976): 51–61; David T. Stanley, "Cities in Trouble," in Charles H. Levine, ed., *Managing Fiscal Stress* (Chatham, NJ: Chatham, 1980); Terry N. Clark and Lorna Crowley Ferguson, *City Money* (New York: Columbia University Press, 1983).

11. See Stephen C. Brooks, "Urban Fiscal Stress: A Decade of Difference," Midwest Political Science Association Meeting, chicago, 1993; Cal Clark and B. Oliver Walter, "Urban Political Cultures, Financial Stress, and City Fiscal Austerity Strategies," *Western Political Quarterly* 44 (September 1991): 676–697; Terry N. Clark and Lorna Crowley Ferguson, *City Money* (New York: Columbia University Press, 1983).

12. Gregory B. Lewis, "Municipal Expenditures Through Thick and Thin," *Publius*, special issue (May 1984): 380–390.

13. *McCulloch* v. *Maryland*, 4 Wheaton 316 (1819).

14. See Elaine B. Sharp, "The Politics and Economics of the New City Debt," *American Political Science Review*, 80 (December 1986): 1241–1258.

CHAPTER 15

1. Quotation in Rufus P. Browning, Dale Rogers Marshall, and David H. Tabb, *Protest Is Not Enough: The Struggle of Blacks and Hispanics for Equality in Urban Politics* (Berkeley: University of California Press, 1984), 17.

2. Carmine Scavo, "Racial Integration of Local Government Leadership in Small Southern Cities," *Social Science Quarterly* 71 (June 1990): 362–372.

3. Lawrence Bobo and Franklin D. Gilliam, Jr., "Race, Sociopolitical Participation, and Black Empowerment," *American Political Science Review* 84 (June 1990): 377–386.

4. Zoltan L. Hajnal, "White Residents, Black Incumbents, and a Declining Racial Divide," *American Political Science Review* 95 (September 2001): 603–615.

5. See Paul Peterson, *City Limits* (Chicago: University of Chicago Press, 1981).

6. See Kenneth R. Mladenka, "Blacks and Hispanics in Urban Politics," *American Political Science Review* 83 (March 1989): 165–191; Thomas R. Dye and James Renick, "Political Power and City Jobs: Determinants of Minority Employment," *Social Science Quarterly* 62 (September 1981): 475–486.

7. C. Vann Woodward, *Reunion and Reaction: The End of Reconstruction* (Boston: Little, Brown, 1951).

8. *Plessy* v. *Ferguson*, 163 U.S. 537 (1896).

9. *Sweatt* v. *Painter*, 339 U.S. 629 (1950); *McLaurin* v. *Oklahoma State Regents*, 339 U.S. 637 (1950).

10. *Brown* v. *Board of Education of Topeka, Kansas*, 347 U.S. 483 (1954).

11. Kenneth B. Clark, *Dark Ghetto* (New York: Harper & Row, 1965), 77–78.

12. The Supreme Court also ruled that Congress was bound to respect the equal protection doctrine imposed upon the states by the Fourteenth Amendment as part of the due process clause of the Fifth Amendment. *Bolling* v. *Sharpe*, 347 U.S. 497 (1954).

13. The Supreme Court declared that the threat of violence was not sufficient reason to deny constitutional rights to black children and again dismissed the ancient interposition arguments. *Cooper* v. *Aaron*, 358 U.S. 1 (1958).

14. *Alexander* v. *Holmes County Board of Education*, 396 U.S. 19 (1969).

15. United States Commission on Civil Rights, *Racial Isolation in the Public Schools*, 2 vols. (Washington, DC: Government Printing Office, 1967). See also James S. Coleman, *Equality of Educational Opportunity* (Washington, DC: Government Printing Office, 1966).

16. *Swan* v. *Charlotte-Mecklenburg County Board of Education*, 402 U.S. 1 (1971).

17. *Milliken* v. *Bradley*, 418 U.S. 717 (1974).

18. *Oklahoma City Board of Education* v. *Dowell*, 498 U.S. 237 (1991).

19. *Adarand Construction Inc.* v. *Pena*, 515 U.S. 200 (1995).

20. *Parents Involved in Community Schools v. Seattle School District No. 1*, June 28, 2007.

21. *Grudder* v. *Bollinger*, 539 U.S. 306 (2003).

22. Michael W. Giles, et al., "The Impact of Busing on White Flight," *Social Science Quarterly* 55 (September 1974): 493–501. See also George M. Metcalf, *From Little Rock to Boston: The History of School Desegregation* (Westport, CT: Greenwood Press, 1985).

23. Howard W. Stanley and Richard G. Niemi, *Vital Statistics on American Politics, 1999–2000* (Washington, DC: Congressional Quarterly Press, 2000), 374–375.

24. Harvard Project on School Desegregation, "Deepening Segregation in American Public Schools," Harvard University, 1999.

25. Opponents of the Civil Rights Act of 1964 argued that Congress unconstitutionally exceeded its delegated powers when it prohibited discrimination and segregation practiced by *privately owned* public accommodations and *private* employers. Nowhere among the delegated powers of Congress in Article I of the Constitution, or even in the Fourteenth or Fifteenth Amendments, is Congress specifically given the power to prohibit discrimination practiced by *private* individuals. In reply, supporters of the act argued that Congress has the power to regulate interstate commerce. Instead of relying upon the Fourteenth Amendment, which prohibits only *state-supported* discrimination, Congress was relying on its powers over interstate commerce. In unanimous opinions in *Heart of Atlanta Motel v. United States* and *Katzenbach* v. *McClung* in December 1964, the Supreme Court upheld the constitutionality of the Civil Rights Act. The Court held that Congress could, by virtue of its power over interstate commerce, prohibit discrimination in any establishment that serves or offers to serve interstate travelers or that sells food or goods previously moved in interstate commerce. This power over commerce included not only major establishments, like the Heart of Atlanta Motel, but also the

family-owned Ollie's Barbecue serving a local clientele. *Heart of Atlanta Motel v. United States*, 379 U.S. 241 (1964); *Katzenbach v. McClung*, 379 U.S. 294 (1964).

26. *Regents of the University of California v. Bakke*, 438 U.S. 265 (1978).

27. Bakke's overall grade point average was 3.46, while the average for special admission students was 2.62. Bakke's Medical College Admissions Test (MCAT) scores were verbal—96, quantitative—94, science—97, general information—72; while the average MCAT scores for special admissions students were verbal—34, quantitative—30, science—37, general information—18.

28. *United Steelworkers v. Weber*, 443 U.S. 193 (1979).

29. *United States v. Paradise*, 480 U.S. 149 (1987).

30. *Firefighters Local Union v. Totts*, 465 U.S. 561 (1981).

31. *Richmond v. Crosen*, 109 S. Ct. 706 (1989).

32. See Justice Antonin Scalia's dissent in *Johnson v. Transportation Agency of Santa Clara County*, 480 U.S. 616 (1987).

33. *Aderand Construction v. Pena* (1995).

34. American Civil Rights Initiative. www.acri.org

35. *Coalition for Economic Equity v. Pete Wilson Ninth Circuit Court of Appeals*, April, 1997.

36. As reported in *The Polling Report*, July 5, 1999.

37. See F. Chris Garcia, ed., *Latinos in the Political System* (Notre Dame, IN: Notre Dame University Press, 1988); Rudolpho O. de la Garza, et al., *Latino Voices: Mexican, Puerto Rican, and Cuban Perspectives in American Politics* (Boulder, CO: Westview Press, 1992).

38. Peter Mathiessen, *Sal Si Puedes: Ceasar Chavez and the New American Revolution* (New York: Random House, 1969).

39. *Plyer v. Doe* 457 U.S. 202 (1982).

40. Caroline J. Tolbert and Rodney E. Hero, "Race/Ethnicity and Direct Democracy," *Journal of Politics* 58 (August 1996): 806–808.

41. *Morton v. Mancari*, 417 U.S. 535 (1974).

42. *Governing* (November 1998), p. 51.

43. See Joseph P. Shapiro, *No Pity: People with Disabilities Forging a New Civil Rights Movement* (New York: Times Books/Random House, 1993).

44. *The Chronicle of Higher Education*, December 8, 2000.

45. *Stanton v. Stanton*, 421 U.S. 7 (1975).

46. *Craig v. Boren*, 429 U.S. 191 (1976).

47. *Dothland v. Raulinson*, 433 U.S. 321 (1977).

48. *Arizona v. Norvis*, 103 S. Ct. 3492 (1983).

49. *E.E.O.C. v. Madison Community School District*, 55 U.S.L.W. 2644 (1987).

50. *Vorcheheimer v. Philadelphia School District*, 430 U.S. 703 (1977).

51. *Rostker v. Goldberg*, 453 U.S. 57 (1981).

52. *Orr v. Orr*, 440 U.S. 268 (1979).

53. See Christopher Z. Mooney and Mei-Hsien Lee, "Legislating Morality in the American States: Pre-Roe Abortion Reform," *American Journal of Political Science* 39 (August 1995): 599–627.

54. *Roe v. Wade*, 410 U.S. 113 (1973).

55. *Harris v. McRae*, 448 U.S. 297 (1980).

56. For a review of state funding of abortions, see Kenneth J. Meier and Deborah R. McFarlane, "The Politics of Funding Abortion," *American Politics Quarterly* 21 (January 1993): 81–101.

57. *Planned Parenthood of Missouri v. Danforth*, 428 U.S. 52 (1976); *Bellotti v. Baird*, 443 U.S. 622 (1979); *Akron v. Akron Center for Reproductive Health*, 103 S. Ct. 2481 (1983).

58. Susan B. Hansen, "State Implementation of Supreme Court Decisions: Abortion Rates Since *Roe v. Wade*," *Journal of Politics* 42 (1980): 372–395.

59. *Webster v. Reproductive Health Services*, 492 U.S. 490 (1989).

60. *Planned Parenthood v. Casey*, 112 S. Ct. 2791 (1992).

61. Ibid.

62. See Robert E. O'Conner and Michael B. Berkman, "Religious Determinants of State Abortion Policy," *Social Science Quarterly* 76 (June 1995): 447–459.

63. *Planned Parenthood of Blue Ridge v. Camblos*, February 27, 1999.

64. *Planned Parenthood of Pennsylvania v. Casey*, op. cit.

65. *Stenberg v. Carhart*, June 28, 2000.

66. *Gonzales v. Carhart*, April 18, 2007.

CHAPTER 16

1. David Osborne, *Laboratories of Democracy* (Boston: Harvard Business School Press, 1988), 92.

2. Paul Brace, *State Government and Economic Performance* (Baltimore: Johns Hopkins University Press, 1993).

3. Kevin B. Smith and J. Scott Rademacker, "Expense Lessons: Education and the Political Economy of the American State," *Political Research Quarterly* 52 (December 1999): 709–727.

4. Thomas R. Dye, "Taxing, Spending, and Economic Growth in the American States," *Journal of Politics* 42 (November 1980): 1085–1107.

5. *Statistical Abstract of the United States, 2004–2005*, p. 165.

6. Administered nationally by the College Board, New York. The SAT was formerly named the Scholastic Aptitude Test.

7. National Commission on Excellence in Education, *A Nation at Risk* (Washington, DC: Government Printing Office, 1983).

8. James S. Coleman, et al., *Equality of Educational Opportunity* (Washington, DC: Government Printing Office, 1966).

9. James S. Coleman, et al., *High School Achievement* (New York: Basic Books, 1982).

10. Eric Hirsch, "A New Chapter for Charters," *State Legislatures* (June 1998): 20–24.

11. Charles Mahtesian, "Charter Schools Learn a Few Lessons," *Governing* (January 1998): 23–27.

12. Pro-voucher arguments can be found in John E. Chubb and Terry M. Moe, *Politics, Markets, and America's Schools* (Washington, DC: Brookings Institution, 1990); Paul E. Peterson and Bryan C. Hassel, eds., *Learning from School Choice* (Washington, DC: Brookings Institution, 1998).

13. Anti-voucher arguments are provided in Kevin Smith and Kenneth Meier, *The Case Against School Choice* (Armonk, NY: M. E. Sharpe, 1995). But see also Robert Maranto, Scott Madison, and Scott Stevens, "Does Private School Competition Harm Public Schools?" *Political Research Quarterly* 53 (March 2000): 177–192.

14. Terry M. Moe, *School Vouchers and the American Public.* Washington, DC: Brookings Institution, 2002.

15. *Zelman* v. *Simmons-Harris* 234 F. 3d, 945 (2002).

16. See Brian Jendryka, "Failing Grade for Federal Aid," *Policy Review* (Fall 1993): 77–81.

17. National Education Association; *Issues in Education*, "ESEA: It's Time for a Change," www.nea.org

18. *Statistical Abstract of the United States*, 2000, p. 172.

19. *Rodriguez* v. *San Antonio Independent School District*, 411 U.S. 1 (1973).

20. *Serrano* v. *Priest*, 5 Cal. 594 (1971).

21. Kenneth J. Meier and Robert E. England, "Black Representation and Educational Policy," *American Political Science Review* 78 (June 1984): 393–403.

22. Trudy Haffron Bers, "Politics Programs and Local Governments: The Case of Community Colleges," *Journal of Politics* 40 (February 1980): 150–164.

23. See Charles Mahtesian, "Higher Ed: The No-Longer-Sacred Cow," *Governing* (July 1995): 20–26.

24. *Pierce* v. *The Society of Sisters*, 268 U.S. 510 (1925).

25. *Cochran* v. *Board of Education*, 281 U.S. 370 (1930).

26. *Everson* v. *Board of Education*, 330 U.S. 1 (1947).

27. *Mueller* v. *Allen* 463 U.S. 388 (1983).

28. Hugo Black, majority opinion in *Everson* v. *Board of Education*, 330 U.S. 1 (1947).

29. *Lemon* v. *Kurtzman*, 403 U.S. 602 (1971).

30. *Mueller* v. *Adams* 463 U.S. 602 (1983).

31. *Tilden* v. *Richardson* 403 U.S. 602 (1971).

32. *Lambs Chapel* v. *Center Moriches Union School District* 528 U.S. 324 (1993).

33. *Rosenberger* v. *University of Virginia* 515 U.S. 819 (1995).

34. *Edwards* v. *Aguillard* 482 U.S. 578, (1987).

35. *Engle* v. *Vitale*, 370 U.S. 421 (1962).

36. Ibid.

37. *Abbington Township* v. *Schempp*, 374 U.S. 203 (1963).

38. *Wallace* v. *Jaffree*, 105 S. Ct. 2479 (1986).

39. *Santa Fe Independent School District* v. *Doe*, 530 U.S. 290 (2000).

CHAPTER 17

1. *Statistical Abstract of the United States*, 2006, p. 476.

2. The original Act did not include disability insurance; this was added by amendment in 1950. Health insurance for the aged, Medicare, was added by amendment in 1965.

3. David Ellwood, *Poor Support: Poverty in the American Family* (New York: Basic Books, 1988), p. 6.

4. *Statistical Abstract of the United States*, 2006, p. 133.

PHOTO CREDITS

INDEX

suburbs, 430–35
sunset laws, 185
Supreme Court, U.S., 61–63, 78, 83, 84, 92, 95, 99–100, 103, 119, 176–77, 197, 307, 309, 311*t*, 314, 316*t*, 333, 543, 574
supreme courts, 317
sustained political participation, 107

T

Takings Clause, 467–69
tax assessor, 356
taxation, 26, 45
tax burden, 499, 501
tax collector, county, 356
taxes, 434, 494–99, 502–5
tax limitations, 502, 504
Temporary Assistance for Needy Families (TANF), 24, 86, 97, 589, 591
Tenth Amendment, 74, 92, 94
tenure, 573
tenure power, 244
term limits, 61–64, 215–16
Thirteenth Amendment, 72
Thornburg v. Gingles, 123
Tiebout model, 441–42
tort, 187
  reform, 187, 301
totality of circumstances test, 123, 372
town meeting government, 365
townships, 357
traditional redistricting principles, 197
train, 204

transportation, 24, 475–83
treasurer, state, 257
trial courts, 304–7, 317
tribal government, 534–36
Truman, Harry, 526
trustees, 214
turnover rate, 210
Twenty-Fourth Amendment, 121
Twenty-Seventh Amendment, 82
Twenty-Third Amendment, 28
two-party states, 217

U

uncontested election, 194
uncontrollables, in spending, 292–93
unemployment compensation, 497, 589
unfunded mandates, 97
Unfunded Mandates Reform Act, 97
unified party government, 161–62, 164*t*
unimodal distribution of opinion, 163
unions, 275–78, 569–70, 573
unitary schools, 520
unitary systems, 68
United States v. Miller, 45
urban county government, 352
urban renewal, 472
U.S. v. Lopez, 99
user charges, 498–99

V

Veterans Administration (VA), 436
veto, 229, 247
victimization, 322
Vietnam War, 122

Villaraigosa, Antonio, 410–11
violence, 138–40
Violence Against Women Act, 100
violent crime, 318
volunteering, as civic participation, 380–81, 421
voter turnout, 107–18, 382, 534
Voting Accessibility for the Elderly and Handicapped Act (VAEHA), 116
Voting Rights Act (1965), 84, 121–22
Voting Rights Act (1982), 123, 200, 372
vouchers, school, 283, 558–60

W

War on Drugs, 57
wealth, 187, 586
welfare, 73, 82, 91, 217, 265, 587–90. *See also* health and welfare
welfare reform, 590–93
  devolution and, 97–99
"white flight," 522
"white primary," 120–21
Wilder, Douglas, 11, 232
women, 125–27, 159, 189–93, 233*t*–234*t*, 274–75, 374*t*, 408–14, 413–14
World Trade Organization, 139
World War II, 122

Z

zero sum game, 291
zoning, city, 462–67